Defeated Leaders

DEFEATED LEADERS

LEADERS

THE POLITICAL FATE OF

CAILLAUX, JOUVENEL, AND TARDIEU

By Rudolph Binion

Columbia University Press   1960

MORNINGSIDE HEIGHTS NEW YORK

This study,
prepared under the
Graduate Faculties of
Columbia University,
was selected by a
committee of those Faculties
to receive one of the
Clarke F. Ansley awards
given annually by
Columbia University Press.

Published 1960, Columbia University Press, New York

Published in Great Britain, India, and Pakistan
by the Oxford University Press
London, Bombay, and Karachi

Manufactured in The Netherlands

Library of Congress Catalog Card Number: 59–14524

Preface

IN THIS BOOK I have attempted to write political history in the form of comparative biography and to write biography of the "life-thought-and-times" variety in the form of continuous narrative. Whether men make history or vice versa, history is not comprehensible unless men are: hence the advantage of approaching the two simultaneously. Likewise, men's thoughts and actions are always bound up with each other as well as with their historical context; to view them under separate heads, though a convenience in the short run, is ultimately a source of confusion. I have chosen the three men Joseph Caillaux, Henry de Jouvenel, and André Tardieu as means to a study of the Third French Republic—three men because, while two would have been less instructive, four would have been a crowd, and these three because they were republicans in conflict with the political regime of the Third Republic, and so their lives are a most revealing commentary on it. I have tried to make each life story, each episode even, intelligible and interesting in itself even if significant only in sequence. Finally, I have written for any reader, not just for specialists: the text tells what I think is a self-explanatory tale, and the notes and other addenda are supplementary, not essential, to it.

For whatever merit my book may have I am much in the debt of Jacques Barzun of Columbia University, who saw it through all the formative stages from conception to completion, and of François Goguel of the University of Paris, who submitted the whole huge first draft of it to his critical scrutiny. Professors Shepard B. Clough, Walter J. Dorn, and John H. Wuorinen of Columbia University graciously pointed out errors and defects in the penultimate version of it, which I defended before them as a doctoral dissertation in November, 1957. My friends Richard Webster, John Michael Montias, and especially Ralph Gladstone also read parts of early drafts of it for me. Finally my wife, Alice, did all in her power to facilitate its composition, which except for her might not have been possible.

Quotations from André Tardieu, *Notes sur les Etats-Unis* (Paris, Calmann-Lévy, 1908), *Le Mystère d'Agadir* (Paris, Calmann-Lévy, 1912), and

The Truth about the Treaty (Indianapolis, Bobbs-Merrill, 1921), and from Alfred Fabre-Luce, *Caillaux* (Paris, Gallimard, 1933), are by special permission of the publishers. Whenever a foreign-language source is quoted in English, the translation is my own.

R.B.

Contents

Introduction

Introduction

THE THIRD FRENCH REPUBLIC was a makeshift: most Frenchmen accepted it in the 1870's only because it satisfied no one. After its acceptance, however, the republicans of France rallied to its defense whenever their adversaries attacked it, and if one of their own party attacked it they ignored him for fear of playing into the hands of their adversaries. In the 1930's, when the need for reforming it grew critical, the problem of reforming it proved insoluble.

Wherein did it need reform? Joseph Caillaux, Henry de Jouvenel, and André Tardieu, republicans though they were, ran afoul of it again and again in striving to serve France: their lives expose dramatically the worst of its defects. But their lives cannot very well be told unless first the regime is introduced. And the best introduction to the regime is a sketch of how it was put together and how it evolved, plus a summary critique of how it worked.

In February, 1871, at the end of the Franco-Prussian War, France elected a national assembly at the behest of Germany to ratify the terms of peace. The Second Empire had fallen five months earlier. Since then a provisional republican government had held power, striving desperately to stem the tide of defeat. Now this government disbanded, and the National Assembly, meeting in Bordeaux, declared itself competent both to decide on the future political regime and to govern until its decision was taken.

Its political composition encumbered it in these tasks. Its seven-hundred-odd members fell into four groups, none of which held a majority. Most numerous were the Legitimists, who advocated a restoration of the grandson of Charles X; next came the Orleanists, or devotees of the grandson of Louis Philippe; then came some two hundred republicans, followed by an ample contingent of Bonapartists. The Assembly chose the veteran statesman Adolphe Thiers to head a provisional government, and it agreed to put off deciding on a new regime until after the financial, administrative, and military reorganization of the country. Then it moved to Versailles.

Its claim to sovereignty did not go unchallenged. In Paris the National Guards refused to surrender their arms at its bidding. When Thiers insisted, the people of Paris rose in insurrection, proclaiming the Paris Commune the lawful government of France. Only after several weeks of bloody fighting did they submit; when they did, the Assembly imposed harsh penalties on their leaders, and thereafter it gradually moved its offices to Paris. The Parisian proletariat, chief protagonists of the insurrection, were the chief victims of the repression. As the republican party had lent support to Thiers, its ties with the labor movement came loose, and, conversely, the privileged classes began to regard the prospect of a republic with somewhat less dread than before.

The two royalist parties struck an agreement on succession to the throne only to fall out bitterly over the flag of France, the legitimists upholding the *fleur de lys* and the Orleanists the tricolor. While they disputed, Thiers held power two years. An Orleanist at first, he became a republican at last—"The republic divides us the least," he said. Cautious, the Assembly put Marshal MacMahon in his place. MacMahon, constitutional monarchist that he was, governed like a constitutional monarch, choosing and revoking his ministers at the pleasure of the Assembly. Meanwhile republicanism and Bonapartism both gained in the country, and early in 1875 the Orleanist deputies, who wanted a parliament even more than they wanted a king, joined forces with their republican colleagues to vote a set of constitutional laws.

These laws, the product of much wrangling and compromising, passed the Assembly by only the slightest of majorities, and then only because they made provision for their own amendment. They gave the power of legislation to two bodies, the Senate and the Chamber of Deputies. The Senate was to be chosen by indirect election,[1] the Chamber by direct; the Senate was to be renewed by one third every three years,[2] the Chamber in its entirety every four years. Both were to have the right of initiative, but the Senate only for laws not of a financial character. The chief executive, the "president of the Republic," was to be chosen every seventh year at a joint session of both houses. His ministry was to be responsible before them both—but should it ever lose the confidence of the Chamber, he might dissolve the Chamber with the consent of the Senate. After the adoption of these laws the National Assembly disbanded. In its place the first Chamber of Deputies came into being, then the first Senate, MacMahon remaining in office as the first president of the Republic.

The constitutional laws of 1875 were shortly to be amended by precedent. The president of the Republic, having the power to appoint his ministers, had also the power to dismiss them—or so it seemed to Mac-Mahon, who on May 16, 1877, served notice on his chief minister to resign. The republicans, now a majority in the Chamber, objected, where-upon MacMahon, with the Senate consenting, ordered new elections to the Chamber. The republicans threatened to win more seats. "And then," said their leader Léon Gambetta, "[MacMahon] will have to give in or get out." They kept just enough seats to compel MacMahon to give in. He got out two years later, having lost his hope of saving France from the Republic.

The incident of the *seize mai* made the president of the Council of Ministers (or *premier ministre*, or, in English, "premier"), who was not even a constitutional entity, the real chief of the government. Collaterally the government lost its authority over the two chambers; thereafter it governed by their sufferance only, at their discretion only, and under their perpetual surveillance. Moreover, as they alone were competent to judge the legality of their own enactments, concentration of powers within them was complete. The constitutional laws of 1875, which had been left fragmentary, were already obsolete. Nonetheless they were amended after 1877 only on a few points of detail, becoming at last, by virtue of their endurance, the sacred scrolls of the Republic and as such proof against revision.

For some years after 1877 the Republic led a precarious existence. It was shaken a few times by scandals and threatened once or twice at the polls. It had its closest call in the late 1880's, when General Boulanger, the idol of the people, became the enemy of parliament; Boulanger, how-ever, turned out to be a timid strong man. Meanwhile the republicans took over from their adversaries key posts in the prefectures and min-istries. And the labor movement began to organize politically: the first Socialists entered parliament in the early 1880's. At first the Socialists in parliament were, like those outside, enemies of the Republic. Under the leadership of Jean Jaurès, however, most of them joined with most of their republican colleagues in demanding a new trial for Captain Dreyfus.

In the long and hard struggle to establish the Republic, the Dreyfus affair was the decisive battle. The controversy over the guilt or inno-cence of Dreyfus took second place to the controversy over whether the judgment of a military court was open to question. Those who saw the interests of the state as above the rights of the individual came to blows with those who saw in the rights of the individual the only justification for the existence of the state. The first view was authoritarian, the second democratic. Some republicans held the first; they found themselves in the camp of the enemies of the Republic. Conversely, the Dreyfusards all found themselves on the side of the friends of the Republic. High-ranking clergymen, noblemen, state officials, and army officers were mostly anti-Dreyfusards. So were, in the main, the privileged classes. But the affair was just as much a battle of the generations: by and large the anti-Dreyfusards were of the old generation, whereas the young generation, which had grown up under the Republic, mostly fought to defend it.

The support given by the Socialists to the Waldeck-Rousseau ministry of 1899 assured the triumph of the *République dreyfusarde*. As a result the old generation was discredited, and along with it the traditional agents of authority: not the army, but militarism; not the church, but clericalism; not the state, but the *raison d'Etat*. The triumph of Dreyfusism made the Third Republic appear for a moment as the definitive regime of France. It had shown itself capable of conciliating the observance of justice with the enforcement of authority, of accommodating peaceably the forces of the future by representing them in its councils, of renewing and revitalizing itself in the process of repairing its own mistakes. No one could decently ask more of a regime, so with the enthusiasm of young manhood the republicans set about ejecting its die-hard adversaries from the administration, securing the loyalty of the army, and breaking the ties between the churches of France and the state.

Contact between the nation and its representatives, so close during the Dreyfus affair, grew gradually more remote thereafter. As the defenders of the old order made themselves inconspicuous, the apostles of the new order grew quiescent; trusting their political affairs to parliament, they went about their other affairs; once an avant-garde of democracy, they became instead an electoral clientele. In parliament, once pressure from the outside had lifted, the battle of ideas gave way to the battle of majorities. This battle seemed to be significant because it was intensive, profitable because France was prosperous, and timely because, as war threatened, the majority shifted to meet the threat.

The First World War brought the chief vice of the regime into prominence. The groups in parliament, after declaring themselves bound in a "sacred union" for victory, left the executive as weak as before. The parliamentary commissions, the administrative bureaus, the general staff all competed with it for authority. The conduct of the war was desultory in consequence. In the final hour, just when the enemies of parliament were becoming the oracles of France, Clemenceau took power. Intent only on victory, he was indifferent to all else. He governed alone. Occasionally he was unjust, sometimes even discourteous. Grudges piled up against him in parliament; his popularity mounted in the country. Victory was won, peace was made—whereupon his own former majority, as if to signify the return to normal, voted him down for the presidency of the Republic.

France emerged from the war deep in debt, her economy disrupted, her population depleted and demoralized. Beset with problems of unprecedented complexity, the regime sank to a new low of inefficiency. Parties grew ever more numerous, governments ever more transient, scandals ever more chronic, debates ever more violent and sterile. The inflation of the 1920's, then the depression of the 1930's, stirred up rumors of revolt. On February 6, 1934, angry mobs and ambitious leagues assailed the Chamber of Deputies, and the guards opened fire. The government of the day resigned, and Gaston Doumergue, hero of the rioters, formed a "national-union" cabinet. "*Pour une constituante!*" and "*A Versailles!*" became the monotonous war cries of French politics. Basic reforms were demanded by all parties and conceded by none. When after nine months in office Doumergue merely moved to move proposals for reform, his cabinet fell apart. Beginning in 1936 a Popular Front government, acting under pressure from labor unions, pushed through parliament a series of social and economic reforms. Its demand for full financial powers, however, met with the intransigence of the Senate, despite clamorous demonstrations in the streets. The Popular Front broke up; the politics of shifting majorities resumed. Then in 1938 the chambers, deadlocked, granted a ministry the authority to govern for three months by decree laws. This ministry undid some of the work of the Popular Front, then broke a general strike of protest. The chambers, in gratitude, twice extended their grant, and in 1940 they invested a new government indefinitely with full legislative power. Thus in the end they went from one extreme to the other—although still refusing, as a matter of republican orthodoxy, to tamper with the "Constitution of 1875."

Their move, for what it was worth, came too late: the prolonged crisis had left France too weak to resist the onslaught of Hitlerism.

After the First World War the Third Republic lost pace with the changing wants and needs of the nation. It failed to put to good use the many resources at its disposal; it relinquished bit by bit what France had gained by the treaty of peace; it resisted reform in the face of the nearly unanimous demands of the people—and of parliament. The vices of the system were older than the war; before the war, however, they had been less evident than afterwards, and they had mattered less.

For these vices to be seen truly, they must be seen at work in the lives of particular men. For them to be seen at all, though, they must first be seen disembodied—in abstractions and generalities, hazy as these may be. And for them to be seen in proper perspective, they should be seen at work in the lives of men active on behalf of the Republic and yet at odds with it—of men whose relationship with it was one of continual tension, of mutual attraction and repulsion. To understand and judge such lives wholly is also to understand and judge the Third Republic as a whole.

The political structure of the Third Republic rested upon the omnipotence of the legislative assemblies.

The tradition of republican thought in France derives originally from Rousseau and the Jacobins rather than from Locke and Montesquieu. According to this tradition, there is no virtue and much danger in the separation of powers.[3] Sovereignty of the people is one and indivisible; the national assembly is its sole depository, the representation and embodiment of the will of the people. The national assembly is therefore itself incapable of abusing power, and only by holding a monopoly of power can it ever insure against such abuse. Even a second assembly was undesirable: the republicans accepted the Senate in 1875 only on the understanding that it would be subservient to the Chamber. Indeed, it *was* subservient until the 1930's, and then, when it made a practice of overthrowing governments, it drew throngs of howling republicans to its doors. Yet whatever the rivalry between them, the two chambers, in so far as they were composed of republicans, were as one in refusing to tolerate the existence of any political power other than their own.

In this refusal the republicans were guided by history as well as by theory, but if they neglected some of the lessons of theory, they also misread most of the lessons of history. Having seen injustice committed by strong governments throughout the nineteenth century, they thought to guarantee the rights of man by keeping the government weak. Seeing the executive power as a potential instrument of oppression, they failed to see it as a potential agency of welfare. The notions of the spirit of laws and of the grandeur and continuity of the state were equally alien to them: to their way of thinking, the law was a creature of the sovereign discretion of the assemblies, and the state their continual improvisation.

If the republicans in the chambers would not admit an independent executive, neither would they invest any government of the day with their confidence: their "votes of confidence" were figurative of their attitude of defiance. So anxious were they to prevent the abuse of power that in the process they did not mind preventing its use; the disuse of power, however, is often the worst abuse of power. "We were in the opposition for so long that we think we are still there," complained Waldeck-Rousseau in 1899;[4] they still thought so even when they had been out of it more than twice as long. Having an inveterate aversion for strong government, they also had one for strong personalities; if Waldeck-Rousseau told them *we* think what *I* know is not so, the solecism was a concession to their cult of impersonality. Wishing power to be exercised exclusively in their sight and under their control, they had the same abhorrence of independent power outside parliament as of occult power behind the government; after about 1900 the most abhorrent, because the most potent, agencies of such power were "high finance" and the "independent press."

Not only as republicans did the republican deputies and senators defend the concentration of powers in the chambers; they did so also as members of the chambers. To strengthen the government would have meant to diminish the power of each member of the chambers. Few ever had an even chance of benefiting by the change, and those few were in a poor position to propose it.

For the people of France, popular sovereignty was the choice legacy of the Revolution; on the other hand, they did not so much cherish representative government as did their representatives. In this the people were closer than their representatives to the teachings of Rousseau, who held the delegation of sovereignty to be the very negation of democracy. Reading the lessons of history after their own fashion, they considered elective chambers to be fully as capable of perverting the will of the nation as single individuals were of realizing its effective expression. And frequently they took as their idols men who stood in defiance of parliament —wherefore after the Boulanger affair parliament, in order to guard against the perversity of the electorate, put an end to the possibility of a deputy's holding more than one seat in the Chamber.

Despite their monopoly of political power the chambers often failed to govern effectively, especially in times of emergency. Two factors together account for their failure: their system of majority rule and their political composition.

Theoretically a government might have sought the support of any majority on each matter of policy in turn, thereby maintaining its independence with regard, if not to the chambers themselves, at least to the various groups in the chambers, while also respecting as closely as possible the will of the electorate. Instead the practice developed—perhaps inevitably, given the interests of the groups as such—of governments' relying for support on some one specific majority. A new government would bid for the confidence of the Chamber on the basis of a full statement of policy, its *déclaration ministérielle*. If a majority gave it a vote of confidence, that majority thereby tacitly contracted to stand by it in return for its standing by its policy as declared. Thereafter, as new issues arose, the government would ask for a new vote of confidence whenever the outcome was doubtful. If it lost the vote, it would resign. If it won, it would remain in office—unless some support from outside its majority had been decisive. In this case it might, of course, attempt to transform the circumstantial majority into a new *majorité de gouvernement*, but to do so would be to defy the dissenters from its old majority, and in this the others would most likely refuse to follow it. Hence generally it would resign instead. In effect, then, the government was responsible before the groups composing its majority, and in practice its policy was the product of their tenuous and fragile compromises on some issues and of their tacit agreement to overlook others.

Why was a stable and coherent *majorité de gouvernement* so difficult to constitute? The answer involves two complex facts about the usual political composition of the chambers: first, the smallness of any one group or faction and great divergence of opinion from one to the next; second, the roughly equal strength of the "right" and the "left" and the basic antagonism between the two. The first fact was an obstacle to the formation of any *majorité de gouvernement*. The second was a further obstacle to the formation of such a majority in the center, the collateral obstacle to its formation on the one side or on the other being the extremists' natural vocation to intransigence.

The distinction between "right" and "left" was fundamental in the political discourse of the Third Republic. In general terms, the right stood for conservation, the left for transformation; the right was the party of the old order (with the emphasis on *order*), the left the party of the new order (with the emphasis on *new*); those who were willing to let well enough alone were on the right, those who were not were on the left. When the Republic was young, to accept the great Revolution whole—as Clemenceau put it—was to be on the left. As time went by, though, Frenchmen who did not see any further than the great Revolution were pushed over to the right by Frenchmen who did. The rallying cry of the left remained nonetheless constant after 1877, when Gambetta first uttered it in the Chamber: *"Le cléricalisme, voilà l'ennemi!"* Secularization of the state was clearly a break with the old order. Certain other crucial differences between left and right did not, however, proceed quite so clearly from definition. For instance, in 1913 some Frenchmen were willing to trust to the future to restore Alsace-Lorraine to France, while others were willing to give the future some help. The first were on the left; the second were on the right.

Though every Frenchman was either on the left or on the right, some Frenchmen were also in the center, and others were also on the extreme left or on the extreme right. In fact, despite the fundamental antagonism between left and right, the most moderate deputies on either side of the Chamber were inclined to draw together and from a majority in the center—a *majorité de concentration*. There were several reasons for this inclination; all of them were arguments in its favor. The moderates on either side were by temperament better suited to work with the moderates on the other side than with the extremists on their own side. Furthermore, the extremists themselves generally refused to share in the exercise of power at the price of compromise; they wanted all or nothing—that is, nothing now and all later. Besides, the closer to the midpoint of the Chamber the "axis of the majority" fell, the less violent was the opposition on either side, and the more it canceled out. Consequently this formula seemed to the deputies in the center to be the geometrical equivalent of the will of the people. They might have been able to apply it had not the electoral laws and practices of the Third Republic interfered.

Under the traditional electoral system of the Third Republic, the *scrutin uninominal à deux tours*,[5] one deputy was elected from each precinct. A majority was necessary for election on the first ballot; if no candidate got a majority, a second ballot was held, and then a plurality was sufficient. When the Republic was young and insecure, "republican discipline" came into use: in the event of a second ballot all but the strongest one of the republican candidates would withdraw in favor of that one. By the time the danger to the Republic was past, withdrawal in favor of the strongest candidate had become standard practice on the right as well as on the left. Except in one case: extremist candidates would refuse to withdraw in favor of any outgoing deputy who in the Chamber had drawn too close to the other side—or, if they did withdraw, their electors would not follow their lead. But the occasion for such refusal was a rare one, as usually any deputy having so compromised himself would be outdistanced on the first ballot by some extremist on his own side. Thus the tendency was for moderate deputies to be replaced by extremists if they did not themselves become extremists, a tendency the more pronounced since senior moderate deputies were favored candidates for the Senate.

As an alternative to the *scrutin uninominal* a form of proportional representation was used in France twice after the First World War.[6] This system provided for the representation of parties in proportion to the relative number of votes polled by each of them on a single ballot. Its adoption left the parties with little incentive to compromise at election time or at any other time, and its effect was to increase the number of opinions represented in the Chamber while leaving the antagonism between right and left intact.

The majority system in use in the chambers might have worked more efficiently had deputies been elected individually, by plurality, on a single ballot. The interest of the two sides would then have been to put up one candidate each, and as moderate a one as possible; the parties on each side would consequently have tended to merge, and the antagonism between the two sides to subside.[7] Ordinarily, however, even moderates shied away from the two-party system, maintaining that its adoption in France would lead not to pacification but to civil war, and that the representation of a broad range of opinions in parliament is, for better of for worse, a special requirement of democracy in France. Perhaps. Indeed there is no telling to what extent electoral laws reflect the political temperament of a people and to what extent they determine it.

Many effects of the majority system were in their turn obstacles to its functioning. Perhaps the most nefarious of these was what might be called the "politicalization" of all policy. No matter how technical the issue, and often purely arbitrarily, every point of policy found its precise place somewhere in the political hemicycle from the extreme right to the extreme left[8]—or, if it did not find its place, it did not stand a chance. In 1913, to build barracks was on the right, to make machine guns was on the left. In the 1920's, fixed defenses were on the right, mobile defenses were on the left. In the early 1930's, to arm was on the right, to disarm was on the left; to arm the League of Nations, however, was nowhere— and when the proposal was made, no party took it seriously. In 1930, to finance public works by means of national loans was on the left, to finance them by means of Treasury funds was in the center, and to finance them by means of the regular budget was on the right; the public works bill failed. Sometimes, it is true, a proposal found support in diverse sectors of the Chambers; such proposals were, however, most often ones involving not policies of government but interests of groups or deputies as such—proportional representation, for instance, which set the small par-

ties against the large. Because new proposals had to find a political location in order for them to be taken up at all, when they were taken up
they were judged first according to their political location and then only,
if ever, on their merits. As for old proposals, they encountered not judg-
ments but reflexes instead. Like every proposal, every deputy too had to
fit in somewhere in order to be taken seriously. As a matter of professional
necessity, for a deputy to be a proponent of income tax in the years after
1900 was for him to be a proponent of state ownership of railways as
well, whereas for him to be strongly anticlerical and nationalistic at once
meant his winning the reputation of a political schizophrenic.

If its practitioners brought out the worst in the system, the system in
turn brought out the worst in its practitioners. All too often they thought
that, freedom of speech being a good, the more freely they spoke the
better; in this they were misled by the famous words of Clemenceau,
"Praise be to countries where men speak! Shame on countries where men
are silent!" All too often they confused the will of the people with the
wishes of their constituents; wrote Alain, himself normally the apostle of
precinct politics: "We asked for statesmen and we got districtmen."[9] All
too often they made of the principle of equality an injunction to despise
superiority of any kind; their motto might well have been the words of
the Ephesians of whom Heraclitus wrote: "They have cast out Hermodorus, the best man among them, saying, 'We will have none who is best
among us; if there be any such, let him be so elsewhere and among
others.'" There were a few such among them; these few fared no better
than did Hermodorus. Their story is, in miniature, the story of the failure
of the Third Republic.

Joseph Caillaux, Henry de Jouvenel, and André Tardieu each had
choice qualifications for serving the Third Republic; each had also choice
qualifications for suffering from it. All were men of strong personality.
All were also by instinct men of the center, men of moderation and balance, as much attached to the past as they were open to the future. All
were independents, refusing to submit to the discipline of coalition
politics; they never worked for France with more spirit than when they
worked farthest from the scrutiny of the chambers—in negotiating, for
instance. They were all enemies of what Jouvenel called *le train des choses*—
the drift of things—which by the time of their political maturity
held ordinary republicans in thrall; they were perpetually thinking,
planning, scheming. All three had attachments to high finance or the
independent press before entering parliament and kept them afterwards.

Finally they had, besides their superiority, the sense of their superiority.

They were all three, though aristocratic by temperament, democratic by conviction. They made their debuts in politics as Dreyfusards, in the entourage of Waldeck-Rousseau himself: Caillaux as his Minister of Finance, Tardieu as his political secretary, Jouvenel as secretary-general of a syndicalist group under his patronage. They too, for a brief moment, felt unbounded confidence in the future of France under the Republic. Although they remained republicans thereafter, they were not to find their place within the Third Republic. Often, inevitably, they came into conflict with it—rejecting it, being rejected by it, sometimes both at the same time. Usually when they came into conflict with it they were acting to make good its deficiencies. Such conflict was the more frequent for their being all three devoted to the interests of the nation over and above the interests of the regime.

Each of them was born into one of the ruling classes; each spent his childhood shut up in a small world of family tradition. But each class and each world was different. Birth made Caillaux a provincial bourgeois, Tardieu a Parisian bourgeois, Jouvenel a lord of the manor. Family tradition pointed the way for Caillaux to public service, for Tardieu to the liberal professions, for Jouvenel to versatile amateurism. And each life was different, for each man had his own way of living.

Joseph Caillaux lived rashly at first, intent on a great future for France and himself, hurrying toward it, never looking back. Men stood aside for him; he took their standing aside for granted. His sins of pride were numerous; he was made to pay for them all—and exorbitantly. Afterwards, to right the balance, men stood aside for him again; by then, however, he had lost the knack of looking forward, and his last years he spent mostly in brooding. In a life such as his, in which retribution was exacted to the full, nothing is too trivial to matter. In fact Caillaux suffered most for things not otherwise worth mentioning.

Henry de Jouvenel lived graciously. He had charm and intelligence to spare, and he had talent and taste for many occupations. Especially for politics—yet he remained all his life on the very periphery of the Republic. His ideals in politics were magnanimity and unanimity. Because he would take power on no other terms, he set himself up instead, after the Roman model, as the censor of the Republic, overseeing the manners and morals of its citizenry, holding up to it standards beyond its reach. He also became its prodigious errandboy, carrying out for it extraordinary missions abroad. And he went on biding his time.

André Tardieu led a charmed life—up to a point. An intellectual colossus, with a capacity for work almost beyond belief, he strode through a third of a century of history wielding more power over the Republic than its constitution-makers had ever dreamed of. At first he wielded his power clandestinely, to the horror of the republicans; later he wielded it openly, again to their horror. He sought nothing less than to renovate France and to reform the Republic. He came close to succeeding; his failure was all the greater, and his fate the more terrible.

Thus to tell the story of these three men properly is not merely to show how the Third Republic worked but to tell a good deal of its history. Indeed, in the life of the Republic after 1900 there were few important events in which they did not take part, few important concerns they did not feel, few important men or institutions they did not know. Nonetheless these are life stories first and foremost, and so they must be told individually and more or less chronologically. The study of Tardieu is the longest, as his public life was the most active; the study of Jouvenel is correspondingly the shortest.

PART I

Joseph Caillaux
on the Brink of the Rubicon

"I couldn't kill the Republic. Joseph will."
Remark attributed to Eugène Caillaux, quoted in [anonymous], *Ceux qui nous mènent.*

CHAPTER 1

"My Ministry"

JOSEPH CAILLAUX was the son of Eugène Caillaux, a civil servant who became a minister, then a political outcast. Eugène was a state engineer for twenty-five years, the last eight or ten of them in the region of the Sarthe, the home of his ancestors. There in 1870, when the Second Empire turned liberal, he was elected town councilor for Le Mans. One year later he entered the National Assembly. He was a republican until the Paris Commune rose in arms; then, counter to the trend of the times, he lost faith in the capacity of a republican regime to preserve France from chaos. He joined the Orleanists, he began to attend mass, and early in 1874 President MacMahon named him Minister of Public Works. He was a skilled technician, and he revered the state; but he had small taste and no talent for politics, being obstinate and—"like his father," wrote Joseph[1]—overbearing; he worked well alone, administered poorly, governed not at all. For two years he held office, while the Republic was founded; he stepped down a senator. On May 16, 1877, he was made Finance Minister by the duc de Broglie, whom President MacMahon took as chief minister after dismissing a cabinet on his own initiative. For six months the *seize mai* government held power in despite of the Chamber; then it was defeated at the polls. Like its other members, Eugène Caillaux never outlived the threat of trial for treason. He also came under suspicion for having, when Minister of Public Works, submitted a faulty estimate of costs in recommending the Louvre as the site of the Cour des Comptes. Again and again the Chamber voted to prosecute him, but the Senate could find no statute to invoke against him, and in 1887 the two houses settled for a vote of censure. By then he had lost his seat in the Senate and had tried once in vain to reenter the lower house. Later he broke with his party over its support of General Boulanger, and in 1892 he gave up all but one of his local offices to become president of the Paris–Lyon–Mediterranean Railway. The one he kept was the mayoralty of Yvré-l'Evêque, a village in the Sarthe department. No one there seems to have minded or even noticed when, as a septuagenarian, he became a republican again.

Eugène Caillaux's first child was born in Le Mans on March 30, 1863 —
Easter Monday. Being a boy, it was called Joseph and baptized a Catholic.
Every firstborn Caillaux was either a Joseph or a Joséphine: Eugène's
grandfather had signed grandly *"Caillaux l'aîné"* ("Caillaux the eldest")
on the ground that his given name was understood.[2] This former royal
notary had speculated in confiscated land after 1789, and the Revolutionary Tribunal by trying and acquitting him had in effect given its sanction
to his huge profits. The eldest of his ten children, Eugène's father, lived
carelessly but married well, affording Eugène the means to fall in love
with Madame Edouard Girard, *née* Cécile Anna Donnet, a wealthy widow,
heiress of several bankers. Although she was a pious Protestant, Eugène
wished to remain in good standing as a Catholic: they were married in
1860, when both their churches agreed to their having only Protestant
daughters and Catholic sons. She brought him two children from her
first marriage, and in 1864 she bore him a second son, Paul.

At first Joseph's childhood was much the same as that of any rich man's
son in the provinces: he had a trip to the seashore and one to Paris every
year, piano lessons and drawing lessons, a governess to care for him with
a whole family of austere and idle women to second her. As for the differences: his governess spoke English to him, and the women on his mother's
side taught him pride in his Huguenot forefathers who, suffering exile for
their beliefs, had won the Lord's bounty in England. He took the differences to heart: he learned Anglomania even as he learned to walk, and he
grew up craving convictions of his own to suffer for.

He was not yet eight years old when France was invaded and defeated.
The invasion meant for him a prolonged holiday in Brittany, the defeat
a trip to Bordeaux and thence to Versailles. There Eugène Caillaux
engaged a tutor for his two sons, and whenever he went home to Le Mans
he would take them and their tutor along with him. Early in 1874 the
family moved into the suite reserved in Versailles Palace for the Minister
of Public Works. Joseph was by then too big to be (as was later said of
him) "brought up in the laps of duchesses";[3] he did, however, make
friends with the sons of dukes, especially with Elie Decazes, whose
father was Foreign Minister. And he learned to be himself with his play-
mates: "If we played soldiers," recalled one of them, "he wanted to be
general. If we played stagecoach, he wanted to be driver."[4] He and his
brother began school at the Lycée Fontanes.[5] To keep them busy between
classes their father engaged—on the recommendation of Monsignor
Dupanloup, the conscience of the center right—a Jesuit forty-five years
old, "long and sad as a cypress, knotty as an olive tree, his face marred

with the pockmarks of fanaticism."[6] For four years the new tutor strove to infect Joseph with his fanaticism; wrote Joseph, "He got the opposite result."[7] Meanwhile in desperation he taught Joseph the humanities.

The humanities, though, were for Jesuits and children, thought Joseph. Grown-ups talked *politics*—and he listened to them at his father's table and eavesdropped on them in his father's drawingroom. He leapt for joy when the duc de Broglie asked Eugène Caillaux's help in maintaining the Moral Order, and the Ministry of Finance became the favorite home of his childhood. After his father was dismissed, he received a vicarious taste of persecution and overheard much bitter talk of how low France was sinking under the Republic. "Why," he wondered, as an old man, "when I think of my dear departed parents, do they appear to me so often against the background of the apartment in the Louvre, which after all they merely passed through in 1877, whereas I just about never see them in the Ministry of Public Works, where we lived so much longer?"[8]

Soon after leaving the Louvre, Joseph entered a boarding school run by secular priests, the Ecole Fénelon, even while continuing to attend the Lycée Fontanes. For seven years he drank a double dose of Greek and Latin, of history and rhetoric. Always among the best in his classes, he was never quite the best.

For a while after getting his baccalaureate he was in danger of becoming an engineer. His father made him enter a preparatory school for the Ecole Polytechnique, and for one year a Jesuit faculty hammered formulas into him. Already sick of clericalism, he now sickened of scientism as well: all his later nightmares took him back to what he called "the rollingmill on the rue des Postes."[9] He passed the written entrance examination, then more or less deliberately failed the oral. His father wanted him next to try the Ecole des Mines; Joseph pleaded well, and went his own way instead. He moved into the Latin Quarter. There he attended the Ecole de Droit and the Ecole des Sciences Politiques; he wrote a few novels, and one or two of them were published; he painted and was painted. Of his subjects he liked economics best—Professor Leroy-Beaulieu taught him that the most economical tax was a tax on wealth, and he never forgot his lesson. In 1886 he received his law degree, and his father summoned him to choose a career.

He chose the Inspection des Finances. Léon Say, who had been Eugène's colleague at Versailles, helped him to prepare for the state examination and recommended him to the Minister. Say also found him a job as clerk in the Caisse des Dépôts et Consignations, and he worked there two years. In 1887 he came out fourth in the competitive examination for the Inspection des Finances—there were, however, only two positions to be filled. The following year he was second and became Deputy Inspector; two years later, after taking a new test, he was promoted to Inspector.

The Inspection des Finances, created by Napoleon I as a kind of public accountants' pool, had come to specialize in fiscal administration. Inspectors audited public accounts in the capital for part of the year; for the rest they toured the country in teams of six or eight, peering into local ledgers, ferreting out errors and fraud. Caillaux got to know what he called the "living administration" of France[10]—men who assessed taxes or who collected them, receivers, controllers, and customs agents. He also got to know the taxes themselves. They were "ineffectual, disparate, and fragmentary."[11] Indirect taxes flourished in wild profusion; the few direct ones struck hard and redundantly at landed wealth, tapped at revenues from some forms of commerce, and all but ignored industry. Two taxes were personal: one on rent, and one—which Caillaux called a tax on hygiene[12]—on doors and windows. The total tax yield, fluctuating from year to year, tended to increase not with national income but with the numbers of persons and of buildings.

Because everyone spoke of reforming the taxes, no one except fiscal agents bothered much to get to know them. In collaboration with two of his colleagues Caillaux began compiling a compendium of taxes for general use; the first volume came out in 1896. Meanwhile, beginning in 1893, he gave a course at the Ecole des Sciences Politiques to prospective finance inspectors. In the capital he lived with his parents, and he chose what friends he had in his parents' milieu. He formed a few *liaisons élégantes* as a pretext for remaining a bachelor, and he frequented one or two salons where literature and politics still mixed. He expressed no political opinions—he may have had none, or he may have been a republican already. He cut a prim and sober figure, except for a pair of woolly poodles perpetually tagging after him. Away from home, on tours of inspection, his manners were different: "He would throw his weight around a little as an agent of the Minister, standing in the main square of some subprefecture to hold up carts transporting alcohol and check the drivers' papers."[13]

Eugène Caillaux died of overwork in 1896, at the age of seventy-four, and Joseph made his debut in politics running to succeed him as mayor of Yvré-l'Evêque; he lost the election. The following year he went to Algeria to audit accounts. Everything Algerian enchanted him except the taxes. He drew up a project for reforming them, and in his spare time he explored the Casbah under the guidance of a petty customs official, François Desclaux. Early in 1898 the republicans of Mamers offered to nominate him for deputy. As they had not won an election yet under the Republic, they saw their only hope in a name like Caillaux. Desclaux persuaded him to rush home and refuse. He left, and on the way he did what he later called "something foolish":[14] he wrote promising the veteran royalist deputy from Mamers, the duc de la Rochefoucauld-Doudeauville, not to run against him and in return won the assurance of succeeding the Duke when the time came. Acceptable to the royalists, he was all the more acceptable to their opponents. Two weeks before the ballot he succumbed to a barrage of petitions and became a Moderate Republican, whereupon his brother Paul, already a retired officer, attacked him publicly for betraying their father's friends. Joseph declared for "No new taxes," "Neither reaction nor revolution," "Order and progress in the Republic." The slogans, rephrased, might have been the Duke's; Joseph kept them all his life. He spoke of economies for France; he hinted at favors for Mamers. He did not mention the Dreyfus affair, which Mamers was not yet fighting, nor did he promise social reforms, which peasants shunned as schemes for fleecing them. He won on the first ballot, some two thousand royalist voters—about one tenth of the electorate—having gone over to his side. "They thought they were voting for his father," whispered the losers.

Soon after the elections Joseph's mother reconciled her two sons, though for her part she was sorry to see Joseph mixed up in *"cette horrible politique."*[15] Some weeks later she died; Paul died two years afterwards. These deaths left Joseph with no close relatives.[16] They also left him with one million francs.[17] He kept the sum intact; he also kept it from growing. A full million, it was to be a badge of distinction; still a full million, a mark of frugality; still only a million, a proof of integrity.

During his first year in parliament Caillaux felt his way cautiously. He sat with the Progressive Republican group in the center. He avoided all political issues but one: when a letter incriminating Captain Dreyfus was produced he voted with the majority to uphold the verdict, and when the letter proved to be a forgery he voted with the new majority to reopen the case. His working time was spent mainly with the Commission for Credits and the Commission for Fiscal Legislation. Maurice Rouvier, who chaired both commissions, soon singled him out to make the interesting reports. Once he was asked to review proposals for introducing the income tax into France: he found them all chimerical. Whenever he spoke, whether in formal debate or in informal discussion, he did so with poise and restraint. He had a few old friends among the deputies on the right; he made a few new ones where he sat, among them Louis Barthou and Raymond Poincaré.

One evening he toasted Waldeck-Rousseau at a banquet and elicited a smile from that solemn jurist, to whom thereafter he paid discreet court. He was secretary to one or two commissions when in July, 1899, premier-designate Waldeck-Rousseau, who "gathered around himself anything and everything he thought capable of restoring order in a threatened Republic,"[18] chose him for Minister of Finance. The Socialist Alexandre Millerand, Minister of Commerce, was at one extreme of the cabinet; at the other extreme were Caillaux and the old aristocrat General Galliffet, Minister of War. Caillaux got a fair press on the left even though he was a novice and his name was against him. His critics were indifferent rather than indulgent, for the government was not meant to last beyond the summer recess. It won a small margin of confidence, the center abstaining. It held power three years.

Rising for the first time as minister to address the Chamber, Caillaux was greeted by applause on the left and by shouts of "Deserter!" on the right. The judgment was premature. In office he continued to avoid politics. When politics intruded on public finance, he responded as a conservative: he opposed a motion to end subsidies to religious bodies, for instance, and another to found a state monopoly on oil. And he was, then and always, an orthodox financier. He was something more besides: as the German Ambassador wrote to the German Chancellor, "He is what his predecessors were not, a specialist. His budget is said to be a master-piece."[19] By a coincidence in dates the Ministry of Finance had devolved upon him along with rest of his patrimony. Quite naturally he took to regarding the public treasury as his own greater purse. He meant to keep the one purse as solvent as the other; better, he meant to prove that the state, like Joseph Caillaux, being rich, could afford to live modestly. Accordingly, he sought to "unify" the budget (that is, to fit it into a single ledger),[20] and to compress and balance it "to the last sou."[21] However, fiscal receipts were as difficult to regulate as were public expenditures, both because the indirect taxes were so many and because the direct taxes, being discriminatory, could not decently be increased. Further, parliament made matters worse year after year by finding new expenditures to dispose of any surplus and new taxes to dispose of any deficit.

To discourage the chambers from voting new appropriations, Caillaux inflated the sinking fund beyond the requirements of the budget, thereby

creating a deficit on paper. As for controlling receipts, he favored simplifying the indirect taxes, and he came to favor replacing them gradually
by a uniform tax on all components of income. By taxing only income at
the source, he reasoned, the state would be able to adjust its receipts
accurately to its needs in the short run, while in the long run the nation
would pay more as it earned more, not as more buildings were built or
babies born; besides, if all income were taxed uniformly at the source,
no one trade or industry would be at a disadvantage with respect to the
others at home or to its competitors abroad. Now, a tax on all incomes is
the equivalent of a tax on all components of income; it is also a shortcut
in a country like the France of Caillaux, where most men were merchants
and peasants, and most merchants and peasant were petty shareholders.
However, most merchants and peasants in the France of Caillaux did not
keep business accounts, and those who did would not confide in their
own brother, much less in the *fisc*. Caillaux drew up a project for an income tax involving the assessment of whole personal income by tax
officials, the taxpayers being entitled to declare their income in protest.
He soon realized, however, that in no time this direct tax on income would
resolve itself into an indirect tax on the items selected as a basis for its
assessment. Besides, in taxing whole incomes rather than income at the
source, the state would be dealing not with large sums and small, but
with rich men and poor; thus the problem was not alone technical, but
also social and political. The income tax was best known in France not
as a potential instrument of fiscal administration but as a potential weapon
of class war. The working classes hoped to make it progressive and so
to wipe out their inequality with the bourgeoisie; the bourgeoisie, however, would sooner risk letting the workers wipe *them* out, while the
peasants for their part were averse to the tax because it was a tax and,
even more, because it was an indiscretion. The Chamber, after having
once accepted the tax in theory, had so far avoided voting on any specific
form of it. The line of political division ran through the Radical party,
which kept class war out of its ranks only by means of a tacit agreement
to accept the tax in any form but to reject all measures for enforcing it.[22]
Caillaux was not prepared to take sides: whenever someone in the
Chamber called for *the* income tax he would ask mischievously, which
one? He drew up his project halfheartedly, as much to exercise his technique as to placate a part of the majority; Waldeck-Rousseau was glad to
have it studied in commission so long as it got no farther. One day in
July, 1901, a voice on the left asked the Minister of Finance to force a
vote on his project by writing it into the next budget. He replied in effect

that the time was not ripe, and won a large vote of confidence. Then, over the signature *"Ton Jo,"* he wrote to his mistress, Madame Jules Dupré, "I crushed the income tax while seeming to defend it." He too neglected to say which one. "Perhaps," he later conceded, "there was just a little foolishness, a little frivolity in my life at the time."[23]

Uncertain how to go about reforming the tax system, he began by touching it up. He transferred to alcohol a tax formerly levied on the alcoholic content of wine, beer, and cider. He canceled a sales tax on sugar and an equivalent subsidy to sugar exports, having first persuaded the rest of Europe to do the same. He ushered in the first progressive tax in France—an inheritance tax, which he had found languishing in one of the commissions: he withdrew it by decree for immediate debate and, with as much roughness of manner as prudence of mind, fought off attempts to magnify the scale of contributions. He also put through the colonial office his plan for a tax reform in Algeria. Bur not only did he do something about taxes; he also spoke about them—sublimely. No one since Turgot had made the subject seem so respectable, nor spiced it with so many Latin phrases.

Foreign trade and foreign loans, too, took up his attention. He fought for free trade, and to the great delight of Italy he removed the tariff from foreign wines; he even tried to exempt them first from the tax on alcoholic content, then from a sales tax he later put in its place.[24] On the advice of the Foreign Minister, Delcassé, he refused a loan to Rumania,[25] encouraged investment in the Ethiopian Railroad,[26] favored a loan to Russia,[27] and made no commitments for a loan to Serbia.[28] Without the advice of Delcassé he opposed a loan to Bulgaria, and great was the annoyance in Saint Petersburg.[29] Throughout he bore himself sedately: to one woman in love with him, he always looked "like a professor going to give his course at *Sciences Po*."[30] While he was Minister many post offices opened in Mamers, and (as was natural) some functionaries from his district advanced more rapidly than others. He was reelected in 1902 by a large majority.

The new Chamber of 1902 was predominantly Radical, with a strong contingent of Socialists eager to help push the Radical program through in order to clear the way for their own. The separation of church and state had been put off so long that it was certain to be brutal. Waldeck-Rousseau and his ministers resigned, leaving their posts free for men who had made a career of priest-baiting. Caillaux too made way for a successor, and as he did so he felt stirring within him for the first time, ever so faintly, the demon of the Rubicon. "It was painful to me, I admit it straight out," he later wrote,

to leave the Ministry of Finance—"my ministry," as I was to call it from then on. I was not sorry to give up my *title*—oh, no, I was quite glad to get my freedom back. I was sorry to leave the *building*. I had spent a few months of my childhood in it, only a few—but at that happy age anything, beginning with the trivialities of everyday life, will make a lasting impression on the mind. When I returned to the Louvre twenty-two years after leaving it, I felt as though I were in my own home again; I recognized the rooms, the paintings, the very furnishings; I went so far as to hunt out a set of books that had been stored away in the attic and whose absence disturbed me.[31]

For nearly four more years Caillaux devoted himself to the problem of fiscal reform, taking small part in the other work of parliament. In 1903 he completed his study *Les Impôts en France*. In a long preface[32] he showed the vanity of any attempt to explain his subject except by "the historical method." "Taxation is linked to the history of a country,"[33] he wrote, hinting at the converse. The Revolution was fought as much over fiscal duties as over human rights, he maintained. After abolishing the old taxes, however, the men of 1789 did not dare to base the new ones on income or wealth; instead they merely made the old exemptions general, declaring things and not persons taxable. At first the revolutionary governments lived on plunder; then they instituted a "single tax" on land, which became oppressive when the plunder gave out; in the end they restored one after another of the former indirect taxes. During the next century the masters of industry and finance, sheltered by the principles of the Revolution, became the new ruling class, and they revived for their own benefit the privileges of the old. They retained the tax on land, of course; whenever possible they enforced import duties, which were simply devices for enabling producers to levy "invisible taxes";[34] and they proliferated indirect taxes, which, being equal for all men, varied in effect inversely with the ability of each to pay.

A progressive tax on all income at the source, Caillaux argued, would not create an injustice, but redress one. He did not, however, make clear how progressive a tax must be in order for it to redress an injustice. "Graduation, without rules or limits, leads to spoliation,"[35] he wrote, disclosing no rules or limits. In fact, Caillaux was less proficient in arguing for just taxation than in arguing for orderly taxation. He argued for fiscal justice on the basis of the revolutionary principle of equality; however, fiscal justice is no nearer to the revolutionary principle of equality than it is to the arbitrary taxation of the Old Regime. Equal taxes are only a monotonous kind of arbitrary taxes: do men who are taxed equally pay equal sums of money? equal portions of their income, or of their fortune? or as much as they are equally reluctant to pay? This last is perhaps the most equitable of equal taxes; it is, however, impossible to assess. Further, all progressive taxation, if it is to redress anything, must affect the spread of net incomes. However, Caillaux did not say what the spread of net incomes should reflect if not, as the classical economists held, differences in the marginal utility of factors of production; nor did he consider to what extent the spread of gross incomes would adapt itself to a progressive scale of contributions, leaving the spread of net incomes unchanged. These omissions are the more notable since Caillaux was professedly a classical economist himself.

But what his arguments lacked in economics they gained in politics. He picked up where the men of 1789 had left off. He denounced the invisible privileges of "a category of citizens,"[36] himself a member of the category. *Privileges!* He had found a new battlecry for the Jacobins just as they were preparing to evict nuns from their convents and monks from their monasteries for want of loftier purpose.

If he had found a battlecry, though, one year later he was still hesitating over the choice of a weapon. Maurice Rouvier having proposed a tax on income as inferred from rent, Caillaux, in a remarkable speech on December 13, 1904, warned the Chamber against one more sales tax on rent. By way of demonstrating the historical necessity for some form of income tax, he traced taxation in France from the Roman occupation to his own administration. The option for France at the time, he maintained, was between the British tax on income at the source and the Prussian *Einkommensteuer;* the second was more apt to be proportional, but in France only the first was likely to be thorough.

After the enactment in 1905 of the final separation of church and state, its fiercer advocates relapsed into obscurity while the *rapporteur* of the law, the tactful anarchist Aristide Briand, stayed on to apply it. With parliament again safe for moderate republicans, Caillaux took part in its debates, speaking on the merchant marine and on the Congo. Again he was available for *his* ministry, and when Sarrien formed a government in April, 1906, everyone "expressed regret, apologized almost," that Poincaré was chosen instead.[37] In the elections a few weeks later Caillaux needed Briand's help to dissuade the Socialists from putting up a candidate against him, and even without an opponent on the left he came close to defeat. Republicans in Mamers were divided on the religious issue, so he had dodged it in parliament, dissatisfying the extremes. Also, he had satisfied only his conscience by voting to tax homemade wines like any other wines. And besides, for four years he had not been in the government; he did not make the same mistake again.

The new Chamber elected Caillaux Vice-President, and the "Democratic Left" (a new small group in the center) chose him for its president. Shortly afterwards, in August, 1906, Madame Berthe Eva Gueydan, the former Madame Jules Dupré, coaxed him into a *"mariage de résignation."*[38] She was a few years his senior, the mother of a grown son. For some years she had been his way of avoiding marriage; then by getting a divorce she had appealed mutely to his honor. He never forgave her his own weakness. Twenty-five years later he cited his nerves:

My life would doubtless have taken another course if at the end of 1905 I had not suffered from a nervous disorder that has recurred periodically but never again with the same violence. It was a real crisis, dragging on and on, aggravated by the irritation due to the 1906 elections. My natural mental unrest was all the greater. Having scruples, like any decent man...[39]

Georges Clemenceau, on becoming Premier in October, 1906, restored Caillaux to the Ministry of Finance. The satanic old Jacobin had entered the Senate four years earlier after first losing his seat in the Chamber during the Panama scandals, then making his name over again in journalism, particularly in defending Dreyfus against the *raison d'Etat*. He had taken his first cabinet post, the Ministry of the Interior, under Sarrien,[40] who had expected the governement to be safer with him on the inside. Now, as he took over from Sarrien, he knew well that if he needed wisdom to govern, he needed tricks to last. In order to keep the Socialists on his side he would let Caillaux propose an income tax; in order to discredit Socialism he would have Caillaux nationalize the Chemin de Fer de l'Ouest, which was operating at a loss; and in each case he would himself act reluctant on the appropriate side of the Chamber.

Caillaux fretted briefly over the railroad purchase; then, to make way for the income tax, he cleared his agenda of everything else. He put through an equal tax on all dividends, so ending the discrimination in favor of foreign stocks—and so losing the favor of the big banks of France. The government had purchased exceptional quantities of armaments during the Algeciras crisis of 1905; gambling—successfully, as it turned out—on a higher tax yield the next two years, he shelved a proposal of Poincaré's for floating a national loan to cover the expenses. To conciliate the staff of his ministry he decreed a mutual security fund for accountants along with an administrative code and an increase in pay for all. Beginning in December, 1906, he was busy encouraging a loan to Russia and discouraging one to Bulgaria as well as preventing French banks from dealing directly with the Bagdad Railway Company.[41]

His income-tax bill was ready by February, 1907. It combined the British system with the Prussian system: to a uniform tax on all income at the source was added a progressive tax on whole personal income as declared. The record of income at the source would provide the means for verifying the declarations of personal income, and the two taxes would be together both proportional and thorough. The cabinet endorsed the bill unanimously. On February 7 Caillaux, after first reading an explanatory statement, deposited it on the bureau of the Chamber. As he did so he set off a frenzy of applause on the left. He had found his political position, and the battle was on.

The Chamber set up a commission to study the bill, and there, day after day, Caillaux fought amendments, counteramendments, and motions to suspend, to interrupt, or to adjourn. He proposed to keep the tax on whole income low, as he had the tax on legacies some years back. He had to fight as hard on the one side to keep it down as he did on the other to keep it at all; in the first fight, however, he had the great help of Jaurès, who knew that any amount of a new thing is revolutionary.[42] For two years he took his bill back and forth through the lobbies between the commissions and the chambers. He took it to the magnates of high finance and the magnates of the press—to less than no avail: seeing a minister actually pushing the income tax, the magnates came out all the more strongly against it. Once he had refused to float a national loan because he preferred to count on surplus revenue; he would no longer even have the choice, for in pushing the income tax he lost his credit at the Bourse. From the first the independent newspaper publishers of the Republic had made a point of hailing the progress of democracy, and as democracy had progressed their private fortunes had escaped scrutiny. The income tax would have defeated their purpose. "Anything but," advised Bunau-Varilla, chief stockholder of Le Matin.[43]

Once the income tax was on the floor Caillaux watched his colleagues from on high: Maurice Barrès, after observing him without malice for the last time, noted in his diary on May 14, 1907, "Caillaux, former finance inspector, ransacks all the benches with his sharp glare, which used to rout out excess packages of tobacco and undeclared assets."[44] It was then, in fighting for his tax, that Caillaux first became his familiar self: his bald pate began to glow insolently, his shrill voice to sound petulantly, and his other accoutrements to fade to indistinctness besides his spats, cane, and monocle.

He did not battle full time. Early in 1908 he entertained the Italian Minister of Finance, Luzzatti, and negotiated with him a monetary convention.[45] Afterwards he went to Budapest and there drew up a project for a loan of 500,000,000 francs to Hungary. In July, atoning for his earlier offense to Bulgaria, he worked out the final terms of the loan to Russia,[46] and in September he took steps to place orders in France for the Russian fleet, which the loan was to finance.[47] He signed the convention with Luzzatti in Paris in November,[48] and then in February, 1909, he acted for his government in rejecting the Turkish state's request to the Ottoman Debt Commission for subsidies to the Bagdad Railway Company in the form of new customs duties.[49]

Clemenceau, however, and not routine, was the chief interference in Caillaux's fight for the income tax. The Premier lost the indulgence of the Socialist group when in 1908 he turned the militia on an army of disgruntled winegrowers from the south after having lighted lanterns to guide them in their march on the capital. All the more harassed by strikes thereafter, he was all the less hesitant in his choice of weapons. Even so he was sure of keeping his majority on the left so long as the income-tax bill was in suspense. Instead of putting the bill through, then, he put it off; he even hinted that he might drop it if it got too far, and so he made up on the right for what favor he had lost on the left. He used the same tactics in reverse with Briand, his Minister of Public Worship, who, after having steered the separation law through the chambers, was applying it so gently as to leave room for doubt whether he was applying it at all. The left charged Briand with inconsistency, and Clemenceau admitted the charge coquettishly. Clemenceau was constant at least, if not consistent: having made a career in the opposition by flirting with his bitterest adversaries, he went on doing the same as premier; having made fun of others' ministers for thirty-five years, he did not spare his own. Accused one day of doing nothing, "It's true," he replied, "but what can I do between Caillaux who thinks he's Napoleon and Briand who thinks he's Jesus Christ?"[50] On March 9, 1909, the Chamber voted to adopt the income tax and to post Caillaux's latest speech about it, and shortly afterwards the government fell in consequence of its own victory.

Caillaux thought the fight nearly over; in fact it had just begun. The Senate was to reject his project; he was to take it back to the commissions, then back to the Chamber, then back to the Senate, again and again. A few months after he had devised it, a conservative Parliament in Great Britain adopted one almost identical. But in France the income tax was on the left, and the right fought it in consequence. Outside parliament the fight against it was led by the Union of Metallurgical and Mining Industries, an offspring of the Comité des Forges which in 1910 created for this purpose the "Committee of Studies and of Fiscal Defense." Raymond Poincaré spoke at the first session of the committee, and thereafter he was its mainstay as well as its legal adviser.[51] In all, its donors probably spent as much in fighting the tax as they would have spent in paying it.

Caillaux had taken up the income tax for technical reasons. He had added reasons of equity for keeping it, though none of these took precedence over his reasons for keeping it at a minimum. Now, however, he had become the "income-tax man," and despite his origins, his ideas, his temperament, his very appearance, he was to follow his tax farther and farther to the left.

CHAPTER 2

Agadir

ARISTIDE BRIAND, designated Premier in July, 1909, invited Caillaux to stay on at the Ministry of Finance. Caillaux by way of refusal demanded the right to oversee expenditures in the other ministries, a right held by Controllers-General under the Old Regime. Briand had taken a "haughty tone of voice" in inviting him, Caillaux explained;[1] besides, Briand was a *politique* and he an *homme de gouvernement*, so the two were not meant to work together.[2] Their temperaments were in truth incompatible. "Briand would rather wait than break a single pane of glass," wrote Briand's biographer; "Caillaux, not to lose time, would smash whole hothouses."[3] Briand, on presenting his government to the chambers, attacked Caillaux's income-tax bill by failing to mention it. Caillaux asked Briand to Mamers for a few days in September—"We will be watching each other," he wrote.[4] Caillaux's absence from his ministry caused some confusion: a few months after his leaving it emissaries of the Greek government, which wanted to float a loan on the Bourse, approached him rather than his successor; he was noncommittal.[5] Meanwhile, a mere deputy again, he "had only to stoop and pick" an honorable avocation.[6] He became president of the Banco del Rio de la Plata and of two mortgage-loan societies, the Crédit Foncier Argentin and the Crédit Foncier Egyptien, with salaries adding up to more than half a million francs a year.[7]

He expected to need the money. A year earlier his butler had brought him, in his wife's presence, a love letter signed *Riri*. He had called it a hoax and cast it aside; she had picked it up and traced it to Madame Henriette Raynouard, previously Madame Léo Claretie. His wife made him confess, then forgave him. When the government fell in July he sent her to Switzerland, promising to join her shortly. She waited there one month. Before returning, she made a point of writing to Briand and not repeating the invitation to Mamers.[8] For a time Caillaux played hide-and-seek with her between Paris and Mamers. When at last she caught up with him in their apartment in Paris, they quarreled, and he made away again to Mamers. There she joined him at the end of September, after first announcing herself by registered mail. She broke into his desk and made off with a whole arsenal of his old letters to her and to Madame Raynouard—letters held by him for safekeeping, and whose precise contents he had forgotten. With elections only six months off he had no choice: he pleaded with her "on his hands and knees" for forgiveness,[9] and wrote to Madame Raynouard: "I give you back your freedom."[10] Fortunately his wife had taken the letters to prevent a divorce, not to obtain one: she consented to burn them all, asking only a writ of apology in return. This double ceremony was performed in the presence of a lawyer on the fifth day of November, 1909, and the following morning the couple left for Egypt—she openly exultant, he secretly. Madame Raynouard followed as far as Rome, the deeper in grief for having just lost her younger daughter. Caillaux wrote begging her to follow no more.

He was in the best of form for the elections. Faithful to his slogan "No new taxes," he defended the income tax to the peasants of the Sarthe as a device for untaxing land. Wrote a visiting reporter from the capital:

One of Caillaux's posters in his precinct bears the title "To My Enemies." He has put in the plural what should be in the singular. He does not have enemies. He has one enemy: himself. That enemy alone has stature and will doubtless play the worst of tricks on him.[11]

On April 25, 1910, he won on the first ballot, his margin greater than ever. He stayed the next week to help out friends less popular than he; then he went back to Paris and filed suit for a divorce.

Briand for his part managed to win the elections while feigning to ignore them. As Premier he extended "appeasement" from religion to politics, heralding a "truce of parties" and a "union of all citizens."[12] One by one the proprietors of the independent press came to his support, forming a shadow cabinet. Until the summer of 1910 Caillaux refrained from taking issue with him. Then, as acting chairman of the Budget Commission, he noticed, camouflaged in the budget for colonies, a payment of 2,393,000 francs to the N'Goko Sangha Company.

The N'Goko Sangha had been formed some years earlier to cultivate a region in the northern French Congo, but instead of cultivating its region it had busied itself suing the governement for not enforcing a customs barrier on the Cameroons frontier. Its suit seemed hopeless until February 8, 1909, when the French government undertook by treaty with Germany to "strive to associate [French and German] nationals" in commercial ventures in return for recognition by Germany of "the special political interests of France [in Morocco]."[13] At once the N'Goko Sangha negotiated a consortium with the German Südkamerun Company, formally sharing with it the privileges it had already usurped. Thereafter, while not actually invoking the treaty of 1909, the N'Goko Sangha pressed its old suit in a new spirit. By 1910 most of the press had a stake in the N'Goko Sangha claim, and Briand did not see fit to turn it down.

The Minister of Colonies having signed a contract for payment, Caillaux in September, 1910, had the Finance Commission declare payments in excess of 100,000 francs subject to the approval of the chambers; then, even as the N'Goko Sangha was discounting the contract privately, Caillaux had the Budget Commission open an investigation. Because parliament, before ratifying the indemnity, would have first to ratify the consortium, Caillaux denounced the consortium relentlessly in the corridors of the Chamber. The prospective partnership was unequal, he argued, since only the N'Goko Sangha's territory was involved; reciprocation was impossible, German colonial concessions being commercial and not territorial;[14] no sacrifice by France was in order, for the treaty of 1909 did not apply outside of Morocco. He was right about the treaty, strictly speaking; however, Briand hoped by encouraging joint ventures in the Congo to release the French government *de facto* from the obligation to encourage them in Morocco. Caillaux dismissed the hope as chimerical, and no doubt he was right again. Besides, even if the treaty were at stake he saw no good reason for saving it. Like most Frenchmen, he feared the Germans no less as merchants than as soldiers, and he did not trust them to distinguish commerce from politics in Morocco or anywhere else. France had bought off all other claimants to Morocco; France would do better, he thought, to buy out the Germans in Morocco with pieces of the Congo than to share Morocco *and* the Congo with them.

In 1909 the director of the N'Goko Sangha boasted of having "two hundred deputies and the whole press" behind him;[15] only the press and the government were faithful to him in 1910. Meanwhile, the policy of appeasement was discredited when the Premier, himself once an advocate of the general strike, put railway and postal employees under martial law to prevent them from striking. Caillaux spoke in Lille on January 8, 1911, stressing nothing in particular; his speech was interpreted as a bid to succeed Briand. After his speech he left for Egypt, where his friend Louis Barthou joined him. Both rushed home as Briand, having lost a few votes on clerical policy, seized this as a pretext to resign. Briand had not dared to submit the N'Goko Sangha consortium to parliament. "I like to think," mused Caillaux in his old age, "that he has since realized what an immense blunder he came close to making,"[16] whereas in 1918 Briand in his diary described Caillaux as "the real author of the war" for having disrupted the 1909 treaty by denouncing the N'Goko Sangha consortium in the corridors of the Chamber.[17]

In March, 1911, the President of the Republic, having three strong candidates for premier—Berteaux, Cruppi, and Caillaux—chose instead a colorless old judge, Senator Monis. While Berteaux became Minister of War and Cruppi Foreign Minister, Caillaux returned to the Ministry of Finance. Concurrently his divorce came through: the court ordered him to pay Madame Gueydan 200,000 francs outright and 18,000 francs a year as alimony.[18] Handing him the bill, his lawyer mentioned another client—Rochette, a financier accused of fraud, who wanted his trial put off long enough to prove his enterprises solvent. The state prosecutor had opposed Rochette's latest request for a postponement even though a certain newspaper most partial to Rochette had so far found no fault with the new government. Caillaux advised the Premier to have a word with the state prosecutor; then he turned his attention to serious matters.

He drew up a convention for a loan to Morocco, making provision in it for an increase in the control by France of the finances and the armed forces of the Moorish Empire.[19] The budget was overdue, and he was busy with it until the middle of April. He had time to make room in it for a single reform, limiting to one chief and two assistants the number of cabinet secretaries allowed to a minister. Meanwhile, the Council of Ministers unanimously voted down the N'Goko Sangha consortium. It also put an end to the negotiations with Germany for a joint railroad enterprise in Morocco by refusing to consider the participation of Germans on the staff. "France... would not stand for having German station-masters in Morocco," Caillaux insisted.[20] However, a secret annex to the treaty of 1909 had designated the posts that Germans were not to occupy in Morocco and so implicitly authorized them to occupy any other posts there. "The failure of the railroad negotiations opened my eyes," said Kiderlen-Wächter, the German Foreign Secretary.[21]

Caillaux went to England for Easter, "summoned," as he cryptically put it, "by a family obligation."[22] His second day away he read in the newspapers that a military expedition had left France to put down a revolt of the Sultan's troops in Fez. Berteaux and Cruppi had decided on the expedition several days earlier without consulting their colleagues. Their decision was dangerous. France was taking her "special political interests" in Morocco for granted just as she was backing out of her obligations towards Germany under the 1909 treaty; besides, by the terms of the Algeciras Act the Sultan of Morocco was a "sovereign ruler" and not a protégé of Paris. Caillaux returned at once to Paris and had Monis call a council of ministers. The council met on April 22; it approved retroactively the decision to send troops to Fez, the Foreign Minister having assured it that, consulted in advance, Germany had not objected and the other signatories of the Algeciras Act had all approved. In fact, however, Bethmann-Hollweg, the German Chancellor, had told the Ambassador of France, "If you go to Fez you will stay there, and then the whole question [of Morocco] will be reopened."[23]

Later the same month the Counselor at the German Embassy, Baron von der Lancken-Wakenitz, called on the Minister of Finance about a new customs law and stayed to suggest a Ubangi–Cameroons railway. Such a joint venture, he dared say, might appeal to the same financiers—a group headed by Semler, vice-president of the Reichstag—as had negotiated the consortium with the N'Goko Sangha; indeed they were still in Paris, so this time the Minister might deal with them himself. The Minister was tempted; on second thought, though, he informed Cruppi, and together the two decided to send instead Fondère, a colonial expert with large holdings in Equatorial Africa. At once the Semler group produced a detailed project. Caillaux disapproved it, as did Cruppi, then the colonial office, and eventually a unanimous Council of Ministers.[24] Semler had not quite finished with the French government, however: Cruppi had to pay him 100,000 francs[25] out of secret funds when Ambassador von Schoen turned up with a letter dated December 15, 1910,[26] from Briand's Foreign Minister, Pichon, undertaking to submit the N'Goko Sangha consortium to parliament for ratification.[27] Meanwhile, Caillaux made "unbinding statements" to Von Schoen about compensation to Germany in central Africa for a free hand in Morocco.[28]

The 1909 treaty was, then, a dead letter in Paris. Rather than propose another, Cruppi chose to wait: he had stolen a virtual protectorate in Morocco, he reasoned, and the longer he held it the lower would be the price of a real one. At an air show on May 19 Berteaux was killed and Monis seriously injured. Cruppi spoke at Berteaux's funeral, "more impressive, more solemn than ever."[29] As he spoke, French troops were entering Fez. "Clearly he considered himself the man of the hour," wrote Caillaux;[30] but as the hours dragged on with not even a threat from Germany, Cruppi lost his nerve.[31] He tried talking joint ventures again, but the Germans had "no instructions."[32] Then Spain ordered troops to Larache and El Qsar, barring the way from Fez back to Tangier.[33] Beside himself, Cruppi instructed Ambassador Jules Cambon to find out "what the Germans have up their sleeve."[34] The Chancellor in Berlin referred Cambon to the spa at Kissingen, and there on June 22 Kiderlen-Wächter told him that if the French wanted Morocco they would have to offer compensation. "Bring us back something from Paris," said the Foreign Secretary, seeing Cambon off.[35]

Cruppi did not look for "something." He did not even inform the government, which was on its way out. The plaster cast Monis wore was of no political importance—the Premier had been ill before, and his ministers had never much consulted him. However, with one triumvir dead and another living down the march on Fez, "Caillaux already appeared as the obvious successor to our weakened government," deemed the Minister of Labor, Paul-Boncour.[36] On June 26 Berteaux's successor told the Chamber in so many words that military authority would supersede civil authority in case of war, and the government fell. Caillaux was called on to set up a new one.

As strike-breaking was then the sorest task of governments in France, the custom was for the Premier himself to move into the Ministry of the Interior, in the Place Beauveau. Caillaux conformed to custom, taking his young follower Jean Louis Malvy with him as Undersecretary of State. For Chief Secretary he chose Desclaux, whom he had been sponsoring ever since Algiers. He left *his* ministry to Louis Lucien Klotz, the least competent qualified man he could find. To avoid seeming to repudiate the Fez expedition, he kept Cruppi on; to avoid seeming to condone it, he switched Cruppi to another post and put a decorous and dull senator, once prefect of Paris, Justin de Selves, into the Quai d'Orsay.[37] He did not know quite how far Cruppi had provoked the Germans already, but he knew enough to want to avoid provoking them any farther—unfortunately, however, he did not know De Selves. For the rest he carried over the old cabinet more or less intact—"Monsieur Caillaux has decidedly no ambition," wrote Gaston Calmette in *Le Figaro*.[38]

The new Premier, meeting the Chamber on June 30, announced "*un gouvernement qui gouverne*";[39] the Chamber understood that he would not hesitate to break strikes with bullets. The railway strikers were demanding a general amnesty; he undertook only to reemploy them at his discretion. The Socialists, in concert with the right, were demanding an electoral reform; he told the Radicals, who were content to do without one, "I'll make the reform *with you*."[40] And in passing he said a word or two about peace and the alliances.

As Caillaux took power, then, foreign affairs were not his prime concern. Lest he forget that they existed, the German government informed the Quai d'Orsay on July 1, 1911, that the gunboat *Panther* was being sent to the port of Agadir in southern Morocco "in order to protect German interests."[41] If the Sultan was incapable of maintaining order himself, said Kiderlen-Wächter in effect, Germany too had the right to assist him— until further notice. Thus restated, the problem of Morocco became critically urgent, and to clear the way for its solution De Selves proposed to send a French gunboat to Morocco. But to send a gunboat to Agadir would have been an act of war, and to send one to nearby Mogador would have been an act of cowardice. As a compromise Caillaux decided not to send one anywhere. Instead on July 4, as acting Foreign Minister, he instructed Jules Cambon to go and ask the German government to explain itself. He gave Cambon nothing to "bring back from Paris"; on contrary, "since *Germany* has invited *us* to talk about Morocco," he maintained, "Germany will have to state her wishes first."[42] And the same day, when President von Gwinner of the Deutsche Bank came to see him about the presidency of the Ottoman Debt Commission and shares in the Bagdad Railway, Caillaux declined to discuss any one of the questions in suspense between France and Germany unless he could discuss them all at once. "But I *am* ready to discuss them all," said Gwinner. "Yes," replied Caillaux, "but I am the Premier of France, and you are not the Chancellor of the Reich," and with a smile he sent the German on his way.[43]

Germany wished the Congo, as Von Schoen hinted on July 8[44] and Kiderlen-Wächter said outright five days later.[45] And of his own accord De Selves tended to be generous with the Congo; whenever the Germans mentioned it, though, he replied with islands in Oceania. All his offers were vague. Some were also vast, and those Caillaux had to retract; generally, though, as Cambon complained, he proposed to pay for Morocco with "scraps."[46] Only by bravado in negotiating, De Selves believed, could France wipe out the shame of negotiating at all, and especially of negotiating in Berlin,[47] while the *Panther* alone lay anchored off the coast of Morocco; his entourage at the Quai d'Orsay urged him on, despising Caillaux for having passed up so splendid a provocation as Agadir;[48] however, knowing neither the Germans nor geography well enough for bravado, De Selves was simply incoherent. Cambon had to write privately to the Premier to have De Selves's instructions confirmed, sometimes to have them interpreted, and as early as July 10 the Ambassador appealed to Caillaux to "have a hand" in the negotiations.[49] He really meant for Caillaux to take over the negotiations from De Selves, not just to butt into them, and from Caillaux he then expected not guidance but leeway. A diplomat in the grand style, Cambon needed the whole French Empire on consignment to negotiate at his ease. He knew no better reason for consulting his government than to stall for time, no better reason for invoking public opinion than to retreat with honor. Only war, to his mind, was not a proper tool of the trade; war was a failure of diplomacy, not a continuation of it or substitute for it. He took it as a personal insult that the Quai d'Orsay should be biding its time for war, and now the prospect of De Selves's bringing on a war by bungling unnerved him altogether.

Elie Decazes, Caillaux's old playmate from Versailles, often met the Kaiser yachting and heard him chatter, and early in July he informed Caillaux that the Kaiser had a confidential agent in Paris—Lancken, the counselor at the German Embassy. Just then Caillaux was about to dismiss an inspector from the Ministry of the Interior for having pleaded a suit against the government. Inspector André Tardieu had pleaded for the N'Goko Sangha. He it was, besides, who had devised the 1909 treaty, then drafted it with Lancken. He was also foreign editor of *Le Temps*, as Caillaux well knew; and the director of this powerful newspaper, Adrien Hébrard, interceded for him. Hébrard argued prescription: in fourteen months the ministry had brought no charges. Besides, now that collaboration between France and Germany in Morocco had failed, Tardieu favored "liquidation" between them, as did Caillaux; he might even support Caillaux, if Caillaux let bygones be bygones. Caillaux scrupled an instant, then gave in: anything but support from Tardieu was, he held, "infinitely dangerous."[50] And Hébrard "rewarded me at once," he recalled, "by taking from his pocket... the résumé of a conversation Tardieu had just had with the counselor at the German Embassy."[51] Lancken, swaggering above his station, had served warning on Caillaux, who "thwarted us in the N'Goko Sangha deal" and "so vigorously opposed the Ubangi–Cameroons railway," not to go on denying Germany's right to compensation for Morocco.[52] However, as Caillaux knew, the German government had taken no official interest in the Congo ventures nor yet mentioned the Congo and Morocco in the same breath. He concluded that the Congo was the Kaiser's own idea, and "Who knows?" he reflected. "Perhaps there [is] a way to... slip in between [the Kaiser] and his government."[53]

It was the Kaiser who, by proxy, came between Caillaux and his government. Lancken invited Fondère to the German Embassy for a chat on July 25, and Fondère called at the Place Beauveau on the way. "Tell him you found me very pessimistic," said Caillaux.[54] The next evening Fondère reported that Lancken demanded the whole Congo, and Caillaux told him to break off the talks. Fondère returned in the morning with a map showing how much Lancken now held Germany's claim to Morocco to be worth. This time Lancken asked less than the whole Congo; Caillaux, while rejecting his terms, welcomed his gesture, and for the whole day Fondère carried on a conversation between them. Whenever Fondère was too tired, Pierre Lenoir, a publisher, replaced him. Caillaux realized that for France to evict her co-tenant from Morocco she would have to cede *some* property in the end. The French people would admit the cession more graciously, he thought, if it were part of a broader settlement "outside of Europe";[55] however, Lancken did not care to discuss the Bagdad Railway at the same time as a real-estate transaction in Africa. He pressed Caillaux for a precise reply on the Congo: how carefully did Caillaux avoid giving one?

Late on July 27 Lancken left for Berlin to make his report, Ambassador von Schoen having wired the Wilhelmstrasse in advance. According to Von Schoen, Caillaux had suggested that France cede territory east of the Cameroons and with it her right of preemption on the Belgian Congo; he had refused the offer of Togoland "in exchange," requesting instead Chad and the North Cameroons; he was very pessimistic, though he sincerely desired to come to terms; finally,

he would rather make a large-scale settlement of all the differences that have arisen between us in recent years. Such a settlement would help him to justify before the public the cession of colonial territories.... He is thinking of... a German president for the Ottoman Debt Commission, the retrocession of the thirty-percent share in the Bagdad Railway to the Paris Bourse, an understanding on the eastern railways. He is also considering the possibility of ceding French possessions in Oceania.... He asks us urgently not to let Cambon know about his offers.[56]

The following morning De Selves showed Caillaux the German Embassy's telegrams, deciphered. Caillaux shrugged them off: he had gathered information for Cambon's use, he said, not negotiated behind his back; Lancken was trying to mystify the Wilhelmstrasse—or the Quai d'Orsay. That afternoon he told Fondère: "Lancken is a double-dealer.... Take care."[57] And the next day he sent Cambon a messenger, François Piétri, to report on the talks with Lancken.[58] Meanwhile, on July 29 Kiderlen wrote to his *confidente*, "I have just received a direct missive from Caillaux that clears the air"[59]—but three days later Cambon, meeting again with him, knew just what concessions to expect from him.[60]

Caillaux was, like Cambon, the more anxious to discuss Germany's demands seriously for knowing that France could not seriously resist them. The Triple Alliance was not a sure prop. Sir Edward Grey, the British Foreign Secretary, saw no reason for England "to go to war in order to set aside the Algeciras Act and put France in virtual possession of Morocco."[61] He even saw no reason not to let the Germans have Agadir if only they promised not to fortify it. "Out of the question," replied Caillaux.[62] Thereupon the Asquith government agreed to refuse to tolerate the presence of Germany in Morocco—and, as Tardieu wrote, "It thus made known to Germany, at least by the evidence of preterition, that England was indifferent to the cessions demanded of France in the Congo."[63] Ambassador Izvolsky advised giving the Germans their "tip" for Morocco, and as time passed he urged making the tip greater and greater:[64] the Russian army was as yet unfit to mobilize, he maintained, and an observer dispatched by Caillaux reported that it would not be fit before "at least two more years."[65] The French themselves were not ready to fight as one man for Morocco, much less for the Ubangi River basin, and though morale had improved greatly in the army since the time of the Dreyfus affair, equipment had not. Caillaux put in an order for heavy cannon, and on August 2 Jules Cambon again called on Kiderlen to offer him *"un gros morceau"* of the inner Congo.[66] This time Kiderlen, at the Kaiser's insistence, accepted the offer as a basis for negotiation.[67] Meanwhile, Caillaux appointed Joffre Commander-in-Chief in place of a nonentity,[68] and in the first days of August he summoned the new Commander-in-Chief before the President of the Republic. *"Général,"* said Caillaux unceremoniously, "they say Napoleon waged war only if he thought he had a 70–30 chance of winning. Have we a 70–30 chance?" *"Non, monsieur le président,"* answered Joffre, after some deep thinking. "Then we'll negotiate," said Caillaux,[69] who yearned to so himself—officially. Lancken returned to Paris with new proposals, and while Fondère fled before him, Caillaux stayed only to retrieve a stretch of the Congo River that De Selves had ceded by an error of syntax;[70] then on August 4 he too left for the seashore.

So ended a month of confusion. André Tardieu summed it up ruthlessly in *Le Mystère d'Agadir:*

To Germany's aggression, no reply: regrets first, then silence. Afterwards, a puerile effort to know what is wanted of us before our stating what we want: a game of half-spoken phrases, worsened by the confused and tortuous mind of the German interlocutor; an imbroglio of incomplete and contradictory plans; inconsistent orders, sent with reservations—the worst way to use an ambassador; no fixed point; no program; velleities, intentions, alternation of confidence and hysteria; shortsightedness, combined with weak will: it is not to this period of our history that tomorrow's diplomats should look for models.[71]

The worst was yet to come. "Our people are losing patience," declared the Kaiser on August 7; "[either] the Gauls will put up something acceptable at once or else we will help ourselves to more";[72] and soon the grimly quixotic monarch was threatening to chase the invaders from Morocco to the last man, "sword in hand."[73] Said Bethmann-Hollweg in confidence: "Germany is unanimous in favor of war, not for Morocco but for the honor and prestige of the German Empire."[74] The Germans in Agadir were reported stirring up an insurrection for the purpose of repressing it.[75] Already in London, Grey had told two colleagues that "the fleet might be attacked at any moment," and "warning orders" were sent.[76] De Selves spoke of convoking the chiefs of staff of the army and navy: "In not sending a boat to Agadir," he wrote to Caillaux, "we made a mistake that must not be repeated."[77] Kiderlen expected the negotiations to break down "if the French do not make some serious proposals,"[78] while Jules Cambon, frantic, begged Caillaux by special messenger to take charge.[79] On both sides of the Rhine the press ran wild and the public followed.[80]

Caillaux hastened back to Paris on August 17, having sent ahead to forbid the chiefs of staff to meet with De Selves. Concurrently the German Foreign Minister took off for a brief holiday, leaving Cambon free to return from Berlin. From then on Caillaux treated foreign policy as an *affaire de gouvernement*. Several times in the next few days he met in his private apartment with a small group of ministers and ambassadors to find a way of retrieving the negotiations. At his request this "small council of ministers"[81] first formulated the demands of France, then agreed on compensation to Germany. First the ministers drafted a treaty whereby Germany surrendered all political rights in Morocco in return for "guarantees of economic equality"; afterwards they mapped out the exchange of a portion of the Congo—about one half, the remainder being two strips joined in the east by the Congo and the Ubangi rivers—for a corner of Togoland and the *Bec de Canard*, a narrow "panhandle" of land south of Lake Chad in the Cameroons. "By a fortunate if tardy return to logic"[82] they proposed to negotiate in the same order—Morocco first, then the Congo. Thus if France did not obtain full satisfaction on the treaty, the map might be adjusted. A full council of ministers unanimously approved the new proposals, and on August 30 Jules Cambon boarded the train for Berlin, his portfolio full.[83] He had grown ill worrying; not until four days after his arrival in Berlin was he fit to resume the dialogue. Then he gave Kiderlen a copy of the draft and a peek at the map. If the German Foreign Minister was somewhat disappointed, the French Ambassador for his part was exultant. That evening he wrote to thank Caillaux for having enabled him "to speak up" at last; "I shall take the liberty of writing to you often," he concluded, "for it is you and you alone who will carry this great venture through to a successful conclusion."[84] In Paris, meanwhile, De Selves acquainted the German Ambassador with the map,[85] and facsimiles were printed in all the newspapers.

The negotiations for Morocco lasted six weeks. Caillaux guided them from Paris, consulting daily with his cabinet. Kiderlen defended an abstruse proposal of his own for a while; then he argued fine points of consular jurisdiction; finally he requested a zone of economic influence.[86] A financial crisis in Berlin weakened his arguments:[87] "When Kiderlen spoke of war," remarked Cambon, "he declared one he did not anticipate."[88] In Paris Caillaux privately invited the Socialists, who were among his fiercest critics just then, to stage a giant peace rally; they announced one for September 23, whereupon Caillaux, having gained at home the benefit of the announcement, forbade the rally and so strengthened his position in Berlin.[89] At one point De Selves inadvertently consented to priority for the construction of a railway between Fez and Tangier, which would have steered traffic away from Algeria; at Delcassé's suggestion, the French government got Germany to agree instead that "no other railway" would have priority over the one from Fez to Tangier.[90] The final text on Morocco differed from the draft in two main respects:[91] the cases in which France would not discriminate against Germany were enumerated, at Germany's request, and the customs franchise, proposed for thirty years, became "perpetual," as the other signatories of the Algeciras Act required—but "in international law," as Cambon pointed out, "perpetual conventions are the only conventions that can be repudiated when the time comes."[92] The treaty was initialed on October 11, the annexes two days later.

By the time the French government had obtained satisfaction in Morocco, public opinion had compelled it to go back on its original offer of compensation in the Congo.[93] Frenchman tended to regard Morocco as theirs in any case, by a sort of historical imperative. Germany, they felt, had a right to be consoled, but not compensated; in offering half the Congo their government was giving in to a threat, not making good a sacrifice. They might have raised no protest had their mere rights somewhere been surrendered; they might even have failed to notice had the whole Congo been delivered up at once. But the longer the negotiations dragged on, the more precious the fated area appeared to them. It was huge; it cut through the other possessions of France in Africa; the great explorer Savorgnan de Brazza was buried in it, and his widow invoked his bones pathetically. The government had to deny the authenticity of the maps as published by the press. Then on October 10 the ministers decided to offer Germany other regions in the Congo. They also agreed unanimously to authorize Jules Cambon to fall back on the original proposals if necessary to avoid a breakdown of the negotiations. Later in the day, however, Caillaux took it upon himself to instruct Cambon to demand at least a corridor along the west bank of the Congo and Ubangi rivers in order to preserve the contiguity of French territory throughout Africa.[94] Cambon was embarrassed, and morbidly skeptical.[95] Kiderlen-Wächter, though, was furious. He had given in completely on Morocco, which was more than ever he had intended or the French expected; and he had not accepted the offer of a *region* of the Congo in the first place, coveting "the *whole* French Congo.... Pieces of the Congo, however nice, with their rubber and ivory, would be of no use to us," he had informed the Chancellor.[96] Thanks to the *West Marokko Deutsch* movement, the German public had not yet adjusted to the loss of Morocco; and the German colonial office demanded nothing more firmly than to "cut through" the French Empire in Africa, having laid plans for railroad lines to cross the two rivers in the east and enter the Belgian Congo.[97] However, the German government was at a disadvantage diplomatically, what with the agreement on Morocco already publicized; worse, war had broken out between Germany's ally Italy and her prospective ally Turkey, and the financial crisis was still raging in Berlin. For five days Kiderlen held his ground; then he agreed to settle for a point of juncture with each river provided that Germany might keep the whole of the Cameroons; in time he backed down on the Cameroons, too, though he then asked France to renounce her preemption on the Belgian Congo; but eventually he agreed instead to leave any future problems of sovereignty in central Africa for a conference of colonial powers to settle, and on November 4, 1911, the Treaty of Frankfurt was signed.[98] In return for a little over one fourth of the Congo, which she already occupied *de facto*,[99] Germany had recognized the equivalent of a French protectorate in Morocco.

At the end of November, at Caillaux's request, Kiderlen recalled the *Panther*. Caillaux promised to acknowledge the gesture, but he did not bother to keep his promise.[100]

So, despite the big guns aimed at Agadir, the French government had struck the harder bargain in Berlin. Cambon had bickered splendidly, even under protest, and circumstances had assisted him; but it was Caillaux who was mainly responsible for the final results. And he could hardly have improved them. He might have intervened earlier instead of just meddling, but until the war scare in August he lacked a real excuse to intervene. Again, as André Tardieu suggested, he might first have established a French protectorate in Morocco and then discussed with Germany the price of recognition.[101] But Germany might not have waited; and as it was, France gained by his not discussing the price until after the goods were delivered. Many Frenchman argued that he should have sent a French gunboat to Agadir before negotiating; however, had he sent a French gunboat to Agadir most likely there would have been no negotiations. When the German government, having other worries, finally settled for part payment on a bad debt, some mistook the abatement for proof that Caillaux had been offering more than necessary all along; and most still regarded the Congo cessions as excessive, whether or not Germany could have been bought off for less. Kiderlen had got 120,000 square miles of primeval forest, just over one fourth of the Congo, in return for foreswearing Morocco, and in the process he had aroused the mistrust of England, thereby strengthening the Entente Cordiale: at least posterity makes him out to be the loser.[102]

Now, there is no exact equivalent in pygmies, tusks, and rubber trees for an outstanding claim to Morocco—though Germany would have alarmed the world by demanding more than the whole Congo, and France by refusing to give up a fourth of it. In the ethics of imperialism, the proper charge for disinterest in one area of the world was reciprocation in another; in the summer of 1911, however, France had nowhere to reciprocate, and Germany was not willing to extend credit. The only "just price" was perhaps a cross ratio of the values normally attached by each country to what was being bought and sold; but the regions ceded in the Congo had never been considered separately before, and in the heat of the dispute France and Germany had both lost their sense of values. Early in September Caillaux told the French Ambassador to impress on his German interlocutor the fact that, in the proposals just formulated by the French government, "the scales are weighted equally";[103] hence surely he thought that France gained more, and no doubt his ministers agreed. He was not cringing. However, he was making no ordinary commercial proposition. Since French troops had occupied Fez without Germany's consent, France had the choice of paying, fighting, or backing out—as Germany had made clear at Agadir. Had he been attentive only to public opinion in France he could not have agreed to pay; but neither could he have agreed to back out, and the country was not fit to fight.

In general the French did not recognize or did not mind the danger. Because Lloyd George said emphatically that peace at the expense of Great Britain's interests "would be a humiliation intolerable for a great country like ours,"[104] the French thought that peace at the expense of their own interests would affect Great Britain similarly; in fact the "just price" for Morocco was set quite as high at Whitehall as at the Wilhelmstrasse.[105] Because Germany had hinted so brutally for them to put or get out of Morocco, at heart the French denied their obligation to do either; in fact their obligation was not much smaller after than before. Hypnotized by the *Panther*, they had lost sight of everything else. However, the Germans too felt cheated in the end—even more so, and after much adding and subtracting of imponderables. When the final settlement was announced in Berlin, the colonial secretary resigned in protest,[106] and the journalist Maximilian Harden could think of no "approximately comparable defeat" in sixty years.[107] By their greater dismay the Germans reconciled the French to the treaty in some measure. Besides, opposing a treaty once it was signed was something quite different from opposing the position of a government in the course of negotiations. After all, France profited by the treaty in any case, whether or not Germany did profit more. France gained Morocco for the loss of a jungle, whereas Germany gained a jungle for the loss of a nuisance value; each got more than it paid for, and a bone of contention between the two was buried; if Germany's interest in Morocco was not worth so much of the Congo, Morocco was. By the time the treaty came up for debate in parliament most Frenchmen realized that, whatever their regrets, there was no turning back—that if the treaty were not ratified, surely no other nation would back France in demanding Morocco anyhow.

Some Frenchmen did not; some hoped at length to sicken the Germans of Morocco, or to incite them to another provocation, and some opposed "on principle" any cessions to Germany. Nationalists had welcomed the 1909 treaty because by it France seemed to be getting something for nothing. "Nothing"—that is, economic cooperation—had proved too costly, and Caillaux had the courage to point out that fact before it became obvious. Because he preferred France to pay Germany off for Morocco once and for all instead of collaborating with Germany in Morocco and elsewhere for ever after, he gained a reputation for docility toward Germany even before Agadir. So, as an alternative to attacking the

Treaty of Frankfurt in itself, its adversaries attacked it as part of a plot to reconcile France and Germany. A campaign ,of whispers and insinuations was waged against Caillaux "by the cabinet of the Foreign Minister," where "subaltern but active elements had on various occasions attempted to prevent agreement."[108] De Selves himself supplied the ammunition. He had been frustrated on losing control of negotiations; afterwards he was frustrated by their success. His *pièces de résistance* were the Lancken telegrams—known as the "green papers" because of a green signet used in the cryptography service of the Quai d'Orsay; to them Bethmann-Hollweg in November added another ending: "I shall never forget Caillaux's contribution to the fortunate outcome of the negotiations."[109] The green papers could not be quoted, of course: they were cited the more freely. Caillaux had negotiated behind the back of his foreign minister, and he had offered better terms. Whatever he had been scheming with Lancken, clearly it was something unsavory or else he would have let his colleagues know of it. So, because he had negotiated secretly with Germany, he was suspected of secretly desiring a reconciliation with Germany. And De Selves related how Caillaux, when first the green papers were shown to him, stormed out of the Quai d'Orsay, leaving behind him a briefcase containing the draft of a treaty of alliance with Germany.[110] But could even Caillaux have expected to put such a treaty through parliament? *Ah, voilà!* He had already set his foreign minister aside; he was just as apt to set parliament aside. His bad manners as a republican seemed to corroborate the charge of disloyalty—if indeed the distinction was ever drawn.

Now, Caillaux did talk business with Lancken. Perhaps, too, he negotiated, though he denied it.[111] Perhaps, too, he offered better terms than De Selves—someone had to. His distrust for his foreign minister showed in his conduct; so did his contempt for parliamentary procedure; so too did his pathological restlessness; and his officiousness, in both senses of the word; and his self-importance, with its disconcerting obverse. But did a desire to reverse the whole foreign policy of France? André Tardieu, who knew where to look, found "no proof, no sign, however weak."[112] However, politics in France is largely a matter of competitive patriotism: in a crisis, a Frenchman who hates Germans unreasonably can make one who hates them reasonably look like a traitor. And wherever Joseph Caillaux was concerned, proof was always irrelevant—where anything is possible, nothing can be certain. The presumption against him caught on; and once it had caught on, trivialities helped it to take hold. He should have been doubly prudent; he was twice as reckless.

Perhaps, too, he did with a sinister inflection tell the British Ambassador that France had "friends in reserve." Certainly he never meant it. His excitement on taking power and his anxiety during the Agadir crisis brought out the swaggerer in him; then, when the treaty was signed, his drop in tension released the "spoiled child" in him. Probably he did threaten Alfonso XIII with arming the Spanish refugees in France and sending them home. As far as the French public was concerned, he was quite capable of having done so; if he had not actually done so, it was an oversight on his part. As far as Alfonso was concerned, too: five years later the Most Catholic King still lived in mortal terror of Caillaux. With Spain Caillaux was his maddest self. At one point in the Moroccan crisis the Spanish government announced its intention of sending troops to the town of Ifni. Like a second Agadir, the move would have weakened the position of France in the negotiations with Germany. Caillaux roared at great length, to no avail; finally he made an end of the matter by asking Kiderlen to intervene for him in Madrid! Again, since France had bought out Germany in all Morocco, Caillaux turned to Spain for compensation when the negotiations were over. However, Spain had not asked France to buy out Germany in all Morocco—Paul Cambon derided "the mad illusions of our Premier."[113] Still Caillaux might have asked for the sand dunes of Ifni, for instance, or a monopoly of fishing rights nearby. He demanded instead the whole Atlantic coast south of Tangier, and he persisted until England called him off.[114] Meanwhile he also made all Belgium tremble when he said at Saint-Calais on November 5, 1911: "Thus I come to another of the main ideas that guided me in these negotiations, the idea that claims in central Africa cannot be regarded as definitively staked out."[115] And he insulted the ambassadors of allied nations—Izvolsky at the opera, Sir Francis Bertie at a hunting party at Rambouillet. Maurice Paléologue fretted over "our Premier's devastating name-calling."[116] Apocryphal, doubtless, but all the more typical is the incident recounted by Charles Benoist:

I can still see the spot on the Boulevard Saint-Germain where, standing up in his car, he repeated the strange words that he boasted of having uttered shortly before to the British ambassador. As, out of politeness or charity, I expressed doubt, he carried on all the more, choking, forcing his falsetto voice, raising his arms higher than the upright cannon behind the statue of Chappe. "*Oui, oui!*" he cried, "*je le lui ai dit! Et ça encore! Et encore ça!*" I hope for his sake that he was exaggerating. Had he said but half the things he claimed, he would have been fit to lock up then and there.[117]

He was not free much longer to boast of having blustered. Whether or not a revision of alliances in Europe was the purpose of his secret diplomacy, argued his adversaries, it would be the consequence of his lack of diplomacy. They exaggerated: all he needed was a good foreign minister. Always behind the accusation of tactlessness, however, was the accusation of treachery. His misfortune was his having come to power while France was so near to war with Germany. Under other circumstances he might have enjoyed the luxury of insulting Germans; as it was, he confined himself to out-negotiating them, which did not count for so much. After the Lancken telegrams the German Embassy did not use the same code again:[118] with calculated verisimilitude De Selves accused him of having complained of the telegrams to Lancken.[119] And so on. The anecdotes were monotonous; they served their purpose. "The *spirit* in which the treaty was negotiated, more than the treaty itself, was intolerable to patriots," wrote one detractor.[120] "His one mistake was in his *manner* of conducting the operation," wrote another.[121] Both meant he was pro-German. The confusion was total.

"Caillaux will probably be voted out on some matter of home policy," wrote Izvolsky to Saint Petersburg on December 7.[122] On December 21, after a week of debate, the Chamber adopted the Treaty of Frankfurt in a spirit of resignation. De Selves had spoken dully for it, and Caillaux with vigor. The extreme right voted against it, and a fourth of the deputies abstained. The deputies from eastern France abstained lest they "seem to be subscribing to a *rapprochement* with Germany."[123] Jaurès abstained: as Socialist Leader he was officially appalled at Caillaux for bartering slices of the world in secret councils. Caillaux lent a Socialist journalist a set of documents on Agadir to show Jaurès. Jaurès refused to see what he might not publish; still he did recognize in Caillaux a man who, in a pinch, would rather negotiate than fight.[124]

"Here, finally, the Chamber of Deputies has accepted the Franco-German agreement," wrote Izvolsky to his government again. "After its acceptance by the Senate, a cabinet crisis may be expected."[125] The Senate set up a special commission to study the treaty, with one of Caillaux's arch-adversaries, Alexandre Ribot, as chairman. Poincaré and Barthou, both of them Caillaux's friends and rivals, were also members; so were Clemenceau and Pichon, who remained faithful to the treaty of 1909. Caillaux appeared before the inquisitors on January 10, 1912, accompanied by De Selves. As he entered the meeting room he was certain that he saw Poincaré, Pichon, and Clemenceau snickering together in a corner.[126] He answered all the questions put to him; then, as the meeting was about to rise, he blurted out, without the least provocation: "And what's more, I never engaged in unofficial negotiations!" At once Clemenceau leapt to his feet, pointed a finger at De Selves, and demanded: "Can you confirm the statement of the Premier?" With an effort at dignity De Selves replied that, between his duty to his chief and his duty to tell the truth, he had to remain speechless; whereupon he resigned. The meeting broke up in great commotion, and Caillaux, De Selves, and Clemenceau went into private conference. Clemenceau said that Caillaux, to keep the matter out of the minutes of the commission, had only to retract his statement. Caillaux retracted, but De Selves sent in his resignation anyhow to the President of the Republic, alleging disagreement over foreign policy.

The government was doomed. Everyone knew it, except Caillaux.[127] He did find someone to replace De Selves: Delcassé, his Minister of the Navy, who had been blacklisted for the foreign ministry since the Algeciras Conference six years earlier—and whom he heartily despised. Then he rushed about frantically trying to find someone to replace Delcassé. Few men were ever as reluctant as Caillaux to cooperate with the inevitable; even in his case, though, the inevitable almost always came to pass. After twenty-four hours he gave up the search, comforting himself with the reflection that he was not the man to get the treaty through the Senate anyhow. Poincaré, who had been serving as *rapporteur* for the treaty in the Senate, succeeded him as premier, becoming foreign minister as well at the same time. Now, there did not seem to be anything underhanded about Poincaré; moreover, patriotism was the most conspicuous thing about him. With him to preside over its execution the Treaty of Frankfurt appeared not an instrument for bringing France and Germany together but a kind of closing of accounts between them. Ribot defended it passionately, and the Senate adopted it in March by a large majority.

After the fall of Caillaux the campaign against him attained its apogee. The prim *Journal des Débats* itself set the tone: "Caillaux's secret negotiations... had, if not as a direct aim, at least as a direct result, the dismemberment of the French empire in Africa with no apparent compensation, the ruin of our influence in the Levant, a rupture with Spain, a quarrel with England, and the subordination of French policy in Europe to Austro-German interests."[128] The right accused him of having striven to make concessions to Germany needlessly, not the greatest of them being the whole Congo. "These accusations, by their obvious exaggeration, fall flat," wrote Izvolsky.[129] Jaurès declared in the Chamber on March 8: "No, I do not agree to throw the whole responsibility for the trials we have undergone, for the difficulties we have gone through, onto the last period of the Morocco affair and in that period onto a single man."[130] But one week later Jaurès added:

France has a right to know by what paths, by what schemes, by what errors, she was led to the edge of the abyss.... I say there is no worse shame than silence. I say that if he persists, if M. Caillaux remains silent, he should be disqualified from parliament.[131]

Monsieur Caillaux persisted, and Poincaré encouraged him to persist. The Senate refused to investigate De Selves's resignation, and Poincaré refused to let the Chamber do so. By a nuance in refusing, however, Poincaré managed to suggest that he wanted to spare the country, above and beyond the fiasco of the green papers' coming to light, the sorry spectacle of a premier in league with Germany—or grovelling before Germany, whichever the case may have been. The phrase "patriotic silence" was coined for use against Caillaux, who "from then on began to take on that outlaw look, which was not unbecoming to his native insolence."[132] He was the income-tax man already; he became the man of secret negotiations with Germany. Even the Germans were fooled in the end: forgetting their dismay over the Treaty of Frankfurt, they came to look on Caillaux as an old friend.

Caillaux did not reply publicly to the accusations against him until the World War had relegated the green papers to the dead-letter file; thereafter he replied for the rest of his life. He replied in his book *Agadir*, which he wrote in first draft between February, 1912, and the end of 1913; then he replied in countless articles and speeches; finally he replied in his memoirs, which read like a vast pretext to tell the story of Agadir once more.

He took up all the petty charges against him. He had talked to Lancken behind De Selves's back? De Selves started, by writing to England on his own for approval to send a gunboat to Agadir.[133] He had insulted Sir Francis Bertie? "He goaded me on."[134] He had insulted Izvolsky? Izvolsky wanted the Dardanelles as "compensation" for Morocco.[135] He had plotted a revolution in Spain? No, it was Tardieu.[136] He had betrayed the Quai d'Orsay's possession of the German code? The Germans knew all along, or else one of De Selves's assistants told them.[137] And even if he was guilty of "venial sins,"[138] he also had his petty merits: for instance, he had set off the Berlin stock-market panic in September, 1911, "by a few phone calls."[139]

And he had greater merits too, he wrote. The term "patriotic silence" might have been used in his favor: not to irritate the Germans by gloating, he had not even impressed on the Chamber the extent of his diplomatic victory.[140] He had squeezed the last possible concession out of Germany—he sensed this intuitively, Cambon's correspondence bore him out, and Kiderlen-Wächter's private letters were to prove him right. Anyhow, there was something more important than one mile more or less of the west bank of the Ubangi River: *peace*. Like the problem of Morocco, all the outstanding sources of conflict with Germany "outside of Europe" might be eliminated by negotiation. He adopted Richelieu's maxim: *"Négocier toujours et en tous lieux."*[141] Negotiate wherever and whenever possible, the Cardinal had meant, but Caillaux understood him to mean: negotiate always everywhere at once. Meanwhile in Europe time would work for France better than any war, thought Caillaux. The Austro-Hungarian Empire was due to disintegrate; so was the Turkish Empire, and Italy might be lured out of the Triple Alliance. A European war, whichever nation were on the winning side, would necessarily be more destructive for France than for Germany, if from the demographic standpoint alone.

His reasons for having negotiated were as compelling as his success in negotiating had been great. They were not reasons of principle, though, or even of politics, but of common sense. And he had settled the problem of Morocco like a shrewd businessman, not like a doctrinaire. He had gambled and rused. He had been lucky, too. Agadir was a *tour de force*— he failed to make a doctrine of it. His whole formula for avoiding war was: Joseph Caillaux in power. He had done it once; he could do it again.

He did not justify Agadir out loud in 1912; instead he let his arguments be felt. While to his adversaries he remained the man of secret negotiations with Germany, to his partisans he became the man of negotiations with Germany. Again his partisans were on the left; for peace, like the income tax, was on the left in France, far on the left, just as *la revanche* was far on the right. *Far* because, if France was unanimous in refusing to do without the "lost provinces," there was a wide range of volition between wanting to fight for them and wanting to wait for them.

CHAPTER 3

Rallying the Left

"Tell me why this aristocrat Caillaux is a leader of advanced democracy."
MAURICE BARRÈS*

IN OCTOBER, 1911, when his divorce from his first wife became final, Joseph Caillaux took time off from the negotiations with Germany to marry Madame Henriette Raynouard. As soon as the debate on the Treaty of Frankfurt was over he took his new wife on a long trip through Egypt, Palestine, and Syria; they met Lord Kitchener in Cairo and Rudyard Kipling on the upper Nile.[1] By the end of May, 1912, he was back in parliament for the debate on proportional representation.

He favored the old electoral system, which was based on local precincts, and he was instinctively suspicious of *"les arguments de justice"* for reforming it.[2] To his mind, men and not parties were the essential components of a democracy. He had a bond with his electors in Mamers stronger and more intimate than a mere party platform: the feudal bond of reciprocal favors. They elected him, he looked after them—"My precinct was very costly," he later wrote.[3] They had elected him as the son of Eugène Caillaux; they would still elect him as the ally of Jean Jaurès. He would have been outraged had he lost their confidence simply for having changed his mind about taxes or made up his mind about peace. Under proportional representation he would be not a lord in his fief but a shareholder in a political corporation, and not an orator but a mouthpiece. With party functionaries for deputies, he thought, parliament would be too obstinately representative; however, besides representing the country, deputies had to govern it, and at times they could not do both. To the tyranny of parties, then, Caillaux preferred the tyranny of men. So did the Radicals, whose "party" was essentially an association of republicans in mutual defense against doctrine and discipline. More than the theory of the class struggle, the issue of the voting system had for years kept the Radicals at daggers drawn with their neighbors on the left, the Socialists, who had the purest party in France. Ideologies apart, what influenced the two decisively was that the Radicals stood to lose by the reform and

* *Dans le cloaque* (Paris, Emile-Paul Frères, 1914), p. 55.

the Socialists to gain by it. Poincaré having declared in favor of it, the Socialists abstained provisionally from attacking him. The Chamber approved it in June, the extremes voting for it in unison.

Caillaux spent the summer of 1912 quietly in Mamers. When parliament reconvened in the fall, one of its commissions investigated rumors that he and Monis had put pressure on a state prosecutor the year before in favor of the financier Rochette; the commission disbanded for lack of evidence. Caillaux barely noticed: the office of president of the Republic was due to fall vacant in January, and already in November the impending vacancy distracted him as well as his colleagues from their other business. For seven years President Fallières had been the very model of a grand elector, at once impartial and intelligent; however, there were only impartial candidates or intelligent ones to replace him. Poincaré was himself a candidate—partial, to be sure, though there was some doubt what he was partial to. For years he had made a career of abstaining. He had abstained in every fashion—modestly, resolutely, audaciously—when he had not abstained by proxy. By preoccupation he was a judge, grave and funless; in the Senate he always looked as though he were between sessions of the Palais de Justice, primarily because he always was. He had a cult of the state and of the statute books. He also had self-restraint, though: he reassured even Briand, who had retained the temperament of an anarchist while renouncing the trade. He played politics by seeming not to: about as much as the Socialists favored the electoral reform the rest of the Senate opposed it, so he held the bill in abeyance and kept his credit with the whole Senate intact. Though professedly he was more on the left than on the right, nationalists supported him for his attitude of defiance toward Germany, for his military parades, for his talk of "strengthening our alliances," for his nostalgia toward his home province of Lorraine. He did not encourage their support; he did not discourage it. Alarmed, Caillaux worked to defeat him—"I lobby tirelessly," he wrote;[4] concurrently the friendship between the two men lapsed into courtesy. Few besides Caillaux then believed Poincaré to be consciously seeking war: Briand maneuvered for him, Jaurès ignored him,[5] and Clemenceau fought him petulantly. Clemenceau wanted the stupidest man for the job, by way of precaution; his candidate—Antonin Dubost by name—was one whit too stupid, though, and Poincaré was elected. Wrote Izvolsky, jubilant: "During the coming years we are completely insured against having such persons as Caillaux, Cruppi, or Monis at the head of the French government or diplomacy."[6]

Briand replaced Poincaré as Premier in January, 1912. Caillaux went to Egypt again, this time for the Crédit Foncier Egyptien; in March, just as Caillaux was returning, Briand was defeated in the Senate over the electoral reform. Briand's ephemeral government had found time to propose increasing the period of military training from two years to three to counter a similar enactment of the Reichstag. Caillaux opposed the "three-years law"—as might have been expected, observed its advocates. Accused periodically of having sabotaged national defense as Minister of Finance or as *éminence grise* of the finance commissions, Caillaux had periodically replied that he simply gave priority to weapons over personnel in the budget. The main item of expenditure under the three-years law was to be new barracks; Caillaux advised spending for airplanes or machine guns instead. Since the law would not mean a larger army in case of war, the real issue was a highly technical one of marginal utilities: so many more man-hours of training versus so many more bombs or bullets. Only after due computation did the general staff take a stand on the bill, favoring it almost unanimously and probably unwisely. Parliament for its part was attentive above all to the problem of how best to reply to the Reichstag. Now, retaliation is an invitation to further retaliation, for not to retaliate to retaliation is as much a confession of fault as it is an act of cowardice. Hence Caillaux saw an opportunity for reuniting the left by basing the opposition to the three-years law on the theme of *peace*.

"You must get me an hour alone with Jaurès," Caillaux whispered to a Socialist one day. A few days later, far away from the Palais Bourbon, he was having lunch with Jaurès. "The difference between these two personalities," wrote their intermediary,

> was such that it stood out at every moment almost as a source of disturbance. These men, who were going to lead a hard fight together and were inspired by an equal devotion to the common weal, took up no problem from the same angle. The one precise, willfully succinct, affirmative, examining the broadest and the most complex problems with a perpetual concern for the actual and the possible; the other always anxious to fit every solution into a vast system and make the whole world participate in the harmony of an ideal philosophy.[7]

Together the two conspirators planned a joint offensive against the three-years law. They agreed to have one of their confederates, the retired army officer Messimy, put up an amendment reducing to thirty months the period of training; if the amendment failed, Caillaux was to move instituting the income tax to defray the expenses of applying the law. The new Premier, Barthou, had taken no firm stand as yet, so the two decided not to attack him unless first they failed to win him to their side. They left their plans at that for the time being. "What for the one was the next thing to do was for the other an inevitable stage in the march forward."[8]

All spring the left behaved with near serenity in the Chamber; a few zealots did strike out against the government, but their leaders fast restrained them. In the army meanwhile the debate was kept alive by a former officer, Robert Nanteuil, who met secretly with Jaurès. The technical issues at stake were taken to parliament by Messimy and to the public by the review *Armée et Démocratie*. The opponents of the bill gained ground, and Poincaré grew nervous. "Foreseeing the possibility of the fall of Barthou and the need to have recourse to a strong man on the left," recalled one of his confidants,

he called Clemenceau to the Elysée.... Clemenceau had just come out in *L'Homme libre* in favor of the three-years law. Poincaré later told me, "I wanted to notify the Chamber that, if it votes out the cabinet over the military question, Clemenceau and not Caillaux will succeed Barthou. I'll see to that by all the powers vested in me by the Constitution. I'll even go so far as to ask the Senate to dissolve the Chamber; then, if the Senate does not back me up, I'll resign." Clemenceau gave his assurances that he could be counted on.[9]

In the end the Messimy amendment failed. Before the law was voted Caillaux read a brief of the arguments of the deputies of the left against it; then he obtained a half-promise from Barthou to support the income tax for financing it, and parliament adjourned.

Caillaux spent a "sad vacation" in 1913, obsessed as he was by the thought of war. "Don't you see where they're leading us?" he would bark at his wife if perchance she smiled.[10]

In October he attended for the first time a congress of the Radical-and-Radical-Socialist party; promptly the party elected him president. Henceforth, with Jaurès for a consort, he was *the* leader of advanced democracy. His gaze riveted on the future, he lost sight of his old group in the center: in an open letter the group baldly reminded him that he had neglected to resign as its president.

As soon as parliament reconvened, Caillaux had two more business lunches: he tried to enlist Briand, then Barthou, under his banner for the spring elections. He regarded these two men as the chief unwitting recruits of a war party headed by Poincaré. Briand was not alarmed by the doings of "his president," however: in place of a big unwieldy peace party he proposed an exclusive Briand-Barthou-Caillaux club, the premiership to rotate among its members.[11] Barthou, when he saw Caillaux, had just asked parliament to cover the three-years law by a national loan with interest exempt from taxation. Caillaux, of course, preferred any tax to a loan, and the income tax to any other tax; he was critical of borrowing even when the Treasury was well-nigh empty, and in 1913 it was full. Besides, the exemption ran counter to a provision of his income-tax bill, which was then before the Senate. He asked Barthou to drop the loan, or at least the exemption. Barthou refused. On November 23 Caillaux attacked the loan in the Chamber; it passed weakly. On November 30, at a banquet of the Radical party, he attacked Barthou on his relations with high finance. He also attacked Briand—that is, he spoke of certain ancient Romans who thought to settle all controversies by lulling the participants to sleep. On December 2—which, it so happened, was the anniversary of the *coup d'Etat* of Louis Napoleon—the tax exemption was up for debate in the Chamber. Of that day Caillaux later wrote: "I am on the rostrum. I overthrow the government."[12]

"Probably Caillaux will be my boss," the nationalistic director of the Quai d'Orsay, Maurice Paléologue, wrote in his diary. "He will not be long in messing up our whole system of alliances."[13] Poincaré, however, having formed the same judgment of Caillaux, did not call him back to the premiership. Caillaux was not sure enough of his following to insist on being called, but he was sure enough of it to demand a premier to his liking. Poincaré first tried two of his own men—Alexandre Ribot, then Jean Dupuy,—but Caillaux held firm. At last Gaston Doumergue was named. Caillaux himself took the Ministry of Finance, even though his wife had mysterious apprehensions about his taking any post.[14] And "M. Poincaré, his face contracted, his teeth clenched, spoke a few words of welcome, sour as vinegar, to the members of the new government."[15]

Thus Caillaux at the end of 1913, when he was fifty years old, was as powerful as any man in France.

Yet his power was mostly illusory. It did not extend much beyond parliament, which in 1913, the year of *La République des camarades*, was truly a world in itself. For all the men in parliament knew, the future of France was hanging on the outcome of the perennial debate between Jaurès and Clemenceau. That debate was symbolic, but it was not vital. The revolutionary party, after first hacking away at tradition for a century, had split into two segments, one of individualists and one of collectivists, and each was preparing to hack away at the other. The energy for the struggle was outside parliament, though, and with regard to the world outside the men in parliament felt a solidarity that transcended all their internecine quarrels. "There is less difference between two deputies

one of whom is a revolutionary," wrote Robert de Jouvenel, "than between two revolutionaries one of whom is a deputy."[16] Caillaux often
addressed himself to the nation at large: for instance, he admonished his
countrymen to stay thrifty much as Guizot had invited them to get rich;[17]
he spoke to the nation at large more by a device of rhetoric, though, than
in an effort to be heard by it. So did Jaurès himself, his golden baritone
luxuriating in Ciceronian periods; but if he too was a stranger to the
world outside, at least he was bound to a part of it by the doctrine of
Marxism and by the Socialist International. Caillaux had no bonds
outside of Mamers, not even with Jaurès. A decision of principle taken
by the Socialist congress at Amsterdam prevented Jaurès from joining a
bourgeois government, and the catechism of the class struggle made it
incumbent on him to snarl at impenitent bourgeois from time to time.
Hence his support of Caillaux was fitful, and his usefulness to Caillaux
was limited.[18] Caillaux, an orthodox financier, had found himself a revolutionary only because he wanted to tax incomes and savings instead of
dividends and spendings; as far as he was concerned, Marxism was so
much mystification, and no doubt he would never have associated with
Marxists in the first place except that they too had found their place on
the left.

If to the proletariat Caillaux was every bit bourgeois, to the bourgeoisie
he was a dangerous renegade. He was rumored to have a tax on capital
up his sleeve, and the ladies and gentlemen of France all trembled at the
prospect of a register of fortunes transforming itself during the next
revolution into a list of suspects. The nationalists also had reason to
despise him, as the Action Française did not cease reminding them. He had
a party behind him, but it was without discipline; he had no newspapers
under his control, no mass movements, no big trusts, and his fortune was
only enough to assure him of independence. Nor was his power secure
even within the *république des camarades*, for to some extent his position
was circumstantial: parliament was, in his own words, "poor in public
financiers,"[19] and he was the only veteran minister available to head the
Radical party. Moreover, whereas he had enough audacity to disqualify
him permanently on the right, he had nothing else to commend him
permanently on the left.

Wherever his ideas were resented, his idiosyncracies were resented
even more. He was notorious for "making faces on the rostrum, spinning
around on his axis, his hands in the armholes of his vest, disdainful, seemingly disgusted with so vulgar an audience."[20] He often behaved as
though what he regarded as genius was a fair substitute for what others

regarded as tact. "Whoever has not heard the theorist of fiscal reform thunder at his interlocutors, 'No! You don't get me,' does not know how far impertinence and disdain for a parliamentary assembly can go."[21] According as he was or was not in power, he regarded the opposition or the governement as a conspiracy to prevent him from doing his job. His fidgety mind was a menace to all, especially to himself: he lived "in a permanent state of fever and delirium," wrote one journalist,[22] and in the summer of 1911 another found him morbidly upset over an anonymous report on the poor state of the army.[23]

Although he had migrated politically, socially he had not budged. He was still a *grand bourgeois*: if he could not have friends of his own sort, he would do without friends. "Don't mind *him*—he's not one of us," he told Joseph Reinach of some Radical colleague.[24] Jaurès alone he admired of his contemporaries;[25] he did not even respect the others. In his eyes Briand was a *parvenu*, Poincaré vain, Clemenceau venal, Barthou vulgar. "I broke with my generation," he wrote, meaning with his set.[26] For want of friends, he fell back on disciples, debtors, and hirelings. Only in spite of him did Madame Caillaux keep some of her own friends, such as Barthou's wife and Poincaré himself.

Having no sure friends and many enemies, Caillaux was vulnerable as 1913 drew to a close. He had been neglectful of little things; the little things in his past were about to catch up with him. Already Madame Gueydan had been espied under a lamppost showing Louis Barthou papers to read.[27]

CHAPTER 4

The Drama

AS DOUMERGUE and Caillaux, on taking power, made cryptic utterances about the three-years law,[1] even Jaurès took them to task in *L'Humanité* for their "ambiguities,"[2] and so the opposition to their government was lively from the first. Briand himself, normally on the reserve, assailed Doumergue in parliament, and at Saint-Etienne on December 23, 1913, he spoke of "some who are feverishly impatient, some demagogical plutocrats who pursue progress so frantically that we lose our breath trying to keep up with them. They want all or nothing."[3] The newspaper *Le Figaro*, long favorable to Caillaux, had been attacking him since October, and late in December the editor, Gaston Calmette, personally undertook a violent campaign against him. First Calmette accused him of secretly retaining his positions with his two *crédits fonciers*, even of taking up the presidency of others; Caillaux issued curt denials, as a matter of form. On January 8 Calmette accused him of having offered the petitioners for the estate of a Frenchman named Prieu, who had died a millionaire in Brazil, the backing of the French Embassy in Rio provided that 80 percent of the proceeds went into the electoral coffers of the Radical party; Caillaux dictated his denial angrily at a cabinet meeting the same afternoon,[4] and as it turned out no one but Calmette had ever heard of Prieu. Undaunted, Calmette accused Caillaux of having embezzled Treasury funds, of having doctored up the accounts of corporations, of having sold the privilege of quotation on the Bourse. Meanwhile, on January 13, "with perfect poise," Caillaux read to the Council of Ministers his financial proposals, which included a tax on fortunes over 30,000 francs[5] on the basis of quinquennial statements by the taxpayers; no one objected.[6] The text day he learned that Calmette had got hold of duplicates of the green papers and intended to publish them. At once he saw Poincaré and asked him to intercede and restrain Calmette. He suspected that Poincaré himself was behind Calmette; he said so by innuendo, and Poincaré denied it the same way. By a devious course the two agreed that Poincaré would ask Barthou but not Briand to have a word with Calmette.[7] Promptly Poincaré saw Barthou and Barthou saw Calmette.

Calmette promised to keep the green papers to himself, and for a few days the attacks in the *Figaro* subsided. Caillaux went to thank Barthou, and the two had a long talk. "I spoke from the heart," wrote Caillaux.[8] The attacks resumed more violent than ever.

At length Caillaux got used to it—"the buzzing of flies about the head of a man at work," he called it.[9] Most of his time he gave to battling for the income tax in parliament. In this battle he

revealed as never before the full measure of his political talent, his financial ability, and above all his indomitable fighting spirit.... .He crushed every opponent by his obviously superior grasp of public finance and his mastery of the intricate details of the French fiscal system. By adroit and supple tactics on the floor, no less than by his courage and promptness of decision, he affirmed his control over Parliament; and by sheer force of his peremptory autocratic manner, his domineering passion for authority, forced a divided and wavering party to accept [his] leadership....[10]

Meanwhile, trusting Doumergue, he gave little of his time to foreign affairs—except when foreign affairs and finance mixed. On December 14 he told an agent of Izvolsky's that he was "absolutely ready" to authorize an issue of Russian railroad bonds.[11] Wrote Izvolsky grudgingly to Saint Petersburg, "The cabinet of MM. Doumergue and Caillaux, damaging as it may be from the point of view of internal French politics, does not so far deserve any reproach on our part as far as our immediate interests are concerned."[12] Then Caillaux gave the loan to Russia priority over Barthou's national loan—"*avec la plus grande complaisance*," reported Izvolsky.[13] On January 21, 1914, he met with ministers from Turkey to attempt to reach an understanding on the perennial problem of the Turkish railways. "On the whole, conversation unsatisfactory," he noted.[14] Two months earlier the Périer Bank had negotiated a loan to Turkey; Russia protested, and Caillaux was able to intervene in time to prevent final payment. Just then Germany was threatening to help Belgium build railroads in the Congo; Caillaux and Doumergue agreed to beat the Germans to it.[15]

Meanwhile solicitors hounded Caillaux, offering to sell him the means of replying to Calmette. Among them was a Hungarian journalist, Leopold Lipscher, who claimed to have proof that the *Figaro* was subsidized by Vienna. Caillaux turned them all away. Some weapons came to him free of charge: for instance, a devotee of his in the Ministry of Finance sent him Briand's tax records—he tucked them away. Political friends came up with even stronger weapons, such as an old letter to Calmette from his mother on the theme: "I would never have thought you capable

of taking money from your mistress, and especially of not returning it."
"I don't use such weapons," said Caillaux proudly.[16]

Calmette's charges, for all their extravagance, won some credence,
and as the campaign developed all Paris took sides—"as at the time of the
Dreyfus affair."[17] Caillaux, however, was attentive only to its effect in
parliament, which was favorable to him; he did not notice its effect
anywhere else, not even in his own home. "It never occurred to me that
someone in my own family might be upset by it," he later wrote.[18] But
his wife was a *grande bourgeoise* by birth and breeding—proud, sensitive,
unused to outspoken nastiness. One day she came home in tears because
at her dressmaker's she had heard a lady whisper, "There's the wife of
that thief Caillaux."[19] A few times she found the courage to ask her
husband, "Are you sure you're not taking the attacks in the *Figaro* too
lightly?" and each time he merely grunted in reply.[20] Slowly her health
gave way; she developed internal pains; she ate and slept less and less.
Soon Caillaux made a point of not noticing. What could he do? To
demand an investigation to clear himself would have meant resigning
his post; however, with the income tax under discussion and no one to
replace him, his colleagues would have thought it insanely touchy of him
to resign. He chose instead to persist in an attitude of "lone and haughty
scorn."[21]

In February, speaking in the Sarthe, he quoted Mirabeau: "In all
countries, in all ages, the aristocrats have implacably pursued the friends
of the people, and if by I know not what secret concordance of circumstances a friend of the people ever turned up in their own midst, he is the
one whom they struck at especially, avid to excite terror by their choice
of victim." And he added: "I shall continue unfalteringly to tread the
clear, straight path that we set out on together more than fifteen years
ago."[22]

Caillaux was not long able to ignore the buzzing about his head. Early
in March Calmette, charging him and Monis with having put pressure
on the state prosecutor Fabre in 1911 on behalf of the financier Rochette,
undertook to publish a complaint drawn up by Fabre at the time. Governments did have the right to give orders to a state prosecutor for
reasons of state; Caillaux was of course suspected of having given an
order for reasons of his own. Calmette did not next produce the Fabre
document; instead, just as Caillaux and Jaurès were working out their
tactics for the final stages of the income tax battle, he wrote in the *Figaro*
of March 10, "Now is the decisive moment; we must not stop short of

any act." Caillaux, on seeing these words, thought at once of his first wife. At their divorce she had sworn that none of the letters stolen by her two years before survived in any form; in fact her sister had taken photographs of them—without her knowledge, she later testified. Since Caillaux's second marriage she had been peddling the copies all over Paris. They contained nothing exactly incriminating that he could remember, except perhaps for some playful allusions to his constituents' animal farms; however, his present wife had a daughter in her charge and a reception by the King of England in prospect, hence she was averse to seeing her old love letters on the front page of the *Figaro*.

The Rochette affair was brought up in the Chamber on Friday, March 13; the discussion was adjourned until the following Monday on a provisional vote of confidence. Also on Friday, March 13, Calmette published Caillaux's letter of 1901 to Madame Gueydan, then Madame Jules Dupré, about how *"Ton Jo"* had defeated the income tax while seeming to defend it; by deleting the date he made the letter timely. Now the campaign, still as base as before, had turned dirty as well. Caillaux issued a press release, dating the letter precisely and explaining it as best he could. Again he complained to Poincaré, but Poincaré pleaded helplessness.[23] Sunday he went to Mamers and found his electors deaf to the charges against him—the *Sarthois* took nothing from the big city seriously, not even slander.

Monday morning, as Caillaux was shaving, his wife approached him, tense and haggard, clutching the *Figaro*, which announced the start of a "Comic Interlude." "Aren't you going to do anything?" she asked. He replied evasively. She crumpled the newspaper, threw it down, and stormed out, slamming the door. "Then—only then—did I realize what a martyrdom the poor creature was suffering," he later wrote.[24] Leaving her to receive in his stead Monier, Chief Justice of the tribunal of the Seine, he went to see Poincaré at the Elysée Palace. Poincaré thought Calmette too gallant to publish a lady's love letters. "If he publishes a single one of them," cried Caillaux, "I'll kill him!" Thereupon Poincaré suggested dryly, as though he were "giving advice to a client,"[25] that Caillaux have his lawyer warn Calmette against publishing them, and he offered to see the lawyer, a good friend of his, himself if Caillaux was too busy. Caillaux left, furious. Later the same morning his wife called on him at the Louvre just as he was discussing Poincaré, Calmette, and injustice with his chief secretary and a Radical colleague. She joined the discussion for a moment; then he took her home. On the way she told him that she had come to him in desperation, Monier having explained to her that the law offers no means of preventing libel. Their only recourse was to wait and later prosecute Calmette, but then their private affairs would become public twice over—and besides, libel suits almost always failed. "You'll have to defend yourselves," the judge had concluded.[26] She had refrained as long as she was able from disturbing Caillaux at the Ministry; by way of refraining she had gone and bought a dress for a reception at the Italian Embassy that evening. Caillaux found no more apt way to reassure her than to growl: "If Calmette publishes any of my letters I'll smash his face in!"[27] Their lunch tasted bad, so they fired the cook—they had already fired one the day before. After lunch Madame Caillaux went back again to the agency for a new cook, and she also did some more shopping for the Embassy reception.

Then she went to buy a revolver. She and her husband were planning a long trip by auto, she explained to the dealer. On the practice target in the basement she made a few bull's eyes and missed a few. By half past three she was back home having tea with a friend, to whom she showed her new dress. At four she handed the maid a note for her husband. "My dearly beloved husband," it began.

When this morning I told you of my conversation with President Monier... you told me you would smash in that wretch Calmette's face one of these days.... France and the Republic need you: I shall do the deed. If you receive this letter I shall have done or attempted to do justice....[28]

Thereupon she had her chauffeur drive her to the offices of the *Figaro*. Calmette was out. Without giving her name she took a seat in the lobby; she waited a full hour, her revolver in her muff, certain of hearing her husband's name whispered sarcastically on all sides. At six o'clock Calmette darted into his office from a rear stairway; the novelist Paul Bourget caught him dashing out again, whereupon an attendant, hearing his voice, brought him an envelope containing Madame Caillaux's card. He was first amazed, then intrigued. To Bourget, who urged him to come along to dinner, he replied that he could not refuse to see a lady. Returning to his office, he found Madame Caillaux there waiting. "You must suspect the reason for my visit?" she asked, as soon as they were alone. "I dare say I do not," replied Calmette; "please be seated."[29] With no further ceremony she drew her revolver and fired six bullets in his direction. He was hit four times. He collapsed to the floor. As the staff came rushing in, Madame Caillaux stood repeating serenely, monotonously: "There is no justice in France. That was the only way."[30] She surrendered her weapon willingly but forbade anyone to touch her.

Caillaux was busy all that afternoon in the Senate, where a motion of

his for restoring the tax on national-bond interest was on the floor. The
motion failed. The police reached him by phone at his ministry soon after
taking Madame Caillaux into custody. He rushed to the prefecture, halting
only at the entrance to snap at the officer standing guard, "You might
salute me: I am the Minister of Finance!"[31] That night Calmette died.
The next morning Caillaux resigned from the government, despite the
protests of his colleagues, and a day later he announced his intention to
withdraw from politics. Meanwhile Madame Caillaux was confined to
the Saint Lazare Prison—"among common-law criminals," wrote Caillaux bitterly.[32]

Caillaux ceased attending parliament or even leaving home except for
questioning at the prefecture or visits to his wife in prison.

The debate on the Fabre affair in the Chamber resumed on March 18.
Pascal Ceccaldi, a Corsican deputy, made a fiery speech of loyalty to
Caillaux, and Doumergue denied the very existence of a "Fabre document." Then Barthou mounted the steps of the rostrum, drew a crumpled
bit of paper from his back pocket and waved it in the air, pronouncing it
the Fabre document. Fabre had waited for Monis to leave office before
writing an account of what he called "the greatest humiliation of my
life"—having received an order from a government. He had given the
document to Aristide Briand, Minister of Justice under Poincaré. Briand,
at a loss what to do with it, had locked it up in a drawer, and on vacating
the premises he had urged his successor, Barthou, to leave the drawer
locked. At once Barthou had unlocked the drawer and pocketed the
document—considering, he said, how he might injure Caillaux needlessly by letting it lie about. He insinuated to the Chamber that Calmette
had been murdered to prevent its publication. The left was dumbfounded;
the right was jubilant—especially Maurice Barrès, who wrote half a book
on the session. Briand, already disgusted with Calmette, was now disgusted with Barthou as well. The Chamber set up a committee to "investigate abusive encroachments of the executive on the judiciary": it
meant Caillaux and secondarily Monis, who at once resigned as Minister
of the Navy. Jaurès automatically was named to chair the committee,
being wary of the temptations of power both as a moralist and as a
Socialist. Within a few days he had called half a hundred witnesses and
tapped as many archives. Rochette wrote from Greece, where he was in
hiding, that Caillaux was blameless; his letter was cited as evidence both
ways. To keep the government from tampering with the findings of the
committee, Jaurès once had to threaten to resign. The committee report

was ready on April 3. Unexpectedly, it first censured Clemenceau and Briand for having manufactured a plaintiff in order to initiate proceedings against Rochette with no clear benefit to the state; then it censured Caillaux and Monis for "deplorable abuse of influence," noting however that the abuse had caused no detriment to the prosecution. The verdict was soft; the Chamber upheld it.

His spirits reviving, Caillaux decided to run in the May elections after all. At first a Radical senator spoke for him in Mamers; then after a few days he went to speak for himself. His adversaries met him with a barrage of obscene tracts and caricatures. He fought them by an old-style campaign. "They said I was washed up, beaten.... Beaten? *Allons donc!*" he told his voters.[33] Posters depicted enemies of peace and of the income tax hunting him down, and mayors boasted that the Sarthe had received extra shares of proceeds from the Pari-Mutuel. He was reelected on the first ballot, his lead over his perennial competitor, M. d'Aillière, almost intact. D'Aillière had abstained from mentioning *the* affair in his speeches, imagining that he did not have to. No doubt the omission made little difference: provincial jurors ran a close second to Parisian jurors for acquitting women who had acted rashly, and the wives of the local woodcutters got up an enormous bouquet of flowers for Madame Caillaux. After the elections, however, D'Aillière made up for his omission somewhat coarsely in an open letter. Caillaux sent seconds, and at dawn on May 4 a pistol duel took place on the outskirts of Paris. "M. d'Aillière missed me. I fired into the air," wrote Caillaux afterwards.[34] "His wife is a better shot than he is," ran the rumor in Paris.[35]

The Fédération des Gauches, the alliance of the center parties under Briand and Barthou, based its campaign on the slogans "Neither inquisition nor vexation," which meant no income tax, and "The three-years law for national defense," which was taken to mean war. It failed to split the leftist vote, and the new Chamber had a large majority of Radicals and Socialists. "We shall see Caillaux back in power, perhaps before long, and that may have rather big consequences," noted Ribot in his diary on May 3.[36] But Caillaux was still busy at the police station: the big consequences would have to wait. At least he got more courtesy from the police in the meantime.

Doumergue resigned shortly after the elections, for no apparent reason, and Poincaré invited a former Socialist, Viviani, to replace him. Caillaux, as a condition for his support, demanded that Viviani undertake to repeal the three-years law; Viviani withdrew. Next Poincaré called his friend Ribot. On May 16 Ribot noted: "Caillaux wishes to return to the pre-

miership. The President knows it and seems to resign himself in advance."
He added: "If Madame Caillaux is condemned, they will ask for grace;
the President does not seem willing to let himself be coaxed."[37] Ribot
could find few men on the left to join his government unless Caillaux's
lieutenant Malvy were kept on as Minister of the Interior;[38] consequently
he chose most of his ministers elsewhere, and the Chamber overthrew
him. Viviani was recalled, and with Malvy at his side he passed the
scrutiny of the Chamber. His government was meant only to last the
summer, and both Ribot and Jean Dupuy asked Poincaré whom he
intended calling afterwards. "Caillaux, if his wife is acquitted," Poincaré
replied.[39]

Caillaux on his side resolved to demand power in the fall, and, if
Poincaré refused, to evict him from the Elysée. Already Poincaré, by his
choice of premiers, had aroused the Chamber's suspicions; he could not
afford another blunder, thought Caillaux. Poincaré was planning a trip
to Saint Petersburg "to strengthen the alliance," and the former Ambassador to Russia, Georges Louis, appealed to Caillaux to prevent it.
Caillaux, though, was not yet ready. One day in June he slipped over to
the Palais Bourbon and sought out Jaurès in the corridors. "We must, as
soon as possible, form a great left-wing government with a foreign policy
of conciliation in Europe," he said, and Jaurès agreed. But, Caillaux
added, "the venture is possible only if the Socialist party enters the
government.... For my part, I would refuse to assume the responsibility
of power...unless you yourself took the portfolio of foreign affairs."
Jaurès, while raising some formal objections, conceded the point that,
"in view of the imminence and the gravity of the danger, the scholasti-
cism of the party would have to be set aside." Caillaux left convinced that
Jaurès was saving his consent until after Madame Caillaux's trial—and
such in fact was the case.[40]

On June 18 the *revanchard* Maurice Paléologue, after attending a council
of ministers, noted in his diary:

We had one subject left to discuss—the President of the Republic's trip to
Saint Petersburg. But at once Viviani broke out insultingly: "Ah yes, let's talk
about that trip!... How idiotic to have chosen July 20 as a date!... The very
day the Caillaux trial is to begin!"[41]

There was excitement the world over as the day of the trial drew near.
Germany made diplomatic capital of the scandal.[42] In Paris feeling ran
against the defendant: every day the press protested anew against her
alleged special treatment at Saint Lazare. Most newspaper editors abused

her in vicarious self-defense. Most columnists found Caillaux guilty of having goaded her on. In June Caillaux asked Briand please to try and get the attacks to tone down; the attacks toned down. A newspaper named the *Bonnet Rouge* came to Madame Caillaux's defense; by way of encouragement Caillaux contributed 40,000 francs.[43] The publisher, a Corsican named Almereyda, was a former convict whose arrest Caillaux himself had ordered in 1911. As for the rest of the staff—"You don't get a tough newspaper going with the recipients of good-conduct medals," Caillaux explained.[44]

The press made out Calmette to have been most upright and patriotic. Caillaux procured a copy of his will. Calmette had started out in journalism thick in debt; he had died a multimillionaire. Lipscher renewed his offer; this time Caillaux accepted, and he even played host to the leader of the Hungarian Independence party, Count Károlyi, who brought the compromising contract from Budapest. The will and the contract were published in the *Bonnet Rouge*. The *Figaro* replied that what looked like a contract for subsidies was in reality part of an old contract for advertising Tyrolian summer resorts; as for Calmette's fortune, it was the product of judicious investment. Meanwhile a princess[45] came forth to testify that Calmette had offered to pay her handsomely to arrange a meeting with Madame Gueydan. From Calmette's former mistresses came evidence that Calmette was no gentleman; Caillaux set the evidence aside—*he* would be a gentleman, though he was fighting for his wife's life. The Action Française organized its toughs to attack him and his partisans in the streets. He had Pascal Ceccaldi fit out a bodyguard of Corsicans—"No doubt they did not all have clean police records," he admitted.[46]

The trial began on July 19, a day before schedule; it lasted nine days. The prosecution charged Madame Caillaux with having murdered Calmette in order to prevent him from publishing either the green papers or the Fabre document; a communiqué from the President of the Republic denied the existence of the green papers, and Caillaux denied having known of the existence of a Fabre document before Calmette's death. He had been apprehensive only lest Calmette publish the letters held by Madame Gueydan, which were compromising for his wife, he declared. Madame Caillaux had meant merely to frighten Calmette; to kill him was necessarily to bring out all the "documents," and to bring them out in the worst light possible; hence she had fired downwards. While the defense spoke of the "deplorable accident," ballistics experts testified that Calmette had either crouched like a coward or else rushed precipitously into her line of fire, and learned doctors testified that the wounds had been harmless but that the surgeon had made a fatal error of diagnosis. Count Károlyi read the contract and Caillaux read the will. In brief: Calmette had provoked Madame Caillaux to shoot him, then he had tried to commit suicide, then his surgeon had killed him inadvertently, and he was a scoundrel anyhow.

Meanwhile the staff of the *Figaro* vouched for Calmette's good moral character; so did his brother Albert and his friends Paul Bourget and Henri Bernstein. The chief witness for the prosecution was Madame Gueydan. She was burning with resentment for the man who had rejected her and spitting with spite for the woman who had taken her place. Flourishing illicit copies of stolen letters, she proclaimed Caillaux deceitful and capable of any crime. In a dramatic gesture she surrendered the copies to the lawyer for the defense, who thanked her tearfully and, amid a hushed silence, read out the two most compromising of them.[47] They turned out to be banal: Calmette had been bluffing.

The defense put on an all-star show; most of the performance backfired. Barthou denied that Madame Gueydan had ever offered him the letters. Poincaré did say that Caillaux had spoken to him of no other documents than love letters the morning of Calmette's death, but he also said that Caillaux had threatened to kill Calmette and had refused to let his lawyer intercede. Neither Barthou nor Poincaré was able to suggest who or what might have been behind Calmette's campaign.

Caillaux was himself in effect the principal attorney for the defense. Whenever he spoke he dominated the hearings; he was never called to order. He proclaimed his wife blameless; he indicted himself for neglect of her feelings. When he was accused of having egged her on, his

bald head was flaming red, and he was fuming with anger.... And then Caillaux talked of love. A thrill ran through the room when, standing between his first and his present wife, he said, "I have been a most unhappy man..." Then he ended his deposition, and kissed his wife's hand.[48]

Madame Caillaux bore up proudly under scrutiny. She showed great courage and little remorse. Her only motive for frightening Calmette, she maintained, was the imminent threat to her reputation as a lady—she was shortly to have been received by the King and Queen of England, who both read the *Figaro*. "*Nous sommes des bourgeois,*" she repeated[49]—she had grown up when the word *bourgeois* was still honorific.

The hearings were tumultuous at times. The Camelots du Roi attempted to terrorize the courtroom, and Caillaux's Corsican devils struck back.

At one point Justice Dagoury accused Justice Albanel of partiality, and Justice Albanel sent seconds; judicial superiors intervened.

On July 28, in his final declaration, the civil plaintiff representing Calmette's two children maintained that Madame Caillaux had murdered Calmette in order to prevent the publication of damning documents; he demanded the death penalty, intimating that she rather than her husband had done the deed because a woman presumably stood the better chance of acquittal. The state prosecutor for his part was willing to recognize extenuating circumstances, and recommended clemency. The chief defense counsel—Labori, one of Dreyfus' lawyers—enumerated precedents for acquittal, then spoke of a poor, tormented soul, and ended up inviting the jury to make a gesture toward reconciling Frenchmen as war clouds gathered. "Paris waited breathlessly for the... verdict.... All thought of war was forgotten."[50]

To the preliminary question, "Did Madame Caillaux kill Gaston Calmette?" eleven jurors out of twelve replied "No," and an hour later Joseph Caillaux, accompanied by a squadron of police and one of Corsican irregulars, escorted his wife home from prison.

The trial of Madame Caillaux threw no new light on the events leading up to Calmette's death. Everyone had agreed from the start that the *Figaro* campaign was no ordinary political campaign: behind it was something more than mere political animosity, and someone more than Calmette. Calmette had never been virulent before, but then he was poisonous. He had never signed his articles before, but then he sprawled out his signature aggressively. No doubt he opposed the income tax and favored the three-years law; that, however, was not reason enough for him to try so relentlessly and so recklessly to discredit Joseph Caillaux. Poincaré gave as his own guess that Calmette, having "let himself be hoodwinked in the Prieu case, wanted to get even [afterwards]";[51] the reasoning does not stand up, for Calmette had most of his ammunition in advance of the campaign. At the time, Parisians imagined a rivalry between Caillaux and Calmette in an *affaire de cœur*.[52] Later, because the campaign had divided and demoralized the country on the eve of war, the enemies of France appeared as its most likely instigators. For several years Caillaux sincerely believed it to have been subsidized by Austro-Hungarian warmongers in their efforts to prevent the formation of a Caillaux-Jaurès government; then, by dropping this hypothesis from his writings, he implicitly recognized that Lipscher had hoodwinked him and Károlyi both.

Caillaux's testimony differed from Poincaré's on several points during the trial, and in later years they carried on a battle of memoirs over the difference. Poincaré made out Caillaux to be all bluff on the surface and cowardice beneath, fitting him out for good measure with the symptoms of a manic depressive. Caillaux for his part made out Poincaré to have been Calmette's chief collaborator, and Barthou merely to have taken the opportunity of the campaign to play a trick on a friend. Poincaré was a little less than half right, Caillaux a little more. Caillaux was no coward; Barthou was no schemer. If Poincaré did not encourage the *Figaro* campaign, he did not discourage it either. Throughout he claimed to have no means of restraining Calmette; afterwards he blamed Caillaux for not having trusted him to restrain Calmette.[53] And he was careful to make fewer mistakes on matters of fact than Caillaux: like all great dissemblers, he was greatly attentive to detail.

Did Madame Caillaux kill Joseph Calmette? Had the jury thought so, the minimum penalty for her would have been life imprisonment. Probably the jury did think so, but not that much. So in a sense the jurors legislated, the force of their verdict being that a man capable of publishing love letters was fair game for those whom he might injure in so doing. Whether Madame Caillaux aimed well or ill, then, her act had one positive result: just as no campaign quite like Calmette's had ever been waged before, none quite like it has ever been waged since.

Caillaux had taken over the defense of his wife both out of affection and out of a natural impulse to preside. In so doing he had assumed the posture of a defendant. Paris condemned him, and in the end the *Figaro* campaign achieved its political purpose. Yet in all the charges against him the truth was at least distorted. The best point against him was the Rochette incident. After it had become an affair he maintained that a government had the right to give a state prosecutor any order;[54] in 1911, however, he did not even stop to think whether a government had that right or not. He had wanted to get rid of a petitioner and back to work, and he was always too busy serving the state after his fashion to trouble much how he found the time to serve it.

Rightly or wrongly, Madame Caillaux had been acquitted. Now what was there to prevent the formation of a Caillaux-Jaurès government?

CHAPTER 5

The Rubicon

JOSEPH CAILLAUX spent the day of July 29, 1914, receiving courtesy calls with his wife on the occasion of her acquittal. At six o'clock, just as the last caller was leaving, Malvy informed him by telephone of a decision of the Council of Ministers to back up a mobilization order given in Russia. Furious, Caillaux spent the whole evening haranguing one after another of the members of the government: at least England should have been consulted, he argued.[1] The following day the Council of Ministers decided to consult England, and for two days afterwards the rumor of war subsided.

On July 31 Jaurès was assassinated. The Prefect of Police notified Caillaux by telephone and advised him to leave Paris at once. He and his wife packed their belongings. The following morning, as they were about to depart, general mobilization was decreed, and all exits from Paris were closed. Caillaux requested a special exit permit; it was several hours in coming. "And," he recalled, "as my wife and I waited, pacing back and forth in our apartment, our automobile at the door, we got one phone call after another, each one a threat of murder."[2]

When in August a new government was formed, no one even notified Caillaux at his retreat in Mamers—he and peace both were obsolete, if not downright unpatriotic.

Caillaux took up active service on August 20, voluntarily. He held the rank of lieutenant in the reserves; because of his grade in the Inspection des Finances he was able to obtain a commission as Paymaster General to the Army with the rank of colonel.[3] On August 24 he left on a mission to the Belgian frontier; as he left, General Messimy, his former confederate in the Chamber, wrote begging Joffre

personally and most urgently to authorize Paymaster Caillaux, accompanied by Corporal Ceccaldi, to be assigned to Sarrail's staff. He agrees to accept them both, I know. There is no use either of us creating political difficulties for ourselves.[4]

Crowds hissed Caillaux wherever he went; again and again he got into fist fights with English officers. Once he found a colonel discourteous and went to headquarters to protest; Galliéni, refusing to see him, had him ordered back to barracks under threat of disciplinary action. In October he was insubordinate, and on October 27 Malvy, as Minister of the Interior, offered him a mission abroad as an alternative to a court-martial.

He chose the mission abroad. He left the army obtrusively: at Paris headquarters on November 6 Lieutenant Tardieu, on an errand for Foch, caught sight of "the Paymaster-with-five-bars Joseph Caillaux gathering crowds in the corridors."[5] On November 14 he sailed with his wife from Bordeaux aboard the *Pérou* to arrange for obtaining food supplies for France in Brazil.[6] Malvy in his haste neglected to notify the French Embassy in Brazil of the mission, and the Brazilian government ignored Caillaux on his arrival. Shortly thereafter orders came from Paris confirming the mission and extending it to Argentina, but simultaneously came instructions from Delcassé, then director of the Quai d'Orsay, to the Ambassador in Brazil, Paul Claudel, to put a close watch on Caillaux. Caillaux kept the Embassy spies busy, for he did not spare his interlocutors his opinions on the war: he called it a big mistake, and he blamed all French governments except his own for having blundered into it gradually since the days when Delcassé had run foreign affairs. Caillaux having once entered Brazilian Railway stock on the Paris Bourse, his host in Brazil was the head of the Brazilian Railway; for the rest he had only chance associates. A certain Count Minotto, an agent for the Guaranty Trust Company, charmed the Caillaux couple in Rio; they ran into him on the train for Sao Paolo; in Montevideo, too, he turned up, and they spent some time with him in Buenos Aires. In Brazil Caillaux told Minotto that the whole present French government except Briand was worthless. In Buenos Aires Minotto mentioned being on friendly terms with Ambassador von Luxburg of Germany; Caillaux, however, had no message to convey to the Ambassador unless it were one of protest against the deference shown him in the German press—praise in Germany, he said, was ruining him in France. News reached him in Argentina late in January that his protégé Desclaux had been indicted for theft of food supplies while serving as Paymaster to the Army; taking the indictment of Desclaux for an attack on himself, Caillaux wound up his business rapidly, and in March he started home. By the time he reached Portugal, Desclaux had confessed and been sentenced to seven years of military prison.

Caillaux and his wife made a brief stay at Biarritz as the guests of Paul Bolo-Pasha, a French financier formerly in the service of the Egyptian government. They did not remain long in Paris, where Caillaux was hissed and threatened. Once back in Mamers, they stayed there for sixteen months, Caillaux abstaining even from attending parliament. Few of his political friends were faithful to him—once Paul-Boncour came on a furlough to see him, and both made a note of the event.[7] His social friends were more attentive: in July, 1915, Minotto, coming from Italy, stopped off in Mamers for a few days, and once or twice Bolo urged the couple to visit Biarritz again. Caillaux kept up acquaintances with the *Bonnet Rouge;* he did not keep up the subsidies, though when the editors started a second paper, *La Tranchée républicaine*, he did send them what he described as a "calling card" of 600 francs.[8] He made a few patriotic speeches in his district, and he wrote a few patriotic letters to newspapers. When he was patriotic in public, however, he excited as much suspicion as when he kept to himself. "I personified a policy opposed to nationalism," he explained.[9]

To Germany as well as to France Caillaux was still the man of negotiations with Germany, whether secret or open. At the outbreak of the war Leopold Lipscher had left Paris precipitously for Belgium, Caillaux still owing him 2000 francs for the Calmette contract. Lancken, in charge of German espionage in France, hired Lipscher in Belgium to sound out Caillaux on the prospects for a separate peace. Lipscher wrote urging Caillaux to meet him in Zurich. Caillaux refused, whereupon Lancken despatched one Thérèse Duverger to Mamers. At the border the Police identified Mlle. Duverger as a spy, then let her through—or escorted her —to Mamers. Caillaux got rid of her with 500 francs[10] of his debt to Lipscher. Lipscher wrote again to Caillaux, and again and again. Caillaux let him write until one day a letter came with the censor's seal on it; then he broke off relations categorically.

Caillaux favored peace, but he was in no position to negotiate it. In April, 1915, he wrote a long pamphlet entitled "Les Responsables,"[11] which no doubt he intended publishing anonymously if the war became unpopular enough: it told how the "war party" of Poincaré had thwarted the "peace party" of Caillaux, and it blamed Poincaré for not having called Caillaux back from Mamers in August, 1914, to take power. In 1915 Caillaux also condensed into a single volume his account of the negotiations with Germany in 1911, closing it with the words, "France was led into the great war. It will be the glory of my life to have, despite the obstacles strewn on my path, prevented it from breaking out in 1911."[12]

If the war dragged on long enough, Caillaux reasoned, eventually Poincaré would have to call either him or Clemenceau to power—Clemenceau if there was some hope left, him if there was none. So he jotted down notes from time to time for use in case he were called. In bold letters he wrote "RUBICON," and underneath:

For a period of x months beginning with promulgation of the present law the President of the Republic is empowered to issue decrees in cabinet with legislative and constitutional effect.

Such decrees as entail an increase of expenditures, the creation of new taxes, or the modification of existing taxes, shall be, though immediately applicable, submitted for legislative sanction to the first session of the chambers held after their enactment.[13]

He would, he wrote, call a joint session of the two chambers and "make them vote (impose on them) the draft law entitled 'Rubicon.' " If the war was still on, his governement would, like the Jacobin government during the wars of the Revolution, send out representatives on mission to the armies to goad on the generals and to report on them. He would also issue a manifesto in favor of peace and of a new constitution, then dissolve the Chamber, dismiss two thirds of the Senate, and call for the election of a constituent assembly. To make sure all went smoothly in Paris he would call in the Corsica[14] and the Mamers regiments; in no case, though, would he make peace "without a special mandate from the country." His peace terms would include, under the guarantee of neutral nations, compulsory referendums on all future treaties and mobilization orders. By the terms of his draft constitution, the referendum would be obligatory in France for "big questions." Senators would be fewer in number and would be elected directly by the people. The Senate would have power only to review the acts of the Chamber; if it twice rejected the same bill, the Chamber would be dissolved, but then the new Chamber would take final action. The Chamber itself would have no say in financial matters and no power of initiative; it might, however, suggest amendments to bills submitted by the government, though not the same amendment more than twice. The Conseil d'Etat would become a "third assembly," but as such it would serve merely to advise the government. None of the sessions of parliament would be publicized, and no official transcript would be made of them. At the beginning of each legislative period, parliament would choose a president of the Republic; the president in turn would choose a premier, who would also be vice-president of the Republic; if the president died or resigned, the vice-president would succeed him. The president would be forbidden to leave the country during his term of office, and after it he might be tried for violation of the Constitution. If a government lost the confidence of the Chamber, new elections would be held immediately—at one writing, however, Caillaux would have had the first president of the Republic announce his intention of refusing to allow a government to resign in the event of a mere vote of no confidence.

Month after month Caillaux drew up lists of prospective collaborators. He would have "a small cabinet, made up of reliable men." He wrote down Malvy's name with a question mark beside it. Barthou and Briand he put down for "Embassies and Administration," Ceccaldi to head the Sûreté Générale and the prefectures. Paul-Boncour he meant to "utilize" and Almereyda to "make use of." Some, too, he put under the head of "Possible Purchase,"[15] and others he meant to "eliminate from the ante-chambers of power," including the staffs of the *Figaro* and of the *Action française*. He would have the "direct and indirect authors of the war" brought to trial along with "the men of the Action Française and certain newspaper publishers." He also drafted a law for "organizing and regulating" the press. It made immediately applicable certain penalties for slander, including imprisonment and fines in some cases, and in all cases damages proportional to the circulation of the offending journal, "with very high minima." It also gave slandered members of parliament the right to send their slanderers to the High Court for trial. Finally, he planned to institute the income tax and a tax on capital, to nationalize the railways, to raise the compulsory school age to seventeen, to suppress religious instruction "by stages," to construct housing for workers, to fight infantile paralysis, infant mortality, alcoholism, and tuberculosis, to institute old-age pensions and unemployment insurance, and to set up an immigration agency.

The "Rubicon" is the expression of a strange blend of respect and scorn for democracy, of self-seeking and of devotion to the common good; it is also a strange mixture of sense and nonsense. The notes on constitutional reform were, as Caillaux himself wrote, "a mass of contradictions."[16] At his best he saw clearly the defects of the Third Republic, particularly the want of an independent executive; even at his best, however, he sought remedies too drastic, because even at his best he did not, as prospective premier, lose sight of his own convenience. Accustomed to wielding power, he did not care how it was legitimated; he could imagine no better way to justify having it than to make good use of it; he did insist, however, that it flow smoothly. His contempt for the republican personnel of his time was constant in his secret thoughts; just as constant, though, and far greater, was his reverence for the state. He thought as a headstrong functionary: his job was to get things done, and his job went on whatever the regime and the tally of wars won or lost.

Once Caillaux, after he had expiated the "Rubicon" in full, lopsidedly explained away the worst of it: "That, giving in to my temperament fond of authority, inclined to rapid solutions, I did at certain moments envisage on paper governmental operations which, face to face with my responsibilities, I would never for an instant have thought of putting into practice, I do not deny."[17] Indeed, the "Rubicon" was more the dream of an unemployed statesman than it was the scheme of an idle Caesar. Statesmen all dreamed of peace at the time—some of exacting it, others of making it. And even a democrat may dream he is a Caesar: such is the stuff most dreams are made of. Caillaux, however, had the bad sense to dream on paper.

CHAPTER 6

The Politician
as Tragic Hero

"A man...who, though not outstandingly virtuous and just, yet falls into
misfortune, not through vice or depravity, but through some tragic flaw;
and moreover he should be drawn from the ranks of men who have enjoyed
great reputation and prosperity." ARISTOTLE (on the tragic hero), *Poetics*.

IN AUGUST, 1916, Caillaux and his wife, tired of their solitary retreat in
Mamers, went to Vichy. There Madame Caillaux volunteered as a nurse
in a militairy hospital; she was booed out of the wards. One day rioters
of the Action Française attacked the couple in the street. They took refuge
in the police station, which then for three hours withstood a veritable
siege. At last reinforcement arrived from out of town, and the assailants
were dispersed. "The chief of the pacifists...is extremely unpopular,"
wrote Izvolsky with delight to Saint Petersburg.[1] Madame Caillaux, her
nerves worn, begged her husband to take her to Italy; he agreed. Just
as they left Vichy, his partisans were organizing a rally of sympathy;
at the request of the mayor he called the rally off and also consented to
waive charges against two rioters "of good family."[2]

Caillaux and his wife next spent a few days on the Italian Riviera under
her maiden name of Raynouard. Then, as she went on to Rome alone,
he returned to Mamers. There in October he was host to Paul Bolo-Pasha
and to Senator Charles Humbert, who were on their way to Spain to
interview Alfonso XIII. For some years Humbert had been the publisher
of *Le Journal* in association with Pierre Lenoir, whose father had assisted
Caillaux and Fondère in their secret talks with Lancken. Bolo had bought
Le Journal from them in March, 1916. Bolo and Humbert were fitted out
with letters from the Quai d'Orsay and—so said Bolo—a word of
greeting for the Spanish king from Poincaré himself. Caillaux coveted the
idea of a union of France, Spain, and Italy, so he asked Bolo to put in a
good word for him with Alfonso. The same month he returned to Italy
with all his papers, some bonds and coupons, two copies of "Les Responsables" typewritten by his wife, Briand's tax records, and a file bearing the caption: "Offers to negotiate peace. My refusals." In Florence

he rented a bank safe in the name of Raynouard and deposited the lot. Afterwards he paid a brief visit to his wife in Rome; she introduced him to a charming friend, Signor Cavallini, who was a friend of Bolo's too. Caillaux was in Paris for the sessions of the Chamber in November. Meanwhile, in Rome, his wife called at the French Embassy on his advice to pay her courtesies. The Ambassador, Camille Barrère, had her informed that she was not welcome. Caillaux protested to the Foreign Minister, Briand, who then ordered Barrère to call at her hotel and apologize. Barrère refused, and Briand told him to send a subordinate. François Charles Roux was sent; not finding Madame Caillaux in, he left his card—whereupon, according to rumor, he offered his resignation, and Briand refused it. Caillaux tried in vain to prevail upon Briand to dismiss Barrère.

While Caillaux was in Paris, Cavallini visited him to suggest their founding a Franco-Italian Bank and a Franco-Italian newspaper. Bolo and Humbert also paid him a call on their return from the Spanish border, where they had seen Alfonso; the Spanish monarch, who had not yet recovered from Agadir, had trembled at the very mention of Caillaux's name. Caillaux again joined his wife in Rome in December, intending to take her to Naples for the duration of the war. Cavallini surrounded the two with his friends, most of whom saw eye-to-eye with Caillaux on the advantages of a negotiated peace. On December 17 Cavallini introduced Caillaux to Martini, recently Minister of Colonies. Caillaux, by his own report, told Martini of his hope for a close union of Spain, France, and Italy whatever the outcome of the war, as well as his doubts about the Allies' chances for total victory—doubts secretly shared by most Frenchmen and Italians at the time. By Martini's report, Caillaux favored an easy peace and was prepared to negotiate it himself—he did not regard even the restitution of Alsace-Lorraine as essential. Meanwhile, Barrère and the other Allied ambassadors in Rome sent home disparaging reports on him and on the company he kept. According to Barrère, he had been to the Vatican to see Monsignor Pacelli, "the most fiery of the pacifists-at-any-price"; also, he had told all comers that Premier Briand, "drunk with his conquests of French and Greek princesses, is using up in worldly pursuits what little energy he has left," that a Clemenceau-Barthou government "to intensify the war effort" was imminent, that it would fail, and that he would himself then return to power and make peace at the expense of England and Russia.[3] The Parisian press, getting wind of the reports, assailed Caillaux for "defeatism." In fact the word "defeatism" was coined then for use against him; although it meant only skepticism about the chances for victory, it connoted a desire for defeat. To the official rumors the press added rumors of its own—rumors of mad things presumably said and done by him. As far as the French public was concerned he was capable of having said and done any one of them, so, as in the case of Agadir, whether he had or not was irrelevant.

Late in January, 1917, a distant cousin of Caillaux's, Lieutenant Henry de Jouvenel, arriving in Rome on mission, warned him that the Cavallini crowd was suspect, especially Cavallini himself, who was a former convict currently under investigation for treason. At once Caillaux returned to Paris. Early in February he asked Briand for access to the file of complaints against him; Briand gently turned him away. A few days later the Sûreté began an investigation of Bolo, whom it suspected of receiving money from Germany through Switzerland. Caillaux, undaunted, volunteered testimony on Bolo, describing him as a patriot and a gentleman incalculably wealthy in his own right.

On February 17 Emperor Charles of Austria-Hungary, having "learned from a reliable source that a Caillaux government was in sight,"[4] recalled his brother-in-law, Prince Sixte de Bourbon, who had been negotiating in secret with Briand. A Caillaux government was not, however, in sight of Poincaré, who in March, when the reports from Italy were all in, asked the Council of Ministers to open an investigation of Caillaux. The Council declined unanimously. The following summer Sixte de Bourbon asked what terms France would offer Austria for changing sides in the war; he received no reply. "Had I been in power I would have jumped at the opportunity," Caillaux later wrote.[5] In July, meanwhile, Lancken engaged a Swiss banker, H. A. Marx, to approach Caillaux; Marx gained entry to Caillaux's home in Mamers on some pretext but was turned out when he made his errand known. Then Lancken made contact with Briand, who reported the contact to Premier Ribot—adding mirthfully that Lancken "had first thought of other political personalities but recognized in the end that these persons no longer had enough authority."[6] Lancken, though he offered Alsace-Lorraine in return for peace, made no headway with Ribot. Briand, wistful, maintained the contact on his own.

In the summer of 1917, as the war went from bad to worse for the Allies, generals came offering their services to Caillaux. He turned them away: Poincaré, he thought, could not put off the choice between him and Clemenceau much longer. On July 22 he made his bid: he spoke in Mamers in favor of Wilson's Fourteen Points, declaring in particular that France would not lay down her arms unless Alsace-Lorraine were restored.

Poincaré, however, had made his choice even before the war. On June 18, 1914, he had remarked in private:

Clemenceau detests me.... He never ceases attacking me, ridiculing me... making me out to be a prisoner of the church and of reaction. But for all his great defects—his pride and jealousy, his hatred and rancor—he has one quality that merits all of my indulgence, one quality in which Caillaux is lacking: he has, to the highest degree, the national fiber.[7]

Clemenceau, moreover, was above suspicion, having for years avoided bad company by avoiding company of any kind.

Marx, it turned out, had brought funds from Germany to the *Bonnet Rouge* at the time of his visit to Caillaux. Early in August the *Bonnet Rouge* was indicted; Almereyda, arrested, hanged himself in prison. Caillaux, in Paris for the preliminary inquest, there wrote encouragingly to Bolo of "my latest intercessions."[8] Probably he interceded for Bolo through Malvy. Malvy, however, under attack by Clemenceau for "laxity," resigned on August 31 as Minister of the Interior. Ribot fell in consequence, and Painlevé took over from him. Late in September Caillaux, in a fit of naïveté, saw the new Minister of the Interior and offered to confine himself to Mamers or else leave France, at the government's pleasure. On October 4 Malvy had to defend himself in the Chamber against an accusation of treason brought by Léon Daudet in *Action française*. Caillaux, on hand for the occasion, spoke up for stricter censorship of the press, concluding with a call for a revival of the spirit of the left. A few deputies applauded him. Later the same month Senator Humbert informed the police that Bolo, in purchasing *Le Journal*, had paid fully in cash; Humbert was just in time, for early in November Washington sent Paris evidence that in April, 1916, Count von Bernstorff, German Ambassador to the United States, had given Bolo a few million dollars. Caillaux testified in favor of the *Bonnet Rouge* on November 6, then again in favor of Bolo two days later. "A man is innocent until he has been proven guilty," he explained, infuriating Poincaré.[9]

Painlevé fell on November 13, and the next day Poincaré called Clemenceau to the Elysée. "On judicial affairs I do not find Clemenceau as determined as I might have wished," noted Poincaré. "He speaks of Malvy with sympathy and even of Caillaux with extreme moderation."[10] Nonetheless, to a friend who warned him a few hours later that a Clemenceau government might mean civil war, Poincaré replied, "I have to choose between Caillaux and Clemenceau. My choice is made."[11] Designated Premier, Clemenceau announced a policy of crushing "pacifism" and "defeatism." Poincaré wrote to him on November 20 to suggest putting Caillaux up for trial: "Fate has placed him at the crossroads of all the paths of treason."[12] And Clemenceau replied: "Caillaux is a bandit. I don't know whether the High Court or the Council of War will try him, but justice will be done." Or so at least recalled Poincaré.[13]

Malvy on November 23 asked the Chamber for an opportunity to clear himself of the charge of treason before the High Court, which was the Senate; the Chamber readily approved his request. Then on December 11 the government asked the Chamber to make Caillaux, too, liable to trial for treason by suspending his parliamentary immunity.[14] A commission set up by the Chamber to study the government's request voted nine to two (Pierre Laval and another Socialist) for the right of the Chamber to suspend a deputy's immunity; then by seven to four it recommended suspending Caillaux's, the government having first agreed not to send him before a military tribunal if the final charges against him were predominantly political. On December 22 Caillaux himself invited the Chamber to suspend his immunity, asking only to be tried by the High Court; while confessing himself guilty of imprudence, he proclaimed himself a victim of persecution—his ideas and not his acts, he said, were at issue. The extreme left applauded him, and the Chamber waived his immunity by 396 to 21, with 115 abstentions.

Caillaux chose as first counsel Maître Charles Demange, dean of Paris lawyers, who had defended Dreyfus, and as second counsel he chose Pascal Ceccaldi. Demange took the case only on the understanding that he would drop it if ever he came to doubt Caillaux's innocence. Then at the end of December Caillaux wrote to Rome asking his wife to remove the contents of the safe in Florence. She in turn telegraphed the bank director forbidding him to open the safe. At once the Italian police were on her heels. Ambassador Barrère authorized them to requisition the contents of the safe, then reported to Paris that they had found plans for a *coup d'Etat* and lists of accomplices together with securities worth 2,000,000 francs and jewelry valued at 500,000 francs,[15] obviously bribes from the enemy. Almost simultaneously Washington sent Paris the text of two telegrams of February, 1915, from Ambassador von Luxburg in Argentina to Bernstorff in the United States. Caillaux, Luxburg had wired, "was sensitive to indirect courtesies from me. Insists how careful he must be, since French government is having him watched here, too. Warns against excessive praise for him in our press."[16] Frank Minotto had been, among other things, a spy for Germany. He had also been James Minotto, an American citizen, and in 1915 he had married the Chicago meat heiress Ida May Swift. Arrested when the United States declared war, he had volunteered testimony on his spying, and Washington passed on to Paris, along with the telegrams, the appropriate parts of his testimony. Briand and Poincaré, taking stock of the new evidence against Caillaux, were both "disgusted."[17] Clemenceau for his part was delighted: "Now we've got him!" he cried, rubbing his hands. "And the two millions in the bank vault! Were they a reserve for flight or a fund for crime?"[18] He decided to have Caillaux arrested, and in true Jacobin style he warned him discreetly, as Danton had been warned. Caillaux, of course, did not take flight; instead, for the first time in years, he attended a salon—the salon of the comtesse Greffulhe, who had invited him knowing of his imminent arrest.[19]

On January 14, 1918, he was confined to the Prison de la Santé, a prison for common-law criminals. In the next cell to his, a man who had raped and murdered a child was awaiting execution. On February 25 he threw up a meal; thereafter, apprehensive, he had his food brought to him from the outside in a locked chest. He was allowed to have visitors at all hours, and eventually his cell was furnished with a bathtub, a radiator, and an easy chair.

Captain Bouchardon, a former magistrate, conducted the interrogation. He strove doggedly to find grounds for keeping the affair under military jurisdiction. "Convinced though he was of your innocence, he wanted to frame you," Bouchardon's nephew later wrote to Caillaux.[20] The evidence did not assist Bouchardon. On a recount the valuables in Florence turned out to be worth only half a million francs. All of them checked with Caillaux's prewar documents such as his divorce papers, even his inheritance—not only had he received no money from Germany, but he had made no profit out of fifteen years of politics.

Bolo was condemned to death, and on April 7 his lawyer easily persuaded Poincaré that he was covering up for Caillaux, "a traitor and a common-law criminal."[21] The police gave him to understand that his life would be spared if he came clean, and at the last minute he sent the newsboys screaming; his revelations fell through, though, and he was shot. Late in April the defense for the *Bonnet Rouge* alleged that Caillaux had commended Marx to the newspaper in 1916. Caillaux swore that he had never even heard of Marx before July, 1917, and the defense did not press the point. One *Bonnet Rouge* editor, Duval, was condemned to death for having taken money from Germany. So was Lenoir at the *Le Journal* trial for having known who paid the bill for Bolo; Humbert, who evidently did not know, was acquitted, and a third associate, who perhaps knew, got five years in prison. At the last minute Lenoir, like Bolo, sent the newsboys shouting, and Maître Demange, consulting with Caillaux in prison, started in alarm as the shouts came through the bars. "There is nothing," said Caillaux with a shrug.[22] Lenoir was shot. In May the state decided to prosecute Malvy. "It will be Caillaux's turn next," noted Ribot. "If he comes before a military court he will quite likely be sent to Vincennes. Will the government call on the Senate to judge? That would be the ugliest gift it could make to the Senate."[23] On August 6 the High Court, finding Malvy guilty of culpable negligence but not of treason, condemned him to five years' banishment. He left at once for Spain.

Captain Bouchardon had failed to link Caillaux with the other treason cases, and at the end of July, with over fifty interrogations to his discredit, he was relieved by a civil prosecutor, Lescouvé. The state formally brought charges of treason against Caillaux on October 29, 1918, and the next day the Senate appointed a committee to examine the charges in case it should itself have to try him. Clemenceau at first favored a military court, but as the months passed and state's evidence failed to pile up he was more and more inclined to have Caillaux cleared of the charges reserved for military jurisdiction. In January Clemenceau's agents had paid dearly in Belgium for a batch of Kiderlen-Wächter's private letters; the letters proved embarrassing to the prosecution, so they were set aside. On August 15 Paul Claudel, in reply to an inquiry, had written from Brazil:

Throughout his entire stay Caillaux did not cease having the most correct attitude and professing the most patriotic sentiments.... In conversation he manifested a certain bitterness due to his thwarted ambition. He pointed out that, had he remained in power and had his policy been followed, France might have avoided war.[24]

At least Claudel knew how to distinguish small talk from big. His report was filed away. Late in November Washington succeeded in deciphering the telegrams exchanged between Ambassador von Luxburg and the Wilhelmstrasse during Caillaux's mission in 1914; as it turned out, they were all about funds for combating Caillaux's influence in South America,[25] so the copies sent to Paris were filed away in their turn.

On November 7, 1918, Ceccaldi died, and Caillaux chose Maurice de Moro-Giafferi, another Corsican, as second counsel. Later he took as third counsel a Socialist, Marius Moutet. By May, 1919, he had found enough peace of mind to put the finishing touches to his book *Agadir*, which was published shortly afterwards. Beginning that spring he was frequently ill, and early in September he was transferred from La Santé Prison to a nursing home in Neuilly, on the outskirts of Paris.

On September 16, 1919, Clemenceau announced his decision to send
Caillaux before the High Court for trial. He first set the date for October
23, then on second thought changed it to the following January 14. January 14, 1920, was the second anniversary of Caillaux's arrest. It was also
two months after the date for the new general elections, and so there
would be time enough in between for a partial renewal of the Senate.
Unlike the old Senate, the electorate was now nationalistic with a
vengeance, and the members of the government did not want to have to
answer to it for an acquittal or even the prospect of one.

On the eve of the trial the Quai d'Orsay bought in Belgium a stolen
copy of Lancken's wartime correspondence with the Wilhelmstrasse.
It expected to find damning evidence against Caillaux; instead it found
damning evidence against Briand. Ribot took the correspondance first
to Poincaré, then to Clemenceau. In his diary Ribot, being honest, wrote
nothing of Poincaré, but of Clemenceau he wrote: "He recognizes that
Briand compromised himself as much as Caillaux, but he is not eager to
have another trial."[26] Clemenceau, on leaving office, turned the correspondence over to Briand in a gesture of generosity. Briand, without even
reading it, returned it to the Quai d'Orsay.

In January the trial was put off once more while the elections to the
Senate were held. Many candidates pledged themselves to find Caillaux
guilty whatever the evidence. Then at the end of the month the National
Assembly met to choose a new president of the Republic. The last time
Clemenceau had wanted it to choose the stupidest candidate, and it had
chosen Poincaré. This time he wanted to be chosen himself; this time,
however, his earlier wish was granted,[27] and he went into retirement.

The trial of Joseph Caillaux for high treason opened on February 23,
1920. In his initial statement to the court, on February 25, Caillaux proclaimed his innocence as he had in the Chamber two years before. The
prosecution first brought up his secret talks with Germany in 1911:
Poincaré told the story of the green papers, after his fashion. Jules
Cambon and Fondère, for the defense, were nervous and evasive. Then
Caillaux had to deny that in fighting for the three-years law he had striven
to demoralize and disarm the country; Messimy bore him out. The next
count on the indictment was treasonable commerce with the enemy in
South America, and the prosecution faltered a little when its chief witness
turned out to be testifying under a false name and never to have been in
South America. According to Luxburg's two telegrams to Bernstorff,
which the state produced, Caillaux resented being lauded by the German

press. According to the same texts, however, he "believes, or professes to believe, in the stories of German atrocities in Belgium,"[28] and nowhere did they state that he had communicated with Luxburg, even if Minotto did say so afterwards. The state offered the "Rubicon" as evidence of a conspiracy to commit treason. The "Rubicon" was irrelevant to the charge of treason, and it was a one-man conspiracy at best; however, if the prosecution could not prove its case, it meant to prejudice the court, and so it made the "Rubicon" serve its purpose. A porter testified that, during a train ride from Milan to Paris, Caillaux had talked about secret peace negotiations, but an American who had occupied the sleeper above Caillaux's called the porter a liar. François Charles Roux denied having resigned from the French Embassy in Rome after having called on Madame Caillaux; on the contrary, he said with merciful cruelty, he would have resigned had it been anyone else's wife in order not to appear to be seeking political influence. The testimony of one witness for the prosecution "proved decisive against the prosecution"[29]—that of Henry de Jouvenel, newly elected senator, who found Caillaux "guilty not of an understanding with the enemy, but of a misunderstanding with the Allies."[30] Not even Barrère brought up Caillaux's supposed visit to Pacelli: the Vatican had denied repeatedly that it would ever have received Caillaux, who was a notorious antichrist, and adulterous besides.[31]

In six years Caillaux had lost none of his skill in debate. He did not apologize for his pacifism; instead he cried out his innocence of treason. On the "Rubicon" his comment was, "My mind wandered";[32] on his opposition to the wartime governments, "They didn't even consult me";[33] on Briand's tax receipts, "*I* don't use such weapons";[34] and, at the mention of Barrère's insult to his wife, he wept. To Senator Delahaye, who said to him, "Sir, I read in the 'Rubicon' that you wanted to 'get rid of' Delahaye: what did you mean?" he replied, with perfect poise, "It's quite simple. I meant to do just what your party associates did to you the other day in refusing to include you on their electoral lists."[35] Moro-Giafferi and Moutet each made fiery statements for the defense, and grey-haired Demange was particularly impressive when, mentioning his compact with Caillaux, he reported that he had found no evidence of treason, only evidence of persecution.[36] Caillaux's own final statement, however, was the best of all. He was on trial for his ideas, not for his acts, he repeated—he was undergoing a *procès d'opinion*. Defiantly he told a jury full of nationalists that time would prove the price of victory to have been exorbitant. Such was his eloquence that, had the vote been taken at once, he would no doubt have been set at liberty then and there.

For a moment the government was desperate; then it got the presiding officer to adjourn the court for a day on the ground that the precise wording of the charges was in doubt. Poincaré and others, even Briand, put the interval to good use, and the feeling grew among the senators that if it would be unfair to Caillaux to find him guilty, it would also be unfair to his accusers to find him innocent. Besides, if he got off scot-free he might return to power, and then he would be greedy for reprisals.

On April 22, 1920, by 213 votes to 28, the High Court found Caillaux innocent of treason, or "intelligence with the enemy" as defined in Articles 77 and 79 of the Penal Code.[37] By a narrow margin, however, it found him guilty of "damage to the external security of the state," which Article 78 defines as "such correspondence with the subjects of an enemy power as, without being directed toward [treason], nonetheless results in furnishing the enemy with information deleterious to the political or military situation."[38] To validate its verdict the court found that he had indirectly but deliberately requested the Germans to cease their praise of him and also held "defeatist" conversations with Italian "neutralists": for the purpose at hand, his request to the Germans was considered "deleterious to the political or military situation," and the Italian "neutralists" were assimilated to the category of "the enemy." He had not been tried under Article 78, of course, and Maître Demange rose in all his dignity and cried: "Remember, gentlemen, you are condemning a man on a count for which he has not been defended!"[39] "An acquittal in cowardice," commented Moro-Giafferi. Caillaux himself defined his crime as *"trahison par imprudence."*[40] The court sentenced him to three years in prison and ten years' loss of civic rights, held him liable for the expenses of the trial, which came out to 53,000 francs,[41] and, in a final, supreme improvisation, inflicted on him a penalty normally reserved for common-law criminals—five years' banishment from all cities of over 50,000 inhabitants except Toulouse.

He had been in prison two years, three months, one week, and one day; his term of prison was mitigated for good conduct, and the morning after the verdict he was home with his wife in Mamers.

Was the verdict just?

Certainly Caillaux was not guilty of treason. In fact the state's evidence weighed in his favor: a man plotting a compromise peace does not proclaim a desire for one. His crime, if he was guilty, was not imprudence but innocence itself. He did not, for instance, even think to notify the police when they let Thérèse Duverger through to him. "Where is it written," he later asked, "that a personality of the class of M. Caillaux—nay, any honest man—should play the part of an informer?"[42] The answer is: in the biography of M. Caillaux. His pacificism made him a rallying point for traitors and spies,[43] but he was too lonely to recognize them for what they were. He was also too naïve: "M. Caillaux, more provincial than all our provinces put together," wrote André Tardieu, "imagined...that he was dealing with a great and mighty lord when he fell into the clutches of the crook-and-spy Bolo-Pasha."[44] He had dreamed of a *coup d'Etat*; his dreams were his own business, though, or at least they did not concern the enemy. Perhaps he did communicate with Luxburg, though there was only a spy's word for it. If he did, the communication was harmless, and his offense was only not stopping to check whether there was anything wrong about communicating harmlessly with the enemy. Laws, however, are presumptuous, especially unwritten ones: they will not excuse a man from the obligation to know them.

If Caillaux had thought ill of the Republic, he had served the state well; yet for what he was merely capable of having said in Rio one day he was condemned as the nearest thing to a traitor that the law lets live. The Radicals and the Socialists had stood by him—many of them sincerely, all of them opportunely. A few individuals had come to his defense spontaneously. As the police car took him to prison, the poetess Anna de Noailles, formerly the mistress of Maurice Barrès but lately attracted to victims of *raison d'Etat*, had thrown herself down before the front wheels —or else, according to another version, clutched the rear bumper and been dragged along.[45] Joseph Reinach, who wrote the history of the Dreyfus case, had appealed to Clemenceau to send Caillaux to the High Court and not to the Council of War. Anatole France, who was a humanitarian late in life, had saluted in Caillaux "the great citizen who vanquished Germany in 1911 without its costing France one drop of blood. The hatred of your enemies makes you greater," he had written to the prisoner of La Santé.[46] By the very ignominy of the sentence Caillaux gained in stature, though the gain was not apparent until he was back on his feet.

Was Caillaux right in his judgment of the war? By making a bid for peace after the victories of the Yser and the Marne, he maintained, France would have gained a "moral hegemony in Europe,"[47] and at any time before 1918 she might quite likely have retrieved Alsace and Lorraine as well. More, what France did gain by the war she would have gained in time without a war, whereas what she lost through the war was not only costlier than what she gained, but it was lost for ever. Such a proposition is undemonstrable, of course, and so it needs to be thought about all the more. Caillaux regarded as inevitable the breakup of the Austro-Hungarian Empire and of the Turkish Empire, along with a consequent weakening of the diplomatic position of Germany; what was not inevitable, to his mind, was the Russian Revolution. In 1920 most Frenchmen thought him culpably wrong; five years later most of the same Frenchmen thought this of his judges instead.

Old-style Radicals, wrote Albert Thibaudet, were "astonished by the contrast between the militant Clemenceau of the Dreyfus affair and Clemenceau the wartime minister who... staged the Caillaux and Malvy affairs like two police operations."[48] Clemenceau, however, never felt the difference. Wrote Ribot in 1924: "Clemenceau had it in especially for Caillaux, whose political fortunes he had launched."[49] Ribot was as wrong about Clemenceau's personal feelings as about Caillaux's political fortunes. Clemenceau remarked in 1925 that he had prosecuted Caillaux without animosity, as he would have prosecuted anyone else whose friends included five or six spies or traitors—in fact, he added, Caillaux was the one man in France with whom he had no quarrel.[50] He did not even pretend at all times to believe in Caillaux's guilt. He had put Caillaux on trial for *raison d'Etat*, the same reason for which others had maintained the sentence against Dreyfus; a Jacobin war lord, he had "discover[ed] traitors because he needed them."[51] Unlike most *raisons d'Etat*, however, his had a certain grandeur to it, for it was not meant to save a caste or a clique, but to lead a nation to victory. If Caillaux and a few others found the price of victory too high, he reasoned, Caillaux and the others would themselves be a fair price to pay for it.

In times of crisis Frenchmen all play roles. For more than a century now they have been reenacting the Great Revolution in politics, just as the Revolutionaries took their models from Greek and Roman history. Caillaux in discussing his trial compared himself with Danton whenever he was not comparing himself with Dreyfus. He may at times have been a poor orator, writer, or thinker, but all his life he was a great actor. He took his parts as they came, and he played them for all they were worth—"a veritable chameleon, and clever the man who could tell his true character," wrote a lifelong acquaintance.[52] He was playing himself as tragic hero when he cried out his innocence in the prisoner's dock while brandishing a briefcase inscribed in letters of gold "*Joseph Caillaux, président du Conseil.*" He was guiltless, yet he had only himself to blame—and that is the very definition of tragedy.

As a tragic hero, however, he was unlucky, for he had no antagonist worthy of him. Clemenceau had as much talent, and at first Clemenceau, too, played his role boldly, in the Jacobin tradition. On November 20, 1917, asking the Chamber to suspend Caillaux's immunity, he exclaimed: "You tell me that *I* have made mistakes! Perhaps you do not know the greatest of them."[53] Superb! However, Clemenceau was too softhearted to be well cast as Clemenceau. He felt sorry for Caillaux because Caillaux was not guilty—Danton at least had embezzled. So he left the Caillaux affair to others, and before it was over he had fallen from power. Later Caillaux, naming himself heroically in the third person, replied to Clemenceau: "When we think how pitilessly they pried into the life of Caillaux, when we think of the innumerable traps they set for him,... does it not surprise us that they should have found so few things to hold against him?"[54] The reply, too, is superb; however, Caillaux had to make it on paper, after the trial, for Clemenceau was not there in the courtroom to hear it.

The trial of Joseph Caillaux was a last act, perhaps a final one. Since April 21, 1920, tragedy has gone out of politics in France. Pétain might have played a tragic role at the Liberation; he did not even try—he played at dignity instead. One man did try, Pierre Laval, but the performance did not come off. Laval was a good showman, but he had two things against him: he was mean, not noble; and he was guilty. Caillaux had no such shortcomings.

CHAPTER 7

The Comeback

"Le banissement a été et reste la consécration de l'homme d'Etat, aujour-d'hui comme il y a vingt-cinq siècles. Notre République, peu propice aux grandes ascensions, subit l'ivresse des grands retours. Ses remords lui tiennent lieu de desseins.... L'erreur politique va de compagnie avec la judiciaire. On ne croit pas à l'innocence, mais on pratique la réhabilitation. Personne ne reste au pouvoir, tout le monde y retourne.... Le sol de la République foisonne de dynasties. Tout bouge, rien ne change. Il est défendu d'agir, et recommandé de vieillir.

"L'homme public qui s'élève de chute en chute gagne le respect en fatiguant l'injure. Un jour vient où il est consacré par les accusations même qui l'ont lapidé au long de la route. Mais ce jour le trouve las, dégoûté de ses con-temporains, découragé de l'avenir. La foi qui transportait sa jeunesse ne soutient plus ses forces, n'inspire plus ses actes. Il a perdu le goût des trans-formations profondes et se résigne aux petits accommodements quotidiens. S'il se souvient de son passé, il ne se reconnaît pas plus en lui qu'en la légende formée autour de son nom par les années de polémiques et de ba-vardages. L'habitude a pris chez lui la place de l'espérance. Sans doute tient-il encore au pouvoir, mais comme le vieillard tient à la vie—quand il ne sait plus qu'en faire."
HENRY DE JOUVENEL[*]

JUST AS DURING THE WAR Joseph Caillaux had attracted spies and traitors to him in spite of himself, so after the war, in banishment and disgrace, he was in danger of attracting deserters and anarchists awaiting an amnesty.[1] This time he was alive to the danger. The first year or two of his exile he spent "shut up with my books, with my files, working, writing."[2] He put the horrors of his imprisonment out of his mind by putting them into a book, *Devant l'histoire, Mes Prisons;* in it he denounced his enemies, then denounced the war, and in October, 1920, concluded by denouncing the peace. He proclaimed the folly of the slogan "Germany will pay":[3] Germany, he argued, could not pay even as much as France owed America, and to try and force payment would be to disrupt the economy of Europe and so increase the dependency of France on America. One year later he completed *Où va la France? où va l'Europe?*, which set forth both more convincingly and with more data his arguments against the Peace of Paris. At the same time it dismissed Soviet communism as a camouflage for "state capitalism," and parliamen-

[*] *La Revue des Vivants*, I (1927), 454-55.

tary democracy as a shield for "privileged oligarchies," though incongruously it concluded with the necessity to "synthesize western-style democracy and Russian Sovietism."[4] This synthesis Caillaux described with
the vocabulary of syndicalism: an "economic state within the political
state," answering the need to "entrust the direction of the economic state
to new organisms" and to "maintain parliamentary assemblies but leave
them with only political rights, only a mission of higher control."[5] He
did not identify the oligarchic privileges to be destroyed, or delimit the
economic state, or describe the new organisms; he did not see the
humorousness of the phrase "only a mission of higher control." He
advised against bloody revolution; to effect the "necessary changes" he
had faith neither in parties, nor in the masses, nor even in classes, but only
in *"individualités de raison désintéressée"*[6]—words difficult to translate, even
into French. Such "individualities," he maintained, were "the source of
all progress. Men of lofty mentality, dispersed throughout the nations
…"[7] *Où va la France? où va l'Europe?* was less an expression of Caillaux's
thought than it was a symptom of his state of mind. It betrays many of his
complex, contradictory emotions: his liking for innovation, which led
him to coin new bits of jargon when in want of new ideas; his pride in his
own singularity, and his lonesomeness withal; his distress at being cut off
from parliamentary democracy by his temperament and from Marxism by
his reason; his reluctance to break old ties, and his nostalgia for the
heroic days when he had led the fight against privileges. Though he did
not later disavow the "economic state," he did not often bring it up again.
Some of the themes of *Où va la France? où va l'Europe?* he retained, however: he had not finished with the struggle against privileges, and with
the *"individualités de raison désintéressée"* he had barely begun.

Having taken a brief glance at the future, Caillaux went back to nursing
old wounds. For the next two years he toiled incessantly at the first draft
of his memoirs, which dealt with the period before 1914. While he was
thus spelling out his bitterness, Madame Gueydan on her side was busy
ransacking back numbers of the *Figaro* and of the *Action française* for
items of gossip about him, which later she strung together to make up a
pretended history of the Third Republic, *Les Rois de la République*. The
marriage of these two, so dreary while it lasted and so dire in its consequences, had a certain grotesque fitness after the fact: she became as much
obsessed with him as he was with himself, and both were resentful enough
at their loss of station not to notice much their other losses.

At times Caillaux grew tired of writing; at times he felt shut up in his
little town of Mamers. "Then I would wander," he recalled.[8] He meant

we: his wife went without saying. By answering for her as he had in 1914, he had made infidelity a dramatic impossibility—for the time being. To strengthen their union they had, moreover, the fellow-feeling of former jailbirds as well as the memory, not of long happiness together, but of long suffering apart. After sharing persecution they shared ostracism, wandering together on the back roads of France. They were turned out of hotels and restaurants; they were insulted in cafés and in the streets. *His* spirit at least was never broken, and his health thrived on a diet of bitter pills. All his life jealous rivals had wanted to do away with him— some crudely, some by due process of law. If he could find no other way of getting even with them, he would at least outlive them.

In the summer of 1921 Caillaux and his wife were the guests of Anatole France in Touraine: "The two friends chatted at length together, sounding the future, foreseeing no good in the fate of Europe."[9] Toward the end of 1921 Caillaux spoke at a Socialist meeting near Grenoble; his hosts applauded him unremittingly, though he warned them that he was no more of a Marxist for being an outcast. Afterwards a band of rowdies armed with clubs and bricks invaded his hotel—thus "he had begun defending himself against his friends even before he was done defending himself against his enemies."[10] In Toulouse in May, 1923, on his way to see his doctor, he was struck over the head with a lead pipe and left lying in the gutter. The blow was almost fatal.

He was not assaulted again. On February 18, 1922, the League for the Rights of Man held a rally in favor of an amnesty for him. Toward the end of 1923 he was able to speak freely in public. His books began to sell. Bankruptcy in Germany, inflation in France, the occupation of the Ruhr as security for reparations payments, all gave currency to his pronouncements. Like Lord Keynes in England, he was actually becoming a prophet in his own country. He was applauded in Agen, Bayeux, Denain, Montpellier—the four corners of France.

In the elections of May, 1924, the Cartel des Gauches, or union of the Radical and Socialist parties, won a decisive victory; even Malvy, back from Spain, reentered the Chamber. Edouard Herriot, forming a new government in June, had Malvy ask Caillaux to suggest a financial policy and a possible Minister of Finance. For two years Poincaré as Premier had been drawing checks against Germany's reparations debt before finally obtaining from the chambers a general tax increase of 20 percent. Caillaux advised Herriot to take inventory of the financial situation at once in order to prepare the public for a new increase in taxes as well as to avoid being blamed for one afterwards. Great Britain and the United States were demanding the evacuation of the Ruhr; Caillaux advised Herriot to demand in return that France not be liable for her war debts to Great Britain and the United States beyond the amount of reparations received from Germany. As for a Minister of Finance, he could think of no one. It was just as well: Herriot, as it turned out, had asked his advice for the sake of asking it, not of taking it.

Speaking in Le Mans on August 17, 1924, Caillaux warned his compatriots that the time had come for "*une grande pénitence économique et financière.*"[11] He no longer proposed to tax their fortunes; instead he proposed to tighten their belts. The phrase "*grande pénitence*," a program in itself, resounded through the country. Caillaux had returned to orthodox finance, if indeed he had ever left it. His credit rose on one side of the political fence without falling off on the other.

Caillaux agreed to be included by special mention in a general amnesty bill. It passed the Chamber on July 14, 1924; in October, however, the Senate amended it, and only on December 17 did the Chamber take final action, then abrogating the sentence of the High Court as of January, 1925. Caillaux's exile was cut short by three months, his loss of civic rights by sixty-three. Meanwhile, by special permission he returned to the capital in October, 1924, to attend the funeral of Anatole France. Murmurs of sympathy greeted him from the crowd: with the financial situation daily deteriorating, his popularity was daily mounting. His legend met all requirements. For men who venerated the state he was the author of the "Rubicon," and for men who dreaded the state he was its most notorious victim. For some he was the "income-tax man," for others he was the man who had "crushed the income tax while seeming to defend it." His exile had added to his appeal: he seemed "constant because he was kept away from whatever changes, independent because he was no longer eligible."[12] He had acquired the mystery that goes with exile: he was the wizard of Mamers, concocting a magic formula in his reclusion for curbing inflation without balancing the budget, for increasing the tax yield without increasing taxes. His popularity intimidated and alarmed the men in power, the Radicals even more than the others: "I fear especially his friends," Anatole France had said.[13] In 1920 Briand had described Caillaux and himself as "irreconcilable opponents";[14] five years afterwards he was saying: "[Caillaux] is somebody. But it's best to keep him in reserve. We'll call him if things go badly."[15] The savior in reserve hesitated a moment before accepting his new role, wondering whether his future was not in exile—whether at 63 he was not too old to start out again in the system he had criticized, among the men who had condemned him.[16] Before he had finished hesitating, however, he had begun acting.

On February 19, 1925, the Radical party held a banquet in Paris to welcome him back to its fold. Of the prominent party members only Herriot did not attend: his absence made the banqueters look like conspirators. Caillaux spoke dolefully of the need for vigorous financial measures but gave no hint of what those measures were. Once he said *"novation de dettes,"* and the press debated whether he meant new loans or new taxes. "Already his slightest utterances made the franc leap."[17] If the franc leaped for Caillaux, though, it dove for Herriot. No budget acceptable to the Cartel was acceptable to the Senate, and when Herriot put a capital levy on the agenda of the Council of Ministers he set off a panic at the Bourse, in parliament, and in the Radical party itself. The Minister of Finance resigned; his successor, seeing no hope of replenishing the Treasury without disrupting the majority, resigned in turn, and in April the government fell.[18]

Painlevé, called to succeed Herriot, invited Caillaux to head a commission of experts on the financial dilemma. Caillaux declined. A few hours later Painlevé gave in and offered him the Ministry of Finance. Caillaux hesitated, for appearance's sake; when he accepted, Painlevé in a symbolic gesture sent a car to fetch him from Mamers. The car broke down on the way to Paris.

Just as Caillaux was the financier in vogue, Briand was the diplomat of the day. The "irreconcilable adversaries" joined hands, and on April 21 the new government appeared before the Chamber. Its fate was uncertain. Caillaux was no more attractive to one half of the Radicals for seeming indispensable to the other half, no more attractive to anyone in parliament for seeming indispensable to everyone outside. His most eloquent defender was a Communist, Marcel Cachin:

At a time when here and elsewhere you were an object of contempt, as you know, there was an uneasy silence throughout this Chamber, even among your friends...and if someone spoke up in your defense it was up *there*, on the Mountain, on the extreme left; and you know too that throughout the country it was the most unfortunate workers who—always generously, always nobly— stood by you.[19]

No less than the Communists, the impenitent Nationalists would have "shut Caillaux up in his past,"[20] and the whole cabinet was needed to restrain him from meeting their attacks. Their most eloquent interpellant, Taittinger, began with a fair estimate of Caillaux's strength:

The Minister of Finance comes to us preceded by all sorts of legends and...

seems to enjoy sympathy in the most diverse quarters. According to some, who are among the greatest magnates of industry and finance,... he is the man of providence...; he alone, it would seem, is capable of destroying the tax on capital while seeming to defend it.... In speculators' circles Caillaux's accession to power is also hailed with I know not what fondness. He is expected to turn all sorts of somersaults to facilitate campaigns for increases and campaigns for decreases.... In certain conservative or Catholic circles, clever propagandists have made out Caillaux to be prepared... to grant all nature of satisfaction and appeasement to those whose consciences have been troubled of late.... Finally, in the eyes of a part of the public, Caillaux arrives as a kind of Treasury magician, capable of turning dry leaves into banknotes, possessing veritable financial panaceas, with the ability to put our budget back in order overnight and to procure for our Treasury the sums that it is lacking.[21]

Taittinger recalled with nostalgia the days when Caillaux was execrated; then, not content with resuscitating the judgment of the High Court, he read into the Court records a supposed confession by Caillaux. As Moro-Giafferi set the records straight, Caillaux exulted in silence. "Better than a retort," wrote Alfred Fabre-Luce,

this error of the interpellant brought to mind the scandals of the prosecution and the iniquity of the sentence. The Minister was saved, and at the same time the trial was revised. This last Nationalist gong, resounding in emptiness, marked the end of an epoch.[22]

The Minister was saved, but the savior was doomed. The Cartel was divided over financial policy, as Herriot had shown in spite of himself. Painlevé had called on Caillaux as the only man capable of holding the Cartel together; however, part of the Cartel accepted Caillaux because of his orthodoxy, part in spite of it. The Socialists accepted him because he had been unjustly condemned by their adversaries; besides, he had once thought of instituting a tax on capital, so they pretended to expect him to expropriate the bourgeoisie. When Painlevé had offered him the Ministry of Finance he had reflected: "It's either too soon or too late."[23] In fact it was both: there were no easy remedies left, and the public did not yet realize the fact. Even so he was not wrong to have accepted the ministry, only to have accepted it without also demanding extraordinary powers. The chambers had never granted extraordinary powers in the past; however, no Minister of Finance had ever had to face such a crisis in the past. Nor was any Minister of Finance ever able to curb inflation and balance the budget with a majority on the left, and no other majority was available to the former inmate of La Santé Prison. No solution could possibly satisfy the whole left, and only until he proposed one would he be the hero of the Cartel and the idol of the country. Refusing him full powers, Painlevé or parliament would have had to contend with the fury of their electoral clientele. Caillaux might have played off the nation against parliament; he settled for accepting the honors of office instead. Perhaps he did not know his own strength; more likely he did not dare test it. He had dreamed once of testing it, but he had been punished for dreaming, and he had recanted. The aspirant Caesar was no more than a legend: "Secret penitence had weakened him"[24]—he had lost his nerve. While now his opponents were realizing that he had once spoken the truth courageously, he was realizing that he had spoken it imprudently; while now they remembered him as fearless, he remembered himself as rash;[25] while now they could not forget how proudly he had borne up under persecution, he could not forget how cruelly they had persecuted him. On the brink of the Rubicon at last, he got cold feet.

All Paris scrutinized the *revenant*[26] as, before having had time to find a private apartment in Paris, he moved into the Louvre once again. He had to improvise an etiquette of rehabilitation: the niceties of readmission among the men who had banished him or even voted for his death; the steps to take, the hands to shake. Most of his colleagues took up with him again as though nothing had changed in ten years—indeed, Paul-Boncour even found him "rejuvenated."[27] He declined no gesture of reconciliation. Anna de Noailles complained: "You meet people at his home whom you've been avoiding on his account."[28] He even shook hands with Barthou, who as president of the Reparations Commission requested an audience with the Minister of Finance—but now they did not call each other *tu*.[29] Only Poincaré kept clear of him. Clemenceau, of course, was keeping clear of everyone.

Caillaux had only to push an armchair or two around and dig out some old books from the basement to feel at home again in his ministry. If the apartment was more or less the same, though, the job had changed altogether. Before the war he had spent his time as Minister of Finance reforming taxes and preparing the next year's budget; since the war Ministers of Finance had been hard put to it to extend the last year's budget from month to month and borrow to sustain the Treasury. For a while he satisfied the public by merely being Minister of Finance; his very name was a program, or a fair substitute for one, and to have asked for more would have been "an insult to his genius."[30] His provisional credit with the public enabled him on April 25 to get provisional credits from parliament for May and June. However, the problem of inflation was far more urgent than that of appropriations. The franc had immediately halted its fall out of deference for the new minister, but it had resumed falling two days later. He was unable to set it at its "real value" as he did not have a balance sheet of debits and credits for the nation. He did not have the past budgets to examine, either—they were still being audited. Because of the war debts, which were due to mature in 1929, the deficit in the budget varied with the exchange rate. The war debts were accounted at 3.5 percent; if honored, they would entail more than half a century of payment. Devaluation, although it would mean an increase in the deficit, would also mean a decrease in the amount of a foreign loan necessary to absorb the deficit. However desirable a new fall in the franc might be, though, public opinion would interpret one as a failure on the Minister's part. "Assuming power with the pound at 90 francs, he became the custodian of that exchange rate in the eyes of the public."[31] "Real" parity was, of course, a mythical entity; however, mythical as it was, it was certainly more than 90 francs per pound. One other thing was certain: in a few days a floating debt of some 50,000,000,000 francs[32] in the form of national bonds would mature. The honest solution consisted in stabilizing the franc and amortizing the debt, and the way to amortize the debt was to cut down on expenditures and find new receipts. In all fairness to the nation, then, he would have to raise taxes. But *voilà!* he had been chosen *not* to raise taxes. As Alfred Fabre-Luce put it: "He is, in the eyes of the public, the man who will know how to remove disagreeable necessities by ingenious artifices, and the confidence shown him is laziness disguised."[33]

What of his old panacea, the income tax? The income tax had been adopted in 1917, and like anything else it had no sooner come into use than already it was obsolescent. Caillaux had championed it in the first place because its yield was most flexible; by 1925, however, its rates were as high as could be. He had expected its adoption to obviate the need for national loans; France had launched more such loans since its adoption than ever before. He had thought it would prove the most economical tax; it was costing inordinate sums to collect, and by discouraging shop-keepers and peasants from keeping accounts it was doing its share in making the economy stagnant. He had expected it to be equitable; not only had fraud and poor accounting restricted its effective action to the salaried classes, which paradoxically had been the first to demand its adoption, but the spread of gross salaries within each class had increased more or less in proportion to the scale of contributions. In later years the government was to fall back on external signs of wealth as a basis for its assessment, making it over in effect into a tax on cars and maids.

Concurrently, indirect taxes were to return to fashion on the left: they almost collect themselves, and while no category of consumer can dodge them they may spare any category of consumption. To be sure, even under the most discriminatory system of indirect taxation the rich pay only insofar as they buy luxury, not insofar as they can afford it; where discrimination is in demand, however, wealth itself is not resented so much as are certain of its uses.

In 1924 Henry de Jouvenel had written: "The men who come to power come to apply ideas or to betray them, never to look for them."[34] Already Jouvenel was wrong: Caillaux was looking anxiously. He did not let on that he was looking, though—"At sixty-two years of age, after ten years of waiting, one does not bungle one's comeback."[35] Instead, giving up on solutions, he sought expedients. When the bonds reached maturity he would have either to pay or to refuse to pay—there was no third course. He wanted to pay the safe way, by setting up a "single ceiling"—that is, by designating some date as a reference date for bond and currency issue combined, the Bank of France being instructed to increase currency issue thereafter only as bond issue decreased. "It would have sufficed for bondholders to be sure of being reimbursed at their convenience for them no longer to want to be reimbursed," asserted one expert.[36] The press, however, denounced the single ceiling as "inflationary," so Caillaux did not dare adopt it. The Bank of France and the Bank of Paris for their part wanted simply to refuse payment; such a refusal then went by the name of "consolidation." Also in favor of consolidation were the Socialists, who took the alternative to be inflation, and inflation to be a wage cut masquerading as a general calamity. Consolidation, Caillaux thought, would ruin the credit of the state, and it would defeat its own purpose by encouraging the public to spend instead of saving.

He had spoken against it in the Chamber on April 21—in fact he had given no more positive hint of his intentions. A few days later he spread the rumor that all bonds would be redeemed; then he denied it.

His temperament tolerates no hesitation, but his intelligence throws him back on hesitation. He thinks aloud, and he translates the progress of his thinking into successive decisions. The misfortune is that each decision spreads at once into the camp it threatens and there stirs up opposition.... If he stuck to one of these heroic resolutions Caillaux would at least have the benefit of audacity before the public. But in the end prudence reappears. Then, after having been frightening, he is disappointing.[37]

At the end of June, when the franc reached 104 to the pound, Caillaux transferred the responsibility for maintaining the exchange rate from the Bank of France to his own cabinet. He also referred the policy of consolidation to an *ad hoc* committee of bankers and financial experts. The committeemen rejected it unanimously but failed to find an alternative. Their failure was merely symptomatic: there was no majority of deputies either for any solution. A campaign against Caillaux began in *Le Journal*. In reaction Caillaux launched an expedient to gain time—a loan with the exchange rate guaranteed, or in effect a national loan in foreign currency. He meant to make the loan a preliminary to stabilization, leaving the national debt constant. It was a judicious gamble. So far Frenchmen had not shown enough confidence in the franc to save it; now if they showed enough defiance toward it, it might be saved. The loan failed.

The Socialists proposed a tax on capital as a panacea. The Treasury had only to help itself to the money of the rich, they argued; tax on capital was equitable by definition, and its yield was infinitely adjustable. Caillaux was still the income-tax man; he ought to be the capital-tax man for the same reasons. At what point does income become capital? For ordinary men as distinct from economists, the question reads like a medieval riddle. The difference in equity between taxing capital and taxing income is, besides, almost imperceptible. However, income and capital are at the two ends of the economic process, and with a tax on each at his disposal a Minister of Finance might regulate the whole economy. But Caillaux held that the time for a tax on capital was past, though the cohesion of the Cartel might depend on his holding otherwise. A tax on capital, he argued, was least practicable precisely when it was most desirable: its introduction in time of inflation would only make matters worse by encouraging conversion into foreign currencies. He was right, but he was too blunt for the Socialists, and by way of protest Vincent Auriol quit the chairmanship of the Finance Commission in the Chamber.

On July 12, 1925, a friend having resigned to make way for him, Caillaux was elected Senator from the Sarthe, and the same day he was also chosen president of the general council of Mamers. The ceremonials done with, he hurried back to Paris, there to learn that his wife had been injured in an auto accident on her way to meet him. For once he did not rush to her side; he had more urgent business. That night, counter to the wishes of the rest of the government, he asked the chamber for a vote of confidence against a proposal to exempt businesses with fewer than four employees from the tax on turnover. The Chamber had voted the exemption once before, and the Senate had rejected it; now most of the

Radicals joined the center right in voting for it while the left wing of the Cartel joined the far right in the opposition. Caillaux had assured himself beforehand of the support of the center. Thus only a few hours after winning a seat among the men who had condemned him he had rehabilitated himself some 60 degrees farther to the right—and a few hours later he was at his wife's bedside commiserating with her over a dislocated hip and broken kneecap.

Called on to mend the Cartel, Caillaux had split it wide open. The contradiction was not his: politics had become so illogical in France that the Cartel was able to survive as a majority only as long as it did not have a policy. Government had become distinct from politics, and as if to show up the anomaly of the distinction the deputies of the left demanded: "What majority does the government intend to lean on in the future?" The question had priority.

The split in the Cartel had been imminent; it rid Caillaux of the need to cater to the Socialists, leaving him free to define a program of austerity. However, the moderates had supported him only to split the Cartel; they were not so eager to let him save the franc. His police record blocked him on the right even while his policies cut him off from the left. In the final reckoning he had not so much shifted his majority as he had reduced it.

Before balancing the budget, before even expressing the budget in so many francs, Caillaux had first to settle the war-debts question. Payments on the war debts to Great Britain and the United States were due to start in earnest in 1929. His hope was first to get Winston Churchill, Chancellor of the Exchequer, to agree to a reduction of the debt to Great Britain, or at least to a linkage of the debt with the reparations payments due from Germany; then, to go to the United States with this example of the magnanimity of John Bull to hold up to the Yankee Shylocks.

In August he met Churchill, and after a brief rumor of deadlock the two negotiators announced their agreement on a reduction of the debt to Great Britain from 1,800,000,000 pounds, which Churchill had at first described as an incompressible minimum, to about 623,000,000 pounds, due in sixty-two annuities ("funded at 2 percent") and payable only so long as Germany met her reparations payments to France—the agreement subject, however, to the proviso that the United States concede to France the same funding terms and the same limitation on liability. Caillaux had achieved more than he had hoped for, even more than he had planned on. Churchill for his part had little apprehension: most likely the United States would decline to match his terms and so both restore France's debt to Great Britain and by the same token take the blame for it.

At the latest reckoning Washington demanded 3.5 percent annual payment on the principal and 5 percent interest besides. To Americans the Caillaux-Churchill agreement appeared as "a conspiracy to cheat America out of her just rights as a creditor of Europe by putting her in the wrong before the eyes of Europeans."[38] On August 31 Caillaux declared that France did not mean to repudiate her debt to America but only to discuss terms within her means. One week later, with the rumor circulating in Washington that Caillaux meant to offer the West Indies in lieu of money, President Coolidge set up the Debt Funding Commission to investigate France's ability to pay. Caillaux on his side picked out a dozen members of his majority, not excluding Vincent Auriol, to advise him in the negotiations with the United States. He met with them several times before leaving, and took small account of their advice. On September 17 he, they, and Madame Caillaux embarked for America. Off Plymouth the Royal Navy gave his ship a twenty-one-gun salute. The United States awaited him with curiosity: on one day the press lauded his "penetrating intellect,"[39] on another it reported him to have drawn up his final plans, on another it recalled his troubles involving the German Embassy in Washington.

He and his party arrived on September 24; they went directly to Washington, where the meetings with the government began the following day. The United States had estimated the total French war debt at 4,300,000,000 dollars. France, replied Caillaux, recognized a debt of only some 4,000,000,000 dollars at the most, and was prepared to pay it in sixty-two gradually increasing annuities. At once the Treasury officials objected that he was overlooking the interest, and they came back with a plan for payments adding up to about 10,000,000,000 dollars. Caillaux replied that he had foreseen the objection but hoped for America to waive the interest. France was poor, he repeated with a sort of personal shame; whenever he spoke of actualities, however, Secretary Mellon replied with potentialities. American banks were forbidden to lend to France so long as the question of the war debts was not settled; Wall Street urged Mellon to give in, and Mellon urged Coolidge; Coolidge, however, was intractable. Apprised of the risks involved in forcing France into bankruptcy he replied: "They hired the money, didn't they?" He was not wholly impervious to sentimental arguments, and he did realize that

America would hardly feel the loss if no payments were made. What with congressional elections pending, however, to waive the debt would have been political suicide: what greater shame for an American than to be played for a sucker by a European?

As the discussions grew technical, the public got bored with them: one Washington news agency started "sending out every night an extra message about the negotiations; forty-eight hours later three fourths of its customers had wired, 'Stop service. No interest.'"[40]

After a few days Caillaux spoke of acceding to Washington's demands provided that France's liability were geared to the receipt of reparations payments from Germany. France, he argued, had contracted her war debts while associated with her creditors in a struggle having as its objective Wilson's Fourteen Points, the eighth of which was reparations payments. What Caillaux proposed was in effect a transfer of the French debt to Germany, and not even Wall Street was willing to underwrite the transfer. By October 1 France had agreed to sixty-eight annuities adding up to 6,200,000,000 dollars. However, on the same terms as the United States had given Great Britain, France would have to pay 10,000,000,000 dollars, and Mellon would go no lower. Wall Street lost all patience. No one seriously expected France ever to meet payment anyhow, so— wondered the well-informed—why not put down just any figure? Mellon hinted at the converse, that France accept any old sum as had Germany, then borrow from New York banks on easy terms. Caillaux refused; and when reminded of the first installment due in 1929 he replied that, like Thiers in 1871, he would launch a "national liberation loan." In a speech to the Lotus Club he appealed to "the heart of America."[41] Meanwhile cordiality flowed: Coolidge asked him for news of Clemenceau and, calling it champagne, served him glasses of Apollinaris.[42] Officially, agreement was imminent until the last moment; then on October 2 the French delegation abruptly packed up and left. America barely noticed. In France the pound, which had not budged since July, shot up to 110 francs.

On October 12 the Council of Ministers in Paris formally rejected the demands of the United States government, and three days later most of its members were in Nice attending a congress of the Radical party. From the very start of the congress Caillaux found himself in opposition to Herriot, who still clung to the Cartel. Already Caillaux had split the Cartel; he was now to split the Radical party. He called on it for authorization to create a sinking-fund office, to establish a single ceiling for bond and banknote issue, then to demand full powers to balance the budget and begin the fight against "the feudalists" ("*les féodaux*"). Also, as the Bank of France was reluctant to extend credit to any left-of-center government, he recommended increasing the government's powers over the Bank; otherwise he would have to resort to foreign credit, "[using] foreign confidence to offset French defiance."[43] He denounced the tax on capital, and Herriot supported it; Herriot won out more or less with the rank and file of the party. Then the two men announced a compromise "tax on all forms of wealth"—a compromise viable only as long as it was not defined. Meanwhile the press ridiculed Caillaux for his timidity. He had lost his prestige as a magician, and the prestige won in resisting Uncle Sam was a poor substitute.

And so he found himself at the right of the Cartel because of his opposition to consolidation and to the tax on capital. In the Assembly, though, he had no troops on the right, where Poincaré was the financier and magician in honor. Only a few memories still bound him to the left; yet Painlevé, who had taken it on himself to fetch him back from Mamers, would not agree to drop him without the whole government's resigning.

On October 26 Caillaux spoke at Château-du-Loir in defense of his projects. He opposed consolidation, he said, because it constituted "a repudiation of the contractual obligations of the state"; instead he wished to suppress "expenditures that might better be avoided." He did not believe in "strokes of the magic wand"—the loan with the exchange-rate guarantee was an expedient, he admitted. What counted was "time, patience, method, and confidence in the men who govern." The magician act was officially over; it was as a magician, however, and not as a politician, that he had been recalled from exile. He posed as the defender of the Republic against the "*réacteurs*" and defender of the state against the "*féodaux*."[44] He was resuming the old fight against privileges with a new vocabulary; the implication was that, given the time and confidence, he would become a Jacobin again.

At the last minute he "clutched nervously at his post."[45] He asked his government for authority to investigate the exchange operations of the Bank of Paris, and he moved to dismiss the director of the Bank of France. "He announced a new plan, then took time submitting it, as though to play at mystery again."[46] He was too late: most of his colleagues threatened to resign individually if they all did not resign collectively, and on October 27 they all resigned. The Cartel was salvaged. The pound rose to 116 francs.

As Painlevé set up a new government without him, Caillaux, no longer cast as a magician, was free to resume the role of a martyr. The Radicals in the government had found his proposals too conservative; he was to criticize theirs in the future as more conservative than his own.

Briand soon succeeded Painlevé as Premier, and one after another all winter long Briand's Ministers of Finance failed. The inflation grew steadily worse, but the Chamber did not dare to vote new taxes. Loucheur thought up the retroactive tax. Paul Doumer could think of nothing. When Raoul Peret took over, the franc fell, and he ascribed its fall to a revolution in Poland; he gave up after a vain attempt to settle the war-debts question. By June Briand had no ministers of finance left; even Caillaux two months earlier had made his conditions unacceptable. Potential ministers, such as they were, had taken to waiting for the worst to pass, leaving it for others to discredit themselves. Fear swept the country. For one week in June Briand tried to form a cabinet uniting men over and above their parties, but the spirit of the Cartel revived against him. Then he tried to reach an understanding with Herriot, but Herriot wanted him to leave the foreign office. Briand, of course, was only staying on as Premier in order to remain as Foreign Minister. The financial crisis distressed him, yes, but it peeved him even more—for all he knew, it was a conspiracy of speculators and warmongers at the Bourse to deter him from his mission of peace among men. Whenever he wearied of forming new governments, President Doumergue urged him to persist. Doumergue had come a long way since 1914, when he had been a front for Caillaux; he was now an impresario for Poincaré, whom he was holding in reserve until things could get no worse and so were bound to get better. He pressed Briand to find other financiers, and at last Briand had to fall back on Caillaux.

This time Caillaux posed his conditions with rigor: full financial powers and the vice-premiership, with the same right to oversee expenditures in all the ministries as Briand had refused him in 1909. In 1926 Briand did not refuse; he merely was shocked. Caillaux regarded the new government as his own in reality: Briand having "courageously resuscitated the policy of Agadir, which today is called the policy of Locarno,"[47] Caillaux in effect relegated him to foreign affairs, using him moreover as guarantor to parliament of the genteelness of his own intentions. Parliament, the press, and the public also regarded the new government as Caillaux's own. Old suspicions were aroused, old charges reiterated—*coup d'Etat*, fiscal inquisition, internationalism. And still the franc rose a few points, defiantly.

The new government did not ask for full powers until the Vice-Premier and Minister of Finance had attended to a few preliminaries. His first day in office he summoned the director of the Bank of France, Robineau, his chief adversary of the year before, and asked him to suggest remedies for the crisis, listened to him an hour or two, thanked him, saw him out, then issued a decree dismissing him from his post. Some weeks earlier Briand had set up a committee of experts to prepare a financial plan. Caillaux was at first inclined to ignore the committee—was he not an expert himself? However, when he found most of his own ideas in the experts' suggestions, he proclaimed his intention of adopting most of their suggestions. The committee was useful for blaming unpopular measures on, and with its advice at his disposal he was able to recommend ratification of a war-debt agreement negotiated in April by a former member of his team in Washington, Senator Henry Béranger.

The government did not even mention taxes at its first appearance before the Chamber; instead it asked for facilities—facilities for credit from the Bank of France, for the issuance of banknotes, for national and foreign loans. The right opposed new currency issues as inflationist and foreign loans as humiliating; the Socialists, faithful to the tax on capital, opposed all alternatives. The imminence of the request for full powers weighed on the debate, encouraging the Socialists in their opposition and driving some Radicals to their side. More than the principle of a financial dictatorship, the person of the prospective dictator was disquieting. Briand was not assurance enough that Caillaux would not "stagger the Republic to save the franc."[48] Attacked by the two extremes, Caillaux stood his ground squarely and proudly between them. On July 10 the government won a majority of 22 votes, "gathered one-by-one by the maneuverer Laval."[49]

Then only did Caillaux request the power to issue decree laws. On July 17, arriving for the debate, he saw the vice-president of the Chamber in the president's seat; evidently Herriot, the president, was going to speak against him. He fought all the more pugnaciously for knowing that the fight was futile. He berated the indecisive deputies collectively from the rostrum; he accosted them individually in the corridors. The Socialist orators denounced the bid for full powers as an attempt to legalize a *coup d'Etat*. Herriot declared that, whatever the emergency, his conscience as a republican forbade him to lend a hand in divesting parliament of its essential function, that of voting taxes. The truth came from the right: Tardieu declaimed the "single article of the draft law entitled 'Rubicon,'" and Louis Marin recalled Caillaux's excuse for it to the High Court—

that his mind had wandered. You don't give full powers to a man whose mind is capable of wandering, said Marin.[50] Neither do you recall a man from exile to power if you do not trust him, yet except for a handful of Radicals the whole left opposed the bid for full powers, and on July 18 the government fell.

Caillaux had split the Cartel in July, 1925; in July, 1926, he had revived its unity against him—for a few days. Herriot, succeeding Briand, strove doggedly to curb inflation with the consent of parliament. Mobs gathered demanding his death. Within one week the Cartel was discredited. Then, with the pound at 235 francs and the Treasury empty, Doumergue called Poincaré. Poincaré invited Herriot to join him; Herriot accepted and, adjusting his scruples, sat by in silence on the ministers' bench as almost without contest the Chamber voted emergency financial powers to Poincaré.[51] The franc was saved.

Joseph Caillaux is evidence that nothing disqualified a man from a political career under the Third French Republic. He engendered and survived every suspicion, even "the suspicion of genius, no more justified than the others."[52] The High Court did not injure his career. On the contrary: had there been no trial he could not have returned to power sooner, for until 1924 the right held control, and had there been no unjust sentence he might never have returned to power at all. By 1924 he had abandoned the capital tax, and the income tax had been voted: like Prometheus having brought fire to mortals, he had exhausted his program. In July, 1926, a collection of his speeches, letters, and essays appeared under the title *Ma Doctrine:* it revealed some thought and much insight, but no doctrine.

The Caillaux program was exhausted earlier, but only in 1926 was the Caillaux legend complete. So far, the most familiar Caillaux had been the paradoxical one: the gentleman with spats, cane, and monocle leading the fight against privileges, or the Anglomaniac leading the search for an understanding with Germany. Often the paradox had not been in him, however; then, reflecting the internal contradictions of the regime, he had been a living indictment of it. Not he but the regime had transformed technical questions into political ones—such as the easiest tax to manipulate or the fairest price for Morocco. Without changing his principles he had gone from the center of parliament leftwards all the way to jail and exile, only to wind up right back where he had started from. Even then he had not finished with paradoxes: within a single day he first took a seat among the men who had condemned him and next split the majority that had called him back to power. But then, in fighting his hopeless battle on two fronts, fighting to save the franc and the center both, he put the finishing touches to the historic picture of himself: the picture of a Caillaux as courageous in the thick of battle as he was frightened in the thin of it; as magnificent in adversity as he was insufferable out; and, like Cyrano, grappling with a hundred enemies at once—most of them imaginary, the others deadly.

CHAPTER 8

Twenty Years More

FOR A FEW YEARS after his failure of July, 1926, Caillaux stood aside. In January, 1927, he was reelected Senator, this time for a full nine years. In November, 1928, taking his revenge on Herriot, he persuaded the Radical congress at Angers to condemn Poincaré's policy of "national union." The Radicals in the government duly resigned, whereupon the *poincaristes* deprived him of a seat on the Finance Commission of the Senate; three years later he became president of the Commission. In October, 1929, he declined an offer to join Daladier, designated Premier, who was looking for a majority on the left. Naturally he knew the financier Oustric, who invested as readily in politicians as in pawn shops, and naturally he took pleasure in shocking the commission set up when the scandal broke. "Please, gentlemen," he implored on January 31, 1931, "let us not be pharisaical! We all know that ministers of finance must have seats on boards of directors to hand out."[1]

Otherwise Caillaux spent most of his time at home, writing. During 1929 and early 1930 he revised and added to his memoirs, bringing their length up to a thousand pages. He had many valuable recollections to record, but he bore too many grudges to record them well. A perennial defendant, reduced from making history to writing it, he was never so much telling his story as pleading his case. He did both best when he digressed—that is, when he was neither vindicative nor vindictive. Similarly, he wrote history best when he wrote it for its own sake, not for his. He, though, did not recognize the distinction. In his view, historiography was only a pretentious and indiscriminate species of biography. History was made, not by the masses, but in spite of them. "The role of men who rule, or of men who may be called on to rule, is not to be led by public opinion, but to restrain it," he wrote.[2] At his hands, however, biography often reduced to a conjunction of anecdotage and gossip. He had none of the makings of a good writer either, and of a great one hardly more than disdain for syntax. His mannerisms on paper were as maddening as his mannerisms off—his relentless quoting, his inept jargon, his cajoling his readers, patronizing them, showing off to them.

He would dialogue with posterity between quotation marks,[3] write "(*sic!*)" after quoting words overheard in childhood,[4] introduce any gratuitous assertion with "Objectively speaking," "Judging from on high," or "Anyone who opens his eyes will see."[5] And his Anglicisms: not content with looking to England for his most fashionable clothing and ideas he would, for instance, come to an "*agrément,*"[6] even with "*reluctance.*"[7] He constantly repeated himself when he was not actually plagiarizing himself, and constantly posed as too naïve to be deceitful when he was not posing as too clever to be deceived. Finally, though his sense of humor was not acute, he used irony and ridicule incessantly on the premise that it was.

Still, the Caillaux story is never dull, even as told by Caillaux. And he told it with spirit, convinced as he was that in telling it he was telling a sizable portion of the story of humanity. "Am I not obsessed with my own person?" he once asked rhetorically,[8] and by way of denial he blamed the *Figaro* campaign against him for having made the First World War possible.[9] Yet his megalomania was mixed with great humility. Two loves had he—Joseph Caillaux, and humanity (not men). And both loves were constant; hence he was egoistic *and* altruistic, selfish *and* selfless.

He did not write only for pleasure. The inflation of the early 1920's had remade his political fortune, but at the same time it had eaten into his personal fortune. Throughout the 1930's he wrote for money in newspapers and reviews. In 1932 he selected several of his articles for publication in book form. Some dealt with peace and some with finance, so he named the selection *D'Agadir à la grande pénitence*. They show him at his worst—he had aged pitifully. His prose was more pompous than ever: in one article, after admonishing André Tardieu for writing foggily of late, he went on to urge the Tardieu government to "contrôler, hors de toute ingérence tracassière, les grandes formations d'affaires dont l'indispensable développement à l'intérieur et à l'extérieur doit être facilité, secondé, mais rigoureusement maintenu sous le signe de l'intérêt général."[10] And some of his arguments made little sense: once, after the inevitable "If we rise for a moment above the prejudices of our times," he ascribed unemployment to population growth, population growth to a rising birth rate, a rising birth rate to increasing "confidence in the future," and increasing "confidence in the future" to "excessive industrialization" —only to conclude that the remedy for the world depression was mass migration from Europe to Africa. In other articles he had other remedies, such as a truce on inventions and a stop to mechanization. As Leon

Trotsky wrote: "It is difficult to imagine a more tragic paradox...: the most enlightened representatives of the liberal doctrine suddenly draw inspiration from the sentiments of those ignorant workers of over a hundred years ago who smashed weaving looms."[11]

The evils of "excessive industrialization" did not shake his faith in "the present economic system," however; on the contrary, he only denounced socialism the more strongly. He ardently desired peace, yet he saw no good in any specific proposal for maintaining it. He opposed multilateral disarmament because Germany had proposed it insincerely as a prelude to rearming; he opposed unilateral disarmament because it would provide other nations with "a temptation." He ignored the League of Nations, remaining faithful to the old secret diplomacy of, say, 1911. He still thought of peace as a conjuror's trick—or at best as the work of a few men whispering, not of assemblies deliberating. The Constitution of 1875 confused the sum of particular interests in France with the general interest, he maintained—in chorus with most of his peers. Had he made any specific proposals for amending the Constitution, his detractors would no doubt have found them in germ in the "Rubicon"; perhaps that is why he made none. He considered the matter of amending it to be urgent, but not especially so. He had lost his power of prophecy: "I shall not dream of bands invading the Palais Bourbon," he wrote. "To my mind, there is no reason to apprehend movements of violence."[12] In his preface he doffed his hat once more to "*individualités de raison désintéressée*, who, now restraining, now leading the masses... are the ferment of all progress, the germ of all civilization."[13] In the essay *Elite et Masses* he declared himself a disciple of Pareto, asserting in italics, with each line a paragraph: "Nothing great in the world, nothing constructive, was ever accomplished except by the elite. Mass movements only destroy."[14] Again, "A democracy, a republic, more than any other regime, has need of an elite"[15]—though in fact not many of the kind have perished for *want* of an elite. Certainly no man, from Plato to Pareto, ever defined the elite to exclude himself, yet by Caillaux's definition it did not clearly include anyone but himself. He defined it by its function only—to guide the rest of humankind—and he proclaimed rather than proved its existence and qualifications. He hailed it loudly, almost on a note of desperation, as a last resort should his membership cards elsewhere be cancelled again.

At a Radical congress in Angers in 1928 a young publisher and editor, Emile Roche, introduced himself to Caillaux as an ardent disciple. Caillaux took a liking to him, and before long Roche was his secretary and collabborator. He filled these functions unfailingly thereafter; more, he was Caillaux's future biographer, and no Boswell was ever more reverent of his Johnson or tagged after him more pertinaciously. His book *Caillaux que j'ai connu* is a huge sample of Caillaux's speeches, articles, letters, and private utterances, all piously annotated. It is also a repertory of Caillaux's day-to-day existence. Even in his seventies Caillaux gave two lectures a month, wrote four articles a week, read a book a day, had an opinion on everything.[16] He worked by schedule, for reasons of intellectual hygiene; he also clung to his bodily health, rising at seven every morning to do calesthenics by an open window. Once Roche caught him simulating a fit of temper, and once meditating on the immortality of the soul.

As the 1930's got started, Caillaux's career might well have seemed to be at an end. He was touching up his memoirs. Two biographies appeared, giving a kind of finality to his life by their very appearance—*Joseph Caillaux* by Gaston Martin in 1932, and in 1933 the superb *Caillaux* by Alfred Fabre-Luce. Even his enemies began treating him with respect: if he was not actually dead, at least he was beyond doing harm. Or so it seemed.

In fact his career was entering on a new course, which it was to follow until the war. He was becoming the terrible old man of the Senate. The Senate was the board of censorship of the Third Republic: traditionally its role was less to undertake than to prevent. Renewed in its membership by one third every three years, renewed by the agency of men elected at four-year intervals, it reflected the oscillations of public opinion with a variable lag, and more often than not its political composition was opposite to that of the Chamber. It offered a great opportunity for obstruction, and because of his years, his services to the state, and the injustice done to him, Caillaux felt entitled to use that opportunity to advise governments, to admonish them, to warn them—and, if necessary, to overthrow them. Through his control over its Commission of Finance he gradually gained a moral ascendancy over the very body that had once condemned him. He did not cease hoping to return to the government—on the contrary, he resolved not to return except as Premier. Just after the general elections of May, 1932, he was mentioned for premier; he was mentioned again on the following December 15, after the fall of Chautemps. Each time President Lebrun, who had been his Minister of Colonies in 1911, abstained from calling him. "A mysterious veto blocks his path," wrote one observer, meaning Lebrun.[17] Daladier offered him the Foreign Ministry on January 29, 1933; he refused, and Daladier fell back on Paul-Boncour. "I supported with all my might [the Four-

Power Pact], prepared... by Henry de Jouvenel, my colleague and my cousin," wrote Caillaux,[18] and Paul-Boncour recalled how in the spring of 1933

Caillaux—who was very attentive to anything that might help the cause of peace, but pugnacious on behalf of that cause, and readily gruff with governments, whose fate he held in his hands through his dictatorship over the Commission of Finance in the Senate—came one day to see me at my seat. "I congratulate you on your efforts," he said, "but tell your government that if it doesn't put the Four-Power Pact through I'll knock it the hell out of office!"[19]

The strange alliance of England, France, Germany, and Italy appealed to Caillaux because it offered diplomats what the League of Nations did not: an opportunity to talk in private. He battled for it long after its authors had forsaken it. "Its adoption would no doubt have forestalled the war," he later lamented.[20]

By the spring of 1935 France was sunk deep in the depression; trade, both foreign and domestic, was almost at a standstill, and the price of gold was soaring. Once more hungry and ragged men were shaking their fists at parliament, and once more in its endemic search for a savior the public singled out Caillaux. President Lebrun designated Fernand Bouisson as Premier, and in May 30 Bouisson gave Caillaux a choice of ministries. Caillaux first made himself "Minister of State with authority over all matters of economy and finance," then on second though took on the Ministry of Finance as well. Louis Marin and Edouard Herriot, in 1926 Caillaux's adversaries on his right and his left respectively, also joined the cabinet; so too did Georges Mandel, who had called for Caillaux's death in 1920, and Pétain, who had hoped for it. From the outset Caillaux demanded full powers. He announced his intention to create a council of bankers and to initiate multinational negotiations for currency stabilization. He also promised to balance the budget, of course, and to defend the franc. The Bourse responded affectionately. On June 4 the government appeared before the Chamber, demanding authority "to take all measures, with effect of law, toward normalizing public finance, reviving economic activity, and removing impediments to public credit." In the course of the debate Caillaux undertook neither to devalue the franc nor to decree an embargo on gold even though he had written in favor of both measures. He also undertook to reform the civil service system, and when someone asked him how he meant to reform it he replied without pause:

I intend... to issue instructions for having... commissioners, chosen even within parliament, sent to all the government services, with full powers, first, to expunge as far as is useful or possible the exaggerated, almost monstrous formalism that exists throughout; then, to ferret out pluralism in office and put an end to the abuses it leads to. The commissioners will, finally, be instructed to demolish...the superfetations and adventitious compounds that have been named "offices" and that generally serve only to provide certain functionaries with an increase in pay on the pretext that these functionaries are the incumbents of those offices.

All that, I expect to do. It will be one of my jobs; there will be others.[21]

At seventy-two he had lost none of his bark. He was applauded on the right; the whole left voted against him, including half the Radicals, and by 264 votes to 262 the Chamber withheld its confidence. "The Chamber ...discerned that, though nominally only Minister of Finance, I was in fact the real head of the government," Caillaux explained.[22] He was right—and many of the same deputies who had applauded him had voted against him. Said one of them afterwards, "I could not, even for discipline's sake, even for the sake of Tardieu or Marin, vote for Joseph Caillaux."[23] The sentence of the High Court was still in force. Pierre Laval formed the new government, with both Herriot and Marin as Ministers of State; Caillaux declined an *invitation de courtoisie* to remain at his post, and the Chamber at once gave Laval full powers by 412 to 137.

Early in 1932, when Pierre Laval permitted Briand to resign from the Foreign Ministry, Caillaux sent his old rival a word of sympathy; Briand replied with an invitation to dinner, and at table the two fell to sentimentalizing—"my friend," wrote Caillaux of Briand thereafter.[24] One day in 1934 well-wishers had Caillaux to dinner with Barthou; the two conversed politely.[25] Meanwhile Caillaux's old ways revived in his old age. He mingled with high society. Actresses visited him in his office in the Senate. The death of the democratic little Countess Anna de Noailles in the spring of 1933 gave him much grief; eventually, though, her place as his inspirer was taken by the marquise de Ludre, "the most accomplished hostess in Paris."[26] Rehabilitation was beyond his reach, but he was moving steadily in its direction.

In March, 1932, as guest lecturer at the Cobden Club in London, Caillaux declared himself a classical economist with some reservations.[27] By 1936, when the Popular Front came to power, he had dropped the reservations—his audacity in fiscal reform, his "economic state," were definitely things of the past. So was the "Rubicon"—"The best constitutions are those that have the greatest flexibility," he told the alumni of the Ecole des Sciences Politiques, and he described himself as a liberal "in the British tradition of the nineteenth century."[28]

Léon Blum, before forming his first government, paid Caillaux a courtesy call. Caillaux kept him to lunch, and when Blum called him more of a writer than a politician Caillaux was so flattered that he made the *"beyliste"*[29] a gift of the complete works of Stendhal. He had not forgotten 1926 and 1935, however, and in September, 1936, he warned Blum from the rostrum of the Senate: "We do not mean to grant the government of today, any more than the government of tomorrow, dictatorial powers."[30] Nonetheless, Blum came to the Senate on June 20, 1937, with his Minister of Finance, Vincent Auriol, to ask for full powers. "Delightful speech for an amateur," remarked Caillaux, when Blum had done; then, his tongue in his cheek, he asked what the government wanted full powers *for;* finally, feigning disappointment at Blum's silence, he had the Senate overthrow the government. Once in the debate he had blundered critically: meaning to ridicule the Jewish Premier as a drawing-room proletarian he had cried, "You do not have the soil of France on the soles of your boots!"

President Lebrun did not offer the new government to his old boss; instead he gave it to a Radical, Camille Chautemps. Chautemps governed with the Socialists seven months, then without them two months. He fell in March, 1938, whereupon Caillaux had his group in the Senate, the Democratic Left, vote a resolution maintaining its opposition to the Popular Front. Blum made a vain effort to set up a national-union cabinet; then he fell back on the Popular Front. He took on a very young Radical, Pierre Mendès-France, as Minister of the Budget. Together the two worked out a plan for economic recovery; it included a 4 percent levy on fortunes of 150,000 francs and over. When this time Blum demanded full powers, mobs gathered in the streets threatening Caillaux. Nonetheless, on April 8, 1938, as a cordon of troops kept order around the Palais du Luxembourg, Caillaux again had the senators overthrow Blum. Two days later, at Caillaux's behest, they unanimously gave full powers to Daladier.

When he was not busy terrorizing the Senate Caillaux was busy gracing the general council of the Sarthe. "No one excels him in presiding over an assembly," wrote one of his general councilors. "He hears everything, knows everything, understands everything, has an answer for everything."[31] Some of his time off he also spent in Paris giving speeches. Usually he was tiresome, as in the Théâtre des Ambassadeurs on January 29, 1937:

Before the war I maintained that, if we wanted to avoid the catastrophe, we had to adopt a different tone of voice [with Germay]. I adopted it, for my part. They didn't listen to me. You know what followed!

When the war broke out I warned them that it would end badly if we did not work out a treaty of conciliation. They threw me into prison.[32]

Now and then he was superb, as in the very same speech:

Eh bien! I am going to tell you a secret. I am not in the least opposed to change. There was slavery; serfdom replaced it, and was swept away in turn; wagedom has taken the place of serfdom, and perhaps wagedom, too, will pass away—doubtless, even. What is important is that this passing from one stage to another should not be brutal, that humanity should not suffer from it.[33]

At the approach of the critical date of March 30, 1937, he grew ill at the thought that no Caillaux had ever lived beyond the age of seventy-four; one year later, however, he was observed "slender, graceful, like a septuagenarian cavalry lieutenant,"[34] and again "prancing with a lively step."[35] He was also seen coming to Paris from Mamers on September 23, 1938, to urge Daladier to negotiate with Hitler;[36] and again, "warmly and proudly" complimenting "a few notorious and... virulent labor leaders," who "shake his hand with evident pleasure, recognizing in him, over and above the social strife of these last ten or twelve years, the aristocrat whom they saved from injustice";[37] and again, at a reception at the Quai d'Orsay on December 8, 1938, giving Ribbentrop "bits of advice for the Reich, if not more directly for Chancellor Hitler."[38]

Caillaux did not follow the government in its retreat from Tours to Bordeaux in June, 1940. Instead he drove up from Tours to Le Mans, against the flow of refugees on the roads—"to be at the head of my region when the enemy gets there," he explained.[39] He did, however, go and vote full powers to Pétain on July 10, 1940.

Under the Occupation he was on his guard. He did not once speak in public. He wrote a few prefaces to books on finance. He also had the first two volumes of his memoirs published—no doubt they disappointed the German authorities. The Vichy government offered him the presidency of the departmental assembly of the Sarthe; he refused even to become a member of it. He communicated with Vichy only once, to appeal to Laval on behalf of a postal clerk, an elderly widow, who had been dismissed without compensation because "she happens to have been born a Jewess."[40] Madame Caillaux died in January, 1943, after a long illness, and Caillaux lived on alone in his great house in Mamers. Later in 1943, in a gesture of protest over the increasing severity of the Occupation, he resigned as president of the general council of the Sarthe; his gesture was imitated throughout France.

In February, 1944, he added a chapter to his memoirs. Embittered, he saw Europe as crushed between the United States and the Soviet Union, and compelled to "unite or perish."[41] Citing George Washington's advice to the American colonies, he advised the nations of Europe, as a first step toward unity, to outlaw customs barriers; however, he saw small hope that Europe would not sooner perish than unite. "We appear as at the twilight of a civilization," he concluded, "in which everything is on the verge of collapsing in ruins."[42]

Early in August, 1944, General de Gaulle, on his way to liberate Paris, called on Caillaux in Mamers. After the Liberation Caillaux expected to return to power shortly. Not to compromise himself, he refused to provide one of the royalist general councilors of the Sarthe with a "certificate of non-collaboration."[43] He was then partly paralyzed and in extreme pain. Gradually he grew delirious. He died on November 22, 1944, at the age of eighty-one, in the home of his birth, calling repeatedly for a new Joan of Arc to "kick the English out of France."[44]

He had outlived his enemies. But in the process he had also outlived his family, his generation, his Republic even. The press took small note of his death, and his funeral was a very sad procession of functionaries and idle passers-by. He had bequeathed his house to the township of Mamers to be converted into a home for old people, but as he did not leave enough money to pay for the conversion, the bequest was refused.

PART II

Henry de Jouvenel
and the Unknown Party

"Henry, with all his brains, was not prepared to take enough trouble to achieve success." LORD ROBERT CECIL, *A Great Experiment.*

CHAPTER 9

Stanislas

BERTRAND HENRY LEON ROBERT DE JOUVENEL
DES URSINS descended from Limousin barons. His name was the
greater part of his patrimony. While rejoicing in its luxury, he resented
its claim on his loyalties and the burden it placed on him to be superior
or else ridiculous. In his first known act of compromise he shortened it.
He discarded all his given names but Henry, which was both easily spoken
and distinctive in print, and, making good use of good usage, retained
only as much of his family name as he thought history justified, his ability
warranted, or democracy was likely to condone.

The name Jouvenel des Ursins had entered history at the end of the
Hundred Years War, in the third generation of Henry's known fore-
bears. His earliest ancestor on record was Pierre Jouvenel, a prosperous
draper and merchant in Troyes toward the end of the fourteenth century.
Pierre provided his son, Jean Jouvenel, with an education in law and a
drapery trade in Paris. Jean embraced the cause of the monarchy from
the first and rose to prominence during the reign of Charles VI, becoming
provost of Paris merchants and, successively, town councilor, king's
advocate in the *parlement* of Paris, president of the *parlement* of Toulouse,
and first president of the *parlement* of Poitiers. His life was exemplary and
his popularity great; he alone of the king's party was loved and trusted
by Charles, who even in madness called for him. Perceiving that the
national and royalist cause could not prevail without the support of the
Third Estate, Jean Jouvenel advised the monarchy to govern assisted by
well-ordered guilds and guided by the duties of kings, the advice of the
States-General, and solid constitutional law. Of his many children the
best known is his namesake Jean, author of the *Histoire de Charles VI*, who
fought under the banner of Joan of Arc and lived to become Arch-
bishop of Reims and peer of France. He it was who, in 1456, established
the orthodoxy of Joan, with the assistance of two bishops and in collaboration with the Grand Inquisitor of Paris. He it was also who, spelling
his name Juvénal, added "des Ursins" to it, in order to signify his descent
from the Italian family de' Orsini; in this he acted in good faith, with the

compliance of the Orsinis and of the pope, but authorities ever since have contested his genealogical claim, among them the duke and peer Saint-Simon, grand master of gossip and pedigree, who taunted "those Juve-nels, so absurdly called des Ursins."[1] One of Jean's brothers was Guil-laume, who, Chancellor under Charles VII, was dismissed on the acces-sion of Louis XI in 1461, only to be called back to office six years later; he is to be seen, portly and wry, in a great portrait of him by Fouquet. Another was Jacque, Bishop of Poitiers, known especially for having aided the ascent to power of the luckless conspirator Cardinal La Balue.[2]

After the death of Jean Juvénal des Ursins the family name reverted to the form *Jouvenel*, the additive *des Ursins* remaining. The family, con-verted to Protestantism early in the reign of Francis I, lost favor with the Court and took refuge in the south of France. Its members who survived the Wars of Religion sank to the condition of the peasantry. One branch alone preserved its identity, having resumed the Catholic faith and settled in a forsaken monastery in Obazine, on a mountain peak in Limousin.

Léon de Jouvenel des Ursins restored his family to prominence in the nineteenth century.[3] First he married a relation of the Casimir-Périers, chief shareholders in the July monarchy; then in 1848, when the monarchy collapsed, he ran as a royalist candidate for the Constituent Assembly. Defeated, he rallied to the Republic at the call of Lamartine. That year he also published a pamphlet on "the suppression of poverty through the collective organization of individual savings," and no doubt it pleased charity-minded Louis Napoleon, for under the Second Empire he was elected deputy from the department of Corrèze. He took his seat on the right of the Chamber and voted with the Orleanists—losing official support, and his seat, in the elections of 1863. His political career resumed in 1871, when, eluding the ban on former official candidates of the Empire, he got elected as an Orleanist to the National Assembly.[4] There he distinguished himself by his proposal to grant heads of families as many votes as they had persons in their legal custody—he was himself a loving family man. He published works on Algeria, on financial and agricultural problems, and—under the pen name Comte Jeneséki (Count Idunnowho) —on "Eve's Granddaughters." He won mundane glory and a wager with Thiers by telling a venerable countess courteously enough to flatter her that she was the ugliest woman in the world.[5]

Léon's son, Raoul, married a daughter of the fiery progressive deputy De Janzé, and became one of the youngest and most lavish prefects of the Second Empire. Like his father, he opted for restoration of the house of Orleans after the abdication of Napoleon III; then, as France settled down under the Republic, he withdrew from public life[6] and returned to his native Corrèze. There, in the town of Brive-la-Gaillarde, on April 2, 1876, his son Henry was born; a second son, Robert, followed five years later. Léon died in 1886. The same year the Count of Paris, Orleanist pretender to the throne, was banished from France, and Raoul wanted to follow with his family into exile. But his wife demurred; perhaps she was reconciled to the new regime by her celebrated sister, Baroness Le Lasseur, who had been so moved on hearing Thiers proclaim the end of the Prussian occupation of Paris in 1871 that she never missed another session of parliament, becoming a fixture in the box reserved for the guests of the chief of state and earning the nickname "Grandmother of the French Parliament" half a century later.[7] Raoul resigned himself at length to witnessing the end of the notables at close range. He sought distraction in writing on Correzians in French history and on fishing regulations in the department of Marne. He also vented his bitterness and frustration on his wife. She pleaded for a divorce; he refused; she deserted him—and even so he went on refusing to the last. Meanwhile monarchism lapsed from a matter of principle to a matter of regret for most of the other noblemen of France: even they came to take the direction of political progress for granted, questioning only how far it was advisable to go in that direction. Not so Raoul.

Henry spent his childhood in Corrèze, in the village of Varetz. He lived surrounded by ancestral relics in his family castle, Castel-Novel,[8] and out-of-doors by slopes of blossom and vine, by distant hills "that the mild winters of the plains of Brive seem to lay bare... only in order to bring out more clearly the graceful harmony of their lines and make the villages that crown their peaks stand out more proudly."[9] In the peace and beauty of the countryside he found relief from the stern rule of his father, as well as solace when his grandfather died, then when his mother departed. His father's ruin did not much affect him, for somehow the ruined noble families of the time brought up their children in the same style as did the unruined ones. Thus in 1893 Raoul took up residence, with Henry, on the fashionable Rue du Faubourg Saint-Honoré in Paris and sent him to the Collège Stanislas to complete studies for a baccalaureate.

The Collège Stanislas, founded by Louis XVIII for the preservation of the faith, was protected against unorthodoxy by the highest tuition rates in the country. Its Jesuit faculty frowned on students who favored Leo XIII and the separation of "throne and altar." Yet the Humanities curriculum, which Henry chose, apparently did not induce intellectual or moral austerity. "Correctness, discipline, classicism, were distasteful to us," recalled one of his classmates,[10] and others enjoyed memories of afternoons spent informally with their masters and evenings at the *café-concert*.

The newcomer to Stanislas soon revealed many of the great talents on which the statesman of later years relied for persuasiveness, especially the talent for being loved. "All my proud friendship went to Henry de Jouvenel," wrote Anatole de Monzie, quoting Montaigne on La Boétie for good measure,[11] and Louis Gillet raved:

Whoever did not see him at that age has seen nothing. The elegance of his slender person, his bearing, his long and rapid stride, his proud head tossing about streams of black hair, the dark lock that fell like a feather over his right eye and that he would brush away with an exquisite motion, his charming eyes that had gold and night, fire and caress in them, everything, even that uneasy look of a lanky and slightly savage wolf's cub, was fascinating: he was already *l'irrésistible*.[12]

His other talents showed in turn. At the end of his first year the head-master of Stanislas described him as "a very intelligent pupil, with a lively imagination and a very great aptitude for literature."[13] And he was as studious as he was gifted. "Adolescence is the time of life when cheating at work is unpardonable," he once remarked. "Later you may be forgiven for wanting to fool people; sometimes it's a professional necessity. But when you're young you work to enlighten yourself by your own efforts."[14] If the young scholar did not cheat at work, though, neither did he care to be caught at work by his fellows:

With moods of whimsicality and fits of nonchalance, he was in reality quite hard-working. His extreme ease in learning could fool people, but he never thought it dispensed him from the need to work.... Pretending to be unconcerned, he always wound up at the head of the class, his proper place.[15]

He studied Greek and Latin, English and German, read the classics avidly, and rebelled all the while against the idea that education consisted solely in acquiring ingredients of knowledge, in finding out secrets preserved in books. Braving his comrades' disdain for physical culture he took fencing lessons, but the only duels he fought were oratorical. In informal discussions he would listen to each speaker in turn and then improvise a scheme for accommodating all the disparate views at once. On the rostrum of the debating society, though, he would do otherwise. His perennial adversary, Marc Sangnier, having addressed their student audience as "friends," Jouvenel would turn to face Sangnier squarely and reply, "Sir!"

How charming he was to see then! Slender, quick, his head high, his arms outstretched toward his opponent as though to touch him with an invisible foil, and then after each thrust stopping with a gentle smile to put his vagrant lock back in place, he would begin the fight with a few stunning passes: he was D'Artagnan, Rastignac, the eternal cadet of Gascony, who is nobody's fool and never caught napping... a mixture of reason and élan, of flame and sobriety...[16]

The apprentice tribune nourished his political imagination by reading the speeches of Mirabeau, Vergniaud, and Lamartine, and dreamed confidently of a future in which his eloquence would overwhelm great assemblies split into hostile factions.

Meanwhile, he employed all his tact to obtain forgiveness for his more conspicuous gifts and all his guile to conceal the others. In one respect he failed, for "though no one made less show of his birth or derived less vanity from it, he was unmistakably well-born. His whole being bore the stamp of his breed."[17] And his schoolmates were not disappointed when they chanced upon his other family secret: genteel poverty.

We had wealthy friends, but he was our great lord. The aura of a king's son and heir radiated from his person, as in tales in which Ali's children, disguised as nomad students, are recognized. He could not help being our Prince Charming. Had he been even poorer than he was he would have been recognized as the favorite of Heaven, made for the table of the gods and the bed of the goddesses.[18]

Indeed, Henry—"fashioned as he was, fair as the day or the night, avid, simmering, with so much grace and wit, caressing, proud, dominating"[19] —was the first in his class in one other respect, and anticipated the future by the same token:

All the women ran after him; he met few cruel ones. He was one of those men who have only to appear in order to triumph. He was torn between his taste for pleasure and his taste for love, between caprice and lyricism, adventure and passion: all the women fought for him, and he drifted from one to the next. At times he showed the cynicism of a roué of the Regency and of a skeptical and disenchanted epicurean; at others he was prepared to do penance for his frivolity and devote himself to a single mistress. These successive and varying states of heart alternated with crises of disgust and what was left of a Catholic feeling of sin.[20]

For Henry, who was of course outwardly pious at Stanislas, was suspected of being secretly pious as well.

In July, 1895, all Stanislas was counting on Jouvenel to win a grand prize for his team at the *Concours général des lycées et collèges de France* in the honored field of French composition, to which he had been assigned by acclamation. He had spent much of his final year sharpening his quill, and so well did he carry out the assignment—a letter, as if by the moralist Joubert to the poet Marie-Joseph Chénier, in defense of Chateaubriand's *Atala*—that his master of rhetoric and his teammates "preferred this pastiche by one of us to all Joubert."[21] Even so he failed to win the favor of the Sorbonne examiners over his rival from the Lycée Condorcet, the *"professionnel du triomphe scolaire"*[22] André Tardieu, and he had to console himself with second prize. Among the reflections with which he had had the wit to credit Joubert the following is characteristic: *"Désormais les écrivains, au lieu de s'amuser de leurs livres, en souffriront"*[23] ("Henceforth writers will derive, not enjoyment, but suffering, from their books"). Another sample of the young author's ability survives—a fragment of a poem, effectively ill-scanned and ill-rhymed, which discloses some of his bafflement and some of his pride at winning love so effortlessly:

> J'ai toujours adoré jusqu'au nom des almées,
> Ces femmes faites pour aimer sans être aimées.[24]

> (I always have adored the very name
> Of *almas*, who are born to love in vain.)

Henry de Jouvenel never outgrew the spirit of his schooldays—his humanism, his enthusiasm for ideas, the original blend of audacity and courtesy in his thinking, his dream of detecting and expressing unanimity amid discord. He matured, not by putting these things aside, but by adding to them. In his "permanent youth"[25] he was suspicious of whatever derived from prescription or authority, while his liberalism always resembled an "adolescent's curiosity of mind"[26] and intellectual hospitality combined in the form of a principle. He nurtured all his early tastes and talents, and in particular he extended to politics and diplomacy the use of his "very rare gift for charming groups of men and even assemblies as surely as persons one by one. For my part," confessed Paul Valéry many years later, "I have never been able to refuse him anything he asked, so pleasantly forceful and indefinably persuasive was his way of speaking."[27]

By the time he left Stanislas, preeminence and independence had become habits with him, and for twenty years afterwards he confined himself to activities in which these two habits of his were secure.

CHAPTER 10

Syndicalism

JOUVENEL ENTERED the Ecole Normale Supérieure in the fall of 1895. He had not been there a year when he was conscripted for military service and ordered to the small garrison town of Bellac, less than a hundred miles from his home in Corrèze.

He donned the uniform without much ambition and doffed it three years later without much regret. In one respect, though, those three years were decisive for him. He went into the army convinced, like so many of his young countrymen, that France had found a system of government capable of assuring the automatic solution of all political problems. The trainees at Bellac "were preoccupied with social questions: we thought we had discovered them and thereby reinvented life."[1] They were patriots as well as social reformers, and they respected the army above all the institutions of the Republic. "The problem of the regime did not arise.... We wanted to change the form of society, not the form of government."[2] But one icy day in January, 1898, Jouvenel, as he was idly thumbing through the newspapers in the barracks, came upon Zola's "J'Accuse."

Until the end of my life I shall feel the blow that was dealt to my convictions, to my habits of mind, to my ignorance, to what I took to be my reason.... Until then, for boys of my age, the Dreyfus affair had not existed. Of course we had been told in school that a Jew had committed treason, and we were indignant for a moment because he had not been shot. Then the incident had slipped our minds.[3]

Day after day Jouvenel—and hundreds of thousands of young men like him—waited for disproof of Zola's accusations; they received instead denials without evidence.

Empty-handed generals invaded the courts. The crowd applauded and left, vaguely uneasy. Ministers, premiers, proclaimed the guilt they did not prove. An atmosphere of frivolity surrounded the most damning of all accusations. Were we some day to enter a war as we had entered this trial?[4]

Little by little the smoke cleared. Dreyfus had been condemned on the strength of evidence neither he nor his lawyer had seen. A new trial was refused. "All the authority of governments pitted itself, more than one hundred years after the Revolution, against the rights of man"[5]—and still most Frenchmen remained indifferent or hostile toward Dreyfus. The day the trainees at Bellac went on maneuvers, news reached them of Colonel Henry's suicide, which they understood to be a confession of forgery. Private Jouvenel lost what faith he had left in the General Staff. He also learned a painful moral lesson:

We shall go on bearing the weight of this sentence... that, like me, the immense majority of Frenchmen had not even noticed. The idea that we had of a France unanimous for justice was shattered. We had thought the moral education of democracy almost complete, but we had met the crowd howling for death. We discovered that it always sides with Barabbas, and that men must be saved in spite of themselves.[6]

Jouvenel was wearing corporal's stripes when he left the army early in 1899. His corporal's stripes and his leaving the army both mightily disappointed his father, who had dreamed of his becoming a cavalry officer. Raoul, however, had the interests of the cavalry at heart as well as those of his son, so on learning Henry's view of the Dreyfus affair he ceased dreaming for him and instead sent him to Paris to go his own way to greatness.

In Paris Henry spent one month writing an article for a philosophical journal, then another writing one for the newspaper *Le Matin*. The first article was formally rejected; the second, though he drew heavily on his family connections and on his savings to invite the editor-in-chief to dinner, was not even acknowledged. Before the year was out he returned to his castle in Corrèze and began preparing his revenge on "a world in which the daily press showed itself so little open to the future,"[7] in the form of a biography of Lamartine. Nothing remains of this inchoate work—"fortunately," commented the author years afterwards[8]—or of the "interminable correspondence" between him and a friend in Paris, Anatole de Monzie, "in which we vented our fury against society— against the society of our relatives, that is, for we knew no other."[9] At length he grew restless, and when, just at the turn of the century, Monzie urged him to return to Paris and meet "an extraordinary being named Paul-Boncour,"[10] he eagerly complied, leaving Corrèze on the pretext of having urgent research to do at the Bibliothèque Nationale.

Paul-Boncour enjoyed heroic stature among young republicans at the time as the author of a dissertation on compulsory trade-union membership and as Waldeck-Rousseau's legal secretary at twenty-six years of age. His neighbor in the Ministry of the Interior, on the Place Beauveau, was the Premier's political secretary, André Tardieu. Jouvenel "would call on me frequently at my office," recalls Paul-Boncour;[11] and Tardieu would always have a good laugh at seeing his colleague finish work and start out with the same friend day after day on the same walk along the Avenue de Marigny and up the Champs-Elysées, theorizing all the while.[12]

By these discussions Jouvenel was trying to define his political convictions. At first he was sure only that, whatever they were, they were ardent and they were on the left. "The youth of 1900," he later recalled,

was full of fight. The Dreyfus affair had divided it into two camps that believed themselves beyond all reconciliation. From time to time we would go down into the street to demonstrate for justice. On such occasions I got to know the "clinks" of the right bank and of the left bank and the stern fists of the central brigades. We *Dreyfusards* would shout: "Vive la loi!" Our adversaries would shout: "Vive l'armée!" And our seditious souls would be content with these testimonials of respect so long as they did not sound contradictory.[13]

His views on social matters were somewhat more precise, for Paul-Boncour had persuaded him of the importance of trade unions in any future society. In 1884, for the first time since the Revolution, professional associations had been recognized by law. National federations of trade unions were springing up, frightening more for their novelty than for anything they did. Jouvenel decided, with Paul-Boncour, to strive to "base a new organization of power on [trade unions]. We would modernize France by syndicalizing the Republic."[14]

Something called syndicalism was beginning to compete with socialism and anarchism for the minds of the ardent young, "promising them a rejuvenated society in which the state would cease to be sovereign master"[15] and seeming to "reconcile their classical taste for ideals with their growing sense of economic realities."[16] Jouvenel resolved to clarify his views on the political function of syndicalism and to incorporate them into a precise program. With Paul-Boncour and a few other young friends he formed a discussion group; it met once a week in the spare room of a club founded by Waldeck-Rousseau, the Republican Circle. Members of the group called themselves "the generation," and their program was to be "the program of the generation." When they were one hundred, they elected a Democratic Conferences Committee, with Paul-Boncour as chairman and Jouvenel as secretary-general. "The regularity of our sessions," Jouvenel later wrote,

the obstinacy with which we refused to rush into life without a doctrine, the method we applied in ceaselessly combining the notion of solidarity with the notion of competence, the conception we formed of a democracy enlightened by technical knowledge, in which services rendered to the community should be the only measure of individual dignity—all that gave our generation a special aspect, which we have since concealed at times, but whose traits may still be discerned after a quarter of a century.[17]

"All that" gave the generation its program as well in a little more than a year, and it provided Henry de Jouvenel with a doctrine for the rest of his life.

Jouvenel's syndicalism was something less than the usual kind, and something more besides. His, too, defined a new organization of power based on trade unions (*syndicats*), but it rejected several characteristic tenets and aims of the syndicalist movement as a whole in an attempt to synthesize syndicalist with republican thought and motivation.

First of all, he did not accept as a basis for class distinction the ownership of the means of production, considering as "the great expedient of Marxism" the separation of society into two classes "doomed to the alternative of victory or defeat and to the sole recourse of force."[18] He advocated "producers' control of production," but he denatured the slogan by according the dignity of "producer" to the capitalist as well as the laborer. Far from proposing to abolish the state, he proposed to aggrandize it by adjoining a "syndical chamber" to the political parliament. The question of whether trade unions ought to serve to improve working conditions under the capitalist and republican system or else to implement social and political revolution, a question that split the syndicalist movement into a reformist and a revolutionary faction, gave him no special concern: recognizing the political potential of the trade-union movement, he sought to transform the Republic in consequence both early and fairly enough to obviate that choice. Indeed, nothing could have been more alien to the gentleman syndicalist Henry de Jouvenel than the notion of the general strike as a salutary social myth: to his mind, that weapon of organized labor fell rather into a category with dynamite and poison gas, because it made the establishment of social peace, just as the latter did of peace among nations, a matter of sudden and dreadful urgency. On the other hand, he shared with orthodox syndicalism its plan for decentralized federations of workers' unions expressing "functional" and not "geographical" interests and excluding consumers as such from control; he did so, however, in a way and with a purpose that require special qualification.

Jouvenel recognized occupational distinctions as valid above all other social distinctions. He distinguished four professional classes or "estates":

industrial workers, farm laborers, intellectual workers, and managers.[19] He also distinguished two valid and compatible methods for representing the people: according to ideas (the extant "political" method) and according to interest (the "social" or "syndical" method). Interests, he argued, are represented by political parliaments in a disorderly and quasi-fraudulent fashion. They are represented in a more orderly fashion by professional unions, but these are politically ineffectual. "The frank and complete representation of interests is a prior condition of the frank and complete representation of doctrines: they must be kept distinct," he wrote,[20] meaning they must be housed side by side within the state. To an "economic parliament" (or "syndical chamber," or "professional chamber," or—most winsomely—"*chambre des compétences*") representing the four estates he ascribed the study of "production problems" and the preparation of social and economic legislation, leaving "the defense of general principles" to the political parliament. Usually he left all final decisions as well to the political parliament, and when once a reporter asked him whether he thought the new parliament should replace the old he exclaimed: "Heavens, no!" as though injured by the suggestion.[21] In fact he often thought of adding a third parliament to be composed of state dignitaries—ambassadors, court presidents, former ministers—and to be charged with preparing all other legislation and acting as High Court in place of the Senate.

The proposed innovation appears moderate enough; Jouvenel defended its adequacy and its urgency in the same breath. He depicted the distress of a cabinet minister and of a "producer" lacking the means to communicate effectively with each other while financial and industrial cartels and organized labor "put production, politics, diplomacy, and the press of whole continents at the mercy of powerful bosses and tend by their very nature to paralyze democracy."[22] The problem, he judged, "consists essentially in determining whether syndicalism will take hold of the state to dismember it or whether the state will adapt itself to syndicalism by organizing it."[23] And, appealing to the sense of modernity as well as to the sense of danger, he wrote:

From now on, there are only technical questions, and politics amounts to finding an economic formula for the mystical ideal of the Nation. We have no need for propensities, but for precision: the parliamentary deficiency is a technical deficiency.[24]

No technician himself, he did not know that economics and the other statistical sciences offer, not precision, but only a more painstaking expression of uncertainty.

Jouvenel employed ingenious arguments and expended much of his idealism and wit in presenting his conception of "a social and political system making it possible for all French citizens to participate, within their field of competence, in the deliberation of laws";[25] yet his reasoning was frequently equivocal and generally inconclusive. He did not, for instance, adduce theoretical grounds for his satisfaction at having classified men by what they do as well as by what they think. He did not justify his distinction of *four* estates of producers, or define them with enough rigor to forego justifying them: they are not, in our century at least, mutually exclusive or collectively exhaustive, nor is the distinction between them natural or abiding. His reference to a "scientific representation of the people" by the two parliaments together[26] is a pretentious play on the word *representation*, and the alleged antithesis between interests and ideas is a fragile basis for political innovation.[27] To prevent his professional parliament from becoming a replica of the political parliament there is only the covert assumption that a citizen would vote one way out of conviction and another out of interest—for to attribute a plural vote to the active population or even to some one of the estates would make far less difference in practice than in theory. Also, the professional chamber would be idle insofar as its members were active in their several professions, and it would embody no less "a sort of abdication of popular sovereignty" than the other unless, simply, its members' mandates were shorter. Finally, the solution Jouvenel proposed is not commensurable with the problem as he stated it. The status of consultant, as one of four estates, could hardly have been expected to appeal to a dynamic proletarian movement as an alternative to demolishing the state; the Conseil National Economique,[28] created in the 1920's along lines similar to those prescribed by Jouvenel, has not had that appeal, much less prevented the representation of class interests in the political parliament.

By calling the Conseil National Economique in 1928 the "embryo" of his syndical parliament,[29] Jouvenel hinted that he had so far been holding back on part of the solution in order not to discourage republicans from taking up the problem rather than that, alternatively, he really expected the syndicalists to be content in the end with only a *sense* of inclusion in the Republic and of effective participation in it—that he was, so to speak, coating the pill for the benefit of a *malade qui s'ignore*, not overstating its potency for the benefit of a *malade imaginaire*. Even so, this original effort to convert syndicalism from a proletarian into a national movement, and from a social and economic system into a political formula, proved inadequate, and it is the most disappointing example of Jouvenel's thought.

True, his purpose was both audacious and reasonable at a time when governments and political parties were blindly encouraging radical syndicalism and so endangering the Republic in their eagerness to suppress— when they could not safely ignore—any movement not accountable before parliament or idea not originating among themselves. It showed, too, the same grand humility that had inspired certain other noblemen to seek the nation in the Third Estate, and it was, for all its modernity, curiously reminiscent of their own conceptions: Jean Jouvenel, who would have founded political order on guilds responsible to the king, or young Mirabeau, who, in Jouvenel's words, "wished to combine liberalism with the feudal system."[30]

Yet Jouvenel's doctrine was impersonal, almost inhuman. "What are we to think," pleaded one critic,

when [Jouvenel], with a personality as pronounced as his, and having no other purpose in life than to be himself... claims to be devoted to "syndicalism"? What! An aristocrat of the intelligence, whose sole value lies in his unique and personal way of thinking, and who calls himself a "syndicalist"?[31]

Recalling the old saying, "The Republic has no need of wise men," this critic added: "Neither has syndicalism any need of Jouvenel—it has its own brute force within." He saw in Jouvenel's doctrine "the transparent painting of an inner conflict" between republican ambitions and syndicalist convictions, and in Jouvenel's loyalty to that doctrine a show of intellectual gallantry toward "a flame of his youth."[32] He did not remark that, by and large, Jouvenel was not critical of the Republic because he was susceptible to syndicalism, but susceptible to syndicalism because he was critical of the Republic; nor that Jouvenel, whatever else he took second-hand from syndicalism, argued out one premise of it—that every regime is predisposed to bureaucratic paralysis—with a genius all his own.

CHAPTER 11

The Republic from on High

"THE GENERATION" delegated Henry de Jouvenel to present a summary of its program to a congress of the Radical party held early in 1902, on the eve of the first general elections since the Dreyfus affair had divided the nation. "I left," he recalled,

my paper in my pocket, proud of my mission. But the moment I entered the room I became aware of my lack of experience. I knew no one. Lost among presidents, members of parliament, veterans of our political battles; unfamiliar with most of the subjects discussed; present by virtue of a mandate conferred by some youngsters without a mandate; moved to respect by the titles and the age of those who rose to speak...I did not dare ask for the floor.[1]

The bashful revolutionary found nothing more politic than to submit his document to the congress secretary, who shoved it deep down into the pocket of his coat. "By the way the leaves crinkled as the abyss of his pocket closed round them I realized that I had just met up with a new kind of waste basket."[2] All was not lost, though, for a Socialist newspaper printed "the program of the generation" in order to show up the timidity of the Radical party.

And the secretary-general of the Democratic Conferences Committee was requited for his brilliance. His speeches in the spare room of the Republican Circle had impressed an occasional visitor from another generation, Alfred Boas, a wealthy Jewish industrialist and an influential habitué of Radical and Freemasonic circles. When the electoral triumph of the parties of the left frightened their moderate leader, Waldeck-Rousseau, out of office, Boas obtained for Jouvenel an appointment as cabinet secretary to the Minister of Justice, Vallé, in the new all-Radical government formed by Combes on June 7, 1902. Jouvenel was then in a better position to renew his application to the newspaper *Le Matin;* this time the proprietor, Maurice Bunau-Varilla, hired him at "an astronomical salary"[3] as associate editor-in-chief. And that same year Jouvenel married Claire Boas, his patron's blonde and beautiful daughter.

Of his three new ventures—into politics, journalism, and marriage—the third was the most disappointing. The couple first moved in with his father; then after one year, having heard enough about Church, Monarchy, and the Jockey Club, they took a house of their own, furnishing it with choice antiques. Both loved antiques; in little else, though, did they agree. She was fond of occultism and of intrigue beyond even his tolerance, and resolute enough in caprice to make even him feel methodical beside her. She bore him a son, Bertrand, in 1903; their marriage broke up soon afterwards, and they were divorced in 1906. She never remarried; instead, with the help of Philippe Berthelot, she rose to "the head of the zealous battalion of Quai d'Orsay ladies," as "a sort of diplomatic and republican squad leader." So at least writes her most prolific detractor, adding:

The conduct of our foreign affairs was for thirty years a perpetual ballet, and Madame Boas de Jouvenel was its principal conductor. Those replies to chiefs of state banefully improvised at bars (the reply to the famous Wilson note in December, 1916) or more tenderly thought out on a boudoir couch, and treaties drawn up amid the hum of alcove secrets or Carbonari conspiracies, had to lead at length to our shame and disaster.[4]

Influential she was: "We obey you blindly," wrote Anatole France.[5] But all was not whimsy with her. In 1917, as the Austro-Hungarian Empire was secretly offering to surrender in return for a guarantee of its integrity, she induced the Czech Beneš, the Slovak Štefanik, and the two Quai d'Orsay specialists in Slavic affairs, Ernest Denis and Louis Léger, to improvise a joint Czech and Slovak state. After the war she founded the organization La Bienvenue Française for the reception of foreign visitors to France, launched the drive La Journée Pasteur to raise money for scientific laboratories, and created exchange scholarships and welfare funds by the dozen. She also wrote maxims and fairy tales, which she signed "Ariel." Berthelot's retirement somewhat curtailed her access to ministries in Paris and to chanceries abroad; what remained of it she used unsparingly for urging war with Hitler.

Claire Boas was to prove no less trying to Jouvenel as an ex-wife than she had been as a wife—but as much as this venture into marriage was a source of regret for him, his venture into journalism was the reverse. When he joined Le Matin it was not yet fifteen years old. Bunau-Varilla had founded it after making a huge fortune overnight at the expense of French stockholders in the Panama Canal enterprise. At first, in order to stave off an inquest into his means of founding it, he had put it at the disposal of successive governments in return for their indulgence. Then, deeming "that [he] had won prescription,"[6] he aspired to put successive governments at his own disposal, and only half in jest did Clemenceau call him "l'Empereur."[7] His megalomania was a match for his means: once, in reply to an innuendo, he said curtly, "Isn't it better for all that money to have gone into *my* pockets rather than those of a lot of shopkeepers and *petits bourgeois* who would only have spent it stupidly?"[8] Having swindled his compatriots, he became conscientiously patriotic. Otherwise, though, he supported the policies of the left—with one exception, which perhaps explained the rule: the income tax. "*Anything* but," he told Joseph Caillaux.[9]

"Anything but" was good enough for Jouvenel, the more so since as editor he sought not to shape but to enlighten public opinion. Only as a contributor did he expose his own views. Half the time, then, he exposed his views. Indeed, *Le Matin* had, in addition to one permanent "editor," two alternating "editors-in-chief." This arrangement could hardly have been devised; most likely it arose spontaneously in answer to Jouvenel's need for occasional stimulus and the staff's need for occasional distraction. Wrote one collaborator, "Taking turns every fortnight had, among other advantages, that of nourishing a little cat-and-dog fight between the two editors-in-chief, Henry de Jouvenel and Stéphane Lauzanne."[10] Lauzanne it was who had not even deigned to reject Jouvenel's first application for a position on the staff. But Jouvenel, by controlling every detail of the copy that he edited (even furnishing "incomparable headlines"[11]) and caring for the interests of every staff member ("with the best part of his earnings"[12]), inspired a tacit conspiracy to fashion the newspaper after his conception of a chronicle of ideas as well as events, with its columns permanently available to his contradictors. By 1914 he had acquired for it a prestige on a par with that of any of its competitors.

"What he liked about journalism," observed Monzie, "was the daily opportunity it provided for squandering nobility."[13] What he liked about editorship, though, was the opportunity of playing host to "the happy diversity of minds," as he wrote. "Many hypotheses are needed to make a science, and many discussions to achieve an average of truth."[14] Of course he liked to decide how a configuration of discussions and hypotheses should be laid out if an average of truth were to emerge from it, but he reserved his editor's veto for "the only grave error, the factual error."[15] So keen was his sense of the responsibility of the press in view of its power that he once proposed, as a means to "outlaw false news," an international agreement for making penal offences of certain forms of misinformation, including tendentious reports, headlines, and even omissions, and for creating leagues to detect and report infractions and a tribunal with supranational authority to pass sentence.[16] But professional manners in any case are not subject to legislation, and the cry once escaped him: "Do we not, oh journalists, see the blood, strength, and faith that are left in this country flow out of the hundred wounds our polemics inflict every day?"[17] He was to remain a journalist all his life, thereby serving the ideal of a republic of the wise and the just, even while in other capacities he served the Republic as it was.

Jouvenel's first direct relations with the politics of his country lasted less than four years. They were confined to the Ministry of Justice until January, 1905, when Combes lost the confidence of the Chamber for tolerating a system of political espionage in the army. Jouvenel then became chief secretary to the Radical-Socialist Dubief, Minister of Commerce in a cabinet formed by Rouvier as the separation of church and state drew to a climax. During these years Jouvenel shunned the usual accessories to an incipient career in politics. He refused to enter a party, or to run for local office, or to sit with the board of directors of any private company, and when the Rouvier government fell in March, 1906, he broke off formal political activity altogether. Journalism was more gratifying. His first expenses as chief secretary had been defrayed by his earnings as editor. Whereas in the ministries he was an exalted hack, by 1907 "he runs *Le Matin*, almost all France, part of the world"—or so wrote one of his prospective contributors.[18] He had, however, passed his apprenticeship in politics, and the obvious sequel, election to the Chamber, was consonant in all respects with his position as editor. His convictions fitted into the parliamentary system a degree or so to the left of the program of the Radical-Socialist party. He might have joined that party, or started one of his own, or run for deputy as an independent candidate. Instead he spent his full time and passion for politics at his editorial desk until, eight years later, war dislodged him. For he had observed the Republic at close quarters and found favor in it artlessly while the danger from the right was noisily passing; so his ardor for it had receded, leaving his convictions intact but disclosing a temperament at variance with them, a temperament averse to much that was requisite for the success of men or ideas under the very regime he sought to reconcile with its antagonists. Estranged from the world of politicians, parties, platforms, and parliaments, the only one where his convictions were valid, Jouvenel expressed his bafflement so articulately that at times *it* resembled a conviction.

The earliest occasion on which Jouvenel declared his reasons for holding aloof from politics was a meeting of a club for aspirant orators, the Conférences Molé-Tocqueville, on March 8, 1907. Proportional representation was up for debate that day, and Jouvenel spoke in support of it against "our local suffrage so pompously called universal suffrage," which, he argued, was conducive to a particularistic outlook and accordingly detrimental to the national interest. For a syndicalist to argue so was already a surprise; but then, in a sudden departure from the issue under discussion, he cried: "France is crumbling, and none of our parties is capable of restoring unity, for some of them deny progress while the others deny history." He did not pause to reconcile his objection to the parties of the day with his support for a voting system designed to augment their influence. Luckily not—for he concluded, projecting his own dismay:

In ancient Greece, after centuries of mythology, there came a day when intelligent men, weary of their local divinities and of a religion that changed from town to town, felt the need for a broader community and, to give form their sorrows and to their hopes, raised an altar to the Unknown God.

Do you not sometimes seem to hear, rising from the depths of our French people—more and more tired of our parliamentary groups and of our local politicians and their calculations in which the fear of reform offsets the fear of the electorate, and more and more eager for a policy at once more audacious and better balanced, one that would guarantee man the right to life, the right to work, and the right to progress, and guarantee the country the right to pride and the right to glory—a cry in which the lassitude and the aspirations of modern France find expression, a muffled and unanimous invocation to the Unknown Party?[19]

This vision of deliverance from a state of servitude by consent distracted Jouvenel and his audience from the topic on the agenda. No one present, it seems, ever forgot the impelling effect of his words as he uttered them, and whoever now tries to speak them intelligibly will realize how great an orator he was. Faithful to the Unknown Party from that time forth, he served it in effect whenever he combated party politics, fell back on it whenever he abstained, and campaigned for it whenever he issued an apologia. Twenty-five years later he wrote, "I go on invoking the Unknown Party."[20]

Nominally the Unknown Party was founded on defiance of only the known parties of the Republic. By the logic of sentiment that defiance extended, however, to the very idea of political parties, which has, perhaps unnecessarily, come to be associated with republican government. Moreover, some of Jouvenel's objections to the parties and politics of his time were also necessarily objections to the republican system of government itself, even to government in general; and so too were some of his objections to the institutions of the Third Republic other than political parties. By conviction he was a republican, and his objections to the Third Republic as a republic followed from this conviction; some of his other objections to the Republic were emotional in origin, though, and often these conflicted with his own better judgment. His critique of the Republic, brilliant as it was on the whole, suffered from the conflict. So too for many years did his political action, which described more or less simultaneously the two main phases of a vicious circle. The regime was, he thought, perfectible with time, and amenable to good use in the meantime, provided only that men like himself were willing to work with it; no sooner would he start to do so, however, or merely think of starting, than feelings of repugnance and of futility would come over him. Then he would contrive pretexts for abstention and motives for despair.

He would say, for instance, that the masses either refuse to accept a superior man or are unable to recognize one, and their chosen rulers are quick to take precautions against having to contend with one:

Of all possible perils, genius is the one against which the nation is most thoroughly insured. The mass of regulations provides a safeguard against initiative, just as the criteria for recruitment and advancement afford protection against originality.[21]

As he saw it, this official conspiracy against initiative and originality operated relentlessly in the higher as in the lower reaches of the state. An offender who had shammed mediocrity all the way to power might not shun it even there, for:

The duration of a republican government is a matter of day-to-day diplomacy based on acquaintanceship with administrative yearbooks, opportune promotions in the Legion of Honor, respect for all sorts of clienteles, and judicious abuse of principles.

The growth of officialdom favors the success of such practices by the multitude of posts that it provides. Thus ministers are bound in solidarity to members of parliament, and these to postmen, right down through the whole official hierarchy. The network is not without a few holes, to be sure, but it is solid enough to safeguard established positions and resist important innovations.

A nation of candidates for civil service, degrees and letters of recommendation in hand, stands ready to guarantee the future of this armature. What danger could then threaten it? If Napoleon came along, he would have to go through channels. When his turn came to reach the heights, he would long since have passed the age of audacity.[22]

Jouvenel of all his contemporaries on the left had the merit of recognizing most clearly the principle of equality for what it was: the corollary and not the denial of the differences among men. For political and administrative purposes, however, "the refusal to accept superiority or the inability to recognize it,"[23] which he ascribed to the masses, is irremediable if indeed it is real. Universal suffrage is admittedly not a fit instrument for detecting superiority—it was not designed for that purpose. And public administrations can hardly be expected to dispense with standards for the selection and advancement of personnel on the off-chance that Napoleon might be kept waiting. The conditions that made Napoleon's career possible cannot be institutionalized, as Napoleon himself demonstrated, and the country could not easily have survived one genius of his kind each generation, much less a regime recruiting them *en masse*. According to proper republican sentiment, Napoleon *should* pass the age of audacity waiting his turn, and according to the ethics of any struggle for recognition, superiority confers its own dispensations and may not plead to be identified by a screening process and accorded a handicap. Then, too, no administration can afford to distinguish initiative and originality from lack of discipline and eccentricity, and any government quite naturally uses what Combes was reproved for calling "the favors at its disposal" to bind it in solidarity with the men on whom it depends for its existence.

Jouvenel, however, also saw in the system, from the evidence of its effects, an incentive to its practitioners to enjoy and enhance the evils they could not avoid. Of course his grievances of this sort cannot be stated convincingly or even meaningfully in the form of an indictment, count by count. They did not have the same validity as the doctrines he defined, or the views he took from day to day toward specific matters of policy. They derived from antipathies, which are not amenable to reason, and they expressed suspicions, as if to legitimate those antipathies. To convert them into postulates is to depreciate them spuriously. Jouvenel of all men knew that superiority, much as it was despised by republicans, was not of necessity an impediment to success among them; however, with mischievous inconsequence, he could not help thinking that it was.

Jouvenel could not help thinking that, as a result of some inherent constitutional defect, "Republics turn into Empires of the Aged."[24] He suffered from an uncanny sensitivity to symptoms of the aging of the population,[25] a demographic process that operates in fact without regard for the form of government. An almost pathological dread of old age pervaded his vision of a whole people adjusting to prolonged life expectancy—and to its obverse, the prolonged expectancy of death. The themes of youth, newness, life, are asserted in everything about the man so aptly named Jouvenel, who grew up in Castel-Novel and founded *La Revue des Vivants*: he loved young people and their activities, and his own youth was the source of his closest friends, his favorite haunts, his only reminiscences. Possibly he continued to associate the dignity of the state with the bushy beards that deputies and ministers had worn in the years of his childhood, and shunned whatever threatened him with success in politics as liable to bring him nearer to beards, to old age, to death. Distorted it is, yet Jouvenel's vision of the Empire of the Aged is just accurate enough to make sanity appear for a moment to coincide with a groping after novelty in any form.

Offices, all the offices of France, are filled with worthy men bent over directories, busily reading the names that come before theirs, taking account of deaths, computing the number of retirements in a year, coveting the places of the old and the dying.

Soldiers, judges, functionaries, and how many businessmen, manufacturers, tradesmen, and how many politicians, and how many sons, live in that way (for that is called living), aging—too slowly for their taste—while watching others grow old, respecting only the hierarchy of age, having as horizons only retirement and death.

And when they "get there," without plans and without programs—for plans and programs are useful only for starting out, and now it is a matter of getting there,—be they senior clerks, generals, prime ministers, what can they do but live from hand to mouth, deal with the problems that they cannot elude, elude those that can still wait, restrain the drive of life with all their might, strive to stay put, to stay put at whatever price?[26]

"I don't think I'll have the supreme talent," Jouvenel once remarked. "Which is...?" "To survive."[27] And when power becomes identified with survival, he wrote, those who hold power cling to it "as an old man clings to life: when he no longer knows what to do with it."[28]

The usual vehicle for exercising the supreme talent in politics is the political party, and Jouvenel's first impulse was to laugh when his son Bertrand, on coming of age, joined the Radical-Socialists; then, thinking it over, he gave the venture his blessings, for (he pointed out) a party judges a man by the length of time he has been inside it.[29] The tendency of youngsters to judge men by other standards, combining with the tendency of remote pretenders to wealth and power to judge differently from their ruling classes, determines continual accretions to the political left and generates an illusion of political progress. "By and large," Jouvenel suspected,

there are bolder minds within the parties of the left not because the individuals there are better, but perhaps simply because they have more to gain than to defend. Established wealth goes hand in hand with established truth: you are less inclined to believe in the second if you do not possess the first. Newcomers feel that they are not continuing, but beginning.[30]

When newcomers have in their turn acquired something to defend, their attitude changes:

We begin by defending our institutions and wind up defending our positions. We confuse the Republic with the place we have taken in it. Whoever disturbs us seems to threaten the regime. We say so, and we think so, for men defend their interests in perfect good faith. To imagine that what *is* ought to be, and that what we *have* is legitimate, is man's natural instinct, the origin of social conservatism, which adjusts easily to the most audacious epithets, preferring them to be, like suits of clothing, cut in the latest fashion.

Soon we protect ourselves against the future as carefully as against the past. The same men will do: trained for combating and not for creating, formed in the opposition and not in the government, accustomed to controversy and not to responsibility, they make of power a weapon and not a tool. They think *against*, they administer *against*, they govern *against*. Fear of successors combines with contempt for predecessors. Wishing the moment to last forever, they baptize it progress. "Stay, oh hour, thou art so fair!" cried Goethe. Members of parliament do not exclaim so poetically: they democratize Goethe...and content themselves with musing, "If only it would last!"

A new idea: danger! A new man: danger![31]

If the conflict of ideas among republican politicians is superficial, the identity of motives, thought Jouvenel, is fundamental. A professional spirit, stronger than the rivalries among them, unites the men in parliament against the outside world. Their dealings with that world are businesslike: "Every four or every nine years[32] [they] would receive from the electorate a kind of *carte blanche*; to have it renewed was their aim, their rule of conduct, they might have almost said their duty."[33] Barring reelection, four or nine years of *carte blanche* is time enough for the representatives of the people to set themselves above the people:

Privilege and not time makes aristocracies: the nobility that abandoned Napoleon at Fontainebleau was not yet fifteen years old. To have managed painlessly to enjoy the advantages of domination and the use of the state as their personal property, to have private officials in the provinces and to support adherents out of the public domain: that is the seignorial system. Has it not been adapted little by little to the parliamentary system?[34]

The function of this aristocracy is, nominally, to express the general will; however, its corporate interest and instinct prompt it to do the reverse.

The castes of nobles and priests continue to thrive in spite of revolutions, but twenty others, a hundred others, have grown up alongside of them, feeding on comparable prejudices, each refusing to know, lest it esteem, the others. On the borders that divide them, and the better to divide them, swarm men of law and men of politics. The latter are recruited for the most part among doctors and lawyers, living off our illnesses and our trials—what a symbol!

How could these specialists in pain and ruin avoid maintaining our state of endemic civil war, what with the chicanery of their consultations and pleadings? They are not dishonest, but their profession has made them pessimistic. To win renown they have had to use all the resources of their minds in discovering the blemishes, vices, and shame of men. They are accustomed to denouncing, not to solving. Confronted with misfortune, they know only how to ask for extensions and delays. Thus a great discovery of modern politics is named "anesthesia" by the former and "moratorium" by the latter. An immense claims office, with a hospital as annex to receive the victims: that is what they instinctively make of national organization.[35]

The complement to this abuse of privilege and power under the Republic is the abuse of persons: "To imagine that every citizen lies, cheats, and steals; to accuse him on a hunch, for safety's sake; to credit him with inborn dishonesty; to spy on him just in case and insult him in any case: that is what, in France, is called politics."[36] And finally, abusing abuse itself, politicians vituperate "only to give tone to their conversation and verve to their style, and to adorn in violent luxury rather modest thoughts whose existence no one would otherwise have noticed."[37]

That is how the Republic appeared to Jouvenel during his protracted moments of discouragement. Gently and impartially he scorned the men and institutions of that unpleasant place, and studiously he confounded what he found wrong with them and what he disliked about them. No one, nothing, was to blame exactly, for the men could not help themselves, and the institutions were what they had to be. What disturbed him was only the hopeless absurdity of it all.

He wrote with the power of inducing in others his own state of mind. As he described them, many activities that are normal and right in a democracy did seem hopelessly absurd, for, without violence to the facts, an appropriate state of mind can make marriage look obscene, or art silly, or life brutish and short. Jouvenel's state of mind could make the men who ruled the Republic, like data that fit a formula, seem insignificant insofar as they ran true to form: whether as republicans, oppressing one another in shifts; or as rulers, devising aristocracies; or merely as men, growing old on the job. "To imagine that every citizen lies, cheats, and steals" perhaps bespeaks a state of mind more suitable than Jouvenel's for men who rule. Even so phrased it approaches an egalitarian form of civic vigilance, and something like "caste spirit" may be saluted as group loyalty or *esprit de corps*. Ordinarily a deputy is praised for striving to please his constituents and for remaining at their service; if it is harmful for deputies to regard reelection as a duty, the harm cannot be avoided within a system of representative government,[38] and if it is injurious for men in public office to "strive to stay put," the injury will be the same whatever the system of government or of administration.

Perhaps the epithets "caste," "aristocracy," "established truth," *are* precise and ugly enough for the regime to be suspected of failing in its purpose if they are apposite to an account of its workings. And of the "hierarchy of age" Jouvenel drew so vivid and dreadful an image that his aversion for it does at first strike us as reasonable: no decent regime, we feel, would have tolerated it. However, so long as he gave no hint of how any regime might have rejuvenated the men who filled "all the offices of France," those men have no proper place in his critique of the Third Republic. More, so long as he gave no hint of how a regime might have encouraged life, newness, and youth in general, those concepts themselves have no proper place there. And surely they are too vague for his purpose: when is a thing no longer young or new? They conflict at times: there is an age at which even Jouvenel decided tacitly whether to do without youth or else without life. They are ambiguous: Jouvenel was known to love "the silks and paintings of old France"[39]—or was it young France? And he himself did not look to the living only: he ceaselessly mourned the great dead, and several years after the First World War he asked,

What other faith is worthy of France than the one whose symbol is, not a single cross, but hundreds of thousands of wooden crosses? What other ideal could a Frenchman accept to live for than the one that for four years so many Frenchmen obstinately held to be worth dying for?[40]

Then, too, the antonym of *novelty* is not pejorative: Jouvenel the editor must have known how good a case can be made for routine in small matters as a condition for freedom in large ones. What he knew, however, was not proof against his perversity, which splendidly contrived laws to hide behind—iron laws of senescence and decay for a regime offensive to him if only in its being what it had to be.

Survival is of course no substitute for ability, but should seniority be penalized? Within a stable regime, what makes the ruling classes old is in the first instance their own longevity, not the exclusion of the young. Men rarely reach power with enough indifference to it to retire at a decent age; collaterally, a political assembly or party that massacred its senior members would find recruitment difficult. However, the dominant pattern of succession—not exactly succession by order of age, but a succession of the old—did seem odd in the case of governing bodies representative in theory and subject to frequent renewal, and as the crew of young republicans that had taken over the prefectures and ministries of France in the 1890's stayed on and on in them, the regime itself and not its duration must have seemed responsible for the incessant sameness of things—of the men, of their ways of working, of the words they used. Sameness, hence worse than sameness, for nothing can last without aging: and to spite that appalling truism, in supreme defiance of men who "protect themselves against the future" for want of a more congenial way of innovating than changing things, Jouvenel once interpreted eight hundred years of French history as a perpetual revolution.[41] Illegality peeps through this study of his as the beneficent demon of history, enabling revolutionary movements to compel progress by threatening destruction. As Jouvenel saw it, to recognize an efficient threat to an established order was a requirement of statecraft, which, he thought, consisted in punishing bluffs but meeting threats half way. Thus he advised the Republic to come to terms with the revolutionary movement based on trade unions. Yet what terms, what mitigated revolution, ever much affected even the most circuitous routines of the most ineffectual incumbents of the most redundant posts of an aging regime?

In time penitence took a place in the midst of Jouvenel's considered opinions. The elite of his time, he then said, in their scorn for politicians, were forgetting that the business of politics "dominates and conditions every other kind of business, and that by neglecting it they were delivering, along with the rights of surveillance and appeal, their fate and that of their time and country, and of generations to come, into the hands of the very men whom they flattered themselves to scorn."[42] Because of his imperfect faith in democracy, though, his attitude was one more of attrition than of penitence, just as for the same reason his "syndicalism" was less a doctrine than a vast expedient. As a young man he had perceived that faith was at the root of every general system of thought: "Faith in historical materialism replaced [among Marxists] the faith that Renan and his contemporaries had in the future of science."[43] To a man who is only *convinced* that democracy is right, a representative of the people will always resemble a self-righteous usurper, and likewise a man who only *consents* to government may well regard politics as a predatory profession.

What Jouvenel almost had faith in was the political value of ideas as measured by their abundance and piquancy. "He conceived easily," wrote Paul Valéry, "and he had a natural relish for ideas";[44] and that was a curse in politics, among men who liked to know just what to expect when they confided power to someone. He lacked the presumption—or the modesty—to identify himself entirely with a few assorted principles, to pin down his ideas to points on a program, to make commitments out of his inclinations. "Parties that teach their doctrine only," he wrote, "financial powers that teach their interest, governments that teach their apology, tend equally to suppress the free quest of truth"[45]—an absurd judgment, unless it was meant to show why men like himself were un-comfortable among parties, financial powers, and governments. Accuracy, "an average of truth," "the free quest of truth": this was as close to truth as ever he claimed or even cared to come, being too happy seeking it to want it—as did Tardieu, or Caillaux—inscribed in the 440 articles of a treaty or locked up in a bank vault in Florence. The cult of ideas exempted his thought from verification and absolved it of inconsistency. And ideas were after all the soul of history, what humanity was always suffering for and glorying in and being brave about—whereas there was never much else to do about truth than to believe it.

The Unknown Party was, then, viable only if immaterial. Universal by definition, it could not have endured the failure to prevail against the real parties of the real Republic; and, deprived of a program of action, it had to rely for sympathy on a mood that even its prophet could not long sustain. As Jouvenel spelled out its somber message, his sense of humor provided a diversion—in the full sense of the term. The internal contra-dictions of a regime whose leaders "inspire confidence insofar as they go back on their word, for they have to prove, not the possibility of doing anything, but the impossibility of doing anything else,"[46] are, paradoxi-cally, masked by the neatness of the paradox, while his aphoristic prose, the high order of generality that he affected, demanded as much con-formity from the politicians of the Republic as he reproved them for de-manding of him. That bizarre and appealing style, which made even nonsense glow, is what gave to everything he wrote its appearance of consistency: not wise enough to resist being clever, he made an exercise in syntax of smoothing over the drama of his life. His playfulness did not deceive his contemporaries: one found his aphorisms "brilliant and cruel,"[47] and another "disturbing, because they reveal the inner struggle of a mind without employment and an ardor burning itself out to no purpose."[48]

Something, though, did fool his contemporaries about him. He was called ambitious at first, because he thought audaciously and refused to wait his turn in the hierarchy of age; and when that turn came anyhow, and he let it go by again and again, he was taxed with indolence. His admirers saw him as a complete and harmonious figure that did not blend, as it were, with the tableau of the Third Republic: he was an Athenian sage, or a man of the Renaissance, or an eighteenth-century *philosophe*. But "nothing amused him more," wrote his son,

than to hear it said of someone, "He belongs to another age. He should have lived in...." "If he had lived in...," Jouvenel would snap back, "he would still have been a man of another age. We owe our age the courtesy of allegiance and presence."[49]

He rejected the system, judged Paul Reynaud: he had "too much pride and joy of thought to partake of the trudgings that lead most surely to power."[50] The system rejected him, wrote Count d'Ormesson:

The very quality of his imagination, with its dash of impulsiveness, while assuring him of success and eminence, seemed to arrest him on the threshold of the highest political offices. This is because, except in rare instances, only conformism and mediocrity put our politicians at their ease. And Jouvenel did not put them at their ease.[51]

Men have abused their pride and joy of thought for less, though, and Jouvenel might well have been a "rare instance" despite his dash of impulsiveness. Nor did he lack the will to power; however, the elements of confusion within him, which impeded his action, were not perceptible at close range—on paper and off, his manner disguised them. "I have never seen him lose his temper with a regime that did not help him to realize any of his far-reaching plans," wrote his son;[52] but not losing his temper was a polite way of losing his temper, and expecting help from that senile, outmoded regime was a haughty confession of helplessness. He rationalized his position pleasantly, coquettishly, unconvincingly. He wanted no post, he said, that could "as well be filled by someone else."[53] The Jouvenels, he would say, "must be uncles to the Republic."[54] Or again, they must play "the thankless part of the husband who repairs the mistakes that others have led his wife to commit."[55] And, with his genial smile and lordly air, he would tell the joke of the husband under the Old Regime who, caught looking lovingly at his wife, was rebuked by her *soupirant*: "Go on, you've had yours."[56]

Without bitterness, then, the fair-haired boy of the Republic lived to become its perennial coming man, loitering year after year on the sidelines of the political scene, testing his talent from time to time while longing always for a magic formula to reconcile his acceptance of democracy with his distaste for it or else a historic moment in which his very record for aloofness would add the decisive touch to his other qualities and single him out for the great role he somehow deserved to play. Meanwhile he *still* believed in the Third Republic—which is to say that he believed in it less and less.

CHAPTER 12

War and Peace

COMPARED WITH the political career he then brilliantly abstained from having, Jouvenel's activities before the war were almost trivial. His time was divided between the capital, where he had his work for *Le Matin*, and Corrèze, which he always regarded as his home. With his first earnings he saw to repairing the family castle even though meanwhile he was breaking with the family. His father died in 1906; before dying Raoul had the child Bertrand baptized on the sly. During his vacations Henry planned and, in 1910, created a *syndicat d'initiative* for encouraging tourist trade in Limousin;[1] when similar associations formed in the neighboring regions he organized them into a federation. In 1913 he escorted the new President of the Republic, Raymond Poincaré, on an official tour of Limousin. For the rest he devoted himself enthusiastically to his private life, which was already as public as anything about him.

He sought out the company of the well-read in preference to that of the well-born. Handsome—"fine face, fine mustaches," chaffed Jules Renard,[2]—charming *and* prosperous, he fast became a lion of the Parisian *gens de lettres*, while the women among them, who held their society together, earned for him the nickname of "the tiger."[3] Among these was the slender and beautiful Madame Pillet-Will, comtesse de Comminges, herself known as "the panther,"[4] who provided him with a second son, Renaud, in 1904. His interest in women as such was, however, inversely proportional to his success with them, and so his prospects for eminence made his second bachelorship trying for him. Though some who courted him had impressive credentials themselves, the one who finally prevailed had no social standing and enough of a past to make her future problematical. Until 1906 she had been the wife and collaborator of the great critic and rose-water novelist Willy. Since then, besides writing on her own with small success, she had earned a living and a reputation by performing—dressed (to some extent) as a cat—a mime and dance at the Folies Bergère; she had, however, abandoned the music hall when the duc and the comte de Morny, nephews of Napoleon III, hurled ripe fruit from the audience one evening, and their sister, the marquise de

Belbœuf, her dancing partner, was taken into protective custody. Then she had become fiction editor of *Le Matin*. She was three years older than Jouvenel, spoke with a lively Burgundian accent, and had an appearance and manner as nearly feline as was humanly possible. She was delighted to change her name—Sidonie Gabrielle Colette—to that of Madame Henry de Jouvenel.

Jouvenel and Colette had a daughter, Colette de Jouvenel, in August, 1913, at the end of their first year of marriage, and while Colette took time off from her domestic hobbies—her cats, her plants, and what she called her "scribblings"—to be a doting mother, her husband dutifully settled down to evenings at home and Sundays in the park. Then, "on our aging society, which believed itself to be at peace because it was tired, disaster fell one day in August, 1914."[5]

Jouvenel was not taken by surprise: two years earlier at the Conférences Molé-Tocqueville he had astounded his friends by leaping onto the rostrum to interrupt a debate on a matter of home policy, crying: "Don't you see the only reality that matters? War is coming!"[6] When it came, he left at once to join his regiment, and within a few days he found himself on the front lines at the Battle of the Marne. Colette for her part volunteered as a nurse, and some weeks later, having located her husband in a besieged town, she succeeded in sneaking through the combat area to spend a few hours with him; another few weeks, however, and, worn by the strain of nursing, she left the hospitals to become war correspondent in Italy for *Le Matin*. Jouvenel, though, remained on the front lines—at the Marne, at Verdun, at the Meuse—almost continuously for four years, rising to the rank of lieutenant in the infantry. Meanwhile he somehow found time and energy to write regularly for his newspaper, and his furloughs were spent behind his editor's desk. Once too—in January, 1917—he went on a mission to Rome for Poincaré. He escaped all physical injury in combat, but because of his passionate abhorrence of waste and destruction and death he suffered morally day after day beyond any reckoning. Patriotism and affection for his comrades gave him courage, and again and again he resolved, like so many other soldiers, to fight for peace as tirelessly all his life as then he was fighting for victory. And whenever he encountered defective supplies or contradictory orders or the grim evidence of carelessness on high, he would reflect: "A regime so ill-suited to organize war would have no excuse for not being dead set on organizing peace."[7] He and his comrades looked forward to playing a decisive role in the politics of their country after the fighting was over—

It did not occur to us thàt soldiers were a minority in France, that the home front saw beauty in the war, that government had never been easier than in the course of these four years, and that victory would not remove the men who, if they were not its authors, had at least the conspicuous good fortune of being its contemporaries and, forgetting the price paid for it, would perceive with the utmost sincerity in this "revenge for 1871" the supreme justification of their routines.[8]

In his impulse to create a new world on the ruins of the old, Jouvenel pursued many and diverse activities in the years after the Armistice, and in their number and diversity he found a safeguard against loss of interest in any one of them. He founded the Federal Union of Veterans; he organized a "States-General of Veterans"; he led a stirring and successful press campaign in November, 1920, for the burial of the Unknown Soldier beneath the Arch of Triumph. Impossible things he preferred doing rapidly, and one day in 1920 he formed the Confederation of Intellectual Workers out of thirty-odd professional unions, which regarded themselves as incompatible, and half a dozen of their federations and confederations, which had sworn "to fight it out to the bitter end— among themselves."[9] A survey conducted by *Le Matin* had revealed the lack of solidarity among intellectual workers in France—journalists, actors, engineers, teachers, scientists, musicians—as well as the rapid decline of their social and economic status in the twentieth century. "Fortunately, Henry de Jouvenel existed."[10] He assembled, by separate invitations, the leaders in the field, and, as most of them were not on speaking terms, he had the floor to himself. Within a couple of hours all their unions—representing forty thousand workers—were federated under the "neutral" auspices of his newspaper. "The most beautiful meeting that we have ever seen," sighed the representative of a group of authors,[11] and Jouvenel later told the delegate of the Society of Composers and Dramatic Authors, "I love the role of break-down mechanic."[12] The Confederation of Intellectual Workers was the first organization of its kind in history. Three years later, when it had a membership of one hundred fifty thousand and had been imitated in twelve other countries, Jouvenel convened an international congress of national confederations of intellectual workers and solemnly confederated them all in the amphitheater of the Sorbonne on April 5, 1923.

In the affairs of the Republic decisive influence was, however, reserved to members of parliament, and the editor and organizer Henry de Jouvenel was only a dignified lobbyist. "On his own initiative he would never have run for election," declared Anatole de Monzie, his closest friend, godfather to both his sons; "it is I who drew him away from journalism and into parliament. I was ambitious for him, being ambitious for the country."[13] Monzie was so ambitious, in fact, that in the autumn of 1919, as the general elections drew near, Jouvenel returned to Corrèze and put in for the Radical nomination for deputy to the Chamber. The Radicals of Corrèze, however, preferred a certain M. Jaubert, a long-standing, dues-paying member, to the proponent of the Unknown Party, who for fifteen years had made a vocation of snubbing them and their kind. Jouvenel conceded the point and ran instead one year later as independent candidate for the Senate and for the general council of Corrèze. He spoke to the city workers and to the peasants about "syn-dicalism" and "organized democracy." The city workers knew that this editor of a progressive Parisian newspaper was speaking in earnest, and the peasants knew that this scion of provincial barons was not speaking in earnest. He was elected to the general council triumphantly, and on January 9, 1921, he won the election to the Senate on the first ballot against several former deputies.

When the general council of Corrèze assembled in January, 1921, it elected Jouvenel president. Regularly thereafter his canton of Saint-Privas reelected him to the council, and regularly the council in turn chose him for its president. Whereas the Republic was for him of the nature of an abstraction, which he treated with due detachment, Corrèze was always apposite in his mind to so many particular men and fields and villages that he loved. He used every official means at his disposal to fit out the region with paved roads, electricity, and even an airport near Varetz, and he gladly drew on his personal fortune, whenever he had one, to round out the local budget. His devotion was repaid in kind by the inhabitants; those of Varetz especially, wrote the local schoolmaster, "all veritably idolized him."[14] Sunday was his favorite day in Corrèze: first came the formal talks, then the informal ones, and often by nightfall several hundred villagers were gathered at Castel-Novel for a "cultural feast"—that is, a feast at which only Limousin was spoken.[15] In the capital, meanwhile, he guarded against nostalgia by heading the Associa-tion for Correzians in Paris.[16]

Jouvenel's first task in the Senate was to testify against Joseph Caillaux, on trial for treason; he made his testimony "decisive against the prosecu-tion"[17] even though he was on the "Rubicon" lists as a prospective minister. Then, as the Senate returned to normal, he elected to sit on the Foreign Affairs Commission. He also registered with the Radical and Radical-Socialist Democratic Left; in time he was to change his status to "unaffiliated," then to settle at last on "*indépendant de gauche*." And he took his bearings, slowly. André Maurois recalls a conversation held many years later with his "clever and brilliant" friend, whom he and his wife would go to see in his old family estate in Varetz.

"The Senate," he told us, in his beautiful, mocking voice, "is a place worth knowing. You are accepted in it only by degrees. The first two years it is wise to remain absolutely inert. Any initiative would be offensive. The third year a clever man may smile, once or twice. The fourth year it is permissible to venture a few remarks. After six years, if you feel the wind in your favor, you make a little speech, wan and modest. After nine years, when you have been reelected, you have the right to be eloquent."

But he had not applied those rules; he had been eloquent from the start, successfully.[18]

And, wrote an English observer, he "quickly made a name by a few speeches which were equally meaningful and thoughtful."[19] He made some twenty speeches in two years, on odd topics ranging from physical education to the Bank of China. He did not speak on general policy: he had not yet adapted his political thought to the welter of confused aspirations and recriminations engendered the world over by the war. His opportunity to adapt them came on August 25, 1922, when Premier Poincaré appointed him French delegate to the League of Nations.[20]

Poincaré's choice of delegate was excellent. In Geneva Jouvenel applied his full enthusiasm and intelligence to the problems of organizing peace, and his colleague Edward Beneš listed his obvious qualifications in describing him as "the model of a French statesman, combining sharpness of judgment, political perspicacity, humanitarian ideals, and love of peace with warm fondness for the small nations."[21] He rapidly acquired an international outlook,[22] a sense of the potential importance of the League, and admirable control of its vocabulary.

His first important work in Geneva was done in the Temporary Mixed Commission,[23] which had been set up in 1921 to consider means of carrying out the disarmament provisions of the Covenant. Though when he joined it its members were agreed only on the complexity of their task, his own differences with the British delegate, Lord Robert Cecil, are generally held to have constituted the main obstacle to an understanding. Lord Robert wanted the nations of the League collectively to guarantee the defense of any one of them that undertook to disarm, while Jouvenel favored the creation of a system of regional defensive alliances prior to disarmament. In reality, as Jouvenel pointed out, the two men argued in common that the problem of security was inseparable from that of disarmament and took precedence over it.[24] Someone moved an order of the day in favor of deferring disarmament until the League was itself capable of assuring the security of its members. Jouvenel objected strenuously: "Conciliation must not be sought in one of those ambiguous texts that satisfy everyone and bind no one," he said.[25] Thereupon he proposed a counterdraft, which the commission adopted unanimously after only changing a word or two. "Material disarmament is impracticable without moral disarmament," it asserted, and governments cannot reduce their armaments without a "satisfactory guarantee for the security of their country... provided by a defensive agreement open to all countries."[26] It was the first formulation at Geneva of the principle of collective security. Jouvenel presented it to the Third Assembly on September 21, 1922, and with great oratorical skill and personal satisfaction he secured its adoption.[27] The Assembly then charged the same commission with preparing a draft of the proposed mutual-assistance treaty, and again Jouvenel's role was decisive in effecting a synthesis of the diverse points of view. The draft treaty embodied his original plan for regional-defense pacts, providing for them to become effective after every signatory nation had reduced its armaments; the League Council was to be responsible for interpreting the treaty and in particular identifying the aggressor nation in case of war.[28] In September, 1923, the Fourth Assembly endorsed the draft treaty, which accordingly went out to the various governments for approval, and Jouvenel was then free to devote more of his time to minor tasks of his choice, such as preparing the admission of Ethiopia to the League.

The draft regional-defense treaty provides a faithful indication of how small an increase in the prerogatives of the League Jouvenel then regarded as sufficient for assuring peace. Nominally he acted under instructions from Poincaré; he was, however, adept in obtaining authority to do as he liked. Paul-Boncour once asked

our beloved Henry de Jouvenel... how he, who was always the first to put forth bold proposals, was able to bear the delegation in those years, when our rulers were so far behind the cause we served together. "I would work things out in such a way that in the instructions I asked of M. Poincaré my questions were so worded that a negative reply had to follow and the *Verboten* played in favor of what I wanted."[29]

"We smiled at the time," added Paul-Boncour, evidently enlightened and satisfied. Yet during this period Jouvenel opposed the idea of a sovereign supranational power at least as zealously as did Poincaré. When a crisis arose over the seizure of Corfu by Italy in the autumn of 1923, Jouvenel wrote in *Le Matin* that sanctions against Italy would drag out a local disturbance and extend it to the limits of the universe...France does not share in this warlike enthusiasm...Between the prestige of the League of Nations and the interests of peace, no hesitation is possible: peace first![30]

In later years he was to say: no distinction is possible. Indeed, in the course of the years he was to define a general theory of peace implying the necessity for the League to acquire full sovereignty over its member states.

Governments in France were generally reticent about long-term commitments to the League: because *they* did not intend to make war, they regarded the predominance of France in Europe as both necessary and sufficient for peace. Their appointees in Geneva were only slightly less reticent, though this differential impassioned French politics for many years. At first Jouvenel himself thought the formula for peace to be intricate patterns of entangling alliances plus an international body to act as supreme arbiter on request. As early as 1925, however, he recognized that the supreme arbiter required supreme force and supreme jurisdiction in order to operate effectively. "To consider sanctions impossible," he remarked, "is to make international law impossible, for law without sanctions is only a verbalism"[31]—an audacious tautology at the time. When he became convinced that the establishment of international law rendered regional-defense pacts and even national armies superfluous, the evolution of his thought was complete.

Disarmament, he argued, was the simple converse, and security the simple corollary, of arming an international arbiter. "Disarmament presupposes general arbitration; or, better, the disarmament problem is involved in that of arbitration with sanctions."[32] He did concede that an international armed force could be created only by stages, that there were material and psychological obstacles to overcome, and that meanwhile every precaution by way of national defense was in order. However, reversing the usual argument, he treated all other proposals for permanent security as unrealistic: "I will not have men called utopian who, having seen civil tranquillity attained insofar as individuals have been disarmed and society armed, believe that international peace will triumph only insofar as nations are disarmed and the League of Nations armed."[33]

Jouvenel was not content with arguing that only an armed League of Nations was capable of assuring perpetual peace; he *defined* peace as "a state of society among nations," then proceeded easily to the conclusion that "when nations shall have accepted laws in common and insured their enforcement, they may deem themselves to be at peace—not before."[34] He distinguished peace from amity: "Peace is made with adversaries; with friends, there is no need for making peace."[35] Once this premise is accepted, his reasoning is irresistible: peace is no longer incompatible with—in fact, it is founded on—latent hostility among nations.

Peace is not based on confidence. What would be the use in society of judges to arbitrate lawsuits, of lawyers to plead them, of attorneys to carry on the proceedings, of notaries to draw up contracts, of revenue officials to detect fraud, of police to repress offenses, if confidence were the foundation of social life? Is it conceivable that the most endangered community, the one that runs the risk not only of individual crime but of a collective crime in which millions of men may participate, should have the right to expose its members to hazards that no city in the world accepts?[36]

If peace were substituted for the mere absence of war, enmity among nations would persist, legitimately and innocuously:

In every town, in every village, neighbors are permitted to hate one another as well as to love one another. Their differences do not disturb the peace in the streets and in the fields: the same law protects them all against their own impulses. At worst their enmity is expressed in lawsuits—that is, in appeals to law—and they are bound to bow down to the verdict of sovereign statutes.[37]

Jouvenel favored, as a step toward world government, a European economic and military union; by 1932, however, when his definitive work on peace, *La Paix française*, appeared, "a state of society among nations" had become an increasingly remote prospect, and the immediate security of France was his overriding preoccupation.

Peace was not opposed to patriotism in his mind: he did not even consider whether France might eventually lose her identity as a nation after relinquishing sovereignty in military or economic affairs. Yet if peace is the *only* object of national policy, it can be assured as well by capitulation; the sacrifice of sovereignty is always regarded by its critics as a capitulation without defeat, and, unfortunately, most men would rather risk war upon war than become part of a national minority in a federation of foreigners. In fact so persuasively did Jouvenel identify peace with the suppression of national states that his arguments were taken up by his contradictors. He might have elucidated the problem had he drafted a new covenant for the League; probably, though, he preferred to let it elucidate itself, considering a federation of nations to be desirable in just about any form, and just about inevitable in one form or another. His notion that the ultimate goal of history was a universal republic was the natural complement to his tendency to look on any other republic as provisional. In modern times, he found, political power has been exercised with greater efficiency and at higher levels from one century to the next, even when nominal absolutism has been replaced by popular sovereignty and multinational empires by national states.[38] This trend, he thought, was enhanced by the requirements of modern warfare, just as the horrors of a world war had enhanced the desire for world government.[39]

To arm the League of Nations may well have been the only realistic proposal for maintaining peace; in France, though, it did not seem even to be real, because it did not fit anywhere in the range of policies on disarmament from the extreme right to the extreme left—that is, from simultaneous multinational armament to simultaneous multinational disarmament. And besides, it ran afoul of the popular practice of gaging the realism of a proposal by the reputation of its author. To be sure, if Jouvenel had been caught dreaming now and again, André Tardieu, who proposed an international army to the World Disarmament Conference in 1932, was a model of this-worldliness; Tardieu's proposal, however, was taken to be a realistic maneuver to disrupt the proceedings.[40]

CHAPTER 13

A Mission to Syria

THE LEAGUE OF NATIONS was not Jouvenel's only refuge from parliament in 1922 and 1923. He still had *Le Matin*, and through it in October, 1922, he launched an appeal for the dissolution of political parties. The political parties of France, he maintained, had in effect declared themselves anachronistic, futile, and dangerous by entering the "sacred union" in August, 1914, just as the privileged estates had done in laying down their prescriptive rights one August day a century and a quarter earlier. He sought the cure for factionalism in a change, not of institutions, but of mentality: he did not appeal to parliament to dissolve the parties, but to the parties to dissolve themselves. His appeal made a great stir; the parties, however, remained intact. He also had as a refuge the avocation of syndicalism, and in the spring of 1923 he assembled representatives of the whole range of political parties, trade unions, syndicates, and civic federations in France, then organized them into a prototype of a syndical chamber, the "Economic States-General," and proposed its adjunction to the political chambers with the power of initiative and of veto in social and economic legislation; despite the enthusiasm of the whole assemblage—especially of the labor leaders and of the royalists[1]—the proposal came to nothing. Meanwhile he presided over countless civic committees and formulated opinions on a variety of subjects—in favor of a national program for mechanizing agriculture, for instance, and of the use of hydraulic energy in view of the shortage of both labor and coal. In striving so energetically to reform France from outside of parliament, he did not precisely flatter the men inside of it. Yet he managed not to offend them either, and in March, 1923, the Radical leader Edouard Herriot, on turning over to him the presidency of a congress of the Latin Press Association, confidently described him as "*le* coming man" of French politics.[2] In the spring of 1924, however, the political behavior of the coming man went from the bizarre to the baroque: being gifted for everything but waiting, he came too soon.

One day in March, 1924, Poincaré, after more than two years as Premier, lost a vote of confidence through an official miscount. The President of the Republic at once reappointed him, whereupon he took the opportunity to make room in his cabinet for some new men acceptable on the left, in the hope of surviving the forthcoming general elections as Premier even if, as was expected, the Cartel des Gauches won ground. He offered Jouvenel the Ministry of Education. No doubt he wished to groom Jouvenel for the foreign office—he himself had begun as Minister of Education thirty years earlier, and as such he had presented a prize in the *Concours général* to the young humanist from Stanislas. Yet patriotism was the nearest thing to a political conviction that the two men had in common: their official relations had benefited decisively from the distance between Paris and Geneva. And Jouvenel, who saw in Poincaré the epitome of what it takes to succeed in a regime insured against genius, despised him moreover for perpetually pleading the case of France instead of pleading her cause. Faced with Poincaré's offer he had the choice between two ways of furthering his political career without modifying his political position: to refuse, or to be a remarkable Minister of Education for one month.

Jouvenel accepted, and on the morning of March 30, 1924, the new Minister of Public Education, Arts, and Technical Instruction started on a tour of the services under his authority, meeting and speaking with the lowliest of functionaries, inspecting every phase of administrative routine. "The progress of science has given rise to a new form of ignorance,"[3] he had once written, decrying the effects of specialization: did he intend to reform the school curriculum? Journalists watched him attentively. He was evidently preparing to revitalize this "second-zone ministry," though his disdain for it—"as formerly M. de Chateaubriand's"—had been taken for granted.[4] Then after a few days he "literally vanished.... He seemed to govern by proxy, to have turned over the conduct of all business to his cabinet."[5] Did he wish by so doing to avoid compromising himself with the government in case it did not survive the elections, observers wondered, or was he "disgusted with a ministry that, more than any other, relies on a past of laws, decrees, imperative circulars, a whole framework of frequently incongruous papers, documents?"[6] He gave proof of his adaptability with respect to minor functions as well as his lack of official preoccupation by organizing lavish garden parties for his cabinet at the estate of the comtesse de Sainte-Aldegonde. He also wrote a brief preface to an elementary-school manual, congratulated Anatole France on his eightieth birthday, and, one week before the elections, suddenly issued a decree creating a Council of Letters composed of 21 members drawn from various academies to advise the Minister.

The Council never met. The electoral victory of the Cartel des Gauches forced Poincaré to resign on May 1, 1924. Herriot overlooked the coming man when he chose his ministers, and Paul-Boncour, who was a Socialist just then, became chief delegate to Geneva in place of the friend who first attracted him there. "My friendship made our keeping him in the delegation—though he had been with earlier delegations, representing governments and a policy that were no longer ours—the condition for my presence,"[7] wrote Paul-Boncour. In fact, Jouvenel had represented one government only, and what the left held against him was not the policy he had pursued but his alleged subservience to Poincaré. He may well have had his own case in mind when he wrote of the great Mirabeau as a hired polemicist: "That he was... an instrument is true. That he wrote against his belief is not true."[8] After his demotion the French delegation carried on the very policy he had launched. In September, 1924, the new Labor government in Great Britain having rejected the Mutual-Assistance Treaty, France supported and the League adopted a substitute proposal, which became the Geneva Protocol. Although it too provided for regional defense pacts, it made their operation contingent on prior efforts at collective action; further, it deferred discussion of disarmament for one year—that is, until the question of security should have been settled. Rejected by the Conservative government in Great Britain, the Protocol was replaced at Locarno by a mutual-defense treaty guaranteeing the western frontiers of Germany with mere token mention of the League and disarmament.

Jouvenel assisted in drafting the text of the Geneva Protocol, and he defended it vigorously in Paris and in Geneva. He also chaired a League committee that drew up a program for the Institute of Intellectual Cooperation, and Paul Valéry then had the opportunity of admiring "his culture ...his manners...his insight...his immediate grasp of opportunities."[9] Informally he acted as press agent for his delegation; wrote one of its members:

We shall never have finished boasting of the prodigalities of mind, the patience, the precision, the good nature, and the tact this master journalist used day by day in answering all the questions, satisfying all the requirements, calming all the impatience, and dispersing all the prejudices of that cohort of other journalists, by whom he was all the better understood for speaking their own language and sympathizing with their state of mind. He was able to win them over to the French viewpoint, and that, I assure you, was no slight victory.[10]

The victory may even have been great; the battle, however, left him with strength in reserve.

Jouvenel paid the penalty for refusing to play the game of left-or-right: he was ostracized by the left without becoming any the more attractive to the right. He had broken the rules of politicalization simply by ignoring them, not by following rules of his own. Thereafter he made a practice of catching the first train to Corrèze whenever a cabinet crisis arose, as a defence both against being accepted or being rejected. Manifestly he was unfit for an ordinary political career; he would have to content himself with an extraordinary one.

On November 6, 1925, the Foreign Minister, Aristide Briand, offered him the post of High Commissioner in Syria. The French had occupied Syria at the close of the First World War, just as the British were taking over the rest of the Turkish Empire in the Levant. The Turks were still not resigned to their loss, and the British and the French were still not content with their respective gains. And if the borders of Syria were contested, so too were the boundaries of the states within, for they cut through a medley of antagonistic tribes and sects. The League of Nations recognized Lebanon as distinct from Syria proper, and France held a mandate for providing each of the two territories with a constitution by September, 1926. The first High Commissioner, General Weygand, failed to fulfil the mandate, though he governed peaceably until April, 1925. His successor, General Sarrail, had little time to fail: hardly had he taken office when he provoked a rebellion in Jabal al Druz by repudiating its special administrative status and making hostages of Druse notables whom he convoked "on the pretext of hearing their complaints."[11] Moslem nationalists opportunely sympathized with the clannish Druse mountaineers and carried the war to the heart of the Syrian state. The truculent general was recalled in October, 1925, after he had submitted Damascus to forty-eight hours of bombardment. Briand knew Jouvenel to be a peacemaker with a talent for improvising durable solutions; besides, he knew of no other able man who might be willing.[12] Jouvenel was willing; however, he did not wish to bind himself to remain in Syria should his proposals fail to satisfy all the parties concerned. He refused to become permanent head of the Syrian government; instead he agreed to act as High Commissioner while conducting an "exploratory mission." When his appointment was announced the press was unanimous in its approval. "The situation is bad, I know," he told the *Figaro*, "but if things were calm I wouldn't have taken the job." Commented the *Figaro*: "He is the man to see it through."[13]

Evil omens attended Jouvenel's departure. First he waited in Paris for Sarrail to return; Sarrail, returning in November 16, brushed past him at the railway station, then the next day at an official meeting gave him little information. Next an envoy from the Syrian insurgents saw Jouvenel to tell him that the condition for peace in Syria was the end of the French mandate in Syria. Afterwards Jouvenel visited the British Foreign Secretary, Sir Austen Chamberlain, for three days to inaugurate a policy of good neighborliness in the Near East—and lost credit at home for conniving with perfidious Albion. He left Paris for Marseille and Syria on November 24; early that morning the government that had appointed him fell, and a small party of friends and officials saw him off in a heavy rain. He sailed by way of Alexandria, and there a high functionary from Beirut met him with the words: *"Monsieur le Haut-Commissaire, there is nothing more to be done for France in Syria."*[14] For a day in Cairo he endeavored vainly to reach an understanding with the Lutfallah family, which was financing the Syrian rebels, and with the Syro-Palestinian Congress, which was pleading the rebel cause abroad.[15]

The record of his first efforts to appease Syria is a memorial to his good intentions. The Lebanese had taken no part in the uprising, and at once he proclaimed their Representative Council a constituent assembly as an example to the Syrian insurgents. Lebanon wanted its rights, however, not a reward for good behavior, just as the insurgents wanted a guarantee for the future and not a prospect of things to come. Convoking the rebel chiefs, Jouvenel promised clemency to those who would surrender and fair treatment for all Syria; they would lay down their arms only for a price, though, and he would concede nothing to men in arms.[16] He gave the order for all Syrians not under martial law[17] to elect local councils, which were to meet together as a constituent assembly after each had decided what powers it wished to retain. The order disfranchised the rebels in effect by failing to induce them to disarm; hence the Nationalists[18] refused to vote before peace was restored, denouncing the plan of election in any case as a maneuver to divide and rule.[19] Jouvenel relaxed press censorship and released the political leaders held in custody. Then he proposed an interim government under Sheik Taj al Din. Though the sheik had the confidence of all, even of the Druses, candidate ministers made it a point of honor to ask too much.[20] Meanwhile, the Nationalists led a rough campaign to boycott the polls, and rebel recruitment rose as Jouvenel attempted to restrain them. No votes were cast in central Syria, and elsewhere candidates who opposed Syrian nationalism vanished at the last minute. The few deputies who emerged on January 26, 1926, "were consequently not heard from again."[21]

Jouvenel realized that he could do nothing with the rebels or without them so long as their defeat was not certain. He ordered an all-out offensive against their stronghold, Suwayda; then he appointed a Frenchman as provisional Administrator of Syria[22] after restoring censorship and extending martial law to half the country.[23] Bitterly he told the Syrian Representative Council at Damascus on February 5, 1926, that France was prepared to bring

to the peoples of Syria and Lebanon every liberty except one, the liberty of oppressing one another....I will concede anything when confronted with arguments of reason; I will concede nothing when confronted with arguments of force.[24]

He supported the military operations inside Syria with adroit diplomacy outside. First he concluded a frontier-guarantee and nonaggression pact with Turkey, thereby relieving a large detachment of troops from border patrol in the north.[25] With the Armenian Patriarch of Antioch he agreed to close the French army to Armenian refugees, thousands of whom were damaging the cause of France by enlisting for purposes of plunder. Then in Jerusalem he opportunely reminded the British High Commissioner of a promise made by Chamberlain to deny the Druses commerce with their neighbors abroad.[26] Suwayda fell on April 2, and victory was assured, though peace was no nearer. The demands of the Nationalists fell in consequence: a treaty defining the mandatory relationship with France became the most fashionable behest in all Syria. Jouvenel himself had always found it the fairest: "I wish to establish, not temporary peace, but permanent peace on the basis of a treaty [with] the diverse regions of Syria and Lebanon," he had declared.[27] Ahmad Nami Bey, having made it a point on his program, succeeded in forming a government with representatives of each of the Syrian parties, and preliminary negotiations for a treaty began. At the same time Jouvenel undertook on his own initiative a program of public works designed to beautify and modernize the country. He also organized fabulous banquets at the residence-general and prevailed on some of the bitterest foes of France to attend.

The attempt to deal with Syria on a national level had given inordinate importance to the Nationalists, whose contempt for minorities was, as Jouvenel saw it, the real political problem in the mandated territory. At the risk of discrediting regionalism by favoring it, he planned to create constitutional governments in six autonomous provinces—the six "lands of Syria"—and defer discussion of an organic law for Syria as a whole. Only in Lebanon, however, did he possess the authority to proceed. On May 15 he instructed the French governor of Lebanon to resign, and he convoked a plenary session of the Lebanese Constituent Assembly. So far, in five months of toil, the Assembly had produced only a disparate mass of recommendations; in three days Jouvenel produced a constitution that it adopted with few changes. On May 24 the Republic of Lebanon was proclaimed. Though the Nationalists "contrived to find more to criticize than to praise" in the constitution of Lebanon,[28] its very promulgation was a decisive argument against them. It created two elective chambers, which in fact did prove too cumbersone and costly. "Had Jouvenel prolonged his mission in Syria," commented one observer, "it would have taken him only a few hours to amend the statute he had so skillfully devised in a few days."[29] By June of 1926, though, Jouvenel's "exploratory mission" was over, and he could not act on his findings without further instructions. He took to Paris his project for political decentralization and his draft of a treaty, having first summoned the Syro-Palestinian Congress to send its representatives along.

The Premier, Aristide Briand, took up the negotiations for a treaty with exceeding caution: at the moment he was as reluctant to indispose the right wing of the Chamber by making concessions to Syrians as he was to indispose the Permanent Mandates Commission of the League by seeming intransigent. This commission, meeting in Rome four months earlier to discuss Syria, had severely censured General Sarrail for his conduct of affairs. Now it had reconvened, and on June 17 Jouvenel appeared before it to plead his cause. He announced confidently that a treaty with the mandated territory was forthcoming and that the few recalcitrant Druses were prepared to attach to it the value of an armistice. He proclaimed his hope of establishing constitutional law thereafter in accordance with the wishes of each of the peoples of Syria. The Commission agreed to recommend to the League Assembly an extension of the mandate; at the same time it addressed a mute rebuke to Jouvenel by stressing the right of mandated peoples to petition the League directly.[30] From Rome Jouvenel went to England, where public opinion was incensed by reports that he had restored the prestige of France highhandedly; Lord Robert Cecil arranged a series of ingratiating public denials. Back in Paris he found the outlook for a treaty dimmed: the rebels would not accept a list of the objectives of France in Syria without a timetable for reaching them. He proposed a schedule of steps to be taken in fulfilling the mandate and a provisional deadline, the termination of the mandate remaining, however, subject to its fulfilment; Briand consented, and in the course of July, 1926, even while the political and financial crises were raging in France, the protocol of a thirty-year treaty took shape along these lines.[31] Then Poincaré returned to power and let it be known that France, being responsible only to the League, had not to subscribe commitments to Syria, and that further he would undertake no political reform until all Syria was prepared to assist him. As the Syrian envoys discreetly reembarked, Jouvenel allowed his mission to expire.

Technically, Poincaré was right: he did not have to make Syria a partner in the mandate. The rebel armies would not submit otherwise, but Jouvenel himself had once merely offered them justice at his own discretion. Then they had asked France to give up the mandate, though, whereas now they were asking France to apply it rapidly; besides, they were on their last legs, and Jouvenel held magnanimity above technicalities. The original rebels, the Druses, were separatists at heart, momentarily suffering from a dramatic distrust for Frenchmen. As much as they wanted France to provide assurances that the mandate would be carried out, the Nationalist party wanted France to refuse. Jouvenel had hoped to end their unnatural fealty to that party by concluding an armistice and granting them autonomy, in both cases without prejudice to the future constitution of Syria. His plan for compounding a nation piece-by-piece instead of step-by-step had the tactical advantage of coaxing the Nationalists into the position of opponents of democracy. Having less patience and more subtlety than Poincaré, he preferred outwitting his adversaries to wearing them down. Poincaré faced the same problems with the benefit of Jouvenel's exhaustive inquiry, and before long Poincaré's envoy did not have to persuade *and* disarm the population at the same time; yet in two years Poincaré, too, failed to provide Syria with a constitution.

Though Jouvenel's mission was rightly regarded in France as an immense personal success, he left his post with a sense of unfulfilment. He had sought to restore confidence rather than discipline in Syria, and to back up his arguments with gracious hospitality in preference to martial law. He had failed, and in failing he had gained the conviction that France could not justify or long maintain her presence in alien territories as a colonial power; that the French Empire, supported by French bayonets, was threatened and not vindicated by the evolution of its subject peoples; that a formula had to be found for replacing a worldwide network of reformatories by a community of free and equal men and nations.

CHAPTER 14

Conciliation: A Personality Becomes a Policy

"AS IN ROME the unrecognized great men of the Republic went to pacify some province or other to prove their worth and, with a firmer stride, returned to trample down the Forum," began a contemporary account of Jouvenel's mission to Syria.[1] In fact Jouvenel in October, 1926, quietly resumed his seat at the Palais du Luxembourg, and afterwards he put his spare time and savings into founding a review. His work with the newspaper *Le Matin*, irregular since his election to the Senate, had ceased altogether during his stay in Syria.[2] At the same time he had withdrawn from a publishing venture begun with Anatole de Monzie soon after the war: the two men had selected and edited more than twenty volumes on current political and diplomatic problems in a series called "Les Petits Guides Politiques." Now he created the *Revue des Vivants*, which appeared monthly beginning in February, 1927. He meant the title to serve as a reminder to the men of his generation that they were survivors of the First World War. He meant the review to serve the cause of European unity, beginning with the reconciliation of France and Germany. Its appeal lay in the variety rather than the uniformity of the views it registered. The eclectic but discriminating editor drew on his wide range of acquaintances in the fields of politics and literature to enlist among its first contributors Joseph Barthélemy, Edward Beneš, Tristan Bernard, Jules Cambon, Austen Chamberlain, Paul Claudel, Marshal Foch, Jean Giraudoux, Léon Jouhaux, Harold J. Laski, Marshal Lyautey, Maurice Maeterlinck, André Maginot, André Maurois, Henry de Montherlant, Anatole de Monzie, Anna de Noailles, Joseph Paul-Boncour, Jérome and Jean Tharaud, Paul Valéry, and General Weygand. A copy of the *Revue des Vivants* numbered some one hundred fifty to two hundred pages, and it was priced inexpensively at five francs.[3] Though its cause made small headway, it was from the start among the most widely read periodicals in Europe. Jouvenel wrote for it himself regularly, though not exclusively. He continued to contribute to other reviews, in particular the *Revue de Paris* and *Revue politique et littéraire*. He also wrote a weekly article on international affairs for the *Telegraaf* of Amsterdam, and even as he founded the *Revue des Vivants* he began work on a biography of Mirabeau, which he completed in 1929.

Like his review, his life itself was devoted to such ideals as tolerance and peace, in contradistinction to all doctrines and all systems of thought. Just as his review lacked unity of argument, so his life lacked unity of action. The one was a collection of articles, the other a collection of incidents. What made the units of both seem to fit together was his personality—and in the end his personality was to give to his political action, diversified as it was, an almost doctrinaire consistency.

Before even having a personality Henry de Jouvenel had a name— necessarily, but also much more than necessarily. Most men are hard put to it to make a name for themselves; Jouvenel, on the contrary, was hard put to it to avoid letting his name get the best of him. It had always been a prominent part of his environment: already as a child he had received from his father, besides fencing lessons, instruction in genealogies. It had been his last surviving link with his father; after his father's death he respected it all the more. He had earned it by 1907, when a freelance writer complained to his diary: "I go to the offices of the newspaper *Le Matin* to turn in an article. What an outfit! I ask for: 'M. Jouvenel.' The office-boys correct me: 'M. *de* Jouvenel.'"[4] His first wife adjusted to it better than he did, for she could never do without it. Toward the end of the war "Madame Boas de Jouvenel" received a writ summoning her to assume a more correct name because of the "persistent confusion brought on by her imposture" and the inconvenience to the only lawful Madame de Jouvenel "to have to continue a witty telephone conversation begun the day before by Madame Boas with the curate of Saint-Eustache, or to turn her home into a perpetual banqueting place for the sake of Madame Boas' guests, who come streaming in every day at mealtime and whom she is often regretfully unable to satisfy because of the reduction of her staff in consequence of the war."[5]

The only lawful Madame de Jouvenel resented the imposture less as her own name, Colette, became famous. Since the war she had developed into that discomforting thing in any household, a great artist. Even so her marriage to Jouvenel remained "seemingly very solid"[6] until he went to Geneva, or—perhaps more pertinently—until her novel *Chéri*, which was published in 1920 and adapted to the stage two years later, gave her private life a notoriety he resented. She reports that he scolded her "judiciously" for refusing to "write a book that isn't about love, adultery, semi-incestuous relations, break-ups: is there nothing else in life?" he would ask; and then, without waiting for a reply, he would hustle off—"for he was handsome and charming, to amorous rendez-vous," leaving her to seek consolation in writing novels "dedicated to love, to love's regret..., entirely blinded by love."[7] From him she learned, with sorrow, the secret of Don Juan, which is his indifference to women. Henry never gave his version of the marriage, and hers is almost too typical of both of them to be true: his frivolity, her self-pity. Still, the remark she ascribed to him *is* judicious, for she did remain uniquely unconcerned with the political and moral problems of her generation, just as she contrived to remove any trace of contemporaneity from her art.[8] The source of their incompatibility was the special genius of each: of Henry de Jouvenel, who was "extraordinarily sensitive to everything that derives from the intelligence,"[9] and of Colette, who was extraordi-narily sensitive to everything else. The cult of ideas never tempted her, while to him passion was at most a private weakness. Their love, and not their marriage, thrived on the contrast. Fidelity in the usual sense was not at issue: Colette, herself a specialist in variety, may have been se-cretly as pleased with him whenever he left her as she was pleased with herself whenever he came back. But vanity and disappointment acted on her with the force of jealousy when she heard, in 1925, that his attachment to a woman whose most signal quality was being *Princess* Bibesco had led him to consider divorce.[10] She filed suit herself, and three years later she spoke of him as "one of my husbands, the second,"[11] then concluded: "Now legally, literarily, and familiarly, I have only one name left, my own."[12]

As Minister of Education in 1924 Jouvenel, even though he was on the left, had—as *De* Monzie, for instance, had not—refrained from abusing his pedigree, signing papers *Jouvenel*—"simply (and correctly)," commented the *Mercure de France*.[13] Matters of styling and breeding still set him off from the political and literary associates of his choice—said one of them: "He remained alien to the very men among whom he fought."[14] If, though, he had retained the manners of his parents' social set, he had discarded its mannerisms, and he had not frequented it in twenty years. Then, after his return from Syria in 1926, as his income from *Le Matin* ceased and his expenses with the *Revue des Vivants* began, he took up residence with his mother, who had some fortune of her own. In so doing he became once again *"Monsieur le Baron"*—first to the servants, then to her friends, then to his own. For a while his new-found dignity was "something of an embarrassment to him."[15] Gradually, however, the embarrassment wore off, and as it did his "class traits" revived.[16] So did his gentlemanly tastes, especially his liking for period furniture and fine tapestries. His mother had a modern house on rue Chardon–Lagache, in the fashionable section of Auteuil; he induced her to purchase in its stead a stately old mansion on rue de Condé, near the Palais du Luxembourg. His associates all visited him there; none felt at home.

Madame Raoul de Jouvenel died in 1929; she was buried in Varetz, beside the family castle. Her legacy did not afford her son the prospect of maintaining the castle and its 240-acre domain much longer. Luxury, however, had again become a way of life with him, and on August 4, 1930, he married the widow of the fabulously wealthy grain merchant Charles Louis-Dreyfus.

Jouvenel's third wife, *née* Germaine Hément, was the daughter of an editorialist for *Le Temps*; she was Jewish, like his first wife, and nearly his own age, like all the women he ever loved. No doubt her fortune enhanced her other charms, and because his marriage to her was so expedient it passed for being little else. A few years after his death Colette depicted Senator Herbert d'Espivant in *Julie de Carneilhan* as less concerned with war and peace than with his health,[17] with his vanity, and with swindling the beautiful heiress who was content to hold him by her money. Yet Paul Reynaud described the marriage without innuendo as "the happiest part of his life,"[18] and André Maurois, who found the bride "beautiful, very beautiful," experienced, watching him with her "in their adorable home in Varetz, an impression of serenity, of perfect understanding, of happiness keen and delicious to the point of anguish."[19] Besides securing his estate in Varetz this marriage brought Jouvenel a villa on the Riviera and, in Paris, Talleyrand's former mansion on rue Férou—an appropriate setting for the "luxurious agapes" described by his neighbor there, who wrote: "Through the window I perceived, in the garden, tables set with flowers and, all around them, the gentlemen of French politics chatting in the artificial cool."[20]

While Jouvenel delighted in luxury more for the sake of sharing it than for its own sake—indeed, he was almost insanely hospitable—he made no more show of it than he did of any of his other assets.[21] In all else, too, he was a perfect *grand seigneur*: discriminating but not exclusive;[22] always active, never busy;[23] somewhat frivolous about serious things and earnest about other things,[24] yet steadfast in everything.[25] With his winsome manner went ingratiating eccentricities, such as smoking rare aromatic cigars and sporting a monocle—"which he took refuge behind whenever someone tried to thank him for something."[26] He impressed all comers, however differently. Some, in fact, he overwhelmed: "This great, strong, magnificent lord," wrote one, "with avid and ferocious eyes—jungle eyes,—marvelously intelligent, marvelously amoral, is a man of the Renaissance, a technician of *virtù*."[27] And, whatever they thought of him, none could help loving him; even for Colette, who had much experience both in love and in forgiving Jouvenel, his one unpardonable fault was his being "what she loved most in the world."[28]

Marked as was his individuality, he was to have posthumous difficulty keeping distinct from his brother, Robert de Jouvenel. There is some sentimental justice in the confusion, for the two were inseparable companions in adult life (when five years of age are no longer a barrier between brothers). Robert, editor-in-chief of the socialistic daily *L'Oeuvre*, was the greater journalist—Albert Thibaudet called him the greatest of his time.[29] He was also the greater author. Whereas Henry produced many wonderful pages and afterwards published them in book form, Robert wrote books: *Le Journalisme en vingt leçons*, and his masterpiece, *La République des camarades*, which appeared when he was thirty years old. Robert's satire was so refined as to be often imperceptible, and he has been taxed with an odd fondness for the foibles he described in the politicians of the Republic. He shared his brother's fascination and distaste for politics; he was a purer rebel by conviction, though, and he remained a journalist all his life. Henry rejoiced in all their differences, of course. Once only was he angry with Robert: after the 1924 elections, when Robert bade Poincaré, who did not rush to resign: "Get out, and fast." Henry would have preferred courtesy.[30] Otherwise he described his brother simply as "the most delightful, the most smiling of human beings."[31] Robert for his part discovered in Henry "curiosity for every question that arises…,the art of listening, the faculty of summing up, political imagination, personal ascendancy over his contemporaries, and eloquence such as influences assemblies of men."[32] Robert died on July 3, 1924, following a long and painful heart ailment, which he had borne serenely, even knowing all the while how it would end. Henry felt the loss deeply the rest of his life.

The three years after Jouvenel's return from Syria Poincaré was in power. Because Poincaré stood for appeasement and stability within France, Jouvenel would not attack him; he would not defend him either, though, and so his work in parliament those years was slight.

One step toward an understanding in Europe he did favor in common with Poincaré: the conclusion of a frontier guarantee between Germany and her eastern neighbors as a complement to the Locarno Pact of December, 1925. The agreement was coincidental: Poincaré considered the sanctification of boundaries to be the condition for peace in Europe, whereas Jouvenel already was looking forward to a European federation in which territorial disputes would be parochial and obsolescent. Both, though, were equally disturbed by the signs of a tacit agreement among the three foreign ministers Briand, Stresemann, and Austen Chamberlain to confine the "spirit of Locarno" to the banks of the Rhine and to settle the affairs of Europe privately, outside the League of Nations. Jouvenel, though officially still a member of the French delegation, did not give much time to the League after his return from Syria; then on August 9, 1927, he publicly announced his refusal to attend its Assembly meeting the following September. The French government, he alleged, was neglecting the Covenant and the rights of small nations; the Locarno Pact had not only created a new Concert of Europe but also in effect called the *status quo* in the East into question by confirming it only in the West.

Jouvenel's resignation—which was concurrent with Lord Robert Cecil's—startled public opinion, delighted Poincaré, and confounded the diplomats of the Palais des Nations. Briand denied Jouvenel's charges, of course. Stresemann rushed to Geneva ahead of schedule and sought further reassurance. His first contacts convinced him "that the bond between the men of Locarno still exists...despite Poincaré and de Jouvenel"; in the general elections of 1928, he reflected, "the French people will decide whether they mean to follow Poincaré and de Jouvenel or (will take their stand behind) the French politicians who are in favor of an understanding."[33] Then he saw Briand alone, and Briand, he wrote, "adopted the attitude that he would in no circumstances agree to an extension of the Locarno treaties to Eastern Europe, after I had explained to him that he would otherwise be playing into the hands of Monsieur de Jouvenel."[34] Meanwhile, Briand gave the League Assembly his assurance that the Great Powers had no other object in meeting confidentially than to prepare themselves for performing their duties as members of the League, and informally he impressed observers with his deep concern over Jouvenel's gesture in resigning.[35]

Jouvenel's behavior "was somewhat painful to Briand," confirmed Paul-Boncour, who observed wisely that Jouvenel "lacked patience, and was irritated by the slowness of an organism necessarily slow in moving."[36]

Indeed, Jouvenel's objections to private consultations among the Great Powers on European affairs, or even to a revival of the Concert of Europe, were not fundamental; in later years he brilliantly overlooked them.[37] Otherwise his criticism of the Locarno Pact was pertinent and timely; it belonged, though, rather on an editorial page than in a letter of resignation from the League. But Jouvenel lacked patience, and after quelling a rebellion and drafting constitutions in Syria for one year he was all the less partial to languorous discussions and timid resolutions. The international body was already a victim of the form of impotence known as standard procedures; its vitality had foundered on a mass of bureaucratic accessories, and its originality had been perverted into a set of formal idiosyncrasies; the variety of languages had become the language barrier, which in turn had yielded an esoteric jargon fit especially for obscuring issues; and Jouvenel felt more inclined to canvass opinions in Europe for his review or to pursue his own thoughts than to deliberate in Geneva, there editing his own opinions and pursuing the thoughts of others.

He soon changed his mind. In Paris in October, 1927, a congress of the Radical party adopted a "party declaration" so similar in parts to the old "program of the generation"[38] that Jouvenel immediately proposed to quit the Senate and to run for the Chamber as a Radical in the next elections. However, the Radicals in Corrèze still had no record of dues paid by him; they knew him to have voted with their party in the Senate only when he had agreed with it; and, though they had no clear idea what "syndicalism" meant, they had been hearing about it long enough to suspect it of being reactionary. Jouvenel was amused, and slightly alarmed. He had used his proposals for "syndicalizing the Republic" as a sort of trust fund, putting a certain amount of thought into them year by year while enjoying his political independence, confident that sooner or later their adoption would become imperative and that he would reap the reward for his sagacity. But there was no copyright on ideas in the Republic, and imperative reforms had no priority over any other reforms; his political independence was turning into political isolation, and he realized that the penalty for defying the common rules for success in public affairs, unless he adhered strictly to some rules of his own, was *only* failure. Impulsive, he had left the League even though he was increasingly convinced of its importance for peace and of the growing danger to peace; before the year was out, then, he returned to Geneva— at the same time as Lord Robert Cecil, and, commented Paul-Boncour,

fortunately for our delegation, to which he brought his ease, his heartiness, and his talent, and to the great satisfaction of the reporters, who adored him, for, being one of them himself, he knew how to assuage their ill-humor when their stay, which only outsiders could imagine was jolly, dragged on too long without sensational news.[39]

He did not withal relinquish syndicalism. On the contrary: in 1928, after completing his study of Mirabeau, he gathered together and revised his best writings on syndicalism for publication in a series entitled "Leurs Raisons," and on October 20, 1929, he was reelected to the Senate as an "independent radical syndicalist." Nor did he break what ties he still had with the parties of the left: campaigning for reelection, he wrote an open letter to Daladier on the need for the whole left, which had been in a minority in parliament since the spring of 1928, to define a common program with constitutional reform in the place of honor. In November, 1929, however, as André Tardieu took power with a majority on the right and a program on the left, the secular animosity between right and left degenerated into a pitched battle in parliament, and Jouvenel found himself in opposition, not to the policies of the Premier, but to the battle itself. At last—on December 4, 1930,—taking his stand high above the battle, he attacked the Premier for provoking the combatants in spite of himself:

...we all feel the need for putting the pieces of the Republic back together again. You too feel it, yet even as you speak of putting them back together again you contribute day after day—far less by the effort of your will than by the impulse of your character—to setting them a little farther asunder.... It is dangerous, it seems to us, to maintain a ministry in office if by its temperament it makes conciliation more and more difficult—if, the prisoners of false positions, we run the risk of jostling one another harder and harder when we should be uniting. Let us guard against dividing the country into two blocs and so someday causing an upset more serious than the upset of a ministry, and this for the benefit of all the extremes and to the detriment of the middle parties—which, to be sure, commit errors, and which must often be saved from themselves, but which in falling would destroy the equilibrium of the nation.[40]

Thereupon the Senate, by a margin of a few votes, overthrew the government. Jouvenel's speech had no doubt been decisive; President Doumergue did not, though, the next day call him back from Corrèze to form a new government. In any case parliament did not want a government in the center: after forcing a new one over to the left, it settled for another one on the right, and Jouvenel turned his attention elsewhere.

Member of the French delegation to the League, he treated the peace of the world as the business of the world, and not something to be taken in and out of Geneva tucked away in a diplomatic portfolio. He made peace the main topic on the agenda of the veterans' groups that he chaired, the Union of Great Associations and the Federal Union of Veterans. He held a contest in 1930 in the *Revue des Vivants* for the best plan for European federation.[41] He formed the French Action Committee for the League of Nations out of the Federal Union of Veterans—which he called "the holy invocation of wounds and hopes"[42]—and two other movements that he led, the French Association for the League of Nations and the University Group for the League of Nations. He was continually invited to lecture and debate, and "crowds of veterans listened to him with delight."[43] He had to refuse most invitations, but early in 1931 he went on a lecture tour from Metz to Bordeaux and thence to Chambéry, taking in as many small communes on the way as his itinerary allowed. At the same time, the defeat of Aristide Briand as candidate for the presidency of the Republic came as a warning that the policy of good neighborliness with Germany was losing ground in the French parliament. Jouvenel confidently proposed holding a "friendship plebiscite" simultaneously in France and Germany. The leaders of the national committees for the League of Nations in Germany and England suggested an international peace congress instead, and Jouvenel agreed to organize it and to serve as secretary-general.

While Jouvenel, assisted by Lord Robert Cecil, was busy inducing illustrious statesmen to take part in the Peace Congress, newspapers the world over discussed its prospects. In Paris, the *Figaro* conducted a virulent campaign against it while the press of the left supported it warmly; only *L'Humanité* ignored it.[44] It was held in Paris in November, 1931. For two weeks, in many orderly and impressive meetings, speakers debated a "peace protocol" drafted by Louise Weiss, a fervent pacifist and a generous patroness of the event. The final evening of November 27 was meanwhile reserved for a crowning ceremony to be attended by the principal delegates and broadcast by short wave to all radio networks. Though by then few practical conclusions had been reached, the general public had responded with enthusiasm to the themes of disarmament and internationalism—in fact on November 26 the former Premier Paul Painlevé was shouted down at a meeting at the Sorbonne when he spoke against pacifism, and Jouvenel was obliged to harangue the assembly of young scholars on freedom of speech.

Exactly what happened at the Trocadéro Palace in Paris on the evening of November 27, 1931, is impossible to determine, though some of the occurrences were striking indeed. A new league founded by Colonel de la Rocque, the Croix de Feu, acting in concert with the Action Française, had evidently succeeded in buying up a large share of the tickets in advance, with the result that more than an hour before starting time the front seats of the meeting hall were occupied by several hundred partisans of international misunderstanding. Edouard Herriot opened the proceedings, greeted by whistling and shouting. Messages of sympathy were read amid a growing commotion. Louise Weiss spoke in vain of pacifism. Herr Joos, the delegate of the Centrist Party of Germany, provoked a violent uproar by merely appearing. By then Jouvenel was horrified: to his mind, even intolerance for an opinion had a kind of dignity compared with intolerance for a German—"*Nous avons la victoire odieuse*," he would say.[45] An Italian delegate was standing speechless before the general clamor when a contingent of *gardes mobiles* arrived to restore order. As Lord Robert Cecil addressed the assembly in English, the turbulent elements began to lose interest; they were completely silent as the voice of Senator Borah was broadcast from the United States. But poor Painlevé was suddenly hailed as a hero, and the representative of an international association of disabled veterans, Henri Pichot, was assailed as a coward. Pandemonium was revived by the pacifistic speeches of Alanson Bigelow Houghton of the United States and Ambassador Madariaga of Spain. As again the police intervened to enforce order, the rioters ominously closed ranks facing the rostrum. Colonel de la Rocque demanded the microphone; Pierre Cot hurriedly conferred with him on behalf of Herriot; Herriot consulted with Jouvenel, who whispered to Pierre Cot, who went back to La Rocque—and somehow La Rocque expected to be recognized as the next speaker. Herriot, although he had lost control of the meeting, had conducted the broadcast in a masterly manner: the howls had sounded like cheers on the radio. But when at 11:30 p.m., with only half the speakers heard from, Jouvenel stepped up to the microphone to take the place of Herriot, the signal was given for a mass assault on the rostrum. The police were overpowered, ministers and ambassadors scampered toward the nearest exit, the rostrum was turned upside down, La Rocque declaimed a "memorandum on the reasons for not disarming," and Jouvenel, left clutching the microphone—his voice "magnificent as ever," affirmed one witness,[46]—uttered the unutterable to the four corners of the world.

The fate of the Peace Congress of November, 1931, is symbolic of what Bertrand de Jouvenel has termed "the disintegration of liberal Europe." The attitude of a few organized rowdies was mistaken abroad for French public opinion, and indignant protests were raised; the French knew better, of course, yet as it turned out the rowdies had been acting with secret orders and secret funds from the chief of the government.[47] Collective security degenerated into a chorus of admonitions after Japan invaded Manchuria in September, 1931. Internationalism, liberalism, parliamentary democracy, were discredited as the great depression spread. Nationalist and authoritarian movements thrived on the misery and discontent, frightening those whom they failed to convince, bewildering those whom they failed to frighten. Most Frenchmen remained republicans, no doubt, but most Frenchman were intimidated, hence the Republic was impaired already: as in a barroom brawl, the number of men defending an opinion mattered less than the violence with which it was defended. Even republicans, though, considered the constitutional laws of 1875 defective and condemned the old parliamentary practices; politicians who had functioned too successfully in the past were mistrusted, while a reputation for dissidence became a political asset. Some moderates spoke of *"l'union nationale"* or *"la trêve des partis,"* longing for someone to command them moderately, reluctantly if possible, until the emergency was past. However, the trend of the times was more nearly the one followed by Henry de Jouvenel's sons, who both began as syndicalists: Renaud was definitively converted to Communism, while Bertrand moved a few years on the fringes of the extreme right.[48]

During this period of turmoil, Henry de Jouvenel's thought and action achieved their greatest consistency and effectiveness. Already the Dreyfus affair had taught him that

it is easy for the caste spirit to be mistaken for the public spirit. A few newspaper articles, a few street demonstrations: that is called Paris opinion, and ministers bow down to it—not to the people, as they believe, but only to a caste.[49]

In opposition to the "caste spirit" in politics and diplomacy, he perfected a method for reconciling antagonists on the basis of some principle of agreement underlying their apparently divergent convictions or interests. His method— once described as *"écarter ce qui divise pour rassembler ce qui rapproche"*[50]—is summed up in the word "conciliation."

Conciliation had always been a habit with Jouvenel, one of his charms. It had also shown in his every policy from his earliest thought on syndicalism and the Republic to his recent mission to Syria. At the Conférences Molé-Tocqueville in 1907 he had spoken as a conciliator, succeeding for a moment of enthusiasm in converting latent disaffection for political parties into an instrument of unanimity. The dynamics of conciliation are implicit in *Huit Cents Ans de révolution française*, and in *La Paix française* he defined progress itself as "a perpetual compromise between the ideal and the possible."[51] His appetence and talent for conciliation showed even in his use of paradoxes and puns, for the paradox is a triumphant scoff at contradictoriness, the pun at incongruity. But he had practiced conciliation most effectively in committee work—when he created a federation of forty thousand "intellectual workers" who had nothing more demonstrable in common than the sense of solidarity that he inspired, or when he discovered a least common denominator among the discordant opinions represented in the Temporary Mixed Commission of the League. "Those who have worked with him," affirmed one colleague, "those who have watched him preside over the numerous committees to which he lent his support and seen him often save nearly hopeless situations, know to what an extraordinary degree he possessed the sense of synthesis and the gift of formulation."[52] And Paul Valéry gave a perfect account of the method of conciliation when he wrote that Jouvenel

seemed to have been born to lead imperceptibly, and to bring to as clear an end as they allowed, the verbal operations of a meeting of strongly dissimilar men and ideas. He knew amazingly well how to cut short and close a debate just when—the necessary uncertainty having been produced by the variety of contradictory arguments, the object of the debate having itself been somewhat obscured by the incoherence of the remarks made— everyone is waiting and hoping for deliverance, and surrenders to the man who presides. He then has to give these generally indecisive resolutions and contradictory wishes their most appropriate formulation. In this Jouvenel always succeeded.[53]

His whole mentality was itself a fusion of opposites: Henry Béranger, comparing him with "Lamartine the orator and man of action," wrote: "He was a Frenchman of the same origin, both a democrat and a gentleman, a poet and a logician, a patriot and a humanitarian, attached to old things by his education and to new things by his idealism."[54] In the chaotic 1930's, when all France seemed to be "waiting and hoping for deliverance," Jouvenel adopted the technique of chairmanship as a political principle and a policy in itself, extending to the nation at large his favorite role of "breakdown mechanic," and after an interval of a century and a half he revived the message of the President of the first National Assembly, who had asked deputies not to stand in the same places every day lest factions form.

To practice conciliation successfully Jouvenel had to be a great orator. He was. The text of his speeches does not itself prove the point: the verbatim transcript of a speech, like the black-and-white reproduction of a painting, isolates unnaturally a single element of the whole. Nature had equipped him for impressiveness with "a large chest, robust shoulders, extremely fine features in a full face,... a strong jaw,... a firm forehead, eyes spread out in broad, very deep orbits,"[55] and for persuasion had provided him with a "warm, musical voice,"[56] which was "nonchalant, always tinged a little with humor, tender inflections stealing into it like fugitives."[57] Oratory found him at his best, moreover:

His glance is [normally] direct, cold, and cutting. The wrinkle that seals his lips is transformed handsomely when they open. A kind of skeptical nonchalance in his movements and bearing is in sharp contrast to the impression that he makes on an audience when he speaks: for then everything changes. His flesh and his attitude harden strangely, everything in him turns solid. He has gathered his nerves, hardened his muscles; his voice sounds at a new pitch.[58]

Wrote another observer: "Tall, a sculptural face livened by a stimulating glance, a well-modulated voice..., his whole appearance, standing and speaking, was that of an aristocratic tribune such as were known under the Revolution."[59] His poise and elocution, even their effect of spontaneity, were studiously cultivated. He would practice declaiming the speeches of the Revolutionary orators, all the while conceiving politics "in the fashion of Athenian assemblies, where general agreement was attained by eloquence."[60]

Again, to be a great conciliator Jouvenel had to appeal to men of all opinions. This too he did, and Marcel Déat, a connoisseur of diverse opinions, wrote in explanation:

[Jouvenel was] not new but not worn out, barely tried out, though recognized among the ablest and worthiest, and held in reserve, like a fine fruit for the winter months...; independent, unique, unclassified, a republican to be sure and on the left; democratic, yet with a taste for grandeur and true hierarchy; accepted as well by the extremes as in the center, exciting hope and reassuring at the same time, disappointing no one."[61]

And Paul Reynaud added: "For such men to be summoned, they must be needed"[62]—in France a tribute, elsewhere a truism.

Jouvenel had also, by the same token, to respect every opinion but his own; sometimes, though, he achieved unanimity rather by distracting from a conflict of opinions than by resolving it. He "sought real agreement, not dialectical triumph," wrote Lord Robert Cecil.[63] The distinction may be factitious; if not, when real agreement is impossible, dialectical triumph is a precious substitute. Jouvenel, wrote another observer, detected and expressed the "general will," which Rousseau distinguished from the sum of particular wills.[64] Though Jouvenel invented as much as he detected, the observation is just for any single act of conciliation; conciliation as a policy, however, is more a localized Hegelian dialectic, the "synthesis" of ideas being performed by a human agent—and history being a series of human improvisations instead of a providential contrivance. Thus it was in periods of chaos and strife, which as a patriot and a gentleman he abhorred, that Jouvenel functioned most effectively.

Conciliation was often at once logically problematical and psychologically valid. "There is an idea on which, I believe, all the parties in France agree," he once told the Senate, characteristically, "that the League of Nations will exist only when it has the power to apply sanctions";[65] a speaker for or against the power of sanctions might have said as much, but only a conciliator could say it conclusively. Again, intervening once in a debate on national defense just as it was approximating a riot, Jouvenel spoke in the same vein:

There should be no right or left in the question before us today. We are all equally aware of our responsibilities, feel the same duties, are haunted by the same memories. We have not to take one another to task before the world, but to stand together.[66]

Conciliation by distraction, at its best! His speech set off a sustained thunder of applause on all sides of the Senate: sounding as a warning from on high that national unity is the soul of national defense, it had shamed the men preoccupied with mere ways and means. Several motions were on the floor, together reflecting the disagreement over the means of assuring both security and peace. At a sign from the president, Jouvenel drafted a motion of his own: "The Senate, having confidence in the government to pursue a policy of national security and to safeguard peace, approves the statements of the government and passes to the order of the day."[67] Then he said:

Gentlemen, my motion has one merit: it comes from a man who belongs to no group, and therefore no group need feel humiliated in accepting it. Certain that I am speaking for us all, I beg the chairmen of the various groups to recognize that we are all agreed on these three principles: confidence in the government, guaranteeing national defense, and safeguarding peace.[68]

His motion was accepted by priority, at almost complete unanimity; military expenditures and alliances were left to the discretion of the government—for a few days. Here at last was the Unknown Party in action, a splendid illusion of unity that Jouvenel revived again and again —and that faded as often, and in fading restored to their natural state so many dour and sullen men.

Having the full force of institutions and of traditions to contend with, Jouvenel could not destroy factionalism by words alone. If majorities were short-lived under the Third Republic, unanimity was stillborn. Achieving it for a moment, he was magnificent; achieving it for a moment, though, he defeated his own purpose. When his colleagues had agreed spectacularly on one occasion, they felt all the less inhibition about disagreeing spectacularly on the next; when they had discovered that they had some ideals in common, the discovery made them rather less than more inclined to compromise on their other ideals. Jouvenel, meanwhile, in winning applause from all of them in general was winning it from none of them in particular; while in getting them to overlook their differences from time to time he was getting them to overlook *him* the rest of the time. This, however, he had the greatness not to mind: it was his free choice to have made unanimity ring glorious a little while rather than to have made a majority stand solid a little while longer.

CHAPTER 15

A Mission to Rome

IN DECEMBER, 1932, when Paul-Boncour became Premier and Foreign Minister, the post of French ambassador to Italy was vacant. "As soon as I arrived at the Quai d'Orsay," he wrote, "my first concern was to send to Rome a man who, by his earlier functions, by his inclinations, by his winning personality, seemed to me to be the man to put an end to the misunderstandings and the latent tension between us and our former ally of 1915, Italy."[1] Indeed, the rift between France and Italy was great: France was committed to the defense of the peace treaties and of the nations created by them in Central Europe, whereas Italy, besides demanding a revision of the peace settlement in Dalmatia and in Africa, was supporting Austria and Hungary in their quarrels with the Little Entente. With nationalism rising in Germany, France faced the prospect of seeing a revisionist bloc form around an Italian-German axis. Since 1930 Jouvenel had been conducting a campaign in the *Revue des Vivants* for better relations with Italy. He greatly admired the Italian people, and he saw some justice and much danger in their grievances. Besides, he was not intolerant of corporatism, with which his own syndicalist doctrine had a certain affinity—though he did not subscribe to the Fascist idea of an absolute and irrevocable ruler or to the philosophy of reverence for power.[2] He accepted the ambassadorship for six months, which was as long as a member of parliament might hold such a post. Paul-Boncour gave him "a free hand to work out as broadly as possible any basis for an understanding that would not imperil...our other alliances."[3]

Jouvenel's appointment caused little surprise in France, and little enthusiasm. The press generally praised the Ambassador and wished him well but regarded the task of transforming the hostility of Italy into friendship as too delicate to entrust to a politician with a deadline.[4] Some comments were less cordial: for instance, in his brother's old newspaper, *L'Oeuvre*, Geneviève Tabouis called him "the Italian Ambassador to Paris."[5] He was received with indifference in Italy, and he elicited no significant response from the *Duce* when, on presenting his credentials, he announced that he had come to negotiate. He had barely settled down in the Farnese Palace when Hitler became Chancellor of Germany. The like ideology of the German and Italian rulers, their common zeal in denouncing the Peace of Paris, did not encourage Jouvenel: "I said to myself, I'm out of luck, and I waited"—and when he was urged to request a special audience with Mussolini, "No, no," he replied, "I'll wait till Hitler comes, till the flourish is past."[6] Meanwhile, his friend Paul-Boncour was replaced as Premier by Daladier, and for a moment the French envoy in Rome thought of abandoning his mission.[7]

On March 2, 1933, Mussolini summoned Jouvenel to his huge private office and confronted him with a plan for associating England, France, Germany, and Italy in a "peace pact" having as its purpose to revise the Versailles settlement without reference to the other nations concerned or to the League of Nations; the alternative for Italy, Mussolini hinted, was an understanding with Germany alone. Jouvenel's first response was adverse. France relied for security on the League of Nations and on the small countries prepared to defend the peace settlement of 1919; besides, he thought, peace could be assured only by an armed League of Nations, and to sacrifice the League in the interests of peace was a contradiction in terms. Yet France could not afford to let Italy conclude an alliance with Germany so long as there existed no effective means of assuring collective security; if a revisionist coalition were inevitable, Jouvenel thought, France would be better off inside than out. So he decided to acquiesce provisionally in Mussolini's scheme and thereafter to strive to blunt its purpose by persuading him to render it compatible with France's other commitments. He still intended to win the Italian government and people over to an alliance with France; meanwhile, however, he would have to accustom his own government to the idea of a transitional period of four-power collaboration.

Jouvenel negotiated with grand diplomatic virtuosity during the weeks that followed. The Italian dictator, he suspected, saw in Hitler a rival rather than a natural ally; he played up the theme of rivalry. In a conversation with the Italian Foreign Minister he made good use of a principle of agreement that he had found in the policies of France and Italy: "The *Anschluss*! We are equally opposed to it."[8] He also found something personal in common with Mussolini: "We're both newspapermen," he told the *Duce* one day, and the *Duce* smiled at last.[9] He induced Mussolini to moderate the references to treaty revision in his draft: "You, a revisionist?" he said. "You're no more of a revisionist than I am." "How so?" "Do you want to revise the Brenner frontier?" Mussolini laughed and replied, "You're right. I'll have to change the wording."[10] And

Jouvenel often invoked the prospect of cooperation in Europe and Africa between their two countries. At length Mussolini was tempted; he would not, however, consider revising the alliances of Italy all at once. Italian public opinion, he alleged, would not follow him; so the French Ambassador multiplied his efforts to earn for France the sympathy of the Italian people. Probably he set a record among emissaries for official appearances and speeches. Certainly he set a record for munificence in entertaining Roman society: "France seemed for a moment to abandon the mediocrity she has assumed," sighed Paul Valéry, "and to return to the tradition of the great embassies of old."[11] Wrote the British Ambassador in Berlin: "The Germans may shortly be faced with a situation comparable to the loss of a second battle of the Marne."[12] Of Jouvenel's ingenious acts of hospitality one at least was permissible only to an amateur diplomat: he invited individually to the same official dinner as many representatives of French and Italian veterans' groups as the Farnese Palace could accommodate. And he was himself a favorite guest; his hosts included the head of the Orsini family, who held a reception "for our French cousin."[13]

At first Daladier left Jouvenel free to negotiate but by the same token did not consider himself bound by the results. All the members of Daladier's government, even Paul-Boncour, were disconcerted by the novelty of the proposed pact and its connotations of power politics. Day by day Jouvenel justified his efforts in a prodigious official and private correspondence. The pact, he argued, offered France the means of reaching an understanding with the two revisionist powers while obviating a direct understanding between them. An alliance with Italy could not be obtained otherwise, and he wrote to Daladier: "I prefer the perilous to the impossible."[14] Concerning the unnatural partnership with Hitler he argued, "The Four-Power Pact is in reality... a pact for holding Germany in check."[15] Occasionally he presented the pact and even the prospective alliance with Italy as expedients for playing off one form of revisionism against another; he was aware, though, that the longer treaty revision were deferred, the more painful it would become. "My feeling is that we can make such a settlement cheaper today than tomorrow," he wrote to Emile Roche,[16] and he pleaded with Daladier: "Need we wait, before dealing with essential difficulties, for our authority in Europe to decline?"[17]

Hitler, of course, welcomed Mussolini's proposal as a means of overriding the League in good company.[18] Ramsay MacDonald and Sir John Simon were also amenable to it when on March 18 they visited Rome fresh from their failure to rescue the World Disarmament Conference in Geneva from inanition—as Sir John put it, "Signor Mussolini's argument fell on willing ears."[19] However, wary of indisposing France, they confined themselves to toning Mussolini's draft down for further discussion.[20] On their way home they conferred with the government in Paris, urging on it the wisdom of Mussolini's words, "Treaties are holy but not eternal."[21] So far the draft had been held secret; by the time they reached London, though, someone—possibly Jouvenel[22]—had made it known to the French press. Its publication caused "an enormous sensation in European chancelleries."[23] All Geneva saw it as "a plot to dish the League of Nations."[24] Its reference to treaty revision elicited a vehement retort from Belgium[25] and from the Little Entente,[26] while in Warsaw it "raised a storm of protest" for branding Poland by implication as something less than a Great Power.[27] MacDonald drew up a formal proposal for emending it[28] after having solemnly assured the House of Commons that he had not promised to retrocede Tanganyika to Germany. In France the government was assailed on all sides for flouting the principle of equality among nations and the policy of respect for the Peace of Paris. Wherefore Mussolini felt "inclined to be pessimistic."[29]

"Unduly pessimistic," commented Jouvenel,[30] and on April 1 he returned to Paris on his own initiative "in the face of withering criticism"[31] to explain and defend his work. His first day he spent in consultation with the government, which he found almost wholly intractable. The next day he declared to the press that Mussolini's intentions had been misconstrued: the pact, he said, was meant to strengthen and not to supersede the League, the consent of the full League Council being required to implement the decisions of the prospective signatories. "The whole question boils down to this: whether it is better for the four countries...to agree or to disagree."[32] Mussolini's intention, he added, was "to create a common safeguard against any attempt to revise the peace treaties by force." Mussolini did not see fit to contradict him. Daladier on his side had to consent to a debate on foreign affairs in the Chamber; on April 6 he won a vote of confidence by declaring: "There is no question of our joining a kind of directory of the Great Powers that would impose its wishes on the rest of Europe."[33] Meanwhile Jouvenel and Paul-Boncour each independently drew up a draft counterproject; the two drafts "coincided in almost every particular."[34] From them the government derived an official counterproposal. The four powers, it said, would consult over matters tending to affect the *status quo* in Europe, then make recommendations to the appropriate organs of the League. It contained no overt reference to treaty revision; in effect it transformed the four-power directory of Europe into an effete discussion group for prominent members of the League.

Jouvenel returned to Rome on April 9, bearing the French counter-proposal. Before presenting it to Mussolini he had to wait two days for a covering letter to arrive from Paris. Mussolini, on reading it at last, showed "evident pleasure."[35] But not so Von Papen, Vice-Chancellor of the Reich, who had arrived in Rome the same day as Jouvenel.[36] Not so Captain Goering, either, who flew in from Germany "hard upon the heels of Von Papen."[37] Soon Mussolini gave signs of wavering.[38] Goering was his house guest, and on April 11 Chancellor Dollfuss of Austria joined his party. And even as Mussolini was signifying his good fellow-ship with the revisionist powers, MacDonald, on seeing the French re-draft, lost interest in the negotiations, and in France Herriot spoke out against the "Holy Alliance" in any form, proposing in its stead an alliance of France, Great Britain, and the United States against treaty revision.[39]

Then Mussolini's guests departed, and for weeks afterwards, patiently, persistently, Jouvenel strove to salvage the negotiations. Together with the British Ambassador and the Italian foreign office he worked out a compromise draft, which on May 1 Italy sent out to the other three powers for approval.[40] By that time Mussolini, despite strong representations from Germany,[41] was again of a mind to come to terms with France,[42] and early in May he twice appealed to the British foreign office to assist him.[43] Then suddenly on May 17 Hitler tearfully told the Reichstag of his will to peace, extolling the prospective pact without even specifying which draft; concurrently Sir John Simon wrote urging Mussolini to "hasten [the] discussions."[44] Two days later Goering again flew to Rome, where at once he took up the negotiations with Mussolini and with the British and French Ambassadors.[45] The negotiators con-sented to one after another of the changes required by France, until by June 5 the French government did not have a single technical objection left to raise. One point suffices to illustrate Jouvenel's skill in negotiating: whereas the pact as originally drafted would have bound the signatories to agree on the rearmament of Germany in the event of a failure of the Disarmament Conference, the final text bound them to agree on dis-armament in the same event.[46] The Little Entente council on May 30 formally approved the final French draft proposal, hence its approval of the pact itself went without question, while Poland, conversely, had been so much offended by the very idea of the pact that its actualization could make no further difference.[47] As it stood, France conceded nothing, the peace of Europe was guaranteed by the nations best qualified to break it, and treaty revision was demoted from a motif of chauvinistic rodomontade to a last recourse for preventing war. Besides, in matters tending to affect the *status quo*, agreement among the four powers or else mute concessions by some of them were in any case the sole alternatives to war.

The more the other negotiators deferred to France, however, the more the Daladier government demurred.[48] The pact had been purged, but its insinuations remained: partisans and adversaries alike in France regarded it as having merely been edited for style. Herriot and Léon Blum, the majority leaders, were against it, and reports on Nazi rule were daily strengthening the objection in France to according Hitler such privileges as had been denied to his predecessors. "The only alternatives now," wrote Jouvenel to Daladier, "are to tear up our text or else to defend it. In the latter case the government will have to take its responsibility before parliament; in the former case it will have to take its responsibility before the world."[49]

His letter did the trick: the next day permission came from Paris for him to initial the pact. "The negotiations...may shortly become conclusive one way or the other," Mussolini told the Italian Senate.[50] Indeed Hitler, exasperated by the eleventh-hour bickering in Paris, was now in turn withholding his approval.[51] For the first time since the war the eyes of the world were on the Wilhelmstrasse; Foreign Minister von Neurath, delighted, sought a delay of twenty-four hours. He was not, he said, free to take it on himself to agree to the "considerable sacrifice"[52] of renouncing the explicit recognition of equal rights in armaments for Germany, and both Hitler and Von Papen were absent from Berlin. For twenty-four hours, then, the wires between Rome and Berlin were busy.

The Italian Senate met the next afternoon at four o'clock, and the senators, their eyes on the empty diplomatic box, began dully discussing a chapter of the budget. Shortly after six o'clock Jouvenel entered, and as he took his seat "a tremor of excitement ran through the Senate."[53] Soon the British, then the German Ambassadors came to their seats beside him. Half an hour later Mussolini arrived: he had just won Hitler's consent by telephone. His appearance spoke for itself; the senators rose at once and cheered loud and long. Only with great difficulty did he restore order; then, after announcing that Europe was about to enter upon a new era of "peace and progress," he remarked, "All Italian-French problems take on a totally new appearance in the light of the pact,"[54] and the cheers broke out anew. In the French Chamber the response was less frenzied: there on June 9 the government won a substantial but somewhat depleted majority on a vote of confidence implying consent to sign the pact.[55] For once Jouvenel was more than content with less than unanimity, and on the evening of June 11

Ambassador and Madame Henry de Jouvenel held a reception and banquet... for whatever the Eternal City had to offer by way of diplomats, statesmen, dignitaries of the new regime, notables of the ancient aristocracy: more than twelve hundred guests. The whole traffic brigade was busy keeping the flow of automobiles in line between the Corso and the Tiber. Opulent Madame de Jouvenel emptied the hothouses of all the florists of Rome to adorn the galleries and the Parlor of Hercules of the Farnese Palace. At the buffet, as champagne-bottle corks popped away, plump chickens alternated with goose-liver *pâté*. A fortune went in a few hours for this Thousand-and-one-Nights feast, for this replica of the legendary banquets at which the Chigi, magnificent, hurled their platters of gold into the Tiber.[56]

At midday on July 15 Jouvenel was the first to arrive at the Palazzo Venezia for the signing of the pact; the crowds cheered him as he drove by. The ceremony was simple and rapid, and with it his mission in Rome came to an end.

He returned to Paris on July 19. Asked on his arrival what the value of the pact was, he said: "Its value will depend on the use to which its signatories put it."[57] Its signatories put it to no use. They did not consult among themselves before the meeting on disarmament in Geneva in September, and within the month Germany, having failed to obtain equality of rights in armaments, withdrew from the League. Thereafter they did not either ratify or repudiate it; they merely spoke no more about it. With Jouvenel no longer briefing his government, its members' agreement on the pact resolved itself into so many contradictory motives: some favored treaty revision and some did not; some favored an alliance with Italy and some did not; and the two whom he had won over to the pact completely, Monzie and Paul-Boncour, turned out to be completely at odds with each other as to its purpose and significance.[58]

For various reasons the pact was objectionable to most Frenchmen. It created a hierarchy of powers in Europe, said some; it recognized one, replied Jouvenel. It seemed to invite treaty revision, said some; it minimized France's losses in case treaty revision were inevitable, said Jouvenel. In the matter of treaty revision, said some, Germany was the natural enemy of France; all the more reason to treat with Germany, said Jouvenel. "You can make war against Germany; you cannot make peace without Germany."[59] This was in fact Jouvenel's greatest lesson in diplomacy: that it is exactly as necessary to make pacts with the devil as it is superfluous to make them with his opposite number. Devil or no, said some, Hitler was no gentleman, hence his signature had no value. This was not certain at the time; it may not even have been true yet—in the summer of 1933 Hitler's course may not have been set. If it was, however, France had all the more reason to signify to him clearly how much of the peace settlement she was willing to defend. Obviously not the reparations clauses: they were dead letter already. Obviously not the disarmament clauses, either: when he scrapped them in October, she merely protested. The case for refusing to revise the treaties was an excellent one; however, if France was not willing to revise any part of them, neither was she willing to defend any part of them. Hence Jouvenel's task had been impossible.

The negotiations had failed in their overt purpose; Jouvenel's covert purpose, *rapprochement* between France and Italy, was more than ever valid. Even while negotiating the pact he had made various trade agreements with Italy and come to an informal understanding on naval armaments. However, the Quai d'Orsay did not follow up its advantages, and Mussolini, after some months of friendliness to France, lost patience at last.

On his mission to Rome Jouvenel had shown himself as unpredictable as the future itself. Sent to smooth over the quarrels between France and Italy, he had sent back what was on the surface an extraordinary scheme for the realignment of the powers of Europe; then almost singlehanded, even while pushing it through to adoption in France, he had brought the other parties around to making it compatible with France's other commitments. Wrote Arnold J. Toynbee: "Its eventual acceptance by all the four signatories had been purchased at the price of emptying the text of almost any meaning that was not already expressed in the other diplomatic instruments that were already in force"[60]—a powerful backhanded compliment to the French negotiator. Exciting mistrust as well as wonderment, Jouvenel lost a little credit on all sides in France. Again he did not mind: he had given himself heart and head to serving France after his fashion—he had even overspent his mother's legacy in the process, thereby becoming financially dependent on his wife. His mission, for all its extravagance and all its futility, remains as an example: it was perhaps the most prodigious stunt of conciliation in diplomatic history. And if the stunt was not a starting-point for peace, the fault was not his.

CHAPTER 16

The Late State

ALL IN ALL, foreign affairs sank disreputably low on the agenda of parliament after the summer of 1933. Daladier, unable to curb the depression, fell on October 24. His successor, Sarraut, fell one month later. Next, Chautemps was overthrown for refusing an investigation of the notorious political and financial scandal, the Stavisky affair, and for attempting to give the *Sûreté générale* control over local prefectures—that is, over the controversial prefect of Paris, Jean Chiappe, who had made himself undesirable by sympathizing with right-wing agitators even as he had made himself indispensable for restraining them. The Cartel des Gauches was fast disintegrating, the groups in parliament were torn by dissension, and unrest in the nation was reaching the danger point when on January 20 Daladier succeeded in forming a new government with the outgoing ministers who had escaped suspicion, a few "wayfarers gathered at random,"[1] and Henry de Jouvenel.

Acting for Jouvenel, absent in Corrèze, his son Bertrand had proposed his appointment either as Foreign Minister, or else as Colonial Minister with jurisdiction over colonies, protectorates, and mandated territories indiscriminately. Daladier chose the second course, and Jouvenel, returning at once to Paris, created the *ministère de la France d'Outre-Mer*. Whereas the traditional policy of France was rather the progressive assimilation of colonial peoples, the League of Nations had decreed their progressive liberation, thereby in effect inviting French colonists to treat Senegalese, Somalis, and Syrians as alien wards and not as potential Frenchmen. As a result, French colonial administrators had come to consider the arrested development of indigenous populations in their custody to be in the best interests of France, while the adolescent nations in turn had adopted hatred for France as a sign of political maturity. Colonial ministers, having too much trouble ever to have a program, merely thanked residents-general to "maintain order." Jouvenel had learned the meaning of that euphemism on his arrival in Syria, and now, by way of adjusting the interests of France to those of the dependent territories, he planned to extend the same rights and obligations to every citizen of the vast French union while allowing each population ultimately to choose between joining metropolitan France or going its own way as a nation. He baptized his ministry and declared his purpose even before the government was complete. The idea of the ministry got a good press in France; so especially did its name, which was praised for poeticality. In French North Africa, however, protests rang loud from the indigenous peoples on their being "lumped together" with Togolanders,[2] and as it turned out Jouvenel did not hold office even long enough to explain to them that they were being "lumped together" with Frenchmen as well.

Except for the creation of the Ministry of Overseas France, the acts of the Daladier government were as pathetic as its existence was brief. His first day in power Daladier proposed to transfer Chiappe to Morocco. The Minister of Overseas France objected: not only was the prefect most needed in Paris, he said, but his removal would provoke his turbulent supporters and impair the morale of the police. Chiappe for his part refused to leave the city while he was under attack; if his reassignment were ordered, he told Daladier by telephone, he would be "out on the street [destitute]." Daladier understood him to say "down in the street [protesting]" and reported the threat to his cabinet.[3] In that case, Jouvenel and his colleagues agreed, Chiappe should be dismissed. The cabinet delegated three of its members to check on the prefect's attitude. Daladier, however, had already ordered Chiappe's transfer—and Chiappe had already resigned.

Part of the government walked out, and as it did so a wave of defiance spread through Paris. On February 6 an unauthorized demonstration of veterans' leagues at the Place de la Concorde turned into an assault on the Palais Bourbon. The police opened fire: twenty rioters were killed and a thousand wounded. Daladier hesitated between martial law and resignation. Jouvenel, though appalled by the event, retained his composure: responsible government, he reasoned, could no more risk civil war over a dubious administrative decision[4] than disavow the Republic by giving in to a street demonstration. Paul-Boncour, who had succeeded the fugitive Minister of War, offered to use the armed forces judiciously in support of a policy of appeasement; however, most of the ministers pressed for immediate resignation as a gesture of conspicuous remorse, and at last Daladier gave in to them. The next morning the ex-government was full of ideas about what might have been done, and Jouvenel spared it a final show of impotence by himself composing the statement of its reasons for resigning; afterwards, worn with anxiety and fatigue, he suffered a mild heart attack, from which he was some weeks in recovering.

In the events of February 6, 1934, Jouvenel's role was small and his attitude irreproachable,[5] but the government had acted so clumsily and expired so grotesquely that no one associated with it escaped altogether the stigma of its disgrace. As the demand for constitutional reform arose on all sides, a "national-union" cabinet was formed under Gaston Doumergue, with Tardieu and Herriot as Vice-Premiers; Pierre Laval succeeded Jouvenel—as Minister of *Colonies*. The *six février* became in time a national symbol, representing for one part of the nation a heroic mass protest against a corrupt regime, and for the other part a signal to the rank and file of the Radical, Socialist, and Communist parties for the spontaneous counterprotest that led to the Popular Front.

The *six février* prompted Jouvenel to reverse his policy toward the vices of political life in France. Until then, except when he tried to set up a syndical chamber, he had fought them solely by appealing for a change in the mentality of republicans; afterwards he fought them by appealing for a change in the structure of the regime as well. He made constitutional revision the theme of the April issue of the *Revue des Vivants*. In his own article, "For a Strong Republic," he wrote that the Stavisky scandal had shown up

the incapacity, the corruption, the impotence of the French state. Parliament stifles power; parties paralyze parliament; groups destroy parties; private interests coalesce to put pressure on groups, then split up among themselves. In this debris, the general interest vanishes; the honest do what they can and the dishonest what they want.[6]

For a government to govern, he went on, it must be competent, it must have autority, and it must last; the governments of France, however, were precarious, weak, and without technical competence. "There is only one way out: to revise the constitution."[7] However,

to reform the Republic without alarming republicans is no easy enterprise. All the more reason for hoping that the present chief of the government will take the initiative of revision and see the job through before, in a welter of passions, the authority of the state gives way to the dictatorship of the mob.... The goal is to resuscitate what a few years ago my brother called "the late state."... Before all else we must fortify the executive power.[8]

Jouvenel took over from Tardieu the proposal that a premier be empowered to dissolve the Chamber in the event of a vote of no confidence; to it he added, however, the proviso that the Premier be, not designated by the President of the Republic, but elected by the chambers—in which case, he thought, parliament might wisely neglect to elect a President of the Republic some seventh year. He proposed further that the Premier be empowered to set a time limit on the discussion of bills, and—following Tardieu, Caillaux, and others—that parliament be deprived of the right to initiate expenditures. These reforms he held to be imperative. "However," he added, "we would err fatally if we limited the reform of the state to a reduction of the prerogatives of parliament and a reenforcement of the executive power... [leaving] aside the real problem, the problem of rejuvenating the regime... by adjoining to it the forces that have gathered in its shadow and that, even as it is sinking, are themselves rising"[9]—the forces of organized labor. And he concluded:

If... the Premier is elected for a term of at least one year with the right to dissolve the Chamber in case, in the course of his term, the Chamber should find itself in disagreement with him, the legislative power will resume its proper function, which is to control the executive under the control of the country, while the executive will also resume its proper function, which is to govern.... What France demands today is, in a word, a strong Republic.[10]

He had quoted Doumergue and Tardieu repeatedly on the need for reform—and this both by way of bearing out his arguments and of exhorting the two to act on their convictions.

Tardieu for one had need of no such exhortation. In return for his agreement not to taunt the Radicals by insisting on new elections he obtained Doumergue's promise to demand constitutional reform in the fall. He made a draft for four constitutional amendments: one empowering the Premier to dissolve the Chamber should he lose its confidence, another forbidding the chambers to initiate legislation entailing expenditures, the third instituting the referendum, the fourth woman's suffrage. Late in September Doumergue, to the dismay of parliament, twice appealed to the nation by radio to support him on this program. He mentioned only its first two points to begin with, on September 23—and Jouvenel meanwhile devoted the October issue of his review to the subject of the referendum. His editorial, "Toward Direct Democracy," began with a critique of political parties and of the traditional electoral system, "precinct bonapartism." "Every four years," he wrote, "the nation, divided into six hundred segments, elects by plebiscite six hundred six-hundredths of a Bonaparte."[11] He argued primarily against a premier's being empowered to dissolve the Chamber in the event of a conflict with it unless he were elected by the chambers in the first place instead of chosen by the President of the Republic, and unless also he were empowered to resort to the referendum as an alternative—that is, to put the issue of such a conflict, instead of the parties to it, on trial before the public. In conclusion Jouvenel proposed, as a compromise:

referendum without the consent of the Senate, dissolution with the consent
of the Senate. This compromise is, I think, more likely to be acceptable to the
National Assembly than the Doumergue proposal of September 23. It is,
moreover, reasonable.[12]

His compromise was in fact a contradiction, the sense of the Doumergue proposal being to release the executive from its fealty to the chambers.
And yet, short of his compromise, his quarrel with Doumergue was not
so great as at first appears—as in fact he meant it to appear. By the time
his article was out Doumergue had proposed the referendum. To be sure,
Doumergue did not give it priority: to Tardieu's mind the referendum
would necessarily complicate the work of the government and of the
chambers both, hence it would be desirable only if the government were
stable and the chambers efficient. The question of priority was, however,
inconsequential, as neither Jouvenel nor Doumergue was willing to
accept the one reform without the other. For the rest, the Chamber did
in effect elect the Premier with its initial vote of confidence, and Tardieu's
intention was clearly to empower him to dissolve the Chamber in case of
a deadlock *thereafter*. Jouvenel's only quarrel with Doumergue was, then,
over the point of whether or not the two chambers, to facilitate their
choice of premier, ought to go on electing a nominating official every
seven years.

But Jouvenel was quarreling for tactical reasons: in rejecting the
Premier's program and yet accepting the meeting at Versailles he was
aiming to set an example for his recalcitrant colleagues on the left.
Whereas in the Chamber the majority was more or less on the left, in the
Senate it was decidedly in the center, hence the left was not eager for
the two houses to meet together. Since the *six février* Jouvenel and Paul-
Boncour had kept in touch with the veterans' groups, which, ignoring the
logic of left and right, were clamoring for reform. The two friends
reckoned that the left need not be outvoted at Versailles even if it was
outnumbered, but also that any reform acceptable there would be better
than no reform at all. Not so the Radicals: when Doumergue asked his
cabinet's permission merely to submit Tardieu's proposals to a trial
vote in Paris, its Radical contingent resigned. Thereupon Doumergue
too resigned, and the Radicals accepted Pierre Etienne Flandin as his
successor upon Flandin's tacit promise not to insist on constitutional
reform.

To reform the Republic without alarming the republicans was indeed
no easy enterprise. "Jouvenel and I plotted to save the day by working
from the Senate itself," wrote Paul-Boncour.

A plan originating in the chambers would not have the same unpleasant connotations for the representatives of the nation as, with great to-do in the press, M. Doumergue had lent to his. Our plot was a bold one; with any help from the government it might have succeeded.

A committee of the Chamber had been desperately enumerating the reforms that parliament might accomplish without actually revising the constitution when

Jouvenel and I drew up a motion proposing a senatorial commission for a reform of the state. We got a certain number of our colleagues to sign our motion, and we asked for immediate debate on it.

Our job was no easy one.... Though all our intentions had not yet been revealed, the syndicalist tendencies common to both of us were well known.... Our motion came under heavy attack on the floor, not only because of syndicalism—true republicans, who had always shown themselves clearsighted and courageous in the crises through which the Republic had passed, obstinately refused to see that the Republic was now threatened from within as well as from without. Jouvenel asked me to intercede; my intransigent republicanism, the equal of theirs, enabled me to give our uneasy colleagues the reassurance they required. The motion was carried, the Commission set up.

When it met, though, it took the counterprecaution of refusing to have either Jouvenel or me as chairman.... Henry Béranger was chosen, flanked by the two of us.... I did not get the impression that he intended going about our business very rapidly.

In the face of timid suggestions for touching up the constitution

I pointed out that, to Jouvenel's mind and to mine, to that of our colleagues who had backed our motion, and still more to that of our comrades the veterans, who were sustaining our efforts from the outside... something new was needed.... Besides maintaining and developing democracy..., besides the syndicalist and professional basis for the new state, on which we were agreed, we all were seeking—more or less, and by different means—to remove the executive, not from the control of parliament, but from a control whose incidence and whose forms paralyzed it and led to the instability that jeopardized the regime and irritated public opinion. A strong power, acting within the laws and funds granted by the representatives of the nation—such was our common ideal.

Prudent, the Commission chose to conduct a preliminary survey of public opinion. Labor leaders, economists, veterans were heard. Then the meetings became less and less frequent, ceasing at last "with the utmost discretion, as is the way in the Senate, among the well-bred."[13]

While the Senate Commission for the Reform of the State was so decorously expiring, Jouvenel put the case for such reform all the more vigorously before the public—and he made his own proposals all the more modest in consequence. Once again he put moral reform foremost. The condition for the survival of the Republic, he said, was "the end of political parties," and he proposed "*la méthode du rassemblement*"[14] ("the method of concourse")[15] as a substitute for "the party method."[15] He did not call on parliament to suppress political parties but rather on men to ignore them. "The agreement of productive forces with intellectual forces," he said, was often and easily reached outside of parliament.[16] Parliament could not govern effectively so long as parties existed to engender discord among men having every reason to agree, and neither could it represent the general will adequately without "the compulsory collaboration of the various professions in an economic assembly."[17] Of his other demands he dropped all but the referendum, in the end even denouncing the right of dissolution as liable "to transform every difficulty between the government and parliament into a national crisis."[18] To no avail: parliament would not follow his lead to Versailles. Bitterly, before the Federal Union of Veterans on April 14, 1935, he appealed to the government to avoid at all costs "reducing the nation to the desperate thought: [the regime] cannot last yet cannot change."[19]

Jouvenel spent the summer of 1935 in Varetz preparing to write a brief history of humanity. "Few names, no anecdotes," he told the erudite *raconteur* André Maurois, "but the great inventions, their consequences, the evolution of the forms of society."[20] Reports of an impending invasion of Ethiopia by Italy brought him back to the capital at the end of September.

He could not have had to face a more terrible dilemma. He had secured the admission of Ethiopia to the League of Nations in 1923, and since then he had defended his work as symbolic of world government whenever men scoffed at guaranteeing the independence of a handful of savages or the integrity of a land fit only to be colonized. Again, no one had contributed more than he to the policy of collective security, and he had called for peace to "put an end to the isolation of nations, bring to the weak the protection of the strong, insure the independence of the smallest governments and the integrity of the smallest territories."[21] But neither had anyone done more than he to reconcile France and Italy; only a few months earlier he had served as *rapporteur* for a treaty settling all colonial litigations between the two countries, and in his last speech to the Senate, amid the wildest ovations he had ever received, he had argued for the friendship of Italy as essential to the security of France. "Another great war will not be possible," he had concluded, "if the peace-loving nations, showing themselves prepared to meet all attempts at justice with more justice, appear equally capable of meeting any act of force with greater force."[22] The two terms of his speech now stood in dramatic contradiction: he had counted Italy among the peace-loving nations. Today it is known that Mussolini began to prepare the invasion of Ethiopia as early as 1933—though it is not known at what point he could no longer have been dissuaded.

Italy invaded Ethiopia on October 3. When the news reached Paris the following day, men found it hard to accept as true, having grown so used to dreading it. Jouvenel saw that a whole era had come to an end, that the construction of a state of society among nations had been post-poned beyond his generation—beyond "the generation," beyond "*les vivants*," who had fought for peace so tirelessly and yet not well enough. True, Ethiopia might still be saved, but only by nations acting each at its convenience, not by the stern command of a higher power; or the same nations might still assure the neutrality of Italy in Europe, but only if they let expediency replace ideals in the conduct of world affairs. Hence-forth the friendship of Italy, essential to the security of his country, was incompatible with peace as he had defined it. In his mind he had to choose between the remnants of a society of nations he had helped to build and the remnants of his work for a vital alliance.

He tried to formulate his thoughts in writing on the morning of Oc-tober 5. That afternoon he gave his instructions for the next issue of his review, and also spent some time eagerly discussing the New Deal with his son Bertrand, who had just returned from America. In the evening he took his family to see the Comédie Française, at the Marigny Theater; afterwards he sent the family home by car, staying himself to stroll awhile, as in his youth, along the Champs-Elysées—as if again in search of a better world. Just before midnight two policemen at the Avenue de Marigny saw "a tall, well-built gentlemen collapse to the sidewalk, visibly in great pain."[23] Finding him unconscious, they hailed a cab and drove with him to an emergency clinic. They got there too late.

"I do not believe," wrote André Maurois, "I will not believe, that jealous gods, watching over the happiness of men, pitilessly make an end of destinies too great, and yet I felt awaken within me an ancient and somber superstition when someone told me one October morning, 'Jouvenel is dead.' "[24] The news competed for space in the press with Laval's plea for "moral disarmament," by which Laval meant for parties to refrain from electioneering over the world crisis: Jouvenel's phrase had come a long way. "At a time when the rivalries of parties and of big groups expose us more than ever before to serious political trouble," wrote *La République*, "Jouvenel would have been one of the few men, if not the only man, to whom we might have appealed."[25] *La République* was right; while alive, however, Jouvenel had given the full measure of what the Republic was content to do without. And so was the *Figaro* right when it wrote: "Death spared Henry de Jouvenel the only trial he never could have borne: growing old."[26] Leaders of political parties, of veterans' groups, of trade unions, of civic organizations, of most of the militant movements of France paid him a last call at the Rue Férou. The most prominent wreath for his hearse came from Mussolini, who assured Madame de Jouvenel that her husband's memory "will remain indelible among us."[27] He was buried beside his brother and parents in Varetz. Anatole de Monzie spoke at his funeral: "Perhaps the young would have upheld him against the cunning of their elders," he said.[28] The *Revue des Vivants* did not survive its editor; in a final copy various public figures mourned "the very man hailed by our chaotic and brutal times to mediate, to pacify, to reunite."[29]

Then gradually that man was forgotten. In October, 1936, the French government saluted his memory, noting that he had died "alas, without fulfilling his destiny";[30] at the same time Louise Weiss commemorated his death in an issue of her review, *L'Europe Nouvelle*. Two years later a monument to him was raised at Varetz, near his castle and near his tomb; Anatole de Monzie inaugurated it on behalf of the government, afterwards noting in his diary:

Until now Henry de Jouvenel's memory has been extolled only in small chapels of friendship. It is as if his fine intelligence and clearsightedness were luxuries, even in death. They who are mistaken still ostracize him who was rarely mistaken.[31]

And Monzie, himself ostracized by patriots five years later, did his friend's memory the injury of extolling it to the last.

PART III

André Tardieu
and His Case against the Republic

"There are the six Great Powers, and then there is André Tardieu."
PRINCE VON BÜLOW

CHAPTER 17

The Prodigy

ANDRÉ TARDIEU was born in Paris. For generations the Tardieus had all made a point of being born in Paris. As far back as the records went they had been *des bourgeois*;[1] and they had been so proudly, even when the word *bourgeois* was faintly seditious. "My ancestors must have taken part in the *Ligue*, in the *Fronde*, in Jansenism," wrote André with assurance.[2]

From father to son they had been painters and engravers. The first of them to achieve eminence was Nicolas Henri, whose wife, Marie Anne, was also an engraver. In 1720 Nicolas became a member of the Royal Academy of Fine Arts. His eldest son, Jacques Nicolas, won acclaim for a series of prophetic works on the horrors of war,[3] and he too entered the Academy; he died during the Revolution, probably a Jacobin. The mantle then fell to Jacques's son Charles Jean, and from Charles in turn to his son Ambroise in the early nineteenth century. Though Ambroise had much competition within the family, his output was unique, including as it did some eight hundred portraits in oils, a *Dictionnaire iconographique des Parisiens*,[4] and several books on the pictorial arts in ancient and modern times. He brought up all but two of his many children to be artists; of these two, Eugène Amédée became instead an attaché in the foreign service, then the librarian of the French Institute,[5] while Auguste Ambroise became a physician, a member of the Academy of Medicine, and eventually Dean of the Faculty of Medicine.[6] Eugène married at twenty;[7] he had two sons, both in his first two years of marriage. His sons digressed in their turn. The first, Jacques, became an official[8] on the chief administrative board of the state, the Conseil d'Etat; later he also gave a course at the Ecole des Sciences Politiques and tutored backward candidates for appointment to the civil service—among them Léon Blum. The second son, André Louis Amédée, became a lawyer. At the age of twenty-one he married an heiress, Marguerite Blot, and in their first year of marriage—on September 22, 1876, the anniversary of the founding of the First French Republic—a son, André Pierre Gabriel Amédée, was born to them. They had a daughter, Elisabeth, one year later.

Young André's family was one of pious women and of men who respected piety. Their fortune was secure; their prestige was great. All were eminently literate and eminently republican: as André later wrote, "They bore Uncle Ambroise, my grandfather's brother, a grudge for having been the Emperor's physician."[9] They lived in the proper part of Paris, in a huge, white, comfortable house built by Eugène Amédée on the Avenue de Messine ten years before André's birth.[10] There André romped amid choice relics of the past: period furniture and first editions, old paintings and engravings, precious miniatures and medallions. Later he went down the street to play amid the colonnades, monuments, and sandbanks of the Parc de Monceau. When he was five his grandfather gave him a whole regiment of lead soldiers for Christmas, and he would march them from room to room with tireless delight. After he was seven his father read him two pages of Bossuet a day; he was attentive to Bossuet, for he revered his father—"I have had several teachers, but only one master, my father," he was to remark.[11] On weekday afternoons he went to catechism at the Eglise Saint-Augustin; the best in his class,[12] he learned his lessons too easily to take them seriously. Then "on Sundays my father would take us to one-o'clock mass in order to please my mother and also to hear the sermons of Abbé Huvelin, whom he suspected of heresy."[13] Finally, in 1888, just as he turned twelve, André began formal studies at the staid Lycée Condorcet,[14] and there the earliest reports on him described his mind as "vigorous and penetrating" and his work as "excellent."[15]

Early in 1889 he had, as he later wrote, his "first political emotion"[16] as General Boulanger, the professional patriot, ran for the Chamber in a by-election in Paris. Boulanger had already been elected deputy by several districts in the provinces, but the capital was to afford the supreme test of his strength. Good republicans put their faith in a workman named Jacques. "My father's and my grandfather's enthusiasm for this Jacques, whom I did not even know, astonished my childish mind," recalled André.[17] Jacques denounced Boulanger copiously; Boulanger in return merely called him "*Frère Jacques*." Boulanger won, and "in the evening at home everyone was sad," wrote André. "So was I."[18] The Republic survived.

For seven years Tardieu was the "*professionnel du triomphe scolaire*"[19] of the Lycée Condorcet. In 1892, in a nationwide contest among fourth-year students, he won the prizes for history, for French composition, and for translation into Latin; the following year he came out first in history, geography, and Latin composition, and again a year later in history and

French composition.[20] He was studious, but not at the expense of his good humor, and his success in school did not prevent him from being popular with his fellows.

In his senior year he represented his *lycée* in a national intercollegiate scholastic tournament, the *Concours général des lycées et collèges de France*. For French composition he had to write a letter such as the moral philosopher Joubert would have written on Chateaubriand; among his competitors was Henry de Jouvenel of the Collège Stanislas. Jouvenel produced 78 lines, many of them exquisite; Tardieu produced 218 lines, all of them correct. His composition shows him to have been, at eighteen, no rebel in thought or in manner. For the thought:

I must dispose in advance of a prejudice that would no doubt make you suspicious of me [he wrote, as Joubert]. I am not one of those bold innovators who, to set themselves off from their predecessors, dismiss the whole past at a single stroke.[21]

And for the manner: "Words fail me as I try to paint his [Chateaubriand's] soul so rich and so proud, attuned to every emotion, vibrating in contact with men and with nature—the soul of a poet who will derive rare enjoyment and refined anguish from life."[22] He wrote to specifications, conscious of his proficiency. As a member of the Stanislas team later remarked:

The compulsion to be original, which commonly takes hold of young people, was then and long remained unknown to him.... [However,] to speak and write like everyone else when you have a temperament and claws of your own takes courage.... At the age of braggadocio André Tardieu had the wisdom to do this. May he forgive us for having misunderstood, for having maligned him as a competitor drunk with textbooks.[23]

Tardieu, indeed, was sobriety itself. In his Latin composition he had Lucilius advise Seneca "to live not happily but well," and he continued:

Evil must not only be denounced; it must be checked. Evildoers must not be merely branded; they must be punished. When the fate of the fatherland is at stake, let us not flee the battle lest the Republic fall a prey to the wicked.[24]

And to his prose composition in Latin he added some Latin verse for good measure.

The results of the *Concours général* were announced in the Grand Amphitheater of the Sorbonne at noon on July 30, 1895. Henri Bergson of the Lycée Henri IV spoke, then Raymond Poincaré, Minister of National Education,[25] handed out the medals. Tardieu won the prize for French composition, as he did also for translation into Greek, for translation into Latin, and for Latin composition; in history he got honorable mention, and in geography, too, he was runner-up—to André Siegfried. Standing at the front of the great old hall, his blond beard trim, his black waistcoat buttoned tight and his collar stiff, he was the very caricature of precocity. While his mother and his sister wept, he perspired, and in so doing made known to the gallery that he was human after all. The next day at the Lycée Condorcet, with the poet Sully Prudhomme presiding, valedictorian André Tardieu took all the prizes for French, Latin, Greek, and history.

"He piled up prizes and diplomas as a juggler piles up eggs—to cast them to the winds without breakage or loss," wrote Jouvenel,[26] aptly. In college he had made plans for studying medicine; once out, he took the entrance examination to the Ecole Normale instead. "He did not have the slightest wish to be a teacher," wrote a schoolmate. "He chose the test because it was reputedly the hardest."[27] Twenty-five candidates passed it; Tardieu was the youngest of them, and he scored highest.[28] At the same time he was also admitted to the Faculty of Letters at the head of the list.[29] After attending the Ecole Normale for a few weeks, he went and enlisted in the Fifty-first Infantry regiment, which had its base at Beauvais, near Paris. As it turned out, his head was literally too big for the army, and he "had to drill for several days in a bowler hat while a military cap was made to order."[30] During spring maneuvers he fell from his bicycle under an ammunition wagon and broke his shoulder; on his recovery a few weeks later he found himself in the inactive reserves. Returning to Paris, he registered at the faculties of Law and of Letters. After a year he took a degree in Letters; by then, however, he had grown restless again. Through his father he met the chief secretary to Gabriel Hanotaux, the Foreign Minister, and in September, 1897, when the Ambassador in Berlin, the Marquis de Noailles, requested a new attaché, Hanotaux recommended Tardieu. Tardieu's grandfather had been the Marquis's good friend, so he took a chance: "Am leaving for Berlin. Trip costly but necessary for future," he telegraphed to his father, then in Italy.[31]

The Marquis accepted him at sight, and already his future had begun. The outgoing attaché, returning from a holiday to take his leave, dined with Tardieu in the company of the Ambassador; he found Tardieu

spic and span, jolly, a good fellow; all his colleagues liked him.

The next morning, still tired, I was sleeping late, facing the wall, when a strong, steady hand drew me from my dreams. It was the "new man," who, laughing heartily by my bedside, reminded me of the embassy schedule.[32]

The Ambassador was the first of a long line of old men to dote on Tardieu. Tardieu found the attitude congenial, and the man no less so. "The Marquis de Noailles," he recalled,

while hating priests and Englishmen with unbounded hatred, was perfectly indifferent to everything else. He took the Emperor William II, a frequent visitor at our embassy, for one of the most perfect fools of his day, and I was more or less of the same opinion.[33]

Before long Noailles had given the new man charge of the diplomatic correspondence.[34] As André was only twenty-one, " 'the career,' so dull in the long run,"[35] fascinated him. So did Berlin: in his free time on weekdays he attended the university,[36] and on weekends he drank beer from dusk to dawn in merry company.[37] After a few months his German was fluent, and useful friends, such as Count Bernard von Bülow, were legion.

In the spring of 1898 he took the foreign service examination in Paris and came out first in the country—"naturally," commented the secretary to the Embassy in Berlin.[38] At once Delcassé, the new Foreign Minister, took Tardieu into his private cabinet. Officially, Tardieu became only second or third assistant to someone; from the start, however, he had the full confidence of the dwarfish Minister meticulously preparing *la revanche*. Late in 1898 the two men drew up a trade agreement with the Italian Minister of Commerce, Luzzatti; afterwards the negotiators celebrated together, and Luzzatti told Tardieu, slapping his back, "We'll end up going side by side to war."[39] That same winter Tardieu, using the pen name Georges Villiers, made his debut as a journalist with a series of articles in the *Figaro* defining and defending the policies of Delcassé after the opportune capitulation at Fashoda. He received the title of Embassy Attaché in December, 1898, and of Embassy Secretary fifteen months later.

In June, 1899, Waldeck-Rousseau became Premier and Minister of the Interior. The new Premier had long known André's father as a colleague and friend, and his nephew, René Waldeck-Rousseau, was engaged to André's sister. On June 23 he appointed André his *agent des Affaires étrangères*, creating for him the title of *secrétaire de la présidence du Conseil*, or political secretary. The *agent's* job was to receive the Premier's visitors, to handle his mail, to sit for him occasionally at the Chamber or at the Senate, sometimes to draft bills for him—Tardieu it was who did the rough copy of the monumental *loi sur les associations*, with which the separation of church and state began. He admired his chief to the point of idolatry; he served him three years, while the Dreyfus affair was settling, and in these years he acquired, as he wrote, "a taste for political battles,

familiarity with the political milieu, acqauintanceship with political lobbies."[40]

In the next office to his in the ministry on the Place Beauveau sat
Waldeck-Rousseau's young legal secretary, Paul-Boncour. Paul-Boncour
later remembered him as an indefatigable worker.[41] And Henry de
Jouvenei, on calling for Paul-Boncour at closing time, "often met
Tardieu, who," he recalled, "filled the ministry with his pranks and the
newspapers with his articles, seeming to be at play as he worked—
rapidly, precisely, joyously."[42] For the two friends Tardieu had affability
to spare, but for their meetings with "the generation" he had only
laughter—as Jouvenel explained, Tardieu disliked "*les soirées doctrinaires.*"[43]

On becoming political secretary to the Premier, Tardieu had gone on
leave of absence from the Foreign Office. In the spring of 1902 he took
the competitive examination for the Ministry of the Interior; he came out
first in the country, and while Waldeck-Rousseau gladly appointed him
Deputy Inspector to the Ministry of the Interior, Delcassé regretfully
added "*honoraire*" to his title of Embassy Secretary. He took up his new
functions after the resignation of Waldeck-Rousseau in June, 1902; he
was to perform them for twelve years, even while pursuing his other
careers. The Interior inspectors spent some three to six months a year,
sometimes in small teams and sometimes singly, inspecting the administrative services in the various departments and communes of France with
a view to assuring centralization and uniformity. As Napoleon had intended, they were the agents of a monolithic conception of law and order;
under Combes and Clemenceau they were official spies as well, also as
Napoleon had intended. Tardieu got to know thoroughly the sanitary
system, the hospitals, the police, and the prisons of France, and in time
his reports, incomparably lucid and instructive, were used as models for
other young inspectors.

Meanwhile he made a great name for himself in journalism—though
he kept his pen name as long as he was in the civil service, even after the
identity of Georges Villiers had become common knowledge. On February 15, 1901, he joined the *Figaro* as a daily columnist on foreign affairs;
with a salary of 12,000 francs a year plus thirty centimes a line[44] he was,
at the age of twenty-four, the highest-paid journalist in France. Through
Delcassé he won easy access to embassies in Paris and even governments
abroad. He made a specialty of interviewing foreign statesmen—or,
more exactly, of writing interviews for their approval. His most famous
was one of Chancellor von Bülow of May 28, 1902, which bore France
an unexpected message of goodwill from Germany; seated on the terrace

of a *Bierstube* on Unter den Linden, he dashed it off "at a single stroke, without erasures," and Bülow found in it "almost nothing to change."[45] While his own personality was admirably absent from his interviews, his articles on foreign policy were distinctive for their vigor and simplicity. Nonetheless his editor, Gaston Calmette, made a practice of touching them up; the result was never an improvement. At length he came to suspect Calmette, who was then still making his fortune, of turning to profit the reputation of Georges Villiers as spokesman for the Quai d'Orsay. Late in the night of August 8, 1902, he sent in an angry letter of resignation, which he followed up with a lawsuit later on.[46] Delcassé congratulated him,[47] and from then on the policy of the *Figaro* was to champion any and every alternative to Delcassé—even Caillaux in 1911.

Tardieu was not a free lance for long: less than two months after his break with Calmette *Le Temps* took him on at the request of its home-news editor, Eugène Lautier. *Le Temps*, even with its small circulation, was the most influential newspaper in Europe. Hotels abroad served it with breakfast; statesmen and scholars cited it for authority; loans failed on the Bourse if they did not have its backing. Its statutes invested a "director" with unlimited power over it, even the power to name his own successor. The director had been gnomish Adrien Hébrard for as long as Paris could then remember. Hébrard was first and foremost a conversationalist, reputedly the wittiest of his time. He never wrote; he did not have to, for all Paris was his stenographer—his *bons mots* fill the memoirs of his contemporaries. Without ever contributing a line of copy himself, he inspired the whole of every issue of *Le Temps*. He demanded that reporters report fully and impartially; as for the columnists, he did not mind what their stand was on any issue so long as they were free from dogma in taking it and clear and cogent in defending it. Wrote Tardieu, reminiscing late in life:

Under the affectionate sway of Adrien Hébrard, *Le Temps* was an irresistible outfit. All of its musty walls exuded an atmosphere of liberal parliamentary tradition. I was able to wage the roughest of campaigns without anyone ever bothering or restraining me.[48]

At first he wrote on miscellaneous topics, among them the religious policies of Combes, which, though himself no devout Catholic, he berated for intensifying discord among Frenchmen. After a few months he got a column of his own, "Propos Diplomatiques," which was tacked on to the "Bulletin de l'Etranger," the editorial by the foreign-news editor, Francis de Pressensé. He dealt with whatever diplomatic news Pressensé did not cover; usually this was news from the Orient, and in explaining it he acquired the art of presenting complex problems simply without ever simplifying them. With the best of his *propos* he made up his first book, *Questions diplomatiques de l'année 1904.*

One day in January, 1905, Pressensé quit *Le Temps*, having become a Marxist. That day Hébrard finished his work as usual; then on bidding the staff goodnight he told Tardieu matter-of-factly to take over for Pressensé in the morning. Tardieu did so, recalled the treasurer of *Le Temps*,

intent on carrying out, with a minimum of breakage and through an ascendancy acknowledged by everyone from the very start, certain essential reforms that the director of *Le Temps* had suggested to him. Enjoying Hébrard's complete confidence, he succeeded without difficulty in getting the foreign corres- pondents to produce more than ever before; he did so by cordial persuasion as well as by his prestige and by his own example.[49]

He organized the foreign correspondents into a veritable espionage ser- vice, and to coordinate their findings he transformed the archives of *Le Temps* from a heap of old dispatches into a reference library. He was Hébrard's "confidant and right-hand man":[50] Hébrard consulted with Lautier in the open, with Tardieu behind closed doors; and while Tardieu might censor Lautier's articles for their effect abroad, Lautier had to put up with the effect of Tardieu's articles at home. Intensive as was his work for *Le Temps*, he soon added to it the functions of columnist for *La France de Bordeaux* and of foreign editor of *Le Petit Parisien*.

From the start his work as foreign editor of *Le Temps* was closely involved with the diplomacy of Europe, which as his work began was itself closely involved with the problem of Morocco.

He had backed Delcassé systematically until the conclusion of the agreement of April 8, 1904, with England, by which France renounced all interest in Egypt in return for support in Morocco; soon afterwards, however, his backing had begun to slacken. Delcassé declined to notify Germany formally of the agreement, even though the German govern- ment, learning of it informally, found it unobjectionable. Thus, thought Tardieu, Delcassé by his obstinacy missed out on the chance of obtaining Germany's tacit acceptance of a future French protectorate in Morocco; worse, by seeming to act in defiance of Germany he encouraged Germany to respond defiantly. When the agreement was signed Delcassé told Tardieu: "I'd like to see William II's face now!"[51] Then, busy gloating, "he let ten months go by without taking any action in Morocco, just as if he were in sovereign command of a serene future. He waited until the rout of the Russians at Liao-Yang...."[52] And meanwhile he shut his eyes to the poor state of the army—"a ruinous aberration of mind in a good Frenchman who, by dint of wishful thinking, had lost all notion of realities and all sense of possibilities."[53] Delcassé did in fact take *some* action in Morocco: he came to an understanding with Spain over zones of influence, meanwhile putting the Sultan a little deeper into the debt of France for troops and money.

In February, 1905, French delegates went to discuss political reform with the feeble Moroccan government; they met with a show of resistance. The next month the Kaiser, visiting the Sultan in Tangier "in his character of independent sovereign," advised him to treat "with great caution" the proposals of France for reform. By way of explanation Ambassador von Radolin, speaking confidentially to Delcassé, set German investments in Morocco at 40,000,000 francs;[54] *Le Temps* printed the preposterous figure, and Radolin had to apologize to Berlin.[55] The German press demanded an international conference on Morocco, the German government took up the proposal, and finally the Sultan, on the advice of his notables, made it his own. Delcassé, questioned by the chambers, at first "feigned not to understand the meaning of the discussion";[56] then he moved to refuse the conference, though France was not armed to refuse. Thereupon a confidant of the Kaiser's, in an interview with *Le Gaulois*, besought France to "give up the Minister whose only aspiration is to trouble the peace of Europe,"[57] and on June 6 the Council of Ministers was unanimous in accepting Delcassé's resignation. France had no choice; three years later Tardieu was to commemorate the anniversary of "an unprecedented humiliation."[58] He did think that the ministers should have resigned collectively; nonetheless he bore them out without protest even while the Kaiser, delighted, made Count von Bülow a prince.

Premier Rouvier himself took over the Foreign Office, and he consented to the conference as soon as Germany had acknowledged the special interests of France in Morocco. Tardieu, though he regretted that France had no alternative, did not despise the prospect of a conference. On the contrary: as he saw it, Germany's sole purpose was to disrupt the alliances of France, hence France, by merely maintaining her alliances, might gain, besides satisfaction in Morocco, a decisive diplomatic advantage.

Dr. Rosen, German Minister in Tangier, came to Paris on September 7 to discuss the conference agenda with Rouvier, and two weeks later Count Witte, Prime Minister of Russia, arrived after signing the peace with Japan at Portsmouth. Witte, in an interview with Tardieu, declared Russia grateful for the sympathy of the Germans in the recent war— "Witte has the bad habit of talking too much to newspapermen," whispered the Russian Ambassador in London to his French colleague.[59] Righting the balance, Witte gave his support to Rouvier in the discussions with Rosen, and on September 28 a protocol was concluded confirming France and Spain in their control of the frontier police and providing for adjudication of economic concessions within the Sultan's empire; the other police and the financial reform were left for the conference agenda.

Early in September Tardieu made a request at the German Embassy for an interview with Bülow; the Embassy put him off,[60] so he took his request "repeatedly and quite insistently" to Rosen.[61] On September 30 Bülow wrote to Rosen: "You may bring me Tardieu, but bring me also a detailed note in French on what I should say to him."[62] Tardieu saw Bülow at Baden-Baden on October 3. At first Bülow spoke in French from his note, then he spoke in German from his heart. France, he said, was attempting to obtain a settlement in Morocco in neglect of the legitimate interests of Germany. "We Germans were obliged to reply to the threat to isolate us"—in the German language, Tardieu later explained, a "threat to isolate Germany" is a "conversational euphemism" for "a grouping of powers outside of Germany's dictation."[63] Bülow expressed the hope that the conference would bring Germany and France closer together; so long as the French respected the interests and dignity of Germany, he added, Germany not only would not annoy them but would be of service to them—in Morocco and elsewhere. The interview appeared in *Le Temps* the following day, and immediately tension dropped throughout Europe. Bülow, who meant well, was quite pleased; having declared himself conciliatory, he actually was conciliatory for a few weeks.

Then Rouvier discreetly asked the German government to agree in advance of the conference to letting France and Spain together have the concession for organizing the police in western Morocco. By admitting Spain to the concession, he argued, Germany would not seem to be conceding so much to France, while France for her part would not have to worry about England's getting in on it. The German government refused, whereupon Tardieu, somehow informed, attacked it violently. The German *chargé d'affaires* in Paris complained to the Chancellor: "Because of your having received the very famous journalist, neither our Legation nor the French government has found the courage to put in a word in our defense."[64] Just after Christmas, the French government having taken out an emergency treasury loan, William II spoke words of appeasement to the French military attaché; the next morning his words appeared in *Le Temps*, and Rouvier had to telegraph Berlin disclaiming responsibility for the leak.[65]

The conference on Morocco opened in Algeciras on January 16, 1906, and for two months thereafter Tardieu gave Rouvier invaluable support in *Le Temps* by seizing on his every sign of weakness. The German government complained of him tirelessly, and one day Radolin "insinuated" to Rouvier "that M. Tardieu came to the foreign office frequently"; Rouvier found the insinuation "drivel unworthy of the two of us"—and besides, he added, he had not seen Tardieu in over a month.[66]

In early March, just as the discussions on the Bank of Morocco and the port police were nearing a conclusion favorable to France, the Chamber overthrew the Rouvier government for roughness in separating church and state. Tardieu was appalled. The Germans put the interregnum in France to use by maneuvering in favor of an Austrian proposal for a compromise between the alternatives of a Franco-Spanish police force or an international police force: a Franco-Spanish police force subject to international inspection. The proposal made headway; the French delegate, Révoil, fought it, but the rumor of a weakening in Paris spread to his detriment. Then on March 13 Tardieu published instructions sent that day by Rouvier to Révoil maintaining in full the demands of France. Tardieu's informant may well have been Rouvier himself; in any case Léon Bourgeois, replacing Rouvier as Foreign Minister the next day, had no choice but to confirm the instructions. In Germany Tardieu's action was denounced with solemn simplicity as a maneuver to prevent a compromise, and in England Foreign Secretary Sir Edward Grey remarked on it wryly to Paul Cambon.[67] Grey sent instructions the same day, March 14, to the British delegate at Algeciras to stand firmly by France; Tardieu published Grey's instructions three days later.

On March 17 Radolin saw Bourgeois on a pretext and got him to talk about Morocco. Then he delivered an ultimatum on the Austrian proposal in what he felt sure was a suave and conciliatory tone of voice—whereupon "I heard with astonishment M. Bourgeois repeat the very words of this evening's *Le Temps*.... Significantly Bourgeois, when I drew his attention to the dangerous interference of Tardieu, made a point of not reacting."[68] The words of *Le Temps* were in the nature of a counterultimatum without being conciliatory in the least. Bülow, beside himself, railed against Tardieu to the Russian Ambassador in Berlin; then he had his own Ambassador in Saint Petersburg arrange for the Russian

Ambassador in Paris, Von Nelidow, to intercede with Bourgeois. Bourgeois expressed regret over the language of *Le Temps* as well as dismay at being powerless to correct it; perhaps, he suggested, the Russian Ambassador might try for himself. Nelidow spoke with Tardieu at the offices of *Le Temps* on March 20, whereupon that afternoon *Le Temps* published a rough résumé of a note of March 19 from the Russian Foreign Minister, Count Lamsdorff, instructing the Russian delegate at Algeciras, Count von Cassini, to "oppose energetically" the efforts of Germany to restrict the control of France and Spain over the Moroccan police. Now the Russian government in its turn was more or less stuck with its instructions. Nelidow, of course, denied the accuracy of the résumé. Lamsdorff, too, described it at first as a "falsification."[69] Von Schoen, who had found Tardieu's articles "intolerable" all along,[70] told Lamsdorff "very precisely" that not only its publication but also its contents "had made a painful impression in our country and would influence public opinion… to the detriment of Russian financial interests."[71] In reply Lamsdorff explained the instructions as necessary "to combat the unfounded rumor of a Russian change of front"; he was, however, unable to account for the leak.[72] Witte, in making his own excuses to Germany, could find no words harsh enough to describe Tardieu's action—that is, he described Tardieu's action as *"unqualifizierbar."*[73] Russia broke off negotiations with France for a loan,[74] and the French Ambassador in Saint Petersburg, Bompard, had to avoid Lamsdorff for several days.[75] Bompard wrote assuring the Quai d'Orsay that the Russian Embassy in Paris was to blame.[76] Bourgeois meanwhile thought it wise to telegraph to Saint Petersburg disclaiming all responsibility,[77] and to Radolin he apologized for Tardieu's "lack of tact," adding that the government of the Republic was not free to interfere with the press.[78] A few days later Von Schoen wrote to Bülow,

Count Lamsdorff says that Nelidow has spoken with an editor of *Le Temps* [Tardieu] who, it seems to him, tried to smooth the matter over by referring casually to instructions to Cassini that he had just been told about and that *Le Temps* had published distortedly. He, Count Lamsdorff, made himself out to be strongly indignant.[79]

The Kaiser, on perusing the report, wrote an exclamation mark next to the word "casually," and beside the word "indignant" he noted: "A poor explanation! and we are supposed to swallow that tissue of lies! That's too much!"[80]

Having failed in her purpose of isolating France, Germany settled for a few token concessions on the Bank of Morocco, and on March 26 the

Algeciras Act was ready. While affirming the independence of the Sultan, it recognized the special interests of France and of Spain in the maintenance of order within his empire and established the principle of the open door in the economic affairs of Morocco. To appraise the work of the conference Tardieu wrote his first great study in diplomacy, *La Conférence d'Algésiras*. It appeared in February, 1907, and even in Germany it was recognized as authoritative.[81] With it Tardieu won his reputation for omniscience, for it contained not only all the well-known facts but, as it seemed, all the others.

Of these others, one was especially striking. Late in February, 1906, while the negotiations were momentarily deadlocked, Witte had written through an intermediary[82] to William II urging him to make every concession to France. Without a drop in international tension, he argued, the Russian government could not hope to float a foreign loan, though it needed one urgently to stave off further revolution. A successful revolution in Russia might well threaten Germany, he added, whereas cooperation with the Czarist government would enable Germany to reduce her land forces and concentrate on naval armaments instead, as the Kaiser would like. The Kaiser's reply was a curt refusal.[83] With mysterious precision Tardieu revealed the circumstances and the substance of the exchange. Izvolsky, "painfully moved," ordered an investigation,[84] only to let it lapse when, like Von Schoen, he found Witte himself the most likely suspect.[85] Meanwhile Jules Cambon, in a talk with a German official, described the revelation as *"une vraie calamité,"* adding, "The foreign office... is worked up against Tardieu as a result: it thinks him a proud and a dangerous man, one striving only for effect and who can be told nothing."[86]

La Conférence d'Algésiras is dramatic in form: first it sets the stage, introduces the actors, and expounds their arguments; then it recounts the negotiations, secret and public; finally it examines the results. France had lost nothing by the conference, Tardieu argued, economic equality for all in Morocco having always been her policy. On the other hand, she had made small but real gains toward political control of Morocco. Moreover, far from isolating her, the conference had served to strengthen her entente with England; it had left her alliance with Russia intact, which was in itself a victory for her; and, thanks to President Roosevelt, it had brought the United States into sympathy with her. Tardieu had full command of his subject and of his style; yet his book, audacious as it was in its revelations, was actually timid in its argument. He barely hinted at what in time he was to express so clearly: that the Algeciras

Act was not practicable, resting as it did on the equivocal distinction between political and economic affairs and the precarious paradox of a sultan independent but incapable of maintaining order on his own.

Tardieu's authority over the foreign policy of France grew steadily after the Algeciras Conference. Stéphen Pichon, who succeeded Bourgeois as Foreign Minister late in 1906, adopted a policy of strict respect for the Algeciras Act; Tardieu, expecting a fair trial for the Act to demonstrate its inadequacy, gave Pichon his support. Next he gave Pichon his advice, and in March, 1907, Radolin to his horror "learned from a very reliable source that M. Tardieu...dominates M. Pichon, that he dictates opinions to him, and that M. Pichon is too weak to resist."[87] In Berlin the Foreign Minister by his own account more than once "quite emphatically advised M. Cambon to make every effort to put an end to the doings of such persons as M. Tardieu,"[88] and one day in London the German chargé d'affaires, after a chat with the French Ambassador, wrote to Bülow: "On saying goodbye...I expressed...the hope of not finding a transcript of our conversation in M. Tardieu's article tomorrow."[89]

When his work was in the capital Tardieu would lead a strenuous existence six days of the week, then on Sundays go off to the country, usually to visit a friend named Mahon, an artillery officer stationed at Orléans. "Mahon," he recalled,

would meet me at Les Aubrais, in a little buggy, with a horse that would lie down and make us get out whenever it passed by the artillery quarters, where its stables were. At the Mahons' home, which was delightfully inviting, we would lunch with Colonel Foch and his wife. Conversation did not lag, I dare say. The Colonel—his eyes clear, his movements brusque, his manner discreetly elegant, his whole person so unassuming as to make him seem even greater than he was—won my respect at once, because I knew that he had been made to suffer without just cause. I knew that in 1901, on a political pretext, he had been dismissed from his post at the Ecole de Guerre, where he had given proof of his creative genius. In the iniquity of his disgrace he was admirable for his serenity, his smile, his sense of humor, his silence about men, his passion for ideas, the peace in his soul and in his thoughts.[90]

Late in 1905 Foch was transferred to the war office, and Tardieu saw him afterwards in Paris. Clemenceau, who in 1906 became Minister of the Interior and then Premier as well, said to the Assistant Inspector Tardieu one day: "My police force assures me that you are well acquainted with this right-wing artillery officer named Foch?" "Yes. Why?" "Because I have heard that he alone is capable of running the Ecole de Guerre... and of preparing us for victory." Tardieu agreed. "Then, if you agree, bring him to me!" "That's not my job. He's on duty at the war office. Have him summoned: he will obey." "It's not a matter of his obeying," Clemenceau explained; "I don't want him summoned through channels. Since he's your friend, you bring him to me. A private visit. Will you?"[91] Tardieu did—and, even though Foch attended mass regularly, Clemenceau put him in charge of the Eccle de Guerre.

In January, 1908, Tardieu went as guest lecturer to Harvard University in the United States. He learned English for the occasion, and he prepared a course of six lectures on France's foreign alliances since her "*mariage de raison*"[92] with imperial Russia fifteen years earlier. His course ran three weeks, and he remained in America seven weeks in all. Certainly he did not sleep a wink during his stay, for he managed to see everything in Boston, where the admixture of "collective pride" and "clannishness"[93] amused him; in New York, where, he noted, the clubs had no "idlers"[94] and the mansions no "setting";[95] and in Washington, where the congressmen struck him as being quite like ordinary businessmen. He took notes assiduously, and in Paris by early May he had four hundred pages of *Notes sur les Etats-Unis* ready for publication. The following summer he made his Harvard lectures into a book, *France and the Alliances*, which appeared in New York in September; a French version came out two years later.[96]

Frenchmen have a natural vocation for interpreting the United States, and Tardieu was very much a Frenchman. Unfortunately he was in a hurry, and he took only a sketchbook back home with him. His sketches are not caricatures, though, for they are drawn to scale and in detail. Some of the details are delightfully dated, such as the height of the highest buildings and the width of the broadest-brimmed hats; others are proof against time, such as the politician's way of declining to comment or the young man's way of resting his foot on the running-board of his girl friend's car. He found out why some American girls were still single at twenty: "An unmarried [American] girl," he wrote, "... has all the advantages that French girls have and also the enjoyments that French girls lack."[97] And he worked out the formula for the musical comedy:

Take an average French vaudeville show. Subtract whatever appeal, in the absence of psychological interest, an ingenious and well-knit plot may have. Mix it up thoroughly by working half-a-dozen irrelevant adventures into the main sequence of events. Imagine that the actors are all acrobats and that on any pretext, or even without pretext, they start turning somersaults, leaping out of windows, or dancing jigs. Flavor the foregoing with songs also having nothing to do with the subject...[98]

Things French had snob appeal in America, but what Americans *admired* in the French, wrote Tardieu regretfully, was "no longer our strength, but our charm.... We hold a strong attraction for them, but we lack authority."[99] He was the more regretful for himself admiring Americans unreservedly.

He found a hero in America—Theodore Roosevelt. At their first meeting Roosevelt impressed Tardieu with his cordiality, his youthfulness, and his excellent French. He invited Tardieu to the White House several times, once—to Tardieu's astonishment—in the company of clergymen of mixed denominations. In his *Notes* Tardieu made a brief study of Roosevelt's life and thought. He saw in him a distinctive fusion of "optimism," "action," and "character."[100] "Mr. Roosevelt has never known discouragement," he wrote;[101] then, expressing the rough-riding colonel's philosophy of life, "Since action is useful, it should be intensive";[102] and, summing up Roosevelt's outspokenness and tolerance, "He is thoroughly healthy."[103]

No less than the person of the President, the political institutions of the country made a lasting impression on Tardieu. The two-party system appealed to his sense of practicality, and he liked seeing politics played as a "sport" instead of being fought with grim earnestness.[104] He lauded the willingness of Americans to hush up partisan quarrels when the interests of the nation were at stake. "Does that mean Americans are our moral superiors?" he inquired. "No. But they have better habits."[105] They had better fundamental laws, too: the president's veto was "an excellent provision,"[106] and so was a cabinet of heads of departments chosen from outside Congress.[107] But the greatest lesson France had to learn from the United States was the virtue of a clear-cut separation of powers. "The right of the chief of state to have a personality," he wrote,

is one of the most striking traits of American democracy, and one we ought to envy. By a decree of fate our history has confused the fight for the Republic with the fight against personal power. Now, there is nothing to prove the two terms inconsistent.[108]

Again:

We have humiliated the executive power in the face of the legislative power; we cannot go on this way with impunity. Our Republic has become a body without a head, and in France the headless never last long.[109]

And again:

The more one studies its functioning, the more one is convinced that the Supreme Court is an indispensable cog in the wheels of a democracy.[110]

In his *Notes* Tardieu also gave a short history of the foreign policy of the United States from the Monroe Doctrine to the dispute over immigration then raging with "*les* Japs." Clearly he had gone to America not only to lecture on the old alliances of France but also to pave the way for a new one. In his lectures he took issue with Washington's Farewell Address, then played up the aggressiveness of Germany and the intervention of Roosevelt at Algeciras. In his *Notes* he wrote, "American patriotism, because it is lively and proud, is egoistic,"[111] trusting to a spontaneous harmony of egoisms to bring France and America together.

By the age of thirty André Tardieu had attained a position of high authority and prestige in journalism and in the civil service of his country. All along, his constant preoccupation had been not his own eminence but the greatness of France, and this even if he did not trust the governments of the Republic to assure the greatness of France without his help. He was critical of the defective organization of power in the French Republic as a patriot even more than as a republican. In his job with the Ministry of the Interior he was able to serve the permanent interests of France as distinct from the political interests of parliament. So he meant to hold on to that job as a sideline; and he meant meanwhile to strive, from his offices at *Le Temps*, to guide the foreign policy of France after his fashion, assuring it of continuity in the face of the capriciousness of the chambers.

Of *continuity*, not of immobility. So far he had sought the diplomatic advantage of France in the diplomatic disadvantage of Germany; for some years after 1907 he was to seek it instead in the common advantage of both countries.

CHAPTER 18

N'Goko Sangha and
Homs-Bagdad

"The role played during the Pichon ministry by a great journalist of *Le Temps*, M. Tardieu, in all of these affairs, in all of these deals, will prove one of the great causes for astonishment and for shame in the history of France." JEAN JAURÈS to the Chamber of Deputies on March 8, 1912.*

BY THE TERMS of the Algeciras Act, the Sultan of Morocco was responsible for maintaining order within his realm, and the signatories were bound to respect his independence. As it turned out, however, the Sultan was unable to assure the protection of foreigners in Morocco by his own devices; in fact the legitimate Sultan, Abdul Aziz, was unable even to assure his own power against his brother, Mulai Hafid, who in 1907 rose in revolt with the backing of the southern kaids. Meanwhile, a Frenchman was killed in Tangier in May, 1906, and France and Spain both sent troops in protest. Ten months later a French doctor, Mauchamps, was murdered in Marrakesh, and French troops from Algeria occupied Ujda. Then in July, 1907, nine European dock workers were massacred by rioters in Casablanca; France sent an army to pacify the entire region. In no case did France act without first obtaining the consent of the other parties to the Algeciras Act; Germany always gave her consent obligingly, waiting to refuse it until refusal should be opportune —and hoping meanwhile for France once to neglect requesting it.

As Clemenceau saw it, no colony, not even Morocco, was worth a quarrel, even a quarrel with Germany, and if Frenchmen could not penetrate into Morocco peacefully, they had only to stay out of Morocco. Hence his government upheld the Algeciras Act at all times, except when Frenchmen in Morocco were murdered; then his sole concern was to get the necessary military action over with as fast as possible. His Foreign Minister, Stéphen Pichon, also favored upholding the Algeciras Act— not for its own sake, though, but in order for France to be in a better bargaining position when the time came for replacing it. Germany, he

* Chambre des Députés, *Débats, 1912*, p. 814.

thought, might eventually let France have political control of Morocco in return for economic advantages. Tardieu thought so too; perhaps he even had the idea first. However, Tardieu also thought that the sooner the time came for replacing the Algeciras Act the better, and that meanwhile France stood to gain more by a show of strength than by an attitude of conciliation. France had sent troops to Morocco not in despite of the Algeciras Act, he held, but because the Algeciras Act was defective; also, suspicious of the success of Mulai Hafid, he argued for the defense of legitimacy in Morocco as incumbent on the great powers by the same token as the defense of legality.

On May 3, 1908, *Le Temps* protested the reception in Berlin of a delegate of Mulai Hafid, whereupon Baron von der Lancken, the German chargé d'affaires in Paris, saw Pichon to complain about Tardieu; Pichon told him reassuringly: "Tardieu is all for an understanding with Germany, only he wants us to be firm in order to reach one."[1] Later the same month, Tardieu having come out for aid to Abdul Aziz, Ambassador von Radolin sought assurances from Pichon that the Algeciras Act would not be set aside; whatever the wishes of Tardieu, Pichon replied, French policy would go on as before.[2] On June 12 Radolin overheard the French Minister of War, Eugène Etienne, "echoing" Tardieu on support for the Sultan,[3] and in Berlin Foreign Secretary von Schoen blamed Tardieu when three days later Jules Cambon told him that France was averse to "rushing into" recognition of Mulai Hafid.[4]

Meanwhile, Tardieu went to the German Embassy on June 11 to complain of the unfriendliness of the German press toward France; Lancken told him he should be the last one to complain, whereupon he conceded the point with a show of contrition. Radolin reported this to Chancellor von Bülow;[5] then from Tangier Dr. Rosen, informed in his turn, wrote to warn the Chancellor against such a show.[6] He had seen Tardieu's true colors in private in Paris and in Baden-Baden, he claimed. Furthermore, Pichon had told only half the truth at most when he denied that the French government took its policies from Tardieu. Perhaps he was right about policy in Europe;

however... anyone who wants to discover the tenor and purport of French policy in Morocco has only to read *Le Temps*. What M. Pichon and M. Clemenceau say from time to time in parliament and what ambassadors communicate to their chancelleries is of no importance.[7]

Rosen pointed prophetically to an announcement by *Le Temps* of an impending triumphal march of Abdul Aziz on Marrakesh even though the French government had repeatedly denied its intention of providing "the landless sultan"[8] with men, money, or arms. As it turned out, however, the triumphal march did not come off, and France eventually joined the other powers in recognizing Mulai Hafid.[9]

Rosen being due for a long vacation, an official from the Wilhelmstrasse, Baron von Wangenheim, left Berlin early in July to relieve him. Wangenheim stopped at the Embassy in Paris on the way and there on July 6 had lunch with Lancken and with Tardieu; afterward he and Lancken each reported the table talk to Berlin. "Tardieu was quite loquacious," wrote Lancken. "Naturally we began with Morocco."[10] For France to restore peace in Morocco, said Tardieu, she would need a free hand in military operations. Peace in Morocco was a prerequisite to good relations between France and Germany; without it "unpleasant incidents would always be cropping up."[11] But peace was not enough, he went on: the two powers had to find a way of eliminating Morocco once and for all as a source of friction between them. Now, since Morocco was vital to France but not to Germany, it was up to Germany to formulate her conditions for renouncing all interest in Morocco—save the privilege of free trade, which was not at issue. "Then by and by we came to speak of Franco-German relations."[12] In a war between England and Germany, Tardieu began, France would remain neutral; whereupon his interlocutors told him that Germany would make neutrality impossible for France—"We made a visible impression on him," boasted Lancken.[13] Then on a note of regret Tardieu spoke of the many lost opportunities for a reconciliation between France and Germany; he wondered why Germany was so suspicious of France, so defiant, so nervous, so prone to "muzzle in"; he saw no obstacles to a better future if only Germany were willing:

It is laughable for us French to go on talking about a *revanche* for Alsace-Lorraine. You make a try for a *revanche* after five years or ten, but not after thirty. So you can be sure that France will not take up the sword for the sake of the lost provinces.[14]

And Germany was just as surely not going to make war for the sake of Morocco, he added—she, too, had passed up too many good pretexts. "Such," concluded Lancken, "is the gist of what Tardieu said. Whether it was all sincere or not is another matter."[15]

The proposal for a settlement in Morocco was sincere. And it proved timely. In September, 1908, a French patrol in Casablanca arrested six deserters from the French Foreign Legion, three of them German, to whom the German consul had given a safe-conduct. Germany demanded an apology from France; France refused. Eventually the two took the dispute to the Hague Tribunal; meanwhile, however, tension rose between them. Then early in October, 1908, Austria-Hungary, without warning even to Germany, annexed the province of Bosnia-Herzegovina from the Ottoman Empire. Germany was diplomatically one down, and Pichon, finding the moment opportune, authorized Tardieu to approach Secretary von Schoen in Berlin on a definitive settlement in Morocco; Tardieu did so on October 10, 1908, and found him receptive.[16] Then in December, in exceeding secrecy, Tardieu and Lancken together prepared a draft treaty on Morocco.[17] Jules Cambon submitted it to the German government, which raised no objections. Clemenceau, informed at the last minute, approved it distractedly, and on February 9, 1909, it was signed in Berlin; the same day *Le Temps* released a statement by Pichon on the harmonious relations between France and Germany, and at the promptings of Tardieu a like statement was issued at the Wilhelmstrasse.[18]

The treaty of 1909, according to the preamble, had as its purpose to clarify the interpretation placed by the two parties on the Algeciras Act. The treaty proper read:

The government of the French Republic, desiring the maintenance of the integrity and independence of the Moorish Empire, determined to safeguard economic equality and consequently not to impede the commercial and industrial interests of Germany; and the Imperial German government, pursuing only economic interests in Morocco, recognizing on the other hand that the special political interests of France in Morocco are closely linked to the consolidation of internal order and peace, and determined not to hinder those interests; declare that they will not pursue or encourage any measure liable to create an economic privilege in their own favor or in favor of any other power, and that they will seek to associate their nationals in such business enterprises as the latter may obtain the right to launch.[19]

On signing the treaty Cambon and Von Schoen exchanged secret interpretative letters specifying the posts to be closed to German nationals in Morocco—and so also, by preterition, those to be left open to them.

The French and German governments, even while saluting economic equality in Morocco and the independence of the Moorish Empire, were in fact trading away a little of each. But political and economic interests, difficult enough to distinguish, were impossible to mete out in equal portions. Moreover, the instrument of exchange was so cryptic that the two parties themselves read it divergently: the German government expected France to assume only enough additional influence in Morocco to create a joint monopoly on public works, whereas the French government expected Germany to acquiesce in a French protectorate over Morocco in return for admission to an investment pool with France.

Paradoxically, with its very lack of precision to prevent it from becoming a solution, the treaty did open the way to a French protectorate. As Joseph Caillaux put it, "By signing the 1909 treaty [Germany] ceases to pose as the defender of the rights of Europe; she proclaims that for her Morocco is only a commercial proposition, only a business deal."[20]

Even cryptic as it was, the treaty was not impracticable. Its single unequivocal message was mutual confidence; haggling, then, was not in order—at least not for a while. Thus it was so worded as not to restrict to Morocco the commitment to encourage joint ventures, though the interpretative letters did take the restriction for granted. Probably Tardieu and Lancken meant to leave a loophole for putting other joint ventures on a par with those in Morocco. For both men were interested in central Africa. Lancken, besides being an *agent confidentiel* for the Kaiser, was an *agent d'affaires* for Semler, the vice-president of the Reichstag, who headed the gigantic Südkamerun Company. Similarly, Tardieu had in mind the N'Goko Sangha Company.

At the beginning of the century, with commercial advertising still in its infancy, newspapers in France had to augment their income from sales by doing favors for private interests; the practice was discreditable, to be sure, but the alternative was fatal; and the closest any newspaper came to being independent was its being sold out on all sides. Among the clients of *Le Temps* was a gentleman named Mestayer, who through high connections obtained a concession of land in the northern French Congo in 1899. To work his concession, he set up a company, which in 1904 merged with another to become the N'Goko Sangha. Then, as *administrateur* of the N'Goko Sangha, he went to Africa to invest in cotton and rubber. The natives resisted his efforts to recruit them for plantation labor; he did not press the point, for, as Joseph Caillaux explained, he soon noticed that, if he worked obscurely to establish and then administer his business seriously, he would reap a modest reward for great labor. His mentality of an idle man-about-town, his past as a prodigal Parisian, had led him to understand business differently. He understood business as it is understood in the circles he moved in, where "to do business" means to make fat sums of money easily, through social connections, and without working. What was the point of stooping to the lowly chores of selling cotton or planting rubber? There was something more profitable to be done.[21]

On his return from Africa Mestayer brought suit against the French colonial office, charging it with failure to enforce civil law in his domain. In March, 1905, he agreed to drop his suit in order to obtain authorization to purchase for the N'Goko Sangha a slice of the northern Gabon; then, the purchase concluded, he brought a new suit against the colonial office, now charging it with having by default allowed German merchants to infringe on his concession. The Südkamerun merchants did in fact have the run of the country: the N'Goko Sangha having made no effort to compete with them, the government of the Congo had made no effort to evict them. To further his suit in Paris Mestayer brought one against the Südkamerun Company in Hamburg in 1907 and requested for it the support of the Quai d'Orsay. Beginning in December, 1907, *Le Temps* periodically reported frontier violations by Südkamerun merchants,[22] and in March, 1908, while Tardieu was absent in America, it made the extraordinary announcement that the French and the German governments "have given up asking each other for indemnities for frontier violations, each party taking on itself the claims of its own nationals"[23]—the two governments did not take the hint. In the fall of 1908 Mestayer, weary of waiting, petitioned the Foreign Affairs Commission and the Colonies Commission of the Chamber for redress of grievances—and, as Tardieu and Lancken then met to negotiate, that was as far as Mestayer's efforts to cultivate his concession had gone.

Not to confine the spirit of mutual confidence to one corner of Africa, Tardieu and Lancken thought of creating a consortium between the N'Goko Sangha and the Südkamerun Company. Germany, given the opportunity to expand her interests in the Congo, might more willingly sacrifice her interests in Morocco. The Südkamerun would be glad of a chance to legalize its encroachment, while the N'Goko Sangha, incapable of competing with it, had everything to gain by merging with it. Besides, the N'Goko Sangha might well find a decisive argument for its indemnity in the diplomatic value of the merger.

In December, 1908, the Foreign Affairs Commission—"which," as Caillaux pointed out, "had nothing to do with the matter"[24]—agreed unanimously that the N'Goko Sangha had suffered damage, hence that compensation was in order; the Minister of Colonies, Milliès-Lacroix, objected, whereupon Mestayer warned him, "I have two hundred deputies and the whole press behind me!"[25] In January, 1909, while the draft treaty on Morocco was still under consideration in Berlin, Semler formally invited the N'Goko Sangha to merge with the Südkamerun. After the treaty was signed Milliès-Lacroix brought up the N'Goko Sangha at a council of ministers, maintaining that not a *sou* was due to it "either in law or in fact"; even Pichon failed to contradict him.

Then Tardieu took over as lawyer for the N'Goko Sangha,[26] and on his advice Mestayer, assisted by the Berlin correspondent of *Le Temps*, began negotiating the consortium. Late in February Pichon wrote assuring the N'Goko Sangha that he was prepared to intercede on its behalf in Hamburg, having waited only for a Congo-Cameroons border commission meeting in Berlin to settle a relevant dispute. One month later the N'Goko Sangha replied that it wished only an indemnity from the French government, not help in Germany, and when the frontier dispute was settled to its detriment it added a charge for loss of territory to the charge for infringements of its territory.

On May 15, 1909, Lancken called at the Quai d'Orsay to suggest to Pichon "the constitution of a sort of Franco-German consortium";[27] he called again a few days later and reiterated this suggestion. Did he represent the consortium officially as an application of the treaty of 1909? The answer, were it known, would serve as a skeleton key to the mystery of Agadir. If, despite Lancken, Semler, or the Kaiser himself, Germany did not recognize the relevance of the treaty to the Congo, Germany would owe France no gratitude in Morocco for the creation of the consortium; then the French government would have to judge the consortium on its own merits, as a business venture. Pichon in any case acted as though the German government considered the treaty relevant. On June 5 he asked Milliès-Lacroix for an opinion on the prospective consortium; Milliès-Lacroix, skeptical, wanted the full details, so on July 2 Pichon wrote asking Mestayer for them. Just then Briand replaced Clemenceau as Premier, and while Pichon kept his post, Milliès-Lacroix made way for a new Minister of Colonies, Trouillot. On August 2 came Mestayer's reply. Begging the question of the form of the consortium he wrote: "The N'Goko Sangha is obliged to subordinate the execution of the plan for a cession that you have invited it to formulate to the decision that the government will take in the matter of the indemnity."[28] Thereupon Pichon undertook to persuade Trouillot of the relevance of the treaty and of the justice of the indemnity, while the N'Goko Sangha, confident of its reward, went ahead with its negotiations.

At the end of 1909 the N'Goko Sangha sent Pichon and Trouillot the details: the two colonial companies were simply to merge their respective concessions on a parity basis. The two ministers, after consulting between themselves, replied on February 5, 1910, provisionally approving the arrangement and, on condition that the N'Goko Sangha go through with it, assenting to the payment of the indemnity.[29] The N'Goko Sangha requested a more precise commitment, Trouillot took up the request with it informally, and eventually both sides agreed to settle the amount of the indemnity by arbitration. Early in March each submitted its claim.[30]

Tardieu, as lawyer for a party to the dispute, had the right to consult the government's file; he had it copied out for future use.[31] On April 5 he settled with the state's advocate on a compromise, which the judge accepted in his arbitral sentence after a formal hearing on April 29: the indemnity was set at 2,393,000 francs[32] plus 150,000 hectares of additional territory in the Congo, the N'Goko Sangha to be authorized moreover to transfer some jungles to another French concessioner for 1,000,000 francs and to issue stock for its share in the consortium to the amount of 2,250,000 francs, of which 1,250,000 francs reserved to the founders —a tidy settlement all in all for a company with a capital of only 2,700,000 francs![33]

On May 11 Trouillot, belatedly prudent, wrote to the N'Goko Sangha denying that the state, in submitting to the arbitral procedure, had contracted a debt; for the indemnity to be payable, he maintained, both the new Foreign Affairs Commission and the Council of Ministers would have to approve it. No doubt he was responding to the turn just taken by the negotiations in Berlin: because the Südkamerun, unlike the N'Goko Sangha, held only a commercial and not a territorial concession, the two had at length decided to restrict the consortium to the N'Goko Sangha area. The justification for the indemnity was now even more problematical than before. If the 1909 treaty was relevant, the French company was now more deserving of compensation, for now it was consenting to share and not merely to pool its concession. Yet even so the indemnity would in a sense be a duplication: as Caillaux put it, "The [French] government was to pay the N'Goko Sangha two and a half million francs for entering into the consortium, and the N'Goko Sangha was to receive an equivalent sum from the Germans as their contribution."[34] And again, if now the indemnity was more justifiable, this was only because the consortium was now more detrimental to France; in effect, wrote Caillaux ironically, the indemnity was now due only "to compensate the N'Goko Sangha for the favor it was doing France in transferring its concession to the Germans, or at any rate in sharing its advantages with them."[35] As Tardieu saw it, however, the consortium was a weapon in the struggle for Morocco; it caught the spirit of the 1909 treaty whether or not it caught the letter as well; and it would cost France nothing, for the N'Goko Sangha had long since lost its concession *de facto* to the Germans anyhow. As for the indemnity, it would be both due compensation for the loss and fair reward to its recipients.

Mestayer wrote incredulously to Trouillot. Trouillot, however, held firm, so Mestayer threatened to call off the consortium—"in which case," he added, "I shall beg the Foreign Minister to explain personally to M. Semler...the new situation created by your recent letter."[36] Wherewith on May 25, 1910, Pichon and Trouillot applied to the Foreign Affairs Commission for approval of the indemnity,[37] and on June 3 Trouillot invited Mestayer to settle with the state's advocate on the mode of payment. Mesayer settled on fifty half-yearly instalments commencing November 10, 1910, plus 4 ½ percent compound annual interest on the running balance; the agreement was signed June 18, Trouillot counter-signing.[38] Afterwards Trouillot requested the Minister of Finance to authorize the payment; next he besought him to approve an advance covering the first instalment; next he appealed to the Treasury itself to make the advance. The N'Goko Sangha meanwhile made haste to negotiate its paper before the new Chamber convened. "First it asked at insurance companies," Tardieu later testified; "[then at] banks...; then finally it found, I don't know how, one M. Vatel-Dehaynin—a capitalist, not a banker—who agreed to take the paper at a discount of 5 percent."[39] Out of its bird in hand the board of directors of the N'Goko Sangha awarded Mestayer a special bonus of 400,000 francs;[40] Tardieu it paid 30,000 francs for his services.[41]

Though Tardieu had earned his fee in full, his job was not yet over. On August 23 the Treasury wrote to Trouillot refusing to honor the funding agreement of June 18: it suggested he try writing the expenditure into the budget for the Congo. He tried—but the acting chairman of the Budget Commission, Joseph Caillaux, detected it with the ease of *expertise* and then made political capital of a bad debt in search of a ledger. The government had hushed up the indemnity; Caillaux and his budgeteers perpetuated the hush-up to the detriment of the government. "It all began by murmurs," wrote Tardieu,

by discreet allusions, whispered on the sly. There was "a scandal to be broken." Private interests had pillaged the Treasury. Corrupting gold was flowing. Only stalwart virtue could resist. No details—there was no hurry. The affair ripened in a haze of equivocation. Responsible ministers felt bearing down on them the unanimous suspicion of the men who did not themselves know but who knew the men who knew. The Foreign Affairs Commission groveled under reprobation. Deputies would point to the meetingroom of the Budget Commission, where behind closed doors the conspirators were sharpening their knives, and in hushed voices they would say: "Momentous things are going on in there!"[42]

Momentous things—or at least things of moment—*were* going on in there. But the Commission did take its time about them; and meanwhile, by way of precaution, it took steps to make the approval of parliament necessary for payments by the state of more than 100,000 francs. Caillaux tormented his old colleague Pichon one day:

"Will you let me take care of it for you? Maybe I can manage it—I have influence in the Budget Commission. On one condition, though: that you drop the consortium." Silence, broken by faint grunts. I caught on: the government was not—was no longer—free.[43]

Even Trouillot again began to doubt whether the consortium in its final form met the conditions for the payment of the indemnity,[44] and finally on October 11 Pichon wrote to Jules Cambon in Berlin that as it stood the consortium was unacceptable.[45]

In November Briand, after breaking a big railway strike, made it up by weighting his cabinet to the left. Trouillot took the opportunity to drop out, and the efforts to pay the indemnity ceased in consequence. Then Semler came to Paris with his associates, and on November 26 Pichon, under pressure from them and from Lancken, had the Council of Ministers agree *"en principe"* to the consortium;[46] he gave his visitors assurances that it would be put to the vote in parliament, and at their departure he sent to Von Schoen, now Ambassador in Paris, reiterating his assurances.[47] And when the German Chancellor mumbled menacingly about Morocco, Tardieu wrote: "In Berlin they do not understand why agreements desired on both sides are being held up [here] by subaltern opposition."[48]

Meanwhile the Bugdet Commission, with a great show of secrecy, had begun hearings on the N'Goko Sangha indemnity. Milliès-Lacroix declared firmly against payment; *Le Temps* described his declaration as "scandalous."[49] Tardieu himself came to testify on December 16, bringing with him *"un dossier d'accusation"*[50] and—"to impress the Commission," wrote its *rapporteur*[51]—a professor of administrative law from the University of Paris. The government, Tardieu argued, had added to its moral obligation a legal one when on February 5, 1910, the Foreign Minister and the Minister of Colonies undertook to obtain payment of the indemnity provided only that the N'Goko Sangha enter into a consortium with the Südkamerun, and it had confirmed this obligation by settling the amount of the indemnity with the N'Goko Sangha in a court of arbitration. These arguments notwithstanding, four ministers came out against the indemnity before the Commission on January 22, 1911,[52] and three days later Pichon himself formally declined to move payment in the Chamber.

Already *Le Temps* had grown more circumspect in its praise of Pichon: "M. Tardieu is in constant and close touch with the foreign office, but he makes no bones about subjecting its activities to very harsh criticism," wrote Izvolsky to Sazonov,[53] and similarly Von Schoen wrote to Beth-mann-Hollweg: "M. Tardieu is beginning to carry out his threat to be unpleasant to the Foreign Minister."[54] Then the axe fell. On January 31, as the Entente powers were negotiating separately with Germany on the question of the Turkish railways, Tardieu inquired:

If the Franco-Russian alliance on the one hand and the Franco-British Entente on the other have not been broken or even relaxed, where does the impression come from that they have? From this, in our opinion: that these combinations, even though they have lasted, have in two years proven almost utterly sterile. They exist, but it is as if they did not exist. They are praised, but they are not used. They are a pretext for compliments, not a basis for action.... They lie idle in the archives.... They have passed the age of fecundity; they no longer create.... From within their majestic frames, a picture of ataxia meets our astonished glances.... In the face of an active Triple Alliance, we have a dor-mant Triple Entente. Peace is not threatened, to be sure. France is not isolated, certainly. But in the bosom of peace, in the heart of our alliances, of our en-tentes, of our friendships, we are not sowing, and tomorrow's harvests will not fill our granaries.[55]

Three days later a senator on the right, Lamarzelle, interpellating the government on foreign policy, remarked:

The day before yesterday, after leaving the Chamber, I had the good fortune to find the newspaper *Le Temps* at home. It contained an article—unsigned, to be sure, but whose author you all know: he has with you, and in all parties, un-disputed authority, which is all the greater in the present debate since M. Tar-dieu (I may as well name him) is an optimist, a man who has consistently supported the policy of the Foreign Minister...[56]

and Lamarzelle read out the article. Pichon replied cavalierly:

... M. de Lamarzelle brought up an article from the newspaper *Le Temps*. One week ago the author of this article found our foreign policy perfect.... Then suddenly he declared that nothing was right with it any longer.... I do not know, I do not care to know, what might have determined so rapid a turn-about.[57]

"You certainly know better than we do," interrupted Lamarzelle,[58] and the Senators all tittered. Some thought of the N'Goko Sangha no doubt, but no doubt the others thought of the Homs-Bagdad.

In the spring of 1909 the Turkish state, lacking the funds necessary to honor its concession agreement with the Bagdad Railway Company, a syndicate of the Deutsche Bank engaged in constructing a railway from the Bosporus to Bagdad, applied to the Ottoman Debt Commission, on which all the Powers sat, for authority to raise customs tariffs in the Ottoman Empire.[59] Great Britain, while withholding her consent to the tariff increase, requested a concession for a railway between Bagdad and the Persian Gulf—without financial guarantees from the Turkish state. The Turkish parliament would have found this request difficult to refuse. However, the German company was coveting a terminus on the gulf for its own railway, and so the Grand Vizier, having no taste for power politics at the expense of his country, besought the Germans to come to terms with their British competitors. Negotiations ensued between the bankers Sir Ernest Cassel and Arthur von Gwinner, and concurrently between the British and German governments. At first Gwinner spoke of admitting the British to a small share in the Gulf sector of the Bagdad Railway "provided the Turks agree";[60] by the end of the year, though, he was offering Cassel a half interest. Cassel expected him to concede even more, and no doubt he would have done so willingly. Gwinner, however, was not the German government, as Caillaux once had to remind him—and besides, the British Foreign Secretary, Sir Edward Grey, was not anxious for even the German government to concede too much. "Grey sought really to delay the building of the railroad, not to participate in it."[61] He held the surrender by the Bagdad Company of its rights in the Persian Gulf area to be a fully adequate *quid pro quo* for the consent of Great Britain to the tariff increase, whereas the German government would consent to the surrender only as part of a general political settlement between Great Britain and Germany.[62]

In December, 1909, Pichon told the British Ambassador in Paris that France too would expect a *quid pro quo* in return for her consent to the tariff increase,[63] and on January 12, 1910, the French government applied in Constantinople for a concession to build and operate a railway from Homs to Bagdad. As Paul Cambon explained to the British foreign office, Pichon really desired the "internationalization" of the Bagdad railway, but knowing the British to oppose it he was demanding the concession instead as "absolutely essential." He proposed making joint ventures of the prospective Homs-Bagdad and Bagdad-Kuweit railways;[64] Grey agreed, so Cambon began negotiating financial terms with him.

Meanwhile, in Constantinople the deputy-director of the Grand Vizerial Archives, Yussuff Said Bey, opportunely drew up a prospectus for a Homs-Bagdad railway and a draft concession agreement to match. Yussuff's railway was to cross the Euphrates close to Homs, with a possible branch line from the point of crossing to the German junction at Aleppo; the Turkish state was to provide, not the usual guarantee of minimum annual receipts per kilometer, in which the British saw only an incentive to sloth, but one of a 4.5 percent annual return on the total investment. Yussuff chose as business agent "that egregious person, Bernard Maimon,"[65] a British citizen of Turkish extraction, whose declared occupation was "occasional correspondent for the *Evening Times*."[66] Maimon won for the project the backing of Sir Ernest Cassel; Cassel formed a group with the British engineering firm of Arthur J. Barry, and in March, 1910, Maimon set out with the approval of the British foreign office to find a French group to join in the venture.

Maimon did not apply directly to French financiers; instead he applied to Tardieu, offering him full powers to constitute a French group plus the chairmanship of the joint board of directors.[67] For years Tardieu had advocated the cooperation of France on the Bagdad railway as one means of inviting concessions from Germany in Morocco.[68] Instead France had generally sought to obstruct the venture, for Russia saw in it a threat to the security of her Caucasus frontier and England a threat to her dominance of the Persian Gulf.[69] However, the railway had long since become inevitable, thought Tardieu, and so the time for obstruction was past and the time for an *"arrangement"* had come.[70] In his eyes the Homs-Bagdad project constituted, "instead of negative grievances, a positive program that might serve either as a counterpart to the German Bagdad or else as a basis for a compromise solution."[71] He was primarily interested in the compromise; the concession, however, impressed him as an excellent alternative. It would extend the French railway system in the Near East from Syria to Mesopotamia; in time of peace it would benefit French shipping in the Mediterranean, and in case of war would permit the transport of French and British troops from Tripoli, Beirut, or Haifa to the Persian Gulf; it "would offset Germany's ambition for a complete control of the highway of Asia Minor"[72]—in short, it would cancel out the chief advantages to Germany of the Bagdad railway.

Tardieu accepted Maimon's offer, and by April 14 he had formed a French group[73] and affiliated it by correspondence with the British group on the basis of strict parity. Then Barry joined Maimon in Paris, and Tardieu took them to see Pichon. "By a stroke of the brilliant journalist's wand the Quai d'Orsay was conquered,"[74] and the next day Tardieu sent the French Ambassador in Constantinople, Bompard, "the plan for a Homs-Bagdad railway, which seems to me to be of great interest, and with which I have been dealing for some weeks in agreement with M. Pichon and Sir Edward Grey."[75] Just as he was concluding the financial arrangements, Bethmann-Hollweg finally wound up the Anglo-German negotiations over the Bagdad-Kuweit line by declaring that, as compensation for the sacrifice demanded by Great Britain, her consent to the tariff increase in Turkey "amounted to nothing."[76] Great Britain had no choice left, reasoned one Whitehall official, but to get "an opposition line" of her own[77]—and then, reasoned another, "We shall be able to bargain on equal terms."[78]

On April 22 Pichon confirmed his approval of the Homs-Bagdad arrangements,[79] whereupon Tardieu went to London to clear them with Paul Cambon and Sir Edward Grey. He left "confident of success";[80] three days later he was back in Paris "hurt and disappointed."[81] As he wrote to Pichon:

[Cambon] does not want a Franco-British affair, but a French one.... He will see you tomorrow.... Your views differ from his, but tomorrow's conversation will be an opportunity for you to win him over.... I shall call on you tomorrow toward 9:15 a.m.[82]

The rest of the week of April 22—the week between the two rounds of the general elections of 1910—he was preoccupied by the arbitration of the N'Goko Sangha indemnity even while Paul Cambon was engaged in disputation with the Quai d'Orsay. Cambon saw the Homs-Bagdad as its own reward for France. Tardieu objected that "the two governments had equally approved the plan of this consortium to use the Homs-Bagdad as a means of solving the problem of the German Bagdad railway," and that the interest of the one as of the other was accordingly to work in concert all the way down the line;[83] to a purely French company, he told Pichon, he would prefer "nothing at all." At Pichon's promptings the disputants eventually settled on a 60–40 division between French and British interests.

Though the venture was saved, the principle was lost, and the compromise led to disappointment on all sides. "The Turks seem never to have seriously considered the [Homs-Bagdad] railroad as a possibility";[84] in their view they could not, as guarantors of the Bagdad railway, afford to license a rival line from Bagdad to the Mediterranean, much less underwrite one. The British in the consortium being the junior partners, their government did not push it very hard. Neither in fact did Ambassador Bompard, lest he compromise his country's credit with the Young Turks—and because he had a project of his own in reserve.[85] Tardieu sent Pichon detailed arguments for Bompard's use; then he wrote and even telephoned directly to Bompard. Bompard was intractable, and Pichon did not force the issue; instead he gave his tacit consent for Yussuff to deal with the Turkish government in his name. "We must rejoice doubly that France has other ways of knowing Turkey than the official ones," wrote Tardieu cryptically in *Le Temps*.[86]

Meanwhile, in view of the failure of the Anglo-German negotiations on the Bagdad-Kuweit line, the Turks came forward with the startling proposal to build it themselves. The British spokesmen in Constantinople found this plan to their liking, and on July 4 the Bagdad Company in turn reported on it favorably to Berlin.[87] That same day in Paris Tardieu went to the German Embassy bearing "the draft for an agreement with Germany suggested by the Anglo-French consortium."[88] Wrote Lancken to Bethmann-Hollweg:

[Tardieu] seems to have had a peculiar fondness for Franco-German collaboration in practical matters ever since he succeeded in getting an agreement underway between the colonial companies of the two countries on the Congo-Cameroons frontier. Already for some time he has been making mysterious insinuations that he is preoccupied with a vast new plan of the sort. Yesterday he told me about his plan at great length.[89]

Tardieu proposed "a sort of compromise between the German Bagdad railway and the French plan for a Homs-Bagdad railway." The German railway would run from Aleppo southeast along the Euphrates instead of along the Tigris; a French branch would link it with Homs by the shortest route, and it would come under joint administration from the point of junction on to Bagdad. The French line from Syria, Tardieu argued, would not be able to compete with the German line from Anatolia for transit from the Mediterranean; on the other hand, because the Euphrates route was shorter than the Tigris route, and because the branch to Homs would promote inland traffic, the arrangement would reduce for Turkey her financial obligations while increasing for her the means with which to meet them. If the arrangement went through, moreover, France and England were to consent to the tariff increase in Turkey, and Bagdad Railway stock was to be admitted for sale on the Paris Bourse.[90] Five years earlier Rouvier had offered Germany the cooperation of France on the Bagdad railway in return for compensation on Morocco; in 1907 Tardieu had proposed renewing the offer,[91] and Caillaux was to renew it after Agadir. Now Tardieu was proposing instead a sort of railway partnership in Mesopotamia, with Germany enabling France to obtain the necessary concession and France enabling Germany to obtain the necessary capital; both partners would profit, but Germany would profit more, hence compensation in Morocco would be for her a moral obligation. Lancken recommended that either the Chancellor or else the Foreign Secretary deal directly with Tardieu:

Even if his plan is not taken as a basis for negotiation M. Tardieu should be allowed to come to Berlin. I do not know whether the prospect of a *rapprochement* between France and Germany fits in with your plans; if it does, here is an excellent opportunity. If M. Tardieu were to find a favorable welcome among us, he would pave the way in France for the realization of our aspirations. To help carry out his plan, which he himself calls very bold, he would have to take the lead in advocating a practical policy of understanding. In my opinion, his motives are not purely idealistic; he wants to satisfy his pride as well, and he sees a very high diplomatic post materializing for himself. That is why, in my opinion, his assurances are quite trustworthy.[92]

Bethmann-Hollweg passed on Lancken's communication to Foreign Secretary von Schoen, who noted on July 8:

There can be no question of a direct understanding between the Imperial German government and M. Tardieu. With M. Tardieu in particular we must stick to our guns in maintaining that the question of the Bagdad railway is one for the relevant financial groups to settle. The Deutsche Bank has already taken up the Tardieu plan, and it intends to drag out the discussions for the time being. The outlook is good for Turkey's soon being in a position to provide the requisite kilometric guarantees, so there is all the less reason for our taking up these proposals just now.

They should be discussed next with the Deutsche Bank and with [the German Ambassador in Constantinople]. The outcome of the discussions will most likely be a friendly, evasive, at the very least dilatory answer for M. Tardieu.[93]

Meanwhile the Turkish Minister of Finance, Djavid Bey, came to Paris to negotiate for a loan to Turkey. Djavid, a Francophile, expected to get the loan on easy terms; while waiting "he daily inquired of Tardieu whether an answer had arrived yet from Germany."[94] Then the Russian government objected to the loan as liable to strengthen the Ottoman Empire, so Pichon set conditions "incompatible with Turkish sovereignty."[95] Djavid went to London. There he found the money market closed to him in solidarity with the Paris Bourse; on the other hand, the foreign office assured him of its willingness to consent to the tariff increase if the Turkish state itself built the rail line from Bagdad to the Gulf. Optimism rose in Berlin, where on July 19 the government formally declined competence to discuss *"den Tardieuchen Plan."*[96] Lancken accordingly

let M. Tardieu know that... to its regret the German government is unable to consider his proposals because it has adopted the policy of not "high-pressuring" the German financial groups concerned.

M. Tardieu was visibly disappointed. Indeed, in his impulsive way he at once replied that [his associates] had forewarned him of the hopelessness of his attempt to come to terms with us in this matter. At the same time he did not conceal his embarrassment at having to admit to them that he had been unable to achieve more than any of the others who had dealt with the same problem in the past—apparently he had boasted far and wide that, with his diplomatic skill, he would succeed in winning us over.

When I pointed out that French capital investment in the present Bagdad railway enterprise was already very high, he replied that only a general and a larger interest in it would prevent France from working to defeat it. He was not the least impressed even by the argument that our agreement with the Porte for construction beyond the junction of the Tigris line with the Euphrates had already rendered his proposal obsolete; he thought that construction was certainly not so far advanced as to make a change in course impossible. He was notably little concerned with discussing objectively the pros and cons of participation by France; instead again and again he made it plain that his main concern was to play a successful part as an intermediary in a world-shaking question and to prove to his French and (as is now obvious) English associates that *he* could do what so far no one else had been able to do—that is, get the Germans to make concessions....

As I, referring to Article Twelve of the Bagdad concession,[97] pointed out that a concession for a Homs-Bagdad railway could be granted only in violation of the contractual rights of the Bagdad Company, he said with a condescending smile that should the attempt to reach an understanding with us fail, authorization would be sought for the construction of a railway from Syria to the Persian Gulf independent of Bagdad and of the Bagdad line, in which case Article Twelve would not be disregarded....

Tardieu was not eager to admit defeat, and his first thought was to arrange to see Herr von Gwinner at the latter's summer residence to discuss the matter further. I did not think it wise to discourage him, though I was clearly aware that his efforts would be futile. What prompted my attitude was mainly the thought that Tardieu, who in his mania for winning his point is occasionally indiscreet, might perhaps give Herr von Gwinner some insight into the economic and political policies of France in the Near East....

A few days after our conversation he called me on the telephone: "someone," he said, had given him to understand that a meeting with Herr von Gwinner did not appear opportune after all. He chose his words quite carefully; there is no doubt, however, that he was alluding not to French financiers but to the French government.[98]

Nonetheless on August 4 Tardieu, by his own report, "strove in the course of a two-hour conversation with M. de Gwinner ... to harmonize the interests of England, France, and Germany in the matter of trans-Asiatic railways."[99] He duly failed: "To a proposal of a private character," he explained, Gwinner "merely replied with a refusal."[100]

If then there was to be an arrangement with Germany, thought Tardieu, the French government would itself have to act, and act in concert with England; but first of all it would have to obtain the Homs-Bagdad concession. The German government did not trust Pichon not to agree with him. "The Deutsche Bank suspects...the French government of using the question of a Turkish loan as a means of pressure in favor of the Tardieu railway project," Gwinner told the new Foreign Secretary of Germany, Kiderlen-Wächter, on September 9,[101] and at once Kiderlen wrote to Ambassador von Marschall in Constantinople:

The acceptance of these projects by the Turks would be incompatible with Article Twelve, Paragraph One of the Bagdad concession agreement and would constitute a manifest violation of the interests of Germany as recognized by contract—and this we cannot allow. Please sound out the government there and, if our suspicions are founded, inform it clearly of our firm expectation that it refuse to act on Tardieu's suggestions.[102]

The Turkish Foreign Minister, Rifaat Pasha, assured the German Ambassador that, as far as the Grand Vizier knew, the Bagdad railway had not been mentioned in the course of the negotiations in Paris. "As I then explained to him," wrote Marschall, "that we were determined not to let our hard-gotten rights under Article Twelve be touched, Rifaat replied that in any case the Porte would reject the French-English plan as inimical to the best interests of the Turkish treasury in consequence of the state guarantees to our Bagdad railway."[103] Meanwhile Marschall was asking Rifaat to obtain from Great Britain a formal commitment to approve the tariff increase if the Bagdad Company surrendered its rights in the Gulf area. The British Ambassador on his side was making the converse request,[104] and Djavid, then in Berlin, told Gwinner that, if the bargain were made, the Bagdad Company might have concessions for branch lines and for a harbor in Alexandretta in addition to the subsidies for the main line as far as Bagdad. Just as the German government was on the point of concluding, Marschall wrote and persuaded it to refuse, a close look at the accounts of the Turkish state having given him reason to expect it soon to be able to afford the requisite "kilometric guarantees" even without the tariff increase.[105]

France was still asking for control over the whole financial system of Turkey as the condition for a loan. "It's pure blackmail!" commented the Kaiser. "The Gauls treat the Turks like a fifth-rate Negro state!"[106] When on October 19 Le Matin reported the French government to have brought its conditions within reason, Tardieu wrote: "The government cannot possibly have contradicted itself so strongly."[107] A week later the president of the Ottoman Debt Commission told Djavid that France was prepared to grant the loan on the sole security of surplus Turkish revenues—but "M. Tardieu was also well informed," wrote Marschall,[108] and indeed Pichon held fast.

In November the German government came to Djavid's rescue by arranging a loan through an Austro-German combine, and negotiations began between the Sublime Porte and the Bagdad Company for a definitive concession. Thereupon the Czar visited the Kaiser in Potsdam, and secretly the two agreed on a juncture of the Bagdad railway with a prospective Russian railway in Persia.[109] For ten years France, out of deference to Russia, had sought to prevent the construction of the Bagdad railway instead of either participating in it or else facilitating it in return for concessions elsewhere, and throughout the past year France and Great Britain had each kept Russia informed of their action in Turkey, promising not to reach a settlement without her consent. Russia, however, suspicious lest her allies come to terms with Germany behind her back, had done so herself at their expense. On January 7, 1911, *Le Temps*, following the *Evening Times* of London, published as "probably authentic" the text of the Potsdam agreement.[110] In Saint Petersburg the Foreign Minister, Sazonov, was barely able to contain his fury;[111] in Berlin Kiderlen-Wächter, blaming Izvolsky for the leak, threw a fit of Russophobia; in Paris Pichon, interpellated in the Chamber, got off without glory. Then Tardieu wrote contrasting Bompard's "negative policy" with Pichon's "constructive policy" on the Turkish railways question. The Potsdam agreement, he argued diplomatically, had not weakened the Entente, but merely shown up its need for a concerted policy in the East. Jaurès quoted him in the Chamber, and Tardieu returned the compliment in *Le Temps*.

In the East the French and British governments went on striving— each for itself, despite Tardieu—to block the concession to the Bagdad Company or else to "force through 'protective' railroad concessions as compensation."[112] Bompard was demanding for France not the Homs-Bagdad line but a line from Homs to Aleppo with an outlet to the Mediterranean[113] plus a monopoly on railway construction in the Black Sea area.[114] Tardieu subjected the Quai d'Orsay to increasingly harsh criticism, charging it on January 29 with ignorance of Russian affairs and on January 31 with letting the alliances of France lie idle. "It is a proof of M. Tardieu's immense authority over French public opinion that his opposition to the Quai d'Orsay, which is founded in part on personal grounds, should meet with so great an echo," wrote Ambassador von Schoen to Berlin on February 2.[115] And when Pichon told the Senate he was unable to account for Tardieu's change of heart, some of the Senators thought of the Homs-Bagdad even as the others thought of the N'Goko Sangha.

On February 6 Tardieu gave a résumé in *Le Temps* of secret proposals made by Bompard in Constantinople, and four days later he published the complete text of a draft railway agreement with Turkey. Thereupon, in a series of articles called "Lettres de Constantinople" in *L'Action Nationale*—a review run by Steeg, the new Minister of the Interior—Tardieu was accused of writing out of personal resentment over Pichon's refusal to back the Homs-Bagdad project and of drawing arguments from the secret correspondence of France, "to which he has access."[116] Then on February 18 the Quai d'Orsay indicted Bernard Maimon, his secretary, and one of its own attachés on the charge of having stolen secret documents from its files; Pichon, more prudent than vindictive, gave an order "himself, in the very office of M. Briand,"[117] for Tardieu not to be interrogated. *Le Temps* had just time enough to cease its attacks on the government before Briand, having lost a few votes on religious policy, seized on the loss as a pretext to resign.

"The first question of foreign policy to arise in the deliberations of the Monis cabinet, which succeeded the Briand cabinet, was the question of the N'Goko Sangha," wrote Joseph Caillaux, the new Minister of Finance.[118] Whereas the new Foreign Minister, Cruppi, had no reason to be partial to the N'Goko Sangha, his colleagues Berteaux, Caillaux, and Messimy, all formerly of the Budget Commission, had good reason not to be partial to it. The consortium was rejected a first time early in March.[119] A few days afterwards, however, the ministers concerned, having been advised by a Quai d'Orsay official that Germany "attached great importance to the consortium," invited the testimony of Jules Cambon, then in Paris. "I don't think the consortium is of any great importance," said Cambon. "There are private interests at stake in it, but they are only private interests"—and, he added, the German government was indifferent to it. Had France been committed officially anywhere along the line? "I was kept out of the negotiations; they were conducted by businessmen, by unofficial agents." The Council of Ministers agreed unanimously to drop the consortium.[120]

On March 23 the Budget Commission released its report on the N'Goko Sangha indemnity. The Commission concluded against the principle of the indemnity, of course; it denied the validity of the arbitral verdict of April 29 and was only faintly embarrassed by the letter of February 5, 1910; finally, it made a big point of condemning the interference of high finance and of the press in the councils of government. That same week the Minister of Colonies, Messimy, told the Commission there would be no indemnity and no consortium, and in the Chamber on April 4 Caillaux corroborated Messimy's statement. The Council of Ministers, said Caillaux, had decided against authorizing "a new concession," and consequently "the government cannot conceive that any payment should be made to the company." Indeed, parliament had long since voted to discontinue the system of concessions in the colonies; by the ingenious device of treating the N'Goko Sangha consortium as a "new concession," which after all it was, Caillaux had rendered the letter of February 5, 1910, invalid. To make doubly sure that everyone had understood him he had himself interrogated the next day, whereupon he reiterated the decision of the Council of Ministers: no consortium, no indemnity. Justice had triumphed—but so had Mestayer, and somewhere in Paris a man named Vatel-Dehaynin was left holding a great big bag.

Meanwhile, in Constantinople on March 21 the definitive concession agreement for the Bagdad railway was signed. Great Britain and France, unable to prevent the agreement, were equally unable to obtain "protective" concessions. Germany, however, not caring or not daring after all to defy Great Britain, surrendered her railway rights south of Bagdad, retaining only an option on a half interest in any future Gulf railway; Turkey, thankful, wrote into the new concession, besides the main line from Bulgurli to Bagdad, a branch line to Alexandretta and a harbor at the terminus. In Berlin Kiderlen-Wächter hailed the conclusion of the new agreement as a *"grossartigen Triumph"* of German initiative over the enemies of Germany, who, he said, had sought to prevent her from reaching Bagdad.[121] The British, who had sought only to prevent her from reaching beyond Bagdad, were on the whole content. Not so the French: as Bompard observed, Germany had turned away from the British sphere of influence only to encroach upon the French sphere.[122]

Spheres of influence in Turkey were not official entities, of course, and so far Germany had refused to recognize them even tacitly—ostensibly out of deference to Turkey, in fact because she saw her own sphere as somewhat greater than those of either France or England. In April, 1911, however, Gwinner, recognizing the detriment to French interests of the new Bagdad convention, proposed to Tardieu's and to other French financial groups

a *formule d'arrangement*.... Instead of affiliation, zones of influence; each side to itself, the sphere of each being defined by mutual agreement, the Germans having their own railway system and the French theirs. Negotiations were conducted on this basis in Paris and in Berlin until mid-May, and already by mid-April the main lines of the division were settled.... The only thing left to do was to conclude the agreement. Such was the purpose of a meeting held in Frankfurt on May 15 and 16, 1911—that is, right in the midst of the Moroccan crisis, a month after the march on Fez and a few weeks before Agadir. This meeting, which the interested parties expected to be a mere formality, turned out to be something quite different. M. de Gwinner, after beating around the bush for some time, wound up telling his audience that he was not, under the circumstances, "authorized to negotiate."

Germany, Tardieu realized, was resuming "her full liberty of maneuver."[123]

On March 30 Bernard Maimon was arrested. Scotland Yard, giving information on him, described him as "far from an amateur" in the theft of state documents.[124] Shortly afterwards in Constantinople Yussuff Said Bey was arrested, also for theft of state documents. Maimon pleaded guilty, stating his motive as "journalism," and on June 3, 1911, he, his secretary, and his accomplice from the Quai d'Orsay were sentenced each to two years in prison.[125] *Le Temps* reported the case sparingly, and for some weeks Tardieu's name appeared nowhere in connection with it. Beginning late in April, however, *Le Rappel*, a newspaper close to the new government, published his correspondence with Maimon and Barry,[126] and two other newspapers reprinted it afterwards.[127] Drawing on the same data, one French review identified him as the evil genius of the Quai d'Orsay,[128] and the London *Daily News* explained in serial form "why wars are fought." References to his role in the N'Goko Sangha affair were still on the level of innuendos—his predecessor on *Le Temps*, Francis de Pressensé, wrote characteristically: "We have seen a professional patriot, one of the high priests of the cult of *revanche*, attempt blackmail for the benefit of Germany in order to grab a few millions from the Treasury of France."[129]

Only ignorance kept his detractors from attacking him for his responsibility in negotiating the treaty of 1909. This treaty, hailed by both parties at its inception, had been left by both thereafter to die of inanition. France had systematically refused, in spite of the interpretative letters, to permit joint enterprises in Morocco with Germans on the staff, while Germany had sought a monopoly of public works with France even though the Sultan was bound by the Algeciras Act to grant all concessions for public works by adjudication. Moreover in April, 1911, France sent troops to occupy Fez without the formal consent of Germany, thereby in effect repudiating the Algeciras Act. The "spirit of mutual confidence" was in hiding, and France was hard put to it to find a new mode of payment for Morocco.

Tardieu for his part saw the urgency of finding one rather more clearly than did Cruppi; he did not, however, think it quite so great as did the German government, which at the end of July, just as Caillaux took power, sent a battleship to Agadir. "What demon pushed you?" Tardieu asked Lancken confidentially on the morrow; and Lancken replied: "The fear that M. Caillaux's government would decline responsibility for the Fez expedition...and refuse to give us the compensation that is our just due." "But what was your big hurry?" asked Tardieu. "Why a show of unfriendliness before even talking to M. Caillaux?" And Lancken retorted: "What could we expect from the man who thwarted us in the N'Goko Sangha deal and so strongly opposed the Congo-Cameroons railway?"[130]

In truth no man had been more instrumental than Joseph Caillaux in preventing the application of the 1909 treaty to central Africa. By the logic of grudges Tardieu had cause to combat him; he had cause to combat him on principle as well, for Caillaux inclined to favor peace on fair terms and Tardieu by then to favor *revanche* on due provocation. Yet though Agadir was just such a provocation Tardieu held his fire; and a few days after Agadir he hailed Caillaux's decision to negotiate. Both Tardieu and Caillaux recognized that the occupation of Fez had given Germany the better legal case in Morocco. Besides, on the morrow of Agadir Caillaux, knowing that he would need whatever support he could get, had moved to dismiss Tardieu from the Ministry of the Interior for having pleaded a suit against the state in a court of arbitration; Adrien Hébrard had interceded, and after a decent interval Caillaux had agreed in the same breath both to drop the charges against Tardieu and to accept his "faithful support."[131]

As Caillaux strove to negotiate a solution in Morocco, then, Tardieu stood by him; at the end of July he even sought to resign his readers to the possible abandonment by France of the whole northern Congo. Early in August *L'Humanité* accused Caillaux of treating with Germany through members of the N'Goko Sangha gang, including the notorious Tardieu; Caillaux discreetly reassured the editors, and the attack ceased. As long as his pact with Caillaux lasted, Tardieu enjoyed immunity from attack on the left—in France; and when in England the humanitarian Edmund Dene Morel wrote to the *Daily News* denouncing the British foreign office for its friendly commerce with the blind *revanchiste* Tardieu in 1910,[132] Tardieu wrote in reply: "I have never acted in an anti-German spirit—quite the contrary."[133] Tardieu lent Caillaux his support against both the demands of Germany[134] and the duplicity of the French Foreign Minister; day after day he bore out the Premier in his newspaper, while privately—wrote Caillaux—"he ceaselessly gave me his excellent cooperation";[135] finally, he backed the treaty of November 4, 1911, wholeheartedly. After Caillaux fell from power Tardieu defended him in retrospect, arguing that, as Premier, Caillaux had had not only the right but also the duty to inform himself by any means of Germany's intentions;[136] then, to vindicate the policies of the former Premier, *Le Temps* began publication of "a sort of yellow book" on Franco-German relations between 1909 and 1911.

With Caillaux out of power, the left broke loose against Tardieu. On March 8, 1912, Jaurès told the Chamber in broken sentences and accents of indignation:

Ah! gentlemen, it is a serious matter if a man having at his disposal day by day as a mouthpiece in the international realm a newspaper that has held the greatest sway in chancelleries for the longest time, it is a serious matter if this man, whose displeasure ministers all too often dread, it is a sad thing that he should have been able—for reasons, for pretexts of national interest—to attempt to put over business deals in which he and his friends were personally involved.

And what turmoil in our diplomacy, what confusion, what wavering, what discredit for our diplomacy abroad when the rest of the world has observed that it is in deals of this sort that official diplomacy darkly winds up....

I do not mean to call into question on this point [on Maimon's theft]—for I do not want to go beyond proven fact—the personal responsibility of Tardieu. M. Maimon was in this affair the correspondent, the partner, the negotiator of M. Tardieu, and it is for him [Tardieu?] that the agent Rouet stole documents from the Quai d'Orsay, which were then commented on in the newspaper *Le Temps*.[137]

Briand entered the debate to hint that the Budget Commission in defeating the N'Goko Sangha consortium had destroyed the 1909 treaty. On March 15 the *rapporteur* of the Commission, Maurice Viollette, replied by denying that the two matters were related; and he added:

I, too, welcome the idea of a greater France, but [shall we] entrust the flag of France to scheming speculators concerned only with the profits of operations that they dare not confess to out loud? Whatever the risks or the dangers I reply: never![138]

The same month appeared a volume by a Socialist, Charles Paix-Séailles, under the tell-tale title *La Diplomatie secrète sous la troisième République, Homs-Bagdad: du Quai d'Orsay à la correctionnelle*. It gave Tardieu's motives in the Homs-Bagdad affair as venality and spite: out of venality he had, by fair means or foul, induced Pichon to make the Homs-Bagdad concession the condition for a loan to Turkey, thereby forcing Turkey into the arms of the Triple Alliance, and out of spite he had worked to ruin his country's chances of reaching an agreement with Turkey thereafter, going so far in this as to arrange for the theft of state documents. "Justice goes on ignoring the obvious complicity of M. Tardieu [in the theft]," Paix-Séailles concluded.[139]

Almost simultaneously Tardieu published *Le Mystère d'Agadir*, which he wrote in the single month of February, 1912, on the basis of his articles for *Le Temps*.[140] In it he told the story of the Agadir crisis from its origins in the failure of the treaty of February 9, 1909, to its resolution by the treaty of November 4, 1911. Obliquely and incidentally he also replied to the critics of his foreign policy by representing the Homs-Bagdad as a gambit for a general settlement in Turkey, which it was, and the Congo venture as an application of the treaty of 1909, which it may not have been. The French government for its part had certainly treated the Congo venture as such; the German government had not certainly done so, though, and therein lay the weakness of his position. In making his point on the Congo, however, or any point in his book, he did not use the facts sparingly or selectively. His critics who called him superficial gave themselves away as not having read him. No observer ever saw deeper into a diplomatic imbroglio; no sleuth ever solved a mystery more perfectly—for a solution, to be perfect, need not be correct. As an object lesson in use of method his book is a masterpiece: he examines his subject minutely in all its parts without ever losing track of the whole, and he reviews the same events again and again without ever repeating himself. History abounds with more interesting facts; few historians have ever made facts as interesting as did Tardieu.

Even if Germany did not recognize the 1909 treaty as applicable outside Morocco, Tardieu was less likely venal than simply wrong. Or perhaps he was willing to gamble on the gratitude of Germany at the cost to France of a small asset in the Congo long neglected. He was, wrote Lancken, "[seeking] to play the leading role in a policy of practical cooperation between France and Germany"—to break the deadlock over Morocco by opposing the reciprocal benefits of businessmen to the mutual distrust of governments. Ambitious for himself, he was no less ambitious for France; intent on long-range objectives, he was heedless of precautions and formalities. The Germans did not want *Morocco*, he reasoned—they wanted new *markets*; give them the markets elsewhere and they will leave Morocco to France. The wishes of Semler or of Gwinner, he was sure, were binding on the German foreign office: in the Reich of William II, as he saw it, the reigning plutocrats made policy, and the governing officials merely defined it. In France, though, his enterprise required, besides the cooperation of businessmen, the compliancy of the government; alone, he could carry it just so far and no farther. The businessmen were cooperative enough; the government, though, was only compliant enough to arouse suspicions, not to effect solutions. In the spring of 1910 his hopes were high and his illusions rife; neither lasted. By the summer of 1910, the Homs-Bagdad was bankrupt, and the N'Goko Sangha consortium, no longer a pawn in a grand design, was only a front for a petty scheme. He, however, as Lancken put it, "was not eager to admit defeat," and so he went on defending ingeniously what he could no longer defend in any other way.

Replies to *Le Mystère d'Agadir* were not wanting: Maurice Viollette, for instance, in a petty argumentative tract, *La N'Goko-Sangha*, made out the Congo consortium to have been all hoax and fraud, and Tardieu no more than its paid apologist. Tardieu was its paid lawyer, of course, but he was its apologist at his own expense. Had his services as apologist been for sale, there were easier ways for him, the foreign editor of *Le Temps*, to earn 30,000 francs. The conclusion was that he *had* found other ways as well; it drew support not from demonstration but from insinuation. To the left in France big business means bad business, and the stigma of *affairisme* clung to Tardieu's name on the left thereafter: twenty-five years later good Socialists still had only to hear the name of Tardieu spoken to reply "N'Goko Sangha" or "Homs-Bagdad," whether or not they knew what those exotic curses meant.

CHAPTER 19

The Seventh Power

HIS OWN POLICY of "cooperation" between France and Germany having failed, Tardieu had given his support to Caillaux's policy of "liquidation" or settling of joint accounts. Liquidation, however, was not a solution in itself. Even when it succeeded, as it had in Morocco, it left a residue of bitterness on both sides. And it was not appropriate to some sources of enmity: as Tardieu told a gathering of alumni of the Ecole des Sciences Politiques in May, 1913: "The generations born since the war still bear the weight of that war, and in everything we do, in everything we undertake, we sense our defeat hovering over us."[1] Increasingly after February, 1912, Tardieu came to regard a new war as the inevitable issue of the rivalry between France and Germany; and believing it inevitable, writing of it as inevitable, he did his share in making it inevitable. He gave his support to Poincaré and the policy of passive provocation, returning by the same token to the good graces of the Quai d'Orsay—"His articles reflect the opinions of Poincaré," wrote Izvolsky on May 23, 1912.[2] With subsidies from Izvolsky, as well as from the Greek, Serbian, and Rumanian governments, he and a few other newspapermen set up the Agence des Balkans for the purpose of pooling information on the Balkans—or, according to another version, "for the purpose of 'fabricating' French public opinion on all Balkan questions" and of preparing "the 'items' of Le Temps that reportedly emanated from special correspondents in Berlin, in Vienna, in Saint Petersburg, in Sofia, in Belgrade, in Bucarest."[3] Boasted Izvolsky, "puffing out his chest, 'The *famous Tardieu*...was eager to put his pen at my disposal.'"[4] In the fall of 1912 Le Temps led a campaign against Austria; the German Embassy in Vienna reported the French Embassy officials to be "unhappy" about it—"They hold the influence of Serbian money on Herr Tardieu responsible for it."[5] Tardieu got for Le Temps the lion's share of the 300,000 francs[6] disbursed by Izvolsky, with Briand's and Poincaré's encouragement, for the campaign in favor of the three-years law;[7] he was, with the Royalist Albert de Mun, the "real leader" of the campaign, wrote its historian.[8] The choice at issue, wrote Tardieu on March 2, 1913, was one "between the convenience of our politicians and the security of our country." He denounced Jaurès, with Caillaux the "real leader" of the campaign *against* the law, as "working against France for the benefit of his party,"[9] and again, in an article "La Campagne contre la patrie" in the *Revue des Deux Mondes* of July, 1913, he described Jaurès as "Minister of the Word"—the Socialists never forgave him so apt an epithet. Also in 1913 he was made *officier* in the Legion of Honor and Inspector General of the Ministry of the Interior.

In the winter of 1913–14 he took a trip through central Europe. In February he had occasion to converse at length with the King of Rumania, Charles I. "I told the King," Tardieu recalled,

that war seemed to me to be near at hand, that it would be general, that it would be long, and that therefore Germany would probably lose it.

The old Hohenzollern grew pale. His fingers seemed to be digging into the wood of the table. And he answered me, "No, sir! Germany cannot be beaten!"[10]

"Tardieu," said Adrien Hébrard one day, as the spring elections of 1914 drew near, "you are not going to do me the offense of letting me die before I have seen you a deputy."[11] Tardieu ran for deputy in the district of Versailles, where he took up residence for the occasion; he ran as a nominee of the Fédération des Gauches, a contrivance of Briand and Barthou to rally part of the left to the three-years law. His chief adversary was a Radical, Emile Laurent; his most vociferous adversary was an anarchist, Duret, an elementary-school teacher by profession, who, Tardieu recalled, "at every meeting, after having roundly insulted 'the renegade Briand, the man with the dirty shirt,' would add, 'And before you, citizen Tardieu, I plant the flag in a dunghill!'"[12] The campaign reached a climax on April 21 as a squadron of Duret's devotees stormed the Café Bilbot, where Tardieu was debating with his opponents; a moment later Tardieu found himself out in the street, bleeding and perspiring, his jaw battered, his clothing tattered, and his monocle still lodged intact in his right eye. He won the election on the first ballot, on April 26, and shortly thereafter Adrien Hébrard died in peace at the age of eighty.

In the years before 1914 André Tardieu was as prodigal with his talent as his talent was great. In the fall of 1909 he took up a professorship in diplomatic history at the Ecole des Sciences Politiques—thereby coming into competition with his uncle, Jacques Tardieu, who gave his course at the same hour.[13] A year and a half later he became professor of diplomatic history at the Ecole de Guerre as well,[14] and consequently a colleague of his friend Colonel Foch. Any one of his positions—with the Ministry of the Interior, with *Le Temps*, as professor—was a career in itself. He was, besides, a ready guest lecturer, often addressing gatherings of diplomats, historians, and students on such topics as the Monroe Doctrine or the history of Egypt. Meanwhile he wrote, voluminously. To write was the regulative function of his mind. He put out an average of a volume a year on current affairs, including a critical study of Prince von Bülow in 1909.[15] He was, besides, the foreign editor of *Le Petit Parisien* and a daily columnist for *La Patrie* of Bordeaux. He contributed regularly to many other newspapers, domestic and foreign,[16] and to just as many periodicals.[17]

More extraordinary than his productivity as a writer was his influence as a writer. On matters of fact his word was authoritative: he knew not only all the dossiers at the Quai d'Orsay but nearly all the statesmen of Europe as well—Asquith whispered confidences to him,[18] and Bülow called him "my friend Tardieu."[19] And on matters of policy no power in Europe was strong enough to ignore him. Said Bülow, "There are the six Great Powers, and then there is André Tardieu."[20] "He wielded more power than a foreign minister," wrote André Siegfried.[21] Gustav Stresemann called him "the cantankerous nursemaid of Europe,"[22] and Maurice Paléologue noted in his diary one day: "*Le Temps*, through André Tardieu's pen, has earned for itself a kind of professorial grand mastership and diplomatic priesthood."[23] His persuasiveness was the bane of his enemies, and the ambassadors of Germany wrote home about it repeatedly—about, for instance, the French Ambassador in Tangier who, "because Tardieu had told him so," would believe nothing else but that Germany would not fight for Morocco.[24] The correspondent of *Le Temps* in Rome wrote a sonnet beginning

Tardieu, terror of the courts and chancelleries...[25]

The treasurer of *Le Temps* knew him to have received "a cigarette-holder in solid gold from Czar Ferdinand of Bulgaria; sumptuous gifts from Gordon Bennett, proprietor of the New York *Herald*, with whom he often went yachting; a monumental inkwell from a Lebanese committee to thank him for a successful campaign."[26] The golden cigarette-holder was for him, along with his lorgnette, a sort of trade-mark; sometimes, though, according to the light of day, the lorgnette would make way for a monocle, whereas the cigarette-holder was a constant fixture of his face, becoming in time an integral part of his profile.

All of his contemporaries knew how great his influence was; few knew how extensive it was. If he had wholesome pride in his work, he had also that supreme vanity, *"le goût de l'anonymat"*:[27] only André Tardieu was capable of writing six hundred pages on "the mystery of Agadir" without once mentioning André Tardieu. In journalism, however, his style was his signature, unmistakable for its terseness, for its clarity, and for its vigor: whenever he was absent from *Le Temps* on a tour of inspection for his ministry, all Europe knew it at a glance.

On a typical day in Paris[28] Tardieu would rise at seven, stroll down from the Avenue de Messine to the Place Beauveau in the company of his pair of dachshunds, call an hour or so later at the Quai d'Orsay—if the Minister was out, the director would rush to receive him—and arrive at *Le Temps* at about 11:30 to "get his article out." He wrote in a large, steady hand, rapidly and without halt, rarely erasing or rewriting. He knew nothing of hesitation or doubt, or of the agony of seeking the *mot juste*. He never read over his own copy—rather than improve one page (or one book) he would write another.

Yet not all of life was work for even Tardieu—far from it. He was a discriminating *bon vivant*; luckily in this "he had, if not a great fortune, a comfortable income, which came to him from his family."[29] His "admirable appetite"[30] was well-known to the restaurateurs of the rue Royale. As a matter of routine he would dine twice of an evening, then carouse half the night with Hébrard. He was also a devotee of the Opéra and a habitué of the aristocratic salons.[31] He would travel on any pretext—"I was in Germany every year before the war," he later told the Chamber. His companions of his own age were all men and all noblemen, so rumor of course made him out a homosexual and a snob. He was a composer of satirical ditties, a first-rate caricaturist, and an indefatigable practical joker[32]—in short, a highly sociable misanthropist. Being prankish, though, was as close as he ever came to being childish.

He had a superb contempt for political office. Often the men who held office held it by his sufferance only; besides, his post was permanent, and from it, with the majesty of a monarch, he would watch them come and go. The real force in a democracy, he thought, was not the men in power but public opinion—and he knew first-hand how that force was generated, how it was distributed, how its expenses were paid. He had no favorite party: parties in France were defined by their stand on home policy, and for him foreign policy was the overriding consideration. However, as the campaign against the three-years law began to approximate a campaign of the left against the right, he took his stand on the right—as far to the left as possible.

Diverse influences combined to produce in Tardieu's thought, rationalistic as it was on the whole, a strain of irrationalism. His favorite author was Bergson, who held instinct and not reason to be the proper faculty of man. All his admiration went to Theodore Roosevelt, from whom he learned that the goal of human life was victory—victory itself, and not the fruits of victory, which were too costly: life is a dangerous game, Roosevelt seemed to be saying, and the condition for playing it properly is to write off the losses in advance. Tardieu also—and even though he was the declared enemy of scientific materialism in any of its forms—came under the influence of Darwinism, an influence almost universal at the time. According to the teaching of Darwin, the economy of nature cannot accommodate all the varieties of animal life in their tendency to multiply; hence some varieties die out, and the obverse of this fact is the principle of "natural selection"—or as he later wrote, in a nefarious tautology, "the survival of the fittest." Materialists at the turn of the century saw in the struggle for survival the source of all progress, human as well as animal. They saw in war a supreme instance of the human struggle for survival, whether the war was fought among men, among classes, or among nations, and even though in war among classes or among nations the fittest men, being the first to fight, are also the first to die. And they glorified struggle for its own sake, even when survival did not depend on it, thereby making the two terms contradictory. Whereas Tardieu knew in his mind that peace was beneficent and that it could be safeguarded by diplomacy, he felt in his heart that the secular conflict among nations was a law of nature, and that if peace was a great good, admirable were the men who did not hesitate to set it aside.

CHAPTER 20

"La Plus Belle Époque"

"The battlefield is a school."   ANDRÉ TARDIEU*

HIS FIRST WEEK in parliament Tardieu broke the golden rule of the *république des camarades* by refusing to meet Jaurès. "You are wrong, *mon petit*," Albert de Mun told him. "You are a deputy: you must adopt the manners of one."[1]

He had not time enough to learn. Almost at once the new Chamber recessed, and in the first days of August, 1914, war came. It did not take him unawares: as early as June 15 he had written in *Le Temps*: "Clearly France, in order to maintain her alliances, must meet certain obligations of a military nature."[2] On August 2, the day after general mobilization was decreed, he enlisted. Because of his rank in the civil service he was commissioned a lieutenant; because of his accident in training, however, he was classified for limited service, and his first assignment was to censor cables at the war office. He requested a livelier job, and on August 5 found himself an interpreter at General Headquarters in Vitry. He got little interpreting to do, but much paperwork: his hands were kept busy while his mind was left idle, so by the end of August he had read a whole library of books on military science in his spare time. Unofficially he was liaison agent between the government and Joffre, the Commander-in-Chief: on August 22 he bore Joffre "a letter from Premier Viviani, who complained—though discreetly—of not being kept well enough informed,"[3] and four days later he took from Poincaré to Joffre the news of the cabinet shake-up.[4] Meanwhile, with the French armies suffering reverses, he was eager to "do some fighting," and his eagerness only grew when he learned how in the great defeat at Charleroi on August 23 Second Lieutenant Duret, the fiery nonpatriot of the April elections, had died bravely in action—"I think of him with the affection of a comrade-in-arms," wrote Tardieu years afterwards.[5]

On August 28 General Foch came to Vitry to get his orders—which were to command a retreat of the center as far as Châlons. Tardieu lay in wait for him outside Joffre's office, caught him leaving, and pleaded to

* *Le Prince de Bülow* (Paris, Calmann-Lévy, 1909), pp. 4-5.

leave with him. "All right," Foch agreed, "I'll work it out at dinner."[6] That evening Joffre summoned Tardieu. "So you want to ditch us and go sightseeing with Foch? Go right ahead!"[7]

Foch left at noon the next day to join his divisions in the Ardennes, taking with him what he described as "the beginnings of a staff"[8]— Lieutenant Colonels Weygand and Devaux plus one major, one sergeant, one orderly, and "Lieutenant-interpreter" Tardieu. The party drove as a convoy along the rear of the battle lines. The first night they slept in an abandoned church at Attigny, and at dawn they rose to survey the battlefield from the roof of the town hall. They saw horses obstructing the retreat, whereupon they spent some hours themselves clearing the roads; then, when the enemy was within half a mile, they drove on as far as Machault. The retreat was everywhere disorderly, but the line was holding; Foch told Tardieu: "Probably all we will lose is the immense advantage of winning the war alone."[9]

By September 1 Foch had established contact with his divisions, and the next four days, after having followed the retreat, he led it. Tardieu was assigned to inspect small units, and once he accompanied Foch on a general inspection. Foch, finding troop morale abysmally low, sent Tardieu on September 2 to warn Joffre against attempting a counter-offensive for the time being.[10] On guard duty that same night Tardieu learned of an enemy advance; rather than awaken Foch he gave the order himself to move headquarters, and was duly reprimanded in the morning. Then, with the retreat growing more chaotic by the minute, Foch sent him on a round of the battlegrounds to encourage the generals to hold on.

On September 4 the "center" became the Ninth Army, and that night it moved its headquarters to Fère-Champenoise. The following morning the Fourth Army was reported in danger of being cut off on the right, and Foch sent Tardieu to General de Langle de Cary with an order to fill in the gap. De Langle was known only to be "somewhere to the southeast,"[11] and Tardieu—kneeling in the rear of his car, armed with a carbine—had his chauffeur drive backwards all along the battle front, through columns of artillery retreating southward. Their car was fired on often, once at close range. Thirty miles from Fère-Champenoise they found De Langle; by the time they got back, Foch had moved on to Plancy. In six days the armies had retreated eighty miles.

The next morning, September 6, the counteroffensive began. It began slowly, for the roads were encumbered with refugees, and hardly had it begun when the Eleventh Corps was ready to retreat again. Foch sent Tardieu to summon the corps commander, General Eydoux, to stand his ground at all costs. Eydoux, on taking the order, told Tardieu how German soldiers in French uniforms had entered his trenches and killed thousands of his men. Everywhere bombardment was breaking the resistance of the troops, and the generals were all skeptical of their chances. Still Foch maintained his orders for an attack. By nightfall the situation had improved on the whole; at Gourgançon, however, Eydoux had fallen back again. Tardieu reported this to Foch, who at once "leaped to a table, tore a page out of his notebook, and wrote, 'General offensive, come what may!'"[12] Tardieu next found Eydoux "seated with his officers, among his dead, on the edge of a burial ditch,"[13] liaison agents accosting him from all sides with pleas for permission to retreat. Eydoux accepted Foch's order in quiet despair. When Tardieu reported again to Foch, Foch sent him back again to Eydoux with the message: "Stick closer to my order than ever. Offensive! Offensive! Offensive!"[14] This time Tardieu found Eydoux jubilant: his troops had broken through. Foch took the news matter-of-factly. "You see?" he said. "Now let's get some supper."[15]

The Germans retreated in haste, leaving even their own dead and wounded lying about untended. In Fère-Champenoise they plundered whatever they did not destroy, and they left the town hall littered with garbage, with the carcasses of horses, and with human bodies. Many prisoners were taken, especially in the wine cellars; they all pleaded not to be shot. Foch, eager to push on, sent Tardieu ahead to set up headquarters at Châlons. There on the main square Tardieu was met by swarms of German soldiers throwing down their arms—they thought the war was over. His first idea for a headquarters building was the town hall; the Germans had left it full of their sick and wounded, though, so he chose the police station instead. There he had dinner that evening with Foch, who afterwards had him receive Léon Bourgeois—"a charming and good-hearted man," he wrote,

but who told me so many stories about Bordeaux [where parliament was meeting], its ministers, and its whores, had so much to say about the displeasure of M. Letellier, director of *Le Journal*, over a certain dinner given for the government by M. Buneau-Varilla, director of *Le Matin*, and asked me with such puerile insistence for a battalion to protect his electors at Fère-Champenoise, that I abandoned him in the waitingroom on the pretext of having some phone calls to make.[16]

On September 12 Major Noulin, Tardieu, and one other interpreter became the "second bureau" of the Ninth Army, in charge of counter-espionage. Tardieu was put to tracing the retreat of the German armies; he traced it by requisitioning the coupons and currency they left behind.

They were retreating from left to right, he found, and in great disorder. After a few days they stopped retreating, though, and dug trenches, leaving him with nothing to do but hunt for spies.

Five times meanwhile he served Foch as liaison with General Headquarters in Vitry—"Foch knew that I had friends there and could talk openly with the Commander-in-Chief." The first time, on September 18, Joffre said to him: "Tell Foch that we won't have to fight on the Aisne, that the next battle will be on the Meuse."[17] The second time, four days later, Joffre said: "The public can't seem to make head or tail of our communiqués. Lieutenant Tardieu, I give you my desk. Resume your profession! Draw up, in one hundred fifty lines, an intelligible account of our victory."[18] In two hours the communiqué was ready, and a few days later it appeared in *Le Temps* under the title "La Bataille de la Marne." On his first two visits Tardieu heard only optimistic small talk, but on September 21 Joffre asked him to tell Foch to return one army corps. "The battle is shifting position," Tardieu reflected:[19] in fact what he was to call "the race to the sea" had already begun. Five days later he went again to Vitry, this time for artillery munitions; he got none. Finally on September 30 he went to ask for more cannon; he was met by Joffre's chief aide, General Gamelin, who asked him in confidence what he thought of the prospective appointment of Foch as second-in-command. Foch was not a man to be stuck at a desk, Tardieu replied, whereupon Gamelin urged him to try and get Foch to accept the command of the armies in the north instead. In this Tardieu succeeded effortlessly—and he got his cannon, too.

Foch's new appointment came through on October 4. Weygand broke the news at dinner, and at 10:00 p.m. the headquarters staff left Châlons in a caravan of four full cars, two empty cars, and two ammunition wagons. They were en route nearly two weeks. At Doullens Tardieu fell out temporarily to restore communications between the Second Army and General Headquarters; for thirty-six hours without a break he coded and decoded messages. By the time they reached Flanders, Antwerp had fallen, and the battle of the Yser was pending.

His first days in Flanders Tardieu assisted Foch with communiqués and served him as liaison with Allied commanders. Once at lunch he met Lloyd George and Sir John Simon; both struck him as unintelligent. Another time he went to Paris to speed up the shipment of maps; he stayed only five hours—"The capital was magnificently calm, but I was assailed with anecdotes about Bordeaux."[20] At dawn on October 24 he accompanied Foch to Cassel, where the battle was starting. That afternoon Foch sent him on to Furnes, the capital of Free Belgium, to take charge of liaison with Belgian troops, and the same evening he stood attention at a review by the side of Albert I. Furnes was flooded, and he spent three days deflecting the flow of water to cut off the enemy. Then on October 28 he went with Foch to Ypres. There they found the battle raging, and the next day Foch put him in charge of moving reserve troops to the front: he borrowed a truck convoy from a British general, and in two hours the job was done. The next day he spent touring the battlefields with Foch; then at midnight Foch got him out of bed for a visit to General French, the British commander, and the three had a few hours of genial conversation. On November 1 Foch took him to a meeting at Dunkirk with Lord Kitchener, the British Secretary of War, which Poincaré, Millerand, Ribot, and Jules Cambon later joined. The soldiers found the politicians insufferable—especially Poincaré, who persistently asked them to set a date for victory. Within an hour the group reached agreement on an order of the day to hold the line at any price, as Foch had intended doing anyhow.

The price was high; the line was held, though, and by the middle of November the battle was won. The first days of November Tardieu had the job of inspecting the towns on the battlefront. Then Philippe Berthelot came from Paris with two attachés, and on November 4 Tardieu took them on a tour of the area; they were all nearly killed. That evening Berthelot made his mission known: Joffre had sent him to fetch Tardieu, who was to have charge of organizing the information services at General Headquarters, now at Romilly. Tardieu left with Berthelot the next morning, and no man ever left a battlefront less willingly.

They reached Romilly on the morning of November 6, and there Tardieu's orders from Joffre were waiting for him. He was to work

for something perhaps impossible: to make the war intelligible to the people here and abroad. If, as now seems likely, the war should drag on, the people will need to understand it all the more tomorrow than they do today.

I put you in charge of creating a service contrary to all the usual practices of the general staff in time of war, and I warn you of opposition to come. I ask you to work with (1) newspapermen, who will pass first through the war office and then through your immediate authority...; (2) our military attachés and diplomatic personnel, who, knowing nothing, no doubt speak a lot of nonsense; (3) our soldiers and their chiefs, who have neither leisure nor means to obtain general information.[21]

Joffre had him to lunch, took him off the limited-service lists, made him a captain, had him to dinner, then sent him to Paris for two weeks to make his arrangements.

He went with Berthelot, and together the two saw Premier Viviani, then visited the war office. A few more calls and Tardieu, nostalgic, sneaked off to Cassel to be with Foch again—"I was deeply fond of that man," he wrote.[22] He returned on November 20, in a few hours worked out with Berthelot his final plans, then went on to Romilly, where the next morning he "set up shop with two secretaries in an office one flight up."[23]

The next few months Tardieu spent nearly all his time reading and writing. He edited the daily bulletins and the official reports on military operations. He wrote some pamphlets for the press and others for the army and the foreign service.[24] Together with General Gamelin he drew up plans for a permanent line of defensive fortifications along the eastern frontier—the future Maginot Line. And some years later a Headquarters official

found among the documents of the Information Section a plan for an armistice written by him about May, 1915, which greatly resembles the one subsequently drawn up by Marshal Foch. In it is to be found the clause providing for the occupation of the Rhine and the bridgeheads on the right bank.[25]

He was permitted a few trips to the front—"too few," he wrote.[26] Several times he risked his life; he was cited in army orders, and he won the *Croix de guerre* for bravery. Once he accompanied Joffre on a visit to Thann in Alsace, and in January he got to see Foch again for two days— "Tardieu, the clever inspirer of the Headquarters press, is sent to Foch to prepare, they say, for him to replace Joffre," wrote resentfully and erroneously the great general Galliéni.[27]

Tardieu took his meals with Joffre and the generals.[28] All Headquarters respected him: to Galliéni he was "the master journalist,"[29] to Gamelin his was "the most perfect intelligence I have ever known."[30] As was usual in his case, his official job description did not suffice to describe his job: according to Gamelin he was "a sort of civilian first secretary to Joffre,"[31] and his nominal superior at Headquarters wrote: "His position was unique and attained by none of his successors. He was, one might say, the General's chief adviser."[32] Joffre trusted him with anything, even his own good name: "By the way, Tardieu," he said one day in January, 1915, as the two were strolling together in the Chantilly forest. "All those documents that pass through your hands in your work for our armies and our embassies—I'd like you to keep copies of them." As Tardieu threw him a questioning glance, "Oh," he went on, "I'm not vain or proud, but I would like the documents of this period to be made public when I'm no longer around, just as I received or sent them." Tardieu promised.[33]

At Headquarters Tardieu was only marking time, however brilliantly. The more he saw of his "papers," the more he longed to see action instead; besides, he had the uneasy feeling "that he might be accused of governing under the cloak of Joffre."[34] Once, at the end of 1914, he asked Joffre to give him a combat unit to command; Joffre refused. The following spring, however, "a great republican power[35] [grew] alarmed by the dictatorship reputedly exercised over France by 'Captain X,' "[36] and Joffre accepted a second request by Tardieu for combat duty.

Tardieu was first assigned to a headquarters division, but he rapidly worked his way down to the command of a company of élite infantry[37]— of *chasseurs à pied* or, as the Germans had nicknamed them, "blue devils." He was happy at last: "I got know the real people and how to talk to them, which was something I had not been taught at home or in the Lycée Condorcet."[38] "Living at close quarters with my men day after day, I spent the most beautiful time of my life."[39]

He fought in the north, under the supreme command of Foch. There he took part in the suicidal mass offensive of September and early October, 1915. On November 29, at Neuville-Saint-Vaast, he was found unconscious in the trenches—"limp, inanimate," wrote a comrade;[40] "gassed," reported the press;[41] "overcome by the cold and by congestion," President Poincaré was told;[42] "seized by a kind of stroke," recalled a Headquarters official, adding: "From the general concern I could judge of the goodwill everyone felt towards him."[43] The doctors thought him lost; after thirty hours, however, he regained consciousness, and by the middle of December he was home on convalescence leave. Poincaré had him to dinner at the Elysée: "He is still as brilliant as ever," observed his host, adding, "He is convinced the war will last another two years."[44] Before the year was out Tardieu, fully recovered, returned to the front "enthusiastically."[45] With the battle then at a standstill, he led his company in reconnaissance work. One of his lieutenants, who often went with him behind enemy lines, had occasion to observe him crawling on his hands and knees hours at a time, his lorgnette perched on the rim of his nose; if he was slightly puffy—"He is no longer thirty as I am, and he holds it against me"—he was no less insensitive withal to fatigue or to danger.[46]

On the front lines Tardieu grew strongly critical of the conduct of the war. He blamed the high command for its defective system of supplies and its macabre taste for premature offensives. The government he blamed for trying to force an early victory—despite Premier Briand, who knew better but "lacked authority." He made no secret of his views, wherefore in the Council of Ministers on February 8 Briand, resentful, "came up with the idea that Tardieu would make an excellent minister of France in Rumania."[47] Rumania's terms for joining the Allies were coming within reason, and France needed someone to conclude the alliance, then help arrange for a prospective offensive through the Balkans. Briand made the offer to Tardieu unofficially, and Tardieu expressed interest. However, "Malvy foresaw serious objections in parliament."[48] A deputation of Radicals came protesting to Poincaré: "They maintained that Tardieu had adopted an anti-parliamentary attitude since the war, and they dug up the old N'Goko Sangha and Homs-Bagdad affairs."[49] Tardieu had other faults besides: in preferring the front trenches of Flanders to the back benches of parliament he had again sinned against the *république des camarades*, and his failure to exude official optimism in discussing the war with civilians had branded him as a dangerous mutineer. On February 17 he was cited in army orders for having captured an enemy trench,[50] while in the Council of Ministers the same day "Sembat, Malvy, Combes, Clémentel made much of the bad impression they thought his appointment would produce in the Chamber."[51] The next day Tardieu, home again on leave, called at the Elysée: wrote Poincaré, "He would like his appointment to Bucarest to be called off or else made without further stalling."[52] Briand, however, did not like to settle things without stalling— in fact he had made procrastination into a policy. On February 22 a Socialist warned Poincaré enigmatically that "the appointment of Tardieu to Bucarest would be fatal."[53] Another ten days and Tardieu told the Quai d'Orsay "that he gives up the legation in Bucarest.... He prefers his battalion of 'blue devils.'"[54]

Tardieu did prefer his "blue devils" to any other devils, and yet he did not return to the front after all. During his leave he had attended one or two meetings of the parliamentary Army Commission, and, as the battle had been raging disastrously at Verdun since February 21, he found his old boss Clemenceau and the Minister of War, Galliéni, alive to the need to reorganize the high command. Before long "the highest military authorities and his closest friends...joined forces to persuade him to resume his seat in the Chamber. General Pétain...found the decisive arguments."[55] His name appeared a last time in army orders early in March,[56] and on March 6 he paid a call to Poincaré in civilian clothing, the ribbon of the *Croix de guerre* peeping through his lapel. Poincaré took down their conversation:

"So," I say to him, "you have given up going to Bucarest?"

"Yes," he replies, "I don't like to be taken for a ride the way Briand took me.

And besides, on second thought, I would not have liked to serve a government as weak as ours."

"Those are harsh words. They seem to me the more unfair since Briand, who met with strong obstacles to your appointment, did not give up the hope of overriding them."

"He would have overridden them by now if he had wanted to. But in any case I'd rather do some work in the Chamber for the time being. I'm attending the meetings of the Army Commission, which interest me greatly. There are errors to be prevented, there is useful advice to be given. The Chamber is far better than the government thinks. If the government would only direct the Chamber! But no..."—and with extraordinary verve he heaps criticism on the government but also on the high command.

"But," I say to him, "you are not one of those who are asking for the Commander-in-Chief to be replaced?"

"I am."

"Replaced by whom?"

"Oh, I don't know."

"So you would want to replace a chief who has so much coolheadedness, thoughtfulness, calm, and balance, and you don't even know by whom?"

"There have been so many mistakes made."

"At Verdun? You know perfectly well that it was General Castelnau who, with full powers from Joffre, saved the day."

"Yes, but does Castelnau have any authority in General Headquarters?"

"Certainly: the proof is that Joffre gave him full powers!"

"But then the government should be defending the command, supporting it, protecting it, whereas the government criticizes it all the time in private, and General Galliéni takes pokes at it in every imaginable way before the commissions."[57]

A day later Galliéni appealed to the Council of Ministers to reorganize the high command, giving all real powers to Castelnau and keeping Joffre on only as a figurehead; Briand stood by Joffre, and after one week Galliéni resigned.

As the fighting at Verdun grew more desperate, the position of the Army Commission in the Chamber grew stronger, and Tardieu, who became its *rapporteur*, gained more and more influence in its secret sessions. "I live like a savage. I work alone," he wrote to a comrade at the front. "*Vae soli!* The government seems to suspect me of being cool, and the opposition seems to suspect me of being soft."[58] On May 16 and 17 two attacks on the high command in *Le Matin* eluded censorship; Briand opined that Tardieu "had certainly suggested the articles to M. Henry de Jouvenel,"[59] and in Headquarters "Tardieu was for a long time spoken of as a model of ingratitude. Those who were inclined to sentimentality described the sorrow of General Joffre at having been abandoned by one whom he loved as a son."[60] Tardieu wrote to Briand advising against a "premature offensive,"[61] and meanwhile he led a campaign in the lobbies for a commission of inquiry into the Verdun disaster. At the end of June he voted confidence to the government—"out of duty," he explained, "having nothing ready to put in its place."[62]

Then in July he drew up a proposal for the "direct," "general," and "permanent" supervision by the Army Commission of the war effort apart from military operations. The Chamber, he argued, had "a right to supervise the government." Such supervision, customary in time of peace, was essential in time of war. In order to exercise it, the Chamber would have to investigate the needs of the army "on the spot." Tardieu proposed that the Commission control "the interior and the zone to the rear of the armies" through its own members, and the battle zone through "inspectors" to be chosen by it from parliament for brief missions. It would act without "the assistance of the government," and he did not define its powers restrictively.[63] His arguments from the Chamber's "right to supervise" were obviously contrived; then only did he ever invoke that right, and what he objected to in Briand's government was its weakness, not its strength. His intention was not for the Army Commission to stand up to a strong government but for it to take over from a weak one.

His proposal, wrote Pierre Renouvin, "recalled to mind the '*Comité de Salut Public*' of 1793,"[64] and the press, seizing its purport, was in the main hostile to it. Joffre for his part opposed it on a point of etiquette: "I would not stand for members of parliament coming into the zone of the armies *without my being previously informed*," he wrote.[65] On July 25, after a week of debate, the Chamber adopted it on first reading; however, "frightened at its own temerity,"[66] it reversed its vote two days later in favor of a counterproposal for strengthening *all* the commissions![67] The need for drastic measures, it seemed, was past. The pressure had lifted from Verdun, and Joffre, pursuing the high strategy of tit for tat, had launched an offensive on the Somme. Optimism soared as parliament recessed for the summer.

The losses on the Somme outweighed the gains, and in the fall the Army Commission resumed its pressure on the government to reorganize the high command. In its secret session of November 28 Tardieu charged the high command with negligence due to excessive optimism, and on December 6, speaking on the need for more heavy artillery, he charged the government with lack of leadership—"A government is not a sum of ministries and administrations," he declared; "it is a head that must direct everything."[68] At length Briand gave in: on December 13, 1916, he made General Lyautey Minister of War in place of General Rocques, a partisan of Joffre, and at the same time he made General Nivelle commander of a new and independent Army of the Orient. Joffre he kicked upstairs as "technical adviser to the government"; nominally, however, Joffre remained Commander-in-Chief, and Tardieu, who preferred the clear-cut to the smooth, challenged the government to explain how it meant to divide authority between Joffre and Lyautey on the one side and the two commanders on the other. "Instead of concentrating responsibility, you are dispersing it," he cried.[69] Briand, devious always, made his answer in a secret meeting of a Senate commission one week later: Joffre would have no real power over the commanders, but power only to make recommendations to the Army Commission, itself an advisory board. Lyautey, arriving from Morocco on December 24, denounced even these functions of Joffre as incompatible with his own, and they were suppressed; at the same time Foch, too, was relieved of his command. All in all, thought Tardieu, the government had gone from bad to worse, and on December 29 he attacked it again vehemently in the Chamber.

In his vehemence there was an echo of the anxiety and sorrow of his private life. Both his parents were ill. His father—"to whom," he later wrote, "I owe whatever I am worth"[70]—was suffering from a heart ailment worsened by his sensitivity to the sufferings of France. Seeing the toll of casualties mount to no avail, he even came to doubt the aptness of the republican regime, at least in time of war. The very last evening of 1916 he died. "It is moral ruination for me," André wrote to a comrade at the front.[71] Then, barely three weeks later, André's mother died, also of a heart ailment. "I am at the end of my strength. Pity me," he wrote again.[72] His grief brought him near to despair; he fought it by losing himself in work.

General Nivelle did not strive to repair the errors of his predecessor, Joffre; instead he strove to beat Joffre at his own game. As Nivelle saw it, Joffre's fault had been, not launching too many attacks, but losing too many. Beginning in January, 1917, Nivelle threw his men into one offensive after another, and the greater his losses were at any one time the harder he hit the next time, hoping each time to make up for the time before. Poincaré and Briand encouraged him: they had been promising a rapid victory for so long already. Many officers from General Pétain down made no secret of their discontent, and in April mutiny broke out in the ranks.

On January 30 Tardieu published in *Le Petit Parisien* an article recommending a switch to defensive action. One week later he wrote another to the same effect, but on the advice of Lyautey the Army Commission forbade its publication.[73] Tardieu suspected the government of covering up for the high command, so he took part in a maneuver to force a showdown. On March 15 Lyautey admitted to the Chamber that he had withheld from it information on national defense; whereupon he resigned, followed four days later by the whole government.

Alexandre Ribot succeeded Briand as Premier and Foreign Minister. Knowing Tardieu to have had a hand in Briand's fall, Ribot was both grateful to him and wary of him; circumstances aiding, he found the perfect solution to his dilemma. On April 6 the United States declared war on Germany, and Tardieu, jubilant, published in *Le Petit Parisien* of April 12 a "program of cooperation" between France and the United States. From America, he wrote, the Allies needed men, money, ships, coal, and steel; even more, though, they needed a long-range program of cooperation—and perhaps also a new organization to apply it, for so far purchasing commissions of the Allied powers, even those of the same power, had been bidding competitively for supplies. The article made a favorable impression in the United States, and at once Ribot offered Tardieu full powers to organize and direct in Washington a French mission to deal with "all matters not strictly a part of diplomacy: questions of supplies, of munitions, of materiel, of raw materials, of transport by rail and by sea, of credits for France."[74] Tardieu hesitated, if only briefly: as he told Poincaré, his English was rusty.[75] A day or two later he was doing research at the purchasing and transport services in Paris. Then he drafted a decree defining his powers; Ribot signed it on April 16, and the same day Poincaré officially appointed him High Commissioner for France in the United States.[76]

He stayed three more weeks in Paris studying the needs of the war services, recruiting his secretariat, and also consulting with the government and with the general staff. The government told him, "Do the best you can"; Pétain, who just then became Commander-in-Chief in place of Nivelle, told him, "Recruit volunteers to plug up the holes in our front," and Foch, whom Pétain made Chief-of-Staff, told him, "Send me regiments for our brigades."[77] If the government had little faith, the high command had little understanding. On May 4 he took leave of Poincaré, who wrote:

He told me of the difficulties that he had encountered in trying to obtain precise information from the various services. On all sides he was beset with requests for supplies exceeding all possibility of shipment. He will have to reduce them and to try meanwhile to get some shipping and some more credits. He seems to have his subject well under control and to be glad of the chance to do something vital.[78]

A few hours later he sailed with his party aboard the "Marseillaise."

He arrived in New York on May 16; as he arrived, former premier Viviani and former commander-in-chief Joffre were just reembarking, having obtained in Washington a loan of 100,000,000 dollars and, they thought, assurances of 150,000,000 dollars more to come each month. Tardieu went directly to Washington; wrote one of the French officials who met him:

Impossible to forget his arrival at the station: his clothes as neat as if they had just come out of the closet; his complexion fresh, not tarnished by a rough crossing; his eye twinkling behind his lorgnette; his cigarette-holder thrusting forth from his lips, which glowed with a smile at one ironical, cordial, and good-humored. His firm gait, his air of resolute calm, inspired us with confidence and infused much-needed hope into our souls.[79]

That afternoon he met General Pershing, who told him simply, "I want to leave [for France]. I am leaving"[80]—and he left. Before he did, though, Tardieu promised him to arrange for France to equip his troops with artillery.

The same evening Tardieu moved into a Louis-XIII-style mansion on Connecticut Avenue, and the following morning he set up his headquarters on Columbia Road. Throughout his stay he kept his mansion "properly and without show";[81] he would offer hospitality in it to Frenchmen on visit to Washington, then put them to work for the mission until they got away. The mission had a budget of 12,000,000,000 francs a year—twice the total budget for France before 1914. Its staff, when complete, consisted of nine hundred English-speaking Frenchmen and three hundred French-speaking Americans. All were devoted to Tardieu; not one left it while he was at its head.[82] He organized it into eleven services, and every morning he held conference with the eleven chiefs of service, the French military and naval attachés, and an adviser from the French Embassy. The chiefs of service would each speak in turn; "Tardieu would listen," wrote the Embassy adviser,

his pencil running over a sheet of paper spread out before him. Most of the time he was sketching the face of some one of his assistants....From time to time he would interrupt, put in a question, ask for more detail, cut short unnecessary elaborations....Never did a meeting degenerate into a chat.[83]

The climate in Washington did not affect his capacity for work. His chief secretary, Louis Aubert, saw him drafting a report on aviation at the end of one hot and busy day in June: "Though he dozed off from time to time, his hand went on writing."[84] His habits of play, too, knew no change. Wrote another witness to his ways: "One evening M. Tardieu brought the Embassy adviser, clad only in pajamas, to a reception of the most elegant sort after first assuring him that the lady of the house was alone in her drawing room."[85]

As early as his second day in Washington Tardieu saw Secretary of the Treasury McAdoo to work out the details of the Viviani-Joffre loan agreement; as it turned out, however, not only did the Secretary know of no such loan agreement, but he had no authority to make one. As long as the war lasted Tardieu had to borrow monthly and even semi-monthly from the Treasury, each time declaring the uses to which the money would be put—McAdoo had all he could do to prevent him from taking out Treasury loans at 5 percent to repay old short-term loans from Wall Street at 10 percent and 12 percent. Every morning Tardieu got the same cable from Paris instructing him to insist on long-term loans; every morning the cable wound up in the same place.

Compared with transport, though, money was no problem. In nearly three years of war France, relying on Great Britain to fill out her needs, had not ordered a single ton of shipping in the United States, even though by 1917 she was receiving from the United States 240,000 tons of merchandise a month. In the first five months of 1917 German U-boats sank 5,000,000 tons of Allied shipping, whereupon Great Britain withdrew 500,000 tons from loan to France. Tardieu brought with him to America urgent requests for an additional 500,000 tons of merchandise a month plus its shipping—even as he landed, 600,000 tons of merchandise bound for France lay idle in the port of New York. He placed an order with the American shipyards; in August the War Department requisitioned his order. He wrote a memorandum to Secretary of War Baker on "the necessity for France to secure ships"; Baker found his tone peremptory.[86] Paris pressed him for results. "I must act with great caution," he replied,[87] and he proposed a Franco-American company to sail the requisitioned ships under the American flag; by October, however, he had made no headway, and his government, incredulous, sent an official to find out why he was stalling.[88]

Of necessity the Treasury and the War Department officials thought him a bit of a nuisance. His relations with President Wilson, meanwhile, were cordial on the surface and chilly beneath: he found Wilson self-righteous, and Wilson found him self-important. With Colonel House, though, he got on famously from the first; as he wrote, "Whenever anything went wrong—recruitment, transport, supplies, finance—I would get in touch with Mr. House. He would say, 'I'll do it,' and then do it."[89] With the British High Commissioner, Lord Northcliffe,[90] a fellow news-paperman, he found himself in "perfect accord": Northcliffe would visit the Treasury officials in his company in order to save himself the trouble of speaking.[91] The French Embassy staff for their part were jealous of him: the long black United States government limousines no longer lined up in *their* yard. Washington society bid for his favor; he gave it to Mrs. Slatter, a Francophile of means, and to her Thursday-evening *soirées dansantes*, at which, wrote an Embassy official, "he liked to stand aloof with airs of dignity and importance."[92]

Meanwhile he bid for the favor of the country at large on a program of "complete cooperation" among the Western Allies.[93] By "complete cooperation" he meant ideally the pooling of all resources—men, weapons, money, food. He meant specifically, as a start, the adoption by each government of measures for controlling prices and requisitioning supplies, as well as the establishment of an intergovernmental committee to coordinate all supply orders and to group them "according to their urgency in relation to military operations."[94] France, being the poorest and hardest-hit of the three western Allies, stood to gain the most from complete cooperation, while conversely the United States, having great resources but as yet poor organization for war, ran the risk of becoming a wealthy satellite of France. "The great duty of the United States at the present time," Tardieu told the Bankers Club in New York, "is to put on the same footing all those who are fighting for the same cause."[95] The bankers applauded; his words must have rung a little false to them, though, just as their applause must have rung a little false to him. He was a soldier; they were businessmen. His country was in the war by immersion, theirs only by contribution. His was fighting for survival, theirs for the right to trade. To him the two were allies first and last; to them the one was, though an ally, no less a customer of the other.

Tardieu, true to his word to Pershing, arranged in July with the War Department for France to furnish artillery for one million American troops in one year. Americans on the whole took the arrangement ill. They wanted their country to have a war industry of its own. They wanted it to have an army of its own, too, and Tardieu was careful not to ask for volunteers to fill in the gaps in the French army. Some Americans even wanted it to have war aims all its own, as Tardieu discovered with dismay. Whereas Nicholas Murray Butler told him in New York, "We Americans want Alsace-Lorraine to become French soon again,"[96] at the Peace Inquiry Bureau in Washington he found Walter Lippmann working out plans for the holding of a plebiscite in each of twelve districts of the two unhappy provinces. "Two hours of conversation were necessary to dissuade him," wrote Tardieu.[97]

While his assistants were spreading goodwill to the tune of some thirty speeches a day, Tardieu was himself even busier being congenial in public than he was pestering the War Department and the Treasury. He had principally to reassure America. In July he declared that the U-boats could not prevent transport across the Atlantic,[98] in August that the casualty rate in the French armies was declining,[99] in October that the German armies were not advancing in Russia.[100] He addressed the American Manufacturers Association on the economics of war, harangued the crowds at City Hall in New York on Lafayette Day,[101] and toasted "the American and French armies, guardians of the traditions and hopes of the two democracies," at the Army and Navy Club.[102] The press made him comment on Bernard Baruch's work with the War Purchasing Commission and Herbert Hoover's work with the Food Administration,[103] the cabinet crisis in Paris in September[104] and the appointment of Viscount Reading to succeed Northcliffe in November. In public he wore the *rosette* of the Legion of Honor or the ribbon of the *Croix de guerre*, depending on the occasion. And he made himself quotable: remarking on the need for speed in training officers he said, "In war, time is not only money—time is blood,"[105] and, asked to explain why America was fighting, he replied, "Read the messages of your President."[106] Even while representing his country's needs as great and urgent he had to combat the rumor of its having been "bled white": he did both at once with facts and figures in a memorandum to the Secretary of War, who published the "superb exposé" in the Official Bulletin.[107] He also wrote an article for *World's Week* on tactical warfare and a preface for a book called *France Bears the Burden*. Yale gave him an honorary degree,[108] and the press gave him many a scrapbookful of publicity.

In addition to cooperating with the British mission he had to compete with it. On the occasion of Lord Balfour's promise of a homeland in Palestine for the Jews he prepared a statement whereby France made the same commitments as England, and he telegraphed it to the new Foreign Minister, Pichon, to sign and return. When Pichon's return cable came he took it to Judge Brandeis, and the judge wept for joy. Then he took it to Wilson, and Wilson said: "I am deeply gratified that France has taken this position in a just cause." Thereupon Tardieu added two rabbis to his staff. "The result was magnificent," he recalled. And to top it off I chose from my eight hundred officers a few Jews duly wounded, mutilated, and decorated, and I had them make the same tour of the Jewish neighborhoods of New York on Saturdays as the English did. It was delirium! My colleague Viscount Reading said to me, laughing, "So you're going to steal Zionism from me, a Jew?" He begged me to let him have in return the use of my Catholic chaplains to go and help recruit for him in French Canada.[109]

Early in November Tardieu—at the same time as Northcliffe, Reading, and Colonel House—left for Paris to attend the first inter-Allied war conference. He arrived on November 14, the day Clemenceau took office as Premier and Minister of War. Poincaré, receiving him the same afternoon, urged him on behalf of Clemenceau to enter the new government as Under-Secretary of State for Armaments. "He replies," wrote Poincaré, "that he prefers to remain in America to carry on the job that he has begun,"[110] and Clemenceau got the same reply on personally offering him the Ministry of Transport and Supplies a few hours later.

Though the meetings of the war conference were secret, Tardieu made the issues public. With some inconsistency: in an official statement he gave unity of command as the sole outstanding problem of inter-Allied cooperation;[111] then he told Le Matin, "The problem of tonnage is the key to all the others";[112] and before the American Club he spoke of the pooling of all resources by the Allies as the condition of victory.[113] On December 2 he declared that the United States was all for unity of command,[114] and on December 10 that France had taken the same stand.[115] The British press protested, primarily because the supreme commander, if there were one, would certainly be a Frenchman. In fact Tardieu had spoken prematurely: the French government had come around to his views, but the French high command, after having given the British and the Americans a share in its front lines, was reluctant to give them a seat in its councils as well. The conference broke down, and Tardieu said to Clemenceau: "They're going to talk to me again over there about unity of command, and no doubt they'll ask me whom we want. Whom should I say?" "Foch," replied Clemenceau.[116]

No easier to achieve than inter-Allied cooperation was intra-French cooperation. Tardieu took before the Council of Ministers draft decrees increasing his powers and defining them with greater precision; the ministers argued with him, and at length Clemenceau said:

They're right: I see no reason for changing things. But since I am a man of decision, and since I have promised you to do as you wish, I'll sign your decrees. You are a Napoleon—but I warn you, I'll have you shot after Marengo.[117]

Tardieu also pleaded with the various state agencies ordering supplies from America to coordinate their activities; the bureaucats merely grinned in reply, and on December 20 he complained to Poincaré "of the anarchy in our bureaus and of the complete lack of system in the orders that they place in America. No program; priorities perpetually changing...."[118] By his crusade for efficiency he earned the nickname *"Tardieu l' Américain."*

In the last days of December he took time off to inspect a detachment of American troops with Foch.[119] Then suddenly Clemenceau said to him: "We have an urgent and immediate need of machine guns for our airplanes. Could you find some in the United States?" So, reported Stéphane Lauzanne,

Tardieu jumped onto a steamer, crossed the ocean, and within a week obtained an option on excellent terms for two thousand machine guns. He cabled Paris, "May I conclude the purchase?" Three weeks later Paris replied, "No, we are not ready." Then, after another two weeks, "No use, we have no credits." Then, after the option had lapsed, "We need the guns right away. What are you waiting for?"[120]

"We are entering the hardest phase of the war," Tardieu declared glumly on his arrival in New York.[121]

In Washington he at once told Wilson of the obstacles to instituting a supreme command. Said Wilson: "You will have to come to it just the same. What does M. Clemenceau think?" "He is all for it." "Whom will he put up?" "General Foch." And from then on Wilson, too, supported Foch.[122] However, Clemenceau, like Foch, had made himself unpopular with the War Department by demanding American platoons instead of an American army, and Tardieu wrote to warn him: "If your aim is really amalgamation, that is, the enlistment of the American army by small units on our front, you will fail."[123]

On the morning of January 8, at 11 o'clock, Colonel House telephoned Tardieu and said: "The President is to read a message to Congress at noon. Come. You will be pleased," and an hour later Tardieu was present for the world première of the Fourteen Points. "I heard President Wilson, before the Senate and the House, which stood to cheer him, utter the famous words, 'The wrong done to France by Prussia in 1871... should be righted.' "[124]

The routine soon resumed. The High Commissioner officiated in Philadelphia at the launching of the third Liberty Loan; he borrowed from Foch for the occasion a company of "blue devils," which he used again to good effect in New York at a meeting of the General Association of Alsatians and Lorrainers in America.[125] With the Alliance Française he commemorated the Treaty of February 6, 1778, between France and the United States,[126] and before the French Institute he saluted simultaneously the Stars and Stripes and the *tricolor*—"the flags of liberty"— for the first anniversary of the entry of the United States into the war.[127] He expressed the gratitude of France to the Central Committee for Franco-American Fraternity for its aid to war orphans;[128] on the occasion of Wilson's appeal for voluntary rationing he spoke to the Southern Commercial Congress in Baltimore about privation in France;[129] he adjured the alumnae of Vassar College: "Remember, it is largely the women of America who today hold in their power the means of victory and the future of the world."[130] He gave the National Lecturers Association, at its request, the catchword for its spring campaign: "Unity."[131]

The game of war left him no leisure even for dismay. On the evening of Saturday, March 22, he had to make merry at a Tricolor Ball in New York just after learning of the retreat of the British Fourth Army to Amiens. The bombardment of Paris began the next day. Promptly on Monday morning there was panic at the Stock Exchange, and he had to throw the whole dollar account of his mission into the balance to maintain the franc at par. By then refugees from Picardy were pouring into Paris, and Clemenceau sent him a cable pleading for a million tons of food. Food-boss Hoover was intractable: France had had her ration for the month. Tardieu issued an appeal for voluntary contributions. Then he went to see the Secretary of the Navy, Josephus Daniels; Daniels delivered the goods at once from naval stores, using his power of requisition the next day to levy the equivalent from Hoover's stocks. Whereas Hoover was furious, Wilson "burst out laughing when he heard the story."[132]

The news of the disaster in Picardy brought with it to London a new spirit of inter-Allied cooperation. Foch became Supreme Commander, and half the British merchant fleet was put to carrying American troops to France. Tardieu was able in consequence to gain for France the use of 680,000 tons of wooden-bottoms, and by June, 1918, shipments of merchandise to France from America reached 500,000 tons a month, or twice what they had been twelve months before.

In May, 1918, because of the German spring offensive, supply orders came in such exceptional confusion from Paris[133] that Tardieu again went to check them on the spot. Arriving in France on May 24, he reported to newsmen with paternal pride on the war effort of the United States. Three days later he saw Poincaré, who wrote: "Tardieu ... is still complaining of the anarchy and contradictions in the Paris bureaus."[134] This time, though, Tardieu did not tarry in the bureaus; instead he consulted on war needs directly with Supreme Allied Headquarters and made several exploratory trips to the front. He also helped the Supreme Commander lay plans: "In collaboration with M. Tardieu," wrote Foch, "I framed a program on the basis of ... eighty American divisions by April and one hundred divisions by July, 1919."[135]

The American Expeditionary Force in France was growing fast: 300,000 troops landed in the course of the single month of June. They mostly landed in the southerly ports and used the southern rail routes for convoy to their sector of the front, steering clear of the other armies in order to avoid the risk of amalgamation by inadvertence. They brought only some equipment and relied on France to provide the rest; the Paris bureaus, however, were hardly able to provide for the French combatants, let alone the American. The General Purchasing Agent for the American Expeditionary Force, General Charles E. Dawes, made contact with Tardieu. Tardieu arranged much for him, including even his appointment to the Military Board.[136] "After having sought in the United States what France lacks, I now have to seek in France what the American army lacks," wrote Tardieu.[137] On June 20 Clemenceau put him officially in charge of relations with American troops on French soil, creating for him the cabinet post of General Commissioner for Franco-American War Cooperation.

Tardieu's new functions, together with his old, kept him too busy to leave Europe for some time. He set up the General Commissariat for Franco-American War Cooperation on the Rue Boccador; it was soon as large as the mission in Washington. Meanwhile, on June 23 he went with Clemenceau, Foch, and Weygand to Chaumont to settle with Pershing on a troop program; Pershing agreed to Tardieu's proposal of one hundred divisions, or three million men, by September 1, 1919, and together the two drew up a transport plan.[138] On June 28 Tardieu was questioned in the Chamber on his persistent attempt to institute a "consortium" or single organ in Paris for notifying all purchase orders to the mission in Washington; such, he replied, was the condition set by the United States for commerce with its Allies in the future—and, the Socialists applauding, he cited the controls on production and distribution in the United States as an example to France. At a meeting of the Supreme War Council on July 3 he came up with a study of tonnage requirements for the hundred-division program. "This seemed greatly to irritate Lloyd George, who said that the question of tonnage did not concern the French, but only the British and the Americans," wrote the American delegate.[139] Tardieu argued with Lloyd George to no avail— "So far as I was concerned," wrote Commander Haig, "it was a complete waste of a couple of hours."[140] The following day Tardieu spoke at an Independence Day banquet at the United States Chamber of Commerce in Paris: "A single watchword," he declared, "We are in it, we must win it."[141] On July 10 he conferred with Dawes on ways of making available in France more equipment for the American Army; "M. Tardieu's organization should be able to save us much tonnage," wrote Dawes to his commanding general.[142] The *Times* of London asked Tardieu for a message for July 14, which had just been made "France Day" in England; he replied: "Henceforth we shall share in our holidays just as we shall share in our mourning."[143] July 14 brought success to the French and American forces in the beginnings of a counterattack on the Marne, and twelve years later Tardieu was to admit before the French Senate: "Victory—oh, believe me, gentlemen, it was hardly certain until July 14, 1918! I was in the government then, and I know!"[144] In mid-July he tried to cut through red tape by communicating directly with Washington on the needs of the American army in France; Wilson resented his initiative, and Pershing threatened to decline to recognize his commissariat if he did not act through Dawes in the future.[145] On July 24, with Baron Edmond de Rothschild, he saluted the passage through Paris of the first volunteers from America for the Palestinian Legion.[146] On August 3, replying to an interpellation in the Chamber, he explained how lucky France was to have obtained the use of even wooden-bottoms from the United States. Then for five days he toured the regions liberated by the counteroffensive on the Aisne and Marne rivers, and for one week afterwards he visited the northern battlefields; there on August 14 King Albert awarded him the Belgian *Croix de guerre*.[147] On August 27 he went to London with his colleague Loucheur, Minister of Munitions, Loucheur to get coal and steel and he to discuss tonnage.[148] After his return he worked several weeks steadily for his commissariat. He requisitioned private homes, hotels, and schools for use as hospitals and for billeting; he also requisitioned equipment of all descriptions, including 90,000 beds and 120,000 horses[149]— Dawes, who had appealed most urgently for the horses, reported: "Tardieu took up the matter with his customary energy."[150] Whenever possible he paid compensation, but he had no scruples about apologizing instead.

Meanwhile the resistance of the German armies gradually wore down, and on October 3 the German Chancellor appealed to President Wilson for an armistice on the basis of the Fourteen Points. Two weeks later, with Wilson's reply still pending, Tardieu left to wind up his business in the United States. While he was at sea, on October 23, the armistice terms were communicated to Germany; he landed on October 28, and by then their acceptance was imminent.

Ill from a rough crossing, he stayed a few hours in New York after landing, while one of his assistants went on ahead to Washington—"as a harbinger," wrote an Embassy official,

to remind our ambassador of the new dignity of the High Commissioner. At once the State Department was advised, and a double row of soldiers presented arms to *M. le Commissaire-général des Affaires de Guerre franco-américaines.*[151]

He did not hold a press conference until November 3; then he declared that he had only to settle a matter of loans with the Treasury before returning to France. "After the battle," he added, "peace will be one more link between us."[152] He witnessed the congressional elections of November 5, which gave a majority in both houses to the Republican party. He made only one public appearance: the Association of Foreign Correspondents in America having chosen him its first honorary member, he delivered an acceptance speech, which was an appeal to the press to support France's reconstruction program. Already Clemenceau was urging him to return and help in preparing the peace, and on November 11, just as the armistice was signed, he reembarked.

His mission was over. In eighteen months he had helped America send 1,600,000 tons of grain, 300,000 tons of sugar, 2,800,000 tons of steel, 170,000,000 75-millimeter shells, 430,000 tons of fuel, and 2,000,000 doughboys to France. In the process he had rubbed a few American officials the wrong way, of course, but he had also done his share in transforming America into something unprecedented in her history. "All my life I shall remember the United States as it then was," he wrote.

A vast war machine, quickened by patriotism; its soul aflame; one hundred million men, women, and children with every nerve strained towards the ports of embarkation; chimneys smoking; trains rushing through the warm nights; women in the stations offering hot coffee to troops on their way to the front; national hymns rising to heaven; meetings for Liberty Loans in every church, in every theater, at every street corner; immense posters on the walls, "You are in it, you must win it."[153]

He was never to see the United States again.

And though a great career lay before him, only during the war—on the the battlefields of Flanders and at his post in America—was he to have known happiness, which the sense of effective participation in a just cause had brought to him. Thereafter all was disillusion.

CHAPTER 21

"Our Treaty"

"...our treaty..."   Clemenceau to Tardieu, on the Treaty of Versailles.*

TARDIEU REACHED FRANCE on November 20, 1918. The day after his arrival he had to defend before the Chamber his policies as Commissioner for Franco-American War Cooperation: challenged on his refusal to seek written pledges from the Americans for future aid, he replied, "The method of distrust is the worst one that can be used with them."[1] A few days later, on Thanksgiving Day, he toasted "the two great friends of France: the people of the United States, and President Wilson."[2]

President Wilson set sail for France on December 4, believing his presence at the Peace Conference to be both necessary and sufficient for assuring the adoption of the Fourteen Points. The peoples of Europe were all eager to welcome him, having read each in its own fashion his message of peace. The statesmen of Europe, however, were on the whole suspicious of his principles and resentful of his popularity. America, they whispered, had made too much profit from the war to be entitled to preach about the peace, and Wilson had too little credit in his own country to deserve any credit abroad. Tardieu, however, realized that France could not do without the United States, and that consequently France had no choice but to do with its only rightful representative.[3] He fought the whispering campaign all around him; he even went to exhort the occupant of that arsenal of whispering campaigns, the Elysée Palace, to do the same—and Poincaré noted, "He does not find it either strange or bad that Wilson should wish to attend the Conference."[4]

Tardieu spent part of every day in December and early January conferring with members of the American delegation, or else wining and dining them.[5] He assisted Clemenceau with the preliminary discussions among the chief Allies, which began with the arrival of Wilson on December 13, and while the discussions lasted he had the task of keeping the other delegations content.

*Introduction to André Tardieu, *La Paix* (Paris, Payot, 1921). The French reads "*notre traité*"; the English translation *(The Truth About the Treaty)* reads "our Peace Treaty."

At the request of Clemenceau he drew up a plan of procedure for the Conference: he enumerated and classified all the topics likely to come up for discussion, and proposed a whole hierarchy of commissions to deal with them. Also at the request of Clemenceau he consulted on the prospective peace settlement with officials from the various French ministries and members of the Study Commission, a group formed by Briand two years earlier to examine that same subject. These consultations were held at the General Commissariat on the Rue Boccador, and the decisions taken, wrote Tardieu, "were put into writing and served as a basis for the French proposals."[6] Briand, however, later charged Tardieu with having ignored the work of the Study Commission, and one of its members, Charles Benoist, wrote of its meetings with Tardieu:

Really it would be difficult to imagine anything more puerile or less serious. M. Tardieu, naturally, would sit at the high end of the conference table. Before him would lie two ashtrays, one containing his watch and the other his cigarette case. As soon as he had finished reading the agenda, General Le Rond on the one side and on the other M. Laroche—and sometimes the two together —would begin to discourse. Now and then M. Tardieu would interrupt them to ask questions—short ones, for he was always in a hurry, as a man who, being in charge of everything, is always expected somewhere else. At any reply he would declare himself sufficiently enlightened and signal for his secretary, M. Aubert, to take a note. The really competent men rarely managed to get in a word edgewise, even if they had been specially convoked.[7]

With Tardieu, however, speed was not a sign of superficiality, and the number and variety of his assignments did not detract from his skill in handling any one of them.

Further to these meetings he prepared briefs on the Saar and on the Rhineland for the French delegation. France, he wrote, demanded restoration of such territory on the Rhine as had been "wrested from her in 1815"; France also demanded ownership of the Saar coal basin, both by way of economic reparation and as insurance against the rearmament of Germany; finally, since the Rhenish territory at issue did not enclose the whole of the Saar coal basin, France demanded a special political status for as much of the territory of the coal basin as would otherwise remain under the sovereignty of Germany. On a cognate issue, Foch had written just after the signature of the Armistice to advise Clemenceau of the military advantages to France of making the left bank of the Rhine the western frontier of Germany; Clemenceau in December summoned Tardieu to find other arguments to justify this proposal, and the result was Tardieu's "Memorandum of the French Government on the Fixation at the Rhine of the Western Frontier of Germany and on the Inter-Allied

Occupation of the Rhine Bridges." Massive, laden with economic and historical arguments, complete with documents and an appendix on the constitution of an independent Rhineland, it neglected no consideration save self-determination of peoples. These two memoranda, together with the proposal for the military occupation of a demilitarized zone of Germany to extend some thirty-five miles east of the Rhine, constituted the initial demands of France in the Rhineland. France's allies were slow in raising objections to the proposals for territorial adjustment;[8] also, they were agreeable from the start to the principle of a military occupation, though they were not eager to take part in the occupation themselves.

Lloyd George arrived from England for the New Year fresh from a triumph at the polls, and on his arrival the Supreme Allied Council convened. After admitting Japan to provisional membership, it agreed to meet as a "council of ten" twice daily for all major decisions, each member state being represented by its chief executive and its foreign minister. Then on January 9 the French delegation was officially constituted under the presidency of Clemenceau; besides its president it included four cabinet ministers—Pichon, Loucheur, Klotz, and Tardieu—and the ambassador Jules Cambon. Tardieu ranked fifth, and he was directly responsible to Pichon; however, he alone of the whole team was the friend and confident of Clemenceau, who in the weeks to come was to rely on him more and more.

Tardieu's first precise assignment as delegate was public relations. Addressing a "distinguished Franco-Anglo-American audience"[9] on January 11, he belittled the rumor of friction among the Allies—they were, he affirmed, "united to organize the victory that the blood of their soldiers had won."[10] At the insistence of Lloyd George and of Wilson, with Clemenceau protesting, the Council decided at the very outset to keep its own proceedings secret and to institute censorship of cables and of the French press for the duration of the Conference; on January 17 it decided further to bar the press from all but the plenary sessions of the Conference and to forbid delegates to give out information unofficially. The job of giving it out officially went to Lord Balfour and to Tardieu; making the best of his job, Tardieu toasted "the prosperity of the press" before a great gathering of Conference reporters.[11]

Ion Bratianu, an old friend of Tardieu's, had arrived in Paris late in December as delegate from Rumania to take part in the preliminary negotiations. Rumania had fought against Germany only a few weeks, toward the end of 1916, then signed a separate peace. Clemenceau, Wilson, and Lloyd George all told Bratianu to go home. Tardieu, however, seeing in Rumania a good prospective ally for France, fought for Rumania about as long as Rumania had fought for the Allies, until at last Bratianu was accredited as representative of an Allied nation.

The Peace Conference opened solemnly in plenary session on January 18, 1919, in the Salle de la Paix of the Quai d'Orsay. Almost immediately it elected Clemenceau its president, whereupon Clemenceau adjourned it for a week. When it reassembled, the small powers made a show of discontent at being brushed off, so Clemenceau told them: "It is my duty to direct our work so that we may get things done."[12] Then the Conference, rejecting Tardieu's plan of procedure, decided instead to create its commissions only as the need for them arose—in the final count it created more of them than Tardieu had proposed in the first place.

For the first few weeks of the Conference Tardieu was busy chiefly with the commissions. He served on the War Guilt Commission until it began collecting documents; then he left it to its own devices, expecting it to bury the issue under the evidence.[13] Early in February he represented France on a commission set up by the Council to discuss the disarmament of Germany; he argued for immediate and forcible disarmament, but the commission was content to recommend a renewal of the Armistice, leaving disarmament for the Technical Commission to handle as a part of the Treaty. The Council appointed him chairman of the Commission for Belgian Affairs, whereupon King Albert told him: "First of all release us from the onerous and sterile Charter of 1839"[14]—the "scrap of paper" guaranteeing the neutrality of Belgium. Next he became chairman also of the Commission on Danish Claims, and the Danish delegates astonished him by requesting a plebiscite in northern Schleswig only. Finally, he was named chairman of a three-power commission on Alsace-Lorraine. This commission held ten meetings of four hours each, fully half of them in reaching the decision to put the contiguous ports of Kehl and Strasbourg under joint management. To the great annoyance of a British member, John Maynard Keynes, Tardieu persuaded the commission to recognize Alsace-Lorraine as a "restored" and not a "ceded" territory.[15]

Meanwhile Tardieu was busy outside the Conference as well. His work with General Dawes went on as before—on February 6 Dawes reported to his superiors "the inestimable advantage" of having to deal with "a man of the commanding ability of M. Tardieu, intensely devoted to the common interests of both France and the United States," and he added: "The earnest thanks of our nation are due to M. Tardieu."[16] Whenever France wished to honor the United States ceremonially, Tardieu was, of course, the master of ceremonies. Early in February he also prepared and published *L'Amérique en armes*, a selection of his speeches and writings as High Commissioner in the United States, in particular those stressing the need for continuing unity among the Allies after the war.

Wilson and Lloyd George had originally expected the Treaty to be ready by February; as it turned out, however, by February 15 the chief peacemakers were only just beginning to realize how far apart they stood in the matters of disarmament, occupation, reparations, the Saar, and the Rhineland, which they had put off to the last. On February 15 both Wilson and Lloyd George left France to consult with their parliaments. Six days later a young man with poor aim took a shot at Clemenceau; the wound was slight, and within a week the Tiger was home convalescing. Tardieu replaced him on the Council, meanwhile visiting him twice daily. Often Colonel House, who was replacing Wilson, would join the two for informal meetings, which were a useful complement to the formal ones.

Lloyd George was absent until the beginning of March, Wilson until March 14; during their absence Tardieu strove to settle the issue of the Rhineland to the advantage of France. First he told House that France did not intend a *permanent* separation of the Rhenish provinces from Germany; in this way, wrote House, Tardieu had relieved his proposal "of one of its most objectionable features."[17] Then Tardieu had two long talks with Balfour, who wrote to House afterwards in support of the proposal as amended. Again Tardieu spoke at length with House, and the two "got nearer together on the question of the Rhenish Republic."[18] A three-power commission was set up, with Tardieu representing France, to delineate the western boundary of Germany—and just then, on March 10, Clemenceau declared bluntly for a permanent separation of the Rhineland from Germany. Tardieu's compromise was compromised. At the first report Wilson cabled to House to withhold consent on even a temporary separation, and Balfour got the same instructions from Lloyd George. Tardieu met with intransigence on the boundary commission, and after two days its meetings ceased.

Germany having waged a war of aggression, Germany was to pay damages to her victims. On this much the Allies agreed; they did not agree, however, either on how much Germany was *liable* to pay or on how much she was *able* to pay. The American member of the Finance Commission, John Foster Dulles, proposed exacting reparation only for war crimes and direct damages to civilian property. His proposal was the most modest one made, and all the other delegates opposed it. Especially did the French delegate oppose it: he wished the Conference to bill

Germany even for the full war budgets of the Allied powers. Dulles stood his ground alone—until suddenly Tardieu, seeing the advantage to France of Dulles' proposals, took them up in a new form. As Tardieu computed it, the total claim of the Allies for damages to persons and property alone amounted to some three hundred fifty billion francs, and for war costs to twice as much again; payable in fifty years, with interest and sinking funds, total reparations so defined would exceed three trillion francs,[19] "a sum so great that it is unreal."[20] Now, the share of France in the total claim for damages to persons and property was sixty-five per-cent; in the total for war costs, on the other hand, it was only twenty-five percent, and in the combined claims it was forty-two-and-one-half per-cent. "Our interest," Tardieu perceived, "owing on the one hand to the danger of an excessive total, and on the other to the play of percentages, was thus to demand, in opposition to the American point of view, damages for pensions in addition to property damages, but, in accordance with that point of view, to leave aside war costs, which ranked us lower among the Allies than the other two classifications."[21] He succeeded by March in making "the play of percentages" intelligible to Klotz, who was chairman of the Finance Commission, and the French delegation changed its policy accordingly.

To coordinate the work of the territorial commissions still active,[22] the Council on February 27 set up the Central Coordinating Commission on Territorial Questions under the chairmanship of Tardieu. On March 8 the Council upheld unanimously the unanimous decision of the Commission for Belgian Affairs in favor of abrogating the status of neutrality of Belgium. Later it adopted with few changes the recommendations of the Commission on Alsace-Lorraine,[23] and Tardieu obtained its agreement for a plebiscite in both the northern and central zones of Schleswig. On March 6 the Technical Commission, despite Foch, its chairman, recom-mended authorizing a German army of two hundred thousand men with enlistments of as little as one year. Tardieu opposed the plan: in ten years, he figured, Germany would have a new army of two million men. The Council requested a new plan, and four days later the commission pro-posed a volunteer army of one hundred fifty thousand men on twelve-year enlistments. Foch and Clemenceau obtained a further reduction to one hundred thousand men, and the plan was adopted.

In arguing for an inter-Allied occupation of the Rhineland Clemenceau had so far represented disarmament, demilitarization, and the League of Nations as inadequate guarantees for the security of France. Disarma-ment, he maintained, would be temporary, demilitarization would be local, and the League of Nations would assure France at best against defeat, not against invasion. Wilson, impressed with his arguments, had impressed them in turn on Lloyd George, and he and Lloyd George on their return offered France, as an alternative to an inter-Allied occupation of the Rhineland, the military guarantee of their two countries against aggression by Germany—"an unprecedented and immensely significant proposal," wrote Tardieu.[24] Clemenceau asked for time to think it over, and the next two days he conferred on it repeatedly with Pichon, Loucheur, and Tardieu. Tardieu advised him to grab the guarantee treaties, but, because they were inadequate in themselves and moreover uncertain of ratification, to insist anyhow on "most of the other guarantees demanded by us, first of all... occupation."[25] So it was decided, and Tardieu drew up a note in consequence—"a masterpiece of precise logic and perfect organization."[26]

Thereafter "the Peace Conference rapidly approached a crisis."[27] Wilson, stung by the ingratitude of the French, suspected them of playing the old game of imperialism at Germany's expense. He had refreshed his idealism back home, and he was certain of having all humanity on his side; Tardieu, meanwhile, chose March 15 to tell the Council, in a report on Poland: "Even with the best will in the world it is materially impossible to set the boundaries of nations according to purely ethnographic principles."[28] Also, Wilson thought of the League of Nations as the central pillar of the peace settlement, while his interlocutors seemed to regard it as a decorative adjunct at best. Just before Wilson's return Tardieu had told the press that the League would be a part of the Treaty. Just after Wilson's return Pichon told the press: "One cannot think of inserting the project of the League of Nations in the Preliminaries of Peace."[29] American headquarters called Tardieu, who rushed over and explained to reporters that "surely the foreign secretary must have been misunderstood," then "obligingly made a round of the French press and kept the Pichon statement from being printed."[30] Thereupon the Council decided—despite the opposition of Clemenceau, the protests of Balfour and Tardieu, and the fury of the pressmen—to authorize no more press conferences in the future.

On March 22 Tardieu wrote privately to House sounding a "cry of alarm"[31] over the increasing tension among the Allies. Three days later Lloyd George sent the French delegation a note urging it to relax its demands; he for his part was as anxious about ratification of the Treaty as Wilson was complacent, and he was fretful to the point of obsession over the prospects of a Bolshevik revolution in Germany if the peace terms were too harsh. Tardieu prepared the reply: Great Britain, he wrote, having herself gained full satisfaction on the high seas and overseas, had no call to counsel moderation in matters involving the security of France on the continent. Clemenceau himself, before delivering the note, toned down its truculence.[32]

Even as Wilson, Lloyd George, and Clemenceau grew more tense in their relations they grew more intimate in their councils. Lloyd George on his return had joined Tardieu and House in their visits to Clemenceau; later Wilson went instead of House, and these meetings continued even after Clemenceau was well enough again to resume his functions in full. By then Japan had lost interest in the work of the Council, and Italy had fallen out with it altogether over her claims on the Adriatic coast; on March 24 the Council of Ten formally reduced itself to a Council of Four, in reality a council of three.

The bones of contention among the three were many. The text of the treaties of guarantee was settled without difficulty;[33] however, while Lloyd George and Wilson proposed two years' duration, Tardieu and Clemenceau defended a counterproposal: "The pledge to continue until it is considered by all the signatories that the League itself affords sufficient protection."[34] Beginning on March 22 Tardieu discharged a whole battery of notes urging a permanent system of verification and inspection of disarmament in Germany; however, the British and American delegations were both reluctant to admit of any interference in the internal affairs of Germany after the signature of the Treaty. The Council, breaking a deadlock in the commissions, agreed on March 26 to have Germany pay reparations only for damage to persons and property, whereupon France proposed leaving the amount of the reparations debt for the Reparations Commission to establish after the signature of the Treaty; Lloyd George did not much mind, but Wilson objected strongly, insisting on the statement in the Treaty of a lump sum within the means of Germany. Tardieu and Loucheur argued France's case concerning the Saar before the Council on March 28; although Lloyd George was willing to allow French ownership of the coal mines and even a special political status for the whole territory but not French sovereignty over the area of the mines, Wilson for his part would admit none of the demands of France, and Clemenceau broke up the meeting by calling him pro-German.[35] Tardieu delivered a note on March 29 requesting for Belgium the privileges of reparation for the indirect costs of the war and of priority in receiving all reparations payments; only France and Belgium defended the request. Foch pleaded with the Council on March 31 for inter-Allied occupation of the west bank and bridgeheads of the Rhine; though neither the Allied generals nor even the King of Belgium bore him out, Tardieu and Clemenceau went on reiterating in innumerable notes their arguments for the occupation.

The crisis came to a head first over the Saar. Tardieu, Loucheur, and Clemenceau, consulting among themselves, decided to limit their demands to ownership of the mines and a special political status for the whole territory, and Tardieu drew up a note to this effect. The last day of March Wilson consented to ownership by France of the mines but at the same time refused to hear anything more about an independent state. In a new note on April 1 Tardieu declared Wilson's concession inadequate: France would not really own the mines, he argued, if Germany had eminent domain over them—in other words, the sovereignty of Germany in the area would have to be annulled. On April 2—"as a means of averting an open break"[36]—the Council set up a committee of three "consulters" on the Saar, Tardieu representing France. The consulters worked halfway through the night, and early the next morning Tardieu went to see Colonel House at American headquarters. A reporter caught him leaving and told him how fine the weather was. "Yes," replied Tardieu, "it's about the only thing that is fine."[37] House, caught in his turn, said: "The burden seems to be getting pretty heavy. Clemenceau has put it on Tardieu, and the President has put it on me, so we are obliged to get together."[38] The three consulters met nine times more, several hours at a time; between meetings Tardieu drew up a new note demanding an independent Saar with a plebiscite after fifteen years. On April 8 they concluded in favor of a "special administrative and political regime" for the Saar, whereupon Wilson angrily called for his ship to go home. Again Tardieu, Loucheur, and Clemenceau resolved to hold firm, and again Tardieu drew up a note explaining their resolve. They were on safe ground—"Wilson could no longer escape the consequences of his concession of the ownership of the coal mines, and French logic had led him straight to the necessity of eliminating German sovereignty in the Saar for fifteen years."[39] A day later Wilson agreed to an independent Saar under the League of Nations; within eight hours more the consulters had drafted the relevant clause, and the Council adopted it the following morning.

The other points at issue were settled no less laboriously. Tardieu, in an effort to meet Wilson halfway on reparations without himself budging, suggested having Germany deliver on account "a single Treasury bond for some billions of gold marks payable on July 1, 1921, under agreement on the part of the Allies to exchange the bond at the above date for a series of bonds of the same nature payable at such intervals as the inter-Allied commission entrusted with fixing the manner of payment shall determine."[40] The American delegation, while endorsing the suggestion, made the point of how much simpler it would be to have the bond correspond to the total reparations debt. The Council debated from April 12 to 15 the matter of a cessation date for the guarantee treaties, agreeing at last to empower the Council of the League to decide their cessation by a majority vote; also, as Wilson and Lloyd George insisted, neither treaty was to become effective until both had been ratified. Tardieu took to the Council on April 16 a proposal of the Commission for Belgian Affairs to give Belgium sovereignty over the left bank of the Scheldt and to compensate Holland with a piece of German territory; the proposal fell before the indignation of Wilson. On the matter of the disarmament of Germany, Wilson on April 17 proposed the clause: "As long as the present Treaty remains in force, a pledge to be taken by Germany to respond to any inquiry that will be deemed necessary by the Council of the League of Nations"; it was adopted, but only after France had obtained an amendment enabling the Council of the League to order such an inquiry "by a majority vote."[41] On April 18 the French delegation broke down and decided to seek as a compromise a *temporary* occupation of the Rhineland. Foch was alarmed: any time limit, he thought, would destroy the value of the guarantee—and deviously he made his thought known to the press. Wilson and Lloyd George protested. Clemenceau covered up for Foch with them, then summoned him privately on April 19; Foch began by denying and ended by apologizing. At the same time Wilson, against his better judgment, agreed to an inter-Allied occupation of the Rhineland on the basis of three military zones, one to be evacuated every five years provided Germany met her obligations under the Treaty; Lloyd George was three days in following suit. Then Wilson gave in on reparations: "The commission of Reparations shall make known to Germany before May 1, 1921, the amount of reparations to be laid to her charge," read the Treaty,[42] and it was so worded that, whereas Germany accepted liability "for all loss and damage," she was held accountable only for damage to civilians and to their property, in consideration of her limited means of payment. The next day—April 25—Foch reiterated to the French delegation his objections to a time limit on the occupation. The guarantees for the payment of reparations, he said, were to decrease in severity with the passage of time even though they would become increasingly necessary as Germany regained strength; worse, they were to cease altogether in fifteen years, whereas Germany would have at least thirty years in which to meet her obligations. These arguments impressed Clemenceau, who thereupon explained to the Council that if either of the treaties of guarantee failed of ratification France would have made the concession of a time limit on the occupation to no purpose. Strenuous bickering ensued; at length on April 29 the Treaty was revised to allow for a continuation of the occupation beyond the term of fifteen years if by then "the guarantees against an unprovoked aggression by Germany are not considered sufficient by the Allied and Associated governments."[43] Finally, on April 29 Tardieu supported before the Council a supreme appeal of the Belgian delegation for privileges in reparation payments; the Council agreed to give Belgium priority for 2,500,000,000 francs and to transfer her war debts to Germany.

The Treaty with Germany was ready by May 1. Tardieu had himself written most of the clauses on the matters closest to the heart of France— "restitution, reparations, guarantees."[44] On major issues France had gained as much satisfaction as was tolerable to her allies—even more, as it turned out. On minor issues, meanwhile, Tardieu had gained some satisfaction of his own: under Article 124 Germany was held liable for all damages wrought by German nationals to French interests in the Congo-Cameroons frontier zone between 1900 and July, 1914.

The Conference met in secret session on May 6 to hear the terms of the Treaty, which were not known to the delegates officially—or, for the most part, unofficially. "As the document is some seventy thousand words," wrote a reporter, "it obviously could not be read to the delegates, so that M. André Tardieu gave a condensed résumé of its main features."[45] When Tardieu was done, the Supreme Allied Commander unexpectedly took the floor and for fifteen minutes aired his stock of arguments against the time limit on the occupation of the Rhineland. He ignored in his remarks the right of the Allies to extend the occupation after fifteen years if they saw fit; besides, there was something even he did not know, and when he had finished speaking Tardieu made "an unexpected announcement that the Treaty did not stand alone as a guarantee of France's security, as an engagement in writing had been made by President Wilson, Lloyd George, and Clemenceau...."[46] While the Conference was given over to a "buzz of comment" on the treaties of guarantee, the Council hurriedly assembled. Again Clemenceau covered up for Foch; this time, though, Clemenceau did not forgive him, and Tardieu, who had originally brought the two together, later wrote: "To him and to Clemenceau, when they started fighting, I owed some of the worst months of my life.''[47] The Treaty was sent to the printer unaltered, and the next day it was handed to the German Foreign Minister, Count Brockdorff-Rantzau, who was given two weeks in which to represent the objections of his government.

For two weeks, then, the pressure was off. During these weeks Tardieu negotiated with Balfour the withdrawal of French troops from Palestine and of British troops from Syria,[48] and with General Dawes he arranged the purchase by France of the surplus materiel of the American Expeditionary Force. Twice the German government protested directly to France over the loss of the Saar mines; once Tardieu wrote the reply himself, and the second time he and an American drafted it, then Wilson and Clemenceau added "the finishing touches."[49] On May 13 Tardieu's two nieces, aged ten and twelve, appeared with him and Clemenceau at a victory celebration at the Etoile; wildly applauded by the crowd, old *Père la Victoire* led the two small girls by the hand up to the Arch of Triumph. During these same two weeks the assembly at Weimar inserted into the new German constitution an article with a loophole for admitting representatives of Austria into the Reichstag. Clemenceau, who had informants everywhere, called Tardieu on the telephone at once: "Prepare the answer," he said. "Make it short and make it pointed." It was two o'clock in the morning, Tardieu recalled, and "at dawn I went looking for our good Allies. After being bawled out by Lloyd George, who always began by getting angry, I managed by the afternoon to get everyone to agree," and a clause was added to the Treaty making the consent of the League necessary for any kind of *Anschluss*. "The Austrians thanked us," added Tardieu.[50]

When its time was up for registering its complaints, the German government requested an extension of one week, and the Council granted its request. By then doubt as to whether it would sign was widespread; this doubt brought on "the second and most serious crisis of the Conference."[51] Lloyd George in his anxiety suggested "unthinkable concessions on almost every point" of the Treaty.[52] He especially wanted the Allies to drop the provision for the occupation of the Rhineland; so in fact did public opinion in France, where the right condemned it as useless and the left condemned it as unjust. Clemenceau, however, with discreet support from Wilson, held out against making any sort of change.

On May 29 Count Brockdorff presented his government's "Remarks on the Conditions of Peace." These included, besides a denunciation of the peace terms in general as inconsistent with the Fourteen Points and consequently with the pre-Armistice agreement, such specific requests for Germany as neutral arbitration of her reparations debt, a six-month limit on the occupation, a plebiscite in Alsace-Lorraine, and the option of making payments of coal in lieu of surrendering the Saar mines. On this same May 29 Tardieu was at the University of Dijon lecturing on the Treaty, and the following day he was busy on the commission for Fiume producing a compromise between the self-determination of the Italians and the self-determination of the Slavs. By then Wilson, although he denied that the pre-Armistice agreement had been violated, was inclined to concede some changes in the Treaty, particularly in the matter of reparations. Brockdorff informally suggested a lump sum of one hundred billion gold marks payable over fifty-six years without interest. Lloyd George saw Brockdorff's point even before Brockdorff had made it. Wilson pleaded with Clemenceau to agree at least to the principle of a lump sum, for technical reasons—"As long as the Germans remain in complete uncertainty as to their obligations," he reasoned, "they will be unable to find any foreign credit," hence France will not be paid.[53] By way of reply Tardieu spoke to the American delegation about canceling the French war debt to the United States and floating the German reparations bond on the American market.[54]

Until June 1 Clemenceau refused to consider any proposals for revising the Treaty; after June 1 he refused even to hear any more of them. Wrote Alexandre Ribot:

[Poincaré] is saddened by the helplessness he feels in trying to make Clemenceau understand that he is doing disservice to the interests of France. Clemenceau has become irritable. He has no one beside him except Tardieu, who is not a sure guide.[55]

Then Wilson proposed modifying not the Treaty but the "machinery of execution," whereupon Tardieu had a talk with two members of the American delegation, McCormick and Lamont. "Mr. Tardieu's position," McCormick explained to Wilson afterwards, "was that they should not agree to a change in the present Treaty; that during these five months the experts have discussed these questions pro and con, and having finally come to a decision it would be fatal to change any principle whatever"[56]—but, Lamont put in, later on Tardieu "came around and said that if it were a question of reparations alone and not a question of the Army of Occupation and these other things, they did not know but that they could devise with us the machinery that could work out the idea of a fixed sum, provided the sum were adequate enough."[57] After six days of devising, however, the sum was still not "adequate enough." Then Lloyd George, in order to strengthen his hand against the army of occupation, withdrew his objections to the reparations clauses. Keynes resigned in horror from British delegation. Wilson for his part only grew more firm, and on June 10 Tardieu had a talk with House in the morning, then wrote to him in the afternoon recapitulating:

The British, who brought forth the first proposal for a modification, are today with us against any modification, and your delegation is offering (with other changes which France could not possibly accept) the figure of one hundred twenty billion, which, as far as France is concerned, would not even amount to one half of that kind of damages, the reparation of which is exacted from Germany by the draft of May 7.

He concluded with a plea for understanding—"You know, dear friend, that I have always talked with you outspokenly"—and at the bottom of his long note, which he had typewritten hastily, he wrote by hand: "I apologize for a very bad copy. A.T."[58] That evening the Council reached a compromise: it decided to maintain the reparations clauses in full but also to instruct the Reparations Commission to fix the annuities with regard for Germany's capacity to pay.[59]

Having himself given in on reparations, Lloyd George held out all the more staunchly against the occupation of the Rhineland—for three days. Then the Council agreed to leave the clauses on the occupation intact, making instead some symbolic (that is, unimportant) changes affecting the eastern boundaries of Germany. It appointed a committee of five under the chairmanship of Tardieu to draft a reply to the "Remarks" of the German government. On June 16 the reply was ready, signed, and dispatched; it ended with the words, "As such the Treaty in its present form must be accepted or rejected."[60]

"There was suspense as Count Brockdorff-Rantzau presented the final terms of the Allies to the German government at Weimar," wrote Colonel House.[61] The German government, unwilling either to sign or to refuse to sign, resigned. Its successor offered to sign at once if the clauses on war guilt and on the surrender of war criminals were dropped; the Allies refused, whereupon the German battlefleet was scuttled by its crew at Scapa Flow. At length the Weimar assembly accepted the Treaty unconditionally, and on June 28 it was signed with great flourish in the Hall of Mirrors at Versailles. The main job of the Conference being then over, the American President and the British Prime Minister went home.

In the disputes among the three chief Allies, almost invariably France had stood alone against both Great Britain and the United States. As far as ideology was concerned, Clemenceau and Tardieu were farther apart from Wilson than they were from Lloyd George, even though they quarreled with Lloyd George more frequently. The French and the British quarreled as rivals; their motives were similar, their interests divergent. The interest of Great Britain was to weaken Germany, not to ruin her—to eliminate her as a competitor on the world market but not as a customer, and as a potential rival on the high seas but not as a potential ally on the continent. On the other hand, there was not so much a conflict of interests between France and the United States as there was a lack of rapport between the chief spokesmen of the two countries. For Wilson, the Allies were primarily peacemakers; for Clemenceau and Tardieu, they were primarily victors. As Wilson saw it, the time had come for justice to prevail in the councils of nations; as his French colleagues saw it, the time had come to settle old accounts. He had reconciliation in his heart; they had reparation on their minds. He was dreaming of the future; they were haunted by the past. He despised them as cynical; they ridiculed him as naïve. He thought they were grabbing from Germany; they thought he was mocking their dead. When he spoke of "self-determination of peoples," they replied "security of France." He wanted a new world order because the old was obviously wrong; and as the old was founded on opportunism, he would have founded the new on principles. In this he was admirable and even sensible; unfortunately he chose his principles more for the sound of them than for their meaning. Clemenceau never even tried to take "self-determination of peoples" seriously.[62] Tardieu did, and he gave up: by the test of self-determination, he found, the nationality of a population will vary with the boundaries of its territory or even with the definition of residence. In fact the very term was a misnomer: there was no question of peoples determining their nationality, but of majorities of inhabitants determining sovereignty over territories. Wrote House of self-determination: "This noble sentiment, carried to its logical conclusion, would have wrecked the governmental machinery of the world"[63]—but to what other conclusion than the logical one did Wilson intend it to be carried? Wilson's principles, being equivocal, were dangerous, and Tardieu fought them even as much as to make fun of them. Wilson had no use for facts that did not fit his principles; Tardieu had no use for principles that did not fit the facts. For their contemporaries, Tardieu came to typify the "realist" and Wilson the "idealist." Both were to die disillusioned.

The reparations question had been the most persistent source of conflict among the Allies during the Conference, and it was to remain such for many years afterwards. Today we regard France as having been savagely unreasonable about reparations. Germany, we say, could never have paid full reparations as defined in the Treaty: we say so because in fact she never did pay a tenth that much, and because moreover Keynes, who was a great economist, said she could not. In fact the position of the French was the only one combining both principle and practicality. If Germany was responsible for the war, Germany was liable for the damages; in this case her debt was what she owed, not what she could afford, and to ask for anything less was to ask for a tribute, not an indemnity. She was, of course, to pay only as she could—but time would tell more accurately than Keynes what rate of payment she could meet. If the total was clearly too great, just as clearly it had to be reduced; but then it had to be reduced discreetly, behind closed doors, and according to some principle defensible as such to the debtors—such was the effect both of Dulles' and of Tardieu's proposals, which distinguished categories of damages. Although Germany's capacity to pay was relevant to the amount of the total debt, her capacity to pay easily was relevant only to the mode of payment, and no more to the amount of her debt than was the capacity of the Allies to forego payment. The danger was, not to establish the amount of the debt in consideration of the debtor's capacity to pay, but to show willingness to do so. The British and the Americans may have been right in wanting to reduce the total further at the very outset; the British were certainly wrong, though, in making a public issue of reducing it, and the Americans in wanting to reduce it arbitrarily. However valid the arguments of Keynes may have been in private discussion among the Allies, in public controversy among the Allies they were valid preeminently as an incentive to Germany to default. Wilson on his side argued to reduce the total not by restricting the definition of war costs but by fixing a lump sum in agreement with the Germans. The debt might well have been more negotiable as a lump sum, but in arguing for a lump sum he was avowedly arguing for an expedient, not for a principle. Arguments from expediency were dangerous, because they gave the Germans grounds for reply—and, by the same token, arguing about expedients with the Germans themselves was fatal. Coming from Wilson, arguments from expediency were incongruous—at first blush; in reality, though, Wilson argued from expediency because, like his countrymen in general, he did not wholeheartedly credit the principle involved. In the eyes of Americans, Germany's reparations debt, though real, was somewhat less real than, say, France's war debt. The first could be fixed by inspiration, they thought, the second only by computation; the first was not legal tender for payment on the second, and if they were willing to waive their share of the one in full, they were not willing to waive a penny of their share in the other.

Clemenceau and Wilson could never have come to an understanding by their own devices. What saved the Conference more than once was the friendship of House and Tardieu. Throughout each crisis, while Wilson was busy evangelizing Clemenceau and Clemenceau blaspheming Wilson, their two confidants were busy compromising.

Compromise saved the Conference, but it stunted the peace. There is no real compromise between forgiving and not forgiving, or between punishing and not punishing. The Germans might have adjusted to one treatment or to the other; they were unable to adjust to a smattering of both. Again, France might have sought her security either in the weakness of Germany or in the strength of her understanding with her allies; she could not do both, and by compromising she failed to do either.

In France the Treaty satisfied no one completely: some found it too hard, some not hard enough. Briand found it too hard—and, having had no part in making it, he was to have no qualms about unmaking it. Tardieu himself found it not hard enough, and for twenty years he was to defend it word for word against revision. Both were wrong, and each was right. Had the Allies put Germany dismembered, dismantled, and disarmed under their perpetual surveillance, quite likely there would have been no *Führer* and no new war; and just as likely there would at least have been no *Führer* had they let Germany off with a light fine and a reprimand. Had the Conference suffered more, then, humanity might have suffered less.

But the Treaty was not the last word. Tardieu himself, who had wanted it to provide for every contingency, wrote: "Treaties, like laws, are worth only as much as the hand that applies them."[64] Was that hand to be his?

CHAPTER 22

L'Expérience Tardieu

"Possibly more than any other man in the history of French politics . . .
André Tardieu came into office with the ability and energy as well as the
desire to achieve something constructive."*

DURING THE SUMMER and early fall of 1919 Tardieu assisted in the
reembarkation of the American Expeditionary Force,[1] took part in the
peace negotiations with Austria, Bulgaria, and Turkey,[2] and campaigned
for France to ratify of the treaty with Germany—with "full confidence,"
he declared, that the United States would follow suit.[3] In October he prepared the instructions for the first French delegation to the League of
Nations. On November 6, the General Commissariat for Franco-American
War Cooperation having gone out of business, Clemenceau created for
him a new ministry, the Ministry of Liberated Regions, with authority
over reconstruction and rehabilitation in Alsace-Lorraine and the regions
of France lately occupied by the enemy. In the general elections a few
days later he ran in the Seine-et-Oise department and won against the
great nationalist orator Franklin-Bouillon.[4] Next he set to work computing war damages and organizing reconstruction in the "liberated
regions" while also assisting Foch to negotiate a military convention with
Belgium.[5] For the moment, then, he gave signs of settling down to an
orthodox political career.

Signs only. The new parliament was pervaded by the disillusionment
that follows victory. Most of its members were newcomers; these held
Clemenceau in suspicion, as a man who had negotiated in secret, while
the others did not forgive him for having won the war and made the
peace without their help. Nearly all were veterans; to them Clemenceau
was a glorious relic, and as such he conjured up bad memories. The old
warlord was undergoing the painful metamorphosis from a great leader
into a great legend. The Chamber belittled him; Briand maneuvred against
him; finally the left itself in a trial ballot turned him down for the pres-

*Robert Valeur, in Raymond Leslie Buell, ed., *Democratic Governments in Europe*
(New York, Nelson, 1935).

idency of the Republic. Tardieu stood by him: "The last debates of the Clemenceau government," he wrote,

the shameful sacrifice of the old chief, the indecent frenzy of the Congress of Versailles in January, 1920, applauding at the sacrifice, would have sufficed to induce me to abandon the parliamentary career had I not still believed in the battle to preserve the results and the spirit of our victory. I led this battle until 1924 against the imbecility of the *Chambre bleu horizon*, against governments that, while reproaching Clemenceau with not having gained enough, abandoned his gains one after the other.[6]

The Clemenceau ministry resigned on January 18, 1920, and Clemenceau went into retirement. Tardieu, refusing to stay on at his post under Millerand, instead founded the *opposition clemenciste*. He had four followers to begin with: Klotz, Loucheur, and two new deputies, Ignace and Georges Mandel. The first two were soon to desert—Loucheur to become a minister again, and Klotz because he was uncomfortable on the right. For the group was on the right, its sole purpose being to preserve the world of 1919, to institutionalize the victory over Germany—alone in the war-weary nation its members argued for the maintenance of a standing army at wartime strength. Tardieu meanwhile became chairman in the Chamber of the Commission on War-damaged Regions, which did much good, hard work compiling figures on destruction and reconstruction; and he continued to advise Foch on the convention with Belgium, which was ready in May.

During the spring of 1920, in a series of articles in the review *L'Illustration*, then in his book *La Paix* (*The Truth About the Treaty*), Tardieu gave a minute account of the preparation of the Treaty of Versailles, defending point by point the work of the French negotiators. His defense is successful on the whole, and his testimony invaluable. Neither, however, can stand alone: he had seen the Conference at too close range to see it as a whole, and in 1920 its controversies were still too vivid in his mind for him to judge their outcome.[7] He sought not so much to analyze the peace settlement as to establish its sanctity; afterwards, in speeches to the Chamber, in articles and lectures, month after month for four years, he was to inveigh against France's successive "abandonments," redundantly and at length monotonously.

The "abandonments" began even as he wrote *La Paix*. In 1920 France agreed first to a reduction of her share of reparations payments from 65 percent to 55 percent, then to a further reduction of her share to 52 percent as well as to a 25—percent reduction of all annuities.[8] In January, 1921, Lloyd George pressed Premier Briand in Paris to agree to a further reduction of the annuities and to a maximum aggregate of 132 billion marks—or about half as much as Clemenceau and Tardieu had expected for France alone. Poincaré joined Tardieu in protest, and John Maynard Keynes fretted: "A breach in the conversations might mean the fall of Briand and the entrance to office of the wild men, Poincaré and Tardieu."[9] Briand met Lloyd George's terms, whereupon Tardieu interpellated him, citing chapter and verse:

The Treaty of Versailles says, "Germany shall reimburse, whatever their amount, the categories of damage written in Annex II"; the Paris decisions do not mention those categories. The Treaty of Versailles says...

"I am an ingenuous man," Briand replied,

and when M. Tardieu let me know that he was going to interpellate me, I allowed myself to feel a little pleased. I said to myself, M. Tardieu is one of the chief architects of the Treaty of Versailles, and as such he knows its good points, but he also knows its bad points, and he will be indulgent with a man who has dutifully applied it to the best of his ability. *Mais voilà!* I did not stop to think that M. Tardieu had already expended his whole stock of indulgence on his own handiwork....[10]

"The flaying of M. Tardieu was intensely dramatic," jubilated the *Times* of London.[11] The French parliament approved the Paris decisions, but the German government refused to subscribe to them—"fortunately," commented Tardieu.[12] The Allies rescinded their concession on the annuities, then threatened invasion, whereupon Germany recognized the maximum aggregate as prescribed.[13]

Tardieu's hostility toward Briand did not abate—on the contrary. In the fall of 1921, when Briand agreed to attend the Washington naval disarmament conference without first seeing the agenda, Tardieu described his policies as those of "a dead dog floating with the current;"[14] neither he nor Briand ever lived the phrase down. In Washington Briand accepted parity with Italy for capital ships; Tardieu attacked him for humiliating France. Meanwhile reparations payments from Germany fell off, and in December the Reparations Commission recommended a moratorium; Tardieu led the Chamber in putting pressure on Briand to reject the recommendation. Briand rejected it, whereupon the Supreme Allied Council met in Cannes in January, 1922, to seek an alternative; failing to find one, it called for a general European economic conference to seek one in its stead. Briand meanwhile began negotiating with Lloyd George a new treaty of guarantee.[15] The Chamber, however, did not trust him to negotiate; on January 12 he was recalled to Paris, and the next day he resigned.

Poincaré, succeeding Briand as Premier, invited Tardieu to join the new government; Tardieu refused on the pretext that Poincaré had kept part of Briand's cabinet. In fact the invitation was only a tease: a few days earlier had appeared the first issue of the newspaper *L'Echo National*, which bore on its masthead, "*Fondateur: Georges Clemenceau. Directeur politique: André Tardieu.*" *L'Echo National* was, simply, the newspaper of the *opposition clemenciste*. Clemenceau confined himself to having founded it; the writing was done by others, principally Tardieu and Georges Mandel. Its choice morsel was Tardieu's editorial, which read like a message from the graves of Flanders. Otherwise it was remarkable chiefly for its accusations: it brought vague but grave charges against Millerand, Briand, and Loucheur for their dealings with the Industrial Bank of China, and it reported Poincaré first to be arming the Little Entente against "the Kemalists and the Soviets,"[16] then to have equipped the Turkish army for its offensive against Greece.[17]

The European economic conference was held in Genoa in April, 1922. The German delegates requested a reparations moratorium; the British supported their request, the French opposed it. As the quarrel persisted, the Soviet and German delegates sneaked off together to Rapallo and signed a commercial treaty, thereby frightening the conference out of existence. Thereafter Germany, remaining in default, periodically asked for a moratorium; each time Poincaré refused, and each time Tardieu accused him of refusing too politely. When at length Poincaré threatened an occupation of the Ruhr, Tardieu urged him to work out an alternative with England. Poincaré tried and failed, and in January, 1923, French troops entered the Ruhr; then all year long Tardieu found fault with the manner of the occupation. Germany meanwhile pleaded for a new assessment of her capacity to pay, and when in November the Chamber gave signs of weakening, Tardieu enumerated the "abandonments" of the past four years—"It is an odd fact," he said, "that this Chamber, which is always and on all questions divided in two…, can achieve great majorities only for voting away the rights of France."[18] Poincaré in self-defense claimed to have striven vainly during the Peace Conference to restrain Clemenceau from giving in on the western frontier of Germany, whereupon Tardieu rushed to see Clemenceau and got from him the reply: "There was *never* any dispute between the President of the Republic and myself on the question of the Rhine frontier."[19] The Chamber was not interested. It gave the government a vote of confidence, and in January, 1924, Tardieu protesting, an inter-Allied commission met under General Dawes to reassess Germany's capacity to pay.

In the general elections of May, 1924, Tardieu was again a candidate in Seine-et-Oise. As usual his campaign was lively: at one meeting, after refusing to surrender the speaker's platform to interrupters, he was thrown off it; he climbed right back up, only to be thrown down again, this time conclusively.[20] He did not mind being beaten conclusively; to be beaten inconclusively, though, was more than he could bear. Through the workings of an incongruous electoral law[21] he lost the election with 76,000 votes while others won it in the same district with as few as 24,000. His defeat completed his embitterment, and in an open letter to his former constituents he announced his decision to retire from public life. The world of 1919 was a fading memory, and he had grown mechanical if not also perverse in his efforts to sustain it. Abandoning his friends, his newspaper, and his city to their fate, he set out with fishing tackle and golf clubs for Saint-Cloud.

For some months he did what was least expected of him—nothing at all. Clemenceau sent him a book inscribed "*A André Tardieu. Souvenirs et regrets*,"[22] and Colette wrote in epitaph, "With Tardieu ends the long line of journalists to be seen at work in cafés."[23]

For distraction from angling and putting, Tardieu at length fell back on writing. He wrote articles on the international situation for an American news syndicate. With a Danish historian he wrote an account of the Schleswig issue at the peace conference, *Le Slesvig et la paix*—he attributed the moderation of the Danish government's demands on Germany to the intimidation of the prime Minister, Zahle, by the very memory of the fearful Second Reich. Finally, in his distress over the estrangement of France and the United States—"Two great nations which I have seen so splendidly able to work together are [today] parted farther asunder than at any time in their history"[24]—he wrote *Devant l'obstacle (France and America)*, which won fair praise in both countries.[25] It begins with an account of the "wartime cooperation" and the "peacetime crisis" between the United States and France, and it ends with a comparative study of the political temperament of the French and of the Americans—Frenchmen, he found, prefer to quarrel over the form of government, Americans over economic welfare. In between is a remarkable history of the people of war-torn Soissonnais and Laonnois, "the most French of the lands of France."

In January, 1926, a seat fell vacant in the Chamber for the electoral precinct of Belfort. For fifty years Belfort had sent only Radicals or Socialists to the Chamber. The challenge was too great for Tardieu to resist, and he gave in to the fifth or sixth petition from the local conservatives. He did not start to campaign until two weeks before the vote; then, fresh from the first long vacation of his life, he campaigned with such verve that Moro-Giafferi and Léon Blum rushed to Belfort to combat him. Their efforts notwithstanding, he won an absolute majority on the first ballot, on February 14. From Clemenceau came the telegram: "You have sought a mandate to speak in the name of France. France is waiting for you. Yours with all my heart."[26] And indeed, he meant to speak in the name of France, not in the name of Clemenceau. He was as anxious as ever to defend the remnants of the Treaty against further "abandonments." Not, however, as the high priest of a cult of conservation, hurling anathema from the gallery—not by renewing what he called "the vain opposition of the years 1920–24." This time he was resolved on taking power himself.

Taking power meant, first of all, finesse and compromise. The "independent deputy from Belfort" took a seat in the center of the Chamber, and there for some weeks he sat in obstreperous silence. He kept in touch with his new constituency through daily articles in *Le Républicain de Belfort*, and never did he write less mordantly. Inflation was then running wild in France, and the game of politics with it. President Doumergue, holding Poincaré in reserve, was exhausting every other possibility for the premiership; his victim of the moment was Briand, who, holding Caillaux in contempt, was exhausting every other possibility for the Ministry of Finance. At last Briand came arm in arm with Caillaux to the Chamber, asking for full powers, and Tardieu broke his silence to read "the single article of the draft law *Rubicon*."[27] Then Herriot, in trying to fight inflation by eloquence, cleared the way for Poincaré, who on July 22 formed a "national-union" cabinet. Briand and Herriot both joined him, and so did Tardieu.

Poincaré kept his cabinet small, making its size a symbol of deflation. Tardieu took over the three ministries of Public Works, of the Merchant Marine, and of the Liberated Regions, which, because they called for administrative ability rather than political *savoir-faire*, bore the trade name of "technical ministries" as opposed to "political ministries." As ministries went they did not rate highly, and the politic thing for Tardieu to do in his position was to *expédier les affaires courantes* with the air of a miscast leading man. Instead he went to work. France had some of the best roads in the world, but France had also some of the worst, and the network was incomplete. He launched a drive for forty thousand kilometers of new or renovated highway; in two years the job was done, whereupon he turned his attention to railways and to bicycle paths. Meanwhile, he maintained a full construction program for light merchant vessels. And on Armistice Day of 1927 he announced the completion of the reconstruction program in the former war zones, which has been called "the greatest economic achievement of postwar Europe";[28] shortly afterwards, eight years after he had set it up, the Ministry of Liberated Regions died of inanition. He gave every sign of good fellowship with Briand and Herriot, both inside the Council of Ministers and outside it. He no longer criticized the Locarno Pact except for applying only to the western frontier of Germany; he endorsed the Kellogg-Briand Pact, though he saw small value in it, and he even swallowed the bitter pill when in September, 1928, Briand promised Stresemann the evacuation of the Rhineland ahead of schedule if a new and definitive agreement on reparations were reached.[29]

In the general elections of the spring of 1928, which were "on the right," he was reelected in Belfort with an increased majority; naturally he got his nose punched and his *lorgnon* shattered in the process.[30] The following November, when the Radicals in the cabinet resigned, he took over the Ministry of the Interior from one of them. This was the "political ministry" *par excellence*. He knew it from long acquaintance, and "he ran it like the headquarters of a huge civil army": when once[31] without his authorization the Communist party called on a half-million suburban workers to manifest their class consciousness, he had the party leaders arrested, not excluding Maurice Thorez—"to the great joy of the Socialists," he wrote, "who pretended to be indignant, but who were delighted."[32] Tardieu stayed on at his post when, in July, 1929, Poincaré withdrew as Premier and Briand took over.

Briand was not Premier for long. Early in 1929 a committee of experts meeting under an American, Owen D. Young, had recommended a reduction of the total reparations debt, an extension to 1988 of the schedule of payments, and the deliverance by Germany of a bond for the whole amount. In a convention signed at The Hague in August, 1929, the Allies, in return for Germany's undertaking to accept the final recommendations of the Young committee, agreed to evacuate the second zone of the Rhineland beginning in September, 1929, and ending in January, 1930, and the third zone beginning eight months after the ratification of the convention—and ending on June 30, 1930. The Hague convention was "the most astonishingly worded paper in diplomatic history," wrote Tardieu,[33] who of the whole arrangment approved only the reparations bond, known as "commercialization of the debt"—his own idea of ten years earlier. The Council of Ministers on August 31 reached unanimity on a single point: there was to be *no* evacuation until the Young Plan had gone into effect. Almost immediately Briand ordered the evacuation of Mainz, the center of the second zone. Foch protested, Tardieu vociferated, and the order was rescinded;[34] nonetheless the cabinet, having lost its support on the right, was doomed.

For weeks alternatives were aired in the corridors, until at last the Cartel des Gauches arranged with Briand to vote against him on the reparations issue as a sign of confidence—to "liberate" him from the right and so clear the way for him to head a left-wing government. On October 22 Briand refused to insist on commercialization of the debt before evacuation even of the third zone of the Rhineland; there were 288 deputies against 277 to demand "commercialization before evacuation," and he fell. The extreme right had voted against him, of course, along with the Cartel des Gauches, yet even so he would have failed to fall on this occasion had not a deputy in the center, François de Wendel, rounded up a few more votes against him.[35]

The interregnum lasted two weeks. While others stayed up nights scheming, Tardieu slept.[36] Daladier, whom President Doumergue called first, failed to find a majority on the left even though Briand agreed to join him and Tardieu not to combat him. Clémentel, a former Radical, failed to find a majority in the center even though Briand joined him and Tardieu accepted the Ministry of the Navy. Then on November 1 Doumergue, having proved his point, called Tardieu.

At once Tardieu sent the Radicals an offer of eight cabinet posts along with the draft of a program including provisions for social insurance, free secondary schooling, veterans' pensions, family allocations, a health campaign, and tariff increases for all agricultural products. Some of these measures were already pending before parliament;[37] most of them were part of the Radical program itself. What was original was their being taken up by Tardieu. "He was resolutely on the left, not out of tactical necessity but out of taste," judged one observer.[38] Perhaps. Certainly, though, having the confidence of the right, he was the very man to put through the program of the left, and at first many Radicals welcomed his offer. Not so the party leaders, though—for party leaders, programs are first and foremost a means of taking power, not of using it. Moreover:

If they let André Tardieu get into race and win it, he would become...the chief toward whom the masses would turn; he would be above the rituals of the game of politics. This was the danger they had to guard against. And so they condemned his offer of collaboration without even taking the trouble to find out more about it. He was the man whom they dreaded, whom they drove off, whom they wanted to put to death.[39]

Herriot called a meeting of his parliamentary group. Sixty out of 265 came; they discussed not Tardieu's program but his personality, and by 40 to 20 they turned his offer down.

The Radicals would not help him apply his program? He would apply it anyhow, without them—even against them. He made his appeal for support to men and not to parties—under constitutional law, he told the reporters, parties did not exist. He began with a telephone call to Briand: Briand agreed to remain at the Quai d'Orsay. Though politically the two still stood far apart, personally they had drawn together. "Briand's charm had worked on Tardieu; Tardieu's intelligence had won over Briand"[40]—and besides, if with him Tardieu failed to find a majority on the right, Briand expected to find one himself on the left more easily. Within twelve hours Tardieu had a full team, which included few former ministers and no party men. He took the Ministry of the Interior himself; he made the venerable Henry Chéron Minister of Finance and the brilliant André Maginot Minister of War, and on November 3 he met with the two at the Place Beauveau.

Considering on the one hand the imminence of three great debates on foreign policy—reparations, naval armaments, air and ground armaments—and on the other hand the recommendations of the finance commissions in favor of a utilization of surplus Treasury funds, we took a decision then and there. It was agreed among us to raise about eight billions[41] from Treasury funds to provide:
(1) The sums necessary for completing our defensive fortifications;
(2) The equivalent for a program of national equipment...[42]

He had given the Radicals a preview of his program; the rumor spread that there was even more to come. He told the press nothing: he merely declared, infuriating Léon Blum, that he would place his government "under the aegis of good humor," leaving France free to "follow in the joyous paths of her destiny."[43]

He made his bid for the confidence of the Chamber on November 7. By then the professionals were giving heavy odds against him—apart from all other considerations, he was a veteran of the World War and a Parisian, and the Republic had never known a premier of either description. Facing his audience proudly, almost defiantly, he declared that so long as world disarmament were not realized he would work to strengthen the defenses and alliances of France, and that meanwhile he would equip the nation economically and give it social peace. After repeating his proposals for social legislation, he outlined a five-year plan for "national retooling"[44]—for the mechanization of agriculture and the modernization of industry; for the construction of houses, schools, hospitals, and research laboratories; for reforestation; for the equipment of all rural communities with railroad and telephone service, with electricity and drinking water. Though he proposed to use Treasury funds to finance his program, he undertook to obtain all manner of tax reduction and tax exemption. "In short," he concluded, "we mean to define and, if you will let us, to introduce into France *une politique de prospérité.*"[45]

His enthusiasm carried conviction, and as he spoke the odds against him fell. One Radical interrupted him to shout: "It's the Radical program!"[46] Franklin-Bouillon was expected to attack him on foreign policy; instead he spoke without malice. Barthou and Briand were expected to combat him behind his back; Barthou did not budge, and Briand for his part declared: "It was all the more agreeable for me to join M. Tardieu since, deliberating side by side in the preceding cabinet, never on any point of foreign policy did we find ourselves in disagreement."[47] While the deputies smiled, Tardieu returned the compliment to Briand by declaring that, as his government read the convention of August 29, the evacuation of the third zone of the Rhineland was to begin only "after the Young Plan had been ratified and put into force"; further, by "put into force" his government understood the deposit by Germany in the future Bank for International Settlements of the full issue of reparations bonds.[48] After thirty-six hours of deliberation the Chamber gave him its confidence by 327 to 256. His majority, astonished at its own strength, broke out into loud and long applause.

Most of the confidence shown him, however clamorous the show, was strictly official, as he well knew. The rest he had won on the strength of his intentions, which was not the same thing as winning it on the strength of his acts. If he was anathema to the left for having stolen its program, he was suspect to the right for the same reason. Still, he *had* made a start; and the same evening he dined out with a few friends, bathed and changed in his apartments at the Ministry of the Interior, had a brief chat with Doumergue at the Elysée, then went back across the Place Beauveau to his ministry and to... work.

Tardieu worked at top speed until the end of the year to put his program through the Chamber. First he had a wheat tariff voted; next a wine tariff; then in consultation with sugar-growers, wholesalers, and retailers he drew up a sugar-tariff act, which the chambers adopted a few days later. Because the vote on the budget for 1930 was bound to be slow, he had the chambers extend the budget year 1929 by three months, expecting thereby to obviate the need for provisional monthly credits.

With Chéron and Maginot he prepared a bill for the construction by January 1, 1935, of a line of defensive fortifications along the northeastern frontier of France. Ever since he and Gamelin had suggested such a line fifteen years earlier it had been under discussion in the commissions; however, there had been no funds available for it, so the discussions had been strictly academic. Tardieu requested 3,300 million francs from Treasury funds, of which 1,000 million immediately; he invoked urgency, the annual contingent of recruits being on the decline. The Chamber approved the plans for the "Maginot Line" by 355–231, the Senate unanimously; then the credits came through on a vote of confidence, and construction began with the new year. The problem of the northern frontier remained, however. The general staff favored extending the Maginot Line along the Franco-Belgian border. The Belgians themselves were not averse to this solution, which they thought would deter Germany from ever invading their country as a shortcut to France. But "Tardieu had another idea," wrote Gamelin, "one that went back to our work together in 1915—that of lending Belgium the sums necessary for setting up a solid defensive system not only from Antwerp to Liège, but also facing Luxembourg as far as Arlon."[49] There was, of course, the risk of offending Belgium by a debate in parliament on the loan. "The idea was attractive," wrote Gamelin. "Was it politically feasible?"[50]

Once the lid of the Treasury was lifted, the clamor for funds arose on all sides. On December 11, after obtaining in the morning a vote of confidence from the Chamber on his refusal of a pay increase for army recruits, Tardieu found himself confronted in the afternoon with the same demand cut in half. *"Ce n'est pas sérieux,"* he said angrily.[51] Thereupon the opposition accused him of making a mockery of its rights; he accused the opposition in reply of practicing "guerrilla warfare at every turn,"[52] and the following day in the Senate, speaking of postwar France, he said:

It is as if the people were holding a perpetual electoral campaign and had given their representatives an imperious and permanent mandate to ambush any and every government.

All too often the result is—and you will not contradict me—that majorities, which ought normally to be instruments for applying policies, become ends in themselves, to the detriment of all policies.

The result is also that often the simplest matters drag on interminably....[53]

What he said was all too true; by saying it he made it all the truer. Four days later an interpellation on his "remarks to the Senate" cut into the budget debate in the Chamber. The parties of the left, considering his remarks to have been directed solely at themselves, accused him of driving a wedge between the left and the right. On the contrary, he replied, he sought unanimity, and so far he had won it on most of his reforms; as for those still under discussion:

Eh bien, messieurs, you'll have to admit that they aren't so bad, since as it happens, according to your own orators and newspapers, it was neither I nor yet some Baron Louis who thought them up: it was *you.* So are you going to shoot at me at the very moment when I come before you bearing your children in my arms?[54]

"*Les enfants sur les bras*" made parliamentary history, becoming the catch-word for what Albert Thibaudet called "the new opportunism...the program of the advanced party carried out by the conservative party at the opportune moment."[55]

On November 24, hardly a fortnight after Tardieu took power, Clemenceau died. Tardieu spent the final hours with his great friend; then, kneeling at the deathbed, he wept bitterly. "The voice of a whole people spoke through the lips of that old man, opening up the paths of hope to the generations of tomorrow," he told the Senate.[56] Ten months earlier Foch too had died; with Clemenceau, then, Tardieu lost his last friend in a generation to which he had been as close in sentiment as ever he was to his own.

Throughout December Tardieu spent his every spare minute preparing for two conferences scheduled for January, the first at The Hague on the Young Plan and the second in London on naval armaments. Occasionally he consulted Briand; Briand, however, was having a serious spell of lethargy at the time. "He can spend hours doing nothing, *nothing*," Tardieu once said. "I don't believe he is even thinking: he is dreaming."[57] On December 24 Briand almost brought down the government by shrugging off a reference to the revival of militarism in Germany. On December 27 Tardieu got a vote of confidence to attend the conferences, and within the next three days he obtained, besides the Maginot credits, a salary increase for civil servants and a series of tax exemptions. Then by decree he dismissed the chambers for two weeks, and on January 2 he left for The Hague.

By decision of the Young committee, Germany henceforth was to make reparations payments in the currencies of the creditor nations, and the Reparations Commission, which then did little more than assure the conversion of payments, was to disappear. At the very outset Tardieu declared the main problem of the conference to be that of determining how, in the absence of an agency of control, the Allies would be able to establish willful default: unless the settlement provided for the application of sanctions in case of willful default, he declared, he would not regard it as definitive. The Young Plan was defective on this point, and for days the German delegates clung to the defect, Tardieu rousing them to fury by his intransigence. He had the edge on them because, being on strong ground, he would not have minded had the conference broken down. The British delegation, after mediating awhile, finally sided with him, and on January 14 all parties agreed to recognize the jurisdiction of the Permanent Court of International Justice in The Hague in cases of default, the creditors of Germany reserving full liberty of action in the event of a verdict against her.

His triumph complete, Tardieu returned to Paris on January 15, just as the chambers reconvened; a few hours later, having obtained their final approval for his stand on naval armaments, he left for London to consult with MacDonald in advance of the conference. He had to break off his consultations once to return and face angry questioning on the appointment as Chief of Staff of General Weygand, who had earned the contempt of the left by defeating the Red Army at Warsaw and the Druses at Suwayda. The conference opened on January 21, and that day Tardieu expressed his customary optimism; his task was, however, quite delicate. Eight years earlier, in Washington, Briand had accepted parity for France with Italy in capital ships; Tardieu was resolved to obtain compensation on other ships.[58] The tonnage requirements of a country, he argued, were relative to the length of its strategic coastline and of the water routes to its territories overseas. On both these counts the requirements of France were greater than those of Italy; besides, France touched on two seas, and so out-and-out parity would mean in effect inferiority for France in the Mediterranean. Italy, meanwhile, had the precedent of Washington in her favor, and the Italian Foreign Minister, Grandi, had also the irrelevant and highly persuasive argument that Italy was willing to accept any absolute low in tonnage if only she were not alone the lowest.[59] The other powers tended to side with Italy: if parity did not mean equality, they said, it meant nothing—and parity, they thought, would deter either country from ever making war on the other.

Until the end of the month Tardieu and Grandi clashed dramatically, both winning popularity at home as a result. For six days afterwards Tardieu was busy in Paris pushing his social-insurance bill through the Chamber. Then he conferred in London for one week with each delegation separately and secretly, seeking a compromise.[60] On February 15 he left again to spend a weekend in Paris; he caught cold on the way, and he was in bed with a 104-degree temperature when on February 17

Henry Chéron asked the confidence of the Chamber against an income-tax exemption for wives who, employed only by their husbands, did not earn enough to bring the household income up to 20,000 francs. The government fell, with a margin of five votes against it. Many deputies, ashamed of themselves, rushed to rectify their ballots, but it was too late.

President Doumergue designated a Radical, Camille Chautemps, to succeed Tardieu. Chautemps first formed an all-Radical cabinet; it lasted three days. Then on a second try he offered Tardieu the vice-premiership and the Ministry of the Navy, inviting him moreover to continue as chairman of the French delegation to London. "Chautemps asked only a very small sacrifice of me," recalled Tardieu, "but one that I judged dishonorable—the repudiation of one of the groups of my former majority.... He never understood my refusal. I never understood his offer."[61] Chautemps's second try failed, and on February 26, the ninth day of the crisis, Doumergue recalled Tardieu to power.

Again Tardieu invited the Radicals to join him; again the Radicals said no. Thereupon he put his old cabinet back into place—with a few additions. He created a Ministry of Public Health, charging it with the jobs of organizing vacation camps for children and of fighting tuberculosis, syphilis, cancer, and infantile diseases; he also resuscitated the ministries of Aviation, of Postal Communications, and of the Merchant Marine. To every minister he assigned an under-secretary of state. Poincaré in 1926 had set the fashion of cabinets of from twelve to fifteen members; Tardieu's now numbered 33—"It's not a cabinet, it's a tribe!" cried Daladier.[62] Two Radicals joined the tribe as under-secretaries of state: a lawyer, Falcoz, and Tardieu's former colleague on *Le Temps*, Eugène Lautier, now editor of the influential newspaper *L'Homme libre*; the renegades were repudiated by their party. Tardieu's program went unchanged—retooling and social insurance, as safeguards for the future. "*Le ministère Tardieu continue*," he told the press,[63] and on March 5 the Chamber gave him its confidence anew with a margin of 53 votes. The crisis, for all its futility, had served at least to prove to the left fringe of Tardieu's majority that no other majority was possible—just yet.

Tardieu had barely hung up his hat again at the Place Beauveau when a catastrophe struck the nation: the whole southwest was devastated by floods. He went at once himself to direct the relief operations, and on his return five days later he obtained the vote of a relief fund of one billion francs. Then on March 15, after having pushed his secondary-schooling bill through the Chamber and sustained eight defeats in one day in a debate on the budget, he returned to London at last—"with a broad smile and an extra-long cigarette holder," wrote one reporter.[64] The flood-relief work went on in his absence, affording by its results the proof of his good intentions: "The attribution of [this] credit...," wrote François Goguel, "besides giving rise to scandalous waste, produced general dissatisfaction in the region, for every victim of the flood considered himself to have been cheated when he compared his indemnity to his neighbor's, and whoever had been spared by the floods got the feeling that he had missed out on a wonderful opportunity for getting rich."[65]

Tardieu resumed the discussions in London at a disadvantage, the other negotiators having in his absence more or less agreed on strict parity for France and Italy as well as on global tonnage limitations such as would have left the French fleet approximately as it then was.[66] Grandi, meanwhile, had dropped hints that Italy might accept something less than strict parity with France in return for compensation in North Africa. Tardieu in his turn dropped hints that he might agree either to an equal rate of naval construction for France and Italy, France preserving her lead of 250,000 tons, or else to equal fleets in the Mediterranean, France being allowed an additional fleet in the Atlantic, provided in either case that a nonaggression pact were concluded among the Mediterranean powers under the guarantee of Great Britain.[67] Provided also that the settlement were definitive: though he was willing to limit future construction, he said, he was not willing to shut down the French shipyards for the sake of a short-term agreement.

He was in London only long enough to drop hints; then Briand took over for him, and he returned to Paris to face questioning in the Senate on the size of his ministry and steer the Hague agreement through the commissions and the chambers. While the questioning meant merely another exercise in repartee, no single task in all his career was so distasteful to him as defending the final evacuation of the Rhineland as a counterpart to a further reduction of the reparations debt. But he had no way out. France had been committed in advance by the convention of August, 1929. Moreover, the other Allied governments were all enthusiastic about the final agreement, and in France the opposition to it was quiescent at best. He was two weeks in getting it past the commissions and the Chamber, then two days in bed with an upset stomach. On April 5 he defended it before the Senate, to cries of "Very good!" from Joseph Caillaux. It was, said Tardieu, "a means of consolidating the peace"; it was "definitive"; and it was "guaranteed"—by the right of the Allies to resort to sanctions in case of willful default, by Germany's own interest in respecting it in order to restore her credit abroad, and by "the undertaking of Germany. Let us take care not to treat too lightly the undertaking of a great country," he said, without even stressing word *too*. The Senate ratified unanimously.[68]

Tardieu spent the remainder of April fighting for his social-insurance bill, his pensions bill, and his budget. The Chamber approved the social-insurance bill nearly unanimously; the pensions bill, however, it rejected, and the budget, despite the extension of the fiscal year by three months, came through only just in time to make a second provisional monthly allowance unnecessary. In London, meanwhile, the negotiators, leaving the dispute between France and Italy in abeyance, settled on a treaty applicable only to Great Britain, Japan, and the United States except in its provisions for the regulation of submarine warfare and for a five-year holiday on the construction of capital ships.[69] Tardieu did not go to London to sign it. He did, however, in May sign the definitive version of the Young Plan, and immediately the final evacuation of the Rhineland began. "Comrades, raise up your spirits—France has need of you once more!" he told a congress of veterans in Lyon the following day.[70] The evacuation was completed by June 30, four and a half years ahead of schedule; it was, he wrote bitterly, "the most generous gesture in French history."[71]

"During the months of June and July parliament will have to discuss the national-retooling bill, which, essential as it is, has been waiting since November," declared Tardieu in Dijon on June 1; and of his other bills in suspense he said: "It is important that these measures be enacted before the summer vacation."[72] Collectively his proposals defined a new doctrine, he added: the doctrine of the welfare state.

The doctrines of yesterday have been outdistanced by events; if we are to have control over events, the time has come to define the doctrine of to-morrow.

The doctrines of yesterday you know. The first is the old and noble doctrine of laissez-faire. Let us pay it a just homage, for it has given rise to much beneficent initiative. But let us recognize that, confronted with the present concentration of capital, size of enterprises, and internationalization of business, it is no longer adequate. Whether we like it or not, the state must henceforth intervene where formerly it did not and take charge of things it used to ignore. ... The other doctrine that has not withstood the test of events is Marxism. No one will deny that, on technical grounds, Marx foresaw clearsightedly the grandiose development of machine industry and the concentration of capital. But he was wrong about the consequences. He prophesied evil effects of the iron law of wages, a relentless class war, the disappearance of the middle classes. Nothing of the sort has come about.[73]

His own economic and social "experiment" was open to all but the impenitent adherents of the old doctrines, he said, and he made a standing offer to admit any non-Marxist groups in parliament to as much share and influence in his government as their numbers warranted.[74]

He did not meet his schedule for the summer months, and his invitation came to nothing. First the public-school teachers and postal workers went on strike for a foretaste of prosperity. He had their strike leaders fired, and at a meeting of the presidents of the parliamentary groups on June 7 the president of the Socialist group asked him to set a date for an interpellation. "Tomorrow, or a week from tomorrow, as you like," he replied.[75] Tomorrow it was, and he came within five votes of being overthrown by the Senate. Two days later there was a fist fight in the Chamber over the issue of whether a government with Tardieu at its head had the moral right to organize the centennial of Jules Ferry's birth; according to one witness: "We saw the respectable old Bracke, a distinguished Hellenist, exchange blows with an obscure Radical deputy, then fall to the floor and roll around the hemicycle with M. Brandon, who had tried in vain to restore order."[76] The fight broke out anew the following day as Léon Blum took a swing at a deputy on the right. Meanwhile specialists in scandal were beginning to whisper about the Oustric bank, which had quite suddenly shut its doors: surely, they were saying, M. Oustric could not have concealed the precarious state of his affairs all along without help from the government. Delegates from Tardieu's majority came to plead with him to adjourn parliament at once, despite his remarks about his schedule. He would never get his retooling law through both houses by August, they argued, and only Marxists or madmen would remain in Paris in August; besides, if he adjourned parliament he would have the whole summer to reach an understanding with Herriot and Blum and so achieve unanimity, whereas otherwise he would run the risk of being overthrown and having to surrender "the powers of the administration" to his adversaries for the summer. "Worn out, sick at heart, I finally gave in to their petitions," wrote Tardieu.[77] On July 11 he read a decree adjourning parliament until November. "This is not the parliamentary regime," cried Herriot in protest,[78] and likewise Léon Blum in Le Populaire the next day wondered "whether our regime is really parliamentary," parliament having been "dismissed brutally, with a kind of insolent derision, in the very course of its deliberations."

Tardieu did not even approach Blum and Herriot on his retooling bill; instead he spent his vacation making speeches throughout the country.

He spoke to veterans repeatedly of his hope for peace. To an assembly of republicans in Belfort he declared, "The Republic has nothing to fear from those who attack it."[79] He told a group of industrialists in Nancy, "I am a *bourgeois* and I don't hide it,"[80] in Alençon he drank to "the unity of the rural folk in France,"[81] and in Saint-Germain and Paris he assured retail merchants that he had *their* welfare too at heart.

In October the rumor spread that he was about to dismiss Briand. Since the evacuation of the Rhineland, 50,000 Stahlhelm troops had paraded near Koblenz and 107 Nazis had been elected to the Reichstag. While the right blamed Briand for the evacuation, the left mischievously praised Tardieu for it—"I couldn't go back on what had been promised!" roared Tardieu, brandishing a Radical review.[82] The chambers reconvened early in November, and for several days afterwards Tardieu defended Briand against the attacks of the right; finally, by declaring the policy of his government to be a fusion of opposites—"disarmament" in Geneva and "military security" at home, "European federation" in Geneva and "financial security" at home[83]—he won the confidence of the Chamber with a majority of 53 votes.

An inquest was opened on Oustric on November 14, despite the furtive efforts of the Minister of Justice, Raoul Peret, to prevent one. The clamor then arose in parliament for an investigation of Oustric's political connections, whereupon Peret resigned his post under heavy suspicion. Tardieu hardly knew Peret—he had taken him into the government by virtue of the principle of *dosage des groupes*, as a representative of the left wing of his majority. He had interrogated him at the first whisper in July, and he did so again at the first clamor in November; Peret confessed to nothing more scandalous than having been Oustric's lawyer five years earlier. Tardieu discussed the case with Blum and Herriot; then on November 17 he had himself questioned and, proclaiming Peret's conduct blameless, won a majority of 43 votes. The demand for an investigation only grew more persistent on the left. The majority gave signs of weakening: a scandal would mean discredit, but it would also mean the prospect of defeating the bill for national retooling without even attacking it.

On Sunday November 19 Tardieu told the Union of Economic Interests, "You are all against state control, but as soon as any one of your activities runs into difficulty you look to the state for help."[84] Then, after denouncing the scandal-hunters as a cabal to defeat his program, he said: "Often saddened, never discouraged, resolved at every moment to hold on till the very end, like Clemenceau I keep on hoping, with the help of my country and of my majority in parliament, to land on the shores of a new France...."[85]

He landed elsewhere. Oustric was arrested on November 21, whereupon Oustric's lawyer went to warn the state prosecutor against causing trouble: Peret, he said, had recently received 100,000 francs from Oustric, and Tardieu's chief secretary was currently receiving 5,000 francs a month. The state prosecutor immediately reported the warning to Henry Chéron, who had taken over the Ministry of Justice; Chéron rushed to inform Tardieu—and Tardieu, informed, "laughed like a child."[86] The same day Falcoz and Lautier, the two renegade Radicals, resigned in their turn from the government. Tardieu, notifying the Chamber of their resignation, himself demanded an investigation—not only of the Oustric affair, though, but of "*all*" scandals.[87] His margin of confidence fell to fourteen votes. Next Georges Monnet and Daladier interpellated him. Monnet, then a Socialist, drew inferences against capitalism from insinuations against Peret. Peret, present for the occasion, made a show of wounded dignity; as Minister of Justice, he maintained, he had shown Oustric no favors—though *while* Minister of Justice he had, he admitted, kept Oustric on as a client. Tardieu blamed him for this, if only for this, saying, "I would rather he had refrained."[88] Then Daladier took up where Monnet had left off: "At the Bourse, since Oustric was indicted, they have been saying that there are 32 members of parliament compromised in the Oustric affair, some of them still sitting on the government benches."[89] The cry arose on all sides, "The names!"[90] Daladier was mute; hence in effect he retracted, and the government's margin of confidence rose to 69 votes. On Sunday, November 26, Tardieu, addressing a local chapter of the Républicains Militants, again denounced the questionings as a maneuver to retard discussion of his retooling law. Twice on Monday he won a vote of confidence as the investigation commission was formed. On Tuesday the commission elected its chairman.[91] On Wednesday it opened its investigation. Then, as it began calling witnesses, legislative work was all but forgotten. Damning evidence was rapidly brought to bear against Peret, Falcoz, Lautier, and Tardieu's chief secretary. Twice a day Tardieu denied rumors of his resignation. On December 4 he had to face questioning in the Senate on his "general policies," and "as I arrived for the debate a man on the left who meant well warned me that my fate was sealed. 'Don't speak,' he said, 'you're all sewed up.' I spoke for two hours, and I said what I felt like saying."[92] He said that his social and economic program was assuring France of prosperity despite the world depression; further, just as his home policy was designed to

organize France, his foreign policy was designed to organize Europe—
"I think that if Europe is not organized in ten years' time, Europe will
not be worth much."[93] At his mention of having consolidated the *école
laïque* a senator on the right shouted, "You should be thrown to the
bottom of the sea with a millstone around your neck, you who dream of
the union of Frenchmen only for the sake of making the souls of their
children rot!"[94] Reproached with encouraging the opposition between left
and right, which was especially articulate that day, Tardieu replied:
"Fighting [with the left] is not a part of my policy or one of my wishes;
I feel only very sincere regret at having to witness the disunity of republicans."[95] Henry de Jouvenel replied to him:

We all feel the need for putting the pieces of the Republic back together again.
You too feel it, yet even as you speak of putting them back together again you
contribute day after day—far less by the effort of your will than by the impulse
of your character—to setting them a little farther asunder.... It is dangerous,
it seems to us, to maintain a ministry in office if by its temperament it makes
conciliation more and more difficult—if, the prisoners of false positions, we
run the risk of jostling one another harder and harder when we should be
uniting. Let us guard against dividing the country into two blocs and so
someday causing an upset more serious than the upset of a ministry, and this
for the benefit of all the extremes and to the detriment of the middle parties—
which, to be sure, commit errors, and which must often be saved from themselves, but which in falling would destroy the equilibrium of the nation.[96]

Thereupon the Senate voted. It overthrew Tardieu by eight votes, which
on a recount came down to three.[97] *L'expérience Tardieu* was over.

To all appearances the Senate voted against Tardieu in the debate on
his general policies because it suspected him of having shielded the
oustricards. In fact it did not suspect him seriously, whereas it did seriously
repudiate his policies. For the senators who swung the balance the Oustric
affair was a convenience, enabling them as it did to vote against Tardieu's
policies without seeming to—even in a vote on his policies. Later in fact
the Senate was to drop the charges against the suspects in the Oustric
affair; as Tardieu put it: "The senators considered that my fall...had
divested the affair of all political interest."[98]

No group approved his plan for national retooling. The Communists
had a vital interest in defending the copyright of the Soviet Union on
five-year plans, and the Cartel des Gauches had a vital interest in preserving
for itself the monopoly on reforms in France. To the men on the right the
plan was acceptable as a trick of demagogy but not as a basis for legislation. They would have wanted the government to use the Treasury

surplus for amortizing the national debt instead of undertaking new expenditures. The Radicals, hoping to encourage them, denounced the appropriation as too small to be useful: "A plan for national equipment at five billions, gentlemen!" scoffed one Radical[99]—and Tardieu aptly replied, "Paltry, the five billions of the Treasury? To be sure, it's less than it would be if it were more, but you must take what you've got...."[100] The Socialists proposed taking more by means of Treasury loans; they also proposed doing nothing without the participation of trade unions, cooperatives, and other "public and private collectivities." For one year parliament contrived to postpone the discussions when it was not dragging them out and to drag them out when it was not postponing them. As Tardieu wrote:

The eternal adversaries of military expenditures were demanding of me an armaments program instead of my public-works program. Parties that had never voted a budget before were invoking the rules of orthodox finance: annual budget, regular budget, special budget. The men who were to pick the lock of the Bank of France in 1936 and remove several dozens of billions were contesting my right to take into account in my plan the three and a half billions of statutory advances guaranteed to the Treasury by conventions. Never has obstruction been pushed further, nor with more cynicism.[101]

The Chamber even gained a few days of delay once by the expedient of demanding to know from the finance commissions whether the same funds were available as when the discussions had begun. Obstruction triumphed. "In the debate on national equipment," wrote Tardieu,

through the fault of the commissions I had to wait six months for a *rapporteur* to be appointed, and through the fault of the Chamber I had to give seventy-five sessions to what could have been done in ten. Forty-one times I had to ask the confidence of the chambers, and after several months I had to leave power without even having obtained the final vote.[102]

Even after his fall the adversaries of his plan did not dare to reject it outright; ten years later, when the war broke out, it was still dragging in the commissions.

Tardieu's policies were not alone at issue. The Senate, wrote François Goguel, held nothing against him so much

as the general spirit in which he governed. The senators, aware perhaps of the danger to the regime of making the division between the two great blocs too sharp, would have wanted the government to try and attenuate it instead of emphasizing it as it had been doing for one year.[103]

Indeed, not since the time of the separation of church and state had parliament been so conscious of its division into left and right, and Tardieu was greatly responsible for the change. The cause was less with his will than with his personality, said Jouvenel[104]—in other words, it was with both, though a little less with one than with the other. Jouvenel was right, but in no simple way.

Since the decision of the Radicals at their party congress of November, 1928, to revive the Cartel des Gauches, the only possible majority in parliament had been a majority on the right. The Cartel was not a third of parliament, and not enough of the center was willing to work with it to form a new majority; such was the lesson of the two cabinet crises before each of Tardieu's two ministries, and such was to be the lesson of the cabinet crisis after his second fall. Tardieu himself was no more at his ease on the right than on the left: once, speaking of "the gentlemen on the right," he told a friend:

Clemenceau used to wonder whether they are stupider than they are mean or meaner than they are stupid. They are both very mean and very stupid: mean without limits whenever their immediate interests are at stake and stupid without limits whenever their immediate interests are not at stake. I will never let myself fall into their grip.[105]

Nor were they at their ease with him: he was a reformer, and conservatives fear reformers even more than they fear reform. It was his boast that he despised party spirit, that in framing his policies he had only the general interest in mind; it was also the truth. His program, as it turned out, was almost a replica of the Radical program, and his first gesture in forming his cabinet was to invite the Radicals to join him. Their refusal did not deter him from seeking their collaboration in the Chamber—and for that matter the collaboration in the Chamber of all the parties of the left. After his first vote of confidence he did not regard his initial majority, such as it was, as immutable, nor did he allow it to pervert his program. Just as he had taken his program where he had found it, on the left, so he took his support where he found it, on the right. In fact he did not follow his majority: he led it—"with an authority such as I have rarely seen in others," wrote Paul-Boncour.[106]

He sought unanimity for a program of reform; however, to his mind the need for reform was more urgent than the need for unanimity, and the choice was fatal to him. He wanted to save France; the Radicals wanted to save their program. If he was sorry to have to face opposition, he was furious to have to face obstruction. He would have wished the chambers to decide issues on their merits; the chambers, however, were not in the habit of viewing issues apart from their political connotations. The distinction between majority and opposition being also the distinction between right and left, in antagonizing the opposition he intensified the conflict between right and left. And he antagonized the opposition by his sharp tongue, his abrupt and defiant manner, his scorn for rhetoric, his impolitic mania for getting things done.

Moreover, even though he held no brief against the parties of the left, the converse was no less false. His whole past stood between him and them: Homs-Bagdad, N'Goko Sangha, the three-years law, "*La Campagne contre la patrie*," the Army Commission, the Treaty, the *opposition clemenciste*. So did his present. He was a *grand bourgeois*, and he was one unashamedly—no doubt, thought the Socialists, the tool of "big interests, which hope to be the privileged beneficiaries of your policies."[107] He was authoritarian by nature, and to the left he was a virtual dictator—he was denounced as a Bonaparte, a MacMahon, a Mussolini. Soon after coming to power he cried to the opposition in the Chamber, "If it's war you want, gentlemen, I'm willing!"[108] And war it was. Parliament was in session eight months while he was in power, and "during these eight months," he computed,

in the course of 329 sessions, I had to reply to 327 interpellations and 62 written questions, to discuss setting a date for 101 of the interpellations, and to debate in detail 93 of the interpellations and 62 of the questions. On these occasions, and in the course of the debates on bills and on the budget, I had to speak at length 172 times and to ask 60 times for a vote of confidence. Including 14 appearances before the commissions, I had to put in a total of 206 appearances at the request of the assemblies, or an average of 25 a month. This average had been 11 a month under the Clemenceau government of 1906, 12 a month under the Méline government of 1896. My own rate was more than twice that of the most hard-fought of my predecessors. And what a pace of living! Statistics cannot describe it.[109]

In this war of attrition the deputies were all the more conscious of their division into right and left for having no great issues to divide them; and the debates of the time, with their myriad invectives and counter-invectives, read like a travesty of themselves. Tardieu witnessed the "division of republicans" only with "very sincere regret," a regret all the more sincere since in his philosophy he did not consider the opposition between right and left to be fundamental. It was only a reality of the moment—a relic of past quarrels, surviving as a bad habit of thought.

Gradually, though, in the course of his year of power, he came to recognize this reality of the moment as too real to ignore. And so he sought to attenuate it—not, however, by smoothing it over, as Jouvenel advised, but by clarifying it. To his mind, the degeneration of the parliamentary system in France—of which the symptoms were not only the intensification of the struggle between right and left but also "the multiplication of parties, the instability of majorities, the inevitable groping of governments"[110]—was a psychological consequence of the war; he strove to remedy it accordingly, by appealing to Frenchmen to revise their habits of thought. He would have had the right think and act *en bloc*, as a single coherent unit; ultimately he would have had France adopt the two-party system, which as he knew was a moderating influence. So he added the effort of his will to the effect of his personality. He was to fail in the end, the groups of the center being reluctant to break their ties on either side, especially at election time. Then, after 1932, he was to regard the vices of the system as older than the war and to ascribe them primarily to the constitutional laws of the Republic.

Tardieu was an outrage to parliament during his year of power in other ways than by dividing it in two. He set at naught the traditions of his office. He took power meaning to use it, not just to hold it—meaning to act, not just to stay put. He had not only policies, but a plan; he faced problems not as they arose or after, but before. Nor did he learn any better with time: no longer in 1930 could Jouvenel write, as he had written in 1928: "The certainty of being *l'homme nécessaire* that takes hold of a premier between his third and his sixth month of power makes him believe that, since now *he* has full charge and control, there is no more need for changing the drift of things."[111] While Tardieu played at statecraft in earnest, he played at politics "the sportman's way. He likes to hit hard, but never below the belt, and when he gets hit he takes it laughing."[112] He refused to court favor, to feign modesty, to mingle in the corridors. More and more arrogant toward the end, he referred in public to "my majority," he spoke to the Chamber of the "other assembly," and addressing the higher assembly itself the decisive day he said "Senators!" instead of "Gentlemen!" The chambers were suspicious of his speech-making outside their doors, resentful of his popularity in the nation at large, fearful lest he play off the people against them.

There was, moreover, something provocative about his whole person: "his forehead—vast, arched, powerful, towering like a bastion against the assaults of mediocrity";[113] his protrusive cigarette holder; "his whiskers golden, a little too golden";[114] even his *embonpoint*, which he bore like an advertisement for prosperity politics. His bejewelled pince-nez, "his modish waistcoats, his impeccable silk hats and jaunty derbies,"[115] were a slap in the face of the left; they were also a thorn in the side of the right, which competed with the left in slovenliness as a sign of democratic sentiment. His colleagues were mostly provincials, and they did not take kindly to his Parisian banter and salacious slang. They were mostly petty bourgeois, and he shocked them when he brought "that big, decorative, and almost symbolic girl, Mary Marquet," to parliament with him.[116] They were mostly single-minded men, proficient in their idealism; he was "cultured, cynical, contemptuous—at least in words."[117] They lived cautiously; he lived intensively: "Doctors told him to eat and drink less or his life would be a short one. 'I don't care,' he would answer. 'Short and sweet!'"[118] Finally, he was a great man, and as is natural the French like their great men best in history books.

Tardieu paid the penalty for his every offense. He wanted a government of men of good will only; he got one rife with men of poor credentials. He cared only for results; instead he got double his share of debates. Majorities, he said, were rightfully "instruments for applying policies"; he had to adjourn the application of his policies four months for the sake of his majority. All his accounts with parliament were in perfect balance when he fell. He had failed to break the system, and the system had failed to break him. The only loser was France.

And France lost incalculably. His financial policies are the neatest case in point. The Treasury having a surplus, he had thought to invest it in the national economy and so forestall a depression. Better than any of his colleagues he realized what had been happening on Wall Street—and what, save prevention, was due to happen on the Bourse. His optimism was not, as Léon Blum thought, a sign of perversity; it was a point in his program. The government had to show confidence if it was to inspire confidence, and to dissuade the people from spending less it had to spend more itself. In the long run, he reasoned, no loss would be involved for the Treasury, for public revenues would follow the course of prosperity. The orthodox protested: with a public debt outstanding, they said, there is no such thing as a Treasury surplus, and for the government to spend as if there were one is deficit finance. Then, after having wept, they took. However, as François Goguel wrote:

From all time many Frenchmen have considered the essential function of the state to be to satisfy their own particular interests, and to do so as far as possible by means of the budget. In 1929–30 this way of thinking became more widespread than ever before because the government seemed in every act to be making a point of justifying it. In the race for subvention and exemption the political divisions of the public mind were wiped out altogether.... In parliament the deputies on the right competed with their colleagues on the left in proposing expenditures. Throughout the nation, in every region and every milieu without exception, unanimity soon reigned supreme for making claims on the Treasury.[119]

Thus did Tardieu appease for a moment the conflict between right and left only at the price of intensifying in its stead the conflict between the devotion of the deputies to the interests of their constituents and their devotion to the interests of the nation as a whole.

The *expérience Tardieu* was a one-man experiment in renovating France against the resistance not of the people but of parliament. Tardieu had the genius to carry it off; he lacked only the tact. Having failed, he went down in legend as an enemy of democracy. In fact he had brought a new conception of democracy home with him from America. In seeking popularity in the nation at large, in attempting to promote economic welfare[120] and the two-party system, he was acting in the spirit of American democracy as he understood it; his French colleagues, however, saw him as defying parliament, despoiling the Treasury, and inciting to civil war. In truth, he maintained, he had spent most of his waking hours with the chambers, he had left the national debt lower than he had found it, and he had won unanimity for nine out of his eleven laws "of a general character."[121] No doubt, but no matter. By the end of 1930 his legend was made: he was a sectarian, a prodigal, and a tyrant—and in politics, legends are truer than the truth itself.

CHAPTER 23

The Hermit of Menton

AFTER THE FALL of Tardieu first Barthou and then Laval tried to set up a government with him in it; finally on December 12, 1930, a Radical, Théodore Steeg, set one up without him, and he left for the Alps with a pair of skis as the chambers recessed for the holidays. He was not gone long. A wheat scandal aiding, the new government fell soon after the chambers reconvened, and Tardieu joined Laval in a government later dubbed the "Laval-Tardieu tandem," which won the confidence of the Chamber on January 30, 1931. He liked Laval, or at least he did his best to: Laval being the son of a peasant, Tardieu took him for a son of the people.[1]

Minister of Agriculture, Tardieu spent the spring of 1931 making the wheat market unsafe for speculation. Concurrently he published a selection of his speeches of 1929–30 under the title L'Epreuve du pouvoir, and he wrote articles deploring the impotence of the executive government in the face of the legislature: "The state," he argued, "must resume consciousness of its duties and of its rights."[2] Also, when that spring Briand was a candidate for the presidency of the Republic, Tardieu took revenge on him for the defeat of Clemenceau ten years before. First he made a show of supporting him, even of coveting the Quai d'Orsay for himself;[3] then he left on a tour of the country. Briand, disarmed, took no precautions: he even spoke to the Chamber of "my excellent colleague and friend M. Tardieu," adding amid smiles: "Though formerly we may have disagreed, [in the goverment] we have always pursued the very same policies in full mutual confidence."[4] Tardieu wound up his tour on May 10 in Lyon at a banquet held in his honor by the mayor, Edouard Herriot; officiating side by side, the two men each expressed their "feelings of esteem and of respect" for one another. The next day in Paris Tardieu quite suddenly led an all-out campaign on behalf of Senator Paul Doumer. At Versailles two days later Doumer won a margin of 41 votes over Briand on the first ballot, and Briand, heartbroken, withdrew. For once the grand elector had failed to swing an election—his own. Some days later, for all his bitterness, he had Tardieu to lunch privately at the Quai d'Orsay. In his six years as Foreign Minister, he whispered, he had saved twenty million francs[5] of secret funds as a reserve in case of war. And he adjured Tardieu, who he thought would soon succeed him: "Watch over my treasure!" Tardieu promised, though only half believing in its existence.[6]

At the end of June President Hindenburg, declaring Germany unable to meet the next reparations payment, appealed to President Hoover for diplomatic support. Hoover proposed a one-year moratorium on all international debts. As France had just paid a biannual installment on her war debt to the United States, Tardieu was for rejecting the moratorium categorically. Not so Laval: by rejecting it, he argued, his government, besides isolating France diplomatically, would get the blame if the depression spread to Germany. He suggested a compromise: asking Germany for the interest on the debt. Tardieu gave in, and as he did he grew nostalgic for the opposition. "In a cabinet," he wrote, "you are never free. For solidarity's sake you agree to measures you do not approve."[7] He defended the compromise in public. It passed parliament, afterwards becoming the basis of the moratorium agreement of July 6. Then on July 18 Chancellor Brüning came to Paris seeking financial assistance for Germany to stave off the depression. On Tardieu's insistence Laval rather than Briand received him with an offer to lend Germany 500,000,000 dollars in return for the German customs duties as collateral[8] and a solemn undertaking to ask no further revisions of the Treaty of Versailles for ten years. Brüning took his petition elsewhere. But when, six months later, he announced that Germany would not resume payments at the expiration of the moratorium, Tardieu could not even protest: the right in France was as much opposed to a reoccupation of the Rhineland as was the left.[9]

France had resumed the policy of abandonments, this time for good. Still Tardieu did not cease his efforts to preserve the peace settlement; he displaced them, though. If France was inept at preserving the peace alone, he meant to enlist all Europe in the enterprise.

In the fall of 1931 he took over the Ministry of the Interior from Laval. Then in January, 1932, when André Maginot died, he also took over the Ministry of War; at the same time Laval coaxed Briand, who was ill, out of the Quai d'Orsay and himself moved in. On becoming Minister of War Tardieu also became French delegate to the World Disarmament Conference, then in its first week of preparation. He left at once for Geneva, which he had never yet seen. Directly on his arrival he met with the French member of the Preparatory Commission, "my friend Paul-

Boncour,"[10] and urged him, a political foe, to remain as alternate for the Conference. Paul-Boncour agreed. "I found Tardieu just as I had left him after the Waldeck-Rousseau government," he recalled,

fiery, peremptory, full of fight; a tireless worker, applying his cerebral mechanism at will to the most diverse tasks at all hours of the day and night, and keeping it always orderly, like a filing cabinet with compartments that open and shut.... He had kept his strength intact, but he had put on a belly.... He was a little gruffer than was usual in Geneva... and his temperament was rather averse to the slowness, to the oratorical precautions, to the somewhat pious phraseology in use there.... He did not withal forget... that the League of Nations was at the very center of the Treaty of Versailles, of which he was, with Clemenceau, the principal architect.[11]

Four days after the Conference opened, on February 5, Tardieu took it by surprise with the most audacious and the only sensible proposal for disarmament ever made.

As the Preparatory Commission saw it, the problem of disarmament was one of deciding what amounts of which arms each nation should destroy and how the destruction might be verified. According to Tardieu, not only would progressive disarmament involve technical problems of hopeless complexity, but even the destruction of all extant armaments would not in itself much reduce the risk of war. In modern warfare most armaments are manufactured in the course of hostilities, and a nation bent on war might well start one with slingshots if there were only slingshots to deter it. So Tardieu proposed, as a complement to the progressive disarmament of the nations, the creation by the League of an international "preventive and defensive army." If only this army were made stronger than any possible combination of national armies, he explained, the question of what quantity of which arms each member was to relinquish would be of no further consequence.

Internationalism was on the left in France; once again Tardieu had taken an idea on the left and, pushing it to its farthest implications, made something new of it. And once again he was provocative instead of suave: reiterating his proposal on February 8, he told the League assembly: "Too often you have taken... the course of least resistance."[12] France, he said, was prepared to transfer to the League any amount of any military weapon or of any instrument capable of military use. And he added:

Equality for individuals in the rules for bearing arms became possible only when, to preside over that equality, there were policemen and judges.... I ask you to believe France when she tells you that there will be no assurance of peace so long as we have not really and truly fortified the League of Nations. If we fail, the result will be... in a word, a great catastrophe.[13]

The professional diplomats in Geneva, such as General Smuts and Lord Robert Cecil, besides being stupefied, were somewhat perturbed: they were not *that* serious about disarmament. The political parties, the press, and the public throughout Europe were unanimous in their enthusiasm, for one day; then gradually they returned to normal. When they did, they saw Tardieu's motion as a maneuver to disrupt the proceedings and so preserve the armaments superiority of France. In France the parties of the left saw it as in addition a maneuver to go one better on them before the spring elections, and their adversaries, agreeing with them, supported it in consequence. The Communists for their part, remembering that the Soviet Union was not a member of the League, saw it as a maneuver to encircle the Soviet Union. Caillaux and Briand discussed it at lunch together: the one called it a "receptacle of ideology," and the other replied, "It's journalism!"[14] Herriot, however, was slow in his reflexes: "This plan is a good one and I say so," he declared on February 13.[15] Wrote Paul-Boncour years afterwards:

I owe it to [Tardieu] to say this much...: the criticism of him at the time, to speak only of the leftist press in France, was unjust.... The position that he took and that I defended with him in Geneva was no different from the one that we [on the left] had been defending all along.[16]

Paul-Boncour was right about the injustice and wrong about the difference. If Tardieu himself spoke of his plan as consistent with the past policies of France at the League, he did so with his tongue in his cheek. Whereas collective security was a magnification of the old system of alliances, the international army was its negation. From the point of view of nationalism versus internationalism the difference was perhaps only one of degree; if so, however, the degree was infinite.

Politics in Paris cut short Tardieu's stay in Geneva. In January a commission of the Chamber had recommended the single ballot for the forthcoming general elections, and Tardieu, seeing in the single ballot a companion piece to the two-party system, had persuaded the government to make its adoption a question of confidence. The Chamber approved it; not so the Senate, however, and on February 13 Laval fell.[17] Doumer asked Tardieu to take over until the May elections. Tardieu, having no long-range program this time, suppressed some cabinet posts and combined others. The Ministry of War, though, he broke up into a Ministry of Ground Forces and a Ministry of Munitions, which, together with the Ministries of Aviation and of the Navy, he put under the supervision of a Minister of State for National Defense; the innovation was criticized on all sides until at length it became an institution.[18] He offered the new Ministry of State to Paul-Boncour; Paul-Boncour, though "touched" by the offer, refused it out of loyalty to his party,[19] and Tardieu took François Piétri instead. Mechanically he invited the Radicals to join him; mechanically they refused. So he carried over most of the Laval cabinet, including Laval. He moved into the Quai d'Orsay himself, and there at once he checked on Briand's treasure. "Briand had made a mistake," he discovered. "There was a reserve of not twenty millions but twenty-three,"[20] and later he told his friend André Maurois: "Say what you will about Aristide—and I fought his policies myself—he was damned honest. Had he cared to spend only a fraction of those millions on press campaigns he would have been President of the Republic."[21] On February 23, presenting his new cabinet to the Chamber, Tardieu declared for maintaining his disarmament plan and for seeking a reparations settlement "allowing of freely negotiated adjustments but excluding repudiation."[22] He won a vote of confidence, and the same evening he returned to Geneva.

As caretaker Premier, Tardieu knew no rest. He was first one week in Geneva conferring with the main delegations, then two weeks in Paris consulting with his government. Briand died on March 7, and Tardieu spoke at his funeral: "His was no doubt the very mean of wisdom."[23] He discussed reparations with Sir John Simon in Paris, then conferred with the lesser delegations in Geneva, and on March 22 was back defending his foreign policy before the Senate. He dismissed the chambers on April 1, and the electoral campaign began. He strove to unite the candidates of the right by proclaiming himself their leader. Likewise he fought the Cartel des Gauches as a unit: "In the Cartel," he said, "the Socialist is master, the Radical prisoner."[24]

Meanwhile he defended his disarmament plan over the radio, and on April 10 he went to defend it again before the League assembly. There the American, then the British, delegates attacked it outright for the first time: they would rather blow up a few guns to start with, they said. Tardieu replied:

There are two main schools of thought. One aims at suppressing certain arms, purely and simply; the other...recommends reserving the use of those arms to the international power and so making it and it alone capable of intervening, in case of aggression, in favor of the victim.... Either we abolish those arms in the case both of the aggressor and of the victim and so run the risk of playing into the aggressor's hands, or else we act to protect the victim by increasing its defensive powers instead of reducing them.... If we wish to face up to the problem there is one way, and we French have found only one: to try to prevent war in all cases and to this end to give the international power weapons more powerful than the weapons of all the other powers put together....Our purpose is to establish the reign of international law.[25]

His reasoning was irrefutable, hence his interlocutors did not even try to refute it. "Don't deal with Tardieu—the leftists are coming," they whispered in the corridors.[26]

The leftists came. On the first ballot, on May 1, they won few seats; however, their composite strength gave them every hope of victory on the second, when their electors would pool their votes. Tardieu reversed his tactics in consequence: for one week he argued the incoherence of the Cartel. Radicals and Socialists, he said, had never succeeded in governing together, and "on nothing that dominates the life of free peoples—the notions of country, of legality, of property—can [they] agree."[27] On May 5 President Doumer was assassinated, and the press of the right, painting the assassin red, summoned Tardieu to postpone the second ballot until the plot against the Republic had been quelled. At that moment Tardieu held all the levers of command in the Republic: what with the police and the army devoted to him, he could have made himself dictator by a few phone calls. All Paris was alert, so strong was his legend. He did make a few phone calls: he gave the prefect of Police, Chiappe, the order to avoid all incidents, described the assassin to the press as a White Russian and a Fascist, and reconvoked the outgoing parliament for May 10 to elect a new President. The victory of the Cartel des Gauches on the second ballot was decisive—whereupon at Versailles two days later the Radicals voted with the center and the right to elect Albert Lebrun.

In the four weeks left to him as Premier, Tardieu strove to wind up two items of business. On May 17 he sent a telegram to the French delegation in Geneva instructing it to demand a showdown on his disarmament plan should the conference resume before June: "The issues are ones on which M. Herriot's stand has always been the same as ours," he wrote;[28] the conference, however, knew better than to resume before June. And on May 28 he called a meeting of the Supreme War Council on the question of defensive fortifications in the north of France. The commissions had already cleared 150,000,000 francs for an extension of the Maginot line along the Franco-Belgian border. Weygand and Gamelin were all for the extension. Pétain, however, favored mobile defenses; most of the civilians on the Council sided with him, and the meeting broke down. Then Tardieu, taking Gamelin by the arm, said to him: "Only my solution of lending to Belgium is left. I'll pass it on to my successor."[29] Weygand and Gamelin, however, urged him to act while the loan could be made to Belgium without public debate, and on June 4, just before Herriot took over, the Supreme Council met again. By 7 votes to 6 it rejected fixed defenses in any form; the credits were lost for good, and the Maginot Line, which then was mostly still unbuilt, lost most of its prospective value.

On June 3, 1932, in his letter of resignation as Premier, Tardieu notified President Lebrun that he would oppose any attempt to form a coalition government in the center of the new Chamber. Having previously failed to unify the right as a majority, he was now to strive to unify it as an opposition bloc; in the process he was to damage his credit with its moderate members, who by force of tradition knew no better reason for opposing any one government than to join the next one. He organized a group in the center right, the "Left Republicans," and on June 7, when Herriot came forth with an all-Radical ministry, Tardieu offered him the support of *"mes amis"* on condition only that the proposal for an international army be upheld in Geneva. The international army was, as Tardieu well knew, unacceptable to the Cartel. It was also unimportant to the rest of the Chamber, though: "Out of the 230 moderates elected in May with my program and with my help," he complained, "there were only... 115 to follow me" in voting against Herriot.[30] His own Left Republicans did not all follow him; resigning on June 10 as their president, he created the "Republican Center" a little farther to the right.

That summer Tardieu attacked Herriot violently for subscribing to Hoover's proposals for a definitive annulment of the reparation debt and for a reduction of each nation's armaments by one third. He also refused to back Herriot's orthodox financial program even though it was causing a split in the Cartel. Meanwhile he published a selection of his campaign speeches, *Devant le pays*—"France needs to be reeducated politically," he wrote in the preface.[31] Then he took an extra-long vacation, returning only on October 26, one month after parliament reconvened. His return was spectacular: wrote the New York *Times*: "André Tardieu appeared in the Chamber today looking more like an American businessman than ever before. He had shaved off his mustache and wore horn-rimmed spectacles, which greatly altered his appearance."[32] His policy of opposition, however, went unchanged. Herriot on December 11 acknowledged Germany's claim to equality of rights in armaments, and his fall became inevitable; he chose to make it noble, and the next day he moved for France to join Belgium, England, and Italy in resuming war-debt payments to the United States. The reparation debt having been annulled at the request of Hoover, the cry went up on all sides: "Not one *sou* for America!" In his heart Tardieu backed Herriot, being loath to see France at odds with her former allies; for tactics' sake, however, he joined the great majority in voting Herriot down.[33] This defeat notwithstanding, and Tardieu aiding, the Cartel was obliged to go on governing as a unit: first Paul-Boncour was Premier, then one month later Daladier replaced him.

In January, 1933, Tardieu began a series of articles in *L'Illustration* on the fifteen years since the war, titled "Fifteen Years of Errors." He was continually amazed, he wrote, to find in the periodical literature of the time

neither thought nor sentiment nor passion.... Looking at France today, one thinks of the Roman Empire of the third century, which, menaced by crises within and attacks without, remained indifferent. If anyone discusses the point he is accused of troublemaking and invited to hold his tongue.[34]

For his part Tardieu refused to hold his tongue. He denounced throughout France "the abusive omnipotence" of the legislative power over the executive and "the servitude of the legislature to... electoral oligarchies." And once when he met with cheers he protested:

Don't be too eager to applaud!... It is you voters who all too often impose on your representatives, and through them on the government, the impossible conditions of existence I have just been describing. *You* have made a general practice of lobbying and of what is known as string-pulling. *You* are stuck on the idea that nothing can be accomplished legally or naturally, and that always, everywhere, you must take steps on your own and bring pressure to bear. Take care lest some day the Republic perish as a result!

Ah! you think your representatives are in office to defend your private interests. You transform their mandate, which is general and national, into a local mandate. By what you make of their job you achieve the dual result of enfeebling and enslaving both the legislative and the executive powers. You are wrong! You lay the way open to the foulest system of three-way bargaining: bargaining by the government, which has need of deputies, by the deputies, who have need of the government, and by the voters, who have need of both. The result is a permanent exchange of services, these services being mostly abuses of power.... I didn't become a deputy for the sake of getting mixed up in such a mess!

Are you not aware that at every period of history the success of dictatorships has always, in all countries, had as its origin the debasement of the executive power and the corruption of civic morality? Do you not realize that the only means of blocking the way of the dictatorships is to reform and rejuvenate the old democracies?... At a time when nearly everywhere, from one end of the world to the other, the idea of liberty, which is the patrimony of France, has been or else is being blotted out, we are doubly duty-bound to provide our

Republic with a free and strong executive power if we wish it to remain a republic.

The political problem is a moral problem. You are the sovereign people. Have you ever thought what duties your sovereignty imposes on you? Every four years you vote. You get worked up in favor of some candidate—or rather against some candidate. Then, when it's all over... you go home and have nothing more to do with politics. For four years you let your elected representatives do whatever they wish with the country as long as they perform in the various bureaus the innumerable little chores with which you burden them. At such times you are deeply convinced—as, alas! you have been taught—that man is the only end of man. You are in unconscious revolt against the powers of the state, which should appear to you as the custodian of the general interest. In your moments of despondency, words of sacrilege—this one, for instance, that patriotism is the instrument of tyranny—win a fair hearing with some of you. And then, all of a sudden, the country is threatened by the invader, whereupon you all cry, "Present!"... Ah! then only do I recognize in you the angry men of Picardy of whom Michelet wrote, the eternal miracle of France![35]

In short, the Frenchman is a good patriot but a bad citizen. Tardieu's audience applauded him throughout despite his protests, thus making his task the harder for him.

Much of the spring of 1933 Tardieu spent in his constituency of Belfort, where he spoke urging the peasants to clamor for high tariffs, the veterans to demonstrate against the proposal to destroy armaments, and France in general to improve her relations with the United States. In Paris, in May, he alone out of 616 deputies voted against the nonaggression pact with the Soviet Union: "The Communist International," he explained, "would not for so small a price give up its sole *raison d'être*, which is to prepare revolutions, even in allied nations."[36] He opposed the Four-Power Pact for being designed to facilitate treaty revision; besides, he argued, "to justify agreements among peoples, a certain minimum of common interests and aims is necessary;... [otherwise] agreements are useless and harmful."[37] He spent the summer and early fall of 1933 travelling incognito, first in Spain and later in Italy. While deploring the absence of civil liberties under the Fascist regime, he was impressed with its economic achievements, its efficient administration, and the seeming contentment of the workers—only in the upper bourgeoisie did he detect signs of discontent.[38]

The following fall and winter brought ample confirmation to his criticism of the French regime. On October 23 Daladier fell; his successor, Sarraut, fell less than one month later. Chautemps took over after two weeks of crisis; in the interim Tardieu, addressing a press convention in Chambéry, declared: "One cabinet crisis is nothing; two of them in a month is too much."[39] Discussing remedies, he remarked that Marxism, if adopted in France, "would very much resemble such dictatorships, different from it in appearance only, as function in Rome and Berlin, and which many Frenchmen would like to see instituted in France." Someone interrupted him to cry: "That's just what we need!" He replied: "Our tradition binds us to humanism, to antiquity, to the individual. We can restore authority without strangling liberty, without departing from our national traditions. We do not wish to be shot or flogged or sterilized."[40] And he did not conclude his critique of the regime without adding, "The men you elect are seriously at fault, but you, the electors, do you think you're any better?"[41]

Early in January, 1934, he published a major study, *L'Heure de la décision* (*France in Danger*), which set forth with force, precision, and a wealth of particulars the problems confronting France. "A great offensive against our civilization is on," he wrote, "and if France is to defend our civilization, France must be in good working condition."[42] The chief ailment of France, he found, was political. He distinguished its symptoms, such as chronic cabinet crises, from the ailment itself, which consisted in an "insufferable hypertrophy of the legislative power to the detriment of the executive" together with its "total servitude... to the demands of electoral oligarchies."[43] Now he gave priority to the need for changing the political institutions of France rather than the political habits of Frenchmen. He made four suggestions for amending the constitutional laws of 1875. The first was "to give the executive and it alone the right to dissolve the Chamber."[44] Once the right of dissolution existed, he argued, the need for its use would diminish: a premier would not be likely to use it if he were not sure of his following in the country, and likewise his adversaries would not be likely to provoke him to use it if they were not sure of theirs. "'Show strength,' said Marshal Lyautey, 'in order not to have to use it.' What holds for Berbers holds for deputies."[45] In defense of this suggestion he pointed to the British system; so too in defense of the second one, which was to deprive parliament of the right to initiate expenditures.[46] "Just as giving the executive alone the right of dissolution will restore its authority," he explained, "so depriving deputies of the right to initiate expenditures will restore their independence."[47] To have taken the American system as his model in proposing the reinforcement of the executive would have been self-defeating, for Frenchmen then saw *le système présidentiel* as equivalent to *le bonapartisme* and shunned it in consequence. Finally he advocated—"in order for universal suffrage to become a reality"[48]—the referendum as in

Switzerland and woman's suffrage as in most other democracies. He distinguished four categories of adversaries that his proposals had so far encountered: the "most ardent" were the "beneficiaries of the abuses I wish to abolish";[49] second in ardor were "the professional skeptics, contradictors, and objectors";[50] next came, "bass trombones foremost, the sonorous mass of over-bidders.... Whatever you propose, they find it inadequate,"[51] while "the last shock troop declares itself in agreement with my proposals but rejects them because they are mine."[52] After recalling the gravity of the threat to civilization, he concluded: "Is what I propose adequate? Perhaps not. But it is certainly necessary. Can we do better? Possibly. However, since no one else is proposing anything, what I propose will have to do."[53]

Few books have ever been so timely. In the last days of January, 1934, as the Chautemps government succumbed to the Stavisky scandal, a rumor of revolt spread through Paris. Chautemps's successor, Daladier, thinking to quell the rumor, dismissed the prefect of police, Chiappe, who was notoriously not a Radical. During the night of February 6–7, as a demonstration of veterans' leagues on the Place de la Concorde was turning into a siege of the Palais Bourbon, Tardieu joined Franklin-Bouillon in an oratorical assault on the government, denouncing the revocation of Chiappe as "the most terrible blow ever dealt to law and order."[54] Even as the palace guards were pacifying the crowds with bullets, Daladier got a vote of confidence. The rest of the night Tardieu walked about the city, noting with astonishment the abrupt decline of apathy among the people.[55] At noon the next day the Daladier ministry, having taken toll of the dead and wounded, resigned, and Gaston Doumergue, cheered by the many, came out of retirement to form a national-union cabinet. Both Herriot and Tardieu joined him as vice-premiers, and on February 15, 1934, the Chamber gave him its confidence, the Socialists and the Communists alone dissenting.

Not for the joy of returning to the ministers' bench did Tardieu agree to join a coalition after all. Immediately he pressed Doumergue to demand new elections on a single ballot. Herriot objected, the Radicals being at the nadir of their popularity. Tardieu accepted a compromise: Doumergue would demand constitutional reform the following autumn.

Until the autumn Tardieu marked time. He took it upon himself to oversee foreign policy: on April 17 he drew up a note for the government refusing to legalize the rearmament of Germany. He also took it upon himself to push the inquest into the Stavisky scandal—he had it in for Chautemps in particular after inquiring of Barthou, Chautemps's successor as Foreign Minister, "about the state of Briand's treasure. 'Eight millions,' answered Barthou."[56] The Radical press on its side sought to implicate him by means of a check stub bearing the notation "Camille A. Tardi" found among Stavisky's effects.[57] The investigation commission called on him to testify on the morning of July 18; to the last man it declared him above suspicion. He, however, he rejoined, had come as "witness-plaintiff and accuser," whereupon he drew from his briefcase a voluminous and scathing indictment of Chautemps; all morning, afternoon, and evening he held forth before the dumbfounded committeemen, winding up late at night in the presence of Chautemps himself, who had come rushing back from vacation.[58] The next day the Radical group ordered the Radical ministers to resign if Tardieu stayed on. A council of ministers met under Barthou, Doumergue having refused to interrupt his fishing for so little. "They all looked at me," Tardieu recalled, "as at an ill-bred child who has said or done something improper in his parents' drawing room. Denouncing nice Camille!"[59] He refused to retract, pretending not to see why his having testified against one Radical should prevent others from collaborating with him. The Council could reach no decision, being as indignant at the ultimatum of the Radicals as it was devoted to the etiquette of the *république des camarades*. Tardieu telephoned Doumergue, offering to resign. Louis Marin telephoned Doumergue threatening to resign if Tardieu did. On July 24 Doumergue broke down and returned to Paris. He censured Tardieu publicly; privately he bade the Radicals in the government all stay or all go—but if they went, he added, he would go too, and for good. Again Tardieu offered his resignation; Doumergue refused it, and on July 25 the Radicals withdrew their ultimatum.

In September Tardieu presented Doumergue with a program of constitutional reform. His program was what it had been in January; as he wrote:

I proposed to restore the balance between the legislative power and the executive power by giving the latter a right of dissolution and depriving the former of the right to initiate expenditures—that is, in both cases by doing as the English do. I proposed to normalize the suffrage by giving women the same rights as men and calling on this enlarged electorate to vote by referendum— to vote not only for men but for ideas as well.[60]

Twice Doumergue appealed by radio directly to the people in support of this program: "Manifest your will without ambiguity," he said. The local elections of October 7 were favorable to him. Herriot spoke against the program at a Radical congress in Nantes on October 24. The Council of

Ministers took it up on November 3; only Doumergue and Tardieu supported it in all its points. Doumergue asked authority to submit it to parliament in his own name and also to request a provisional budget for the first three months of 1935. The Council consented unanimously; on second thought, however, the Radical ministers were alarmed, and on November 4, after an all-day meeting with their parliamentary groups, they decided to resign. They were two days in announcing their decision, two more in acting on it; Doumergue did nothing to dissuade them, and on receiving their resignation he handed in his own.

The Radicals had hesitated to the last, wondering—as all France was wondering—what would happen if ever Doumergue resigned. "Nothing happened, either in the chambers or in the streets," wrote Tardieu;[61] even the toughs of the Croix de Feu, who had been receiving secret funds to act as bodyguard and cheering squad for the government,[62] made no more virile a protest than "to lavish on Doumergue their sterile regrets and stage the vainest of parades beneath his windows."[63] Flandin took over the remnants of the Doumergue cabinet, and the old routine picked up where it had left off nine months earlier, when it had been so rudely interrupted from the street.

Tardieu refused to pick up where he had left off. He had been unable to reform the regime from the inside; he would work to reform it from the outside. The people were apathetic again; he would rouse them to revolt. He would quit the government, quit Paris—but first he would enlist the collaboration of a few friends.

I invited to dinner, to make my views known to them, some of the men who had been with me in the Doumergue government....

We ate at Prunier's. The oysters were frozen. So were the glances when I had spoken.

They wondered whether I had gone mad. They were certain that I had turned dangerous. I paid the check.[64]

At the end of the month, just as Flandin was assuring the Senate Commission for the Reform of the State that the change of a few procedural rules would be reform enough, Tardieu left Paris for the Riviera to prepare his revolution alone. He built a palatial villa atop a hill called *Tête du commandant*, overlooking Menton. He filled his huge new study with books and decorated it with the photographs of five men: Adrien Hébrard, Clemenceau, Lyautey, André Maginot, and—"a mute rebuke for his illusions"[65]—Gaston Doumergue. Up at six, to bed at ten, he worked twelve to fourteen hours a day, taking time out only to play with his two bulldogs, Oscar and Maboul,[66] or feed the squirrels in his garden.

In April, 1935, he published a selection from his recent speeches, *Sur la pente*; in the preface he wrote: "Proof piles up to no effect. No one wishes to understand that, what we call the crisis being intellectual and moral in origin, intellectual and moral action are needed to resolve it."[67] Returning to Paris briefly in June, 1935, he supported Caillaux, then Laval, in their bids for full financial powers, but he would join neither government. In the last days of 1935 he resigned from the Republican Center—he had quit as its president on entering the Doumergue government. Then on March 10, 1936, he announced to his constituents of Belfort his decision not to run for reelection: "For a form of action I know to be futile I am substituting another I hope will be effective.... I believe in the force of ideas."[68] He visited Paris again that spring and twice lectured on the new revolution to a full and fashionable house at the Salle Pleyel. "I have begun a rough task," he declared, "and I will see it through to the end if heaven grant me the life it has so far generously supplied."[69] Then the first Tardieu ever to leave Paris made of Menton his permanent residence.

Already the paperwork on his revolution had begun. "You are not sovereign. You are not free. You are not equal. You are neither represented nor protected. You are living by lies,"[70] he told his countrymen in a pamphlet, *Alerte aux Français*, published in March, 1936. "If you want a change, first your minds must realize what is wrong. Then your consciences must realize wherein you are guilty. Then your wills must realize the necessary revolution."[71] He announced a five-volume study, *La Révolution à refaire*, for their guidance in revolution. Two volumes appeared: *Le Souverain captif* in March, 1936, and *La Profession parlementaire* one year later. The first was a poor start; he made up for it with the second.

The style of *Le Souverain captif* is polemical and often defective. Tardieu wrote it hastily, with the echoes of partisan quarrels still in his ears. In his desire to reach as large a public as possible he was prone to mistake repeating an argument for reinforcing one and to aim at overwhelming his readers instead of convincing them.

Le Souverain captif begins with a brief history of the running debate on the meaning and value of liberty, equality, and popular sovereignty. Then it states its theme: whether or not democracy is defensible in theory, the French are convinced that they are living in a democracy—that since the 1870's "they have been in effective possession of the democratic prerogatives they had sought gropingly for eighty years to acquire. The question is... whether they are right or wrong in this conviction."[72] By way of providing an answer Tardieu cited innumerable instances of abuse of the principles of liberty and equality under the Third Republic and of defective electoral laws and practices; in so doing he defeated his own purpose. Like the documentary proofs of the war guilt of Germany, "the numerical arguments of M. Tardieu"[73] were beside the point; the more there were, the less they proved. "To be sure," Alfred Fabre-Luce had once remarked, "our precincts are unequal, our electoral system is unjust, our women are deprived of political rights; but with this sort of reasoning we could wind up proving that we have never known democracy. Yet we did know democracy once."[74] Virtually, that is: men never *know* democracy, but only tend either toward or away from it. Liberties are always getting in one another's way, and equality is rarely unequivocal. The enumeration of cases in point does not suffice to convict a regime of false pretences to democracy unless the proof is also made that its policy persistently failed to conform to the general will, the first and ultimate democratic sanction.

Did the policies of the Third Republic conform to the general will? Here Tardieu's judgment suffers from a neglect of extenuating circumstances. In theory, the general will means the will of the whole social body; in practice, however, it must mean the will of the majority. And the rule of the majority, besides being at best only an approximation of democracy, must also be somewhat arbitrary, for wherever there is a broad dispersion of opinions there is also a plurality of majority opinions. Finally, popular sovereignty necessarily entails delegation of sovereignty, and no representative assembly can be fully representative. Though Tardieu saw these points he did not face them, and as a result his indictment of the Third Republic was quarrelsome and inconsequential. The separation of church and state, he pointed out, was enacted by a relative majority in parliament representing only 2,600,000 Frenchmen; true, but was it contrary to the general will? Frequently majorities in parliament were constituted arbitrarily, frequently they oppressed minorities, frequently they were themselves only minorities in the nation. Necessarily. But no doubt more than necessarily: and had Tardieu conceded throughout that the defects of the regime were necessarily great, he might have made out a good case for their being greater than necessary.

He repeated his earlier proposals for reform with the addition of popular initiative, and though he described them as tentative and inadequate, the sense of his effort is unmistakable. If he knew no formula for detecting the general will, he did know one for preventing the systematic abuse of it: the balance of powers. He sought to make democracy work more; primarily, though, he sought to make it work more efficiently. Perhaps unruly chambers embody the will of the people best, even though the people dislike unruly chambers. Tardieu, however, saw no virtue in an omnipotent parliament incapable of governing. To make the executive independent would perhaps not in itself have increased democracy; but it would have cleared the way for such increase, just as referendum and popular initiative, however slight their practical effects, would have restored to the captive sovereign a sense of freedom if not of majesty.

Did government under the Third Republic serve the general interest? Manifestly not, said Tardieu, and few would quarrel with him. The interest of all, he was fond of repeating, is not an aggregate of the interests of each; however, something about the French parliament prevented its members from seeing beyond the interests of each. That certain something is the theme of *La Profession parlementaire*.

La Profession parlementaire begins:

Political life in France suffers from two kinds of debasement. On the one hand the principles France believes to be at the basis of her political life are outrageously violated, and the people are deprived by the men whom they elect of the powers with which they are themselves credited. On the other hand the men whom they elect, who hold these powers, behave not as representatives, but as professionals of the parliamentary trade. To what the people are reduced by the chambers, you already know. What the chambers are, you shall see.[75]

And later Tardieu gives as his purpose "to enter the house, follow its tenants in their everyday activities, observe their inclinations, describe the milieu they compose, note how great are the despotism they wield and the bondage they bear."[76]

As professions go (writes Tardieu), the parliamentary profession is unique, for its members need have no special qualifications, and it sets no limit on their tenure of office or on the number of other jobs they may hold. It provides them with regular pay and good retirement benefits, and they may grant themselves privileges and immunities as they see fit. In return they have only to apply the two rules of the trade: the "static rule," which is to get reelected, and the "dynamic rule," which is to get into power—that is, to replace the men in power.[77] These two rules comprise "the substance of the trade."[78] In order to get reelected a deputy must procure jobs and do other favors for constituents and lobbies. In order to become a minister he must enter a coalition and so sacrifice a first part of his program and ideas—"coalitions are great for blunting ideas."[79] He must also cultivate skill in oratory and a feeling for the Chamber as a theater with its public galleries; in this lawyers excel, for they tend to think that once they have spoken their job is done. Finally, he must convince himself that the so-called historic movement to the left is concomitant with progress and in the nature of things, whereas in fact it is a "law of the profession,"[80] to wit, the perpetual adjustment of the profession to the perpetual revolt of the electorate.

"Parliament undeniably has a great force of attraction,"[81] for it recruits from all walks of life. To belong to it is to be an object of flattering solicitation. Moreover, it is the setting for an amusing game, a stage for histrionics,[82] a place where "things happen."[83] "Finally, parliament is enticing because eternal. Regimes come and go; the chambers remain."[84] Its attractiveness is as great for senior members as for newcomers or outsiders. The *esprit de corps* of its members is of the strongest, being a form of "*solidarité dans le privilège.*"[85] A spirit of equality and of camaraderie makes of it "a sort of ill-tended club, but one pleasant in its informality."[86] During off hours professionals exchange shoptalk about reelection, advancement, favors procured; on this level there is a community of sentiment among them all—"in short, they feel solidary, even if they do not like each other."[87] The sentiment is only skin deep, of course: "They rub elbows, they talk familiarly, they remain strangers."[88] "The press is the big bass drum that sends resounding throughout the country the echoes of what is said in the house without windows";[89] it is, "in its corporative totality, inexhaustibly favorable to the profession,"[90] even though bribery or blackmail may occasionally strain the relations between them. Congenial as the parliamentary milieu may be, its congeniality is offset by the egotism, the bad faith, and the ferocity of its members when their professional interests are at stake; the disloyalty of parties to their leaders, to their supporters, to their ideals; and the systematic duplicity of the heads of governments.

An account of the "mediocrity of parliament"[91] completes Tardieu's description of the "*milieu parlementaire.*" Professionals who are not mediocre to begin with become so in consequence of "the nature of their work"[92]—debating for the sake of debating, running errands for constituents, attitudinizing for the press. "Omnipotent clichés" conceal the absence of ideas: "When they have spoken of *social justice* and *the secular state* on the one side and of *union of right-thinking citizens* and *France above all* on the other, they have nothing left to say."[93] Since no quorum is required for sessions and votes may be cast by proxy,[94] there is little risk of deputies' having to decide issues on their merits. Fisticuffs have become an acceptable expression of opinion. Under the circumstances, parliament toils confusedly and "with fearful slowness,"[95] its enactments being regularly overdue and regularly in need of amendment. Consequently, despite its attractiveness, the profession has fallen into disrepute, and

there has come into being in France a curious state of mind, which is in certain respects inexplicable. The French are anxious to keep their representatives; ordinarily, though, they neither esteem nor trust them. They admit that the less their representatives sit the better, that parliamentary vacations set the country at rest, and that the stoppage of legislative work is one work-stoppage to the good. Nothing gives them more pleasure than to hear ill spoken of those whom, however, they believe themselves to have chosen.[96]

The "despotism of the legislative assembly" is "the direct consequence of the disfranchisement of the people by their elected representatives and the substitution of a trade for a mandate."[97] There is no basis for this despotism in the writings of the eighteenth-century *philosophes* and no example of it outside of France; it owes its existence to the circumstance that, to the French mind, "the division of power is more repugnant than the abuse of power."[98] The legislature exercises its tyranny over the executive by means of interpellations, written questions, and the deposit and defense of bills of a "professional" character, particularly ones involving expenditures in the absence of corresponding receipts. The executive has also to contend with commissions, which, being agencies for reelection and for accession to power, function rather to hold up work than to prepare work; with the consultations and interrogations of its majority groups on policy and on administrative appointments; with the "pressure"[99] of individual favor-seekers. Distracted from its work, it must risk its existence at all hours of the day or night, and for its harassed chief

a permanent alternative is open concerning the application of his ideas. For their application to be thorough, he must resist; for it to be possible, he must last. Where does his duty lie? Every morning he asks himself the same question. Often, after ten years, he finds it hard to answer.[100]

This despotism of the legislature knows "no checks or bounds."[101] The chief of state is a figurehead, a master of ceremonies. The existence of the premier is precarious. "In the sight of the chambers, which are an immense potentiality, the government, a mere actuality, counts for very little";[102] it must maneuver for survival, dissipating what power it has among those who would otherwise work against it. The chambers need fear neither referendum nor popular initiative: "It is understood that the people shall vote only... for or against the elective tradesmen, never on issues or ideas."[103] Petition and dissolution are also unknown, and the judiciary is not competent to pass on the constitutionality of laws "for many reasons, the first of which is that France has no constitution."[104] There is, to be sure, a Senate, and the Senate has encroached on many of the prerogatives of the Chamber; it is, though, "only a duplication of the Chamber,"[105] composed for the most part of senior members of the profession.

Ministerial instability is the first product of the despotism of majorities, which is itself "both a condition and a consequence of the profession."[106] Ministerial instability leads in its turn to government by expedient and improvisation. It makes the civil service refractory to the orders of the government of the day, which will be gone tomorrow. "Ministerial responsibility, as it operates, is but an ingenious device for avoiding real responsibility."[107] If no one inside the ministries feels any real responsibility, no one outside does either. Deputies feel none, being collectively sovereign and individually helpless; of course they are responsible to their constituents under threat of non-reelection, but "non-reelection, before being a punishment, is a normal occupational hazard with which they must reckon *whatever* they do. *What* they do is therefore secondary and does not give rise to a feeling of personal responsibility."[108] As for the captive sovereign, his responsibility is limited to paying the bills; he pays them "with his misery...with his blood...with his despair."[109] Thus do majorities oppress minorities and vice versa in a spirit of anonymous responsibility, or general irresponsibility.

"Nothing in life is free. The price of the despotism of the elected is their servitude."[110] The deputy is a slave locally "to his electors and election-fixers"; he must satisfy their little wants, and in so doing "he enslaves himself to the government and to its agents."[111] He is a slave to the parties, groups, and clubs whose assistance he needs. "Even short of any personal failings" he is enslaved through his party to the "moneymen" who finance it.[112] He may also, if he is not otherwise able to keep up with the profession, have to exchange favors with moneymen directly:

He can be of use for the placing of an order, the award of a decoration, the vote of a tariff or of a tax of exemption. The moneyman on his side can easily be obliging: pay an old bill for printing, buy stock in a down-and-out newspaper, organize a cruise to the Isle of Elba.[113]

These are mere courtesies; sometimes, though, there is corruption. Corruption may come to deputies "from on high," from the government;[114] more frequently it comes to them "from the outside,"[115] services on the inside being paid for on the basis of reciprocity. Corruption is inseparable from the parliamentary profession, its members being possessed of despotic power without intellectual, moral, or financial resources to match. "When this diffuse and subjacent corruption comes to the surface, then we cry scandal!"[116] Parliamentary scandals are "the critical form of the permanent abuse of power and unlawful despotism on which the profession is founded."[117] When they break out, they invariably follow six laws of growth and decay—"adjournment, denial, repudiation, diversion, counterattack, invocation of democracy"—all of which are "inspired by the conscious or unconscious desire to protect those who, in carrying on their trade, have gone perhaps a little too far."[118] Repression, too, "has its rites. Their purpose is to afford—with the least possible harm to the guilty parties and the greatest possible benefit to the party in power...—satisfaction to public opinion, which moreover is not very demanding."[119]

Tardieu concludes:

For more than a century, government of the people by their representatives has been confused with self-government.... The nation does not see that those whom it calls its delegates, and whose master it thinks itself, are in fact professionals who have become its masters. It does not know that the trade they carry on is contrary to the mandate it thinks it has given them.... Our people have, in politics, habits and not principles.... The problem is not alone political; it is also moral.... In saying that a new revolution is needed I am not thinking of institutions only. I believe, with Bergson, that France needs "more of a soul."[120]

Tardieu's account of the behavior of the members of parliament is a brilliant *tour de force*. He adduces no end of evidence to indict them collectively, and his indictment is the more effective for his treating them as individually blameless. The more he pardons each of them, the more he damns them all. To be sure, he does not pardon sympathetically, but with the scorn of the *grand bourgeois* for men who reckon and compute, the scorn of the *grand solitaire* for men whose job it is to talk together, the scorn of the thinker for men with whom opinions count only in the sense that they are counted. Here and there, moreover, his erudition is so conspicuous as to obscure an argument, leaving his readers more sure of his having proved his point than of their having understood it. And now and then he relapses incongruously into professional jargon to regret that the profession exists, pleading for principles that have lost their meaning in words that have lost theirs. Then his style oddly conceals what he has discovered, that a barrier between the people as sovereign and the people as subject has arisen within parliament itself, in the professional character of its membership. His failings, though, are as slight as his discovery is great. No researcher before him had delved so deep into the minutiae and paraphernalia of power, nor come up with so much. And he made an indictment out of his inventory merely by showing how each one of the items on it, however defensible in its own right, helped transform representatives into tradesmen and their any ideas or ideals into professional liabilities.

In his two volumes of *La Révolution à refaire* Tardieu declared himself an enemy of the tradition in France known as radical, and he took issue repeatedly with its most qualified exponent, Alain. To Alain the state, even a democratic state, appeared as the greatest threat to the freedom of the individual. Of itself the state tended, not to wither away, but to proliferate foul excrescences.[121] The interest of the sovereign individual was to keep close watch on it, conceding to it only what it required to subsist and rescinding his concessions if ever they were abused or even taken for granted. Ideally the deputy was a local envoy defending his constituents against the state and subject to their tireless vigilance.[122] His functions, as Alain prescribed them, resemble that "precarious and revocable mandate" the notion of which, Tardieu wrote regretfully, had "given way to a feeling of lawful possession and eminent domain."[123] The resemblance is, however, superficial. Tardieu deplored the "usurpation" by the chambers of the full sovereignty of the people not because the chambers gained in power as a result, but on the contrary because government was inoperative as a result. Similarly, if both men regarded the state as a necessary adjunct to the life of a free man, Tardieu also held its possibilities of beneficent action to be practically unlimited, whereas for Alain its proper function was not intervening in the affairs of men but assuring men against such intervention. For Tardieu did not trust individuals to act always in accordance with their best interests, whereas Alain conceived the best interests of individuals to lie in their acting always as they saw fit. Again, both considered the individual and not the collectivity to be the greatest good. Tardieu, however, held that only in serving their common interests did men serve their individual interests best; hence he rejected as vicious the radicals' conception of "man as the only end of man," upholding the ideal of the nation in its place.[124] This last difference is not fundamental, but it can lead men far apart.

All Tardieu's writings show how extreme was his faith in rationality. For a problem to be solved, he thought, it need only be stated properly, and no proposition is true except in so far as it accords with a general system of truth. Even in France republicanism is a sentiment, however, not a system of thought, and those who profess it loathe final answers even as they love freedom. They are rebellious when they see corruption or feel oppression—not, however, when they read about the perversion of principles. Besides, no revolution has yet been made in consideration of so little as the need for one. André Maurois, who visited Tardieu in Menton, noted:

> He was writing books about politics and believed he could transform France with a pen. "Then," he said, "I'll return to power, but in a regenerated France." For an old hand at politics it was a conception of surprising naïveté. Poor Tardieu, like many men who are too intelligent and believe in the primacy of the intelligence, had astonishing illusions.[125]

Such illusions *are* astonishing—as astonishing as civilization itself. No man is wise to have them, but without them no man is great.

Tardieu's retirement and the appearance of *Le Souverain captif* intrigued the political world. The press of the right thought him to be in league with the left, and the press of the left made him out to be recruiting shock troops on a blank check from the Comité des Forges. Parents frightened naughty children with pictures of him grinning his Mephistophelean grin. Laval spoke with the voice of the profession: "Clever of him! He attracts attention and makes himself wanted."[126] Month after month he sustained his siege of the Republic, waiting for friends to join him. None came. No committees sprang up in his name, no howling throngs troubled his seclusion. *La Profession parlementaire* aroused little comment; by the time it appeared Tardieu, once "the prince of the Republic," was known to France as "the hermit of Menton."

Tardieu in his hermitage was no less attentive to the threat to France from without than to the threat from within.

The occasion for his resigning from the Republican Center at the end of 1935 had been the reaction of its president, Paul Reynaud, to the Italian conquest of Abyssinia. To the colonial powers in 1935, the acquisition of colonies appeared as an ugly anachronism, and the argument of a civilizing mission of Europe as proper only in the case of present holdings. When Premier Laval and Foreign Secretary Sir Samuel Hoare moved to recognize this conquest despite the vote of sanctions against Italy by the League, a wave of indignation in England forced Sir Samuel out of office, and Reynaud, in a stirring speech to the Chamber on December 27, proposed as a foreign policy for France resistance to all acts of aggression. In his letter of resignation Tardieu charged Reynaud with antagonizing Italy to no purpose. "This frightful confusion in world affairs has but one cause," he wrote, the attempt to apply sanctions without having first organized them, the sanctions being consequently both ineffectual and dangerous.... If the threat of sanctions organized in advance, hence total and massive, can by its clarity prevent war, the improvisation of sanctions—that is, the partial and gradual application of sanctions,—by its equivocal character, on the contrary leads to war.[127]

The British, he added, were hypocritical, for they had opposed every effort to organize sanctions or to apply them to Germany and Japan. Besides, the empire of Haile Selassie was of small concern—and later he wrote, "The house in Geneva took fire over a slave trader who ought never to have been admitted in the first place."[128] Reynaud missed his whole point: "André Tardieu... secret admirer of Fascism," he wrote.[129]

When on March 7, 1936, during the electoral campaign in France, Hitler ordered the remilitarization of the west bank of the Rhine, Tardieu declared: "The League and the Locarno guarantors have their responsibilities to take—especially, it seems to me, those of them who for four months have been demanding sanctions against Italy for a mere colonial expedition."[130] And he added:

I perceive three dangers to the future of Europe. The first danger: we go on using, as if it were new, that broken tool known as the League of Nations.... Second danger: preparation is being made in one or another form for negotiating and signing new treaties. Now, there is no point in exchanging signatures with countries for which—or at a time when—signatures have no more value. Third danger: there is no reason to believe that a logical idea will stop dead in its path.... After the military sacrifices we will, if we want to keep Germany happy, have to come around to making territorial sacrifices.

In the chain of sacrifices, he concluded, "The last link is liable... to be... war."[131]

Beginning in 1936 Tardieu contributed a column on foreign policy, "La Note de la Semaine," to *Gringoire*, a popular weekly on the extreme right. When in October, 1936, Belgium unilaterally repudiated her military alliance with France, regarding it as more of a risk than a guarantee, he wrote: "Never has France undergone a worse setback."[132] In November Germany, in a symbolic gesture, repudiated the clauses of the Treaty of Versailles on international waterways; Tardieu wrote: "Everything proves that war is certain, and only madmen could argue the point," and he described Germany as "mistress of the hour at which it will break out."[133] Then early in 1937, in an essay published posthumously, *Le Communisme et l'Europe*, he distinguished the interests of Russia from the interests of the Communist state and analyzed the interaction of the two: "Between what Moscow represents and what western Europe represents," he concluded, there is, I believed, no possible conciliation. In order to destroy what we represent, Communism will use either alliances or war, but its will to destroy us will not weaken. For in Communism the will to destroy is much the same as the will to live.[134]

On February 25, 1938, anticipating the *Anschluss*, he wrote in *Gringoire*: "No question... involved more strongly European public law, of which the independence of Austria was one of the essential foundations."[135] And on April 8, commenting the death of Colonel House: "Everything we fought for—he, I, and many others—has been destroyed."[136] All spring and summer of 1938 he urged France to take a firm stand on Czechoslovakia; then came the Munich agreement, which he described as "the greatest success for Germany in all the years since the war."[137] In May, 1939, *Gringoire* having made light of Beneš and the alliance with Czechoslovakia, he broke with it after attacking it mercilessly in its own columns: both the duty and the interest of France, he maintained, bound her to stand by Czechoslovakia unconditionally.

Three times during his retreat Tardieu attracted the attention of the public.

On May 29, 1937, he was reported engaged to one Julie Angélique Largenton. Journalists investigated the two addresses given by the fiancée to the mayor of Chaumont-sur-Taronne, where the bans were published; finding Julie Angélique unknown at both of them, they concluded that the "ironclad bachelor" was having a misogynous laugh at the world.[138] Nonetheless the ceremony took place, and the bride, a middle-aged school teacher, went with her husband afterwards to share his seclusion.

In the spring of 1937 *Gringoire* joined a few other publications of the extreme right—*La Liberté*, *Le Jour*, *Choc*, *L'Action française*—in a campaign to discredit the Croix de Feu for the benefit of a rival league, the Cagoule. The editor of *Gringoire*, Horace de Carbuccia, charged La Rocque with having received secret government funds for his league, and in July Tardieu confirmed the charge in an interview with the editor of *Choc*, Duke Pozzo di Borgo. After the failure of a mysterious attempt to murder the Duke, La Rocque brought suit in Lyon against the two newspapers, charging them with libel. Tardieu testified that while in office he had given La Rocque 20,000 francs[139] twenty-six times; moreover, he had paid arrears in February, 1932, Laval meanwhile having cut the allowance in half. Confronted with Tardieu, La Rocque was tongue-tied. Condemned to pay expenses, he appealed the judgment in Paris. There on the witness stand Tardieu gave full particulars of the mode and dates of payment to La Rocque, whom he called "a good and true servant." La Rocque was utterly quashed. The press protested in delight against the revelation of amounts and uses of secret funds. Naturally an effort to link Tardieu with the Cagoule ensued; it failed, Tardieu having obviously as much contempt for one league as for another.[140]

On October 15, 1938, Tardieu's one-time assistant Louis Aubert wrote on behalf of the Radical and Socialist leaders Yvon Delbos and Léon Blum to invite him to join a national-union cabinet, "the question of Communist participation being reserved."[141] Both men were themselves willing to have Tardieu for premier, Aubert added, even though Blum thought his party would most likely object. Blum had come a long way since shouting at Tardieu in the Chamber one day: "I hate you!"[142] Tardieu too had come a long way, though: he would not even consider "resuming the vain palaver on which I squandered so many years," and he bade Aubert tell whomever it might concern to put away the idea

that for four years in Menton I have been engaged in a tactical retreat.... I believe that our institutions and our customs need to be made over. My ideas on this subject are perfectly clear. I have my conclusions in my head, only I have not yet been able to put them into writing. They are far removed from what you are offering me.[143]

One month later Blum himself sent out a second feeler; Tardieu rebuffed it just as categorically. Rumors spread.[144] Tardieu had himself interviewed by *Gringoire*; naming no names, he told of the offer, his refusal, and the courteous regrets "of the authors of the offer."[145] Delbos and Blum, the obvious suspects, denied everything.

In the first months of 1939 Tardieu wrote a series of articles about his wartime service with Foch; later he published them in book form, along with—in fulfillment of an old promise to Joffre—copies of orders sent by General Headquarters to Foch in 1915. His devotion to his subject was complete: "None can contest that this was the greatest general the world has known since Napoleon," he wrote;[146] and again: "When a country can produce at just the right time a mind and character of such a mold, it is assured of eternity."[147] *Avec Foch* tells its story simply and vividly: in twenty-five years the experience of his service at the front had lost none of its freshness for him. Obsessed now with the imminence of a new war and with the certainty of the defeat of France, he looked on those months as *"la plus belle époque de ma vie."*[148] Then heroism had been a way of life in France, and no hope for the future had seemed too high; since then, however, the future had come and gone, leaving him in despair.

His career had been great. He had been born to a head start; circumstances had aided him, and so had men—old men especially. Yet if ever success was inevitable, his was. Henry de Jouvenel once said that, given his pick of brains, he would have chosen Tardieu's for his children if not for himself, *"car on pense toujours à la carrière de ses enfants."*[149] But if Tardieu's own success was inevitable, the success of his ideas was not: rarely has so much of the one kind of success gone with so little of the other. His career had been great, but his life, he thought, had been futile; he had spent it fighting, and the fighting had been in vain. His "policy of practical cooperation with Germany" before the war had come to nothing. "Total cooperation among the Allies" had not survived the victory. Of the victors' peace, such as it was, only the memory remained. By his first efforts to preserve it he had only isolated himself from his compatriots, and now every month brought fresh evidence of its failure and his own: the remilitarization of the Rhineland, the return of Belgium to neutrality, the *Anschluss*, Munich. In lieu of a line of defensive fortifications against Germany, France had got half a line, and the World Disarmament Conference had led to the creation not of an international army but of a new *Reichswehr*. His attempt to renovate France had gone down in bickering; republicans had thought the Republic too weak to survive his program of reform; then in striving to make a revolution he had found himself a hermit. He saw France, twenty years after her victory, without security in her defenses or her alliances, with the vices of her political regime intact.

Frenchmen, even while resisting the influence of Tardieu, had always held him in the highest awe. Already when he first took power his detractors wrote of him not as *M. Tardieu*, but as *André Tardieu*, or as *Tardieu* alone—as of a great artist, or a dead man. He was a mystery to all around him; none ever felt close to him in heart and mind. He had his idols: Waldeck-Rousseau, Theodore Roosevelt, Clemenceau, Foch —all men who refused to do things the comfortable way. His kinship, however, was with others. It was with men whom he names often in his writings—often with censure, but often: Benjamin Constant, Royer-Collard, Tocqueville. Such men are conscious of belonging, by birthright almost, to a political class and tradition of their own. They are aristocrats of democracy. They love the people as an abstraction; they are ill-at-ease with real men and women. They command respect without commanding obedience. They have few confidants and fewer friends. Cosmopolitan because curious, they assimilate new languages and cultures easily, but without changing in consequence. Restless, they suffer over things ill done and time ill spent; principled, they behave deliberately, as though their demon (or their biographer) were always at their elbow; exclusive, they fight great battles all alone. They are ironic, and humorless; irritable, solitary men; men of quick tongue, fond of silence. Such men are dreaded wrongly: their grand egoism naturally engenders the suspicions of others intent on smaller things. They people the margins of our histories, issuing solemn warnings, leaving caustic memoirs.

From his retreat Tardieu perceived clearly the needs of France; the more clearly he perceived them, however, the less heed he gave to the wants of Frenchmen. In the end France became for him a collective ideal of which he held individual Frenchmen unworthy. He saw France as suffering in her grandeur from the baseness of Frenchmen. By then his mind was weakening.

In February, 1939, on his return from a brief visit to Paris, he noted in his diary, "Ill."[150] He had a bad case of influenza. A few days later he replied to a friend who had complimented him on an article, "When I wrote that one, I had a temperature of more than 103 degrees."[151] He did not fully recover his health. Maurice Maeterlinck, visiting him in June, was "struck by the abnormal swelling of the veins in his forehead";[152] he urged Tardieu to accompany him to Royat for treatment, but Tardieu refused. Later the same month Gamelin and his wife were Tardieu's guests at Menton. The general spoke of taking a trip to Corsica shortly: "You will not go to Corsica," Tardieu assured him.[153] "He had dug his old blue-devil's uniform out," wrote Gamelin.[154] As late as July 15 he had a friend to dinner—the Rumanian statesman Titulescu.[155] On July 22 he spent the whole day trying to turn out an article "that he had composed in his mind but that his hand refused to write."[156] Then he suffered a stroke: in an instant the angry patriot was transformed into a mute and paralyzed old man.

For one month the news of his illness did not reach the press. Conversely, newspapers were hidden from his sight; on November 6, however, he caught sight of a copy of L'Eclaireur, and "this proud man... collapsed on the spot. For a moment his despair made him conscious of his condition."[157] Somehow he got across to his doctor his wish to be with his sister in Nantes. The doctor saw the Minister of Public Works, Anatole de Monzie, to request transportation; Monzie promised to help "my old friend,"[158] but failed to keep his promise.

Strapped in a wheelchair, fed on pills and injections, his eyesight dimming steadily, Tardieu lived to witness from his terrace the defeat and occupation of his country. Gradually inflation combined with doctors' bills to eat away his fortune, and only the hard-found charity of a few neighbors kept him out of the poorhouse. For a while in 1941 his condition showed improvement; then on January 1, 1942, hearing Pétain speak on the radio of the freedoms still left to France, he wept aloud, and some days afterwards he suffered a relapse. A bulletin on July 14, 1942, described him as "out of danger." He lived on for more than three years longer; his mind, however, gave way almost completely. It is not certain whether or not he comprehended the news of the Liberation. He died on September 15, 1945, unmourned. His obituary was all but crowded out of the newspapers by tidings of the future Fourth Republic.

In Conclusion

In Conclusion

CAILLAUX, JOUVENEL, AND TARDIEU had certain like policies: they stood close on reform of the state in particular, and Tardieu and Jouvenel alone among the statesmen of their time argued for an international army. Yet at least the rationale of their policies was always different. For instance, while both Jouvenel and Tardieu made a strong issue of the freedom of the press, Jouvenel saw the usefulness of the press in its informing the public, Tardieu rather in its guiding the public; as for Caillaux, who suffered from the freedom of the press, he saw it as a source of annoyance to great men. Again, if Jouvenel and Caillaux were both pacifists, Jouvenel was one primarily because he found war repugnant, Caillaux primarily because he thought it futile. Tardieu for his part did not find war repugnant, and if the Great War had been futile, he thought, it had been so only because the peace, imperfectly made, had been progressively forsaken—he sought to perpetuate the peace settlement of 1919 for the sake not of peace, but of France. And even if all three men had a like conception of the ultimate interests of France, their starting points were not the same: Caillaux's was strong government and amity among nations, Jouvenel's was just government and peace among nations, Tardieu's was orderly government and the permanent victory of France. Each man also, whatever his policies, had a manner and a motive distinctively his own: Caillaux nervous and impulsive, Jouvenel lordly and gracious, Tardieu pugnacious and self-assured; Caillaux eager to be right, Jouvenel eager to be agreeable, Tardieu eager to be effective. Jouvenel, moreover, never did his talents justice. With Caillaux it was the reverse: his life was greater than he was. But Tardieu was no more nor less than were his actions, which followed one another like steps in an argument.

All three lives, different though they were, show up the same vices of the Third Republic. One such vice was "politicalization." The politicalization of peace and the income tax made of Caillaux, moderate and bourgeois though he was, the hero of the revolutionary proletariat. Jouvenel, in making his ideas proof against politicalization, found himself without a following and without a program. Tardieu, in breaking the laws of politicalization, came under fire from the very men whose children he bore in his arms. Again, all three men were victims of their colleagues' dread of strong personalities, a dread that condemned Caillaux to the role of martyr, Jouvenel to the role of dilettante, Tardieu to the role of hermit.

In the case of Caillaux, this dread brought on its own sufficient cause. His dealing in secret with Germany convinced the chambers that they were wrong to have entrusted the government to a man like him; their cashiering him afterwards convinced him of the need to set the government free from their control; then his planning to set it free convinced them that men like him were as much of a menace out of power as in; and so forth. Only when prison and old age had somewhat mellowed him did this self-reinforcing mechanism come to a halt—and only then, when it no longer mattered, did it occur to some of them what a splendid job of negotiating he had done in the first place.

To see the faults of the Third Republic through the lives of these men is not, of course, to see the men themselves as faultless. However, any tension between a regime and its vital elements argues first against the regime; and such faults as these three men committed they committed in reaction to those of the regime, which is why their lives are especially instructive. The Republic was consciously in need of such leadership as they had to offer it. Rarely, however, did it call on them to act but it withheld from them the means of acting or else repudiated their actions afterwards. They, meanwhile, instead of limiting their objectives accordingly, urged them all the more exclusively. Any simple judgment of their lives must, then, be ambiguous—that is, it must point to two complementary facts at the same time. Thus, they were the lost leaders of the Third Republic: the Republic lost them as leaders, and as leaders they got lost.

What brought them most into conflict with the regime was also what they shared most fully: their sense of the state—of the state as distinct from parties, from parliament, from the Republic itself; of its grandeur, its strength, its continuity. To their minds the rights of the state, even if subordinate to the rights of man, were no less real and imperious. Neither were the rights of the nation, and at his best each of the three men aspired to save the nation from a perversion of democracy. In this they were handicapped by their patrician breeding, their scorn for standard procedures, the sound of authority in their voices. And to some extent each threw his chance away—Tardieu defiantly, Jouvenel carelessly, Caillaux compulsively. But the Republic threw its chance away more surely than they did theirs: it let their ability as statesmen go to waste just when its need for such ability was greatest. Their frustration was a symptom and a symbol of the plight of their country, so productive of able men and so needful of able performances. Their frustration was not so notable as their failure, though, for frustration might well have been their lot in any case: the urge to save a nation does not presuppose the talent to live in it when it no longer needs saving. The proper picture of each of them is, then, a picture of failure—of their own failure, and of the failure of the Republic: Caillaux in his prison cell, railing against the ingratitude of the Republic; Jouvenel in his castle, taking refuge from the Republic in boredom; Tardieu in his wheelchair, watching the Republic crumble, as it were on schedule.

Appendix

Background to
the Homs-Bagdad:

THE BAGDAD RAILWAY 1888–1909

IN OCTOBER, 1888, the Turkish government granted the Anatolian Railway Company, a syndicate of the Deutsche Bank, a concession to build and operate a railway from the Bosporus to Angora under a guarantee of 15,000 francs per kilometer in annual receipts. The railway, begun the following year, was completed by 1893. Sultan Abdul Hamid then invited the German company to extend it transversely across Asia Minor via Bagdad to the Persian Gulf. The Company hesitated, being short of funds. The German government, however, pressed it to accept. In matters of imperial policy, Kaiser William II always saw big. The railway would open up to Germany a vast area for investment, trade, and colonization. Besides, as Alexander had shown by demonstration and Napoleon by default, "The control of this highway is the key to the East."[1]

France and Great Britain for their part were seeking concessions for railways in Syria and southern Anatolia. Railway investment in Turkey was not likely to be profitable in itself; however, France and Great Britain, like Germany, had vested interests in Turkey, and such concessions were a means for them of improving the Turkish economy while increasing their control over it. Meanwhile they strove, each for reasons of her own, to obstruct the concession to the German company. In the 1870's Great Britain had herself prospected for a railway to run from the Syrian coast across the Euphrates Valley to Bagdad; since then, however, secure in the possession of the shortest water route to India, she had come to regard the land route as a menace. France, on the contrary, was anxious to prevent the Germans not from opening up the "short cut to India," but from claiming it for themselves alone. She might normally have asked to participate in the German concession; instead, out of deference to Russia, she chose to combat it. The interest of Russia was for the Ottoman Empire, which shared her Caucasus frontier and held the Dardanelles, to go on being weak indefinitely; in consequence, "it was her policy to prevent railways being built [there],"[2] especially railways between the Black Sea and the Persian Gulf.

While the Bagdad concession was pending, then, "Constantinople was again a nest in intrigue."[3] The British did the most conniving to obstruct it. To some avail: the new concession to the Anatolian Railway Company, which came through in February, 1893, was for a line to run southwards only as far as

Konia, with a kilometric guarantee slightly lower than the one before. Concurrently the French Ambassador, Paul Cambon, won for his country an option to extend the Syrian railways from Homs across the Euphrates to Bagdad.

The world depression of 1893 hit the Deutsche Bank and the Paris Bourse with equal force. The option to France was allowed to expire. The German line was more than three years in construction, and when it was built the Anatolian Railway Company was not eager to push on to Bagdad. The Kaiser, however, was eager for it to do so. Already, by merely being more tolerant than Gladstone of the massacre of Armenians, he had won for Germany the place of honor in the councils of "the unspeakable Turk"; then in Damascus in 1898 he proclaimed himself "friend and protector of the three hundred million Mohammedans" and so won the devotion of the two hundred million Mohammedans. The Sultan renewed his old offer to the German syndicate. The Deutsche Bank, unable to see its way clear to financing the venture, held out for some time against the pressure of the German government; at length it agreed to accept, provided it might admit French and British financiers to joint participation. The German government was willing: by its willingness it hoped to gain the cooperation of the French and British governments, perhaps to obtain a terminus on the Gulf, eventually even to transfer the railway guarantee to the Ottoman Debt Commission if Turkey defaulted, and all the while to exchange German steel for French and British capital.

Now, while the German bank still had to count its *Groschen*, French banks again had capital in abundance; besides, having large investments in Turkey, they were all the more eager to protect them by further investments. Early in May, 1899, French bankers agreed to participate with the Deutsche Bank in the Bagdad railway on a 40–40 basis, the remaining interest going to Austrian and Swiss groups in alliance with Germany; Delcassé, misunderstanding the arrangement, was satisfied with it.

In November, 1899, the Sultan, in order to shut out other competitors, granted a tentative concession for the Konia-Bagdad line to the Anatolian Railway Company. At once Russia, protesting strenuously, exacted from Turkey by way of precaution the exclusive right to build railways in northern Anatolia, which she took with the express purpose of reserving it forever. Great Britain for her part suspected Germany of coveting the Persian Gulf; to allay her suspicions Germany represented the railway to her as a threat against Russia and offered her a proportional share in it. Meanwhile Germany strove to reassure Russia; finding her efforts vain, she prevailed upon France to assist her. In Saint Petersburg early in 1901 Delcassé won the consent of the Russian government for the railway, and in Danzig the following September the Kaiser told the Czar that there was a place waiting for Russia in the railway syndicate. Then in January, 1902, after countless delays *à la turque* and handouts to match, the Sublime Porte made the concession to the Anatolian Railway Company definitive.

Immediately the British foreign office announced: "The maintenance of the *status quo* in the Persian Gulf is incompatible with the occupation by any Power of a point on those waters,"[4] whereupon British troops occupied Kuwait on the Gulf; Turkey and Germany, taken unawares, acknowledged the *fait accompli*. Then as Russia, ignoring her prior consent, denounced the railway project all over again, Delcassé, exasperated, wrote the obvious to Saint Petersburg:

The Bagdad railway is inevitable—it will be built by the Germans alone, or by an Anglo-German consortium. It would be better, then, for France and Russia to join the enterprise and secure for themselves the influence belonging to a group which participates in the control.[5]

Russia, however, was not to be misled by the obvious: she would perhaps be willing to pay to prevent the Bagdad railway from being built, said Witte, but she would not pay to help build it.[6] Then the Bagdad Railway group, through the British Ambassador in Constantinople, won the consent of the British Foreign Secretary, Lord Lansdowne, to a prospective participation of British capital; in nine months, however, Lansdowne found no British financiers willing to participate. Gwinner went to London to see what was amiss, and Lansdowne told him with sudden nostalgia: "Until now England held the shortest route to India."[7] Lansdowne consenting, Gwinner himself found two British financiers who were willing: Sir Ernest Cassel, chief of the new Ottoman National Bank, and Sir Clinton Dawkins of Morgan and Company. The various participants formed a new syndicate, the Bagdad Railway Company. The British, French, and German groups were each to subscribe capital in equal shares; of the eleven directors, however, three were to be German and another three under the control of the German group.

By a convention of March 5, 1903, with the new Bagdad Railway Company,[8] the Porte made its concession more precise and more advantageous. The railway was now to run beyond Bagdad to Basra, and thence to a terminus on the Persian Gulf "to be determined," all under a guarantee of 15,000 francs per kilometer. It was to be built in four main sections, one at a time, and as each section came under construction the Porte was to issue bonds for one fourth of the estimated costs of the whole line, or four series at 54,000,000 francs each; the interest of 4 percent on the bonds was to be guaranteed by the surplus of revenues ceded to the Great Powers. Under Article Twelve the company won priority for the building of branch lines to the Mediterranean. It also won mining and oil rights, the right of navigation on the Tigris and Euphrates, franchise for imports of equipment, and concessions for ports at Bagdad, at Basra, and on the Persian Gulf. So much for what Turkey conceded; as for what she exacted in return, except for the highest officials the employees of the railway were to be Turks, and *every* employee was to wear a fez.

While all Germany jubilated at the news of the new arrangement, in France and in England the public raged in protest—with encouragement in England from "the financiers" and in France from "the politicians."[9] Rumors ran wild about the concession; Gwinner optimistically sent a copy of it to the London *Times*—"Wherefrom it appeared that all the anathema heaped upon it was abundantly justified."[10] The provisions for joint administration were denounced as a mockery: obligingly the company amended its statutes to put the French and British directors in a majority. Still the British public was not satisfied: it was suspicious of Cassel for his German origins and of Dawkins for his affiliation with Morgan; besides, at the moment it did not trust the French any more than it did the Germans. In Turkey the Lynch steamship company, which held a monopoly on inland navigation, staged patriotic protests of Turks along the banks of the two rivers. Lansdowne, after defending participation for some weeks, backed down at last, whereupon Delcassé, under strong pressure from his *revanchard* following and from Russia, took the opportunity to demand a half interest for the French group as a condition for its remaining.[11]

The British and the French had been too indignant over the very idea of the Bagdad railway to see where their best interests in it lay. The British saw it as a threat to their mercantile supremacy in the East, and the French saw it as a threat to the strategic position of Russia. It was both these things, no doubt; but it was also inevitable, and by their refusal to participate in it they were only to delay, not prevent, its construction. To delay its construction was in some ways to their advantage; however, just as their refusal to participate left Germany alone in control of the main highway of Turkey, so their policy of obstruction was inevitably to drive Turkey into closer and closer sympathy with Germany. Tardieu, by way of consolation, saw in the common opposition of France and Great Britain to the Bagdad railway, rather than in any mutual affection, the origin of the *entente cordiale* of 1904.[12]

The Bagdad Railway Company began construction early in 1904, and by October of that year the first rail section, which ran from Konia to Bulgurli, was complete. The second, however, fell entirely within the Taurus mountain range, and the company, though over half the value of the first series of bonds was left to it, found that even after the sale of the second series it would not have enough money to go on building. It therefore requested the Turkish government to issue all the bonds at once. The Turkish government in turn asked leave from the Ottoman Debt Commission, on which all the Great Powers sat, to raise tariffs from 8 percent to 11 percent in order to guarantee the interest on the bond issue. Rouvier tried to negotiate the consent of France against concessions from Germany in Morocco; Germany, however, stood firm in her demand for an international settlement in Morocco. Lansdowne saw no reason for British exports to Turkey to suffer for the sake of the Bagdad railway, so Germany prevailed upon the Turkish government to refuse a concession for a British railway from Smyrna to Aden. Lansdowne was then ready to reconsider participation in the Bagdad railway. This time, however, the German government made a point of the "essential German character" of the enterprise, which it was willing to sacrifice only in the Gulf area. Again Gwinner went to London, again to no avail.[13] In April, 1907, the Great Powers gave Turkey authority to raise her tariffs provided that three fourths of the proceeds went for reforms in Macedonia and not a *piastre* of them for the Bagdad railway—the uncommitted balance went finally for a German concession to irrigate the Konia plain.[14]

In 1907 the stalemate over the Bagdad railway was complete. Tardieu, reviving Rouvier's idea of 1905, urged France to offer Germany the means of completing the railway in return for compensation in Morocco:

The Act of Algeciras must be set aside and France must have a free hand in Morocco! An agreement upon the Bagdad question would be mischievous if it concerned Bagdad alone, for, the Germans having the concessions in their pockets, the position of the negotiators would not be equal. On the other hand, if the agreement is for two purposes, if it refers to Bagdad *and* Morocco, I believe, I repeat, it would be both practicable and desirable.[15]

In the Reichstag the leader of the National Liberal Party urged the government to rebuff any such proposal, and the government acquiesced in silence.[16]

On June 2, 1908, the Turkish government agreed to issue conjointly the second and third series of the Imperial Ottoman Bagdad Railway bonds, covering construction from Bulgurli across the Taurus range and thence to El Helif within two hundred fifty miles of Bagdad, the additional guarantees to become effective in 1911, when three fourths of the surplus of revenues ceded to the Ottoman Debt Commission would be once more available to the Turkish state. With prospects good for negotiating the bonds at a small discount, Germany spoke proudly once more in the chancelleries of Europe. Then in July, 1908, Abdul Hamid was dethroned by the Young Turks, and Germany, the most favored nation of the old regime, was discredited. The Young Turks even spoke of repudiating the Bagdad concession, and in desperation Germany again sought an understanding on the railway with Great Britain. Only for a moment: early in 1909 she regained some of her former preeminence in Constantinople when the military clique of the Young Turk party won control. By then, however, the Turkish state was deeper in debt than ever: if it was to honor the Bagdad concession, it would have to raise tariffs again.

Notes

LIST OF ABBREVIATIONS

BD   *British Documents on the Origins of the War, 1898–1914.* Edited by G. P. Gooch and Harold Temperly. 11 vols. London, H. M. Stationery Office, 1926–38. Note references are to volume and document number.

DBFP   *Documents on British Foreign Policy, 1919–1939.* Edited by E. L. Woodward and Rohan Butler. London, H. M. Stationary Office, 1947. Note references are to series, volume, document number.

DDF   *Documents diplomatiques français (1871–1914).* Paris, Imprimerie Nationale, 1929–. Note references are to series, volume, document number.

GP   *Die grosse Politik der europäischen Kabinette, 1871–1914.* Edited by Johannes Lepsius, Albrecht Mendelssohn-Bartholdy, and Friedrich Thimme. 40 vols. Berlin, Deutsche Verlagsgesellschaft für Politik und Geschichte G.m.b.H., 1922–27. Note references are to volume and document number.

LJ   *Documents diplomatiques 1912, Affaires du Maroc VI, 1910–1912.* Paris, Imprimerie Nationale, 1912. Also published as *Livre jaune: Affaires marocaines (1910–1912).* Note references are to document number.

LN   *Un Livre noir, Diplomatie d'avant-guerre d'après les documents des archives russes (1910–1917).* 3 vols. Paris, Librairie du Travail, 1922–192(?). Note references are to volume and page.

Notes

NOTES TO INTRODUCTION

1. By the Chamber itself voting jointly with certain local elective officials.

2. A provision for some lifelong senators was repealed after a few years.

3. In some passages of the *Social Contract*, to be sure, Rousseau upholds the principle of the separation of powers. His disciples in France, however, generally discount those passages, finding them incompatible with his main argument. His critique of representative government is likewise discounted as obsolete.

4. Quoted by André Tardieu, *La Révolution à refaire* (2 vols., Paris, Flammarion, 1936–37), II, 189.

5. My account of how this system worked follows roughly Charles Seignobos, *L'Evolution de la 3e République, 1875–1914* (Paris, Hachette, 1921), pp. 116–17.

6. There was also the *scrutin de liste*, which, except that it enabled each voter to vote for some few deputies rather than for a single one, was like the *scrutin uninominal* in its workings.

7. In fact the single ballot was used once—in 1871. Because it then yielded a majority of monarchists, it was anathema to the left thereafter. When once (in January, 1932) it won the approval of the Chamber, it was rejected by the Senate as too favorable to the right, which, the senators thought, was more apt to agree on a single candidate.

8. Tardieu made this point once in connection with political favor-seeking. Of the *Administration* (civil service) he wrote: "Il lui faut en toute matière, si technique que soit cette matière, soumettre aux ministères deux éléments de décision, qu'elle aligne avec déférence: la valeur propre de cette décision, et sa valeur parlementaire, laquelle se peut interpréter soit du point de vue de la majorité, soit de celui de l'opposition. Point de caniveau à creuser ni de tuyau à poser qui n'offrent ce double caractère." *L'Heure de la décision* (Paris, Flammarion, 1934), pp. 127–28.

9. Alain, *Politique* (Paris, Presses Universitaires de France, 1951), p. 271.

NOTES TO 1: "MY MINISTRY"

1. Joseph Caillaux, *Mes Mémoires* (3 vols., Paris, Plon, 1942–47), I, 30.

2. *Ibid.*, p. 4.

3. Alfred Fabre-Luce, *Caillaux* (Paris, Gallimard, 1933), p. 13, and (Laurance Lyon), *The Pomp of Power* (London, Hutchinson, 1922), p. 178, both quoting Joseph Reinach.

4. Fabre-Luce, *Caillaux*, p. 13, quoting Guy de Pierrefeux, *Le Revenant, Propos et anecdotes autour de Caillaux* (Strasbourg, Hiller, 1925).

5. The Lycée Fontanes changed its name to Lycée Condorcet a few years later.

6. Caillaux, *Mémoires*, I, 67.   7. *Ibid.*, p. 68.   8. *Ibid.*, p. 201.

9. *Ibid.*, p. 71.   10. *Ibid.*, p. 75.   11. *Ibid.*, pp. 193–94.

12. Chambre des Députés, *Débats, 1904*, p. 3019; Joseph Caillaux, *Les Impôts en France* (2 vols., Paris, Pichon, 1911), I, xxi and lxxxiv.

13. Octave Homberg, *Les Coulisses de l'histoire, Souvenirs 1898–1928* (Paris, Fayard, 1938), p. 136.

14. Caillaux, *Mémoires*, I, 87 (*"un geste d'étourderie"*).

15. *Ibid.*, p. 89*n*.

16. His half-sister lived until 1914, but the contact between them was slight.

17. Approximately $575,000 in the United States in 1960. (I obtain this rough equivalence by "deflating" the francs on the basis of the French cost-of-living index, then converting them into dollars.)

18. Joseph Paul-Boncour, *Entre deux guerres, Souvenirs sur la IIIème République* (3 vols., Paris, Plon, 1945), I, 96.

19. *GP*, Vol. XIII, no. 3644.   20. Caillaux, *Mémoires*, I, 184.

21. *Ibid.*, p. 185 (*"ric et rac"*).

22. For an excellent résumé of the attitude of the Radicals toward the income tax between 1899 and 1914 see T. H. Thomas, "Caillaux," *The Atlantic Monthly* (June, 1925), pp. 832–35.

23. Quoted by Paul Vergnet, *Joseph Caillaux* (Paris, Renaissance du Livre, 1918), p. 97.

24. *DDF*, Ser. II, Vol. I, nos. 13, 73.

25. *Ibid.*, no. 531.   26. *Ibid.*, no. 309.   27. *Ibid.*, no. 251.

28. *Ibid.*, nos. 49, 200.   29. *DDF*, Ser. II, Vol. II, nos. 234, 244.

30. Fabre-Luce, *Caillaux*, p. 31, quoting Madame Gueydan.

31. Caillaux, *Mémoires*, I, 201.

32. Pierre Mendès-France, speaking at Caillaux's tomb on November 21, 1953, declared: "This preface does more than just sum up: it presents a philosophy of taxation along with the whole political and social contents of a fiscal system." *Les Cahiers du Cercle Joseph Caillaux*, 2ème année, numéro 2 (premier trimestre, 1954), p. 53.

33. Caillaux, *Impôts*, I, xxxi–xxxii.   34. *Ibid.*, pp. cxiv–cxv.

35. *Ibid.*, p. xiii.   36. *Ibid.* A term used throughout the Preface.

37. Caillaux, *Mémoires*, I, 226.   38. *Ibid.*, p. 229.   39. *Ibid.*

40. The story goes that Premier-designate Sarrien, meaning to offer Clemenceau a drink, asked him, "What'll you have?" Replied Clemenceau, "The Interior."

41. *DDF*, Ser. II, Vol. X, *passim.*, especially nos. 355, 360.

42. For Jaurès' cooperation in this with Caillaux, see Mendès-France, in *Les Cahiers du Cercle Joseph Caillaux*, 2ème année, numéro 2 (premier trimestre, 1954), p. 55.

43. Caillaux, *Mémoires*, II, 27.

44. Maurice Barrès, *Mes Cahiers* (13 vols., Paris, Plon, 1929–50), V, 114.

45. *DDF*, Ser. II, Vol. XII, no. 350, note.

46. *DDF*, Ser. II, Vol. XI, no. 409.   47. *Ibid.*, no. 447.

48. *DDF*, Ser. II, Vol. XII, no. 350, note.

49. *DDF*, Ser. II, Vol. XI, no. 643.

50. Quoted by Charles Benoist, *Souvenirs* (3 vols., Paris, Plon, 1934), III, 144.

51. See Georges Michon, *La Préparation à la guerre, La Loi des trois ans (1910–1914)* (Paris, Rivière, 1935), p. 30.

NOTES TO 2: AGADIR

1. Joseph Caillaux, *Mes Mémoires* (3 vols., Paris, Plon, 1942–47), II, 6.

2. *Ibid.*, p. 4.   3. Georges Suarez, *Briand* (6 vols., Paris, Plon, 1938–52), II, 111.

4. Caillaux, *Mémoires*, II, 7.

5. *DDF*, Ser. II, Vol. XII, no. 405.   6. Caillaux, *Mémoires*, II, 8.

7. That is, more than $300,000 in 1960 dollars (see Note 17, Chapter One).

8. Suarez, *Briand*, II, 234–35.

9. Paul Vergnet, *Joseph Caillaux* (Paris, La Renaissance du Livre, 1918), p. 112, quoting testimony of Madame Gueydan.

10. *Ibid.*, p. 106.

11. Stéphane Lauzanne, *Sa Majesté la presse* (Paris, Fayard, 1925), p. 147.

12. Speech at Périgueux, August, 1909.   13. See p. 217.

14. This was Caillaux's rebuttal to the German Embassy counselor Lancken's assurances that Germany would consent to an equivalent Franco-German consortium in the Cameroons (*DDF*, Ser. II, Vol. XIII, no. 155).

15. Caillaux, *Mémoires*, II, 36.   16. *Ibid.*, p. 38.

17. Quoted by Suarez, *Briand*, II, 329.

18. In 1960 dollars, about $100,000 and $9,000 (see Note 17, Chapter One).

19. *DDF*, Ser. II, Vol. XIII, no. 186 and annex (March 13).

20. Caillaux, *Mémoires*, II, 63.

21. Quoted by Joseph Caillaux, *Agadir, Ma Politique extérieure* (Paris, Michel, 1919), pp. 90–91, from a report by Jules Cambon.

22. Caillaux, *Mémoires*, II, 66.

23. *DDF*, Ser. II, Vol. XIII, no. 241. Remark quoted by Caillaux, *Agadir*, p. 96. See also *DDF*, Ser. II, Vol. XIII, no. 364, and *GP*, Vol. XXIX, no. 10535.

24. *DDF*, Ser. II, Vol. XIII, no. 317, notes and annexes.

25. In 1960 dollars, about $50,000 (see Note 17, Chapter One).

26. *DDF*, Ser. II, Vol. XIII, no. 86.

27. Caillaux, *Mémoires*, II, 58–59. See also Caillaux, *Agadir*, pp. 77–86, and *GP*, Vol. XXIX, nos. 10573, 10574.

28. Erich Brandenburg, *From Bismarck to the World War, A History of German Foreign Policy 1870–1914*, trans. by Annie Elizabeth Adams (London, Milford, 1927), p. 372. Brandenburg says that Caillaux offered "whatever we [the Germans] wanted." See however *GP*, Vol. XXIX, nos. 10554, 10555.

29. Caillaux, *Mémoires*, II, 67.   30. *Ibid.*

31. In the estimate of Paul Cambon, Cruppi was—besides being "inexperienced"—merely "tired." *DDF*, Ser. II, Vol. XIII, no. 329.

32. Caillaux, *Mémoires*, II, 68. See also *GP*, Vol. XXIX, no. 10563.

33. *LJ*, nos. 337–39 (June 3), 352–54 (June 9), 357 and annex.

34. Caillaux, *Mémoires*, II, 68.   35. *DDF*, Ser. II, Vol. XIII, no. 364.

36. Joseph Paul-Boncour, *Entre deux guerres, Souvenirs sur la IIIème République* (3 vols., Paris, Plon, 1945), I, 220.

37. Caillaux shrewdly ignored the curious request of the Kaiser and of Bethmann-Hollweg to reinstate Delcassé, who had been removed from the Quai d'Orsay at the behest of Germany in June, 1905 (*DDF*, Ser. II, Vol. XIII, no. 367). See however p. 49. For Kiderlen's explanation of the request, see Caillaux, *Agadir*, p. 275.

38. *Le Figaro*, June 28, 1911.   39. Chambre des Députés, *Débats, 1911*, p. 2537.

40. *Ibid.*, p. 2536, as freely quoted by Caillaux, *Mémoires*, II, 94.

41. Memorandum of the German government, delivered to the French governement on July 1, 1911. *GP*, Vol. XXIX, no. 10578; *LJ*, no. 418; *DDF*, Ser. II, Vol. XIV, no 1.

42. *LJ*, no. 426 (July 4); *DDF*, Ser. II, Vol. XIV, nos. 22 and 18; Caillaux, *Agadir*, p. 116; *GP*, Vol. XXIX, no. 10592.

43. André Tardieu, *Le Mystère d'Agadir* (Paris, Calmann-Lévy, 1912), p. 437.

44. *GP*, Vol. XXIX, nos. 10595–97; *LJ*, no. 439; *DDF*, Ser. II, Vol. XIV, no. 43.

45. Alfred von Kiderlen-Wächter, *Kiderlen-Wächter der Staatsmann und Mensch, Briefwechsel und Nachlass*, ed. by Ernst Jäckh (2 vols., Stuttgart, Deutsche Verlags-Anstalt, 1925), II, 126; Caillaux, *Agadir*, pp. 293–94; *LJ*, no. 452, 455; *DDF*, Ser. II, Vol. XIV, no. 65; *GP*, Vol. XXIX, no. 10607. According to Bethmann (*GP*), Jules Cambon "almost fell over backwards" when Kiderlen made known Germany's demands, "and [Cambon] explained 'that even a partial cession of the Congo territory would be very difficult for the French government to defend before its parliament.'" Four days earlier, however (July 9), Kiderlen had written to his *correspondante* Madame Marina de Jonina that at his mentioning to Cambon, who had just returned from

Paris, the "hypothesis... of our giving France *carte blanche* in Morocco and claiming in return not moral but real compensation in the colonial realm, Herr Cambon interrupted me quite vivaciously with the words, '*On a parlé du côté du Congo*.' I told him that I did not consider it as out of the question." (*Kiderlen-Wächter*, II, 125; Caillaux, *Agadir*, pp. 278–83; *GP*, Vol. XXIX, no. 10598). In either case Jules Cambon was a good actor: as the Kaiser noted in the margin of Bethmann's dispatch of July 15 (*GP*, Vol. XXIX, no. 10607), "*spielt gut Comödie*." Kiderlen had to contend with the Pan-Germanists, led by the Crown Prince, who vehemently opposed the principle of compensation in lieu of partition; nonetheless as early as July 6 Cambon was expecting him to bring up the Congo (*DDF*, Ser. II, Vol. XIV, nos. 37 and 64), and according to Cambon the first mention of the Congo on July 9 came from Kiderlen (see *DDF*, Ser. II, Vol. XIV, no. 51; *GP*, Vol. XXIX, no. 10598, note, and no. 10600 and notes).

46. Quoted by Caillaux, *Agadir*, pp. 160, 302, and *Mémoires*, III, 283 (Cambon's letter of July 24). Caillaux called this style of negotiating "putting our family trinkets in hock" (*DDF*, Ser. II, Vol. XIV, no. 144). Cambon's correspondence with Caillaux during the Agadir affair is reprinted *in extenso* in Caillaux, *Mémoires*, III, 281–326, and partially in *DDF*, Ser. II, Vol. XIV, *passim*. See also *DDF*, Ser. II, Vol. XIV, no. 99; *GP*, Vol. XXIX, nos. 10600–13, 10674 and note, 10677, 10679, 10683.

47. See *DDF*, Ser. II, Vol. XIV, nos. 40, 43.   48. See *Ibid.*, no. 274, pp. 759–60.

49. Quoted by Caillaux, *Agadir*, pp. 158, 286, and *Mémoires*, III, 283; *DDF*, Ser. II, Vol. XIV, no. 53. Cambon urged Caillaux in particular to see Von Schoen in Paris—professedly at the bidding of Kiderlen, though Kiderlen's correspondence with Madame de Jonina reports no such request.

50. Caillaux, *Mémoires*, II, 109.   51. *Ibid.*, p. 108.

52. *Ibid.*, p. 109. See also *DDF*, Ser. II, Vol. XIV, no. 105—which, however, places this conversation at July 26.

53. Caillaux, *Mémoires*, II, 111.

54. Caillaux, *Agadir*, p. 163; *DDF*, Ser. II, Vol. XIV, no. 105 (Fondère's notes on his conversations); *GP*, Vol. XXIX, nos. 10675, 10676. Kiderlen thought that the initiative for the meeting had come from Caillaux (*GP*, Vol. XXIX, no. 10675, note 2).

55. Caillaux, *Mémoires*, II, 159. Cambon had urged this line of negotiation on Caillaux, arguing that it alone would keep the other powers from cutting in on the conversations (*DDF*, Ser. II, Vol. XIV, nos. 17 and 21). Fondère (*ibid.*, no. 105) does not mention the reservation "outside of Europe," but even Von Schoen reported an equivalent one (see Note 56).

56. *GP*, Vol. XXIX, nos. 10675 and 10678; quoted by Caillaux, *Agadir*, pp. 303–5, 306–7, and by Charles Paix-Séailles, *Jaurès et Caillaux* (Paris, Figuières, 1919), pp. 174–75. Compare *DDF*, Ser. II, Vol. XIV, nos. 105, 144. On the subject of whether these were formal offers or merely suggestions, see also *GP*, Vol. XXIX, no. 10713.

57. *DDF*, Ser. II, Vol. XIV, no. 105.

58. Fondère prepared the report for Piétri; it is given *ibid*.

59. Quoted by Caillaux, *Agadir*, p. 320, and *Mémoires*, II, 156; also by *GP*, Vol. XXIX, no. 10679, note. Kiderlen did not doubt the veracity of the telegrams: for his surprise and perplexity at Cambon's seeming to know what Caillaux had presumably urged be kept secret, see his letters of August 2 in Caillaux, *Agadir*, pp. 332–35. Though he thought Lancken "stupid" to have had the telegrams sent instead of waiting to make an oral report, he may have suspected Lancken of having meant them to be deciphered by the Quai d'Orsay, for he wrote, "The embassy used an old code that the French must once have stolen"; in *GP*, Vol. XXIX, no. 10717, Lancken seems to be defending himself against such a suspicion. Kiderlen also thought that Caillaux had sent Piétri to Berlin only in desperation. Caillaux, in *Mémoires*, II, *passim*, and *Agadir*, pp. 247–368, *passim*, quotes extensively from the French edition of Kiderlen's correspondence with Madame de Jonina, *Kiderlen-Waechter intime* (see p. 83); the German edition, cited previously, is relatively incomplete.

60. Caillaux, *Agadir*, pp. 166, 172, 324–30 (quoting Piétri and Cambon). See also *LJ*, no. 480, and *DDF*, Ser. ii, Vol. xiv, no. 134: Kiderlen reduced his demands to "territorial access [from the Cameroons] to the Congo river."

61. *BD*, Vol. vii, no. 405.

62. *Ibid.*, no. 408; Caillaux, *Mémoires*, ii, 133–34. See also *DDF*, Ser. ii, Vol. xiv, no. 36.

63. Tardieu, *Mystère d'Agadir*, p. 468. For the refusal of Great Britain to back France, see further A. J. P. Taylor, *The Struggle for Mastery in Europe, 1848–1918* (Oxford, Clarendon, 1954), pp. 470–72. "The British cabinet would not pledge themselves to France" (p. 470). Of Lloyd George's famous Mansion House speech of July 21, 1911, in which he declared that England would not be treated as of no account "where her interests are vitally affected," Taylor writes: "In essence, this was not a pledge to support France against Germany; it was a warning that Great Britain could not be left out of any new partition of Morocco. It was directed against Caillaux, not against Kiderlen" (p. 471). It is no less true, though, that Kiderlen and with him all Germany took this warning to be directed against themselves. See also *GP*, Vol. xxix, nos. 10633, 10634; *BD*, Vol. vii, nos. 407, 408; and between the lines of *DDF*, Ser. ii, Vol. xiv, nos. 19, 22, 26, 36, 37 (especially Caillaux's notations), 87, 88, 106.

64. Caillaux, *Mémoires*, ii, 140, and *Agadir*, p. 142. See also Ernest Judet, *Georges Louis* (Paris, Rieder, 1925), p. 156; *GP*, Vol. xxix, no. 10593 and note; *DDF*, Ser. ii, Vol. xiv, nos. 200, 201, 234, 236, 241.

65. Quoted by Caillaux, *Mémoires*, ii, 144, and *Agadir*, p. 144.

66. *GP*, Vol. xxix, no. 10683, note. Cambon also threw in some Oceanic islands, and he gave Kiderlen to understand that no mock exchange of territories would be necessary.

67. *Ibid.*, no. 10685.

68. Technically there was no commander-in-chief in time of peace; Caillaux wrote assuring Joffre of the appointment in case of war, meanwhile naming him vice-president of the Conseil supérieur de la Guerre. See Alexandre Zévaès, *Histoire de la IIIᵉ République* (Paris, Nouvelle Revue Critique, 1946), p. 258*n*.

69. Joseph J. C. Joffre, *Mémoires du maréchal Joffre (1910–17)* (2 vols., Paris, Plon, 1932), i, 15–16.

70. Caillaux, *Agadir*, pp. 172–73, 332, and *Mémoires*, iii, 284–86 (Cambon to Caillaux, August 2, 9); *DDF*, Ser. ii, Vol. xiv, nos. 135, 136, 137, 140, 148, 152.

71. Tardieu, *Mystère d'Agadir*, pp. 446–47.

72. *Kölnische Volkszeitung*, August 7, 1911; quoted in *GP*, Vol. xxix, no. 10699, note, and Caillaux, *Mémoires*, ii, 164.

73. Quoted in Caillaux, *Mémoires*, ii, 165.

74. Quoted by the Spanish ambassador in Paris in a dispatch of August 6, deciphered by the French Ministry of the Interior (Caillaux, *Agadir*, p. 341).

75. *BD*, Vol. vii, nos. 416, 488; *DDF*, Ser. ii, Vol. xiv, nos. 167, 169, 170, 175, 198.

76. Winston Churchill, *The World Crisis, 1911–1914* (New York, Scribner, 1924), p. 44, and *GP*, Vol. xxix, no. 10626, note. The British recalled their fleet from maneuvers off Norway, and Kiderlen had all he could do to restrain the Kaiser from reciprocating and thereby provoking a war: see Caillaux, *Agadir*, pp. 333–34.

77. Caillaux, *Agadir*, p. 176. See also *GP*, Vol. xxix, nos. 10686 and note, 10688, 10689. The Kaiser, believing a false report that Caillaux himself had threatened to send a French gunboat to Agadir, described his absence from Paris as *"eine neue Unverschämtheit!* When you are involved in such serious negotiations and make such threats you don't go off on a picnic.... [My informant in Paris] will have to find Caillaux immediately and make it clear to him that within 24 hours he will have apologized for having been so fresh to me or else I'll break off the negotiations! That

should make it pretty hot for him!" (*GP*, Vol. xxix, no. 10694; see also nos. 10695–98). The Kaiser's informant next claimed to have been set right by Caillaux at a second meeting (Caillaux, *Mémoires*, ii, 163); Caillaux himself knew nothing of this second meeting *(ibid.)*.

78. Quoted in Caillaux, *Mémoires*, ii, 168. Kiderlen was urged to intransigence especially by the Secretary of State for Colonies, Von Lindequist, a spokesman for the Pan-Germanists: see *GP*, Vol. xxix, nos. 10690, 10702, and Caillaux, *Agadir*, p. 337.

79. Caillaux, *Mémoires*, ii, 168, and *Agadir*, pp. 176–78.

80. See *GP*, Vol. xxix, nos. 10705, 10715; *DDF*, Ser. ii,, Vol. xiv, nos. 144, 198. Wrote Kiderlen-Wächter: "Public opinion here has been slowly... but powerfully aroused by the growing insolence of our neighbors across the Rhine and across the sea, and, intent though I am on peace, I could not restrain it if the insults were to continue" (quoted by Caillaux, *Agadir*, p. 339).

81. Tardieu, *Mystère d'Agadir*, p. 485 (*"conseil des ministres restreint"*).

82. *Ibid.*, p. 481.

83. For the instructions to Cambon, see *LJ*, no. 520 and annex; *DDF*, Ser. ii, Vol. xiv, no. 223, and map facing p. 760.

84. Quoted by Caillaux, *Mémoires*, iii, 291 (letter of September 4). See also *LJ*, no. 529.

85. *GP*, Vol. xxix, nos. 10719, 10729; *DDF*, Ser. ii, Vol. xiv, nos. 254, 305, 306, 387, 393.

86. *LJ*, nos. 536–76; *DDF*, Ser. ii, Vol. xiv, nos. 260–416, *passim*; *GP*, Vol. xxix, nos. 10735–44.

87. *BD*, Vol. vii, Appendix i; *DDF*, Ser. ii, Vol. xiv, nos. 256, 262, 264, 288, 296, 303, 312, 326, 333, 372.

88. Quoted by Caillaux, *Agadir*, p. 351, and *Mémoires*, ii, 170–71; *DDF*, Ser. ii, Vol. xiv, no. 326.

89. Paix-Séailles, *Jaurès et Caillaux*, pp. 38–39.

90. Caillaux, *Agadir*, p. 210. See also *LJ*, no. 574; *DDF*, Ser. ii, Vol. xiv, nos. 380, 381, 388 (especially annex ii), 409, 416.

91. Compare *GP*, Vol. xxix, no. 10772 with 10734.

92. *DDF*, Ser. ii, Vol. xiv, no. 398; Caillaux, *Agadir*, p. 205, and *Mémoires*, iii, 317 (letter of October 4).

93. *GP*, Vol. xxix, nos. 10754–60; *LJ*, no. 583; *DDF*, Ser. ii, Vol. xiv, no. 420.

94. Caillaux, *Agadir*, pp. 229–30; *LJ*, no. 577; *DDF*, Ser. ii, Vol. xiv, no. 420 and notes.

95. *LJ*, no. 583; *DDF*, Ser. ii, Vol. xiv, no. 427.

96. *Kiderlen-Wächter*, ii, 129 (July 17); quoted by Caillaux, *Mémoires*, ii, 153. See also *GP*, Vol. xxix, nos. 10607, 10719–21, 10728–31; Caillaux, *Agadir*, pp. 293–94 (Kiderlen to Madame de Jonina, July 17, 1911).

97. For the pressure on Kiderlen in the colonial office, the Reichstag, and even the foreign office, see *DDF*, Ser. ii, Vol. xiv, nos. 463, 466, 479, 506.

98. *GP*, Vol. xxix, nos. 10754–69; *DDF*, Ser. ii, Vol. xiv, nos. 431–522, *passim*.

99. See Tardieu, *Mystère d'Agadir*, pp. 170–87.

100. Brandenburg, *German Foreign Policy*, p. 383. It was, more exactly, the *Berlin*, which had replaced the *Panther*: see *DDF*, Ser. iii, Vol. i, nos. 5, 6, 144, 145, 159, 216, 224, 233.

101. Tardieu, *Mystère d'Agadir*, pp. 588–605.

102. See for instance Brandenburg, *German Foreign Policy*, pp. 286, 383–85.

103. *DDF*, Ser. ii, Vol. xiv, no. 250; Caillaux, *Mémoires*, iii, 287, and *Agadir*, pp. 186–87 (letter of September 3).

104. Speech at Mansion House, July 21; *BD*, Vol. vii, no. 412.

105. See Note 63, Chapter Three.

106. See *Kölnische Volkszeitung*, November 4, 1911; *DDF*, Ser. III, Vol. I, nos. 2, 3, 4, and notes.

107. *Die Zukunft*, December 2, 1911.

108. Tardieu, *Mystère d'Agadir*, p. 533. See also *DDF*, Ser. II, Vol. XIV, no. 274, pp. 759–60.

109. Caillaux, *Agadir*, p. 312, and Paix-Séailles, *Jaurès et Caillaux*, p. 176. (Not in *GP*.)

110. See Suarez, *Briand*, II, 358.

111. Lancken's telegrams provide the only evidence that Caillaux negotiated—that is, made or approved any formal proposals. Most likely Caillaux, as he himself consistently maintained and as Fondère's report indicates (*DDF*, Ser. II, Vol. XIV, no. 105), wanted only to sound Lancken out. No doubt Lancken, too, at first intended not more than to sound Caillaux out and only later saw his opportunity to disrupt the French government under discreditable circumstances. As effective in this as his telegrams was his comment to a Quai d'Orsay official on August 19 concerning De Selves's offers, "*On nous a déjà offert davantage*" (*DDF*, Ser. II, Vol. XIV, no. 194). On August 23 Delcassé remarked to Jules Cambon on the growing tension between Caillaux and De Selves (*ibid.*, p. 756). Cambon having in his letter of July 10 to Caillaux (Note 49, Chapter Three; *DDF*, Ser. II, Vol. XIV, no. 53; Caillaux, *Agadir*, p. 158, and *Mémoires*, III, 282) urged him to consult with Von Schoen, Caillaux on seeing Cambon in Paris asked him to arrange a meeting. Accordingly Cambon, coming upon Von Schoen in De Selves's office on August 24, asked him to call on Caillaux the next day. Naturally De Selves called at the same time—whereupon he had a spat with Caillaux over the Lancken-Fondère conversations, in the very presence of the German ambassador. A day later De Selves denounced Caillaux to Paul Cambon for having made bold commitments to Germany, and in the same vein on August 28 he mentioned the "green papers" to both Paul and Jules Cambon. Long afterwards (March 2, 1912) Von Schoen, discussing the Fondère-Lancken talks with Jules Cambon, admitted: "Much more was made of them than was warranted." (*DDF*, Ser. II, Vol. XIV, pp. 756–58.)

112. Tardieu, *Mystère d'Agadir*, p. 597.

113. Paul Cambon, *Correspondance, 1870–1924* (Paris, Grasset, 1940), p. 355.

114. *BD*, Vol. VII, no. 337 and *passim; DDF*, Ser. III, Vol. I, references listed pp. xii–xiii.

115. *DDF*, Ser. III, Vol. I, no. 38 and note.

116. Maurice Paléologue, *Journal, 1913–1914* (Paris, Plon, 1947), p. 206. See also *BD*, Vol. VII, nos. 337, 618, and *passim*.

117. Charles Benoist, *Souvenirs* (3 vols., Paris, Plon, 1934), III, 167.

118. The telegram of November was in *another* code, also one that had not been used for some time before and was not used again. See *GP*, Vol. XXIX, no. 10675, note.

119. According to Kiderlen-Wächter's correspondence (Caillaux, *Agadir*, pp. 314, 333, and *Mémoires*, II, 151n), Fondère let the cat out of the bag by begging the German Embassy not to reveal that he had been an intermediary.

120. Daniel Halévy, *La République des comités* (Paris, Grasset, 1934), p. 122.

121. Benoist, *Souvenirs*, III, 163.   122. *LN*, Vol. I, p. 170.

123. Quoted by Georges Michon, *La Préparation à la guerre, La Loi des trois ans (1910–1914)* (Paris, Rivière, 1935), p. 79.

124. Paix-Séailles, *Jaurès et Caillaux*, pp. 57–59.

125. *LN*, Vol. I, p. 174. Izvolsky hoped "to see someone at the foreign office who knows more about what is going on around him than that poor fellow De Selves."

126. Caillaux, *Mémoires*, II, 205–6. This is also as good a reference as any for the rest of this paragraph.

127. Even the Kaiser noted on January 10: "*Er liegt bereits im Graben*"—and added, "*Gut*" (*GP*, Vol. XXIX, no. 10793).

128. *Journal des Débats*, January 12, 1912. In Paris only *Le Temps* (Tardieu) and *Le Matin* (Jouvenel) took Caillaux's defense. See *GP*, Vol. xxix, nos. 10796, 10797.

129. *LN*, Vol. ii, p. 192.   130. Chambre des Députés, *Débats, 1912*, p. 641.

131. *Ibid.*, p. 771 (March 15). Jaurès said this of Cruppi too.

132. Halévy, *République*, p. 123.

133. Caillaux, *Mémoires*, ii, 120; *DDF*, Ser. ii, Vol. xiv, no. 1, note, bears Caillaux out. See also Caillaux, *Agadir*, p. 110; *GP*, Vol. xxix, no. 10586 and note; *DDF*, Ser. ii, Vol. xiv, nos. 19, 25, 26, 46. For Caillaux's counter-order, see *LJ*, no. 427; *DDF*, Ser. ii, Vol. xiv, no. 18.

134. Caillaux, *Mémoires*, ii, 192.   135. *Ibid.*, p. 194.   136. *Ibid.*, p. 189*n*.

137. *Ibid.*, pp. 150–51; Caillaux, *Agadir*, pp. 310–13, 315–16.

138. Caillaux, *Mémoires*, ii, 199.

139. *Ibid.*, p. 170. Caillaux said as much by insinuation in *Agadir*, p. 350.

140. Caillaux, *Mémoires*, iii, 343, quoting (*in extenso*) his own essay *Les Responsables*.

141. *Ibid.*, p. 88.

NOTES TO 3: RALLYING THE LEFT

1. Joseph Caillaux, *Mes Mémoires* (3 vols., Paris, Plon, 1942–47), iii, 15–16.

2. *Ibid.*, ii, 94.   3. *Ibid.*, p. 8.   4. *Ibid.*, iii, 33.

5. The Socialists abstained from the preliminary vote of the "republicans" in parliament for the choice of a common candidate, then in Versailles they put up a candidate of their own without a chance of success.

6. *LN*, Vol. ii, p. 19.

7. Charles Paix-Séailles, *Jaurès et Caillaux* (Paris, Figuières, 1919), pp. 86–88.

8. *Ibid.*, p. 89.

9. Maurice Paléologue, "Comment le service de trois ans fut rétabli en 1912: ii," *Revue des Deux Mondes*, xxvii (May 15, 1935), 318 (conversation of May 24, 1913).

10. Caillaux, *Mémoires*, iii, 71.

11. Paix-Séailles, *Jaurès et Caillaux*, pp. 101–3.

12. Caillaux, *Mémoires*, iii, 78.

13. Maurice Paléologue, *Journal, 1913–1914* (Paris, Plon, 1947), p. 247.

14. Caillaux, *Mémoires*, iii, 83–84.   15. *Ibid.*, p. 84.

16. Robert de Jouvenel, *La République des camarades* (Paris, Grasset, 1913), p. 17.

17. Joseph Caillaux, *Les Impôts en France* (2 vols., Paris, Pichon, 1911), i, cxxix.

18. See Caillaux, *Mémoires*, iii, 101–5.   19. *Ibid.*, p. 80.

20. Charles Benoist, *Souvenirs* (3 vols., Paris, Plon, 1934), iii, 165.

21. (Anonymous), *Ceux qui nous mènent* (Paris, Plon, 1922), p. 93.

22. Georges Suarez, *Briand* (6 Vols., Paris, Plon, 1938–52), ii, 343.

23. Stéphane Lauzanne, "Will M. Caillaux Come Back to Power?" *The English Review*, XL (January–June, 1925), 474.

24. Quoted by (Laurance Lyon), *The Pomp of Power* (London, Hutchinson, 1922), p. 178.

25. See Caillaux, *Mémoires*, iii, 91–100.   26. *Ibid.*, p. 3.

27. See John N. Raphael, *The Caillaux Drama* (London, Goschen, 1914), p. 97.

NOTES TO 4: THE DRAMA

1. See Georges Michon, *La Préparation à la guerre, La Loi des trois ans (1910–1914)* (Paris, Rivière, 1935), p. 180.

2. Quoted *ibid.*, p. 110.

3. Quoted by Charles Paix-Séailles, *Jaurès et Caillaux* (Paris, Figuières, 1919), p. 104.

4. Raymond Poincaré, *Au service de la France* (10 vols., Paris, Plon, 1926–33), iv, 31.

5. About $15,000 in 1960 dollars (see Note 17, Chapter One).

6. Poincaré, *Au Service*, IV, 32.   7. *Ibid.*, pp. 33–35.

8. Joseph Caillaux, *Mes Mémoires* (3 vols., Paris, Plon, 1942–47), III, 110.

9. *Ibid.*, p. 111.

10. T. H. Thomas, "Caillaux," *The Atlantic Monthly* (June, 1925), p. 839. Thomas, judging Caillaux to have been "the most unpopular figure in France" at the time, finds his "*tour de force*" all the more remarkable.

11. *LN*, Vol. II, p. 206.   12. *Ibid.*, p. 222.

13. *Ibid.*, p. 228 (Izvolsky's French); see also p. 245.

14. *DDF*, Ser. III, Vol. IX, no. 119.   15. *Ibid.*, no. 165.

16. Paix-Séailles, *Jaurès et Caillaux*, p. 110; Caillaux, *Mémoires*, III, 111.

17. Poincaré, *Au service*, IV, 32.   18. Caillaux, *Mémoires*, III, 111.

19. *Ibid.*, p. 112.   20. *Ibid.*   21. *Ibid.*, p. 114.   22. *Ibid.*, p. 115.

23. Poincaré, *Au service*, IV, 79–88.   24. Caillaux, *Mémoires*, III, 120.

25. *Ibid.*, p. 121.   26. *Ibid.*, p. 122.

27. *Ibid.*, p. 123; see also John N. Raphael, *The Caillaux Drama* (London, Goschen, 1914), p. 14.

28. Quoted by Paul Vergnet, *Joseph Caillaux* (Paris, Renaissance du Livre, 1918), pp. 170–71.

29. Quoted *idid.*, p. 173.

30. Quoted *ibid.*, pp. 173–74; Raphael, *Caillaux Drama*, p. 7.

31. Quoted by Vergnet, *Caillaux*, p. 175; Raphael, *Caillaux Drama*, p. 9.

32. Caillaux, *Mémoires*, III, 148.

33. Quoted by Alfred Fabre-Luce, *Caillaux* (Paris, Gallimard, 1933), p. 104.

34. Caillaux, *Mémoires*, III, 147.   35. Fabre-Luce, *Caillaux*, p. 104.

36. Alexandre Ribot, *Journal de Alexandre Ribot et correspondances inédites, 1914–1922* (Paris, Plon, 1936), p. 2.

37. *Ibid.*, p. 6.   38. *Ibid.*, p. 11.   39. Caillaux, *Mémoires*, III, 152.

40. Paix-Séailles, *Jaurès et Caillaux*, pp. 139–40.

41. Maurice Paléologue, *Journal, 1913–1914* (Paris, Plon, 1947), p. 311.

42. See *DDF*, Ser. III, Vol. X, no. 95.

43. About $20,000 in 1960 dollars (see Note 17, Chapter One).

44. Caillaux, *Mémoires*, III, 156.

45. Princess de Mesogne-Estradere.   46. Caillaux, *Mémoires*, III, 156.

47. Reprinted in Vergnet, *Caillaux*, pp. 103–10.

48. Geneviève Tabouis, *They Called Me Cassandra* (New York, Scribner, 1942), p. 36.

49. Fabre-Luce, *Caillaux*, p. 113. See also Vergnet, *Caillaux*, p. 183.

50. Tabouis, *Cassandra*, p. 36.   51. Quoted by Ribot, *Journal*, p. 6.

52. One curious fact gave rise to even wilder conjectures about the shooting: Calmette died only a few hours before his divorce was to become final, and so his wife succeeded to his entire fortune.

53. Ribot, *Journal*, p. 6.   54. Caillaux, *Mémoires*, III, 143.

NOTES TO 5: THE RUBICON

1. Joseph Caillaux, *Mes Mémoires* (3 vols., Paris, Plon, 1942–47), III, pp. 170–72.

2. *Ibid.*, p. 179.

3. Octave Homberg, *Les Coulisses de l'histoire, Souvenirs 1898–1928* (Paris, Fayard, 1938), p. 134.

4. Quoted by Joseph J. C. Joffre, *Mémoires du maréchal Joffre (1910–1917)* (2 vols., Paris, Plon, 1932) I, 316.

5. André Tardieu, *Avec Foch* (Paris, G. D., 1939), p. 136.

6. From here on, my chief source for Caillaux's wartime activities is Paul Vergnet, *L'Affaire Caillaux* (Paris, Renaissance du Livre, 1918).

7. Joseph Paul-Boncour, *Entre deux guerres, Souvenirs sur la IIIème République* (3 vols., Paris, Plon, 1945), I, 221.

8. Caillaux, *Mémoires*, III, 380 (letter from Poincaré to Clemenceau quoting Caillaux). The equivalent in 1960 dollars of Caillaux's "calling card" is about $250 (see Note 17, Chapter One).

9. *Ibid.*, p. 186.   10. About $200 in 1960 dollars (see Note 17, Chapter One).

11. Printed in annex to Caillaux, *Mémoires*, III, 331–60.

12. Joseph Caillaux, *Agadir, Ma Politique extérieure* (Paris, Michel, 1919), p. 243.

13. Quoted by André Tardieu in Chambre des Députés, *Débats, 1926*, p. 2973. Most of the "Rubicon" is given in Vergnet, *L'Affaire Caillaux*, pp. 82–91.

14. Caillaux was especially fond of Corsicans because of their "well-known loyalty to their chief" (*Mémoires*, III, 156), perhaps also because Napoleon was one. Almereyda, Ceccaldi, and Piétri in his entourage were Corsicans.

15. Not in Vergnet, *L'Affaire Caillaux*. Quoted by Alfred Fabre-Luce, *Caillaux* (Paris, Gallimard, 1933), p. 39.

16. Joseph Caillaux, *Devant l'histoire, Mes Prisons* (Paris, Sirène, 1921), p. 73; see also pp. 211, 215.

17. *Ibid.*, p. 216.

NOTES TO 6: THE POLITICIAN AS TRAGIC HERO

1. *LN*, Vol. III, p. 170.

2. Paul Vergnet, *L'Affaire Caillaux* (Paris, Renaissance du Livre, 1918), p. 42.

3. Alexandre Ribot, *Journal de Alexandre Ribot et correspondances inédites, 1914–1922* (Paris, Plon, 1936), p. 38.

4. *Ibid.*, p. 61.

5. Joseph Caillaux, *Mes Mémoires* (3 vols., Paris, Plon, 1942–47), III, 192.

6. Ribot, *Journal*, p. 216.

7. Quoted by Maurice Paléologue, *Journal, 1913–1914* (Paris, Plon, 1947), p. 139.

8. Caillaux, *Mémoires*, III, 374 (letter from Poincaré to Clemenceau quoting Caillaux).

9. *Ibid.*

10. Raymond Poincaré, *Au service de la France* (10 vols., Paris, Plon-Nourrit, 1926–33), IX, 368.

11. *Ibid.*, p. 370.   12. Quoted by Caillaux, *Mémoires*, III, 379.

13. Poincaré, *Au service*, IX, 382.

14. The statement of the charges against him was signed by General Dubail, Military Governor of Paris, who had been his and Messimy's envoy to Russia in 1911. In *Devant l'histoire, Mes Prisons* (Paris, Sirène, 1922), Caillaux maintained that Dubail had been given the statement to sign without being allowed to read it first.

15. In all, about $700,000 in 1960 dollars (see Note 17, Chapter One).

16. Quoted by Vergnet, *L'Affaire Caillaux*, p. 16.

17. Georges Suarez, *Briand* (6 vols., Paris, Plon, 1938–52), II, 329; Poincaré, *Au Service*, X, 7.

18. *Ibid.*, pp. 7–8.

19. Both her gesture and his struck the fancy of Marcel Proust, who was using her as a model for his duchesse de Guermantes. See André Germain, *Les Clés de Proust* (Paris, Sun, 1953), p. 44.

20. Quoted by Caillaux, *Mémoires*, III, 203.

21. See *ibid.*, p. 381 (letter of April 7, 1918, from Poincaré to Clemenceau).

22. Alfred Fabre-Luce, *Caillaux* (Paris, Gallimard, 1933), p. 170.

23. Ribot, *Journal*, p. 249.

24. Caillaux, *Mémoires*, III, 384, quoting Claudel's telegram.

25. *Ibid.*, pp. 384–85, quoting telegram of November 25, 1918, to Paris from the French Ambassador in Washington.

26. Ribot, *Journal*, p. 282.

27. For how the new President of the Republic, Paul Deschanel, met Clemenceau's specifications, see Richard Walden Hale, Jr., *Democratic France* (New York, Coward-McCann, 1941), p. 318.

28. Quoted by Vergnet, *L'Affaire Caillaux*, p. 16.

29. Caillaux, *Devant l'histoire*, p. 299.   30. Fabre-Luce, *Caillaux*, p. 179.

31. Though Poincaré spent years doctoring up his memoirs, his mood of the first hour often survived his hindsight, as in his comment on someone who "has got it into his head that Caillaux was not in contact with the Holy See…[simply] because… Monsignor Pacelli told him, with a strong accent of sincerity, that he had never received M. Caillaux's visit" (Poincaré, *Au service*, IX, 39).

32. Quoted by Louis Marin in Chambre des Députés, *Débats, 1926*, p. 2973.

33. Quoted by Fabre-Luce, *Caillaux*, p. 12.   34. Quoted by Suarez, *Briand*, V, 72.

35. Maurice de Moro-Giafferi in *Les Cahiers du Cercle Joseph Caillaux*, année 2, numéro 2 (premier trimestre, 1954), p. 13. Delahaye did not open his mouth again in court.

36. Demange was unable to attend court to deliver a final statement; Moro-Giafferi spoke in his place.

37. Among the 28 was one Senator who, at Caillaux's first appearance before his judges, had seized his hands and cried, "Ah, my dear friend! If only you knew how distressed I am to see you here!" (Moro-Giafferi, *Les Cahiers du Cercle Joseph Caillaux*, année 2, numéro 2 [premier trimestre, 1954], p. 12).

38. See *ibid.*, p. 11. This article of the Code of 1810 had been drawn up for use in enforcing the continental system; it did not even appear in standard editions of the Code any longer, so the prosecution had been obliged to go to great pains to find an official copy of it.

39. Quoted by Fabre-Luce, *Caillaux*, p. 181. According to Moro-Giafferi, *Les Cahiers du Cercle Joseph Caillaux*, année 2, numéro 2 (premier trimestre, 1954), p. 10, the three defense attorneys knew from rumors several days in advance that Article 78 would be invoked, and he himself wished to defend Caillaux on this count but was overruled by his two colleagues.

40. Caillaux, *Mémoires*, III, 211. Fabre-Luce, *Caillaux*, p. 181, attributed the expression to Maître Demange.

41. In 1960 dollars, about $7,000 (see Note 17, Chapter One).

42. Caillaux, *Mémoires*, III, 200.

43. Or, as T. H. Thomas put it ("Caillaux," *The Atlantic Monthly* [June, 1925], p. 841), "a vague headquarters for all the political underworld of Europe, that queer wartime stratum of bungling spies and informers, German agents and defeatist propagandists, crooks and grafters of every description, and all the riffraff of French politics."

44. André Tardieu, *La Révolution à refaire* (2 vols., Paris, Flammarion, 1936–37), II, 311.

45. She also brought him flowers as he was leaving the Senate after his trial.

46. Quoted by Caillaux, *Mémoires*, III, 209.   47. Caillaux, *Devant l'histoire*, p. 35.

48. Albert Thibaudet. *Les Idées politiques de la France* (Paris, Stock, 1932), p. 134.

49. Alexandre Ribot, *Lettres à un ami* (Paris, Bossard, 1924), p. 153.

50. Jean Martet, *Clemenceau*, trans. by Mellon Waldman (London, Longmans, 1930), p. 79n.

51. Henry de Jouvenel in *Vu*, II (December 4, 1929).

52. Octave Homberg, *Les Coulisses de l'histoire, Souvenirs 1898–1928* (Paris, Fayard, 1938), p. 134.

53. Quoted by Caillaux, *Mémoires*, III, 202.   54. *Ibid.*

NOTES TO 7: THE COMEBACK

1. Alfred Fabre-Luce, *Caillaux* (Paris, Gallimard, 1933), p. 199 (not quite a direct translation). Much of the biographical material in the present chapter as well as several points of interpretation are drawn from this excellent source.

2. Joseph Caillaux, *Mes Mémoires* (3 vols., Paris, Plon, 1942–47), III, 212.

3. This phrase derives from Tardieu: in the Chamber on September 2, 1919, to the question "Who will pay [for reconstruction]?" he replied, "Germany."

4. Joseph Caillaux, *Où va la France? où va l'Europe?* (Paris, Sirène, 1922), p. 271.

5. *Ibid.*   6. *Ibid.*, p. 286.   7. *Ibid.*   8. Caillaux, *Mémoires*, III, 212.

9. Jacques Suffel, *Anatole France* (Paris, Myrte, 1946), p. 361.

10. Fabre-Luce, *Caillaux*, p. 199.

11. Quoted by Joseph Caillaux, *Ma Doctrine* (Paris, Flammarion, 1926), p. 243.

12. Fabre-Luce, *Caillaux*, p. 221.   13. Quoted by Caillaux, *Mémoires*, III, 213.

14. Letter to *Le Figaro*, December 23, 1920.

15. Raymond Escholier, *Souvenirs parlés de Briand* (Paris, Hachette, 1932), p. 50.

16. Fabre-Luce, *Caillaux*, p. 205.   17. *Ibid.*

18. The decisive cause of the fall of Herriot was rather complex. His government had made a practice of borrowing from the Bank of France beyond the limits authorized by law and, by means of twenty-four-hour loans from credit establishments, reimbursing the Bank for the day on which it published its quarterly accounts, thereby disguising the operation. For April 1, 1925, however, the government could not raise the necessary credits; consequently the Bank statement showed an excess both of loans and of fiduciary circulation, and the Senate overthrew Herriot for having "*crevé le plafond.*" See François Goguel, *La Politique des Partis sous la IIIème République* (2 vols., Paris, Seuil, 1946), I, 264–65.

19. Chambre des Députés, *Débats, 1925*, p. 2218.

20. Fabre-Luce, *Caillaux*, p. 210.

21. Chambre des Députés, *Débats, 1925*, p. 2221.

22. Fabre-Luce, *Caillaux*, p. 210.   23. Caillaux, *Mémoires*, III, 214.

24. Fabre-Luce, *Caillaux*, p. 204.   25. *Ibid.*, p. 221.

26. *Le Revenant* is the title of a book by Guy de Pierrefeux on Caillaux's return from exile to power.

27. Joseph Paul-Boncour, *Entre deux guerres, Souvenirs sur la IIIème République* (3 vols., Paris, Plon, 1945), II, 40.

28. Quoted by Fabre-Luce, *Caillaux*, p. 211.   29. Caillaux, *Mémoires*, III, 132n.

30. Fabre-Luce, *Caillaux*, p. 213.

31. Raymond Philippe, *Le Drame financier de 1924–1928* (Paris, Gallimard, 1931), p. 80.

32. About $6,000,000,000 in 1960 dollars (see Note 17, Chapter One).

33. Fabre-Luce, *Caillaux*, p. 215.

34. Quoted by Alfred de Tarde and Robert de Jouvenel, *La Politique d'aujourd'hui* (Paris, Renaissance du Livre [1925]), p. 281.

35. Fabre-Luce, *Caillaux*, p. 216.

36. Philippe, *Drame financier*, p. 76. Philippe was a member of the experts committee of 1926 (see p. 105).

37. Fabre-Luce, *Caillaux*, pp. 217–18.

38. New York *Times*, August 31, 1925.   39. *Ibid.*, September 5, 1925.

40. André Tardieu, *Devant l'obstacle, L'Amérique et nous* (Paris, Emile-Paul, 1927), p. 297.

41. New York *Times*, October 3, 1925.

42. (Soda water—prohibition was in effect at the time.) Fabre-Luce, *Caillaux*, p. 225.

43. *Ibid.*, p. 223.   44. Caillaux, *Doctrine*, p. 279.

45. Fabre-Luce, *Caillaux*, p. 228.   46. *Ibid.*   47. Caillaux, *Mémoires*, III, 217.
48. Fabre-Luce, *Caillaux*, p. 239.   49. *Ibid.*, p. 241.
50. Chambre des Députés, *Débats, 1926*, p. 2973.
51. Poincaré obtained the power to augment most extant taxes within the limit of six times what they had been on July 31, 1914; Caillaux had requested the power to augment the same taxes within the limit of only five times what they had been on the same date (neither man asked for the power to create new taxes). Poincaré also received authority, such as Caillaux had requested, to effect economies in public services and to take steps toward repatriating French capital. Finally, all measures decreed by Poincaré were to be—also as Caillaux had requested in his own case—subject to legislative approval in 1927 though effective until then without such approval.
52. Henry de Jouvenel, in *Revue des Vivants*, I (1927), 454.

NOTES TO 8: TWENTY YEARS MORE

1. Quoted by Jacques Debû-Bridel, *L'Agonie de la Troisième République* (Paris, Bateau Ivre, 1948), p. 120.
2. Joseph Caillaux, *Mes Mémoires* (3 vols., Paris, Plon, 1942–47), II, 199.
3. *Ibid.*, III, 159–62.   4. *Ibid.*, I, 53.   5. *Ibid.*, *passim.*   6. *Ibid.*, II, 60.
7. Joseph Caillaux, preface to Emile Cazalis, *Syndicalisme ouvrier et évolution sociale* (Paris, Librairie des Sciences Politiques et Sociales, 1925), p. xii.
8. Caillaux, *Mémoires*, III, 87.   9. *Ibid.*, pp. 159 ff.
10. Joseph Caillaux, *D'Agadir à la grande pénitence* (Paris, Flammarion et Durand-Auzias, 1933), p. 126.
11. Leon Trotsky, "Nationalism and Economic Life," *Fourth International*, XVII, 1 (Winter, 1956), p. 19; reprinted from *Foreign Affairs* (April, 1934).
12. Caillaux, *D'Agadir à la grande pénitence*, p. x.   13. *Ibid.*, p. 105.
14. *Ibid.*, p. 190.   15. Caillaux, *Mémoires*, I, 72.
16. See Emile Roche, *Caillaux que j'ai connu* (Paris, Plon, 1949), p. 35.
17. Octave Homberg, *Les Coulisses de l'histoire, Souvenirs 1898–1928* (Paris, Fayard, 1938), p. 139.
18. Caillaux, *Mémoires*, III, 240.
19. Joseph Paul-Boncour, *Entre deux guerres, Souvenirs sur la IIIème République* (3 vols., Paris, Plon, 1945), II, 349.
20. Caillaux, *Mémoires*, III, 240.   21. Chambre des Députés, *Débats, 1935*, p. 1774.
22. Caillaux, *Mémoires*, III, 239.
23. Quoted by Debû-Bridel, *Agonie de la République*, p. 306.
24. Caillaux, *Mémoires*, III, 389.   25. Roche, *Caillaux*, pp. 91–92.
26. André Germain, *La Bourgeoisie qui brûle* (Paris, Sun, 1951), p. 192.
27. See Roche, *Caillaux*, pp. 325–45 (Caillaux's speech).
28. *La Réforme de l'Etat*, ed. by Société des anciens Elèves et Elèves de l'Ecole libre des Sciences politiques (Paris, Alcan, 1936), p. 53.
29. Blum was the author of a volume on Stendhal (Henri Beyle).
30. Quoted by Roche, *Caillaux*, p. 171. For relations between Caillaux and Blum see *ibid.*, pp. 171 ff.
31. Roger de Fleurieu, *Joseph Caillaux au cours d'un demi-siècle de notre histoire* (Paris, Clavreuil, 1951), p. 239.
32. Quoted by Roche, *Caillaux*, p. 190.   33. *Ibid.*, p. 192.
34. Anatole de Monzie, *Ci-devant* (Paris, Flammarion, 1941), p. 34.
35. *Ibid.*   36. *Ibid.*   37. *Ibid.*   38. *Ibid.*, p. 67.
39. Roche, *Caillaux*, p. 300.   40. *Ibid.*, p. 306.
41. Caillaux, *Mémoires*, III, 259.   42. *Ibid.*, p. 274.
43. Fleurieu, *Caillaux*, p. iv.   44. Letter to myself from François Goguel.

NOTES TO 9: STANISLAS

1. Quoted by M. N. Valois, "Note sur l'origine de la famille Jouvenel des Ursins," *Bulletin et Mémoires de la Société nationale des Antiquaires de France*, sixième série, IX (1898), 77–88. See also Jean Herluison, "Jean Juvénal des Ursins," *La Revue critique des Idées et des Livres*, XI (1902), 584 ff. Péchenard, *Jean Juvénal des Ursins*, appeared in 1876, and Louis Batiffol, *Jean Jouvenel*, in 1894. The movement Action Française in its journal of the same name "recruited" Jean Juvénal des Ursins on June 8, 1910, in an article, "Un ancêtre de l'Action Française," signed Démocrite.

2. Cardinal La Balue spent fifteen years in an iron cage for having conspired with Charles the Bold.

3. Abbé L. Berty, *Vie de Léon de Jouvenel, Député de la Corrèze (1811–1886)* (Chastrusse, Praudel, 1931, no place of publication noted), pp. 25–28, traces the Jouvenels in Corrèze back to Jean Jouvenel, notary in Cosnac, 1582–89, and Dejovenel, hereditary notary and scrivener royal in Cosnac, 1591. Léon's father was a geometer in the civil service.

4. J. Nouillac, preface to Berty, *Vie de Jouvenel*, p. 14.

5. Henry de Jouvenel, *Pourquoi je suis syndicaliste*, in the series "Leurs Raisons," ed. by André Billy (Paris, Editions de France, 1928), p. 33.

6. He was prefect last in Côtes-du-Nord.

7. Geneviève Tabouis, *They Called Me Cassandra* (New York, Scribner, 1942), pp. 136–37.

8. A castle acquitred by Léon. A photograph of it faces Berty, *Vie de Jouvenel*, p. 165.

9. Henry de Jouvenel, *Pourquoi je suis syndicaliste*, p. 8.

10. Anatole de Monzie, *L'Entrée au forum (vingt ans avant)* (Paris, Michel, 1920), p.25.

11. *Ibid.*, p. 18 (Montaigne: "Parce que c'était lui, parce que c'était moi").

12. Louis Gillet, "Souvenirs de Stanislas," *Revue des Vivants*, IX (November-December, 1935), 1655.

13. Quoted by Alphonse Olivieri, "André Tardieu et Henry de Jouvenel peints par eux-mêmes," *Revue contemporaine*, LXXI (March, 1923), 322–28.

14. Bertrand de Jouvenel, "Henry de Jouvenel parmi les jeunes," *Revue des Vivants*, IX (November–December, 1935), 1699.

15. Gillet, "Souvenirs de Stanislas," *Revue des Vivants*, IX (November–December, 1935), 1658.

16. *Ibid.*, p. 1663.   17. *Ibid.*, pp. 1655–56.   18. *Ibid.*, p. 1657.   19. *Ibid.*

20. *Ibid.*, p. 1655.   21. Monzie, *Entrée au forum*, p. 20.   22. *Ibid.*

23. Quoted *ibid.*, p. 19; composition quoted in full by Olivieri, "André Tardieu et Henry de Jouvenel peints par eux-mêmes," *Revue contemporaine*, LXXI (March, 1923), 322–28. The awards in the *Concours général* were conferred by the Minister of Education, Raymond Poincaré, at a ceremony at which Henri Bergson presided.

24. Quoted by Gillet, "Souvenirs de Stanislas," *Revue des Vivants*, IX (November–December, 1935), 1666.

25. Maurice Sarraut, "Henry de Jouvenel, journaliste," *Revue des Vivants*, IX (November–December, 1935), 1650.

26. André Maurois, "Notre Voisin," *Revue des Vivants*, IX (November–December, 1935), 1667.

27. Paul Valéry, "Henry de Jouvenel, homme de l'esprit," *Revue des Vivants*, IX (November–December, 1935), 1640.

NOTES TO 10: SYNDICALISM

1. Henry de Jouvenel, *La Paix française, Témoignage d'une génération* (Paris, Portiques, 1932), p. 61.

2. *Ibid.*, p. 63.   3. *Ibid.*, p. 61.   4. *Ibid.*, p. 64.   5. *Ibid.*   6. *Ibid.*, p. 65.

7. Henry de Jouvenel, *Pourquoi je suis syndicaliste*, in the series "Leurs Raisons," ed by André Billy (Paris, Editions de France, 1928), p. 8.

8. Henry de Jouvenel, *Paix*, p. 63.

9. Henry de Jouvenel, *Pourquoi je suis syndicaliste*, p. 9.   10. *Ibid.*

11. Joseph Paul-Boncour, *Entre deux guerres, Souvenirs sur la IIIème République* (3 vols., Paris, Plon, 1945), I, 95.

12. Paul-Boncour, private letter to myself.

13. Henry de Jouvenel, *Pourquoi je suis syndicaliste*, p. 10.

14. *Ibid.*   15. *Ibid.*, p. 11.   16. *Ibid.*   17. *Ibid.*, p. 12.

18. Quoted by José Germain, *Le Syndicalisme et l'intelligence* (Paris, Valois, 1928), p. 90.

19. Jouvenel used the designation *patronat* to include capitalists, though his style often betrays embarrassment on this point (the word is equivocal because owners were also managers to an unusually great extent in France). Sometimes he gave "commerce" instead of "management" as a fourth category. For his abortive "Economic States-General" of 1923 he proposed the powers of initiative and of veto in social and economic legislation, with the government as arbiter between the two parliaments in case of deadlock.

20. Quoted by Alfred de Tarde and Robert de Jouvenel, *La Politique d'aujourd'hui* (Paris, Renaissance du Livre [1925],) p. 285.

21. Georges Suarez, "Chez Monsieur Henry de Jouvenel," *Revue de Paris*, xxxv (January–February, 1928), p. 462.

22. Henry de Jouvenel, *Pourquoi je suis syndicaliste*, p. 61.

23. *Ibid.*   24. De Tarde and Robert de Jouvenel, *Politique*, p. 282.

25. Henry de Jouvenel, *Pourquoi je suis syndicaliste*, p. 13.

26. De Tarde and Robert de Jouvenel, *Politique*, p. 283.

27. Jouvenel himself made this point ironically on inaugurating the International Congress of National Confederations of Intellectual Workers (see p. 148): "In our times, when philosophy itself is becoming somewhat elementary, we have so well and so often contrasted *interests* and *ideas* that it is beginning to look as though ideas have no interest."

28. Today, the Conseil Economique et Social.

29. Suarez, "Chez Monsieur Henry de Jouvenel," *Revue de Paris*, xxxv (January–February, 1928), p. 462.

30. Henry de Jouvenel, *The Stormy Life of Mirabeau* (Boston, Houghton Mifflin, 1929), p. 62.

31. Louis Planté, "Grands maîtres de l'Université: Henry de Jouvenel," *Revue politique et littéraire, Revue bleue*, LXVII (January, 1930), 15.

32. *Ibid.*

NOTES TO 11: THE REPUBLIC FROM ON HIGH

1. Henry de Jouvenel, *Pourquoi je suis syndicaliste*, in the series "Leurs Raisons," ed. by André Billy (Paris, Editions de France, 1928), p. 14.

2. *Ibid.*   3. Bertrand de Jouvenel, private letter to myself.

4. André Germain, *Les Grandes Favorites 1815–1940* (Paris, Sun, 1948), p. 175. Pages 165–74 provide a pleasantly unscholarly account of her marriage and subsequent career.

5. Anatole France, Preface to Ariel [Claire Boas], *Des Histoires pour grands et petits* (Paris, Excelsior, 1929).

6. Joseph Caillaux, *Mes Mémoires* (3 vols., Paris, Plon, 1942–47), II, 28.

7. *Ibid.*   8. *Ibid.*, p. 29.   9. *Ibid.*, p. 27.

10. Colette, *L'Etoile vesper* (Geneva, Milieu du Monde, 1946), p. 55.

11. José Germain, *Le Syndicalisme et l'intelligence* (Paris, Valois, 1928), p. 63.

12. Paul Reynaud, "Henry de Jouvenel au parlement," *Revue des Vivants*, IX (November–December, 1935), 1679.

13. Anatole de Monzie, "Adieux à mon ami," *Revue des Vivants*, IX (November–December, 1935), 1636.

14. Henry de Jouvenel, "Dialogue d'un lecteur et d'un auditeur," in Société des Nations, Institut international de Co-opération intellectuelle, *Cahiers I, Le Rôle intellectuel de la presse* (Paris, Société des Nations, 1933), p. 67.

15. *Ibid.*, p. 77.

16. Address to the French National Commission for Intellectual Cooperation, March 17, 1929; quoted by Wladimir d'Ormesson, *Pour la paix* (Paris, Spes, 1929), pp. 63–69.

17. Henry de Jouvenel, *Pourquoi je suis syndicaliste*, p. 27.

18. Jules Renard, *Journal* (Paris, Gallimard, 1935), p. 754. Renard added, oddly, "It's very funny."

19. Henry de Jouvenel, *La Paix française, Témoignage d'une génération* (Paris, Portiques, 1932), pp. 14–15.

20. *Ibid.*, p. 15.   21. Henry de Jouvenel, *Pourquoi je suis syndicaliste*, p. 20.

22. *Ibid.*, pp. 21–22.   23. *Revue des Vivants*, I (1927), 454.

24. *Revue des Vivants*, IV (1930), 733.

25. This expression was coined by the demographer Alfred Sauvy in *Richesse et Population* (Paris, Payot, 1944) to designate an increase in the proportion of old men and women within a total population consequent on a decline both of the death rate and of the birth rate. Sauvy's analysis provides an instructive background to Jouvenel's. "The hierarchy of command," writes Sauvy, "corresponds to a pyramid with a very broad base. The number of directors and of colonels is far smaller than that of clerks or of second lieutenants.... A change in the age distribution of a population is an obstacle to personnel advancement. A broad pyramid [a pyramid, in demography, is a figure obtained by the piling up of bars of standard height, the width of each being proportional to the number of persons in each specific age group of the population] corresponds either to a high death rate and hence a more rapid advancement, or to a high birth rate and hence a general expansion involving in particular the creation of new businesses. In an army constantly receiving new recruits, advancement is rapid. As a result of a decline in the birth rate, the old businesses are sufficient, and young men have no choice but to get in at the bottom and wait their turn. The lowering of the death rate further slows down advancement; despite its advantages, appearances are against this form of progress, for survivors do not realize that, in former times, advancement would certainly have been faster but, as on a battlefield, for some of them only. As a result, in certain careers the young have a sense of being blocked" (pp. 103–4). The French population "aged" earlier than any other in modern times, with effects visible to Stendhal, for instance, nearly half a century before the Third Republic came into being. (Stendhal also blamed the regime—then the monarchy.)

26. *Revue des Vivants*. IV (1930), 732–33.

27. Bertrand de Jouvenel, "Henry de Jouvenel parmi les jeunes," *Revue des Vivants*, IX (November–December, 1935), 1703.

28. Henry de Jouvenel in *Revue des Vivants*, I (1927), 455.

29. Bertrand de Jouvenel, private letter to myself.

30. Henry de Jouvenel, *Paix*, p. 23.

31. Henry de Jouvenel, *Pourquoi je suis syndicaliste*, pp. 21–22.

32. Deputies were elected for four years, senators for nine.

33. Henry de Jouvenel, *Pourquoi je suis syndicaliste*, p. 31. This passage was written to describe conditions prevailing before the First World War—hence the past tense. It concludes, "Nothing has changed."

34. *Ibid.*, p. 31.   35. *Ibid.*, p. 27.   36. *Le Matin*, November 11, 1907.   37. *Ibid.*

38. That is, unless deputies are elected for life or ineligible for reelection. Both solutions tend to impede popular sovereignty. In his essays on syndicalism Jouvenel implied preference for brief mandates (see Chapter Ten, above), although on March 22, 1932, he addressed the Senate in favor of extending deputies' mandates to six years (Sénat, *Débats, 1932*, p. 418). On the other hand, historians have, I believe, been unanimously critical of the first National Assembly of France for declaring its members ineligible for reelection in 1791, when it disbanded.

39. Reynaud, "Henry de Jouvenel au parlement," *Revue des Vivants*, IX (November–December, 1935), 1679.

40. Speech to the Federal Union of Veterans at Le Touquet, April 24, 1935; *Revue des Vivants*, IX (November–December, 1935), 1787.

41. Henry de Jouvenel, *Huit Cents Ans de révolution française, 987–1789* (Paris, Hachette, 1932).

42. Henry de Jouvenel, *Pourquoi je suis syndicaliste*, p. 31.

43. Henry de Jouvenel, *Paix*, p. 62.

44. Paul Valéry, "Henry de Jouvenel, homme de l'esprit," *Revue des Vivants*, IX (November–December, 1935), 1641.

45. Henry de Jouvenel, "Dialogue d'un lecteur et d'un auditeur," in *Cahiers I, Le Rôle intellectuel de la presse*, pp. 67–68.

46. *Revue des Vivants*, IV (1930), 733.

47. Robert de Saint-Jean, "Pourquoi je suis syndicaliste," *La Revue hebdomadaire*, XXXVII année, VII (July, 1928), 99.

48. Louis Planté, "Grands Maîtres de l'Université: Henry de Jouvenel," *Revue politique et littéraire, Revue bleue*, LXVII (January, 1930), 15.

49. Bertrand de Jouvenel, "Henry de Jouvenel parmi les jeunes," *Revue des Vivants*, IX (November–December, 1935), 1700.

50. Reynaud, "Henry de Jouvenel au Parlement," *Revue des Vivants*, IX (November–December, 1935), 1680.

51. Wladimir d'Ormesson in *Le Figaro*, October 6, 1935.

52. Bertrand de Jouvenel, "Henry de Jouvenel parmi les jeunes," *Revue des Vivants*, IX (November–December, 1935), 1702–03.

53. *Ibid.*, p. 1702.   54. *Ibid.*   55. *Ibid.*   56. *Ibid.*

NOTES TO 12: WAR AND PEACE

1. The departments of Corrèze and Haute Vienne together correspond to the former province of Limousin. The provinces have had no legal status since the Revolution but survive as geographical expressions.

2. Jules Renard, *Journal* (Paris, Gallimard, 1935), p. 754.

3. André Germain, *Les Clés de Proust* (Paris, Sun, 1953), p. 236.   4. *Ibid.*

5. Henry de Jouvenel, *Pourquoi je suis syndicaliste*, in the series "Leurs Raisons," ed. by André Billy (Paris, Editions de Paris, 1928), pp. 31–32.

6. Quoted by Wladimir d'Ormesson in *Le Figaro*, October 6, 1935.

7. Henry de Jouvenel, *La Paix française, Témoignage d'une génération* (Paris, Portiques, 1932), p. 77.

8. Henry de Jouvenel, *Pourquoi je suis syndicaliste*, p. 37.

9. José Germain, *La C. T. I.* (Paris, Renaissance du Livre, n.d.), p. 20.

10. José Germain, *Le Syndicalisme et l'intelligence* (Paris, Valois, 1928), p. 60.

11. José Germain, *C. T. I.*, p. 22.

12. Romain Coolus, "Henry de Jouvenel, animateur," *Revue des Vivants*, IX (November–December, 1935), 1714.

13. Anatole de Monzie, "Adieux à mon ami," *Revue des Vivants*, IX (November–December, 1935), 1636.

14. Jean Farges, "Henry de Jouvenel en Corrèze," *Revue des Vivants*, IX (November–December, 1935), 1708.

15. Minstrel poets of the Middle Ages regarded Limousin as the purest form of Provençal; no longer a written language today, it survives only as a regional dialect. The Third Republic discouraged the use of any language but French in schools.

16. L'Association corrézienne de Paris was founded by Henry's grandfather Léon in November, 1870.

17. Caillaux, *Devant l'histoire, Mes Prisons* (Paris, Sirène, 1921), p. 299.

18. André Maurois, *Mémoires* (New York, Maison Française, 1942), II, 137–38.

19. [Laurance Lyon], *The Pomp of Power* (London, Hutchinson, 1922), p. 175.

20. In place of René Viviani, who had resigned.

21. Edward Beneš, "L'Œuvre d'Henry de Jouvenel en Europe," *Revue des Vivants*, IX (November–December, 1935), 1671.

22. According to Monzie, *Ci-devant* (Paris, Flammarion, 1941), p. 58, Jouvenel never could resist "ideological cosmopolitanism" (whatever that is).

23. Also known as the Third Commission.

24. In his book *A Great Experiment* (New York, Oxford University Press, 1951), p. 140, Lord Robert Cecil describes Jouvenel as "my greatest ally" and affirms that "we cooperated vigorously." The two men were close friends outside the Commission.

25. Quoted in *Revue des Vivants*, IX (November–December, 1935), 1741.

26. Quoted by André Gardes, *Le Désarmement devant la Société des Nations* (Paris, Pedone, 1929), pp. 90, 88. Gardes also (pp. 69–84) gives a documentary account of the controversy between Cecil and Jouvenel.

27. It was adopted as a series of sixteen resolutions, of which one quoted above— Resolution XVI—became known as the "moral-disarmament resolution."

28. If one belligerent nation refused the arbitration of the Council, that nation was to be regarded as the aggressor. See Maurice Fanshawe, *Reconstruction* (London, Allen & Unwin, 1926), p. 108, or Charles M. Levermore, *Third Year-Book of the League of Nations* (New York, Brooklyn Daily Eagle, 1923), p. 302, for a brief appraisal of Jouvenel's work on the mutual-assistance treaties.

29. Joseph Paul-Boncour, *Entre deux guerres, Souvenirs sur la IIIème République* (3 vols., Paris, Plon, 1945), II, 141.

30. *Le Matin*, October 1, 1923.

31. Alfred de Tarde and Robert de Jouvenel, *La Politique d'aujourd'hui* (Paris, Renaissance du Livre, [1923]), p. 202.

32. Henry de Jouvenel, *Paix*, pp. 340–41.   33. *Ibid.*, p. 29.

34. *Ibid.*, pp. 32–33.   35. *Ibid.*, p. 32.   36. *Ibid.*, pp. 33–34.   37. *Ibid.*, p. 35.

38. Henry de Jouvenel, "L'Evolution du pouvoir vue par un politique," *Encyclopédie française*, ed. by Anatole de Monzie (Paris, Larousse, 1935), X, 10.62–8—10.62–13.

39. Henry de Jouvenel, *Paix*, *passim*. Carrying Jouvenel's thought a step further, one arrives at a comforting, if tenuous, paradox: if the growth of the power of the state over its citizens and the development of supra-national authority are complementary aspects of the same historical process, and if the odium of war derives from the first and lasting peace from the second, then as war becomes more odious, lasting peace draws nearer.

40. For a contemporary comparison of the views of Jouvenel and Tardieu on this subject, see the conclusion of Georges Suarez, *Les Hommes malades de la paix* (Paris, Grasset, 1933).

NOTES TO 13: A MISSION TO SYRIA

1. See New York *Times*, March 11, 1923.

2. Quoted by Alphonse Olivieri, "Henry de Jouvenel," *La Revue contemporaine*, III (1923), 52.

3. *Le Matin*, October 23, 1922.

4. Louis Planté, "Grands Maîtres de l'université: Henry de Jouvenel," *Revue de Paris*, xxxv (January–February, 1928), 12.

5. *Ibid.*   6. *Ibid.*

7. Joseph Paul-Boncour, *Entre deux guerres, Souvenirs sur la IIIème République* (3 vols., Paris, Plon, 1945), II, 141.

8. Henry de Jouvenel, *The Stormy Life of Mirabeau* (Boston, Houghton Mifflin, 1929), p. 165. Before the Revolution Mirabeau was for several years a paid pamphleteer for the Finance Minister Calonne.

9. Paul Valéry, "Henry de Jouvenel, homme de l'esprit," *Revue des Vivants*, IX (November–December, 1935), 1639.

10. Maurice Sarraut, "Henry de Jouvenel, journaliste," *Revue des Vivants*, IX (November–December, 1935), 1649.

11. Written instructions from General Sarrail to a subordinate; the French government established their authenticity by failing to deny it when they were quoted in parliament: Chambre des Députés, *Débats, 1925*, pp. 4437–52 and 4501–56, *passim*.

12. Already Paul Doumer, approached for the high-commissionership, had declined.

13. *Le Figaro*, November 9, 1925.

14. Henry de Jouvenel, *La Paix française, Témoignage d'une génération* (Paris, Portiques, 1932), p. 97.

15. The Syro-Palestinian Congress, a group of Arab exiles from Syria and Palestine, had the full support of the rebels in demanding for them an unconditional amnesty and a war indemnity, and for Syria certain disputed areas of Lebanon, a centralized government, the termination of the mandate, and admission to the League. The Congress was aspiring overtly to reunite the two territories of Syria and Palestine and covertly to realize a pan-Islamic federation. The Lutfallahs, merchant princes of Egypt, were for their part aspiring to the crown of Syria.

16. The Druses would in no case *give up* their arms, which they needed to defend their farms against marauders. They also demanded, not clemency, but an amnesty to include rebel leaders and even common-law criminals; however, when Jouvenel proposed an amnesty (December 22), they replied that they could not trust him to respect it. In view of his attitude and theirs, the specific demands then made and rejected are of secondary importance. They included the political centralization of Syria and evacuation by France, both before the election of a constituent assembly. They also included rectification of the Lebanese boundary in favor of Jabal al Druz, and Jouvenel advised the rebels to think of organizing their country before thinking of enlarging it. According to Arnold J. Toynbee, *Survey of International Affairs, 1925*, Vol. I, *The Islamic World Since the Peace Settlement* (London, Oxford University Press, 1927), p. 450: "This refusal may have been essential if France was to retain the goodwill of the Christian Lebanese; but it was perhaps the principal cause of M. de Jouvenel's failure to overcome the hostility of the Sunnis and the Druses, who constituted the majority of the population in the mandated territory." Jouvenel's "advice" was indeed ill-advised, for the populations in the disputed area were predominantly Druse; however, his mission would have ended then and there had he consented to put a Christian minority under the jurisdiction of Druses or, worse, of a centralized Moslem state. In fact the one objection of the venerable Patriarch of the Maronite (Lebanese Christian) Church to Jouvenel's policies was, "You don't do enough hanging."

17. The inhabitants of Damascus and of the Hauran were under martial law; Jabal al Druz was, of course, altogether out of French hands.

18. Members of the Nationalist or Syrian People's Party.

19. Jouvenel replied that he was not trying to obstruct the general will but to detect it (speech of February 5 to the Representative Council of Damascus). In fact his order for elections conformed to instructions issued by Briand and confirmed by the French Senate on December 17 (Sénat, *Débats, 1925*, pp. 1746–47) and by the Chamber on December 20 (Chambre des Députés, *Débats, 1925*, p. 4538). Later, however, Jouvenel did favor dividing the country—not the better to rule, though, but the more rapidly to institute self-government (see p. 161).

20. The Nationalists demanded, for instance, the incorporation of the Alawi state and of Jabal al Druz into the Syrian state, the attribution to Syria of the disputed areas of Lebanon, the substitution for the mandate of a treaty between France and Syria (this proposal, advanced by the rebels, had Jouvenel's personal approval: see p. 160), the admission of Syria to the League, evacuation by the French army, an indemnity to war victims, and an indemnity to Syria for a disadvantageous currency reform.

21. Elizabeth P. MacCallum, *The Nationalist Crusade in Syria* (New York, Foreign Policy Association, 1928), p. 183.

22. The jurisdiction of the provisional Administrator, Pierre Alype, did not cover the Alawi state, where a representative council had resumed its sessions.

23. That is, the regions of Homs and Hama were added to Damascus and the Hauran under martial law. The Alawi state remained under civil law, as did Dayr al Zur, Aleppo, and Alexandretta.

24. Quoted in *Revue des Vivants*, IX (November–December, 1935), 1756.

25. The "De Jouvenel Agreement" primarily settled a litigation concerning the use and defense of the Bagdad Railway, part of which ran along the Syrian border. It took effect for all practical purposes the day it was initialed (February 18), though it was not signed until May 30, when the Turkish government agreed that the validity of the nonaggression clause was limited by the prior commitments of France to the League. See Toynbee, *Islamic World*, pp. 457–64.

26. England was officially neutral in the war, but local British officials were often patriotic beyond the call of duty in courting favor with Arabs at the expense of France. The Druses had probably been receiving supplies through Transjordan and Palestine; even for some time after Jouvenel's visit to London of November 19–21, 1925, they counted on being able to retreat southwards across the border in case of defeat.

27. Quoted in *Revue des Vivants*, IX (November–December, 1935), 1757.

28. MacCallum, *Nationalist Crusade*, p. 190.

29. Pierre Lyautey, *L'Empire colonial français* (Paris, Editions de France, 1931), p. 258.

30. The following September Jouvenel charged the Commission with having "somewhat prolonged the revolt in Syria" by seeming to offer the rebels a better hearing than did France. For a strong objection to this charge see Arnold J. Toynbee, *Survey of International Affairs, 1928* (London, Oxford University Press, 1929), p. 129.

31. No details of the draft treaty are known. Evidently it provided for the eventual withdrawal of French troops and independence of Syria; it seems also to have guaranteed the territorial unity of greater Syria (mandated Syria minus Lebanon), though certainly without limiting the special rights of the various minorities. See for instance MacCallum, *Nationalist Crusade*, pp. 192–94; Nadar Kuzbari, *La Question de la cessation du mandat français sur la Syrie* (Paris, Pedone, 1937), p. 14.

NOTES TO *14: CONCILIATION: A PERSONALITY BECOMES A POLICY*

1. Louis Planté, "Grands Maîtres de l'université: Henry de Jouvenel," *Revue de Paris*, xxxv (January–February, 1928), 14.

2. He remained chief editor until the end of 1922; thereafter he was chairman of the editorial board until his departure for Syria in 1925.

3. About 40 cents in 1960 United States currency (see Note 17, Chapter One); most comparable reviews at the time cost 8 or 10 francs.

4. Jules Renard, *Journal* (Paris, Gallimard, 1935), p. 822.

5. Quoted by André Germain, *Les Grandes Favorites, 1815–1940* (Paris, Sun, 1948), pp. 171–72.

6. André Germain, *Les Clés de Proust* (Paris, Sun, 1953), p. 236.

7. Colette, *Oeuvres complètes*, Vol. viii, *La Naissance du jour* (Paris, Flammarion, 1949), pp. 17–18.

8. I refer in particular to the *nouvelles* she wrote during this period, *Chéri* and *Le Blé en herbe*. Of all her works of fiction the one real exception is *Julie de Carneilhan*, which she wrote in 1941 about Jouvenel.

9. Paul Valéry, "Henry de Jouvenel, homme de l'esprit," *Revue des Vivants*, ix (November–December, 1935), 1641.

10. For Colette's side of the estrangement see also her novel *La Seconde*.

11. Colette, *Naissance du jour*, p. 7.   12. *Ibid.*, p. 18.

13. *Mercure de France*, clxxiii, 772.

14. Jules Jeannenay, in *Sénat, Débats, 1935*, p. 834.

15. Bertrand de Jouvenel, private letter to myself.   16. *Ibid.*

17. Jouvenel, like his brother, suffered from heart trouble.

18. Paul Reynaud, "Henry de Jouvenel au parlement," *Revue des Vivants*, ix (November–December, 1935), 1679.

19. André Maurois, "Notre Voisin," *Revue des Vivants*, ix (November–December, 1935), 1667–68.

20. Anatole de Monzie, *Ci-devant* (Paris, Flammarion, 1941), p. 58.

21. "He knew many things, but he also knew how to make you forget that he knew them"—Henry Béranger, "Henry de Jouvenel à la commission sénatoriale des Affaires étrangères," *Revue des Vivants*, ix (November–December, 1935), 1676.

22. He was most respectful of what came least naturally to him, wrote Monzie: "statistics, numerical reasoning, political economy in a tuxedo" (*Ci-devant*, p. 58).

23. "This very great worker made it a point of pride to appear nonchalant"—Béranger, "Henry de Jouvenel à la commission sénatoriale des Affaires étrangères," *Revue des Vivants* ix (November–December, 1935), 1676.

24. He once browbeat his elder son, then ten years old, for being unable to summarize a novel after reading it: "'What's the use of reading,' he cried furiously, 'if what you read doesn't imprint itself on your brain in a few large, simple strokes? Reading isn't an amusement—it's training for the mind!'"—Bertrand de Jouvenel, "Henry de Jouvenel parmi les jeunes," *Revue des Vivants*, ix (November–December, 1935), 1699.

25. "He went to the bottom of things, a thoroughbred you often had to restrain not by pulling the reins but by stroking the mane"—Joseph Paul-Boncour, *Entre deux guerres, Souvenirs sur la IIIème République* (3 vols., Paris, Plon, 1945), p. 348.

26. Georges Huisman, speech to the French Association for Artistic Expansion and Exchange, November 18, 1935; in *Revue des Vivants*, ix (November–December, 1935), 1720.

27. Pierre Pasquier, *Les Etapes de la défaite* (Montreal, Zodiaque, 1941), p. 137.

28. The last words of *Julie de Carneilhan*.

29. Albert Thibaudet, *La République des professeurs* (Paris, Grasset, 1927), p. 38.

30. Bertrand de Jouvenel, private letter to myself.

31. Henry de Jouvenel, *La Paix française, Témoignage d'une génération* (Paris, Portiques, 1932), p. 97.

32. Alfred de Tarde and Robert de Jouvenel, *La Politique d'aujourd'hui* (Paris, Renaissance du Livre [1925]), pp. 200–1.

33. Eric Sutton, ed. and trans., Gustav Stresemann, *His Diaries, Letters and Papers* (London, MacMillan, 1940), III, 186 (private report of September 5).

34. *Ibid.*, p. 209 (letter of September 21).

35. C. Howard-Ellis, *The Origin, Structure and Working of the League of Nations* (London, Allen & Unwin, 1928), p. 455.

36. Paul-Boncour, *Entre deux guerres*, II, 150.

37. See Chapter Fifteen (Four-Power Pact). Further, on January 6, 1934, Jouvenel called on the French government to inaugurate a policy of preliminary negotiations among the Great Powers in order to facilitate the work of the League (Sénat, *Débats, 1934*, p. 49).

38. See Chapter Ten. The section devoted to trade unions in the Radical and Radical-Socialist Party Declaration of October 29, 1927, read in part: "For some fifty years associations have been surging forth on all sides, and every day they are growing in number and in strength.... What will their role be with respect to parliament? Will they fight it, replace it, second it? This is a serious problem, and its solution is a difficult task for the coming years. Our party has confidence in professional associations; it does not believe that labor can be organized or the civil service reformed properly without their support. It thinks that they have their part to play along side of parliament, to inform it as it prepares laws and to help it in applying them."

39. Paul-Boncour, *Entre deux guerres*, II, 150.

40. Sénat, *Débats, 1930*, pp. 1756–57.

41. The five prize-winning essays were published with a preface by Jouvenel in *La Fédération européenne* (Paris, Revue des Vivants, 1930).

42. Quoted by Henri Pichot, "Henry de Jouvenel parmi les anciens combattants," *Revue des Vivants*, IX (November–December, 1935), 1695.

43. *Ibid.*

44. The Communist newspaper explained its attitude on November 27, 1931: it favored disarmament but expected no good from a meeting of men like Jouvenel, who was "known for his great plan for a French-German-Polish alliance" directed against the Soviet Union! The allusion was probably to the "Locarno of the East."

45. Bertrand de Jouvenel, private letter to myself.

46. André Germain, *Les Grandes Favorites*, p. 178.

47. See M. E. Ravage, "Why France has No Dictator," *The Nation*, February 5, 1938, p. 152.

48. Bertrand de Jouvenel was associated with the Doriot group until it came out in support of the Munich Pact; none of the violent "activism" of his youth survived the war, as is evident from his great treatise *On Power*. Renaud de Jouvenel has remained a loyal Communist; one of his books, *L'Internationale des traîtres*, was the subject of a famous trial a few years ago.

49. Henry de Jouvenel, *Paix*, p. 65.

50. Georges Suarez, *Les Heures héroïques du cartel* (Paris, Grasset, 1934), p. 310.

51. Henry de Jouvenel, *Paix*, p. 97.

52. Romain Coolus, "Henry de Jouvenel, animateur," *Revue des Vivants*, IX (November–December, 1935), 1715. The groups not already mentioned of which Jouvenel was president include the Union of Great (veterans') Associations, the French Association for Artistic Expansion and Exchange, the Committee for Artistic Action,

the Union of Frenchmen Living Abroad, the Group for the Expansion of Thought (in charge of cultural exhibits for the 1937 World's Fair), and the Council of State Radio Broadcasts. In February, 1935, when Louis Barthou was assassinated in Marseilles, Jouvenel was unanimously elected to succeed him as president of the Association of Parisian Journalists. Except for the Senate Commission for Reforming the State (see Chapter Sixteen), the only commission on record that he belonged to but did not preside over was the Senate Foreign Affairs Commission, whose perennial president, Henry Béranger, wrote, "In this major constellation Henry de Jouvenel shone like a star of the first magnitude"—Béranger, "Henry de Jouvenel à la commission sénatoriale des Affaires étrangères," *Revue des Vivants*, IX (November–December, 1935), 1676.

53. Paul Valéry, "Henry de Jouvenel, homme de l'esprit," *Revue des Vivants*, IX (November–December, 1935), 1639.

54. Béranger, "Henry de Jouvenel à la commission sénatoriale des Affaires étrangères," *Revue des Vivants*, IX (November–December, 1935), 1677.

55. Suarez, "Chez Monsieur Henry de Jouvenel," *Revue de Paris*, XXXV (January–February, 1928), 456.

56. Wladimir d'Ormesson in *Le Figaro*, October 6, 1935.

57. Maurois, "Notre Voisin," *Revue des Vivants*, IX (November–December, 1935), 1668.

58. Suarez, *Cartel*, p. 228.

59. Marcel Prévost, "Henry de Jouvenel, orateur," *Revue des Vivants*, IX (November–December, 1935), 1644.

60. Bertrand de Jouvenel, private letter to myself.

61. Marcel Déat, "Un Chef," *Revue des Vivants*, IX (November–December, 1935), 1652.

62. Paul Reynaud, "Henry de Jouvenel au parlement," *Revue des Vivants*, IX (November–December, 1935), 1680.

63. Lord Robert Cecil, "L'Oeuvre d'Henry de Jouvenel à Genève," *Revue des Vivants*, IX (November–December, 1935), 1673.

64. José Germain, *Le Syndicalisme et l'intelligence* (Paris, Valois, 1928), p. 60.

65. Sénat, *Débats, 1934*, p. 49.

66. Sénat, *Débats, 1935*, p. 331.   67. *Ibid.*, p. 334.   68. *Ibid.*

NOTES TO 15: A MISSION TO ROME

1. Joseph Paul-Boncour, *Entre deux guerres, Souvenirs sur la IIIème République* (3 vols., Paris, Plon, 1945), II, 337.

2. Jouvenel's contacts with Mussolini were allegedly facilitated by a common friend, the syndicalist theorist Lagardelle, then a resident of Rome. Georges Suarez and Guy Laborde, *Agonie de la paix, 1935–1939* (Paris, Plon, 1942), p. 72.

3. Paul-Boncour, *Entre deux guerres*, II, 338–39.

4. See for instance *Journal des Débats*, December 30, 1932, and January 5, 1933; *L'Ordre*, January 4, 1933; *Le Figaro*, January 15, 1933.

5. Quoted by Geneviève Tabouis, *They Called Me Cassandra* (New York, Scribner, 1942), p. 164.

6. Quoted by Maurois, "Notre Voisin," *Revue des Vivants*, IX (November–December, 1935), 1668; see also *DBFP*, Ser. II, Vol. V, nos. 37, 79.

7. *Ibid.*, no. 37.

8. Letter of February 10 to the French government; quoted by Monzie, *Ci-devant* (Paris, Flammarion, 1941), p. 48.

9. Wladimir d'Ormesson, "Henry de Jouvenel à Rome," *Revue des Vivants*, IX (November–December, 1935), 1690.

10. Quoted by Maurois, "Notre Voisin," *Revue des Vivants*, IX (November–December, 1935), 1669.

11. Paul Valéry, "Henry de Jouvenel, homme de l'esprit," *Revue des Vivants*, IX (November–December, 1935), 1641.

12. *DBFP*, Ser. II, Vol. V, no. 101. Evidently Frick, Nazi Minister of the Interior, urged Hitler to visit Rome and London by way of reprisal (*ibid.*).

13. Bertrand de Jouvenel, private letter to myself.

14. Letter of March 3, 1933; quoted by Monzie in *Journal officiel, 1938*, p. 12532.

15. Letter of March 22 to Emile Roche; quoted in Roche, *Caillaux que j'ai connu* (Paris, Plon, 1949), p. 66. Henry Béranger, Emile Roche, and a few others visited Jouvenel in Rome to obtain a confidential account of the four-power negotiations, after which Béranger and Caillaux became Jouvenel's staunch partisans in the Senate (see *ibid.*, pp. 66 ff.; Paul-Boncour, *Entre deux guerres*, II, 337–61; Joseph Caillaux, *Mes Mémoires* [3 vols., Paris, Plon, 1942–47], III, 239–40).

16. Quoted by Roche, *Caillaux*, p. 65 (letter of March 10).

17. Quoted by Monzie in *Journal officiel, 1938*, p. 12532 (letter of March 3).

18. See for instance *DBFP*, Ser. II, Vol. V, nos. 61, 69.   19. *Ibid.*, no. 204.

20. *Ibid.*, no. 44 and enclosures; no. 45.   21. *Ibid.*, no. 46.

22. Norman Hillson, *The Geneva Scene* (London, Routledge, 1936), p. 128.

23. *Ibid.*   24. *DBFP*, Ser. II, Vol. V, no. 53.   25. *Ibid.*, no. 68.

26. *Ibid.*, no. 54 and enclosure, no. 56 and enclosure, nos. 57, 84.

27. Arnold J. Toynbee, *Survey of International Affairs, 1933* (London, Oxford University Press, 1934), pp. 218–19; Toynbee adds, wryly, "This was perhaps the principal positive result which the Four-Power Pact produced." See also *DBFP*, Ser. II, Vol. V, nos. 58, 67, and especially 206.

28. *Ibid.*, nos. 64, 66.   29. *Ibid.*, no. 52.   30. *Ibid.*; see also no. 60.

31. New York *Times*, May 21, 1933.   32. Quoted *ibid.*, April 2, 1933.

33. Chambre des Députés, *Débats, 1933*, p. 1690.

34. *DBFP*, Ser. II, Vol. V, no. 79; see also no. 216.

35. *Ibid.*, no. 79; see also no. 78.

36. Papen did also at first show himself to be "agreeably surprised" (*ibid.*, no. 78); not for long, though (*ibid.*, nos. 80, 82). He went to Rome primarily to negotiate a concordat with the pope; in his *Memoirs*, Briand Connell, ed. and transl. (London, Deutsch, 1952), he betrays no recollection of the Four-Power Pact.

37. New York *Times*, April 11, 1933.

38. *DBFP*, Ser. II, Vol. V, nos. 82, 90.   39. New York *Times*, April 12, 1933.

40. *DBFP*, Ser. II, Vol. V, nos. 148, 216.   41. See *ibid.*, no. 97.

42. *Ibid.*, no. 144.   43. *Ibid.*, no. 148.   44. *Ibid.*, no. 149.

45. *Ibid.*, nos. 165, 216.

46. For the successive drafts of the Four-Power Pact see *Documents on International Affairs*, ed. by John W. Wheeler-Bennett (London, Oxford University Press, 1934), pp. 236–49.

47. Paul-Boncour suggests (*Entre deux guerres*, II, 346–47, 350–51, 353) that Poland was more or less reconciled to the pact; he was, however, evasive when questioned on this point in the debate of June 9 in the Chamber, and all other testimony points the opposite way (see for instance *DBFP*, Ser. II, Vol. V, nos. 178, 206).

48. See *DBFP*, Ser. II, Vol. V, nos. 159, 171, 178, 186, and especially 195 and 216. Evidently some of the delay was due to a (legitimate?) misunderstanding in Paris as to which draft was under discussion at one point: see *ibid.*, no. 216.

49. Quoted by Monzie in *Journal officiel, 1938*, p. 12532.

50. New York *Times*, June 7, 1933.   51. See *DBFP*, Ser. II, Vol. V, no. 216.

52. Quoted by New York *Times*, June 7, 1933.

53. *Ibid.*, June 8, 1933.   54. Quoted *ibid.*

55. In the night of April 6–7 the Chamber had given Daladier authority to conclude the pact by a vote of 430 to 107; the vote of June 9 was 347 to 245.

56. Pierre Pasquier, *Les Etapes de la défaite* (Montreal, Zodiaque, 1941), pp. 137–38.

57. Quoted by *Le Temps*, July 20, 1933.

58. Monzie: "The issue then at stake was to restore to the great and true nations their freedom with respect to the small ones" (*Ci-devant*, p. 39); and again, "On the morrow of Munich I am pleased to give my friend credit for the method by which we have clung to peace" (*ibid.*, p. 49). Monzie's judgment of the significance of Jouvenel's work in Rome is hardly defensible, and Paul-Boncour (*Entre deux guerres*, II, 337–61, especially 357) refutes his conception of Jouvenel's purpose in negotiating the pact.

59. Quoted by *Le Temps*, September 18, 1933.

60. Toynbee, *Survey of International Affairs, 1933*, pp. 218–19.

NOTES TO *16: THE LATE STATE*

1. Georges Suarez, *Les Heures héroïques du cartel* (Paris, Grasset, 1934), p. 188.

2. New York *Times*, February 4, 1934.

3. "*A la rue*" (Chiappe) versus "*dans la rue*" (Daladier). Most Frenchmen believed one version or the other; the hypothesis of a misunderstanding is weak, but it is an "average of truth."

4. "Weak governments imagine that repression will spare them the necessity of having a program," Jouvenel had written of the Necker government of May, 1789. *The Stormy Life of Mirabeau* (Boston, Houghton Mifflin, 1929), p. 208.

5. As far as I know, Jouvenel was the only minister to oppose resignation after having opposed the removal of Chiappe. His position now appears as the only reasonable one, but at the time any position was equivocal.

6. *Revue des Vivants*, VIII (April, 1934), 487–88.   7. *Ibid.*, p. 490.   8. *Ibid.*

9. *Ibid.*, p. 495.   10. *Ibid.*, p. 498.

11. Henry de Jouvenel, "Pour le référendum, Vers la démocratie directe," *Revue des Vivants*, VIII (October, 1934), 1480.

12. *Ibid.*, p. 1482.

13. Joseph Paul-Boncour, *Entre deux guerres, Souvenirs sur la IIIème République* (3 vols., Paris, Plon, 1945), II, 313–18.

14. Jouvenel originated this slogan, which De Gaulle took up in 1947.

15. Quoted in *Revue des Vivants*, IX (November–December, 1935), 1779.

16. *Ibid.*, p. 1780.   17. *Ibid.*, p. 1783.   18. *Ibid.*, p. 1785.   19. *Ibid.*

20. André Maurois, "Notre Voisin," *Revue des Vivants*, IX (November–December, 1935), 1667.

21. Henry de Jouvenel, *La Paix française, Témoignage d'une génération* (Paris, Portiques, 1932), p. 33.

22. Sénat, *Débats, 1935*, p. 390 (March 26)—a variation on a theme by Pascal.

23. *Le Temps*, October 6, 1935.

24. Maurois, "Notre Voisin," *Revue des Vivants*, IX (November–December, 1935), 1667.

25. *La République*, October 6, 1935.   26. *Le Figaro*, October 6, 1935.

27. Quoted by *Le Temps*, October 7, 1935.

28. Monzie, "Adieux à mon ami," *Revue des Vivants*, IX (November–December, 1935), 1636.

29. Marcel Déat, "Un chef," *Revue des Vivants*, IX (November–December, 1935), 1651.

30. *L'Europe Nouvelle*, XIX (October 10, 1936), 1007, quoting Pierre Viénot.

31. Anatole de Monzie, *Ci-devant* (Paris, Flammarion, 1941), p. 49.

NOTES TO 17: THE PRODIGY

1. Since 1674. See Michel Missoffe, *La Vie volontaire d'André Tardieu* (Paris, Flammarion, 1930), p. 14, and Tardieu, *La Révolution à refaire* (2 vols., Paris, Flammarion, 1936–37), I, 9.

2. *Ibid.*   3. New York *Times*, November 24, 1929, Sec. III, p. 7.

4. Or, as the author explained, "a general list of persons born in Paris of whom there exist portraits in lithograph or engraving, with a biography of each person named (around three thousand names)." Ambroise Tardieu, *Dictionnaire iconographique des Parisiens* (Herment [Puy-de-Dôme], Ambroise Tardieu, 1885), title page.

5. Eugène Amédée Tardieu was also a geographer, his most important work in this capacity being *Sénégambie et Guinée* (Paris, Didot, 1847).

6. Auguste Ambroise Tardieu was also private physician to Napoleon III and the author of a *Dictionnaire de l'Hygiène publique*; moreover, he was at one time municipal councilor in Paris, and in 1876, the year of André's birth, he rose to the rank of Commander in the Legion of Honor.

7. His wife was Charlotte Elisabeth d'Arpentigny de Malleville, an amateur instrumentalist and composer of no mean talent: see Missoffe, *Vie de Tardieu*, p. 13. For Eugène, as well as for Tardieu's ancestry in general, see also Victor Goedorp, *Figures du temps* (Paris, Michel, 1943), pp. 221-22; Goedorp, however, is sometimes at fault, particularly in his confusion of André's father, André Louis Amédée, with André's uncle Jacques.

8. A *maître des requêtes.*   9. Tardieu, *Révolution*, I, 9.

10. At 26 Avenue de Messine, opposite a Carmelite convent.

11. On June 30, 1895, to the marquis de Beauchesne, examiner in history at the Sorbonne, who inquired of him about his early education; quoted by Missoffe, *Vie de Tardieu*, p. 21.

12. Tardieu, *Révolution*, I, 10.   13. *Ibid.*, pp. 9–10.

14. Formerly the Lycée Fontanes, or Collège Fontanes et Bonaparte. Like Caillaux, he entered it as a day student.

15. Alphonse Olivieri, "André Tardieu et Henry de Jouvenel peints par eux-mêmes," *Revue contemporaine*, LXXI (March, 1923), 323.

16. Tardieu, *Révolution*, I, 10.   17. *Ibid.*   18. *Ibid.*

19. Anatole de Monzie, *L'Entrée au forum (vingt ans avant)* (Paris, Michel, 1920), p. 22; quoted by Missoffe, *Vie de Tardieu*, p. 19.

20. For the complete record of his prizes see Missoffe, *Vie de Tardieu*, pp. 20–21.

21. Quoted by Monzie, *Entrée au forum*, p. 22. For long excerpts from Tardieu's composition see also Olivieri, "André Tardieu et Henry de Jouvenel peints par eux-mêmes," *Revue contemporaine*, LXXI (March, 1923), 324-26.

22. Quoted by Monzie, *Entrée au forum*, p. 24, and by Olivieri, "André Tardieu et Henry de Jouvenel peints par eux-mêmes," *Revue contemporaine*, LXXI (March, 1923), 325.

23. Monzie, *Entrée au forum*. pp. 24–25.

24. Quoted by Missoffe, *Vie de Tardieu*, pp. 27, 27–28. Missoffe saw in the phrase "*ne fugiamus certamina*" (let us not flee the battle) a motto for Tardieu's life.

25. Poincaré had been a household name at the Tardieus' since November 28, 1883, when André Tardieu *père*, his colleague at the bar, was elected to sit with him as secretary of the *Ordre des avocats à la Cour d'appel de Paris.* Of the four secretaries, Poincaré was the first and Tardieu the fourth; the third was Alexandre Millerand.

26. Henry de Jouvenel, *Pourquoi je suis syndicaliste*, in the series "Leurs Raisons," ed. by André Billy (Paris, Editions de France, 1928), p. 9.

27. Octave Homberg, *Les Coulisses de l'histoire, Souvenirs 1898–1928* (Paris, Fayard, 1938), p. 15.

28. Missoffe, *Vie de Tardieu*, p. 23.   29. *Ibid.*

30. Maurice Privat, *Les Heures d'André Tardieu et la crise des partis* (Paris, 1930), p. 111.

31. Quoted by Missoffe, *Vie de Tardieu*, p. 33.

32. Maurice Cassenave, "André Tardieu—souvenirs d'Amérique," *Correspondant*, VIII (1930), 892.

33. Tardieu, *Révolution*, I, 11.

34. Missoffe, *Vie de Tardieu*, p. 36.

35. André Tardieu, *Le Prince de Bülow* (Paris, Calmann-Lévy, 1909), p. 4.

36. Chambre des Députés, *Débats, 1930*, pp. 1896–97.

37. Missoffe, *Vie de Tardieu*, p. 34.   38. Homberg, *Coulisses de l'histoire*, p. 15.

39. André Tardieu, *Notes de semaine 1938*, *L'Année de Munich* (Paris, Flammarion, 1939), p. 116.

40. Tardieu, *Révolution*, I, 11.

41. Joseph Paul-Boncour, *Entre deux guerres, Souvenirs sur la IIIème République* (3 vols., Paris, Plon, 1945), I, 95, and II, 213.

42. Henry de Jouvenel, *Pourquoi je suis syndicaliste*, p. 9.

43. *Ibid.*, p. 11.

44. In 1960 dollars, about $7,000 a year plus $.18 a line (see Note 17, Chapter One).

45. Homberg, *Coulisses de l'histoire*, p. 16.

46. The suit dragged on some years, and the verdict was indecisive: see *Plaidoirie prononcée par Me Bourdillon... pour M. André Tardieu contre M. Calmette... et Jugement rendu par la 3e Chambre du Tribunal civil de la Seine le 17 juin 1904* (Auxerres, Lanier, 1904).

47. Joseph Caillaux, *Mes Mémoires* (3 vols., Paris, Plon, 1942–47), III, 107n.

48. Tardieu, *Révolution*, I, 11.

49. Goedorp, *Figures du temps*, pp. 231–32.   50. *Ibid.*, p. 232.

51. Tardieu, *Notes de semaine 1938*, p. 132.

52. André Tardieu, *France and the Alliances* (New York, MacMillan, 1908), p. 181.

53. *Ibid.*

54. About $22,000,000 in 1960 dollars (see Note 17, Chapter One).

55. *GP*, Vol. xx, no. 6567.   56. Tardieu, *Alliances*, p. 181.

57. Quoted *ibid.*, p. 185.   58. *Le Temps*, June 5, 1908.

59. *DDF*, Ser. II, Vol. VII, no. 446.

60. *GP*, Vol. xx, no. 6802.   61. *Ibid.*, no. 6833.   62. *Ibid.*, no. 6834.

63. Tardieu, *Alliances*, p. 191.

64. *GP*, Vol. xxi, no. 6901.

65. *DDF*, Ser. II, Vol. VIII, no. 289; Rouvier blamed General Galliffet.

66. *Ibid.*, Vol. IX, no. 176; *GP*, Vol. xxi, no. 7001.

67. *DDF*, Ser. II, Vol. IX, no. 443.   68. *GP*, Vol. xxi, no. 7114.

69. *Ibid.*, no. 7123 and note.

70. André Tardieu, *La Conférence d'Algésiras* (Paris, Alcan, 1907), p. 196.

71. *GP*, Vol. xxi, no. 7123.   72. *Ibid.*   73. *Ibid.*, note.

74. *DDF*, Ser. II, Vol. IX, no. 629.   75. *Ibid.*, no. 549.   76. *Ibid.*, no. 629.

77. *Ibid.*, no. 557.   78. *GP*, Vol. xxi, no. 7124.   79. *Ibid.*, no. 7125.

80. *Ibid.*, note.   81. See *ibid.*, no. 6949, note.

82. Prince zu Eulenburg, the former Chancellor.

83. See *GP*, Vol. xxi, no. 7027 and insert.

84. *Ibid.*, note.   85. *Ibid.*   86. *Ibid.*

87. *Ibid.*, no. 7251.   88. *Ibid.*, no. 7327.   89. *Ibid.*, no. 7329.

90. Tardieu, *Avec Foch (août-novembre, 1914)* (Paris, G.D., 1948), p. 2.

91. *Ibid.*, pp. 2–3.   92. Tardieu, *Alliances*, p. 1.

93. André Tardieu, *Notes sur les Etats-Unis* (Paris, Calmann-Lévy, 1908), p. 37.

94. *Ibid.*, p. 15.   95. *Ibid.* p. 14.

96. *La France et les Alliances* (Paris, Alcan, 1910).

97. Tardieu, *Etats-Unis*, pp. 52–53.   98. *Ibid.*, p. 81.   99. *Ibid.*, p. 89.

100. *Ibid.*, pp. 102–3.   101. *Ibid.*, p. 103.   102. *Ibid.*   103. *Ibid.*, p. 135.

104. *Ibid.*, pp. 136–64.   105. *Ibid.*, p. 31.

106. *Ibid.*, p. 195.   107. *Ibid.*, p. 202.

108. *Ibid.*, p. 205.   109. *Ibid.*, p. 207.   110. *Ibid.*, p. 230.   111. *Ibid.*, p. 371.

NOTES TO 18:
N'GOKO SANGHA AND HOMS-BAGDAD

1. *GP.*, Vol. xxiv, no. 8335.   2. *Ibid.*, no. 8337.

3. *Ibid.*, no. 8344.   4. *Ibid.*, no. 8345.

5. *Ibid.*, no. 8344, note.   6. *Ibid.*, no. 8348.   7. *Ibid.*   8. *Ibid.*

9. Months later—in January, 1910—as Mulai Hafid was "stalling for time in the matter of [a] Moroccan loan," Tardieu thought of preparing public opinion in France for the use of pressure on him by producing "irrefutable proofs" that he "bears the chief guilt in the murder of Mauchamps and in the Casablanca massacre." He consulted the German Embassy, which consulted Berlin; Secretary von Schoen replied, "Germany would not welcome such revelations if they are made by Tardieu," and the matter was dropped. See *ibid.*, Vol. xxix, nos. 10494, 10495.

10. *Ibid.*, Vol. xxiv, no. 8350.   11. *Ibid.*   12. *Ibid.*

13. *Ibid.*   14. *Ibid.*, no. 8351.   15. *Ibid.*, no. 8350.

16. Ostensibly he went to urge the German government to agree to make a joint declaration with the French government of their common approval of the Young Turk movement in order to distract public opinion from their quarrel over the six deserters; Von Schoen passed the suggestion on to Bülow, and it came to nothing. *Ibid.*, Vol. xxvi, no. 9021.

17. Tardieu considered the prospect of an Austro-French *rapprochement* on Morocco to have been the decisive factor in bringing Germany to accept the negotiations. On the evening of October 3, 1908, the Austrian Ambassador in Paris, immediately after announcing the annexation of Bosnia-Herzegovina, saw Tardieu privately to suggest to him an Austro-French entente on Morocco. Pichon was absent from Paris, and Tardieu could not get Clemenceau interested in the offer; at length he mentioned it opportunely to Lancken, who cried angrily: "What, those pigs of Austrians did that?!" And "a few days later," wrote Tardieu, "began the conversations that…led to the agreement signed by the Clemenceau cabinet on February 8, 1909." Joseph Caillaux, *Mes Mémoires* (3 vols., Paris, Plon, 1942–47), I, 273–75n (letter from Tardieu to Caillaux).

18. *GP*, Vol. xxiv, no. 8494.

19. Quoted by Joseph Caillaux, *Agadir, Ma Politique extérieure* (Paris, Michel, 1919), pp. 33–34.

20. *Ibid.*, p. 41.   21. *Ibid.*, pp. 57–58.

22. *Le Temps*, December 8, 1907.   23. *Ibid.*, March 9, 1908.

24. Caillaux, *Agadir*, p. 60.   25. Caillaux, *Mémoires*, II, 36.

26. The N'Goko Sangha took at the same time a second lawyer—Jean Dupuy's son-in-law, Pierre Arago.

27. Quoted by Charles Paix-Séailles, *Jaurès et Caillaux* (Paris, Figuières, 1919), p. 158.

28. Quoted *ibid.*, p. 161.

29. They had taken their decision some weeks before writing, though: see *DDF*, Ser. II, Vol. xiii, no. 178.

30. See *ibid.*, Vol. xii, nos. 451, 452 and annex, 465, 501 and annexes (documents

relevant to the arbitral procedure). The state's advocate was the Governor-General of French Equatorial Africa (Merlin); the state designated as arbitrator the first president of the Cour des Comptes (Hérault).

31. Maurice Viollette, *La N'Goko-Sangha* (Paris, Larose, 1914), p. 79.

32. About $1,300,000 in 1960 dollars (see Note 17, Chapter One).

33. For the arbitration agreement see *DDF*, Ser. II, Vol. XII, no. 501, and Vol. XIII, no. 178.

34. Quoted by Paix-Séailles, *Jaurès et Caillaux*, p. 165.

35. Caillaux, *Agadir*, p. 66.   36. Quoted by Viollette, *N'Goko-Sangha*, p. 45.

37. *DDF*, Ser. II, Vol. XII, no. 501 and annexes.   37. *Ibid.*, Vol. XIII, no. 178.

39. Quoted by Viollette, *N'Goko-Sangha*, p. 192. See also *DDF*, Ser. II, Vol. XIII, no. 178.

40. About $200,000 in 1960 dollars (see Note 17, Chapter One).

41. About $15,000 in 1960 dollars (see Note 17, Chapter One).

42. Tardieu, *Le Mystère d'Agadir* (Paris, Calmann-Lévy, 1909), pp. 328–29.

43. Caillaux, *Mémoires*, II, 37.   44. *DDF*, Ser. II, Vol. XII, no. 571.

45. *Ibid.*, no. 591.   46. *Ibid.*, Vol. XIII, no. 53; see also no. 41 and notes.

47. *Ibid.*, no. 86.   48. *Le Temps*, December 11, 1910.

49. Quoted by Viollette, *N'Goko-Sangha*, p. 79.   50. *Ibid.*   51. *Ibid.*, p. 181.

52. Charles Paix-Séailles, *La Diplomatie secrète sous la Troisième République, 1910–1911* (Paris, Courrier Européen, 1912), p. 97. See also *DDF*, Ser. II, Vol. XIII, no. 178. The Commission on Colonial Concessions of the Chamber also had pronounced against the indemnity if not against the consortium: see *ibid.*, nos. 9, 18.

53. *LN*, Vol. I, p. 128.   54. *GP*, Vol. XXVII, no. 10181.

55. *Le Temps*, January 31, 1911.   56. Sénat, *Débats, 1911*, p. 124.

57. *Ibid.*, p. 128.   58. *Ibid.*

59. For the background to this request see Appendix.

60. Quoted by Maybelle Kennedy Chapman, *Great Britain and the Baghdad Railway* (Vol. XXXI of "Smith College Studies in History," Menasha [Wisconsin], Banta, 1948), p. 105.

61. *Ibid.*, p. 108. See also *ibid.*, p. 124; *BD*, Vol. VI, no. 384. Chapman differs on this point from John B. Wolf, "The Diplomatic History of the Baghdad Railroad," *The University of Missouri Studies*, XI, No. 2 (April 1, 1936): as Wolf saw it, the British were "sorely tempted" by the prospect of an understanding with the Germans on the Gulf segment.

62. Chapman, *Britain and Baghdad Railway*, p. 110; *BD*, Vol. VI, no. 317. See also *GP*, Vol. XXVII, no. 9990.

63. *BD*, Vol. VI, no. 303.

64. *Ibid.*, nos. 320, 321. In fact Pichon was acting under pressure from Cambon himself, who had a personal interest in the Turkish railways. See André Gérard, "The Story of the Baghdad Railway," *The Nineteenth Century and After*, no. 448 (June, 1914), p. 1318.

65. Gérard, "The Story of the Baghdad Railway," *The Nineteenth Century and After*, no. 448 (June, 1914), p. 1321.

66. *Le Temps*, April 8, 1911.

67. According to his detractors, Tardieu was to receive a bonus of 1,000,000 francs (about $500,000 in 1960 dollars) if and when the concession came through. See for instance Félicien Challaye, "Politique internationale et journalisme d'affaires," *Revue du Mois*, XI (June 10, 1911), 749–57; Paix-Séailles, *Diplomatie secrète*, p. 28; Frederick L. Schuman, *War and Diplomacy in the French Republic* (New York, Whittlesey House, 1931), p. 393. No evidence was ever adduced to support this allegation; it was no doubt in the first instance a misconstrual of the normal and unobjectionable provision

in his agreement with Barry for a perpetual right of option on 1,000,000 francs worth of the shares reserved to the French founders should any of them ever come up for resale.

68. See for instance *GP*, Vol. xxiv, nos. 8350, 8351; also Appendix.

69. See Appendix. In December, 1909, Pichon, at the request of the British Ambassador, attempted once again to convince Izvolsky that, the Bagdad railway being inevitable, the interest of the Entente powers was to obtain a share in it. He failed. See *BD*, Vol. vi, no. 303.

70. See Appendix.   71. Tardieu, *Mystère d'Agadir*, p. 403.

72. Morris Jastrow, *The War and the Bagdad Railway* (Philadelphia, Lippincott, 1917), p. 111.

73. Tardieu's group included the Société financière d'Orient, the Régie générale des Chemins de Fer d'Orient, and the Bardac bank.

74. Gérard, "The Story of the Baghdad Railway," *The Nineteenth Century and After*, no. 448 (June, 1914,), p. 1321.

75. Paix-Séailles, *Diplomatie secrète*, pp. 33–34; Challaye, "Politique internationale et journalisme d'affaires," *Revue du Mois*, xi (June 10, 1911), 751.

76. Quoted by Chapman, *Britain and Baghdad Railway*, p. 112.

77. *BD*, Vol. vi, no. 348.

78. Quoted by Chapman, *Britain and Baghdad Railway*, p. 112.

79. Challaye, "Politique internationale et journalisme d'affaires," *Revue du Mois*, xi (June 10, 1911), 751.

80. Quoted *ibid.*   81. Paix-Séailles, *Diplomatie secrète*, p. 41.

82. Challaye, "Politique internationale et journalisme d'affaires," *Revue du Mois*, xi (June 10, 1911), 751–52.

83. Tardieu, *Mystère d'Agadir*, p. 404.

84. Wolf, "The Diplomatic History of the Baghdad Railroad," *The University of Missouri Studies*, xi, no. 2 (April 1, 1936), 82; Louis Ragey, *La Question du Chemin de Fer de Baghdad, 1893–1914* (Paris, Rieder, 1936), p. 98, agrees.

85. Wolf, "The Diplomatic History of the Baghdad Railroad," *The University of Missouri Studies*, xi, no. 2 (April 1, 1936), 82.

86. *Le Temps*, June 10, 1910.

87. Chapman, *Britain and Baghdad Railway*, p. 118.

88. Tardieu, *Mystère d'Agadir*, p. 404.   89. *GP*, Vol. xxiv, no. 10004.

90. For full details of these proposals see Tardieu, *Mystère d'Agadir*, pp. 404–5.

91. See Appendix.

92. *GP*, Vol. xxvii, no. 10004.   93. *Ibid.*, no. 10005.   94. *Ibid.*, no. 10009.

95. Wolf, "The Diplomatic History of the Baghdad Railroad," *The University of Missouri Studies*, xi, no. 2 (April 1, 1936), 61.

96. *GP*, Vol. xxvii, no. 10005.   97. See Appendix.

98. *GP*, Vol. xxvii, no. 10009 (order of paragraphs altered).

99. Paix-Séailles, *Diplomatie secrète*, p. 80, quoting a letter written by Tardieu in October, 1911, to the *Daily News* of London.

100. Tardieu, *Mystère d'Agadir*, p. 405.

101. *GP.*, Vol. xxvii, no. 10010.   102. *Ibid.*

103. *Ibid.*, no. 10011. Wolf, "The Diplomatic History of the Baghdad Railroad," *The University of Missouri Studies*, xi, no. 2 (April 1, 1936), 83—following in this Tardieu's critics—gives the French government as having tied the concession to the loan.

104. *GP*, Vol. xxvii, nos. 10007, 10012; *BD*, Vol. vi, no. 388.

105. *GP*, Vol. xxvii, no. 10015.   106. *Ibid.*, no. 10051, note.

107. *Le Temps*, October 20, 1910; quoted by Paix-Séailles, *Diplomatie secrète*, p. 86.

108. *GP*, Vol. xxvII, no. 10057.

109. *DDF*, Ser. II, Vol. xIII, nos. 32, 36, 37, 39, 40, 44, 46, 49, 60, 71, 72.

110. Challaye, "Politique internationale et journalisme d'affaires," *Revue du Mois*, xI (June 10, 1911), 753.

111. *GP*, Vol. xxvII, no. 10199 and note.

112. Wolf, "The Diplomatic History of the Baghdad Railroad," *The University of Missouri Studies*, xI, no. 2 (April 1, 1936), 61.

113. The plan of one M. Ornstein; according to Wolf (*ibid.*, p. 82) it was objectionable both to Turkish and to German observers.

114. *DDF*, Ser. II, Vol. xIII, nos. 109, 128. In these dispatches Bompard represents the Turkish ministers as reiterating incessantly their opposition to the Homs-Bagdad concession but not to the principle of compensatory concessions to France.

115. *GP*, Vol. xxvII, no. 10183; see also Vol. xxIX, no. 10519.

116. *Action Nationale*, February 10, 1911; quoted by Paix-Séailles, *Diplomatie secrète*, p. 107.

117. *Ibid.*, p. 112.   118. Caillaux, *Agadir*, p. 73.

119. At this time certain Quai d'Orsay officials were pushing for a new solution involving the transfer at a very high price of most of the N'Goko Sangha concession (including the 150,000 acres "awarded" to the company on June 18, 1910) to the French Sangha-Ubangi Forest Company, which would in turn enter into the consortium with the Südkamerun: see *DDF*, Ser. II, Vol. xIII, no. 178.

120. Caillaux, *Agadir*, pp. 74–75. On the alleged disinterest of the German government see, however, *DDF*, Ser. II, Vol. xIII, no. 41 and notes, nos. 53, 67, 130.

121. *GP*, Vol. xxvII, no. 10038.   122. *Ibid.*, no. 10037.

123. Tardieu, *Mystère d'Agadir*, pp. 405–6. Tardieu is, I believe, the only source for this meeting, though *DDF*, Ser. II, Vol. xIII, no. 282 (of May 5, 1911), establishes Gwinner's intention to hold it.

124. Paix-Séailles, *Diplomatie secrète*, p. 108.

125. Later the court of appeals added a year to Maimon's sentence and reduced his secretary's to one month.

126. *Le Rappel*, beginning April 23, 1911.

127. *Le Courrier Européen* and *Le Cri de Paris*.

128. *La Revue de Mars*, June, 1911.

129. *Mouvement socialiste*, February, 1911, p. 135; quoted by Challaye, "Politique internationale et journalisme d'affaires," *Revue du Mois*, xI (June 10, 1911), 755.

130. Quoted by Caillaux, *Mémoires*, II, 109–10. See also *DDF*, Ser. II, Vol. xIV, no. 105—which, however, places this conversation at July 26.

131. Caillaux, *Mémoires*, II, 108.

132. October 3, 1911: see Edmund Dene Morel, *Ten Years of Secret Diplomacy* (London, National Labor Press, 1915), p. 119.

133. Quoted *ibid.*

134. Cambon, like De Selves, did not appreciate Tardieu's devices, which included sending out feelers on the intentions of the French government, publicizing the concessions made by Germany, and listing the further demands of France as categorial: see *DDF*, Ser. II, Vol. xIV, nos. 37, 111, 120, 313. His information on the concessions made by Germany came, not from Caillaux, but from Lancken: see *ibid.*, nos. 111, 120.

135. Caillaux, *Mémoires*, II, 189*n*.   136. *Le Temps*, January 13, 1912.

137. Chambre des Députés, *Débats, 1912*, p. 815.

138. *Ibid.*, p. 768 (March 15).   139. Paix-Séailles, *Diplomatie secrète*, p. 118.

140. Maurice Privat, *Les Heures d'André Tardieu et la crise des partis* (Paris, Portiques, 1930), p. 112.

NOTES TO 19: THE SEVENTH POWER

1. André Tardieu, "L'Egypte," in Société des anciens Elèves et Elèves de l'Ecole libre des Sciences politiques, *L'Afrique du Nord* (Paris, Alcan, 1913), p. 207.

2. *LN*, Vol. I, p. 255.

3. Federico Curato, "La Storiografia delle Origini della prima Guerra mondiale," *Questioni di Historia contemporanea*, ed. by Ettore Rota (Milan, Marzorati, 1952), p. 456; Curato gives as his source Henri Pozzi, *Les Coupables* (Paris, 1935), pp. 137, 157–58, 165, 173, 177, 178, 216.

4. Quoted by Ernest Judet, *Georges Louis* (Paris, Rieder, 1925), p. 72.

5. *GP*, Vol. xxxiii, no. 12358. See also *ibid.*, Vol. xxxiv, no. 12558, and *LN*, Vol. I, p. 371.

6. In 1960 dollars, about $150,000 (see Note 17, Chapter One).

7. *L'Humanité* published the list of recipients on the eve of the general elections of 1924: see *L'Humanité*, December 14 and 25, 1923, and January 1–16, 1924. In the judgment of Frederick L. Schuman, *War and Diplomacy in the French Republic* (New York, Wittlesey House, 1931), p. 204, "The facts of the situation have been established beyond reasonable doubt."

8. Georges Michon, *La Préparation à la guerre, La Loi des trois ans (1910–1914)* (Paris, Rivière, 1935), p. 137.

9. *Le Temps*, March 2, 1913; quoted by Michon, *Préparation*, p. 139.

10. André Tardieu, *Notes de semaine 1938, L'Année de Munich* (Paris, Flammarion, 1939), p. 106.

11. Fidus, "M. André Tardieu (silhouettes parlementaires)," *Revue des deux Mondes*, 102ème année (February 1, 1932), p. 647.

12. André Tardieu, *La Note de semaine 1936* (Paris, Flammarion, 1937), pp. 120–21.

13. Michel Missoffe, *La Vie volontaire d'André Tardieu* (Paris, Flammarion, 1930), p. 84.

14. By appointment of Eugène Etienne, Minister of War, a few days before the Briand government fell.

15. Bülow was then still commanding figure in the diplomacy of Europe. Tardieu had once described him, after a long acquaintanceship, as "disappointing" (*La Conférence d'Algésiras* [Paris, Alcan, 1907], p. 72). Tardieu's book is no less disappointing than his subject. It is more a compendium of documents than a study of character and thought: he made the life of the Prince available without actually writing it.

16. These included the New York *Herald*, *La Dépêche marocaine*, *Le Bulletin de l'Afrique française*, *Le Journal des Balkans*, *L'Indépendance roumaine*, *Das Neue Wiener Tagblatt*, and *Die Neue Freie Presse*.

17. Such as especially *La Revue diplomatique*, *La Revue bleue*, and *La Revue des deux Mondes*.

18. *DDF*, Ser. iii, Vol. iv, no. 169.   19. *Ibid.*, Ser. ii, Vol. xi, no. 319.

20. This phrase is quoted in nearly every article on Tardieu; I do not know its source.

21. Ditto.

22. Ditto. Georges Suarez claimed to have heard Stresemann utter it (*Les Hommes malades de la paix* [Paris, Grasset, 1934], p. 128).

23. Maurice Paléologue, *Journal, 1913–1914* (Paris, Plon, 1947), p. 146.

24. *GP*, Vol. xxiv, no. 8355.

25. Sonnet by Jean Carrère; quoted by Maurice Privat, *Les Heures d'André Tardieu et la crise des partis* (Paris, Portiques, 1930), p. 112.

26. Victor Goedorp, *Figures du temps* (Paris, Michel, 1943), pp. 243–44.

27. Anatole de Monzie, *L'Entrée au forum (vingt ans avant)* (Paris, Michel, 1920), p. 23.

28. See Goedorp, *Figures du temps*, pp. 231 ff.   29. *Ibid.*, p. 244.

30. Pierre Mille, *Mes Trônes et mes dominations* (Paris, Portiques, 1930), p. 160.

31. His choice of salons was, by name of hostess: for politics, the duchesse de Rohan, Boulevard des Invalides, and princesse Murat, Rue de Monceau; for pleasure, the comtesse de Fitzjames, Rue de Constantine, and the comtesse Jean de Castellane, Rue Brignoles.

32. For samples see Mille, *Trônes et dominations*, frontispiece and pp. 160–67.

NOTES TO 20: "LA PLUS BELLE ÉPOQUE"

1. André Tardieu, *La Révolution à refaire* (2 vols., Paris, Flammarion, 1936–37), II, 109.

2. Article written on the occasion of an increase of the annual contingent of recruits and length of military service in Russia.

3. Joseph J. C. Joffre, *Mémoires du maréchal Joffre (1910–1917)* (2 vols., Paris, Plon, 1932), I, 293.

4. *Ibid.*, p. 320.

5. André Tardieu, *La Note de semaine 1936* (Paris, Flammarion, 1937), p. 121.

6. André Tardieu, *Avec Foch (août-novembre, 1914)* (Paris, G.D., 1948), p. 38. The details of Tardieu's early wartime experiences are drawn mainly from this source.

7. *Ibid.*

8. Ferdinand Foch, *The Memoirs of Marshal Foch*, trans. by Col. T. Bentley Mott (New York, Doubleday, Doran, 1931), p. 44.

9. Tardieu, *Avec Foch*, p. 41.   10. Joffre, *Mémoires*, I, 372.

11. Tardieu, *Avec Foch*, p. 47.   12. *Ibid.*, p. 53.   13. *Ibid.*

14. *Ibid.*, p. 55.   15. *Ibid.*, p. 57.   16. *Ibid.*, p. 68.

17. *Ibid.*, p. 77: Tardieu described Joffre's message as an *"erreur formidable."*

18. *Ibid.*, pp. 77–78.   19. *Ibid.*, p. 79.   20. *Ibid.*, p. 107.

21. *Ibid.*, pp. 134–35.   22. *Ibid.*, p. 36.   23. *Ibid.*, p. 137.

24. These included "Quatre Mois de guerre," "La Bataille de Flandre," "La Guerre, du 2 août 1914 jusqu'au premier février 1915," "La Condition de l'armée allemande," and histories of various individual armies.

25. Jean de Pierrefeu, *French Head Quarters 1915–1918*, trans. by C. J. C. Street (London, Bles, 1924), p. 85.

26. Tardieu, *Avec Foch*, p. 156.

27. Joseph Galliéni, *Les Carnets de Galliéni* (Paris, Michel, 1932), p. 139.

28. Pierrefeu, *French Head Quarters*, p. 85.   29. Galliéni, *Carnets*, p. 154.

30. Maurice Gamelin, *Servir* (3 vols., Paris, Plon, 1946–47), II, xxix.   31. *Ibid.*

32. Pierrefeu, *French Head Quarters*, p. 85.   33. Tardieu, *Avec Foch*, pp. 7–8.

34. Pierrefeu, *French Head Quarters*, p. 86.   35. Poincaré?

36. Tardieu, *Avec Foch*, p. 156.   37. The 7th Company, 44th Battalion.

38. Tardieu, *Révolution*, I, 13.   39. Tardieu, *Avec Foch*, p. 156.

40. Michel Missoffe, *La Vie volontaire d'André Tardieu* (Paris, Flammarion, 1930), p. 135.

41. See *Le Monde*, September 10, 1945.

42. Raymond Poincaré, *Au service de la France* (10 vols., Paris, Plon, 1927), VII, 345.

43. Pierrefeu, *French Head Quarters*, p. 86.   44. Poincaré, *Au service*, VII, 345.

45. *Ibid.*, p. 365.   46. Missoffe, *Vie de Tardieu*, p. 143.

47. Poincaré, *Au service*, VIII, 63.   48. *Ibid.*   49. *Ibid.*, p. 69.

50. *Ibid.*, p. 63, and Missoffe, *Vie de Tardieu*, p. 141. For Tardieu's other war citations see Missoffe, pp. 140–50.

51. Poincaré, *Au service*, VIII, 69.   52. *Ibid.*   53. *Ibid.*, p. 80.
54. *Ibid.*, p. 97.   55. Missoffe, *Vie de Tardieu*, p. 151.
56. Missoffe, however, describes in great detail (*ibid.*, pp. 142–49) a reconnaissance mission carried out by him with Tardieu during the night of March 29–30; only on April 3, when his division was replaced on the front by another, did Tardieu (according to Missoffe) consent to quit the army for the Army Commission (*ibid.*, p. 149).
57. Poincaré, *Au service*, VIII, 102–3.
58. Missoffe, *Vie de Tardieu*, pp. 154–55 (letter of May 15).
59. Poincaré, *Au service*, VIII, 216. See also Suarez, *Briand*, III, 295.
60. Pierrefeu, *French Head Quarters*, p. 86.
61. Georges Suarez, *Briand* (6 vols., Paris, Plon, 1938–52), III, 299.
62. Missoffe, *Vie de Tardieu*, p. 155.
63. Quoted by Pierre Renouvin, *The Forms of War Government in France* (New Haven, Yale University Press, 1927), pp. 131–32.
64. *Ibid.*, p. 133. Charles Benoist, "Chronique de la Quinzaine," *Revue des deux Mondes* (August 1, 1916), p. 714, considered that Tardieu's "inspectors" might become "commissars comparable to the representatives on mission in the period of the Convention."
65. Joffre, *Mémoires*, II, 393; see also 395–99.
66. Renouvin, *War Government in France*, p. 133.
67. See Jere Clemens King, *Generals and Politicians* (Berkeley, University of California Press, 1951), pp. 123–25.
68. Quoted by Missoffe, *Vie de Tardieu*, p. 160.
69. Chambre des Députés, *Débats, 1916*, p. 3632.
70. Tardieu, *Révolution*, I, 10.
71. Missoffe, *Vie de Tardieu*, p. 163.   72. *Ibid.*, p. 166.
73. Poincaré, *Au service*, IX, 59.
74. Alexandre Ribot, *Lettres à un ami* (Paris, Bossard, 1924), p. 172.
75. Poincaré, *Au service*, IX, 113.
76. The appointment was made in the first instance for one year; it was renewed on April 16, 1918, with some flourish.
77. André Tardieu, *Devant l'obstacle, L'Amérique et nous* (Paris, Emile-Paul, 1927), p. 218.
78. Poincaré, *Au service*, IX, 128.
79. Maurice Cassenave, "André Tardieu, souvenirs d'Amérique, "*Correspondant*, VIII (1930), p. 894.
80. André Tardieu, *Notes de semaine 1938, L'Année de Munich* (Paris, Flammarion, 1939), p. 237.
81. Cassenave, "André Tardieu, Souvenirs d'Amérique," *Correspondant*, VIII (1930), p. 898.
82. *Ibid.*, p. 895.   83. *Ibid.*, p. 896.
84. R. de Villeneuve-Trans, *A l'ambassade de Washington* (Paris, Bossard, 1921), p. 11, quoting Louis Aubert.
85. *Ibid.*, p. 189.
86. Frederick Palmer, *Newton D. Baker, America at War* (2 vols., New York, Dodd, Mead, 1931), I, 403.
87. Quoted by J. G. Harbord, *The American Army in France, 1917–1919* (Boston, Little, Brown, 1936), p. 139.
88. Poincaré, *Au service*, VIII, 318.   89. Tardieu, *Notes de semaine 1938*, p. 241.
90. Northcliffe arrived in Washington in June.
91. Cassenave, "André Tardieu, Souvenirs d'Amérique," *Correspondant*, VIII (1930), p. 897.
92. Villeneuve-Trans, *A l'ambassade*, p. 21.

93. His program was first announced in the New York *Times*, June, 8, 1917.

94. *Ibid.*, July 12, 1917.   95. *Ibid.*   96. *Ibid.*

97. André Tardieu, *The Truth About the Treaty* (Indianapolis, Bobbs-Merrill, 1921), p. 240.

98. Washington *Post*, July 20, 1917.   99. New York *Times*, August 12, 1917.

100. *Ibid.*, October 11, 1917.   101. *Ibid.*, September 7, 1917.

102. André Tardieu. *L'Amérique en armes* (Paris, Fasquelle, 1919), p. 17.

103. New York *Times*, October 10, 1917.   104. *Ibid.*, September 23, 1917.

105. *Ibid.*, July 1, 1917.   106. Tardieu, *Amérique en armes*, p. 37.

107. Quoted *ibid.*, p. 45 (Baker's letter of August 2).

108. New York *Times*, June 21, 1917.

109. Tardieu, *Notes de semaine 1938*, p. 148.   110. Poincaré, *Au service*, IX, 372.

111. Statement to Agence Havas, November 19, 1917.

112. *Le Matin*, December 1, 1917.   113. New York *Times*, November 30, 1917.

114. *Le Petit Parisien*, December 2, 1917.

115. New York *Times*, December 11, 1917.

116. Tardieu, *Truth About the Treaty*, p. 37.

117. Poincaré, *Au service*, IX, 425.   118. *Ibid.*, p. 424.

119. New York *Times*, December 28, 1917.

120. Stéphane Lauzanne, *Les Hommes que j'ai vus* (Paris, Fayard, 1920), pp. 139–40.

121. New York *Times*, January 2, 1918.   122. Tardieu, *Devant l'obstacle*, p. 235.

123. André Tardieu, *France and America* (Boston, Houghton Mifflin, 1927), p. 219.

124. Tardieu, *Truth About the Treaty*, p. 241; see also Tardieu, *Notes de semaine 1938*, p. 241.

125. Tardieu, *Truth About the Treaty*, p. 240.

126. Tardieu, *Amérique en armes*, p. 152; New York *Times*, February 7, 1918.

127. Tardieu, *Amérique en armes*, p. 169.   128. *Ibid.*, pp. 179–85.

129. New York *Times*, March 19, 1918.   130. *Ibid.*, January 20, 1918.

131. Tardieu, *Amérique en armes*, p. 178.

132. Tardieu, *Notes de semaine 1938*, p. 234; quoted by Josephus Daniels, *The Wilson Era, 1917–1923* (Chapel Hill, University of North Carolina Press, 1946), p. 321.

133. For instance, at the same time as Clemenceau made his request for a million tons of food, another bureau in Paris sent Tardieu the cable, "Have urgent need fifteen–twenty tons pork, lard, dehydrated vegetables, to make up for losses due to offensive. Please ship at once." When this order was ready for shipment another cable came to Washington, "No need to follow up our order." Lauzanne, *Hommes vus*, pp. 138–39.

134. Poincaré, *Au service*, x, 191.   135. Foch, *Memoirs of Foch*, p. 345.

136. Charles E. Dawes, *A Journal of the Great War* (2 vols., Boston, Houghton Mifflin, 1921), I, 126.

137. Tardieu, *Devant l'obstacle*, p. 223.

138. Tardieu, *Notes de semaine 1938*, p. 237.   139. Palmer, *Baker*, II, 259.

140. Duff Cooper, *Haig* (2 vols., London, Faber and Faber, 1936), II, 316.

141. Tardieu, *Amérique en armes*, p. 241.   142. Dawes, *Journal of War*, I, 148.

143. Tardieu, *Amérique en armes*, p. 241.

144. Sénat, *Débats, 1930*, p. 966. See also Tardieu, *Truth About the Treaty*, p. 87.

145. Dawes, *Journal of War*, I, 151–52.

146. Tardieu, *Notes de semaine 1938*, p. 149.

147. New York *Times*, August 15, 1918.   148. Poincaré, *Au service*, x, 320.

149. Tardieu, *France and America*, p. 224.   150. Dawes, *Journal of War*, I, 178.

151. Villeneuve-Trans, *A l'ambassade*, p. 187.

152. Tardieu, *Amérique en armes*, p. 271.

153. Tardieu, *France and America*, p. 238.

NOTES TO 21: "OUR TREATY"

1. Chambre des Députés, *Débats, 1918*, p. 3102; quoted by André Tardieu, *L'Amérique en armes* (Paris, Fasquelle, 1919), p. 300.

2. Tardieu, *Amérique en armes*, p. 304.

3. André Tardieu, *The Truth About the Treaty* (Indianapolis, Bobbs-Merrill, 1921), p. 216.

4. Raymond Poincaré, *Au service de la France* (10 vols., Paris, Plon, 1922), x, 435.

5. See for instance James T. Shotwell, *At the Paris Peace Conference* (New York, MacMillan, 1937), *passim*.

6. Tardieu, *Truth About the Treaty*, p. 86.

7. Charles Benoist, *Souvenirs* (3 vols., Paris, Plon, 1934), iii, 331–32.

8. Tardieu, *Truth About the Treaty*, pp. 171, 262.

9. George Bernard Noble, *Policies and Opinions at Paris, 1919* (New York, MacMillan, 1935), pp. 93–94. See also *Le Temps*, January 13, 1919.

10. Tardieu, *Amérique en armes*, p. 307.

11. *Ibid.*, p. 318; see also Tardieu, *Truth About the Treaty*, p. 111.

12. Quoted *ibid.*, p. 100.

13. Tardieu blamed Poincaré for having begun the practice of "substituting documents for evidence": André Tardieu, *Avec Foch (août–novembre, 1914)* (Paris, G.D., 1948), p. 136.

14. André Tardieu, *La Note de semaine 1936* (Paris, Flammarion, 1937), p. 175.

15. A preamble to the relevant clauses of the Treaty was to proclaim the "moral obligation" of the signatories to "redress the wrong done by Germany in 1871"; the option of inhabitants in favor of the "ceding" nation was to be denied and sentences passed by German courts suspended; France was to assume no share of Germany's public debt and pay no indemnity to Germany for public properties in the two provinces, which moreover would enjoy, in addition to other economic advantages, five years of special customs treatment by Germany without reciprocity.

16. Charles E. Dawes, *A Journal of the Great War* (2 vols., Boston, Houghton Mifflin, 1921), ii, 39–40.

17. Paul Birdsall, *Versailles Twenty Years After* (New York, Reynal and Hitchcock, 1941), p. 202, quoting House's diary.

18. *Ibid.*

19. About $600,000,000,000 in 1960 dollars (see Note 17, Chapter One).

20. Tardieu, *Truth About the Treaty*, p. 290.   21. *Ibid.*, p. 292.

22. These were the commissions for Alsace-Lorraine, Belgium, Denmark, the Saar, Czechoslovakia, Poland, Rumania, Greece, Albania, and Yugoslavia.

23. In order to avoid setting a precedent for central Europe it refused to bill Germany for the losses sustained either by the French government in redeeming German currency in the provinces at par or by individual Alsatians and Lorrainers in consequence of the war.

24. Tardieu, *Truth About the Treaty*, p. 177.

25. *Ibid.*, p. 178.   26. Birdsall, *Versailles*, p. 208.   27. *Ibid.*, p. 209.

28. Tardieu, *Notes de semaine 1938*, *L'Année de Munich* (Paris, Flammarion, 1939), p. 216.

29. Quoted by Noble, *Policies and Opinions*, p. 128.

30. Charles T. Thompson, *The Peace Conference Day by Day* (New York, Brentano, 1920), pp. 247–48. In fact the statement did appear in two papers, *L'Oeuvre* (on the far left) and *La Libre Parole* (on the far right): see Noble, *Policies and Opinions*, pp. 128–29.

31. Tardieu, *Notes de semaine 1938*, p. 242.   32. Birdsall, *Versailles*, p. 186.

33. Tardieu, *Truth About the Treaty*, p. 205.

34. *Ibid.*, p. 208.
35. Birdsall, *Versailles*, p. 209.
36. Thompson, *Peace Conference*, p. 282.   37. *Ibid.*, p. 283.   38. *Ibid.*, p. 284.
39. Birdsall, *Versailles*, p. 235.
40. Tardieu, *Truth About the Treaty*, p. 310 (translation slightly altered).
41. Quoted *ibid.*, p. 140.
42. Quoted by Philip Mason Burnett, *Reparation at the Paris Peace Conference* (2 vols., New York, Columbia University Press, 1940), I, 1136.
43. Quoted by Tardieu, *Truth About the Treaty*, p. 211.   44. *Ibid.*, p. 115.
45. Thompson, *Peace Conference*, p. 356.   46. *Ibid.*, p. 357.
47. Tardieu, *Avec Foch*, p. 36.
48. According to Georges Suarez, *Clemenceau (soixante années d'histoire française)* (Paris, Editions de France, 1932), Tardieu discovered suspicious inaccuracies in the maps in use, which were of British make, and intruded on a cordial meeting of the Council to whisper his discovery to Clemenceau: in an instant the Tiger was at Lloyd George's throat, while Wilson sat primly by.
49. Thompson, *Peace Conference*, p. 381.   50. Tardieu, *Notes de semaine 1938*, p. 170.
51. Tardieu, *Truth About the Treaty*, p. 120.   52. *Ibid.*
53. *Ibid.*, p. 299.   54. *Ibid.*, pp. 343–44.
55. Alexandre Ribot, *Journal de Alexandre Ribot et correspondances inédites, 1914–1922* (Paris, Plon, 1936), p. 273.
56. Burnett, *Reparation*, II, 114, quoting minutes of American delegation meeting.
57. *Ibid.*, p. 111.   58. Quoted *ibid.*, pp. 178–79.
59. The Council also decided that Germany would receive an invitation—"hedged round with many conditions," wrote House—to make an offer of a lump sum herself, and that the reparations bond issue would be set at 100,000,000,000 gold marks. Edward M. House, "Conference of Paris," *Encyclopedia Britannica*, Fourteenth Edition (London, Encyclopedia Britannica Company, 1929), XVII, 302.
60. Quoted by Tardieu, *Truth About the Treaty*, p. 123.
61. House, "Conference of Paris," *Encyclopedia Brittannica*, XVII, 304.
62. He referred to it and to the League of Nations as "only clever slogans for making the balance of power weigh in one's own favor": quoted by Georges Michon, *Clemenceau* (Paris, Rivière, 1931), p. 240. See also *ibid.*, pp. 215–54, especially 240 ff.
63. House, "Conference of Paris," *Encyclopedia Britannica*, XVII, 304.
64. Tardieu, *Avec Foch*, p. 36—paraphrasing Waldeck-Rousseau's famous words to the same effect on laws alone.

NOTES TO 22: L'EXPÉRIENCE TARDIEU

1. He paid tribute to its units and commanders as they left, and he obtained French university scholarships for 7,000 of its veterans.
2. For Tardieu's work at the Peace Conference after June, 1919, see *DBFP*, Ser. 1, Vol. I, *passim.*
3. "The immense majority" in that "great democracy" wished to assert its "solidarity with Europe," he declared. Chambre des Députés, *Débats, 1919*, p. 4542 (September 24).
4. Tardieu headed a list of independents, Franklin-Bouillon a list of Radical-Socialists; Tardieu's list won all the seats.
5. André Tardieu, *La Note de semaine 1936* (Paris, Flammarion, 1937), p. 173.
6. André Tardieu, *La Révolution à refaire* (2 vols., Paris, Flammarion, 1936–37), I, 14.
7. He was even apt to confuse in his memory the spirit with the letter of the decisions taken: the United States Senate having rejected the guarantee treaties, he maintained that the occupation of the Rhineland was *ipso facto* to last indefinitely, and

two years were necessary for Poincaré to make him see his error. See Raymond Poincaré, *Histoire politique* (4 vols., Paris, Plon, 1922), IV, 244 ff.

8. The first reduction on the initiative of the Reparations Commission in February, the second at the inter-Allied conference at Spa in July. See Pierre Rain, *L'Europe de Versailles* (Paris, Payot, 1945), pp. 154–59.

9. John Maynard Keynes, *A Revision of the Treaty* (London, MacMillan, 1922), p. 21.

10. Quoted *ibid.*, p. 23.   11. Quoted *ibid.*, p. 24.

12. André Tardieu, *The Truth About the Treaty* (Indianapolis, Bobbs-Merrill, 1921), p. 473n.

13. Rain, *Europe*, pp. 160 ff.

14. Chambre des Députés, *Débats, 1921*, p. 3678 (October 25).

15. Rain, *Europe*, p. 167.   16. September 28, 1922.   17. February 16, 1923.

18. Chambre des Députés, *Débats, 1923*, pp. 3695–96 (November 23).

19. Quoted by Jean Martet, *Clemenceau*, trans. by Mellon Woldman (London, Longmans, Green, 1930), p. 149.

20. In the suburb of Sartrouville; he was thrown down by André Marty. See New York *Times*, April 28, 1924.

21. By the terms of the electoral law in effect in 1924, candidates ran on district lists, each list having as many names and each voter as many votes as there were seats for the district; as many of the candidates having obtained the most votes on each list were elected as the total number of votes cast for that list contained the quotient of the total number of voters in the district divided by the total number of seats for the district, the remaining seats going all to the next strongest candidates on the list that with these seats obtained the highest quotient of the total number of votes cast for all the candidates on it divided by the total number of candidates elected from it. Generally a voter cast all his votes for the candidates of the same list, and the candidates on Tardieu's list, which came out first in the district, each got approximately 76,000 votes. Officially Tardieu's list had the patronage of Poincaré; as rumor had it, however (see Maurice Privat, *Les Heures d'André Tardieu et la crise des partis* [Paris, Portiques, 1930], p. 116), Poincaré discreetly encouraged some voters of Seine-et-Oise to vote for all the candidates on the list except Tardieu, who consequently got a few dozen votes less than those of his *co-listiers* who were elected. Thus he was defeated with 76,000 votes, while the top man on the weakest list to obtain the "quotient" once was elected with 24,000 votes.

22. Quoted by Charles Benoist, *Souvenirs* (3 vols., Paris, Plon, 1934), III, 469.

23. Colette, *L'Etoile vesper* (Geneva, Milieu du Monde, 1946), p. 53.

24. André Tardieu, *France and America* (Boston, Houghton Mifflin, 1927), p. 258.

25. For this country see Bernard Baruch in New York *Times*, June 5, 1927.

26. Quoted by Michel Missoffe, *La Vie volontaire d'André Tardieu* (Paris, Flammarion, 1932), p. 222.

27. Chambre des Députés, *Débats, 1926*, p. 2973.

28. Francis J. Tschan, Harold J. Grimm, and J. Duane Squires, *Western Civilization Since 1500*, ed. by Walter Consuelo Langsam (Chicago, Lippincott, 1947), p. 1341.

29. He swallowed it at the Council of Ministers of September 17.

30. At Belfort, by his opponent André Miellet. See New York *Times*, April 9, 1928.

31. August 1, 1929.

32. André Tardieu, *Le Communisme et l'Europe* (Paris, G.D., 1948), p. 26.

33. Tardieu, *Révolution*, I, 41.

34. Later—on November 8, 1929—Tardieu denied that an evacuation order had ever been given (Chambre des Députés, *Débats, 1929*, p. 3064); no one believed him.

35. Privat, *Heures de Tardieu*, p. 79. François de Wendel, besides being a deputy, was an industrial baron of Lorraine. His industries fed on iron mines of his own and on coal from the Ruhr, which he handled as his own. Consequently he had a direct

interest in the maintenance of the occupation, and in arguing his point he drew heavily on the resources of the coal-and-steel trust, the Comité des Forges, over which he had lately won control from the Creuzot group. In 1925 and 1926 Wendel had helped to sustain the financial crisis until Poincaré—and Tardieu—came to power; not until the crisis of October, 1929, though, did he act in concert with Tardieu. Thereafter the two were notoriously in touch.

36. *Ibid.*

37. Poincaré had proposed social insurance in 1924, and Herriot himself had proposed free secondary schooling in 1927 under Poincaré.

38. Privat, *Heures de Tardieu*, p. 100.   39. *Ibid.*, p. 106.

40. Georges Suarez, *Briand* (6 vols., Paris, Plon, 1938–52), VI, 308.

41. About $700,000,000 in 1960 dollars (see Note 17, Chapter One).

42. Tardieu, *Note de semaine 1936*, p. 228.

43. Victor Goedorp, *Figures du temps* (Paris, Michel, 1943), p. 205.

44. Variously, *plan d'équipement national, de rééquipement national, d'outillage national,* or *de réoutillage national. Equipement national* was Tardieu's own favorite; the relevant documents of the Chamber appear under the head *Outillage national*.

45. Chambre des Députés, *Débats, 1929*, pp. 2999–3001; quotation from p. 3001.

46. *Ibid.*, p. 3000.   47. *Ibid.*, p. 3050.   48. *Ibid.*, p. 3064.

49. Maurice Gamelin, *Servir* (3 vols., Paris, Plon, 1946–47), II, 69,   50. *Ibid.*

51. Chambre des Députés, *Débats, 1929*, p. 4265.   52. *Ibid.*

53. Sénat, *Débats, 1929*, p. 1255.

54. Chambre des Députés, *Débats, 1929*, p. 4385.

55. Albert Thibaudet, *Les Idées politiques de la France* (Paris, Stock, 1932), p. 69. To his dying day, in spite of the context of his remark, Tardieu maintained that the children he meant were not the social insurance bills but the laws already voted unanimously by the left, and he complained: "Many good folk, thanks to others less good, know me as the man whose policy has consisted in holding other people's children in his arms—that is, in deserting his own ideas for those of his adversaries and surrendering to the enemy out of moral and intellectual turpitude." Tardieu, *Révolution*, I, 32.

56. Sénat, *Débats, 1929*, p. 1140.

57. Quoted by Jacques Debû-Bridel, *L'Agonie de la Troisième République* (Paris, Bateau Ivre, 1948), p. 143.

58. Specifically, on light cruisers, destroyers, and submarines.

59. Alexander Werth, *Which Way France?* (London, Harper, 1937), p. 36, called this argument "a bluff put up by Grandi at France's expense." See also Werth, *France in Ferment* (London, Harper, [1935]), p. 41.

60. See *DBFP*, Ser. II, Vol. I, nos. 145, 146.   61. Tardieu, *Révolution*, I, 51.

62. Quoted by Debû-Bridel, *Agonie de la République*, p. 90.   63. Quoted *ibid.*

64. New York *Times*, March 16, 1930. This article provides an excellent résumé of Tardieu's position on naval armaments.

65. François Goguel, *La Politique des partis sous la IIIème République* (2 vols., Paris, Seuil, 1948), I, 379.

66. At a meeting with Tardieu on March 16 MacDonald denied approving Italy's claim but then refused to make his denial public. See *DBFP*, Ser. II, Vol. I, no. 155.

67. France had launched the idea of a Mediterranean pact already during the preliminary consultations (see *ibid.*, nos. 77–141, *passim*). Great Britain opposed any such pact entailing military commitments (see *ibid.*, no. 168).

68. Sénat, *Débats, 1930*, pp. 960–68, *passim*, especially p. 963.

69. See *DBFP*, Ser. II, Vol. I, no. 184 and Appendix I.

70. Quoted in André Tardieu, *L'Epreuve du pouvoir* (Paris, Flammarion, 1931), p. 82.

71. *Ibid.*, p. 72.   72. Quoted *ibid.*, pp. 50–51.   73. Quoted *ibid.*, pp. 52–53.

74. His exclusion of the Marxist groups was gratuitous if only for the reason that both of them then had an iron law against participating in any coalition government.

75. Quoted in Tardieu, *Révolution*, I, 27.

76. Debû-Bridel, *Agonie de la République*, pp. 96–97.

77. Tardieu, *Révolution*, I, 27.

78. Chambre des Députés. *Débats, 1930*, p. 3140.

79. Quoted in Tardieu, *Epreuve du pouvoir*, p. 64.

80. Quoted *ibid.*, pp. 98–99.   81. Quoted *ibid.*, p. 97.

82. Quoted by Debû-Bridel, *Agonie de la République*, p. 76.

83. Chambre des Députés, *Débats, 1930*, pp. 3383–90, *passim* (November 13).

84. Quoted in Tardieu, *Epreuve du pouvoir*, p. 125.

85. Quoted *ibid.*, p. 129.

86. Debû-Bridel, *Agonie de la République*, p. 110, quoting the testimony of the state prosecutor Donat-Gignes before the investigation commission.

87. Chambre des Députés, *Débats, 1930*, p. 3529.

88. *Ibid.*   89. *Ibid.*, p. 3531.   90. *Ibid.*

91. It elected Louis Marin; his election was denounced by the left as a maneuver to hush up the scandal.

92. Tardieu, *Révolution*, I, 53.   93. Sénat, *Débats, 1930*, p. 1751.

94. *Ibid.*, p. 1746.   95. *Ibid.*, p. 1750.

96. *Ibid.*, pp. 1756–57.

97. Caillaux as well as Jouvenel voted against him.

98. Tardieu, *Révolution*, II, 345.

99. Sénat, *Débats, 1930*, p. 1740.   100. *Ibid.*, p. 1746.

101. Tardieu, *Révolution*, II, 198.

102. Tardieu, *L'Heure de la décision* (Paris, Flammarion, 1934), p. 125.

103. Goguel, *Politique des partis*, II, 336.

104. Vincent Auriol had also said as much once, even if ironically. See Chambre des Députés, *Débats, 1929*, p. 4265: "Gentlemen, the temperament of the Premier has no doubt led him farther into violence than he cared to go."

105. Debû-Bridel, *Agonie de la République*, p. 95.

106. Joseph Paul-Boncour, *Entre deux guerres, Souvenirs sur la IIIème République* (3 vols., Paris, Plon, 1945), II, 214. Paul-Boncour goes on:"... nor I dare say use myself— and I regret it, for he was right, and I was wrong."

107. Chambre des Députés, *Débats, 1929*, p. 4383.

108. *Ibid.*, p. 4265 (December 16).

109. Tardieu, *Révolution*, I, 49.   110. Sénat, *Débats, 1929*, p. 1255.

111. Henry de Jouvenel, *Pourquoi je suis syndicaliste*, in the series "Leurs Raisons," ed. by André Billy (Paris, Editions de France, 1928), p. 21.

112. Henry de Jouvenel in *Revue des Vivants*, III (1929), 561.

113. Georges Suarez, *Les Heures héroïques du cartel* (Paris, Grasset, 1934), p. 263.

114. Colette, *Etoile vesper*, p. 53.

115. Geneviève Tabouis, *They called Me Cassandra* (New York, Scribner, 1942), pp. 122–23.

116. André Germain, *Les Grandes Favorites 1815–1940* (Paris, Sun, 1948), p. 164; for further details see *ibid.*, pp. 163–64.

117. André Maurois, *Mémoires* (3 vols., New York, Maison Française, 1942), II, 132.

118. *Ibid.*   119. Goguel, *Politique des partis*, I, 380.

120. Tardieu's social-insurance law, which went into effect on July 1, 1930, was "a prototype for the American Social Security legislation of 1935." Tschan, Grimm, and Squires, *Western Civilization*, p. 1342.

121. Tardieu, *Révolution*, I, 49.

NOTES TO 23: THE HERMIT OF MENTON

1. Jacques Debû-Bridel, *Agonie de la Troisième République* (Paris, Bateau Ivre, 1948), pp. 129–30. According to Paul Reynaud, *Au Cœur de la mêlée* (Paris, Flammarion, 1951), p. 105, Laval was "imposed" on Tardieu by the proprietor of a newspaper whose support Tardieu needed.

2. Tardieu in *L'Illustration*, January 31, 1931.

3. François Goguel, *La Politique des partis sous la IIIème République* (2 vols., Paris, Seuil, 1946), I, 338.

4. Chambre des Députés, *Débats, 1931*, p. 2655.

5. About $3,000,000 in 1960 dollars (see Note 17, Chapter One).

6. André Tardieu, *La Note de semaine 1936* (Paris, Flammarion, 1937), p. 91. The Foreign Minister had an allowance of 1,000,000 francs per month in secret funds; thus Briand had received in six years a total of 72,000,000 francs.

7. André Tardieu, *La Révolution à refaire* (2 vols., Paris, Flammarion, 1936–37), I, 26.

8. To prevent the formation of an Austro-German customs union. This time France was treating not Turkey but Germany *"wie einen Negerstaat fünfter Güte."*

9. Among other reasons, French banks had subscribed to the German reparations bond in 1930 and did not wish to see its value fall to nothing.

10. André Tardieu, *Devant le pays* (Paris, Flammarion, 1932), p. 50.

11. Joseph Paul-Boncour, *Entre deux guerres, Souvenirs sur la IIIème République* (3 vols., Paris, Plon, 1945), II, 213.

12. Quoted in Tardieu, *Devant le pays*, p. 46.   13. Quoted *ibid.*, pp. 58–59.

14. Joseph Caillaux, *Mes Mémoires* (3 vols., Paris, Plon, 1947–47), III, 390.

15. Quoted by André Tardieu, *L'Heure de la décision* (Paris, Flammarion, 1934), p. 85.

16. Paul-Boncour, *Entre deux guerres*, II, 213.

17. The immediate occasion for his fall was the fixing of a date for a question period on general policy; the issue of the electoral reform was, however, decisive against him.

18. Tardieu's first idea was to transform the original three ministries into undersecretariats of state under the authority of a Minister of National Defense; however, the chiefs-of-staff insisted on having a full-fledged minister to deal with in the war office.

19. Paul-Boncour, *Entre deux guerres*, II, 216.

20. Tardieu, *Note de semaine 1936*, p. 92.

21. André Maurois, *Mémoires* (3 vols., New York, Maison Française, 1942), II, 61; quoted by Georges Suarez, *Briand* (6 vols., Paris, Plon, 1938–52), VI. 368.

22. Chambre des Députés, *Débats, 1932*, p. 738.

23. Quoted by Suarez, *Briand*, VI, 372.

24. Quoted in Tardieu, *Heure de décision*, p. 107.

25. Quoted *ibid.*, pp. 75, 78, 83.

26. *Ibid.*, p. 105.   27. Quoted *ibid.*, p. 107.   28. Quoted *ibid.*, p. 85.

29. Maurice Gamelin, *Servir* (3 vols., Paris, Plon, 1946–47), II, 71.

30. Tardieu, *Révolution*, II, 137.   31. Tardieu, *Devant le pays*, p. xxiv.

32. New York *Times*, October 27, 1932.

33. Debû-Bridel, *Agonie de la République*, p. 191.

34. Quoted in Tardieu, *Heure de décision*, p. 33.

35. Address of March 26, 1933, to the general assembly of the Groups for Social and Republican Action; quoted in André Tardieu, *Sur la pente* (Paris, Flammarion, 1935), pp. 39–42.

36. André Tardieu, *Le Communisme et l'Europe* (Paris, G.D., 1948), p. 29.

37. Tardieu, *Heure de décision*, p. 90.

38. Debû-Bridel, *Agonie de la République*, p. 204.
39. Quoted in Tardieu, *Sur la pente*, p. 84.
40. Quoted *ibid.*, p. 94.   41. Quoted *ibid.*, p. 95.
42. Tardieu, *Heure de décision*, p. vii.   43. *Ibid.*, pp. 111–12.
44. Article v of the constitution of 1875 read: "The president of the Republic may, with the consent of the Senate, dissolve the Chamber of Deputies before the expiration of its legal mandate." Tardieu proposed instead: "The president of the Republic may, at the request of the premier,'dissolve the Chamber..." (*ibid.*, p. 187). The word "may" would, of course, have left the president of the Republic free to refuse; in practice, however, he would most likely have refused about as often as the king of England. As Tardieu explained his purpose, "Il s'agit de donner aux chefs du gouvernement français...la certitude d'obtenir du chef de l'Etat, s'ils la lui demandent, la dissolution de la Chambre des Députés" (*ibid.*, p. 188).
45. *Ibid.*, p. 189. Jouvenel, commenting on Tardieu's proposals immediately after the *six février*—that is, before revising his position for tactical reasons—judiciously pointed out that the threat of dissolution, although it would reduce the frequency of cabinet crises, would not reduce *obstruction*, from which Tardieu and France had suffered so much together; consequently he suggested as an additional reform a limitation on the length of time a bill might remain in suspense. See Chapter Sixteen.
46. He proposed the following draft: "Proposals for the appropriation of funds and for the reduction of receipts may be made only by the executive power" (*ibid.*, p. 202).
47. *Ibid.*, p. 204.   48. *Ibid.*, p. 205.   49. *Ibid.*, p. 240.   50. *Ibid.*, p. 242.
51. *Ibid.*, p. 243.   52. *Ibid.*, p. 245.   53. *Ibid.*, pp. 280–81.
54. Chambre des Députés, *Débats, 1934*, p. 411.
55. Debû-Bridel, *Agonie de la République*, pp. 246–47.
56. Tardieu, *Note de semaine 1936*, p. 92.
57. The name of a former editor of *La Liberté*, a newspaper to which Tardieu had contributed funds and articles in the past, was Camille Aymard.
58. Tardieu's testimony is reprinted in his *Sur la pente*, pp. 115–243.
59. Camille Chautemps, that is. Quoted by Debû-Bridel, *Agonie de la République*, p. 268.
60. Tardieu, *Révolution*, I, 18.   61. Tardieu, *Sur la pente*, p. lvi.
62. See pp. 333–34.   63. Tardieu, *Sur la pente*, p. lvi.
64. André Tardieu, *Notes de semaine 1938, L'Année de Munich* (Paris, Flammarion, 1939), p. 49.
65. Louis Guitard, Preface to Tardieu, *Communisme*, p. 16. The information in this paragraph is drawn from the same source.
66. *Maboul* is French slang for "crazy."   67. Tardieu, *Sur la pente*, p. xxiv.
68. Reprinted in Tardieu, *Note de semaine 1936*, p. 12.
69. Quoted by Guitard, Preface to Tardieu's *Communisme*, p. 15.
70. André Tardieu, *Alerte aux français* (Paris, Flammarion, 1936), table of contents.
71. *Ibid.*, p. 42.   72. Tardieu, *Révolution*, I, 121.
73. Alfred Fabre-Luce, *Le Secret de la République* (Paris, Grasset, 1932), p. 81.
74. *Ibid.*   75. Tardieu, *Révolution*, II, 13.
76. *Ibid.*, p. 39.   77. *Ibid.*, p. 33.   78. *Ibid.*, p. 40.
79. *Ibid.*, p. 52.   80. *Ibid.*, p. 75.   81. *Ibid.*, p. 95.
82. Tardieu writes in this connection: "Voyez M. Caillaux pointer de sa place une jumelle de théâtre sur les spectatrices des galleries: le geste de ce vieillard vous donnera la mesure du cabotinage parlementaire, qui est l'un des charmes du métier." *Ibid.*, p. 100.
83. *Ibid.*   84. *Ibid.*, p. 101.   85. *Ibid.*, p. 103.   86. *Ibid.*, p. 107.
87. *Ibid.*, p. 108.   88. *Ibid.*, pp. 108–09.   89. *Ibid.*, p. 111.

90. *Ibid.*, p. 116. 91. *Ibid.*, p. 151. 92. *Ibid.*, p. 153. 93. *Ibid.*, p. 154.

94. The Palais Bourbon, Tardieu points out, has a total seating capacity smaller than the number of deputies. At the prospect of a "crisis"—that is, when professional interests are at stake—deputies crowd the hemicycle and are obliged to sit in one another's laps. Otherwise sessions are only sparsely attended—except those "qu'on appelle les grandes séances, pour les distinguer des autres" (*ibid.*, p. 101).

95. *Ibid.*, p. 167. 96. *Ibid.*, p. 178. 97. *Ibid.*, p. 181. 98. *Ibid.*, p. 184.

99. *Ibid.*, p. 207.

100. *Ibid.*, I, 28. (Tardieu makes his point better, I think, in this passage from *Le Souverain captif* than in any equivalent passage in *La Profession parlementaire*: hence the switch.)

101. *Ibid.*, II, 214. 102. *Ibid.*, p. 232. 103. *Ibid.*, pp. 237–38.
104. *Ibid.*, p. 241. 105. *Ibid.*, p. 245. 106. *Ibid.*, p. 249.
107. *Ibid.*, p. 258. 108. *Ibid.*, p. 262.
109. *Ibid.*, p. 263. 110. *Ibid.*, p. 273. 111. *Ibid.*, p. 274.
112. *Ibid.*, p. 287. 113. *Ibid.*, p. 292. 114. *Ibid.*, p. 306. 115. *Ibid.*, p. 295.
116. *Ibid.*, p. 323. 117. *Ibid.*, p. 324. 118. *Ibid.*, p. 334. 119. *Ibid.*, p. 342.

120. *Ibid.*, pp. 357, 358, 362. Tardieu was quoting from Bergson's famous phrase, "Le corps de l'homme, aggrandi par la science, attend un supplément d'âme."

121. See Alain, *Politique* (Paris, Presses Universitaires de France, 1951), p. 88.

122. See *ibid.*, pp. 9, 74. 123. Tardieu, *Révolution*, II, 37.

124. For Tardieu's profound abhorrence of the cult of the state, see for instance *Heure de Décision*, pp. 264–70. This is the point on which his thought has been most consistently misrepresented.

125. Maurois, *Mémoires*, II, 132.

126. Quoted by Debû-Bridel, *Agonie de la République*, p. 312.

127. *Le Temps*, December 29, 1935; quoted in Tardieu, *Note de semaine 1936*, pp. 151–53.

128. Tardieu, *Notes de semaine 1938*, p. 122.

129. Paul Reynaud, *La France a sauvé l'Europe* (Paris, Flammarion, 1947), p. 171. Reynaud deleted this phrase from the later edition of his book, *Au Cœur de la mêlée*.

130. Interview with the North American Newspaper Alliance; quoted in Tardieu, *Note de semaine 1936*, p. 154.

131. Quoted *ibid.*, pp. 157–58. 132. *Ibid.*, p. 172. 133. *Ibid.*, p. 201.

134. Tardieu, *Communisme*, p. 29.

135. Tardieu, *Notes de semaine 1938*, p. 169.

136. *Ibid.*, p. 243. 137. *Ibid.*, p. 233.

138. See New York *Times*, May 30, 1937.

139. About $1,600 in 1960 dollars (see Note 17, Chapter One).

140. On this point see Tardieu, *Révolution*, II, 88–89. For the Tardieu-La Rocque affair see M. E. Ravage, "Why France Has No Dictator," *The Nation* (February 5, 1938), and Alexander Werth, *France and Munich* (London, Harper, 1939), pp. 265–66.

141. Quoted by Tardieu, *Notes de semaine 1938*, p. 245.

142. Quoted by Victor Goedorp, *Figures du temps* (Paris, Michel, 1943), p. 205.

143. Quoted in Tardieu, *Notes de semaine 1938*, pp. 246–47.

144. See New York *Times*, December 23, 1937.

145. Quoted in Tardieu, *Notes de semaine 1938*, p. 245.

146. Tardieu, *Avec Foch (août–novembre, 1914)* (Paris, G.D., 1948), p. 14.

147. *Ibid.*, p. 36. 148. *Ibid.*, p. 156. 149. *Revue des Vivants*, III (1929), 561.

150. Guitard, Preface to Tardieu, *Communisme*, p. 8. 151. *Ibid.* 152. *Ibid.*

153. Gamelin, *Servir*, II, xxxi. 154. *Ibid.*

155. Guitard, Preface to Tardieu, *Communisme*, p. 8. 156. *Ibid.*

157. Anatole de Monzie, *Ci-devant* (Paris, Flammarion, 1941), p. 161. 158. *Ibid.*

NOTES TO APPENDIX: BACKGROUND TO THE HOMS-BAGDAD RAILWAY 1888–1909

1. Morris Jastrow, *The War and the Bagdad Railway* (Philadelphia, Lippincott, 1917), p. 115.

2. A. J. P. Taylor, *The Struggle for Mastery in Europe, 1848–1918* (Oxford, Clarendon, 1954), p. 504.

3. J. B. Wolf, "The Diplomatic History of the Baghdad Railroad," *The University of Missouri Studies*, XI, no. 2 (April 1, 1936), p. 16.

4. Quoted by Jastrow, *War and Bagdad Railway*, p. 100.

5. *DDF*, Ser. II, Vol. III, no. 76 (February 11, 1903); quoted by Wolf, "The Diplomatic History of the Baghdad Railway," *The University of Missouri Studies*, XI, no. 2 (April 1, 1936), p. 38.

6. *DDF*, Ser. II, Vol. III, no. 135.

7. Quoted by Wolf, "The Diplomatic History of the Baghdad Railway," *The University of Missouri Studies*, XI, no. 2 (April 1, 1936), p. 39.

8. See Foreign Office, "Convention of March 5, 1903," *Bagdad Railway, no. 1 (1911)* (London, His Majesty's Stationer's Office, 1911).

9. Taylor, *Struggle for Mastery*, p. 411*n*.

10. David Fraser, *The Short Cut to India* (Edinburgh, Blackwood, 1909), p. 41.

11. *DDF*, Ser. II, Vol. III, nos. 260, 374; *GP*, Vol. XVII, no. 5263. More exactly, the French government demanded "equal rights" for the French group.

12. André Tardieu, *France and the Alliances* (New York, MacMillan, 1908), pp. 48–57.

13. See Wolf, "The Diplomatic History of the Baghdad Railway," *The University of Missouri Studies*, XI, no. 2 (April 1, 1936), pp. 49–50.

14. *Ibid.*, p. 52.

15. André Tardieu, "La Politique extérieure de l'Allemagne," *Questions diplomatiques et coloniales*, XXIII (1907), 340–41; quoted by Edward Mead Earle, *Turkey, the Great Powers, and the Baghdad Railway* (New York, MacMillan, 1923), p. 170.

16. Earle, *Baghdad Railway*, p. 170.

Bibliography

Bibliography

A NOTE ON SOURCES

THE NOTES to this study provide more or less complete bibliographical references; nevertheless, certain sources and certain problems of documentation merit special attention.

I.   My basic sources included the following. For general history: newspapers (especially *Le Temps, Le Journal des Débats, Le Matin, Le Figaro,* and the New York *Times*) and reviews (especially *La Revue de Paris, La Revue des deux Mondes, La Revue politique et littéraire: Revue bleue, La Mercure de France,* and *La Revue des Vivants*). For political history: the *Journal Officiel.* For diplomatic history in the period before the First World War: France, Ministère des Affaires étrangères, Commission de Publication des Documents relatifs aux Origines de la Guerre de 1914–1918, *Documents diplomatiques français (1871–1914)* (Paris, Imprimerie Nationale, 1929–); France, Ministère des Affaires étrangères, *Documents diplomatiques 1912, Affaires du Maroc VI, 1910–1912* (Paris, Imprimerie Nationale, 1912), also published as *Livre jaune: Affaires marocaines (1910–1912)*; Germany, Auswärtiges Amt, *Die grosse Politik der europäischen Kabinette, 1871–1914,* edited by Johannes Lepsius, Albrecht Mendelssohn-Bartholdy, and Friedrich Thimme, 40 vols. (Berlin, Deutsche Verlagsgesellschaft für Politik und Geschichte G. m. b. H., 1922–27); Great Britain, Foreign Office, *British Documents on the Origins of the War, 1898–1914,* edited by G. P. Gooch and Harold Temperly, 11 vols. (London, H. M. Stationery Office, 1926–38); U.S.S.R., Ministère des Affaires étrangères, *Un Livre noir, Diplomatie d'avant-guerre d'après les documents des archives russes (1910–1917),* 3 vols. (Paris, Librairie du Travail, 1922–192[?]). A good companion piece to the diplomatic documents is Luigi Albertini, *The Origin of the War of 1914,* 2 vols. (London, Oxford University Press, 1952). Of the primary sources for diplomacy between the two wars, only Great Britain, Foreign Office, *Documents on British Foreign Policy 1919–1939,* edited by E. L. Woodward and Rohan Butler (London, H. M. Stationery Office, 1947–), was much relevant to my subject. The best political histories of the Third Republic are Charles Seignobos, *L'Evolution de la 3e République (1875–1914),* Vol. VIII of "Histoire de France contemporaine depuis la révolution jusqu'à la paix de 1919," edited by Ernest Lavisse (Paris, Hachette, 1921), which covers the period before the First World War, and François Goguel, *La Politique des partis sous la IIIème République,* 2 vols. (Paris, Seuil, 1946), which emphasizes the later period; I have made frequent use of both.

II.   There is no dearth of material on Caillaux. Alfred Fabre-Luce, *Caillaux* (Paris, Gallimard, 1933), is invaluable, especially for Caillaux's financial policies in 1925–26. Roger de Fleurieu, *Joseph Caillaux au cours d'un demi-siècle de notre histoire* (Paris, Clavreuil, 1951), is mostly defamation, and Gaston Martin, *Joseph Caillaux* (Paris, Alcan, 1931), is mostly adulation; both are quite useless. Paul Vergnet, *Joseph Caillaux* and *L'Affaire Caillaux* (both: Paris, La Renaissance du Livre, 1918), published successively while the Caillaux treason trial was pending, are indictments; they present their one side of the story fully and accurately. Berthe-Eva Gueydan (the first Madame Caillaux),

Les Rois de la République, 2 vols. (Paris, Perrin, 1925), based almost exclusively on back numbers of the *Action Française*, is a protracted insult to Caillaux and to history. Of the more restricted studies, Emile Roche, *Caillaux que j'ai connu* (Paris, Plon, 1949), on Caillaux's last years, is most useful (see pp. 110–11). Severance Johnson, *The Enemy Within* (New York, McCann, 1919), on Caillaux's wartime activities, is vile, and Henri Bernier, *La Raison des fous* (Paris, Les Etincelles, 1930), ostensibly on the same subject, is pathetic. Maurice Barrès, *Dans le cloaque* (Paris, Emile-Paul, 1914), on the Rochette affair, and *En regardant au fond des crevasses* (Paris, Emile-Paul, 1917), on the question of Caillaux's loyalty to France, are impressionistic slander, as is Léon Daudet, *Le Poignard dans le dos* (Paris, Nouvelle Librairie Nationale, 1918), which deals with Malvy and Caillaux. John N. Raphael, *The Caillaux Drama* (London, Goschen, 1914), published on the eve of the Calmette murder trial, is a dramatic presentation and judicious appraisal of the evidence, and Gustave Binet-Valmar, *Une Femme a tué* (Paris, Flammarion, 1924), is a bitter protest against the verdict. Charles Paix-Séailles, *Jaurès et Caillaux* (Paris, Figuières, 1919), is a sympathetic account of the joint maneuvers of the two occasional allies (the style of the Appendix, which is on the Congo ventures, as well as of certain portions of the narrative itself, smacks suspiciously of Caillaux). Tardieu's *Le Mystère d'Agadir* (see Section IV, below) is still the best history of the Agadir crisis and of Caillaux's action in resolving it. Geraud-Bastet, *Une Transformation sociale, M. Caillaux et l'impôt sur le revenu expliqués* (Paris, Tallandier, 1909), on Caillaux and the early stages of the income-tax battle, presents the facts and documents appealingly and well, but Albert Letellier, *Joseph Caillaux, L'Empereur des crédules* (Roanne, Editions des Imprimeries réunies, 1922), a critique of Caillaux's postwar program, has little substance or coherence, and Guy de Pierrefeux, *Le Revenant, propos et anecdotes autour de Caillaux* (Strasbourg, Hiller, 1925), is similarly disappointing. Of the brief studies, the best is Major T. H. Thomas, "Caillaux," *The Atlantic Monthly* (June, 1925), pp. 832–42. The several essays in the collection *Caillaux* ("Les Ecrits pour et contre"; Paris, Delpeuch [1925]), as well as the chapters on Caillaux in [anonymous], *Ceux qui nous mènent* (Paris, Plon, 1922), Sisley Huddleston, *Those Europeans* (New York, Putnam, 1924), and [Laurance Lyon], *The Pomp of Power* (London, Hutchinson, [1922]), are so many divergent estimates of his character and value; all attest at least to the fascination he held for his contemporaries. *Les Cahiers du Cercle Joseph Caillaux, Revue d'études politiques et sociales*, which appeared sporadically for two years (1953–55) under the direction of Emile Roche, contains some interesting reminiscences.

Of Caillaux's publications, the following were available to me (by chronological order of their first appearance):

1910   *L'Impôt sur le revenu.* Paris, Berger-Levrault.

1911   *Les Impôts en France, Traité technique.* 2 vols. Paris, Pichon.

1913   Preface to Maurice Ajam, *Problèmes algériens.* Paris, Larose.

1914   Preface to René Besnard and C. Aymard, *L'œuvre française au Maroc, avril 1912–décembre 1913.* Paris, Hachette.

1916   *La Guerre et la république.* Paris, Vervoort.

1919   *Agadir, Ma Politique extérieure.* Paris, Michel.

1921   *Devant l'histoire, Mes Prisons.* Paris, Editions de la Sirène.

1923   *Où va la France? où va l'Europe?* Paris, Editions de la Sirène. *Whither France? Whither Europe?* Translated by Helen Byrne Armstrong. New York, Knopf, 1923.

1925   Preface to Emile Cazalis, *Syndicalisme ouvrier et évolution sociale.* Paris, Librairie des Sciences politiques et sociales.

1926   *Ma Doctrine.* Paris, Flammarion.

1932   *The World Crisis.* Translated by Hamilton Marr. London, Cobden-Sanderson. (The original of this speech to the Cobden Memorial Association is appended to Emile Roche, *Caillaux que j'ai connu.*)

1933 *D'Agadir à la grande pénitence.* Paris, Flammarion et Durand-Auzias.
1936 Speech in Société des anciens Elèves et Elèves de l'Ecole libre des Sciences politiques, *La Réforme de l'Etat.* Paris, Alcan.
1942 *Mes Mémoires.* Vol. I. Paris, Plon.
1943 *Mes Mémoires.* Vol. II. Paris, Plon.
1947 *Mes Mémoires.* Vol. III. Paris, Plon.

I did not have access to the records of either Caillaux trial; also, the publication of the Ligue des Droits de l'Homme on the treason trial was not available to me, and neither was the appropriate one tenth of *Destins hors série* by Anatole de Monzie.

Of Caillaux's writings, *Agadir, Mes Prisons,* and of course *Mes Mémoires* are chiefly autobiographical.

III. There *is* a dearth of material on Jouvenel. His private papers and family documents disappeared during the Occupation, when the Germans plundered the baronial residence in Corrèze, which they suspected of serving as a cover-up for various underground movements. Similarly, the archives of the two Senate commissions on which he sat—the Foreign Affairs Commission and the Commission for the Reform of the State—were evacuated from Paris to Tours in 1940, and later the same year, when the Senate withdrew to Bordeaux, they were destroyed, whether by the air raids of June or voluntarily is not known. The only source for his whole life is *La Revue des Vivants,* IX (November-December, 1935), a collection of reminiscences on him by his friends; it is insubstantial. One chapter in his life has been well covered: his mission to Syria. The most authoritative account—and also the most disparaging—is Elizabeth P. MacCallum, *The Nationalist Crusade in Syria* (New York, Foreign Policy Association, 1928), pp. 148–94; excellent though it is, it is systematically anti-French and often falls into the error of identifying the Syrian People's Party with the Syrian people. Arnold J. Toynbee, "The High Commissionership of M. Henry de Jouvenel and the Investigation of the Permanent Mandates Commission of the League of Nations," in *Survey of International Affairs, 1925,* Vol. I, *The Islamic World Since the Peace Settlement* (London, Oxford University Press, 1927), pp. 439–57, while it is thoroughly disorderly and suffers from an odd mixture of anti-imperialism and anti-French-imperialism, has the merit of providing an exhaustive bibliography of the periodical literature of the time. For Jouvenel's role in the negotiation of the Four-Power Pact and for the corresponding controversy in the French government, Paul-Boncour (see section V, below) is the best source, to which *DBFP,* Ser. II, Vol. V, is the best supplement. The relevant documents and a commentary are given in *Documents on International Affairs,* edited by John W. Wheeler-Bennett (London, Oxford University Press, 1934), pp. 236–49, and Toynbee, "The Little Entente Pact and the Four-Power Pact," *Survey of International Affairs, 1933* (London, Oxford University Press, 1934), pp. 203–23, provides a full account of the negotiations in their public stage; however, Wheeler-Bennett and Toynbee, like most contemporary observers, saw the origin of the pact in the MacDonald-Mussolini conversations of March, 1933, whereas in fact Mussolini had discussed the prospective pact earlier with Jouvenel (see *DBFP,* Ser. II, Vol. V, nos. 37, 43, 44 [enclosure 4], 216, and above, pp. 179–80). U.S. Department of State, *Documents on German Foreign Policy, 1918–45,* Ser. C, Vol. I (U.S. Government Printing Office, Washington, D.C., 1957), became available too late for my use; it supplements my account of the negotiations (especially nos. 68, 109, 117, 153, 165, 190, 258, 282, 287, 291, 303, 320, 343). Alfred de Tarde and Robert de Jouvenel, *La Politique d'aujourd'hui* (Paris, La Renaissance du Livre, [1923]), generously quotes Henry de Jouvenel's remarks on sundry topics. Two monographs deserve mention: Louis Planté, "Grands Maîtres de l'université: Henry de Jouvenel," *Revue politique et littéraire, Revue bleue,* LXVIII (January, 1930), which deals with

Jouvenel's brief term as Minister of National Education; and Georges Suarez, "Chez Monsieur Henry de Jouvenel," *Revue de Paris*, xxxv (January- February, 1928), which concentrates on his doctrine of syndicalism.

Of Jouvenel's publications, the following were available to me (by chronological order of their first appearance):

1924   Speech in Ecole des Hautes Etudes sociales, *Les Réformes politiques de la France* ("Bibliothèque générale des sciences sociales"). Paris, Alcan.

1925   Speech, "La France devant les échanges internationaux," in Société des anciens Elèves et Elèves de l'Ecole libre des Sciences politiques, *Notre Diplomatie économique*. Paris, Alcan.

1928   *Pourquoi je suis syndicaliste* ("Leurs Raisons," edited by André Billy). Paris, Editions de France.

1929   Preface to André Gardes, *Le Désarmement devant la Société des Nations*. Paris, Pedone.

1929   *La Vie orageuse de Mirabeau*. Paris, Plon. *The Stormy Life of Mirabeau*. Boston, Houghton Mifflin, 1929.

1932   *La Paix française, Témoignage d'une génération*. Paris, Editions des Portiques.

1932   *Huit Cents Ans de révolution française, 987-1789*. Paris, Hachette.

1933   "Dialogue d'un lecteur et d'un auditeur," Cahier 1 of Institut international de Co-opération intellectuelle, *Le Rôle intellectuel de la presse*. Paris, Société des Nations. *The Educational Role of the Press*. Paris, League of Nations, International Institute of Intellectual Cooperation, 1934.

1935   "L'Evolution du pouvoir vue par un politique," *Encyclopédie française*. Edited by Anatole de Monzie. Paris, Librarie Larousse. X, 10.62–8 to 10.62–13.

1935   "La Révolution," *Encyclopédie française*. Edited by Anatole de Monzie. Paris, Librairie Larousse. X, 10.62–13 to 10.62–15.

A few pages of *La Paix française* and of *Pourquoi je suis syndicaliste* are autobiographical in character.

IV.   There is no full-length biography of Tardieu; however, Jacques Debû-Bridel, *L'Agonie de la Troisième République* (Paris, Editions du Bateau Ivre, 1948), picks up the story of his career where Michel Missoffe, *La Vie volontaire d'André Tardieu* (Paris, Flammarion, 1930), leaves off—in 1929, at the beginning of the *expérience Tardieu*—and Louis Guitard in the preface to Tardieu's *Le Communisme et l'Europe* (see below) adds a few words on his retirement, illness, and death. Missoffe, though informative, is puerile and affected; Debû-Bridel, like Missoffe a strong partisan of Tardieu, is by comparison sober and objective. Neither covers any phase of Tardieu's career satisfactorily—Debû-Bridel because Tardieu was not really his subject, Missoffe even though Tardieu was his whole subject. Unfortunately, *André Tardieu, par Louis Aubert, Ivan Martin, Michel Missoffe, François Piétri, Alfred Pose; introduction par Gabriel Puaux; hommages de Bernard Baruch, Lord Vansittart, Paul van Zeeland* (Paris, Plon, 1957) appeared too late for me to make use of it: it provides much valuable information and commentary on the various aspects of Tardieu's career, especially on his governmental work ("Tardieu au ministère," by Ivan Martin). Félicien Challaye, *Un Aspirant Dictateur, André Tardieu* (Paris, Editions de "la Révolution Prolétarienne," [1930]), and P. L. Darnar, *Tardieu* (Paris, Les Publications révolutionnaires, 1934), both of them pamphlets, are merely diatribes.

A few works deal singly with certain of Tardieu's diverse activities. The chapter in Victor Goedorp, *Figures du temps* (Paris, Michel, 1943), on Tardieu's editorship of *Le Temps* is long but meager; the one in Pierre Mille, *Mes Trônes et mes dominations* (Paris, Editions des Portiques, 1930), is short and meager. Charles Paix-Séailles, *La Diplomatie secrète sous la IIIème République, 1910-1911; Homs-Bagdad, Du Quai d'Orsay à la correctionnelle* (Paris, Courrier Européen, 1912), presents Tardieu's correspondence in the Homs-Bagdad affair along with a derogatory commentary; likewise, Maurice Viollette, *La N'Goko-Sangha* (Paris, Larose, 1914), offers a non-random sample of documents on the N'Goko Sangha affair, as does the appendix to Paix-Séailles's *Jaurès et Caillaux* (see Section II, above). Maurice Cassenave, "André Tardieu, Souvenirs d'Amérique," *Correspondant*, VIII (1930), is a brief appreciation of Tardieu's high commissionership in the United States. On the Peace Conference of 1919 as well as on Tardieu's contribution to it, by far the best work is Paul Birdsall, *Versailles Twenty Years After* (New York, Reynal and Hitchcock, 1941). Maurice Privat, *Les Heures d'André Tardieu et la crise des partis* (Paris, Editions des Portiques, 1930), is an artful analysis of the cabinet crisis between the fall of Briand in October, 1929, and the formation of the first Tardieu government. The first part of Georges Dovime, *Leurs Finances (de Tardieu à Daladier)* (Paris, A l'Etoile, 1933), nominally about Tardieu's financial policies, in fact hardly mentions them. Paul Creyssel, *La Rocque contre Tardieu* (Paris, Sorlot, 1938), is only the futile plea of La Rocque's lawyer in his libel suit against *Gringoire*. Of the brief character studies, Fidus, "M. André Tardieu (silhouettes parlementaires)," *La Revue des deux Mondes*, 102ème année (February 1, 1932), is perhaps the best.

Of Tardieu's publications, the following were available to me (by chronological order of their first appearance):

1905 *Questions diplomatiques de l'année 1904*. Paris, Alcan.

1907 *La Conférence d'Algésiras*. Paris, Alcan.

1907 Speech in Société des anciens Elèves et Elèves de l'Ecole libre des Sciences politiques, *Les Questions actuelles de politique étrangère en Europe*. Paris, Alcan.

1908 *Notes sur les Etats-Unis*. Paris, Calmann-Lévy.

1908 *France and the Alliances*. New York, MacMillan. *La France et les alliances*. Paris, Alcan, 1910.

1909 *Le Prince de Bülow*. Paris, Calmann-Lévy.

1911 Preface to A. Cottes, *La Mission Cottes au Sud-Cameroun (1905–1908)*. Paris, Leroux.

1911 Speech, "La Doctrine de Monroë et le panaméricanisme," in Société des anciens Elèves et Elèves de l'Ecole libre des Sciences politiques, *Les Questions actuelles de politique étrangère dans l'Amérique du Nord*. Paris, Alcan.

1912 *Le Mystère d'Agadir*. Paris, Calmann-Lévy.

1913 Speech, "L'Egypte," in Société des anciens Elèves et Elèves de l'Ecole libre des Sciences politiques, *L'Afrique du Nord*. Paris, Alcan.

1917 Preface to Nikola Stojanovič, *La Serbie d'hier et de demain*. Paris, Berger-Levrault.

1919 *L'Amérique en armes*. Paris, Fasquelle.

1921 *La Paix*. Paris, Payot. *The Truth About the Treaty*. Indianapolis, Bobbs-Merrill.

1921 Speech in Société des anciens Elèves et Elèves de l'Ecole libre des Sciences politiques, *Les Conséquences de la guerre*. Paris, Alcan.

[1923] Preface to *France* ("The Nations of the World," edited by Lord Albert E. W. Gleichen). London, Hodder & Stoughton.

1926 (with Franz v. Jessen) *Slesvig paa Fredskonferencen, Januar 1919–Januar 1920*. Copenhagen. *Le Slesvig et la paix*. Paris, Meynial, 1928.

1927 *Devant l'obstacle, L'Amérique et nous*. Paris, Emile-Paul. *France and America*. Boston, Houghton Mifflin, 1927.

1931 *L'Epreuve du pouvoir*. Paris, Flammarion.

1932 *Devant le pays*. Paris, Flammarion.

1933 Speech in Fédération républicaine et sociale du Massif Central, *4 juin 1933, Le Président André Tardieu à Aubert, Un Discours-programme*. Clermont-Ferrand, Imprimerie moderne.

406   BIBLIOGRAPHY

1934   L'Heure de la décision. Paris, Flammarion. France in Danger. London, Archer, 1935.
1934   La Réforme de l'Etat, Les idées maîtresses de "L'Heure de la décision." Paris, Flammarion.
1935   Sur la pente. Paris, Flammarion.
1936   Alerte aux Français. Paris, Flammarion.
1936   La Révolution à refaire. Vol. I, Le Souverain captif. Paris, Flammarion.
1937   La Révolution à refaire. Vol. II, La Profession parlementaire. Paris, Flammarion.
1937   La Note de semaine 1936. Paris, Flammarion.
1939   Notes de semaine 1938, L'Année de Munich. Paris, Flammarion.
1939   Preface to Charles d'Ydewalle, Vingt Ans d'Europe, 1919–1939. Paris, Flammarion.
1948   Avec Foch (août-novembre 1914). Paris, Editions G. D.
1948   Le Communisme et l'Europe. Paris, Editions G. D.

Tardieu's publications not available to me include A la jeunesse française (Paris, 1919) and La Note de semaine 1937 (Paris, Flammarion, 1938). Notes sur les Etats-Unis alone among Tardieu's earlier works contains a smattering of autobiographica material. Tardieu was also necessarily a part of the subject of his La Paix. His later works contain occasional reminiscences, especially his "Notes de semaine" (his articles for Gringoire, reprinted in book form); and his last book, Avec Foch, is his diary of the first months of the First World War.

V.   I have drawn heavily on other miscellaneous sources too diverse to classify and too numerous to list.

Of these, the most useful were: Raymond Poincaré, Au Service de la France—neuf années de souvenirs, 10 vols. (Paris, Plon-Nourrit, 1926–33), the full political chronicles of the President of the Republic of 1913–19, who was painstakingly accurate in all verifiable matters of fact; Joseph Paul-Boncour, Entre deux guerres, Souvenirs sur la IIIème République, 3 vols. (Paris, Plon, 1945), reminiscences on his long and active career (1899–1939) by the gentle partisan of collective security and the syndicalist state; Georges Suarez, Briand, 6 vols. (Paris, Plon, 1938–52), the standard biography of Briand and the one serious work of an immensely talented scoundrel; Georges Michon, Clemenceau (Paris, Rivière, 1931), a brilliant scholarly critique, especially of Clemenceau's persecution of Caillaux and of his Realpolitik at the Peace Conference of 1919. Also especially useful were: Maurice Paléologue, Journal, 1913–1914 (Paris, Plon, 1947), and Georges Michon, La Préparation à la guerre, La Loi des trois ans (1910–1914) (Paris, Rivière, 1935), for militarism versus pacifism in pre-First-World-War France; Ferdinand Foch, The Memoirs of Marshal Foch, translated by Col. T. Bentley Mott (New York, Doubleday, Doran, 1931), Joseph Galliéni, Les Carnets de Galliéni (Paris, Michel, 1932); Joseph J. C. Joffre, Mémoires du maréchal Joffre (1910–1917), 2 vols. (Paris, Plon, 1932), and Jean de Pierrefeu, French Head Quarters 1915–1918, translated by C. J. C. Street (London, Bles, 1924), for the military conduct of the war; Alexandre Ribot, Journal de Alexandre Ribot et correspondances inédites, 1914–1922 (Paris, Plon, 1936), and Pierre Renouvin, The Forms of War Government in France (New Haven, Yale University Press, 1927), for the political conduct of the war; Maurice Gamelin, Servir, 3 vols. (Paris, Plon, 1946–47), likewise for the First World War but also for military affairs between the two wars; Charles Benoist, Souvenirs, 3 vols. (Paris, Plon, 1934), Octave Homberg, Les Coulisses de l'histoire, Souvenirs 1898–1928 (Paris, Fayard, 1938), and André Maurois, Mémoires, 2 vols. (New York, Editions de la Maison Française, 1942), for anecdotes; Albert Thibaudet, Les Idées politiques de la France (Paris, Stock, 1932) and La République des professeurs (Paris, Grasset, 1927), for insights; Anatole de Monzie, *Ci-devant* (Paris, Flammarion, 1941), for incidental intelligence; Etienne Chichet, *Quarante Ans de journalisme, Feuilles volantes* (Paris, Nouvelles Editions Latines, 1935), Colette, *Œuvres complètes* (Paris, Flammarion, 1949), *passim.*, André Germain, *Les Grandes Favorites 1815–1940* (Paris, Sun, 1948), *La Bourgeoisie qui brûle* (Paris, Sun, 1951), and *Les Clés de Proust* (Paris, Sun, 1953), and Geneviève Tabouis, *They Called Me Cassandra* (New York, Scribner, 1942), for gossip and for diverse impressions of men and events.

OTHER WORKS CITED

Alain. *Politique*. Paris, Presses Universitaires de France, 1951.

Berty, Abbé L. *Vie de Léon de Jouvenel, député de la Corrèze (1811–1886)*. Preface by J. Nouillac. N. p., Chastrusse, Praudel, 1931.

Brandenburg, Erich. *From Bismarck to the World War, A History of German Foreign Policy 1870–1914*. Translated by Annie Elizabeth Adams. London, Milford, 1927.

Burnett, Philip Mason. *Reparations at the Paris Peace Conference*. 2 vols. New York, Columbia University Press, 1940.

Cambon, Paul. *Correspondance 1870–1924*. Paris, Grasset, 1940.

Cecil, Lord Robert. *A Great Experiment*. New York, Oxford University Press, 1951.

Challaye, Félicien. "Politique internationale et journalisme d'affaires," *La Revue du Mois*, xi (June 10, 1911), 749–57.

Chapman, Maybelle Kennedy. *Great Britain and the Baghdad Railway*. Vol. xxxi in "Smith College Studies in History." Menasha (Wisconsin), Banta, 1948.

Curato, Federico. *La Storiografia delle origini della prima guerra mondiale* ("Questioni di historia contemporanea"). Milan, Marzorati, 1952.

Dawes, Charles G. *A Journal of the Great War*. 2 vols. Boston, Houghton Mifflin, 1921.

Earle, Edward Meade. *Turkey, the Great Powers, and the Baghdad Railway*. New York, Macmillan, 1923.

Escholier, Raymond. *Souvenirs parlés de Briand*. Paris, Hachette, 1932.

Fanshawe, Maurice. *Reconstruction*. London, Allen & Unwin, 1925.

Gérard, André. "The Story of the Baghdad Railway," *The Nineteenth Century and After*, No. 448 (June, 1914).

Germain, José. *La C.T.I.* Paris, La Renaissance du Livre, n.d.

— *Le Syndicalisme et l'intelligence*. Paris, Librairie Valois, 1928.

Halévy, Daniel. *La République des comités*. Paris, Grasset, 1934.

Harbord, J. G. *The American Army in France, 1917–1919*. Boston, Little, Brown, 1936.

Hillson, Norman. *The Geneva Scene*. London, Routledge, 1936.

House, Edward M. "Conference of Paris," *Encyclopedia Britannica*. 14th ed., Vol. xviii. London, Encyclopedia Britannica Company, 1929.

Howard-Ellis, C. *The Origin, Structure and Working of the League of Nations*. London, Allen & Unwin, 1928.

Jastrow, Morris. *The War and the Bagdad Railway*. Philadelphia, Lippincott, 1917.

Judet, Ernest. *Georges Louis*. Paris, Rieder, 1925.

Keynes, John Maynard. *A Revision of the Treaty*. London, Macmillan, 1922.

Kiderlen-Wächter, Alfred von. *Kiderlen-Wächter der Staatsmann und Mensch, Briefwechsel und Nachlass*. Edited by Ernst Jäckh. 2 vols. Stuttgart, Deutsche Verlags-Anstalt, 1925.

Kuzbari, Nadar. *La Question de la cessation du mandat français sur la Syrie*. Paris, Editions Pedone, 1937.

Lauzanne, Stéphane. *Les Hommes que j'ai vus*. Paris, Fayard, 1925.

— *Sa Majesté la presse*. Paris, Fayard, 1925.

Lyautey, Pierre. *L'Empire colonial français*. Paris, Editions de France, 1931.

Martet, Jean. *Clemenceau*. Translated by Mellon Woldman. London, Longmans, Green, 1930.

Monzie, Anatole de. *L'Entrée au forum (vingt ans avant)*. Paris, Michel, 1920.

Noble, George Bernard. *Policies and Opinions at Paris, 1919*. New York, Macmillan, 1935.

Olivieri, Alphonse. "André Tardieu et Henry de Jouvenel peints par eux-mêmes," *Revue contemporaine*, LXXI (March, 1923).

— "Henry de Jouvenel," *Revue contemporaine*, III (1923).

Ormesson, Wladimir d'. *Pour la Paix*. Paris, Editions Spes, 1929.

Palmer, Frederick. *Newton D. Baker, America at War*. 2 vols. New York, Dodd, Mead, 1931.

Pasquier, Pierre. *Les Etapes de la défaite*. Montreal, Zodiaque, 1941.

Philippe, Raymond. *Le Drame financier de 1924–1928*. Paris, Gallimard, 1931.

Ragey, Louis. *La Question du chemin de fer de Bagdad, 1893–1914*. Paris, Rieder, 1936.

Rain, Pierre. *L'Europe de Versailles*. Paris, Payot, 1945.

Renard, Jules. *Journal*. Paris, Gallimard, 1935.

Reynaud, Paul. *Au coeur de la mêlée, 1930–1945*. Paris, Flammarion, 1951.

— *La France a sauvé l'Europe*. 2 vols. Paris, Flammarion, 1947.

Ribot, Alexandre. *Lettres à un ami*. Paris, Bossard, 1924.

Schuman, Frederick L. *War and Diplomacy in the French Republic*. New York, Whittlesey House, 1931.

Stresemann, Gustav. *His Diaries, Letters and Papers*. Edited and translated by Eric Sutton. 3 vols. New York, Macmillan, 1935–40.

Suarez, Georges. *Clemenceau (soixante années d'histoire française)*. Paris, Editions de France, 1932.

— *Les Heures héroïques du cartel*. Paris, Grasset, 1934.

— *Les Hommes malades de la paix*. Paris, Grasset, 1933.

Suarez, Georges, and Guy Laborde. *Agonie de la paix, 1935–1939*. Paris, Plon, 1942.

Taylor, A. J. P. *The Struggle for Mastery in Europe, 1848–1918*. Oxford, Clarendon Press, 1954.

Thompson, Charles T. *The Peace Conference Day by Day*. New York, Brentano, 1920.

Villeneuve-Trans, R. de. *A l'ambassade de Washington, octobre 1917–avril 1919*. Paris Bossard, 1921.

Werth, Alexander. *Which Way France?* New York, Harper, 1937.

Wolf, John B. "The Diplomatic History of the Baghdad Railroad," *The University of Missouri Studies*, Vol. XI, No. 2 (April 1, 1936).

For works cited only once, the facts of publication are available in the place of citation.

My inventory of useful sources would be deficient without due mention of Bertrand de Jouvenel's having by letter very kindly filled for me the most critical gaps in my information on his father's life and of François Goguel's having likewise answered all of my requests for specific information not available from any source in the United States.

Index